Scott of the Antarctic

I may not have proved a great explorer but we have done the greatest march ever made and come very near to great success.

Robert Falcon Scott

Scott of the Antarctic

We Shall Die Like Gentlemen

Sue Blackhall

Pen & Sword

First published in Great Britain in 2012
and reprinted in this format in 2021 by
Pen & Sword Discovery
an imprint of
Pen & Sword Books Ltd
47 Church Street
Barnsley
South Yorkshire
S70 2AS

ISBN 978 1 52679 665 3

A CIP catalogue record for this book is available from the British Library.

Typeset in 11pt Ehrhardt by
Mac Style, Beverley, E. Yorkshire

Printed and bound in the UK on FSC accredited paper by
4edge Ltd, Essex, SS5 4AD

Pen & Sword Books Ltd incorporates the Imprints of Pen & Sword Aviation, Pen & Sword Family History, Pen & Sword Maritime, Pen & Sword Military, Pen & Sword Discovery, Wharncliffe Local History, Wharncliffe True Crime, Wharncliffe Transport, Pen & Sword Select, Pen & Sword Military Classics, Leo Cooper, The Praetorian Press, Remember When, Seaforth Publishing and Frontline Publishing.

For a complete list of Pen & Sword titles please contact
PEN & SWORD BOOKS LIMITED
47 Church Street, Barnsley, South Yorkshire, S70 2AS, England
E-mail: enquiries@pen-and-sword.co.uk
Website: www.pen-and-sword.co.uk

Contents

Chapter 1

The Moulding of an Explorer

One could never have imagined that Robert Falcon Scott, the day dreamer with his childhood discomfort of blood and seeing animals suffer, would one day have to confront both of these great anxieties in a most tragic and legendary way. But then the young Scott with his rather awkward approach to life could never have envisaged embarking on an adult venture that would immortalise him as a great British hero.

Scott was born on 6 June 1868 into the privileged background of a family with a large estate and a father who was a magistrate. He was one of six children, with younger sisters Katherine ('Kitty') and Grace ('Monsie'), younger brother Archibald (Archie) and two older sisters Ettie and Rose. Scott's parents were John Edward and Hannah. John came from a large family and was the youngest of eight children. He had four older brothers, one of whom died young, two who went into the Indian army and the other who became a naval surgeon. John himself was blighted with poor health, which prevented him from following the family tradition of entering the services. But he was fortunate to inherit a small brewery in Plymouth that his father Robert and uncle had bought for £4,782 out of prize money received during the Napoleonic wars. In fact, Robert Scott senior was the first of the family to settle in Plymouth. He was of Scottish descent with an ancestry full of military service. Oatlands, the family estate, was bought in 1819 and for a while was home to three generations of Scotts (and a great aunt) until John inherited it upon his father's death.

Outlands provided a most pleasant life for the Scott family. Situated near Stoke Dameral, just outside Devonport in Devon, it boasted a stream at the bottom of the garden, three large greenhouses, peacocks on the lawn and a small staff of maids and gardeners. John had married Hannah Cuming, the daughter of William Bennett Cuming of Plymouth, in 1861. It was a highly respectable match as Hannah's father was a Lloyd's surveyor, Commissioner of Catwater Pilotage, Commissioner for the Catwater Improvement and a member of the Chamber of Commerce. The naval link between the two families (Scott's grandfather and four uncles had all served in the army or navy) was further forged when one of Hannah's brothers, Harry, became a Vice-Admiral.

Life for the Scotts was to change dramatically but during their childhood it was idyllic. John was an easy-going and patient father – despite the occasional outburst of temper – and Hannah, a woman of strong religious principles, was adored by her children. Even in adult life Robert referred to her as 'the dear mother.'

In accordance with family tradition Robert and Archie were destined for careers in the armed services. Robert was educated first in the nursery at home and then for four years at a local day school. He was also a choirboy at St Mary's Church in Ford. Nicknamed 'Con' by his family, little Robert would often go into silent flights of fancy (whether any of these daydreams involved one day being an Antarctic explorer one will never know), and despite his best efforts, concentration would often be interrupted by private thoughts. He was also shy and diffident, and according to one biographer was 'small and weakly for his age, lethargic and backward'. Not an auspicious beginning for a man who was to become a schoolboy hero.

Robert was later sent to Stubbington House School in Fareham, Hampshire, a 'cramming' establishment that prepared candidates for the entrance examinations to the naval training ship HMS *Britannia* at Dartmouth. (The first of the two HMS *Britannias* that served as naval training ships was in operation between 1859 and 1909. Scott trained on the second, which came into service in 1869). Stubbington House School was founded as a boys' preparatory school in 1841 by Reverend William and became known as 'Foster's Naval Academy'. It gained a reputation in the late nineteenth century as the 'recognised place for coaching towards a naval cadetship'. Indeed, as well as Robert Scott the academy boasted Andrew Cunningham, 1st Viscount Cunningham of Hyndhope and First Sea Lord, Lieutenant-Colonol Angus Falconer Douglas-Hamilton VC, army officer and posthumous winner of the Victoria Cross, fellow Victoria Cross winner Sir Anthony Cecil Capel Miers and, in latter years, John Sandy Woodward, naval officer and Falklands Task Force Commander as its former cadets. The school moved to Ascot in Berkshire in 1966 and eventually closed its doors on 7 July 1997. The former school site in Stubbington has been redeveloped as a community centre. The school's name has been preserved and re-registered as a limited company by one of the school's former assistant masters in the expectation of it one day being re-established as a traditional boys' prep school.

The young Scott passed his examinations in July 1883 – coming seventh out of a class of twenty-seven – and emerged from HMS *Britannia* as a midshipman, thus becoming equipped to begin his naval career as a cadet. By October he was en route to South Africa to join HMS *Boadicea*, the flagship of the Cape Squadron and the first of several ships on which he served during his midshipman years. HMS *Boadicea* was one of four ships to bear that name. The first was a 338-gun fifth-rate launched in 1779 and used for harbour service from 1854 until being broken up in 1858. Scott's *Boadicea* was a Bacchante class corvette launched in 1975 and was to be his home for two years while he served as a midshipman earning around £30 a year. It was a hard life and training under naval instructors was intense for the cadets, with beatings and extra drill as the punishment for misdemeanours. The young lads were 'up aloft' (working in the rigging 120ft above deck) in all sorts of weather and away for long hours in boats – 'under oars and sail'. There were no bathrooms and bed was a hammock. One can only imagine how this harsh regime took its toll on a sensitive boy who had known only great comfort and privilege. Robert had to grow up fast, taking his beatings like a man, learning how to obey orders without question and overcoming his weaknesses and homesickness. His reputation as a bit of a day dreamer earned him the nickname 'old mooney'.

Despite his sometimes slovenly appearance and quick-fire temper, Scott shaped up into an excellent student as he climbed the lower branches of the navy. After a brief tour with HMS *Liberty*, he served for a year on HMS *Monarch*, whose captain rated him as an 'intelligent and capable young officer of temperate habits'. At the end of 1886 Scott joined HMS *Rover* (an iron screw corvette launched on 12 August 1874 and completed in September 1875). By now Scott had moved from the Royal Artillery to the post of Aide-de-Camp and private secretary to the Governor of Lagos, Sir Gilbert Carter. The pay was better and living expenses were less. A year later he transferred to the Hausa Force, which was engaged in bringing law and order to warring tribes of the interior of the Oil Rivers Protectorate (a British Protectorate in Nigeria).

Scott was just eighteen when the Royal Navy's Training Squadron, to which HMS *Rover* belonged, was cruising in the Caribbean. A group of midshipmen decided to race four cutters across the bay at St Kitts in the West Indies, with Scott narrowly emerging the victor. A few days later he was invited aboard HMS *Active* to dine with the Commodore, Albert Markham. Present at the dinner was Albert's cousin, a middle-aged geographer named Clements Markham, secretary of the Royal Geographical Society. That meeting on 1 March 1887 would change Scott's life, for little did he know but Markham's habit was to 'collect' likely young naval officers with a view to their undertaking polar exploration work in the future. Clements was so impressed by Scott's intelligence, enthusiasm and charm that he later wrote: 'My final conclusion was that Scott was the destined man to command the Antarctic expedition.'

Scott spent nine months aboard the *Rover* before going on to spend the winter of 1887–8 at the Royal Naval College in Greenwich. In March 1888 he passed his exams for Sub-Lieutenant and was awarded four out of a possible five first-class certificates in pilotage, torpedoes and gunnery, coming in with the highest marks in his class in his year of seamanship. At the end of 1888 he was instructed to join the cruiser HMS *Amphion* stationed near Vancouver, Canada. He had to make his own way across North America with the last stage of his trip being a long journey in a tramp steamer from San Francisco to Esquimault, British Columbia. Robert Scott's career progressed smoothly, with service on various ships and promotion to Lieutenant in 1889.

After a tour of service in the Pacific, Scott briefly joined HMS *Caroline* in the Mediterranean. The summer of 1891 was spent on leave with his family at Outlands. This was a most carefree time of life for twenty-two-year-old Scott with his Lieutenant's salary of £182 10s a year providing him with financial independence. That summer was spent playing golf with his brothers and tennis with his sisters. It was to be the last blissfully happy interlude of Scott's life.

In September 1891, after a long spell in foreign waters, Scott applied for the two-year torpedo training course on the depot ship HMS *Vernon*, marking an important career move. He graduated with first-class certificates in both the theory and practical examinations.

It was in 1894, while still serving as Torpedo Officer on HMS *Vulcan*, that Scott learned of the financial disaster that had befallen his family. After selling his Hoegate Street brewery, John Scott had not invested the proceeds wisely and was now almost bankrupt. It was a major shock to Hannah and the rest of the family who believed there were funds enough for John to enjoy his retirement pottering in his greenhouses, and that interest income from the brewery sale would provide a comfortable life in their older years. In this dramatic change of lifestyle and in poor health, John was forced to swap the role of brewery owner to brewery manager at the age of sixty-three. He also had to leave his beloved home of Outlands and move his family to a £30 per year rented property, Holcombe House in Shepton Mallett in Somerset. After hearing of his family's misfortunes, Robert applied for a transfer to HMS *Defiance*, stationed at Devonport, so that he could assist in the sale of Outlands and help relocate his mother and sisters into Somerset. Once they were settled he applied for another seagoing post and was appointed torpedo lieutenant on battleship HMS *Empress of India* in the Channel Squadron.

Now destitute, the Scott family was dependant on Robert's service pay and that of his younger brother Archie, who left the army for a post in the colonial service in a bid to boost his earnings. It was a challenging time for Robert and life, instead of being sociable and full of promise, became frugal and isolating. He did not have enough money to cover his living expenses or to enjoy shore leave (partaking of a glass of wine or taking a young woman out to dinner was impossible in his financial state). Scott became distanced from his friends and colleagues who had the money to enjoy life's simple pleasures. For the first time in his life Robert discovered what poverty really was and though bowed, he did not allow himself to wallow in self-pity, more concerned that his beloved family should survive.

Grace and Katherine moved to a room over a shop in London's Chelsea and went into the conventional women's trade of the time, dress making. Rose went on to find a job at Nottingham Hospital and Ettie, thirty-two and attractive, went on to become an actress. She joined a touring company whose leading lady was Irene Vanbrugh, an acclaimed actress of the time.

John Scott died of heart disease aged sixty-six in 1897 while Robert was serving as Torpedo Lieutenant on the Channel Squadron flagship HMS *Majestic*. The death created a new family crisis. He had left them with no support of life insurance and Hannah had to leave Holcombe House and lodge with Grace and Katherine. Archie managed to contribute £200 a year to his mother to keep her afloat. This amount was nearly as much as Robert's entire salary but he still managed to send £70 a year. By this time Ettie had married an up-and-coming politician, William Ellison-Macartney, and was now one member of the family who was financially stable. Her husband was not wealthy – further burden coming with the arrival of three children – but he was a compassionate man and furthered Grace and Kate's seamstress careers by giving them a loan to study fashion in Paris. He also helped to support Hannah. Rose left her British nursing position and bravely took on one in the Gold Coast (then known as 'The White Man's Grave'). She worked hard to save money and in 1899 married Captain Eric Campbell of the Royal Irish Fusiliers, one of her brother Archie's fellow officers in the Hausa Force.

Running parallel with the upheaval in Scott's life at this time was the suggestion that he was involved in a scandal. During the research for his 1979 dual biography of Scott and rival explorer Roald Amundsen, author Roland Huntford picked up the rumour that Scott 'disappeared' from naval records for eight months from mid-August 1889 until 24 March 1890. Huntford hints at Scott's involvement with a married American woman, of a cover-up, and protection from senior officers. Huntford was never able to confirm all this. Another biographer, David Crane, said Scott's 'disappearance' was actually around eleven weeks. He too was unable to prove or disprove the speculation but did not accept the theory that senior officers offered protection to Scott as he was not important enough or so well-connected to warrant this. But mysteriously, documents that may have offered explanations are missing from Admiralty records. Around this time too there was a report that in the summer of 1893 Scott blotted his hitherto exemplary service record by running aground a torpedo boat he was commanding. It was only his previous excellent record that saved him from a severe reprimand and he instead received a mild rebuke.

That same year oceanographer Professor John Murray gave a lecture to the Royal Geographical Society urging 'an expedition to resolve the outstanding questions in the south'. Murray's plea was answered two years later when the RSG hosted the sixth International Geographical Congress. The Congress unanimously passed the resolution that:

The exploration of the Antarctic Regions is the greatest piece of geographical exploration still to be undertaken. That, in view of the additions to knowledge in almost every branch of science [that] would result from such a scientific exploration, the Congress recommends that the scientific societies throughout the world should urge, in whatever way seems to them most effective, that this work should be undertaken before the close of the century.

In the autumn of 1898 Archie came home on leave and Robert from a cruise off the Irish coast in HMS *Majestic*. Robert was extremely proud of his brother, describing him as: 'absolutely full of life and enjoyment and at the same time so keen on his job. He deserves to be a success. Commissioner, Consul and Governor is the future for him I feel.' But again, any secure life for the Scotts was short-lived. Unbeknown to him Archie had contracted typhoid fever. A little over a month after an outing with his brother he went to Hythe in Kent to play golf, became ill and died within the week. Hannah was devastated and felt fully responsible for his death believing that Archie's decision to serve in West Africa solely to earn extra money that he could send home to his family had been a fatal one – leading first to poor health and then his early death. Robert wrote to her offering reassuring words: 'Don't blame yourself for what happened, dear. Whatever we have cause to bless ourselves for, comes from you. He died like the true-hearted gentleman he was, but to you we owe the first lessons and example that made us gentlemen. This thing is most terrible to us all but is no penalty for any act of yours.'

Chapter 2
The First Steps

Now the young Scott had a tremendous financial and emotional responsibility to his family. His earlier weakness gave way to ambition and the realisation that higher income would only be earned by promotion or by taking on a new challenge. This was to come his way by a chance meeting in Buckingham Palace Road in London with Clements Markham (now Sir Clements and RGS President) early in June 1899, when Scott was home on leave from HMS *Majestic*. At that meeting, and recalling how impressed he had been during their first encounter, Markham informed Scott that there was an imminent Antarctic expedition. This had not materialised with ease and getting financial backing and support for such a venture was tortuous. In 1894 Markham had invited the Royal Society (RS) to join with the Royal Geographical Society (RGS) to finance the Antarctic project he had long dreamed about. He would later feel this was a mistake as he was essentially snubbed by the RS whose members felt the RGS was beneath them. Markham was then put off by the First Lord of the Admiralty and, worse, by the Prime Minister, Lord Salisbury, who 'regretted that he was unable, under existing circumstances, to hold out any hope of HMG [Her Majesty's Government] embarking upon an expedition of this magnitude'. Markham fought on by lobbying his friends, addressing meetings and writing to the newspapers. But all was in vain. He became furious and frustrated at the thought of other countries 'beating' him to glory. To add further insult to injury, in 1895 a wealthy British publisher, George Newnes, put up the money for Norwegian Carsten Borchgrevink's 1898 expedition – even though Markham's planned expedition was winning all the attention. Born in 1864, Borchgrevink had migrated to Australia in 1888 where he later became a teacher. In 1893 he signed on as a 'useful hand' with a Norwegian sealing and whaling expedition to the Antarctic. The crew landed on Cape Adare on 24 January 1895 – the first confirmed landing on the Antarctic continental mainland. Over the next two years the team visited Tristan da Cunha, the Prince Edward islands, Illes Crozet, Illes Kerguelen, the Balleny islands, Campbell Island and Possession Island. Borchgrevink later decided to launch a second expedition to the Antarctic and returned home to Australia to raise funds. Eventually George Newnes agreed

to finance the expedition and gave £40,000. It was no wonder the RGS was furious
– they declared that sum would have got the National Expedition 'on its legs'.
Borchgrevink bought a fifty-two-ton ship, which he renamed *Southern Cross*. It set
off from London on 23 August 1898 and although Borchgrevink's expedition
contributed greatly to knowledge of the Antarctica, he did not receive a warm
welcome back to Britain, with the general feeling of annoyance at his finance
coming from one of their own countrymen when they had had to fight so hard to
get their own backing. But Borchgrevink later went on to become a Fellow of the
RGS and was awarded the Patron's medal of the RGS. Years later the then
president had to admit: 'When the *Southern Cross* returned, this society was
engaged in fitting out Captain Scott to the same region, from which expedition
much was expected and the magnitude of the difficulties overcome by
Borchgrevink were underestimated. It was only after the work of Scott's Northern
Party on the second expedition of 1912 that we were able to realise the
improbability that any explorer could do more in the Cape Adare district that Mr
Borchgrevink had accomplished. It appeared then that justice had not been carried
out under the British flag and at the expense of a British benefactor.'

But at the time Markham was incandescent that an ordinary teacher in Australia
was securing good British money while he, with all his influence, was failing in his
mission. Finally, in 1897, the Council of the RGS pledged £8,000 – its largest
single contribution to any expedition to that date – and a further £5,000 came from
Alfred Harmsworth, later Lord Northcliffe, who had earlier financed the Jackson-
Harmsworth expedition to the Arctic, 1894–97. Markham persevered with his own
fund-raising, writing letters to wealthy people and begging their support.
Eventually RSG member Mr Llewellyn Longstaff, a paint manufacturer living in
Wimbledon, pledged £25,000. This surprisingly generous gift caught the attention
of the Prince of Wales, who had previously declined to associate himself with the
expedition 'until public feeling was manifest'. With a Royal seal of approval other
benefactors soon followed. And so this was the optimistic situation when Markham
bumped into Scott that day in London. Scott saw the expedition as the chance for
early command and to distinguish himself – together with an opportunity perhaps
to improve the fortunes of both himself and his family and to enjoy some glory too.
A few days after the meeting, on 11 June, Scott arrived at Markham's home and
volunteered to lead the expedition. Recalled Scott of the meeting: 'I espied Sir
Clements Markham and accompanied him to his house. That afternoon I learned
for the first time that there was such a thing as a prospective Antarctic Expedition;
two days later I wrote applying to command it.' As Scott later wrote in *The Voyage
of the Discovery*, 'I may as well confess that I had no predilection for polar
exploration.' This was backed up by sister Ettie who agreed Scott 'had no urge
towards snow, ice, or that kind of adventure', but had grown restless with the navy
and 'wanted freedom to develop more widely'. She said he had 'developed great

concentration, and all the years of dreaming were working up to a point'. After his meeting with Markham, Scott went back to sea and resumed his duties aboard HMS *Majestic*.

In July 1899, the government finally announced it would make a grant of £45,000 towards the proposed expedition – provided that private sources matched it with an equal amount. By that time Markham had already raised £42,000 in pledges – the rest was raised from smaller donations. The expedition also benefited from significant commercial sponsorship. Colman's provided mustard and flour, Cadbury's gave 3,500lb of chocolate, fashion house Jaeger gave a 40 per cent discount on special clothing, Bird's gave baking powers and Bovril supplied its famous beef extract. Other sponsors too made significant contributions. The total estimated £90,000 cost of the expedition may sound small today, but it was equal to nearly £7½ million at the time of the 100th anniversary of Scott's tragic second expedition in 2012.

A joint committee of the RS and the RGS was formed to plan the expedition, acquire a ship and assemble team members. The joint involvement did not work well. From the very beginning the two societies disagreed over the aim of the expedition. The RS saw it as an opportunity for extensive scientific research, while Markham and the RGS declared it an opportunity for the research and advancement in scientific knowledge specifically concerning magnetism, meteorology, biology and geology. Eventually the two main objectives of the expedition were summarised in the joint committees' 'Instructions to the Commander'. These were to 'determine, as far as possible, the nature, condition and extent of that portion of the south polar lands which is included in the scope of your expedition' and 'to make a magnetic survey in the southern regions to the south of the fortieth parallel and to carry out meteorological, oceanographic, geological, biological and physical investigations and researches'. The instructions stipulated that 'neither of these objectives was to be sacrificed to the other'. The instructions concerning the geographical objective then became more specific. 'The chief points of geographical interest are to explore the ice barrier of Sir James Ross to its eastern extremity; to discover the land [that] was believed by Ross to flank the barrier to the eastward, or to ascertain that it does not exist [...] If you should decide to winter in the ice [...] your efforts as regards geographical exploration should be directed to [...] an advance to the western mountains, an advance to the south, and an exploration of the volcanic region.'

Actually the *real* aim to Markham was twofold: geographical discovery *and* opportunities for young naval officers to win distinction in times of peace. The RS felt the expedition leader should be a scientist while Markham felt he had to be a naval officer in the regular line (and *not* in the surveying branch), and he must be young. 'These are essentials', he stressed. Markham was soon in for a serious struggle as the scientists joined forces with the 'hydrographic clique' to put forward the names of those they wanted to lead the expedition. They did not object to a naval officer commanding the ship, but they expected him to simply ferry the scientists to the ice, drop them off for their year of work and come back the following year to pick them up and bring them home. He was not expected to actually take part in the innovative project. The RS wanted eminent geologist John Walter Gregory, Director of the Scientific Staff, to take command. Although Gregory's scientific ability could not be faulted, Markham felt he was unsuitable as commander of such an expedition. Actually he was well qualified as he had not only been on safari in East Africa's Rift Valley in 1896 when it was wild, unmapped and dangerous, and was the first to lead a specifically scientific expedition to Mount Kenya where he made some key observations about the geology that still stand today, but he had scaled Alpine peaks and explored Spitzbergen within the Arctic circle too. He later became professor of geology at Melbourne University.

The joint committee began its search for an expedition leader the same month that Markham invited Scott to apply for the position. Gregory was appointed Scientific Director in February 1900, four months before Scott was named the expedition's naval commander. Markham then sent a request to the First Lord of the Admiralty for the release of two young officers, one to lead and the other to be second-in-command. He stated: 'The work involved in the stress of contest with the mighty powers of nature in the Antarctic regions calls for the very same qualities as are needed in the stress of battle. Our application is that a young commander should be allowed to take charge of its executive work [...] Youth is essential in polar service. No efficient leader of *Discovery* in icy seas has ever been over forty, the best have been nearer thirty.'

Markham offered three names: Commander John de Robeck, aged thirty-eight, an admiral in the British Royal Navy (and who later went on to command the allied naval force in the Dardanelles during the First World War); Royal Naval officer Charles William Rawson Royds, aged twenty-four; and Robert Falcon Scott, aged thirty-two. Robeck's request to the Admiralty to be released for the expedition was denied but Scott and Royds were approved for release from service on 5 April 1900. The joint RS and RGS committee met on 18 April 1900 when it was officially told by Markham that Scott and Royds were available to embark on the venture. Sir William Wharton of the joint committee and its fellow members were angry at Markham for going over their heads and assuming charge for naming leadership. Scott's appointment became a matter of controversy. Another committee was appointed at the next meeting on 4 May in a bid to settle the matter once and for all. Six members were on Markham's side and six on the side of the 'hydrographic clique', who wanted to secure a job for the survey department with 'obstinate perversity'. But at the next committee meeting on 24 May, two of the 'hydrographic clique' representatives did not turn up, which placed the majority with Markham. With Scott's appointment confirmed, the tussle was over. On 9 June 1900 Scott received his letter of appointment and two days later wrote a formal letter of acceptance to the committee. A follow-up letter arrived on the desk of the two society presidents soon after. In it, Scott stipulated his 'terms' exactly:

1. I must have complete command of the ship and landing parties. There cannot be two heads.
2. I must be consulted on all matters affecting the equipment of the landing parties.
3. The executive officers must not number less than four, exclusive of myself.
4. I must be consulted in all future appointments, both civilian and others, especially the doctor.
5. It must be understood that the doctors are first medical men, and secondly members of the scientific staff, not vice versa.
6. I am ready to insist on these conditions to the point of resignation if, in my opinion, their refusal imperils the success of the undertaking.

Scott went on leave for a few weeks and then started preparational work for the expedition by taking a course in magnetism at Deptford. Living with his two sisters and mother over the shop in Chelsea, he started his day by jogging across Hyde Park for exercise. He plunged himself into the planning of the expedition. Extraordinary details had to be worked out and even Hugh Robert Mill, then, distinguished librarian of the Royal Geographical Society, thought that Scott 'if anyone, could bring order out of the chaos [that] had overtaken the plans and preparations'.

Professor Gregory arrived in Britain from Australia in December 1900 to organise his side of the expedition. When he turned up in London he was shocked to learn of his 'number two' position on the team because as far as he had been concerned he would be the Antarctic command leader. He expected to take the expedition on the ice while Scott wintered over in Melbourne. According to Markham, instead of going to work on his scientific program, Gregory set about conspiring with the hydrographers to have Scott's leadership role overturned. But despite his best efforts Gregory was unsuccessful. In May 1901 Gregory was sent a telegram with a choice to either serve under Scott's command or resign. Gregory chose to resign – and in great disgust. Dr George Murray, head of the botanical department of the British Museum, was appointed in his place on the condition that he went only as far as Melbourne to give scientific advice and training to the other scientists and then return to his duties at the museum.

In October 1900, Scott and the Markhams went to Christiania (later to become Oslo) in Norway for discussions with Fridtjof Nansen, a scientist who had undertaken a scientific and exploratory trip to the Arctic in the *Fram*, which had served as an oceanographic-meteorological-biological laboratory and was saucer-like in design so it could be lifted above the ice floes. Ironically, Scott's rival

Amundsen later borrowed the *Fram* from Nansen and sailed it to Antarctica and across the Ross Sea. Nansen had been away for nearly three years, during which time he discovered that the Arctic region was an ocean rather than a continent. He later published six volumes of scientific observations made between 1893 and 1896.

Nansen's main advice to Scott was to do what he had done and get his dogs for the trip from Russia. Originally Scott was going to get them from Greenland as these were bigger and better, but they were hard to get as the many Arctic expeditions of the previous fifty years had denuded the supply of these dogs. In the end Scott chose twenty dogs and three bitches, which were sent to London Zoo where they were kept until they could be shipped to New Zealand. Following their meeting Scott was left greatly in awe of Nansen and wrote to his mother: 'He is a great man, absolutely straightforward and wholly practical, so our business flies along apace. I wish to goodness it would go as well in England.' The two men had obviously gelled as later Nansen paid an equally positive compliment about Scott saying: 'I see him before me, his tight, wiry figure, his intelligent, handsome face, that earnest, fixed look, and those expressive lips so seriously determined and yet ready to smile – the features of a kindly, generous character, with a fine mixture of earnestness and humour.'

Chapter 3

An Expedition in the Making

Excitement about the proposed expedition was gathering.

During the next four or five years there promises to be a renewal of the siege of the two great Polar areas, which has not had its parallel since the forties and fifties of the last century [...] our National Antarctic Expedition has been making steady progress since its commander, Captain Robert Scott, became at liberty to devote himself to the active work of preparation a few months ago [...] Many important matters with reference to scientific work and equipment have been settled, and the scientific staff is all but filled up. It would, of course, be a mistake and, indeed, useless to draw up a hard-and-fast programme as to the course of the expedition and as to the details of the methods by which its great objects are to be carried out. These objects are clearly enough laid down. In brief, they are the exploration, as far as may be practicable, of the unknown area, and the making of scientific observations and collections in all the departments of science concerned. How this work is to be accomplished can only be finally determined when the actual conditions are faced, and much must be left to the discretion and judgement of the commander who, we may be sure, will, as far as he considers it safe, give every possible facility to the scientific staff...

The Times – 22 January 1901

Even as the heated debates raged between the RS and RGS members over the expedition's leader and intent, a team was quietly being assembled.

Albert Armitage
On 28 May 1900, Lieutenant Albert 'The Pilot' Armitage was appointed to serve as second-in-command and navigator. Armitage, thirty-six, came from the Merchant Navy and had already spent many years at sea since joining the training ship HMS *Worcester* in 1887. He was still employed by P&O when he was approached by Scott and Markham, although he had previously been given leave to be navigator on the

Jackson Harmsworth Expedition to Franz Josef in 1894, where he took charge of the magnetic, meteorological and astronomical work and gained useful experience in sledge travel. This expedition's main goal was to determine if Franz Josef was part of a continent that might extend all the way to the North Pole. Armitage and seven others landed at Franz Josef Land and spent three years in a hut within the 80°N circle, shooting polar bears and doing scientific research. Franz Josef Land was simply a series of scattered islands that had been incorrectly mapped by their discoverer, Julius Payer. One day Armitage was searching the area with his field glasses when he spotted someone approaching on skis. The man was covered in oil and grease and black from head to foot. It was Fridtjof Nansen. He and a companion had left the *Fram* and her crew to make a dash for the North Pole. But they too soon discovered the impossibility of such a journey and had wintered in a tiny hut, living on bear meat in the latitude of 86°13'N, the farthest-north record until American explorer Robert Edwin Peary claimed to be the first person to reach the North Pole in April 1909. Coming across Armitage had saved the lives of Nansen and his team. For having eaten all their dogs by that time, they had dragged sledges and two kayaks across nearly 700 miles of ice in the hope of reaching Spitzbergen, where whaling vessels occasionally called. But the trip across the open seas in kayaks would have resulted in certain death. They eventually got back to more friendly climes in July 1896. On his return Armitage was presented with the Murchison Award from the RGS. Both Markham and Scott wanted their expedition to be manned entirely by members of the Royal Navy, but Sir Alfred Harmsworth, who had donated such a large sum, made the condition that Armitage be on it together with Koettlitz. In the end, Scott and Armitage got on well – though they later fell out – and Armitage was certainly ready for another challenge. He said: 'Twenty-eight years since I was entered on the books as a cadet, twenty-one of which have been, with the exception of such time as my poor person had been loaned to the polar people, in the service of the P&O. A long time to wait, to work, and strive for. Many grow weary of waiting, many grow stale and grooved by so many years of little varied routine, many sicken and die from the result of striving apparently so fruitless.'

Reginald Koettlitz

Reginald 'Cutlets' Koettlitz, thirty-nine, was also chosen for the team in 1900. He had been on the Jackson-Harmsworth expedition as the doctor. (He brought back a polar bear, which became the stuffed pride of place exhibit at Dover Museum.) Other expeditions followed: to Abyssinia, Somaliland and Brazil. Markham described Koettlitz as 'a very honest food fellow, but exceedingly short of commonsense'. (However, Koettlitz was in agreement with other notable doctors that scurvy, the plague of all polar expeditions, was caused by a poison resulting from putrefaction of preserved food. The remedy was absolutely pure food.) Born in Ostend, Koettlitz then settled in Hougham in Kent, attended Dover College and then London's Guy's Hospital before taking up a post as country doctor in Ireland.

Edward Adrian Wilson

The assistant surgeon was Edward 'Billy' Adrian Wilson, son of a Cheltenham doctor and a deeply religious man with a talent for drawing and water colours. Wilson had passed his Oxford and Cambridge exams with honours in science and went on to Gonville and Caius College in Cambridge where he read Natural Sciences and obtained a first class degree. It was while at Cambridge that Wilson encompassed the Christian faith. He studied for his Bachelor of Medicine degree at St George's Hospital Medical School in London and undertook charitable work in London's slums. When Scott met him in 1900, Wilson still had his arm in a sling from treatment for an abscess in his armpit after contracting blood poisoning while working as a junior house surgeon. Wilson had also spent two years in sanitariums in Norway and Switzerland with pulmonary tuberculosis. He was a heavy smoker, ate poorly, preferring to give his money to beggars and buy books, and spent many a cold night bird-watching, as well as working amongst the slum-dwellers. Nevertheless, Scott invited him on board. Wilson's poor health history meant he had to pass an Admiralty Medical Board. He failed twice because of disease in his right lung. But Scott told Markham he had to have Wilson who himself confessed: 'I quite realise it will be kill or cure, and have made up my mind that it will be cure.' Wilson married Oriana Souper just three weeks before setting off with Scott's team. His contributions to the expedition were enormous and he left the legacy of a collection of artwork, which today is highly prized.

Charles Royds

Charles William Rawson Royds was appointed as First Lieutenant. Born in Rochdale, Lancashire, he was a career Royal Navy officer who had become a naval cadet in 1892 and then served on several vessels. In September 1896 he had been commissioned as a sub-lieutenant and the next year was appointed to the cruiser HMS *Champion* in the training squadron. In 1898 Royds was awarded early promotion to lieutenant for his skilled command of a boat that picked up a man who had fallen overboard in the Baltic Sea. When he met up with Scott, Royds had recently returned from the West Indies on HMS *Crescent* and spent the winter of 1900 studying meteorology at the Ben Nevis Observatory. He would later find posterity when Cape Royds in the Antarctic was named after him.

Michael Barne

Michael Barne was Second Naval Lieutenant. At the time he was serving on HMS *Crescent*, flagship on the North America station. Barne was born at Sotterley Park, Suffolk, the son of Frederick Barne and his wife Lady Constance Adelaide

Seymour, daughter of Francis Seymour, 5th Marquess of Hertford. Like Scott, Barne had been educated at Stubbington School in preparation for the navy (the two served together on HMS *Majestic*) and entered the service as midshipman in 1893, being commissioned to serve aboard HMS *Porcupine* in 1898.

Reginald Skelton
Chief engineer was Reginald 'Skelly' William Skelton who had the heavily responsible job of supervising the building of *Discovery*, the ship used on the expedition. Born in Long Sutton, Lincolnshire in 1872, Skelton was educated at Bromsgrove School before joining the navy as an engineer student in 1887. He entered the RNE College, Devonport in 1891 and once commissioned served in various ships on various stations (including HMS *Centurion* from 1894 to 1897) and HMS *Majestic* with Scott, who had been impressed by Skelton's engineering abilities. Skelton was also to act as expedition photographer.

Thomas Vere Hodgson
Thomas 'Muggins' Vere Hodgson was appointed naturalist and at thirty-seven was one of the oldest members of the team. The job was initially offered to William Speirs Bruce, but he turned it down as he was organising his own Scottish National Antarctic Expedition in the *Scotia* which set off in 1902. Born in Birmingham, England, Hodgson had initially pursued his interest in marine biology and scientific study in his spare time before joining the Marine Biological Station in Plymouth and becoming director. He had worked on collections from the Southern Cross expedition. Markham described Hodgson as 'young to have a polished bald head, sometimes needing a skull cap, but otherwise apparently strong and healthy'. Cape Hodgson, the northernmost point of Black Island in the Ross Archipelago, is named after Thomas Hodgson.

Hartley Ferrar
Irish-born Hartley 'Harry' Travers Ferrar, twenty-two, raised in South Africa and recently graduated from Cambridge with an honour's degree, was the geologist. The son of a bank official, he was sent to England to be educated at Oundle School before going to Sidney Sussex College, Cambridge to study geology and natural science. An excellent sportsman, Ferrar was rowing at Henley when he received a telegram offering him the place on Scott's team in 1901. He was the youngest member of the scientific staff. Markham felt that though capable, Ferrar was 'very young, very unfledged, and rather lazy', but could be 'made into a man in this ship by the young lieutenants'.

Louis Bernacchi

The physicist on the expedition was Louis 'Bunny' Bernacchi, twenty-five, who was appointed late in the proceedings and had to join the ship in New Zealand. He had just spent two years with Borchgrevink's Southern Cross expedition and had wintered over in the hut at Cape Adare. He later published his account called *To The South Polar Regions*. Born in Belgium, Bernarcchi later moved to Maria Island in Tasmania. A great admirer of explorer Sir James Clark Ross, Bernacchi moved to Melbourne to study astronomy, magnetism and meteorology at the Observatory and then joined Kew Laboratory in London. Markham declared him 'always grown up – never a boy'. Bernacchi's childhood had been spent on a mountainous island that was uninhabited except for his family and their dependents. His father was a silk merchant from Lombardy, Italy and had bought the island from the Tasmanian Government for £20,000. Bernacchi was the only member of the expedition to have prior experience in the Antarctic.

Ernest Shackleton

Ernest Henry 'Shackle' Shackleton was taken on as third lieutenant with his particular duties listed as 'In charge of seawater analysis; ward-room caterer. In charge of stores and provisions [...] he also arranges the entertainments'. Shackleton was born in 1874 in County Kildare, Ireland, the son of a doctor and one of ten children. The family moved to London when he was ten years old and he started at Fir Lodge Preparatory School in West Hill, Dulwich before going on to Dulwich College. Despite wanting Shackleton to follow in his footsteps as a doctor, his father managed to secure him a berth with the North Western Shipping Company aboard the square-rigged sailing ship *Hoghton Tower*. (The family was not able to afford for Shackleton to undertake a naval cadetship.) In August 1894 Shackleton passed his examination for second mate and accepted a post as third officer on a tramp steamer of the Welsh Shire Line. Two years later he obtained his first mate's ticket, spent some time in the Pacific and in 1898 was certified as a Master Mariner. Shackleton joined the Union-Castle Line, the regular mail and passenger carrier between Southampton and Cape Town. His passion for reading caused one shipmate to describe him as 'a departure from our usual type of young officer'. Following the outbreak of the Boer War in 1899, Shackleton transferred to the troopship *Tintagel Castle* where, in March 1900, he met an army lieutenant, Cedric Longstaff, whose father, Llewellyn Longstaff, was the main financial backer of the National Antarctic Expedition. Shackleton asked Cedric to ask his father to set up a meeting with Albert Armitage. Armitage was impressed and recommended Shackleton to Scott and Markham, who appointed him Third Lieutenant in February 1901. For one so keen on joining such an ambitious project, Shackleton had not had an auspicious start, admitting he was not much good at school. 'I never learned much geography at school.' Shackleton was to leave the *Discovery* expedition in 1903. Some say it was through poor health, others that another man, George Mulock was wanted on board. The rift between Shackleton and Scott spurred Shackleton to mount his own expedition in *Nimrod* between 1907 and 1909. Although he carried out a scientific programme, his main aim was the one shared by Scott – to be the first man to reach the South Pole. His privately-funded expedition nearly achieved just that. But his flag was planted 100 miles away from his goal as to push on to the Pole would have meant certain death and the four-man team had to return.

George F.A. Mulock

Mulock was only twenty-one and a Sub-Lieutenant, but he had received excellent instruction as a surveyor on HMS *Triton*. His services were to prove invaluable. George Francis Arthur Mulock was born in Fleetwood, Lancashire and educated at Stanmore Park and HMS *Britannia* at Dartmouth. Mulock replaced Shackleton when he left the expedition in 1903 and was given primary responsibility for holds, stores, provisions and deep-sea water analysis. Reginald Skelton was less than impressed saying: 'Mulock is distinctly peculiar for such a youngster, a mixture of sulkiness, attempts at sarcasm, great readiness to take offence where none is meant, a little conceit.' But Scott had a very high opinion of Mulock and frequently recorded praise of him in his diaries. One entry read: 'Mulock was then only twenty-one years of age but [...] having a natural bent for his work, his services proved invaluable.'

The navy also released three warrant officers and six petty officers, including Edgar Evans and David Allan from HMS *Majestic*. The full list of the crew on this first expedition was:

Officers
Robert F. Scott, Cdr RN
Albert B. Armitage, Lieutenant RNR, Navigator and Second-in-Command C
Charles W.R. Royds, Lieutenant RN, First Lieutenant
Michael Barne, Lieutenant RN
Ernest H. Shackleton, Sub-Lieutenant MM*
George F.A. Mullock, Lieutenant RN
Reginald W. Skelton, Engineer Lieutenant RN, Chief Engineer

Scientists
Reginald Koettlitz, Surgeon and Botanist
Edward A. Wilson, Surgeon, Zoologist and Artist
Thomas V. Hodgson, Marine Biologist
Hartley T. Ferrar, Geologist
Louis C. Bernacchi, Physicist

Warrant Officer's Mess
Thomas A. Feather, Bosun PO1, RN
James H. Dellbridge, 2nd Engineer RN
Fred E. Dailey, Carpenter RN
Charles R. Ford, Chief Steward Dom 1, RN

Mess Deck

Petty Officers
Jacob Cross PO1, RN
Edgar Evans PO2, RN
William Smythe PO1, RN
David Allan PO1
William Macfarlane PO1, RN*
Gilbert Scott, Pte RMLI
A.H. Blisset, Pte, RMLI

Civilians
Charles Clarke, Ship's Cook
Clarence H. Hare, Domestic*
H.C. Buckridge, Laboratory Attendant*

Seamen
Arthur Pilbeam, LS RN
William L. Heald AB RN
James Dell AB RN
Frank Wild AB RN
Thomas S. Williamson AB RN
George B. Croucher AB RN
Ernest E.M. Joyce AB RN
Thomas Crean AB RN
Jesse Handsley AB RN
William I. Weller AB, Dog Handler
W. Peters AB RN*
J.D. Walker AB RN*
J. Duncan MN, Carpenter's Mate*
H.R. Brett MN, Cook*
Thomas Kennar, PO2, RN
George T. Vince AB RN, died at Danger Slopes March 1902
Charles Bonner AB RN (died in December 1901 as the ship left Lyttelton).

Stokers
William Lashly, Lg stoker RN
Arthur L. Quartley, Lg stoker RN
Tomas Whitfield, Lg stoker RN
Frank Plumley, Stoker RN
W. Page RN*
William Hubert M.N., Donkeyman*

*Returned on the *Morning* in March 1903.

The *Discovery*

The vessel that was to take the crew was the *Discovery*, the sixth ship to bear that name and the first to be specifically designed and built for scientific work. On 14 December 1899, a contract with the Dundee Ship Building Company was signed. The keel was laid on 16 March 1900. The *Discovery* was itself modelled on the design of a whale ship also called *Discovery* (ex *Bloodhound*) that had been on an Arctic expedition in the 1870's. Fridtjof Nansen had recommended that the ship be a duplicated design of the *Fram*. The Ship Committee of the expedition, however, decided that a conventional whaling hull would be more appropriate as the ship would have to cross the ominous Southern Seas to get to Antarctica.

Finding a yard to build the *Discovery* was not easy, as wooden hulls of that size had become rarities by 1900, the year she was put out to tender. She was almost built in Norway but it was decided that a ship for a British expedition should be built in Britain.

The ship had a massive wooden hull which was designed to withstand being frozen into the ice. The propeller and rudder could be hoisted out of the way to prevent ice damage. Iron shod bows were severely raked so that when ramming the ice they would ride up over the margin and crush the ice with deadweight. She was also, at the time, the first ship ever built in Britain specifically for a scientific expedition, and cost over half of the total budget of £92,000.

Much thought went into the creation of *Discovery*. She had to be a wooden ship (steel would buckle) and built from a variety of timbers, including a framework of English oak 11 inches thick, Riga wood – also 11 inches thick – for the lining and Honduras mahogany, all sheathed in 26 inches of solid wood. In short, the *Discovery* had to be mightily strong to withstand the pressure of the ice and her bow was particularly robust with some of the bolts 8½ inches long. The ship was 172ft long and 34ft wide, of 485 tons register and a displacement of 1,620 tons. She also had to be a sailing ship, but with auxiliary engines. She had to have room to store fuel, oil, 350 tons of coal, ample fresh water, dog food, medical supplies, scientific instruments, axes and saws, a sectional wooden hut, a piano and a library. The final cost, including engines, was £49,277. On 21 March 1901, Lady Markham cut the tape in front of the *Discovery* with a pair of golden scissors and the vessel was launched. Food for the forty-seven crew was stored aboard – and what a store it was. There were 150 tons of roast pheasant, 500 of roast turkey, whole roast partridges, jugged hare, duck and green peas, rump steak, wild cherry sauce, celery seed, blackcurrant vinegar, candied orange peel, Stilton and Double Gloucester cheese, 27 gallons of brandy, 27 gallons of whisky, sixty cases of port, thirty-six cases of sherry, twenty-eight cases of Champagne, lime juice, 1,800 pounds of tobacco, Pemmican (a concentrated mixture of fat and protein), raisins, chocolate and onion powder.

Further, as *The Times* newspaper reported: *The ship will be supplied with books of all kinds and with every sort of amusement suited to the conditions, and with every appliance that can be thought of to make life through the long Antarctic nights as endurable as possible.*

Pemmican was to become a big part of the staple diet of polar explorers. The word comes from the Cree word pimihkan, derived from the word pimi 'fat grease'. It was invented by the native peoples of North America and was adopted as a high-energy food by Europeans involved in the fur trade. The ingredients were basically whatever was available. The meat used was often bison, elk, deer or moose and fruits such as cranberries, raisins and saskatoon berries were sometimes added.

With much fanfare and a Godspeed service on board, the *Discovery* left the Dundee shipyard on 31 July 1901, paused at Spithead to correct her compasses, and then proceeded to Cowes on the Isle of Wight to receive the royal blessing from the new King and Queen – the yet uncrowned Edward VII and Alexandra – on 5 August. The next day the *Discovery* passed the Needles at the start of her journey to the wild, Antarctic territory. Markham said of the crew on board: 'Truly, they form the vanguard of England's chivalry. No finer set of men ever left these shores, nor were men ever led by a finer Captain.'

Like other ships designed for ice, before and since, the *Discovery* rolled terribly at sea. The flat, shallow hull with no protuberances that works so well in ice provides minimal stability in normal, and particularly in heavy, seas.

Scott was initially unimpressed with the ship in the English Channel, pronouncing her sluggish, short-masted and under-canvassed. By the time she had reached the *roaring forties* (the name given to the strong westerly winds in the Southern Hemisphere) these same characteristics had become virtues. She could sail through the worst gales with a considerable amount of canvas aloft in winds that would have stripped the sails from more conventional ships.

Chapter 4

The *Discovery* Expedition

New Zealand was 14,000 miles away but the *Discovery* was so heavy in the seas that she could not make more than seven knots. Her first stop was at Madeira Island and upon leaving the crew was shocked to see that their ship was leaking water into the hold and that a large food supply had been ruined. They saved whatever they could and the rest was thrown overboard. *Discovery* arrived in Cape Town on 3 October 1901. Because the going was so slow, Scott decided to cut the Melbourne leg of the journey and sail directly to Lyttelton, New Zealand. Dr Murray was left in Cape Town so that he could return to his post at the British Museum.

Undoubtedly strong, the *Discovery* was flawed in many ways during her building. Once she reached Lyttelton at the end of November, she was put into dry dock for repairs (there was no time for these in Britain before her departure). The ship's carpenter signed a damning report with such details as numerous empty bolt holes and improperly clenched bolts being uncovered. Six feet of seawater had seeped into the hold since leaving Britain. Many harsh exchanges ensued between the Dundee shipyard and the RGS headquarters in London.

Meanwhile, the hospitality offered to the men during their stop-off often lead to heavy drinking. Scott wrote: 'They disgust me, but I'm going to have it out with them somehow. There are only a few black sheep but they lend colour to the flock.' A few of the crew were discharged and replaced. But Scott was to receive some good news from Markham; the relief ship they needed to bring more supplies was on its way, courtesy of their great benefactor Llewellyn Longstaff, who had contributed £5,000. In September 1901 the *Morgene* sailed from Norway to England where she was refitted and renamed the *Morning*. Lieutenant William Colbeck, RNR, who had had Antarctic experience as magnetic observer on Borchgrevink's *Southern Cross* expedition, was appointed her commander.

Unless the unexpected happens, the Morning *should reach Lyttelton in November. There she will refit, make good defects, and fill up with coals and provisions, especially with as large a supply as possible of meat and fresh butter for the* Discovery's *people. The* Morning *will leave Lyttelton in December, and Captain*

Colbeck's previous experience of the Antarctic pack will enable him to choose the best time to advance and the best meridian along which to effect a passage. On reaching open water to the south he will proceed at once to Cape Adare. It is known from Captain Scott's reports that it is his intention to leave records at Cape Adare, Possession Island, Coulman Island, Wood Bay, Frankland Island, and Cape Crozier. Exact directions have been given by Captain Scott as to the localities where the records are to be deposited, and it will be Captain Colbeck's duty to search all these places or such as he is able to reach, in order to find those records. He will examine all the coast from Cape Adare to Cape Crozier with great care, to find the Discovery *in the event of her having wintered anywhere between these points. Of course, should he find the* Discovery *anywhere along the east coast of Victoria Land, Captain Colbeck will use his best endeavours to communicate with her, to assist in extricating her from her winter quarters, and to transfer the coals and provisions and all on board the* Morning *will then be under the command of Captain Scott.*

The Times – 2 July 1901

On 21 December 1901, *Discovery* was escorted by HMS *Ringarooma* and HMS *Lizard* out of the harbour in front of cheering crowds. And it was here that tragedy struck. A young able seaman, Charles Bonner, fell to his death from the top of the main mast where he had climbed to acknowledge the applause. He was buried at Port Chalmers two days later.

On reaching Antarctica, and after some initial explorations along the coast, *Discovery* made her way to McMurdo Sound where winter quarters were to be established. Soon after crossing the Antarctic Circle the vessel entered the ice pack. Shortly before midnight on 8 January 1902, Charles Royds sighted land and they headed for Cape Adare, where Borchgrevink's party had previously wintered. From Cape Adare they sailed along the shore of Victoria Land and eventually landed at Cape Crozier on the northeastern tip of Ross Island. Royds and Wilson climbed to 1,350ft and viewed the Great Ice Barrier stretching as far as the eye could see. From Cape Crozier they steamed along the eastern edge of the Barrier and on 30 January, after suffering a whiteout in a snowstorm, the crew reached the eastern extremity of the Barrier. Scott named the new discovery King Edward VII Land. The team then turned about and retraced their route back to McMurdo Sound to set up their winter quarters. Huts were put up to house the magnetic instruments and the dogs were moved into their kennels. It was too late in the season for any long-distance sledge trips so Scott planned a few short practice trips to test the equipment and men. The first of these was a three-day one to White Island by Wilson, Shackleton and Ferrar. They believed the island could easily be reached in a day and a half of sledging and decided to haul the sledge themselves. It was two days before they reached the island and they then became overwhelmed by a blizzard and suffered frostbite to their hands and feet. They were learning more about the unforgiving Antarctic every day as Scott recorded:

The ice was breaking up right across the strait, and with a rapidity that we had not thought possible. I have never witnessed a more impressive sight; the sun was low behind us, the surface of the ice-sheet in front was intensely white, and in contrast the distant sea and its forking leads looked almost black. The wind had fallen to a calm, and not a sound disturbed the stillness about us. Yet in the midst of this peaceful scene was an awful unseen urgency rending that great ice-sheet as though it had been naught but the thinnest paper...now without a word, without an effort on our part, it was all melting...and we knew that in an hour or two not a vestige of it would be left, and that the open sea would be lapping on the black rocks of Hut Point.

On Easter Monday one more sledging trip was made before winter came. Scott headed the twelve-strong party, which included Armitage, Wilson and Ferrar, and which had three sledges and nine dogs. The aim was to lay depots towards the south for the spring's sledging parties. It was another failure with the dogs becoming agitated and the temperatures dropping fiercely. Eventually the men took refuge in their sleeping bags with Wilson recording: 'Once in, one can do literally nothing but lie as one falls in the tent. Reindeer skin hairs get in your mouth and nose and you can't lift a hand to get them out.' After two days Scott made the decision for the men to pack up and return to *Discovery*.

On 23 April 1902, the sun sunk and the four-month winter had begun.

This winter darkness saw the men establishing a routine, trying to carry on life as much as normal in the extreme conditions. They read, played cards and chess, celebrated birthdays, carried out scientific studies and had a rota for chipping off blocks of ice around the ship, which was melted in the boiler. Time was taken out every Sunday to hold a religious service. During this time Shackleton edited his very own *South Polar Times* with the men submitting contributions.

Sledging resumed on 2 September when Scott and eight others set out to lay a depot. They were back in three days – again beaten by the merciless conditions that were the Antarctic; hardships that the men recorded in diaries, telling of their small tents just about accommodating three men, the skin on their hands literally sticking to their metal cooker, having to thaw out clothes, and of their frozen breath. Answering the call of nature was a nightmare with Bernacchi writing many years later of 'no matter how quick you were, your clothes would fill with snow and for the next few hours you would walk around with a wet, cold bottom'.

Venturing out on a trip on 17 September with Barne and Shackleton, Scott was hit by a blizzard and all three men suffered frostbite. On 2 November Scott, Wilson and Shackleton went on another sledging trip with a supporting party led by Barne. The aim was to 'get as far south in a straight line on the Barrier ice as we can, reach the Pole if possible, or find some new land'. Another blizzard, more frostbite and Shackleton was showing early signs of illness. But on 11 November photographs were taken at the 79th parallel before half of Barne's supporting party turned back. The rest pushed on until 15 November, but it was yet another unhappy trek blighted by setbacks with the men taking over the hauling when their dogs gave up. But there was one great achievement on 25 November when the party became the first ever to cross the 80th parallel, a victory prompting Scott to write: '*It has always been our ambition to get inside that white space and now we are there so the space can no longer be a blank. This compensates for a lot of trouble.*' There was more trouble to come. Food rations had to be reduced (though Christmas Day was celebrated with double rations – and a Christmas pudding Shackleton had kept for the occasion), hungry dogs fed off the body of one of their number – provoking the bitter decision to slay the weaker dogs to feed the strongest – Shackleton showed signs of scurvy, the men were desperately hungry and Wilson was forced to haul his sledge blindfolded because of snow-blindness. The men eventually reached a massive mountain that they named Mt Markham. They had travelled 300 miles further south than anyone and were less than 500 miles from the Pole.

But it was all at a price. Shackleton's deteriorating health forced them to camp out for several days from 18 January 1903. They finally reached a depot 60 miles from the *Discovery* on 28 January. The party eventually reached the ship on 3 February 1903, after covering 960 miles including relays, in ninety-three days, at a daily average of just over 10 miles. By this time, relief ship *Morning* had arrived and, following a heated discussion amongst the officers, Scott decided that Shackleton should return home on it. It was a decision Shackleton was never to forgive Scott for. Neither would Armitage.

A riotous farewell party was held on the *Morning* on 1 March 1903 and it set sail the next morning, but not before one of its crew, twenty-one-year-old Sub-Lieutenant George Mulock disembarked to take Shackleton's place.

The next trip was on 4 March when four officers and eight men – Royds as the leader (taking over from Scott who had injured his knee in a skiing accident) accompanied by Quartley, Vince, Weller, Wild, Barne, Skelton, Evans, Heald, Plumley, Koettlitz and Hare – set off with four sledges heading for the penguin rookery at Cape Crozier. It was a disastrous venture. The men suffered from frostbite, the soft snow hindered progress (one day they only made 5 miles), some of the dogs got lame and rations including sugar and cheese somehow got mixed meaning strange and unappetizing meals were cooked up. With fatigue hitting the group so early, on the fourth day Royds sent the men back to the ship and pushed ahead with Koettlitz and Skelton. The returning party did not have an easy time. Just 4 miles away from the *Discovery* they were hit by a blizzard and were forced to stop and pitch tents. It was a miserable time and getting colder by the minute, they decided once more to forge ahead with Evans, Quartley and Barne all tumbling within inches of a precipice above the sea, saved only by a mound of soft snow. They could only watch in horror as one of their dogs tumbled over the edge. Wild took charge of the remaining group at the top of the slope in a bid to get them back to the safety of the ship. But tragedy hit when Vince, who was wearing fur-soled boots with little grip, lost his footing and wandered onto a snow slope, tumbled over the cliffs and fell into the pounding sea below. He was the first man to lose his life in McMurdo Sound. His body was never recovered. The slope was later to be named 'Danger Slopes' and Vince was commemorated by a wooden cross erected by the crew. The fatal incident was recorded by Scott:

Tuesday 11 March 1903

The cold and the snow drift were now very intense, so that sitting in the tents the men were getting frostbitten at their lunch. But being, as they knew, only a few miles from the ship, rather than put on their furs and camp till the wind dropped, they decided to leave all their sledges and camping gear and get home. This was the mistake. For the blizzard was now so thick that all well known landmarks were blotted out; Vince and Hare were in finnesko, fur boots. All the others were in ski boots, leather soles. I believe Wild was the only one who had nails in his ski boots. Barne gave special orders for everyone to keep together and that no one should go off by himself. This was all right, but the unfortunate thing was that not one in the whole party knew the piece of country they were on. A landmark that was dimly seen in the snow drift was mistaken for a totally different hill and the whole party went on to a gradually increasing snow slope on the north side of this hill instead of on the south and safe side. This snow slope they got on to was a clean slip of some five or six hundred feet down to the sea, with an ice foot or precipice of 20 to 30ft. at the bottom. Only here and there on this slope was a flatter terrace of snow drift, and here and there a still steeper slip of blue ice, in one place reaching the very edge of the ice foot. It was a regular death trap in this weather and how anyone, let alone a whole party, ever escaped having once got into it, is beyond understanding. Soon after leaving the sledges the drift got so thick that no one could see more than a few yards and it was very hard to keep together. Then Hare, finding he had no hold on this hard snow slope in fur boots went back or tried to, to get his ski boots from the sledges they had left. His leaving was reported to Barne, who immediately turned to look for him. This soon proved utterly useless. No sign of him could be found nor the camping place, and there was every chance of more men going adrift. So once more they turned on to the slope that they thought led down in the direction of our winter quarters. No one as yet dreamed that the sea was anywhere near them, and the roar of the wind in such weather is such that it is only by shouting your shrillest you can make anyone hear a word, even when you are face to face. So there was no possibility of discriminating the waves' wash against the ice foot so far below. So Hare was of necessity left to shift for himself and find his own way home. Then Evans slipped and shot down out of sight. Quartley followed him in the same way, and then Barne followed to see if he could help them up. They all disappeared out of sight in a second. Wild, seeing this, determined to try and go down diagonally with the rest of the party now reduced to four, but in a few seconds they all went and all, except Vince, held up on one of these drift terraces. Vince, in fur boots, with no foot-hold whatever, shot on and disappeared over the edge. This was the first indication that any of them had that the sea was anywhere near.

After another five days and in bitter temperatures, the party led by Royds was abandoned and the three men decided to head back too.

Meanwhile, Wild, Weller, Heald and Plumley made it back and reported on the missing men. A search party headed by Wild was organised and rescued a dazed Barne, Evans and Quartley. Royds' party eventually returned too. But that left one man missing – Hare, who had last been seen making his way towards the men's abandoned sledges to retrieve his ski boots. Incredibly, he turned up two days later having fallen down and gone to sleep in a snow-covered bed.

The winter of 1903 saw more strain amongst the crew. Scott and Armitage continued their hostility, Royds wanted to return to Cape Crozier to collect penguin eggs and Armitage wanted to follow Scott's trek south across the Barrier – only in better time. Scott refused him.

The sun reappeared on 21 August 1903 and two sledging trips with supporting parties were planned to lay depots. The first, comprising six men and led by Royds and Wilson, set off for Cape Crozier on 7 September and returned some time later without too much mishap, apart from the routine rigours of frostbite. The second, led by Scott with Skelton and four other men, set off on 9 September. It was another miserable venture, with the team at one point having to trek back nearly 90 miles to their ship for repairs to their sledges before ploughing on yet again. Before this trek, Scott had written of the discomfort the cold was causing:

Tuesday 2 September 1903

Wind and drift again this morning and the temperature hovering about zero…It was a beastly day to start, everything full of drift snow, a very biting wind and every promise of a lot more of both…It was not very long before we had the dogs fixed up for the night, and the tents pitched and I as cook got the lamp going and the cooker full of hot pemmican. After that we had some cocoa and then out all cooking apparatus and in with the three man reinskin sleeping bag, change socks and finnesko (reinskin fur boots) and snuggle down in the bag to shiver for an hour or two, when all your clothes begin to thaw out and you get wetter and wetter and gradually warmer and warmer, and you doze off to wake at fitful intervals to wonder whether you have been to sleep or not. The strangest thing about sleeping in this cold in a tent is that one sleeps a good deal, but one can never say whether one has been asleep or not. One never stops thinking, but one gets far away from all thoughts of cold and discomfort, tents and sledging, till a fall of hoar frost rime off the tent drops on some part of one's face, which has got accidentally uncovered in one's dreamy desire for a little fresh air outside the bag. One doesn't take long to realise where one is and then begins another period of shivering till one drops asleep again...

They reached the summit on 14 November and Scott wrote: 'I don't know where we are but I know we must be a long way to the west. As long as I live, I never want to revisit the summit of Victoria Land.' The party turned back on 1 December but got lost two weeks later, eventually returning to the *Discovery* on Christmas Eve.

The *Morning* returned in January 1904, this time accompanied by another ship the *Terra Nova*. After long and heated debates with Sir Clements Markham, the British government had decided that the Antarctic party had been away long enough and that their expedition was proving costly – having been relieved once a year by a hugely expensive relief ship – and wanted them all brought back whether or not the *Discovery* had to be abandoned in the process (the *Morning* had reported the previous year that the *Discovery* was still frozen in and could only be removed with great difficulty). It took the combined efforts of the two relief ships and the use of explosives to free *Discovery* from the ice.

Scott decided to take the Discovery *around Cape Adare and explore to the west along the northern coast of Victoria Land. The* Morning *was to head straight for the Auckland Islands where the three ships would rendezvous and sail together to Lyttelton. After two years in the ice, the* Discovery *was far from seaworthy; water poured into the holds, the pumps wouldn't work, gales came up and subsequently everyone got seasick since they'd been landlocked for so long. The rudder was in such poor shape that it was ready to fall off; they had a spare but it was only half as big. The farther west they went, the thicker the ice became. Becoming short of coal, the ship turned north to find open water so they could use the sails. By this time she had lost touch with the* Terra Nova. *She was pushed so far north that she missed land altogether and instead rediscovered the Balleny Islands. On March 14 they reached the Auckland Islands with only 10 tons of coal left aboard. Neither of the other ships were there so while they waited, some of the crew cleaned and painted the ship while others went ashore and shot anything that looked edible, including wild cattle and pigs. The New Zealand Government maintained a depot of emergency supplies for the use of shipwrecked sailors (called by sealers* Sarah's Bosom*). The other* *vessels showed up a few days later and after three days sailing, on Good Friday, April 1, 1904, they reached Lyttelton Harbour.*

The Times – 19 February 1904

The home-coming was marred when a newspaper reporter claimed to have overheard Scott criticising the decision to send the *Terra Nova* to bring them back. The report, by Reuter's news agency stated:

Commander Scott emphatically protests against the dispatch by the Admiralty of the Terra Nova, *which he declared to have been a wasteful expense of money. He says that had the proper position of the* Discovery *been made known, it would have been obvious that she was perfectly safe, and no assistance beyond that which the* Morning *could render was requisite.*

Did Scott really make such a remark? Commented Royds: 'Although it was the truth, he never said it…'

Back home matters for Scott weren't much better. Together with his brother-in-law he was still supporting his mother. His two sisters were having a difficult time in the dressmaking industry, as his mother wrote: 'It is really a bad season, and no money going.' Scott felt if he was not promoted a life of poverty would return, airing his fears to his mother: 'If they wait till we get home, then two or three persons will inevitably leap over my head. The question is whether they will pass me over in June. It is such a close thing that it must make a great deal of difference.'

Meanwhile, the *Discovery* was in need of repairs and yet money was so tight that Scott only paid the regular crew members while the officers were left to fend for themselves.

The *Discovery* finally returned to Britain on 16 September 1904, with the team being hailed as heroes – especially Scott. Markham declared: 'Never has any polar expedition returned with so great a harvest of scientific results.' Loyal Wilson wrote: 'Without a doubt he Scott has been the making of the expedition and not one of us will feel more and more grateful to him for the way he has acted throughout. Notwithstanding that it is a difficult thing, at least I imagine it is, for the Captain to make intimate friends with anyone, I feel as though we were real friends and I need hardly say I am proud of it.' But Scott was determined his team should win acclaim too, stating: 'An Antarctic expedition is not a one-man show, not a two-man show, nor a ten-man show. It means the co-operation of all […] There has been nothing but a common desire to work for the common good.'

Scott was promoted to the rank of Captain and received many honours, including the Officer of the Legion of Honour. But he was most proud to receive an honorary degree of Doctor of Science from Cambridge University

On 4 November 1904, an expedition exhibition at London's Bruton Galleries attracted around 10,000 people who were enthralled by the drawings, photographs, equipment used and the model of the *Discovery*. Items collected by the scientists went to the Museum of Natural History and their data to the Royal Society. Scott gave a lecture on his adventure on 7 November at the Albert Hall in front of a selected audience of 7,000. More lectures in Scotland followed and Scott was joined by Shackleton on tour after the two men put their differences behind them. Scott's book *Voyage of the Discovery* was published on 2 October 1905, and was described by the *Times Literary Supplement* as 'a masterly work'.

With public praise being heaped upon him and now often mixing in Royal circles, Scott returned to a full-time naval career in January 1906, first as assistant to the Director of Naval Intelligence at the Admiralty and then as Flag-Captain to Rear-Admiral Sir George Egerton on HMS *Victorious*. Both were welcome promotions, not just for the kudos but for the financial reward as Scott was still supporting his mother.

The *Discovery* went into dry docks for two months for a complete overhaul. Markham pleaded with the government to retain her for future polar work but was refused. She was sold to the highest bidder, the Hudson's Bay Company, for £10,000 – about one-fourth of her original cost.

A few months' after the *Discovery's* return, Sir Clements Markham, then aged seventy-five, announced his retirement as RGS president after twelve years in the post – the longest-serving president on record. Markham said he felt his 'active geographical life had closed' and that he 'could do no more in that particular direction'. He kept the member position of vice-President. He also, of course, kept a keen interest in exploration of the Antarctic.

The expedition scientists all went their separate ways and the servicemen returned to their posts. Some of the men got engaged and married.

But it would not be long before Scott's wanderlust for the Antarctic took hold of him again.

Antarctica

Antarctica is an enormous continent. Britain could fit into it more than fifty times. More than ninety-nine per cent of it is covered by ice, which in some places is more than 3 miles thick. Antarctica is completely surrounded by the vast Southern Ocean, half of which freezes in winter. It is high, windy and extremely cold. There is no indigenous human population and no life forms at all except around the coast.

The area was first described more than 2,000 years ago when Greek writers wrote of a large mass of land in the south of the world. Even though they had never seen it they believed it must exist so that it could 'balance' the land they knew about in the northern half of the world. They named this imagined land 'Anti-Arkitos', meaning the 'opposite of the Arctic'.

In 1769 Captain James Cook was officially sent by the Royal Navy to Tahiti to observe the transit of Venus across the face of the sun. But his real mission was to discover this fabled southern continent. This first attempt was not a success. For two years from 1772 he made another expedition, venturing even further south in HMS *Resolution* and HMS *Adventure*. This time Cook managed to cross the Antarctic Circle but was forced back by pack ice. Cook decided that people would probably never travel further south than latitude 71°, the position he reached. This was still more than 1,000 miles from the Pole.

Until the end of the nineteenth century, only sealers and whalers had set foot on the desolate terrain and it was the last unexplored continent on earth. In 1819 a British merchant ship, the *Williams*, blown off course round Cape Horn, stumbled on the South Shetland Islands. Another trip was made in the *Williams* by Edward Bransfield in 1820. Bransfield landed briefly on the Graham Land peninsula, making the first landing on the Antarctic Continent.

In the early years of the twentieth century, rich Western nations began to take an interest with Britain, Japan, Germany, Sweden, Norway, France and Belgium all planning expeditions

Captain Robert Falcon Scott was the first person to explore Antarctica extensively by land.

Chapter 5
Plans to Conquer the South Pole

THE SOUTH POLE EXPEDITION

At a meeting of the Royal Institution last night Captain R.F. Scott described the plans for his forthcoming expedition to South Polar regions. Captain Scott warned those who were interested in the subject that circumstances might upset some, if not all, his calculations and cause the results of the expedition to be very different from those which he proposed to foreshadow. He had arranged for a scientific staff larger than that carried by any preceding expedition and for the carriage of a very extensive outfit of scientific instruments. The Terra Nova *would leave London on June 1 and sail to Portsmouth for the adjustment of her compasses and thence to Cardiff to complete her cargo of coal. She would go from Cardiff on June 15 and, after a call at Madena, would reach Cape Town about August 1. After a week's stay there she would sail for Melbourne, reaching that port about September 13 and would afterwards call at Sydney and Lyttelton, New Zealand, where she was due to arrive about October 13. A few stores [that] had not been shipped at London, such as petrol for the motor sledges, would be taken on board at Lyttelton, as well as the 20 ponies and 30 dogs [that] Mr Meares was shipping from Vladivostok. Hitherto Antarctic expeditions had sailed to the South in the latter part of December, but with a large ship like the* Terra Nova *it was hoped to penetrate the pack ice at an earlier date than it had been possible for previous expeditions to do that, and accordingly they would leave New Zealand towards the end of November, and probably reach McMurdo Sound about the end of December. Immediately on arrival in McMurdo Sound the hut, provisions, and equipment of the western part would be landed. The party would consist of from 22 to 25 persons, and as soon as the winter station had been thoroughly established, the greater number of these would proceed to the south to lay depots. He hoped that it would be possible to start this party off not later than the third week in January, when 60 or 70 days would remain for travelling [...]*

The Times – 28 May 1910

It was early in 1906 that Scott approached the RGS about the funding of a second Antarctic expedition. The RGS wanted this expedition to be 'scientific primarily, with exploration and the Pole as secondary objects', but Scott had his own ideas. And this time he was in charge. Then he heard some devastating news – Ernest Shackleton, the man with whom he had a tenuous friendship, had announced his own plans to make the trek to the *Discovery's* old McMurdo Sound base and make a bid to the South Pole. Scott felt the need to claim the area as his own – telling Shackleton in one letter that it was his own field of work and that he had the rights to it. He went further by telling Shackleton to undertake his scientific work somewhere else. Shackleton finally agreed to avoid the first expedition's old hunting ground – but unable to find suitable alternative landing grounds had to base himself at Camp Royds with his *Nimrod* expedition team and accompanying horses. In the end Shackleton returned, having narrowly failed to reach the Pole. He crossed the Great Ice Barrier and discovered the Beardmore Glacier route to the Polar Plateau but had been forced to turn back 100 miles from his goal. Relationships between the two men were severely strained and in April 1906 Scott petulantly announced to the RSG that 'in all probability I shall not return to those regions'. By the end of that month he had changed his mind confirming Markham's remark that he had been 'bitten by the Pole mania'.

By the beginning of 1907 Scott was making plans for his new Antarctic expedition – despite meeting the woman who would become his wife. Sculptor Kathleen Bruce was one of the many socialites Scott was now mixing with, his new-found public acclaim opening the doors to Edwardian society. He first met Kathleen, the youngest of eleven children of Canon Lloyd Stuart Bruce and Jane Skene, at a lunch party. Kathleen had attended the Slade School of Fine Art and then the Academie Colarossi in Paris where she studied under Auguste Rodin. She also included dancer Isadora Duncan and artist Picasso in her social circle. Scott and Kathleen's paths crossed a few months later and after seeing off Kathleen's other suitor, novelist Gilbert Cannan, Scott finally married her at the Chapel Royal, Hampton Court Palace, on 2 September 1908. Their only child, Peter Markham Scott was born on 14 September 1909. None of this was to halt Scott's determination to reach the South Pole and to 'secure for the British Empire the honour of this achievement'. It was, of course, to go fatally wrong.

Scott took up the London-based post of Naval Assistant to the Second Sea Lord on 24 March 1909, but he was not to remain there for long. By December that year he was released on half pay to take over command of the 1910 British Antarctic expedition – later to be known as the *Terra Nova* expedition after its ship. Despite Scott's initial approach to the RGS, this expedition was eventually organised as a private venture at a cost of around £40,000 – equal, on the 100th anniversary of the trek, years on, to more than £2m. Half of this was raised by a government grant and the rest made up from public subscriptions and loans.

In all, sixty-five men were chosen from more than 8,000 applicants. Amongst the team were six men who had been on the *Discovery* and five who had accompanied Ernest Shackleton on his trek. The crew was divided between 'officers', 'scientific staff', and 'men'. Five of the shore party's seven officers came from the Royal Navy. The *Terra Nova*'s Second-in-Command was an ambitious young lieutenant, Edward (Teddy) Evans, who was persuaded by Clements Markham to abandon his own Antarctic plans and join forces with Scott. Evans was joined by Lieutenant Victor Campbell and two Royal Naval surgeons, George Murray Levick and Edward Atkinson. Twelve of the shore party were either serving or had served in the Royal Navy, including petty officers Thomas Crean, Edgar Evans and Thomas Soulsby Williamson who had been with Scott on the *Discovery*, and petty officers Frank Browning, Robert Forde and Patrick Keohane who had served under Teddy Evans on HMS *Talbot*. This strong Royal Naval contingent was in contrast to the largely civilian crews of the *Nimrod*, the later *Endurance* expedition of 1914–17 and Antarctic expeditions organised by Shackleton on the *Discovery*. Scott had been stung by criticisms of the *Discovery's* scientific results, and so appointed seven professional scientists with academic qualifications. The staff were led by Scott's old friend from the *Discovery*, Edward Wilson, who was joined by biologist Edward William, meteorologist George Simpson and geologist Raymond Priestley. This team was completed by Canadian physicist Charles Seymour Wright and geologists Frank Debenham and Thomas Griffith Taylor, both graduates of the University of Sydney. Scott felt that these last three recruits would emphasise the expedition's 'imperial' character.

The scientists and naval seamen in the shore party were joined by Cecil Henry Meares in charge of the dogs, who in turn recruited Russian dog-driver Demetri Gerof, groom Anton Omelchenko and photographer Herbert Ponting. Scott appointed two more officers, Lieutenant Henry Bowers and old Etonian Captain Lawrence Oates. Oxford graduate Apsley Cherry-Garrard offered £1,000 to join the expedition but Scott initially turned him down. However, he was so impressed when the young landowner donated the money in spite of his rejection, he signed him up as assistant zoologist. The shore party was completed by Norwegian ski expert Tryggve Gran – recommended by Fridtjof Nansen – and mechanic Bernard Day.

Among the serving Royal Navy personnel released by the Admiralty was Lieutenant Harry Pennell, who would serve as navigator and take command of the ship once the shore parties had landed.

Cecil Meares

Cecil H. Meares was responsible for buying the thirty-four expedition dogs and twenty ponies from Siberia. He was also chief dog handler and Russian interpreter. The animals were transported from Siberia via Japan to New Zealand. Meares travelled first to Nikolayevsk, Siberia to choose the dogs and met up with experienced dog driver Dimitri Gerof who helped with his selection (and was subsequently invited to join the expedition). Meares also recruited Russian jockey Anton Omelchenko as a groom. The ponies were chosen from Vladivostok. Scott specifically requested white ponies as these had lived longer than darker ponies on Shackleton's *Nimrod* expedition. Meares was born in 1877 in County Kilkenny, Ireland, the son of an army officer, and had lead a colourful life before coming across Scott – including being a British military officer, fur trader and seeing action in the Russo-Japanese War and Boer War.

Edward Evans

Lieutenant Edward Ratcliffe Garth Russell 'Teddy' Evans, who had been the Navigating Officer on relief vessel *Morning* during the *Discovery* operation in 1904, was Scott's Second-in-Command. He was initially in charge of Scott's motor-sledge party. Born in London in 1881, the son of a barrister, Evans' early start did not look promising. He had been expelled from Merchant Taylor's School for truancy but managed to secure a place on the Mercantile training ship HMS *Worcester* and obtain a naval cadetship in 1896. Evans attended the Royal Naval College for two years from 1900, was promoted first to Acting Sub-Lieutenant and then Lieutenant before serving as second officer on the *Morning*. Evans found himself on Scott's expedition by default – being offered the position to dissuade him from embarking on his own expedition to explore King Edward V11 Land. Scott would forever view Evans as a something of a rival.

Henry Bowers

Henry Robertson 'Birdie' Bowers was appointed storekeeper in March 1910. He had been introduced to Scott by Markham. Birdie (so nicknamed because of his beaky nose) was born in 1883 at Greenock, Scotland. He had entered HMS *Worcester* as a cadet and went on to serve on a sailing barque to Australia. Bowers was later appointed Sub-Lieutenant in the Royal Indian Marines, serving in Burma and Ceylon.

Wilfred Bruce

Kathleen Scott's thirty-six-year-old brother and another Worcester Cadet. He was instructed to go to Vladivostok and meet with Cecil Meares.

Lawrence Edward Grace Oates

Lawrence 'Titus' Oates won special sanction from the War Office to join the expedition and was taken on to be in charge of the ponies. He heard about Scott's plans and volunteered to take part, taking leave to attend the expedition interview. He also contributed a large sum towards the tragic journey – £1,000, equal to around £50,000 100 years later. Oates was born in Putney, London in 1880, the son of William and Caroline Oates. His uncle was the naturalist and African explorer Frank Oates. Oates was educated at South Lynn School, Eastbourne and Eton College. In 1898 he joined the 3rd West Yorkshire (Militia) Regiment and then served as a junior officer with the 6th Inniskilling Dragoons, being promoted first to Lieutenant in 1902 and then Captain in 1906. Oates had served during the Second Boer War during which he suffered a gunshot wound to his left thigh that left it shattered and the leg one inch shorter than his other. Oates got his the nickname 'Titus Oates' after the historical figure, an Anglican minister, who was imprisoned after announcing a Catholic plot to kill Charles II and replace him with his Roman Catholic brother James.

Edward Atkinson
Edward Leicester 'Naitch' Atkinson was taken on as surgeon, parasitologist and bacteriologist (he later took on command at Cape Evans). Leicester was born in the Windward Islands in 1882 before going to London and attending Forest School in Snaresbrook. He then went on to St Thomas's Hospital in London and qualified in 1906. (He also became the hospital's heavyweight boxing champion.) Atkinson had also had a paper published on gonorrheal rheumatism. He was on the staff of the Royal Naval Hospital *Haslar* in Gosport, Hampshire when he was appointed to the *Terra Nova* team.

Edward Wilson
Dr Edward Adrian 'Billy' Wilson was Scott's choice as Chief of Scientific Staff and zoologist. He was also a veteran of the *Discovery* expedition. (See earlier listing.) Born in Cheltenham in 1872, the son of a doctor, Wilson had become fascinated with nature and drawing and studied natural sciences at Cambridge. He then studied medicine but in 1898 discovered he had tuberculosis. He recovered and volunteered to join the *Discovery*. He became a close friend and confidante of Scott's, refusing to join Shackleton's *Nimrod* expedition out of loyalty.

George Simpson
George Clarke 'Sunny Jim' Simpson, meteorologist. He had visited Lapland in 1902 to investigate atmospheric electricity and in 1905 joined Manchester University as the first person to lecture in meteorology. He joined the Indian Meteorological Service as an Imperial Meteorological Service at their HQ in Simla and inspected stations in India and Burma. Simpson was born in Derby in 1878, the son of a department store proprietor. He was educated at Derby School (where his homosexuality made him a target of bullies), Owens College, Manchester and the University of Gottingen. Another *Discovery* veteran.

Thomas Taylor

Thomas Griffith 'Griff' Taylor, senior geologist, was working as a physiographer at the Australian Weather Service when he joined Scott. He was born in Walthamstow, London, in 1880 and was the son of a metallurgical chemist. The family moved to Serbia where his father was manager of a copper mine, and then returned to England where Taylor senior became director of analytical chemistry for a major steelworks company. The family emigrated again, this time to New South Wales, and Thomas attended The King's School in Sydney. In 1899 he enrolled in arts at the University of Sydney, later transferring to science and achieving his Bachelor of Science in 1904 and Bachelor of Engineering in 1905. Two years later he was awarded a scholarship to Emmanuel College, Cambridge where a mutual passion for the Antarctic led to a friendship with Raymond Priestley, Canadian explorer Charles Wright and Australian Frank Debenham. Taylor was elected a fellow of the Geographical Society.

Edward Nelson

Edward William 'Marie' Nelson joined the expedition as biologist. Educated at Clifton, Tonbridge and Cambridge, Nelson was working at the Plymouth Marine Laboratory when he was recruited. There, together with fellow biologist J. Allen, he developed a simple method for culturing phytoplankton.

Frank Debenham

Frank 'Deb' Debenham was one of the three geologists. He was born in Bowral, New South Wales, Australia in 1883, the son (one of twins) of Rev John William Debenham. He attended his father's school and then went on to The King's School, Parramatta, where he excelled both academically and as a sportsman. Debenham graduated from the University of Sydney with a BA in English and philosophy. He then joined the staff at the Anglican Armidale School in New South Wales before returning to his studies – geology under Sir Edgeworth David. He was also Emeritus Professor of Geography at Cambridge University and was to become the first director of the Scott Polar Research Institute.

George Wright

George Seymour 'Silas' Wright, physicist. Born in Toronto in 1887, Wright was educated at Upper Canada College. He was an undergraduate at Gonville and Caius College, Cambridge and did research at the Cavendish Laboratory between 1908 and 1910. After a distinguished career in World War I, during which he gained the Military Cross and OBE, he became Director of the Admiralty Research Laboratory and then Director of Scientific Research there. His nickname came from the American novelist Silas K. Hocking.

Apsley Cherry-Garrard
Apsley George Benet Cherry-Garrard, assistant zoologist, and at twenty-four one of the team's youngest members. He had no scientific training but had been introduced to Scott by Edward Wilson who considered him his protégé. Cherry-Garrard also contributed £1,000 towards the trip – an offer he still stuck by even when Scott initially turned him down for the expedition. Cherry-Garrard could well afford the generous offer. He was born in Bedford, Hertfordshire in 1886, the son of Major General Apsley Cherry of Lamer Park, Hertfordshire and Denford Park, Berkshire, and High Sherriff of Hertfordshire. Garrard's surname was changed from Cherry to Cherry-Garrard under the terms of an aunt's will through which his father inherited enormous estates near Wheathampstead, Herfordshire. Cherry-Garrard was educated at Winchester College and Christ Church, Oxford, and had always been looking for a venture that would equal his father's achievements. Scott's biographer David Crane would later describe Cherry-Garrard as 'the future interpreter, historian and conscience of the expedition'.

Herbert Ponting
Herbert George 'Ponco' Ponting, expedition photographer. He had already made his mark in this profession, covering the Russo-Japanese war of 1904–5 after which he travelled around Asia photographing Burma, Korea, Java, China and India. Ponting compiled his photographs of Japan into a 1910 book, *In Lotus-land Japan*. He sold his pictures to some of London's most highly-regarded periodicals including the *Illustrated London News* and *Strand Magazine*. Born in 1879 in Salisbury, Wiltshire, Ponting moved to California lured by tales of the American West. He took up freelance photography after a fruit farm he took on failed. His natural flair for telling a story in a single picture led to his recruitment on the *Terra Nova* – the first professional photographer ever to go on an Antarctic expedition. He was elected a Fellow of the RGS (FRGS).

Tryggve Gran
Gran was introduced to Scott by Fridtjof Nansen while he was testing a motor tractor in Norway. He was recruited as ski instructor after impressing Scott with his skiing techniques and was one of the most-travelled members. Gran was born into an affluent ship-building family in Bergen, Norway in 1889. He was educated in Switzerland and served as a member of the Nygaards Battalion, one of Bergen's Buekorps. (Buekorps – literally Bow Corps or Archery Brigade are traditional marching neighbourhood youth organisations peculiar to Bergen. The tradition dates back to the nineteenth century when children would imitate the adult militia soldiers performing close order drill.)

It was his meeting with family friend German Emperor William II, that encouraged him to be a naval officer and he entered naval college in 1907, graduating in 1910. Arriving in Antarctica in early January 1911, Gran was one of the thirteen expedition members involved in the laying of the supply depots needed for the attempt to reach the South Pole later that year.

George Levick

George Murray Levick was appointed as surgeon. He was to serve with the northern party under Victor Campbell, spending the first year at Cape Adare and the second exploring and sledging along the Victoria Land coast. The party wintered for seven months in a snow cave on Inexpressible Island without adequate supplies before returning safely to the base at Cape Evans. While at Cape Adare he studied the behaviour and breeding biology of Adélie penguins, which became the material for a scientific report and popular book on their natural history. Levick was born in 1877 and studied medicine at St Bartholomew's Hospital, London. He qualified in 1902 and joined the Royal Navy where he became a specialist in physical and recreational training.

Raymond Priestley

Raymond Edward Priestley was one of the geologists and wintered at Cape Adare and Inexpressible Island. He was in the second year of his studies when he was taken on as a member of the *Nimrod* team with Shackleton, during which he worked closely with renowned geologists Sir Edgeworth David and Douglas Mawson Priestley was born in Tewkesbury, Gloucestershire, in 1886, the second of eight children of Joseph Priestley, headmaster of Tewkesbury Grammar School. He was educated at his father's school and taught there for a year before reading geology at University College, Bristol.

Bernard Day

Bernard C. Day was to take charge of the motor sledges. Born in Wymondham, Leicestershire, in 1884, he was employed by the New Arrol Motor Car Company before joining Shackleton's *Nimrod* expedition.

William Lashly

Lashly was serving as an instructor at the Royal Naval College, Osborne on the Isle of Wight when he was recruited as Chief Stoker. He had also accompanied Scott on the *Discovery* expedition, an involvement which had him described by Reginald Skelton as 'the best man far and away in the ship', recruited from his job as leading stoker in the Royal Navy on the HMS *Duke of Wellington*. Lashly, a non-smoker and teetotaller, was born in 1867 in Hambledon, Hampshire, the son of a farm worker.

Harry Pennell
Harry Lewin Lee Pennell, Lieutenant and Commander of the expedition. Born in 1882 and educated at Exeter School, he joined the Navy as a cadet on HMS *Britannia* in 1898. The following year he went to sea as a midshipman and by 1903 had been promoted to Lieutenant. In addition to his duties as navigator, Pennell was responsible for conducting magnetic observations and as an amateur naturalist, he also assisted Edward Wilson and Dennis Lillie in their studies of birds and whales. On 22 February 1911, Pennell made the first sighting of Oates Land, named after Captain Lawrence Oates.

Edgar Evans
Edgar 'Taff' Evans was Petty Officer, veteran of the *Discovery* expedition. Born in Rhossili, Wales in 1876, he had joined the Royal Navy in 1891.

Robert Forde
Petty Officer and Sledge Officer in the second western party led by Griffith-Taylor. Born in Moviddy, near Cork, Ireland in 1875, Forde had joined the Royal Navy at sixteen, rising to the rank of Petty Officer First Class. Forde was part of a group that headed out from Cape Evans in January 1911 to explore the polar capes and took part in two depot-laying journeys. He suffered severe frostbite during the expedition and was eventually ordered back by Captain Scott for medical treatment.

Thomas Crean
Petty Officer Crean joined the *Terra Nova* from HMS *Bulward*. Another veteran of the *Discovery* expedition, Crean was born on a family farm in Annascaul, County Kerry, Ireland in 1877 but left to join the Royal Navy in England aged fifteen. It was while serving on HMS *Ringarooma* in New Zealand that he volunteered for the *Discovery*. Crean's *Terra Nova* feat of making a 35-mile walk on his own across the Ross Ice Shelf to save the life of Edward Evans led to him receiving the Albert Medal.

Patrick Keohane
Petty Officer Keohane joined the *Terra Nova* from HMS *Repulse*. He had also served on HMS *Talbot* with Edward Evans. He was a member of Scott's supporting party back from the head of the Beardmore Glacier in December 1911. He would also become a member of the search party that found the bodies of Scott, Wilson and Bowers. Born in Courtmacsherry, County Cork, Ireland in 1879, he joined the Royal Navy and rose to the rank of Petty Officer.

Frederick Hooper
Frederick J. Hooper, born 1891, joined *Terra Nova* as a steward but was transferred to the shore party. He was also a member of the search party that discovered Scott, Wilson and Bowers.

Thomas Williamson

Thomas Soulsby Williamson was another Petty Officer who had been with Scott on the *Discovery*, joining while serving on the HMS *Pactoius*. He was born in 1877 in Sunderland.

Anton Omelchenko

Anton Lukich Omelchenko was the expedition's groom. He met Scott through his agent Wilfred Bruce and was involved in purchasing ponies for the trek. Born in 1883 at Bat'ki, Russia, Omelchenko was the seventh son of a poor farmer and worked from the age of ten, acquiring much experience at handling horses.

Demetri Gerof

An experienced dog-driver, Demetri Semenovich Gerof was recommended to Meares to help buy the thirty sledge dogs for the trip. Gerof was born Girev in 1888 in Sakhalin, Eastern Siberia.

Victor Campbell

Victor Lindsay Arbuthnot – known as 'The Wicket Mate' – was First Officer on the *Terra Nova* and leader of the eastern party that left Cape Evans in January 1911 to help set up base in King Edward VII Land. Born in 1875 in Brighton, Sussex, the son of Hugh Campbell.

George Abbott

G P Abbott joined *Terra Nova* from HMS *Talbot*. He wintered at Cape Adare and Inexpressible Island.

Harry Dickason

Harry Dickason joined the *Terra Nova* from HMS *Defiance* and wintered at Cape Adare and Inexpressible Island.

Frank Browning

Frank Browning joined the *Terra Nova* from HMS *Talbot*. He wintered at Cape Adare and Inexpressible Island. Browning was born in Devonshire in 1882.

Thomas Clissold

Cook. Joined *Terra Nova* from HMS *Harrier*.

A month after setting off, ship's commander Wilfred Bruce made a list of all those on the trip, with their occupations and their destination on the voyage – with 'S' meaning 'ship' or 'shore' (the latter divided into 'E' (Eastern), 'W' (Western) and 'Far W' for those who would be going west to carry out geology surveys in Victoria Land.

The Crew of the 1910 British Antarctic Expedition

Wardroom
Officers
Robert Falcon Scott, Captain, RN CVO; Leader – W
Edward R.G.R. Evans, Lieutenant, RN; Captain – W
Harry L.L. Pennell, RN; Navigator – Ship – W
Henry Robertson Bowers, Lieutenant, RIM; Watchkeeper – S
Wilfred Bruce, Commander, RNR
Rennick, Henry – Lieutenant, RN
Victor Campbell, Lieutenant, RN; No 1 – E

Scientists
Edward Adrian Wilson, BA, MB (Cantab), Chief of Scientific Staff and Zoologist
George C. Simpson, DSc, Meteorologist – W
Thomas Griffith Taylor, BA, BSc, BE, FGS Senior Geologist – Far W
Edward W. Nelson, Biologist – W
Frank Debenham, BA, BSc, Geologist – Far W
Charles Seymour Wright, BA, Physicist – Far W
Apsley G.B. Cherry-Garrard, BA, Assistant Zoologist – W
Dennis G. Lillie, Biologist – S
Raymond Edward Priestley, BA, Geologist – E

Surgeons
George Levick E – E
Edward L. Atkinson, Surgeon, RN, Parasitologist – W

Others
Lawrence Oates, Captain 6th Iniskilling Dragoons; In Charge of Ponies – W
Herbert G. Ponting, FRGS, Camera Artist – W
Cecil H. Meares, In Charge of Dogs – W
Anton L. Omelchenko, Groom – W
Demetri Gerof, Dog Driver – W
Tryggve Gran, Sub-Lieutenant, Norwegian, NR, BA, Ski Expert – W
Bernard C. Day, Motor Mechanic – W
James R. Dennistoun, In Charge of Mules in the Ship – W

Messdeck
William Lashly, Chief Stoker, RN – W
W.W. Archer, Chief Steward, Late RN – S
Thomas C. Clissold, Cook, Late RN – S

Edgar Evans, Petty Officer, RN – W
Robert Forde, Petty Officer, RN – W
Thomas Crean, Petty Officer, RN – W
Thomas S. Williamson, Petty Officer, RN – S
Patrick Keohane, Petty Officer, RN – W
Frederick J. Hooper, Steward, Late RN – W
Frank Browning, Petty Officer, RN – E
Harry Dickason, Able Seaman, RN – E

Ship's Party
George P. Abbott, Petty Officer, RN
William A. Horton, Engine Room Artificer, RN. 2nd Engineer
William Williams, Chief engine room artificer, RN Engineer
Albert Balson, Leading Seaman, RN
Robert Brissenden, Leading Stoker, RN
William Burton, Leading Stoker, RN
Edward A. McKenzie, Leading Stoker, RN
Bernard Stone, Leading Stoker, RN
Alfred B. Cheetham, Boatswain (Bosun), RNR
Francis Davies, Leading Shipwright, RN
Bruce Wilfred, Leading Shipwright, RN
Francis Drake, Assistant Paymaster, RN (retired) Secretary and Meteorologist
    in ship
William Heald, Late P.O., RN
W.H. Neale, Steward
Arthur S. Bailey, Petty Officer, 2nd class, RN
John Hugh Mather, Petty Officer, RNVR
Frederick Parsons, Petty Officer, RN
William Knowles, Able Seaman
Joseph Leese, Able Seaman, RN
Mortimer McCarthy, Able Seaman
Williams, Charles, Able Seaman
Thomas F. McLeod, Able Seaman
William McDonald, Able Seaman
Robert Oliphant, Able Seaman
James Paton, James, Able Seaman
James Skelton, Able Seaman
Charles Lammas, Fireman
Angus McDonald, Fireman
Thomas McGillon, Fireman

The *Terra Nova*

Arrangements have been made for the purchase of the steamship Terra Nova for the British Antarctic Expedition, 1910. The Terra Nova is the largest and strongest of the old Scottish whalers, built at Dundee in 1884. She is 8ft in length and 31ft in beam, that is 11ft longer, but 22ft narrower than the Discovery...Of late years, consequent on some decline in the whaling business, she has been occupied in seal hunting in the northern waters, sailing regularly from St Johns, Newfoundland. The Terra Nova, however, has not confined herself to the humdrum of trading. In 1903 she was purchased by the Admiralty as relief ship for the Discovery expedition, and after being considerably strengthened, duly made her appearance in the Ross Sea...The year 1905 saw her in the service of the North Polar Expedition, on a visit to Franz Josef Land. Thus, she has ranged from the Great Ice Barrier in the south to the North Polar pack – from extreme to extreme of the navigable waters of the globe. The size and strength of the ship make her a fitting receptacle for the extensive equipment – which it is necessary she should carry for the full success of the plans of the expedition. After being duly inspected on behalf of the expedition in Newfoundland, she will sail for England and, it is hoped, reach the Thames about the end of October or early in November. The Terra Nova is bought, but not yet paid for, and such an arrangement for acquiring the vessel is only possible because the vendors, Messrs Bowring Brothers of St Johns, Newfoundland, are as sanguine as Captain Scott that the British public intends that his expedition shall start in August, 1910. Not only has the ship been obtained on most reasonable terms, but in addition to this, the Liverpool and London directors of C. T. Bowring and Company (Limited) have promised a donation of £600 to the funds of the expedition, and the brokers, Messrs. David Bruce and Son, have also promised to the expedition a large proportion of their commission on the transaction, which practically amounts to a gift of £160 to the funds. It is certainly most gratifying to think that the expedition will sail in a ship that is both British built and British owned. Captain Scott stated yesterday that the Terra Nova is a great deal larger than the Nimrod. The increased size is necessary for the more extensive plant of the expedition. He had already expressed the opinion that Mr Shackleton's 'Furthest South' can only be surpassed by taking more men and more equipment. Further, it is to be remembered that the programme of the expedition includes two bases for the purpose of scientific work and geographical exploration, and, of course, this also necessitates a large vessel. The Terra Nova is of the ordinary whaler type. She is a sailing ship with auxiliary steam power. Most of these ships are comparatively poor sailors, but in making long passages with a fair wind the sails are, of course, an enormous advantage, and in going to the south they are a great aid in saving coal. The officers and crew for the expedition have now been selected and it is understood that no further applications for service can be entertained.

The Times

The *Terra Nova* was a 750 ton three-masted barque built in 1884 for Dundee's whaling and sealing fleet (of which she was the biggest) and was later used for ten years in the annual seal fishery in the Labrador Sea.

She was ideally suited to the polar regions – her first scientific venture being as the relief ship for the Jackson-Harmsworth Arctic expedition from 1894 to 1897. In 1898 she was bought by Bowring Brothers – a private company set up in 1811 and which went on to own several shops and department stores, later going on to become ship owners, general merchant and a steamship agent – and sailed under the command first of Nicholas Kennedy and latterly Captain Abram Kean. Later, she was equipped with an auxiliary steam engine and an iron-sheathed bow for her first trip to the Antarctic, as a relief ship in 1903–4 when she sailed in the company of ex-whaler *Morning* to help in freeing the *Discovery* from her ice trap.

She was bought from Bowring Brothers in 1909 for £12,500 specifically for Scott's second Arctic expedition. He described her as a 'wonderfully fine ice ship…as she bumped and flowed with mighty shocks, crushing and grinding a way through some, twisting and turning to avoid others, she seemed like a living thing fighting a great fight.'

Scott wanted to sail the *Terra Nova* as a naval vessel under the White Ensign and to make this happen he had to obtain membership of the Royal Yacht Squadron for £100. This also meant he was able to impose naval discipline on the expedition and also that the vessel was exempt from Board of Trade regulations.

The ship was reinforced from bow to stern with oak and sailed to Cardiff's Roath Dock in early June 1910. The *Terra Nova* and her crew were given a particularly warm and generous welcome in Cardiff with an expedition office being found on the dock and all docking fees and routine repair costs being waived, 300 tons of patent fuel donated by Crown Patent Fuel, and 100 tons of coal and 500 gallons of engine and lamp oil donated by Welsh coal companies. The cooking utensils were provided without charge by the Welsh Tin Plate Company of Llanelli and even Scott's sleeping bag was bought with money raised at a local school for the *Terra Nova*. There was so much support in Wales for the expedition that Cardiff was designated the *Terra Nova*'s home port and it was to Bute Dock that she returned at the end of the expedition on 14 June 1913.

Indeed, the crew had been the subject of the city's amazing support and generosity. When word got round that Edward Evans had abandoned his own plans to lead a Welsh expedition and teamed up with Scott, the two men were invited to Cardiff for a farewell banquet at the Royal Hotel's and attended by the Lord Mayor and other local prominent figures. The event was a huge success, with rousing speeches made, singing from the Royal Welsh Choir and general exuberance carrying on until late into the night (with Evans needing the support of six men to get him back to his ship). But around £1,000 was raised. At another luncheon, Evans was given £22 17s by a local businessman. Leading Cardiff ship owners

Daniel Radcliffe and William Tatem played an important role in fund raising and obtained sponsorship from throughout the South Wales business community, and in the provision of the crew's dock facilities. Also, William Davies, editor of the *Western Mail*, felt it a worthy project to support a fellow Welshman and his team (including another Welshman, Edgar Evans, from Rhossili, Gower) and not only won public support, but got Chancellor of the Exchequer David Lloyd George to provide a government grant of £20,000. In all, the good people of Cardiff raised and donated around £26,000 for the *Terra Nova* expedition – more than the rest of the country put together. Scott was so touched that he re-registered the *Terra Nova* with Cardiff as her home port and promised the people of the city that it would be the first port of call when they returned – a promise, of course, that he himself would never fulfill.

The final preparations for the British Antarctic Expedition are in such a forward state that Captain Scott's ship, the Terra Nova, will, Reuter's Agency learns, sail from the Thames next Wednesday. The old Dundee whaler of 749 tons, built 26 years ago, has been transformed into a model yacht and is undoubtedly the most efficiently equipped vessel ever employed in Arctic or Antarctic work. Her engines are capable of developing 10 knots. The vessel, which was formerly a schooner, has been rerigged as a barque, and interior alterations have been of a very extensive character. The small wardroom, formerly only capable of accommodating six men, has been rebuilt and enlarged so as to be able to hold four times that number. The forecastle has been extended, and the crew space so improved as to accommodate all the men in comfort. A warrant officers' mess has been built and below the wardroom large stores for scientific instruments, clothing, tobacco, etc, have been constructed, while magazines for acetylene and petrol have been added. On deck great improvements have been effected. Very little tinned meat will be employed, and with a view to using fresh provisions as much as possible, a hundred carcasses of beef and mutton are being taken out, and a large ice chamber has been constructed for their reception. Stores for three years are being taken, and the work of stowing and marking these has been a matter of the greatest care. All provisions, etc, have been packed in specially devised veneer wood cases, very light and strong, bound with metal, each weighing not more than 60lb – a one man load. On board the Terra Nova are also stowed 60 sledges of Norwegian niake, two large huts for winter quarters, and a hut for the scientific observers. The motor sledges will be sent out by ordinary steamer to New Zealand and, together with the dogs and ponies that are being collected by Mr C. H. Meares in Siberia and Manchuria, will be shipped on board the Terra Nova at Christchurch.

The Times – 26 May 1910

The fund raising was all pretty much down to Scott who spent months and months on it. Promises of financial backing were still coming in from South Africa, Australia and New Zealand as the *Terra Nova* set sail. So Scott did not go with her then but left her at Greenhithe where he was presented with two flags by the Queen – one to be planted at the farthest point south he reached and the other to be hoisted there, but then brought back to England. Scott then set off for South Africa, reaching Cape Town on 2 August, thirteen days ahead of the *Terra Nova*, with wife Kathleen on HMS *Saxon*.

The *Terra Nova* had stopped first at Madeira and then sailed on to the uninhabited South Trinidad Island, around 700 miles from Brazil. Wilson and Cherry-Garrard hunted for a new species of petrel bird named *Estrelata wilsoni* after Wilson, who discovered it on the *Discovery* expedition of 1901. There were also treks to seek out plants, rocks and fish. Five new species of spiders and a new moth were collected. The *Terra Nova* arrived in Simon's Bay, Cape Town on 15 August 1910. Although not happy about it, Wilson was ordered to take an ocean liner to Melbourne with his wife and Scott's and Evans' wives on board. Scott took over command of the *Terra Nova* as an experiment to see how he got on with the crew, to assess their characters and to select members of the two shore parties. One party would remain at the expedition's base near McMurdo Sound carrying out scientific research, while a second party would make the ultimate assault on the South Pole. A breakaway party of six men (the Eastern Party) led by Victor Campbell would be dispatched to the unexplored King Edward VII Land, 4 miles to the east. Pennell and Rennick would remain in charge of the ship.

The *Terra Nova* reached Melbourne on 12 October 1910, where Kathleen was reunited with her husband after a short journey in a motor launch – not a welcome trip by her companions in the pitch black of night. She wrote: 'I heard my good man's voice and was sure there was no danger, so insisted, getting more and more unpopular...we at last got close to the beautiful *Terra Nova* with our beautiful husbands on board. They came and looked down into our faces with lanterns.'

It was while staying behind to fundraise in Australia that Scott received a telegram from Amundsen saying he was 'proceeding south'. It was the first time Scott became aware there was a race on. When tackled by the press, he said he had no intention of changing his plans and that the expedition's scientific goals 'should not be sacrificed for a desire to be an Antarctic victor'. But Scott was privately angry that Amundsen's intentions had been so secretive. Further, all monies raised had been to fund an expedition to the Arctic not the South Pole and Amundsen had even secured the *Fram* from Fridtjof Nansen at no expense. The outrage was shared by the general public. Sir Clements Markham poured scorn on Amundsen's goal saying: 'She (the *Fram*) has no more sailing qualities than a haystack. In any case, Scott will be on the ground and settled long before Amundsen turns up, if he ever does.' On 15 October 1910, Markham reported to the RGS that Amundsen had: 'quietly got a wintering hut made on board and 100 dogs and a supply of tents and sledges. His secret design must have been nearly a year old. They believe his mention of Punta Aranas and Buenos Aires is merely a blind, and that he is going to McMurdo Sound to try to cut out Scott...If I were Scott I would not let them land, but he is always too good-natured.'

Scott and Kathleen arrived in New Zealand on 27 October and were greeted by Clement Markham's sister, Lady Bowen, and her husband Sir Charles. The Scotts were guests of the expedition's agent Joseph J. Kinsey in Lyttelton. It was a happy two weeks as Kathleen chronicled: 'There we were for a happy fortnight working and climbing with bare toes and my hair down and the sun and my Con and all the expedition going well. It was good and by night we slept in the garden and the gods be blest.'

The *Terra Nova* was put into dry dock to fix her leaks and also so that the stores could be re-arranged and re-packed for the journey ahead. They were labelled red for the main party and green for the eastern one. Scientific instruments were checked and the party's hut was erected on land in a practice run. The motor sledges were lashed to the deck and, at Oates's insistence, 45 tons of food were loaded for the ponies (who were waiting with the dogs and looked after by Bruce and Meares on Quail Island in Lyttelton Bay). Oates also managed to smuggle another two tons of food on board for the ponies without Scott's knowledge. Stalls were built for the ponies and chained bolts for the dogs. Around 430 tons of coal were packed into the holds and 30 more tons were stacked in sacks on the upper deck. In the ice house were three tons of ice, 162 lumps of mutton and three of beef, together with cases of sweetbreads and kidneys. There was little room left for the human cargo.

And all was not well amongst everyone on board. Petty Officer Evans got drunk and disgraced himself and Scott's wife and Evans' wife had a fight. Oates was forced to report: 'Mrs Scott and Mrs Evans had a magnificent battle; they tell me it was a draw after fifteen rounds. Mrs Wilson flung herself into the fight after the tenth round and there was more blood and hair flying about the hotel than you see in a Chicago slaughter-house in a month, the husbands got a bit of the backwash and there is a certain amount of coolness, which I hope they won't bring into the hut with them, however it won't hurt me even if they do.' Kathleen Scott later remarked: 'If ever Con has another expedition, the wives must be chosen more carefully than the men...better still, have none.'

The *Terra Nova* sailed for Port Chalmers, Dunedin, New Zealand. The Scotts did not sail with her, but returned to dry land in a tug and spent two quiet days together. Then it was time to bid each other farewell. Cheering crowds lined the shore as the three wives were taken off the *Terra Nova* for the last time and she was ready to set forth. Kathleen Scott wrote: 'I didn't say goodbye to my man because I didn't want anyone to see him sad. On the bridge of the tug Mrs. Evans looked ghastly white and said she wanted to have hysterics but instead we took photos of the departing ship. Mrs Wilson was plucky and good...I mustered them all for tea in the stern and we all chatted gaily except Mrs Wilson who sat looking somewhat sphinx-like.' Wilson wrote of seeing his wife go: 'There on the bridge I saw her disappear out of sight waving happily, a goodbye that will be with me till the day I see her again in this world or the next...I think it will be in this world and some time in 1912.' The *Terra Nova* left Port Chalmers at 4.30pm on 29 November 1910, three days after Scott had made the following journal entry:

The first three weeks of November have gone with such a rush that I have neglected my diary and can only patch it up from memory.

The dates seem unimportant, but throughout the period the officers and men of the ship have been unremittingly busy.

On arrival the ship was cleared of all the shore party stores, including huts, sledges, &c. Within five days she was in dock. Bowers attacked the ship's stores, surveyed, relisted, and restowed them, saving very much space by unstowing numerous cases and stowing the contents in the lazarette. Meanwhile our good friend Miller attacked the leak and traced it to the stern. We found the false stem split, and in one case a hole bored for a long-stem through-bolt, which was much too large for the bolt. Miller made the excellent job in overcoming this difficulty, which I expected, and since the ship has been afloat and loaded the leak is found to be enormously reduced. The ship still leaks, but the amount of water entering is little more than one would expect in an old wooden vessel.

Scott wanted this expedition tailored exactly to his demands; he would have dogs (chosen from Siberia), Manchunian ponies and motor sledges. All seemed to be going well – but Scott was to find out that he was not the only one embarking on the journey...there was a Japanese expedition being muted, the Australasian Antarctic expedition led by Douglas Mawson was set to leave in 1911 – and Roald Amundsen had announced his own plans for an Antarctic voyage...

Reuter's Agency learns that the first member of the British Antarctic Expedition under Captain Scott left England yesterday. He is going to Siberia to obtain dogs and ponies for use in the expedition. Except that he is to make a brief stay at Moscow. Mr Meares travels direct to Vladivostok. Thence he will proceed north to the Aniur and by means of sledges will press further north to Yakut, a great sabio centre. In Yakutsk, where animals will probably be procurable. Later he may have to go to Okhotslt and on to the Verkholansk Mountains, a region which is described as being almost, if not quite, the coldest in the world. Mr Meares intends to get most of his dogs, particularly the main team leaders, in Siberia. This part of the work is likely to occupy between three and four months. Mr Meares will then begin the collection of ponies in the country round Harbin and, with his animals will join the min body of the expedition on board the Terra Nova in New Zealand in December.

The Times – 15 January 1910

Chapter 6

The First Stage

Thursday 1 December 1910

The month opens well on the whole. During the night the wind increased; we worked up to 8, to 9, and to 9.5 knots. Stiff wind from NW and confused sea. Awoke to much motion.

The ship a queer and not altogether cheerful sight under the circumstances.

Below one knows all space is packed as tight as human skill can devise – and on deck! Under the forecastle fifteen ponies close side by side, seven one side, eight the other, heads together and groom between – swaying, swaying continually to the plunging, irregular motion.

Despite this uneventful entry by Scott it was not to be an easy start to the long journey. On 2 December 1910, the *Terra Nova* encountered a huge storm that loosened cargo on the deck, making it hazardous. The sea crashed over the decks causing the dogs to be tossed from one side to the other with one being lost overboard. The ponies were terrified and two had to be killed. Water poured into the engine room and cabins below. It got mixed with coal dust causing a sludge that choked the bilge pumps. The water rose rapidly to the furnaces and the men had to resort to using buckets to bale it out by hand. Mercifully, come the next morning, the sea was calmer enabling repair work to be carried out. Teddy Evans managed to clear the pumps. Around 10 tons of coal, 65 gallons of petrol and a case of biologists' spirits were lost. Scott described the nightmare storm:

Friday 2 December 1910

A day of great disaster. From four o'clock last night the wind freshened with great rapidity, and very shortly we were under topsails, jib and staysail only. It blew very hard and the sea got up at once. Soon we were plunging heavily and taking much water over the lee rail. Oates and Atkinson with intermittent assistance from others were busy keeping the ponies on their legs. Cases of petrol, forage, etc, began to break loose on the upper deck; the principal trouble was caused by the loose coal-bags, which were bodily lifted by the seas and swung against the lashed cases. You know how carefully everything had been lashed, but no lashings could have withstood the onslaught of these coal sacks for long; they acted like battering rams. There was nothing for it but to grapple with the evil, and nearly all hands were labouring for hours in the waist of the ship, heaving coal sacks overboard and re-lashing the petrol cases, etc, in the best manner possible under such difficult and dangerous circumstances. The seas were continually breaking over these people and now and again they would be completely submerged. At such times they had to cling for dear life to some fixture to prevent themselves being washed overboard, and with coal bags and loose cases washing about, there was every risk of such hold being torn away.

No sooner was some semblance of order restored than some exceptionally heavy wave would tear away the lashing and the work had to be done all over again. The night wore on, the sea and wind ever rising, and the ship ever plunging more distractedly; we shortened sail to main topsail and staysail, stopped engines and hove to, but to little purpose. Tales of ponies down came frequently from forward, where Oates and Atkinson laboured through the entire night. Worse was to follow, much worse – a report from the engine-room that the pumps had choked and the water risen over the gratings.

From this moment, about 4am., the engine-room became the centre of interest. The water gained in spite of every effort. Lashley, to his neck in rushing water, stuck gamely to the work of clearing suctions. For a time, with donkey engine and bilge pump sucking, it looked as though the water would be got under; but the hope was short-lived: five minutes of pumping invariably led to the same result – a general choking of the pumps.

The outlook appeared grim. The amount of water that was being made, with the ship so roughly handled, was most uncertain. We knew that normally the ship was not making much water, but we also knew that a considerable part of the water washing over the upper deck must be finding its way below; the decks were leaking in streams. The ship was very deeply laden; it did not need the addition of much water to get her water-logged, in which condition anything might have happened. The hand pump produced only a dribble, and its suction could not be got at; as the water crept higher it got in contact with the boiler and grew warmer – so hot at last that no one could work at the suctions. Williams had to confess he was beaten and must draw fires. What was to be done? Things for the moment appeared very black. The sea seemed higher than ever; it came over lee rail and poop, a rush of green water; the ship wallowed in it; a great piece of the bulwark carried clean away. The bilge pump is dependent on the main engine. To use the pump it was necessary to go ahead. It was at such times that the heaviest seas swept in over the lee rail; over and over [again] the rail, from the forerigging to the main, was covered by a solid sheet of curling water that swept aft and high on the poop. On one occasion I was waist deep when standing on the rail of the poop.

The scene on deck was devastating, and in the engine-room the water, though really not great in quantity, rushed over the floor plates and frames in a fashion that gave it a fearful significance.

The afterguard were organised in two parties by Evans to work buckets; the men were kept steadily going on the choked hand pumps – this seemed all that could be done for the moment, and what a measure to count as the sole safeguard of the ship from sinking, practically an attempt to bale her out! Yet strange as it may seem the effort has not been wholly fruitless – the string of buckets, which has now been kept going for four hours, together with the dribble from the pump, has kept the water under – if anything there is a small decrease.

Meanwhile, we have been thinking of a way to get at the suction of the pump: a hole is being made in the engine-room bulkhead, the coal between this and the pump shaft will be removed, and a hole made in the shaft. With so much water coming on board, it is impossible to open the hatch over the shaft. We are not out of the wood, but hope dawns, as indeed it should for me, when I find myself so wonderfully served. Officers and men are singing shanties over their arduous work. Williams is working in sweltering heat behind the boiler to get the door made in the bulkhead. Not a single one has lost his good spirits. A dog was drowned last night, one pony is dead and two others in a bad condition – probably they too will go. Occasionally a heavy sea would bear one of them away, and he was only saved by his chain. Meares with some helpers had constantly to be rescuing these wretched creatures from hanging, and trying to find them better shelter, an almost hopeless task. One poor beast was found hanging when dead; one was washed away with such force that his chain broke and he disappeared overboard; the next wave miraculously washed him on board again and he is now fit and well. The gale has exacted heavy toll, but I feel all will be well if we can only cope with the water. Another dog has just been washed overboard – alas! Thank God, the gale is abating. The sea is still mountainously high, but the ship is not labouring so heavily as she was. I pray we may be under sail again before morning.

The *Terra Nova* came across its first iceberg on 7 December and hit the southern ice pack on 10 December where it was forced to stop. It was there for twenty days before breaking clear and continuing, finally coming into the open water of the Ross Sea. In his diary Scott wrote of the gruelling experience: 'We are out of the pack at length and at last one breathes again.'

The delay, which Scott said was 'sheer bad luck', had consumed 61 tons of coal and put the team well behind schedule.

Wilfred Bruce wrote to his friend Lilian Knowles in March 1911 about the storm:

We met a gale three days out and the complete extinction of the great expedition was very nearly a fait accompli *in the first chapter. She was loaded very deeply and her decks were fearfully lumbered up with motor-sledges, ponies, dogs, coal, petrol, etc. She leaked so much above and below in the terrific sea, that the engine fires were put out and all our pumps choked. We kept her afloat till the gale was over by baling with buckets up the perpendicular engine room ladders. Sixteen blooming hours did we learned scientist, naval lieutenants, seamen, cooks and servants – pass buckets of filthy oily water over each others' heads and pour them over the side [...] We clear with the loss of two ponies, one dog, half our bulwarks and much coal and petrol, all washed over the side. Our cabins, bunks and clothes were all wet.'*

Bruce also described an attack by killer whales which nearly cost the life of the expedition photographer Herbert Ponting:

...we had an attack of whales, on our dogs really, but it threatened much more than the dogs, four 'killer whales' chasing penguins, sighted some of our dogs tied up to a mooring wire near the edge of the floe. They tried to get at them on the ice, coming half out of the water in their endeavours. I was working stores on the ice and had big heaps of petrol cases ready to be sledged on shore. I called to Ponting, our photographer, to come and snap the wonderful sight and he went quite close to the whales, who just at this time changed their mode of attack and dived under the ice, charging up from underneath and breaking the 4 feet thick ice into fragments. Huge panic and excitement. The ship was adrift, (her ice anchors being now fast to loose ice), the stacks of petrol on loose floes amid waves of ice 4 feet high. Ponting was isolated on a 5 yards square floe and a 'killer' put his head out between him and the ship and only a few feet from him and stared at him. I was about 15 yards away. I've seen men scared before but never a man as scared as that. Well luckily they cleared off for a few minutes and when they came back we dosed them with a fusillade of rifle shots and eventually saved everything, dogs, petrol, Ponting and all.

On New Year's Day, 1911, Mount Erebus came into view. A few days later the crew attempted to land the *Terra Nova* at Cape Crozier, where they had planned on setting up winter quarters, but the seas were too rough. Their next option was McMurdo Sound where both *Discovery* and *Nimrod* had previously landed. Rounding the north-west tip of Ross Island, they proceeded down the coast past Cape Royds, Inaccessible Island and Cape Barne. When they arrived at the Skuary (renamed Cape Evans) Scott, Evans and Wilson made the joint decision that this was where they would make their winter camp. After their ordeal at sea, the ponies were particularly happy to finally be on firm ground, showing their pleasure by rolling and kicking in the snow. There was around a mile-and-a half of ice between the shore and open sea and about 15 miles north of the base that Scott had made before at Hut Point. He hoped it would be ice free in the Antarctic summer so that the *Terra Nova* would be able to move around freely with ready access to Hut Point and the Barrier.

On 4 January the *Terra Nova* was anchored to the ice and the unloading began. First came two motor sledges put to use hauling stores to the camp. It took twenty men to haul the third and largest sledge, which crashed through the ice and sank deep into the water. Scott recorded:

The work of landing stores for the western party was at once commenced. How arduous it was may be imagined from the fact that a distance of a mile and a half from the ship; half sea and half ice, had to be traversed. The ponies, the motor-sledges, the dogs, and the men were all employed in the work of transportation, which was completed in a week, though not without a great misfortune in the loss of one of the motor sledges, which dropped through a hole in the ice. The next business was the building of a house as the expedition station, and as soon as it was built it was occupied and put into proper order, all in a fortnight, accommodation being found for fifteen ponies, thirty dogs, and one of the rabbits. The situation is a comfortable one, and very convenient for scientific work. We have already obtained a rich biological collection. So far the weather has been very changeable, and the strong winds that have prevailed have made it a matter of considerable difficulty to keep the ship anchored safely amidst the ice. Once, indeed, she was driven, on a shoal, but happily she was re-floated without damage. I am now departing on a sledge journey to the south, with twelve men, eight ponies, and two teams of dogs, and expect to be cut off from Cape Evans for two months. We hope to return over new ice early in April, and in the meantime the ship will have proceeded west to land a geological party, and then east, in accordance with our pre-arranged programme to put a small party ashore on King Edward's Land for exploration purposes. The men and the animals are in excellent health.

The men's 50ft by 25ft hut was put up. It stood 9ft tall, was insulated with seaweed and lined with matchboard. Lighting came by way of acetylene gas and a stove and a cooking range was installed. Keeping to his 'on ship' discipline, on completion of the hut on 18 January Scott oversaw the erection of a partition to divide the nine crew men from the sixteen officers and scientists. The accommodation was divided by crates with a wardroom and a mess-deck. In the many debates that were to follow about Scott's fated expedition, this arrangement had both its critics and supporters, with some saying the division of social classes was wrong, and others that it helped to create a naval vessel atmosphere that was familiar to the men.

Before starting the depot-laying trek across the Barrier and towards the Pole, Scott and Meares travelled 15 miles south to revisit his old Hut Point. He threw a temper when he discovered a window had been left open letting in snow which had in turn frozen into a solid pack of ice. Scott immediately put the blame on Shackleton as he was the last man to use the hut when he had been based at Cape Evans three years earlier. Scott wrote: 'It is difficult to conceive the absolutely selfish frame of mind that can perpetrate a deed like this…finding that such a simply duty had been neglected by one's immediate predecessors disgusted me horribly.'

Depot laying across the Glacier Tongue and on to the Barrier got underway on 24 January 1911 and used all the dogs and eight ponies. Scott went back to the *Terra Nova* to bid farewell to Lieutenant Pennell and his crew, for he figured that by the time he returned from depot laying, the vessel would be on its way back to New Zealand after dropping off Campbell, Priestley, Levick, Browning, Dickason and Abbott at King Edward VII Land. Also on board were Taylor, Debenham, Wright and Edgar Evans, who were to carry out scientific work in the mountains of Victoria Land.

The base hitherto used in British expeditions has been McMurdo Sound but, in the cause of science and the desire to investigate a virgin area, a second base will be established in King Edward VII Land, 400 miles to the east of McMurdo Sound. The new base may be difficult to establish, and it will certainly be exposed to the full rigour of the Antarctic climate; but on the other hand its distance from the Pole will be no greater than that of the McMurdo Sound base, and the region about it is entirely unknown. The advance to the Pole will be made from one or other of these bases according to circumstances. The track to the Pole from McMurdo Sound traverses at first the extensive plateau of the Great Barrier, maintaining approximately the level of the sea, it then rises gradually on the surface of a long glacier, and finally, in its third and most difficult phase, it traverses an inland plateau, which probably maintains a great altitude. The track to the Pole from King Edward VII Land may be expected to include similar phases; but in all probability it will continue longer on the sea level, meet the mountains in a more southerly latitude, and consequently leave a shorter distance to be traversed on the lofty inland plateau.

The Times – 1911

Two days later, the depot-laying party was on the Barrier and establishing a camp called Safety Camp, far enough from the edge not to become victim of breaking ice. From here were made the final plans for the push to the Pole. The first concern over the presence of ponies came when they sank into the soft snow and Meares and Wilson headed back to base camp at Cape Evans to collect special snow shoes for the animals. But on arrival they discovered that the sea ice had broken away and there was no 'path' to the camp. The two men made the trip back to Safety Camp without the crucial snow shoes.

The work carried on, laying depots that would provide accommodation and supplies on the Barrier from its edge of Safety Camp down to the south for use on the polar journey the following spring. The work was carried out by a team of twelve men and eight of the fittest ponies, and did not involve the motor sledges because of the ice conditions. Scott had made the decision to set off without Atkinson, who was suffering with a bad foot, and instructed Crean to stay to look after him. Cherry-Garrard wrote of a 'state bordering on panic' as they set off. Things did not go smoothly. Progress was slow – only around 10 miles a day – with the ponies hindered because the Norwegian snow shoes they needed had been left behind at Cape Evans. The dogs proved stronger – and a wiser choice – for the expedition. Though at one point, when they broke loose, they savaged a pony nicknamed 'Weary Willy', which caused Scott to write:

Tuesday 14 February 1911

Oates and then I hurried back. I met Meares, who told me the dogs of his team had got out of hand and attacked Weary Willy when they saw him fall. Finally they had been beaten off and W.W. was being led without his sledge. W.W. had been much bitten, but luckily I think not seriously: he appears to have made a gallant fight, and bit and shook some of the dogs with his teeth. Gran did his best, breaking his ski stick. Meares broke his dog stick – one way and another the dogs must have had a rocky time, yet they seem to bear charmed lives when their blood is up, as apparently not one of them has been injured.

The party set up Corner Camp, 40 miles from Hut Point. There they were held up for three days by a blizzard before resuming their trek. Scott was becoming concerned over the welfare of the ponies. He sent three of the weakest animals back on 13 February, one dying on route, and Scott realised that the rest would not make it back unless he and his men turned north. The situation reached crisis point and Scott made a list of jobs to be done:

Wednesday 15 February

Mems. – Storage of biscuit next year, lashing cases on sledges.
Look into sledgemeter.
Picket lines for ponies.
Food tanks to be size required.

Oates advised Scott against a change of direction, saying they should carry on forward to the original site and kill the ponies for meat as they collapsed. But Scott, torn between what he saw as unnecessary slaughter and the need for ponies to get him to the Pole, insisted on his plan, urging his men to struggle on for twenty-four days to lay 'One Ton Depot', which boasted a ton of food and supplies – hence its name – making it the largest of all the depots. It was, however, over 30 miles north of its original location, a fact that was to add to the final, fatal outcome. Oates is reported to have said to Scott: 'Sir, I'm afraid you'll come to regret not taking my advice.' Scott continued his planning:

Friday 17 February 1911

Camp 15. Lat. 79° 28' S. It clouded over yesterday – the temperature rose and some snow fell. Wind from the south, cold and biting, as we turned out. We started to build the depot. I had intended to go on half a march and return to same camp, leaving Weary Willy to rest, but under the circumstances did not like to take risk. Stores left in depot:

Lat. 79° 29' Depot.

lbs.
245 – 7 weeks full provision bags for 1 unit
12 – 2 days provision bags for 1 unit
8 – 8 weeks tea
31 – 6 weeks extra butter
176 – 176 lbs biscuit (7 weeks full biscuit)
85 – 8 1/2 gallons oil (12 weeks oil for 1 unit)
850 – 5 sacks of oats
424 – 4 bales of fodder
250 – tank of dog biscuit
100 – 2 cases of biscuit
– –
2181
1 skein white line
1 set breast harness
2 12 ft sledges
2 pair ski, 1 pair ski sticks
1 Minimum Thermometer
1 tin Rowntree cocoa
1 tin matches

With packing we have landed considerably over a ton of stuff. It is a pity we couldn't get to 80°, but as it is we shall have a good leg up for next year and can at least feed the ponies full up to this point.

Our Camp 15 is very well marked, I think. Besides the flagstaff and black flag we have piled biscuit boxes, filled and empty, to act as reflectors – secured tea tins to the sledges, which are planted upright in the snow. The depot cairn is more than 6 ft above the surface, very solid and large; then there are the pony protection walls; altogether it should show up for many miles.

I forgot to mention that looking back on the 15th we saw a cairn built on a camp 12½ miles behind – it was miraged up.

It seems as though some of our party will find spring journeys pretty trying. Oates's nose is always on the point of being frostbitten; Meares has a refractory toe, which gives him much trouble – this is the worst prospect for summit work. I have been wondering how I shall stick the summit again, this cold spell gives ideas. I think I shall be all right, but one must be prepared for a pretty good doing.

On 17 February Scott decided to turn back. He wanted to get back to Cape Evans to see if there was any news left there by Pennell concerning Campbell's party at King Edward VII Land.

On the return trip when they were about 12 miles away from Safety Camp, Wilson saw Meares's and Scott's dogs simply 'disappear': 'Exactly like rats running down a hole – only I saw no hole. They simply went into the white surface and disappeared.' The team was faced with the horrific sight of a sledge hanging dangerously at the edge of a crevasse with eight dogs howling and struggling in terror as they dangled above the abyss. Wilson and Cherry-Garrard managed to haul the dogs to safety but two others had fallen some 65 feet onto a ledge. Scott insisted on retrieving them, which somehow he did after being lowered onto the ledge. He wrote about the rescue:

Tuesday 21 February 1911:

New Camp about 12 miles from Safety Camp. 15½ miles. We made a start as usual about 10pm. The light was good at first, but rapidly grew worse till we could see little of the surface. The dogs showed signs of wearying. About an hour and a half after starting we came on mistily outlined pressure ridges. We were running by the sledges.

Suddenly Wilson shouted 'hold on to the sledge', and I saw him slip a leg into a crevasse. I jumped to the sledge, but saw nothing. Five minutes after, as the teams were trotting side by side, the middle dogs of our team disappeared. In a moment the whole team was sinking—two by two we lost sight of them, each pair struggling for foothold. Osman the leader exerted all his great strength and kept a foothold—it was wonderful to see him. The sledge stopped and we leapt aside.

The situation was clear in another moment. We had been actually travelling along the bridge of a crevasse; the sledge had stopped on it, whilst the dogs hung in their harness in the abyss, suspended between the sledge and the leading dog. Why the sledge and ourselves didn't follow the dogs we shall never know. I think a fraction of a pound of added weight must have taken us down.

As soon as we grasped the position, we hauled the sledge clear of the bridge and anchored it. Then we peered into the depths of the crack. The dogs were howling dismally, suspended in all sorts of fantastic positions and evidently terribly frightened. Two had dropped out of their harness, and we could see them indistinctly on a snow bridge far below. The rope at either end of the chain had bitten deep into the snow at the side of the crevasse, and with the weight below, it was impossible to move it.

By this time Wilson and Cherry-Garrard, who had seen the accident, had come to our assistance. At first things looked very bad for our poor team, and I saw little prospect of rescuing them. I had luckily inquired about the Alpine rope before starting the march, and now Cherry-Garrard hurriedly brought this most essential aid.

It takes one a little time to make plans under such sudden circumstances, and for some minutes our efforts were rather futile. We could get not an inch on the main trace of the sledge or on the leading rope, which was binding Osman to the snow with a throttling pressure. Then thought became clearer. We unloaded our sledge, putting in safety our sleeping-bags with the tent and cooker. Choking sounds from Osman made it clear that the pressure on him must soon be relieved. I seized the lashing off Meares's sleeping-bag, passed the tent poles across the crevasse, and with Meares managed to get a few inches on the leading line; this freed Osman, whose harness was immediately cut.

Then securing the Alpine rope to the main trace we tried to haul up together. One dog came up and was unlashed, but by this time the rope had cut so far back at the edge that it was useless to attempt to get more of it. But we could now unbend the sledge and do that for which we should have aimed from the first, namely, run the sledge across the gap and work from it.

We managed to do this, our fingers constantly numbed. Wilson held on to the anchored trace whilst the rest of us laboured at the leader end. The leading rope was very small and I was fearful of its breaking, so Meares was lowered down a foot or two to secure the Alpine rope to the leading end of the trace; this done, the work of rescue proceeded in better order.

Two by two we hauled the animals up to the sledge and one by one cut them out of their harness. Strangely the last dogs were the most difficult, as they were close under the lip of the gap, bound in by the snow-covered rope. Finally, with a gasp we got the last poor creature on to firm snow. We had recovered eleven of the thirteen.

Then I wondered if the last two could not be got, and we paid down the Alpine rope to see if it was long enough to reach the snow bridge on which they were coiled. The rope is 90 feet, and the amount remaining showed that the depth of the bridge was about 65 feet. I made a bowline and the others lowered me down. The bridge was firm and I got hold of both dogs, which were hauled up in turn to the surface.

Then I heard dim shouts and howls above. Some of the rescued animals had wandered to the second sledge, and a big fight was in progress. All my rope-tenders had to leave to separate the combatants; but they soon returned, and with some effort I was hauled to the surface.

All is well that ends well, and certainly this was a most surprisingly happy ending to a very serious episode. We felt we must have refreshment, so camped and had a meal, congratulating ourselves on a really miraculous escape. If the sledge had gone down Meares and I must have been badly injured, if not killed outright.

The dogs are wonderful, but have had a terrible shaking — three of them are passing blood and have more or less serious internal injuries. Many were held up by a thin thong round the stomach, writhing madly to get free. One dog better placed in its harness stretched its legs full before and behind and just managed to claw either side of the gap — it had continued attempts to climb throughout, giving vent to terrified howls. Two of the animals hanging together had been fighting at intervals when they swung into any position that allowed them to bite one another. The crevasse for the time being was an inferno, and the time must have been all too terribly long for the wretched creatures. It was twenty minutes past three when we had completed the rescue work and the accident must have happened before one-thirty. Some of the animals must have been dangling for over an hour. I had a good opportunity of examining the crack.

The party finally reached Safety Camp where Teddy Evans, Ford and Keohane were waiting for them.

* * *

Campbell's expedition set off on the *Terra Nova* on 26 January. He was forced to go to Victoria Land when King Edward VII Land proved inaccessible. Returning westward along the Barrier edge, the team came across Amundsen's expedition vessel the *Fram* and his group of eight men camped in the Barrier inlet of the Bay of Whales. They were treated with courtesy and hospitality by Amundsen who although politely made it clear he was out to reach the Pole first, even offered to lend some of his 100 dogs and who was more than willing to let Campbell's team camp nearby. But Amundsen's offers were declined and Campbell was anxious to return to Cape Evans to inform his team of Amundsen's presence.

The brief narratives from Captain Scott and Lieutenant Pennell as to the fortunes so far of the British Antarctic Expedition can easily be followed, and little by way of elucidation is necessary. Without doubt the most significant feature of the situation is that, as was feared, there is a rival expedition in the field, that of Captain Amundsen in the Fram. *There were no signs of the Japanese having arrived. It was at first thought that Captain Amundsen, who had a good start of Captain Scott, might fix his headquarters somewhere in the neighbourhood of McMurdo Sound. Fortunately such an awkward situation has been avoided by Captain Amundsen's establishing his base at Balloon Bight, on the Great Ice Barrier itself, some 400 miles to the east of McMurdo Sound...It may be admitted that no nation and no individual has any monopoly of a particular route to the South Pole, yet it is certainly a pity that with such an enormous continent to explore there should be any rivalry of this kind, or any appearance of one explorer encroaching upon what may be regarded as the field of another. Captain Amundsen, instead of going to the Ross Sea, might well have gone to the Wyeddell Sea and endeavoured to make his way with his hardy companions and his 116 dogs across to the Pole from Coats Land. However the situation being as it is must be made the best of. Naturally the sympathies of Englishmen at least will be with Captain Scott. Unfortunately when he started on his southern journey he was unaware of the presence of Captain Amundsen anywhere in the vicinity. Means may have been taken after Lieutenant Pennell's departure in the* Terra Nova *of letting Captain Scott know, but probably this would not make any difference in his plans. It is doubtful whether, even if he had known, he would have made any serious attempt during the present season to reach his goal. Lieutenant Pennell does not say that he gathered any information as to the intentions of Captain Amundsen; he himself does not appear to have been at Balloon Bight when the* Terra Nova *called there. The determination and powers of endurance of Norwegians are well known, and their capacity for putting up with discomforts and hardships [that] others might not care to face. It is hard to say what course Captain Amundsen may pursue when he is aware that the British expedition is at work in the same field. Whether with a selection of his eight men and his 116 dogs, he has attempted to push on at once for the South Pole is impossible to say.*

The Times – 30 March 1911

Chapter 7
Bitter Times

After leaving news of Amundsen's arrival at Cape Evans, Campbell's eastern party became the northern party. It sailed northwards on 9 February 1911, arriving at Robertson Bay, near Cape Adare, on 17 February, where the men built a hut close to Norwegian explorer Carsten Borchgrevink's old quarters.

The party spent the 1911 winter in their hut. Meanwhile the Motor Party (Lieutenant Evans, Day, Lashly and Hooper) had started from Cape Evans on 24 October with two motor sledges, their objective being to haul loads to latitude 80°30'S and wait there for the others. The bitter temperature was noted in Scott's diary:

> *The temperature on the march tonight fell to −21° with a brisk SW breeze. Bowers started out as usual in his small felt hat, ears uncovered. Luckily I called a halt after a mile and looked at him. His ears were quite white. Cherry and I nursed them back whilst the patient seemed to feel nothing but intense surprise and disgust at the mere fact of possessing such unruly organs. Oates's nose gave great trouble. I got frostbitten on the cheek lightly, as also did Cherry-Garrard.*
>
> *Tried to march in light woollen mits to great discomfort.*

On their return to base, Scott and his men learned of the presence of Amundsen in the Bay of Whales, 200 miles to their east. Scott's first reaction was reportedly to hasten to the Bay of Whales and 'have it out' with Amundsen, but then he reconsidered and decided not to amend his schedule, noting in his journal: 'One thing only fixes itself in my mind. The proper, as well as the wiser, course is for us to proceed exactly as though this had not happened. To go forward and do our best for the honour of our country without fear or panic.' Edward Evans later said that Scott was actually bitter that Amundsen had secretly made his way south and to the Ross Sea, Scott's own goal. Should Scott have continued with a dangerous race he had no way of winning? Writing to a friend in New Zealand, he said: 'I am fully alive to the complication of the situation by Amundsen, but as any attempt at a race might have been fatal to our chance of getting to the Pole at all, I decided long ago to do exactly as I should have done had Amundsen not been down here. If he gets to the Pole, he is bound to do it rapidly with dogs, but one guesses that success will justify him, and that our venture will be out of it. If he fails, he ought to hide [...] meanwhile, you may be sure we shall be going the best way we can to carry my plan.' To Nansen he wrote: '[...] it is evident that Amundsen has left everyone in ignorance of his intentions and if that is so, I am sure you will agree with me in deploring the fact. I do not believe the reports that he is going to McMurdo Sound – the idea seems to me preposterous in view of his record – but the fact that he departs with so much mystery leaves one with an uncomfortable feeling that he contemplates something that he imagines we should not approve [...] However, it's no use discussing the matter till more is known. I hope to sail on the 25th and to be in the ice early in December. Everything has worked out well and the spirit of enthusiasm is very fine – as you know, this expedition is on a very big scale. We may have made a mistake in having such an extensive organisation, but I am most anxious to get really good scientific results and for that one ought to have a number of experts. As to the travelling, we might have improved matters by having more dogs and fewer ponies. It is difficult to say – the animals we have are splendid and all in good condition.'

So Scott did admit to regret over his choice of taking so many ponies. But this realisation came too late. He would have no choice ultimately but to depend on man-hauling – and this would not be enough.

Scott wanted to get everyone back to Cape Evans. On the last day of February the move began with Meares and Wilson leading off with the dog teams. Wilson went round by Cape Armitage and arrived safely at Hut Point. The others followed with the ponies and had to follow the sea-ice route. Faithful and stalwart pony Weary Willy collapsed and died. Scott, Oates and Gran stayed at the pony's deathbed while Bowers, Crean and Cherry-Garrard went on ahead with the four surviving ponies. They dropped off the Barrier onto sea ice and started to make their way around Cape Armitage. When the ponies could go no further they made camp and fell into a deep sleep, only to be awoken by the sound of ice breaking up and the discovery they were now adrift on a floe. One pony disappeared and now, left with just three, the men had no option but to try to make their way back to the Barrier by hopping from floe to floe. It took them six hours during which time the men used their sledges as ladders – and could only watch as a floe carrying the remaining horses drifted away from them in full view of killer whales. The next morning Bowers spotted the animals still on the floe and attempted to rescue them with Oates. But one hapless animal fell in the water and Oates had to summon up all his courage to end its misery with a pick axe. Another pony kept slipping into the water and this time it was Bowers who used a pick axe to prevent it being attacked by the ever-present whales. The remaining pony was rescued – just one of the two out of the original eight that had started off on the depot-laying journey. Scott wrote of his sadness:

Friday 3 March 1911

I was interrupted when writing yesterday and continue my story this morning… In the middle of the night at 4.30 Bowers got out of the tent and discovered the ice had broken all round him: a crack ran under the picketing line, and one pony had disappeared. They had packed with great haste and commenced jumping the ponies from floe to floe, then dragging the loads over after – the three men must have worked splendidly and fearlessly. At length they had worked their way to heavier floes lying near the Barrier edge, and at one time thought they could get up, but soon discovered that there were gaps everywhere off the high Barrier face. In this dilemma Crean, volunteering, was sent off to try to reach me. The sea was like a cauldron at the time of the break up, and killer whales were putting their heads up on all sides. Luckily they did not frighten the ponies.

He travelled a great distance over the sea ice, leaping from floe to floe, and at last found a thick floe from which, with help of ski stick, he could climb the Barrier face. It was a desperate venture, but luckily successful.

As soon as I had digested Crean's news I sent Gran back to Hut Point with Wilson and Meares and started with my sledge, Crean and Oates for the scene of the mishap. We stopped at Safety Camp to load some provisions and oil and then, marching carefully round, approached the ice edge. To my joy I caught sight of the lost party. We got our Alpine rope and with its help dragged the two men to the surface. I pitched camp at a safe distance from the edge and then we all started salvage work. The ice had ceased to drift and lay close and quiet against the Barrier edge. We got the men at 5.30pm and all the sledges and effects on to the Barrier by 4am. As we were getting up the last loads the ice showed signs of drifting off, and we saw it was hopeless to try and move the ponies. The three poor beasts had to be left on their floe for the moment, well fed. None of our party had had sleep the previous night and all were dog tired. I decided we must rest, but turned everyone out at 8.30 yesterday morning. Before breakfast we discovered the ponies had drifted away. We had tried to anchor their floe with the Alpine rope, but the anchors had drawn. It was a sad moment. At breakfast we decided to pack and follow the Barrier edge: this was the position when I last wrote, but the interruption came when Bowers, who had taken the binoculars, announced that he could see the ponies about a mile to the NW. We packed and went on at once. We found it easy enough to get down to the poor animals and decided to rush them for a last chance of life. Then there was an unfortunate mistake: I went along the Barrier edge and discovered what I thought and what proved to be a practicable way to land a pony, but the others meanwhile, a little overwrought, tried to leap Punch across a gap. The poor beast fell in; eventually we had to kill him – it was awful. I re-called all hands and pointed out my road. Bowers and Oates went out on it with a sledge and worked their way to the remaining ponies, and started back with them on the same track. Meanwhile Cherry and I dug a road at the Barrier edge. We saved one pony; for a time I thought we should get both, but Bowers' poor animal slipped at a jump and plunged into the water: we dragged him out on some brash ice – killer whales all about us in an intense state of excitement. The poor animal couldn't rise, and the only merciful thing was to kill it. These incidents were too terrible.

At 5pm we sadly broke our temporary camp and marched back to the one I had first pitched. Even here it seemed unsafe, so I walked nearly two miles to discover cracks: I could find none, and we turned in about midnight.

So here we are ready to start our sad journey to Hut Point. Everything out of joint with the loss of the ponies, but mercifully with all the party alive and well.

Scott's team waited at Hut Point for the sea ice to freeze over again so they could continue to Cape Evans. On 15 March they were joined by Taylor, Debenham, Wright and Edgar Evans, who had been exploring the western mountains in Victoria Land. On 11 April Scott and half his team set off for Cape Evans leaving instructions that the rest were to follow. Arriving at the camp they discovered another pony and dog had died.

Scott's faith in and dependence on ponies for the gruelling trek have latterly been questioned. Extracts from his diaries show that the animals were just not up to the extreme demands made upon them:

Friday 3 February 1911

It is pathetic to see the ponies floundering in the soft patches. The first sink is a shock to them and seems to brace them to action. Thus they generally try to rush through when they feel themselves sticking. If the patch is small they land snorting and agitated on the harder surface with much effort. And if the patch is extensive they plunge on gamely until exhausted.

Most of them after a bit plunge forward with both forefeet together, making a series of jumps and bringing the sledge behind them with jerks. This is, of course, terribly tiring for them. Now and again they have to stop, and it is horrid to see them half engulfed in the snow, panting and heaving from the strain.

Now and again one falls and lies trembling and temporarily exhausted. It must be terribly trying for them, but it is wonderful to see how soon they recover their strength. The quiet, lazy ponies have a much better time than the eager ones when such troubles arise.

Wednesday 8 February 1911

The ponies were much shaken by the blizzard. One supposes they did not sleep – all look listless and two or three are visibly thinner than before. But the worst case by far is Forde's little pony; he was reduced to a weight little exceeding 400lbs on his sledge and caved in altogether on the second part of the march. The load was reduced   to 200lbs, and finally Forde pulled this in, leading the pony. The poor thing is a miserable scarecrow and never ought to have been brought – it is the same pony that did so badly in the ship.

Friday 10 February 1911

With numbed fingers on our horse's bridle and the animal striving to turn its head from the wind one feels resentful. At last all is ready. One says 'All right, Bowers, go ahead', and Birdie leads his big animal forward starting, as he continues, at a steady pace. The horses have got cold and at the word they are off, the Soldier's and one or two others with a rush. Finnesko give poor foothold on the slippery sastrugi and for a minute or two drivers have some difficulty in maintaining the pace on their feet. Movement is warming, and in ten minutes the column has settled itself to steady marching

Sunday 12 February 1911

The surface is getting decidedly worse. The ponies sink quite deep every now and again. We marched 6¼ miles before lunch, Blossom dropping considerably behind. He lagged more on the second march and we halted at 9 miles. Evans said he might be dragged for another mile and we went on for that distance and camped.

The sky was overcast: very dark and snowy looking in the south – very difficult to steer a course. Mt Discovery is in line with the south end of the Bluff from the camp and we are near the 79th parallel. We must get exact bearings for this is to be called the 'Bluff Camp' and should play an important part in the future. Bearings: Bluff 36° 19'; Black Island Rht Ex. I have decided to send E Evans, Forde and Keohane back with the three weakest ponies that they have been leading. The remaining five ponies, which have been improving in condition, will go on for a few days at least, and we must see how near we can come to the 80th parallel.

The surface was wretched today, the two drawbacks of yesterday (the thin crusts that let the ponies through and the sandy heaps that hang on the runners) if anything exaggerated.

Tuesday 14 February 1911

Memo – Arrangements for ponies.

1. *Hot bran or oat mashes.*
2. *Clippers for breaking wires of bales.*
3. *Pickets for horses.*
4. *Lighter ponies to take 10ft. sledges?*

Wednesday 15 February 1911

Bowers' pony refused work at intervals for the first time. His hind legs sink very deep. Weary Willy is decidedly better. The Soldier takes a gloomy view of everything, but I've come to see that this is a characteristic of him. In spite of it he pays every attention to the weaker horses. We had frequent halts on the march, but managed 4 miles before lunch and 3½ after.

The temperature was −15° at the lunch camp. It was cold sitting in the tent waiting for the ponies to rest. The thermometer is now −7°, but there is a bright sun and no wind, which makes the air feel quite comfortable: one's socks and finnesko dry well. Our provision allowance is working out very well. In fact all is well with us except the condition of the ponies. The more I see of the matter the more certain I am that we must save all the ponies to get better value out of them next year. It would have been ridiculous to have worked some out this year as the Soldier wished. Even now I feel we went too far with the first three.

Thursday 16 February 1911

The surface is a good deal better, but the ponies running out. Three of the five could go on without difficulty. Bowers' pony might go on a bit, but Weary Willy is a good deal done up, and to push him further would be to risk him unduly, so tomorrow we turn.

Wednesday 22 February 1911

Everything much the same. The ponies thinner but not much weaker. The crocks still going alone…There is rather an increased condition of false crust – that is, crust that appears firm till the whole weight of the animal is put upon it, when it suddenly gives some 3 or 4 inches. This is very trying for the poor beasts.

We reached Safety Camp. Found Evans and his party in excellent health, but alas, with only one pony. As far as I can gather, Forde's pony only got 4 miles from the Bluff Camp; then a blizzard came on and in spite of the most tender care from

Ford, the pony sank under it. Evans says that Forde spent hours with the animal trying to keep it going, feeding it, walking it about; at last he returned to the tent to say that the poor creature had fallen; they all tried to get it on its feet again but their efforts were useless. It couldn't stand, and soon after it died...Then the party marched on some 10 miles, but the blizzard had a bad effect on Blossom – it seems to have shrivelled him up, and now he was terribly emaciated. After this march he could hardly move. Evans describes his efforts as pathetic; he got on 100 yards, then stopped with legs outstretched and nose to the ground. They rested him, fed him well, covered him with rugs, but again all efforts were unavailing. The last stages came with painful detail. So Blossom is also left on the Southern Road.

The last pony, James Pigg as he is called, has thriven amazingly – of course great care has been taken with him and he is now getting full feed, so he ought to do well. The loss is severe, but they were the two oldest ponies of our team and the two which Oates thought of least use.

Friday 24 February 1911

Since the junction with the motor party the procedure has been for the man-hauling people to go forward just ahead of the crocks, the other party following two or three hours later. Today we closed less than usual, so that the crocks must have been going very well. However, the fiat had already gone forth, and this morning after the march poor old Jehu was led back on the track and shot. After our doubts as to his reaching Hut Point, it is wonderful to think that he has actually got eight marches beyond our last year limit and could have gone more. However, towards the end he was pulling very little, and on the whole it is merciful to have ended his life. Chinaman seems to improve and will certainly last a good many days yet. The rest show no signs of flagging and are only moderately hungry. The surface is tiring for walking, as one sinks 2 or 3 inches nearly all the time. I feel we ought to get through now.

Wednesday 1 March 1911

Our pony died in the night. It is hard to have got him back so far only for this. It is clear that these blizzards are terrible for the poor animals. Their coats are not good, but even with the best of coats it is certain they would lose condition badly if caught in one, and we cannot afford to lose condition at the beginning of a journey. It makes a late start necessary for next year.

Well, we have done our best and bought our experience at a heavy cost. Now every effort must be bent on saving the remaining animals, and it will be good luck if we get four back to Cape Evans, or even three. Jimmy Pigg may have fared badly; Bowers' big pony is in a bad way after that frightful blizzard. I cannot remember such a bad storm in February or March: the temperature was −7°.

Monday 17 April 1911

Two of the ponies hauled the sledges to within a mile of the Glacier Tongue; the wind, which had been north, here suddenly shifted to SE, very biting. (The wind remained north at C Evans during the afternoon, the ponies walked back into it.) Sky overcast, very bad light. Found the place to get on the glacier, but then lost the track – crossed more or less direct, getting amongst many cracks. Came down in bay near the open water – stumbled over the edge to an easy drift. More than once on these trips I, as leader, have suddenly disappeared from the sight of the others, affording some consternation till they got close enough to see what has happened.

Sunday 28 May 1911

Quite an excitement last night. One of the ponies (the grey, which I led last year and salved from the floe) either fell or tried to lie down in his stall, his head being lashed up to the stanchions on either side. In this condition he struggled and kicked till his body was twisted right round and his attitude extremely uncomfortable. Very luckily his struggles were heard almost at once, and his head ropes being cut, Oates got him on his feet again. He looked a good deal distressed at the time, but is now quite well again and has been out for his usual exercise.

Thursday 1 June 1911

I have today regularised the pony 'nicknames'; I must leave it to Drake to pull out the relation to the 'proper' names according to our school contracts!
    The nicknames are as follows:

James Pigg Keohane
Bones Crean
Michael Clissold
Snatcher Evans (PO)
Jehu
China
Christopher Hooper
Victor Bowers
Snippets (windsucker)
Nobby Lashly

Monday 31 July 1911

The ponies are getting buckish. Chinaman squeals and kicks in the stable, Nobby kicks without squealing, but with even more purpose – last night he knocked down a part of his stall. The noise of these animals is rather trying at night – one imagines all sorts of dreadful things happening, but when the watchman visits the stables its occupants blink at him with a sleepy air as though the disturbance could not possibly have been there!

Saturday 26 August 1911

The ponies are very buckish and can scarcely be held in at exercise; it seems certain that they feel the return of daylight. They were out in morning and afternoon yesterday. Oates and Anton took out Christopher and Snippets rather later. Both ponies broke away within 50 yards of the stable and galloped away over the floe. It was nearly an hour before they could be rounded up. Such escapades are the result of high spirits; there is no vice in the animals.

Friday 1 September 1911

There is no choice but to keep the rest at home to exercise the ponies. It's not going to be a light task to keep all these frisky little beasts in order, as their food is increased. Today the change in masters has taken place: by the new arrangement

Wilson takes Nobby
Cherry-Garrard takes Michael
Wright takes Chinaman
Atkinson takes Jehu.

Thursday 26 October 1911

Forty minutes after PO Evans, his driver, came in almost as hot; simultaneously Wilson arrived with Nobby and a tale of events not complete. He said that after the loads were removed Bowers had been holding the three ponies, who appeared to be quiet; suddenly one had tossed his head and all three had stampeded – Snatcher making for home, Nobby for the Western Mountains, Victor, with Bowers still hanging to him, in an indefinite direction. Running for 2 miles, he eventually rounded up Nobby west of Tent Island and brought him in. Half-an-hour after Wilson's return, Bowers came in with Victor distressed, bleeding at the nose, from which a considerable fragment hung semi-detached. Bowers himself was covered with blood and supplied the missing link – the cause of the incident. It appears that the ponies were fairly quiet when Victor tossed his head and caught his nostril in the trace hook on the hame of Snatcher's harness. The hook tore skin and flesh and of course the animal got out of hand. Bowers hung to him, but couldn't possibly keep hold of the other two as well. Victor had bled a good deal, and the blood congealing on the detached skin not only gave the wound a dismal appearance but greatly increased its irritation. I don't know how Bowers managed to hang on to the frightened animal; I don't believe anyone else would have done so. On the way back the dangling weight on the poor creature's nose would get on the swing and make him increasingly restive; it was necessary to stop him repeatedly. Since his return the piece of skin has been snipped off and proves the wound not so serious as it looked. The animal is still trembling, but quite on his feed, which is a good sign.

Wednesday 14 November 1911

Huge icicles under their noses during the march. Victor generally rubs his off on my sleeve.

Sunday 19 November 1911

Camp 15. We have struck a real bad surface, sledges pulling well over it, but ponies sinking very deep. The result is to about finish Jehu. He was terribly done on getting in tonight. He may go another march, but not more, I think. Considering the surface the other ponies did well. The ponies occasionally sink halfway to the hock, little Michael once or twice almost to the hock itself. Luckily the weather now is glorious for resting the animals, which are very placid and quiet in the brilliant sun.

Tuesday 28 November 1911

'The Thunderbolde' has been shot tonight. Plucky little chap he has stuck it out well and leaves the stage but a few days before his fellows...

Wednesday 29 November 1911

The men-haulers started 1½ hours before us and got here a good hour ahead, travelling easily throughout. Such is the surface with the sun on it, justifying my decision to work towards day marching. Evans has suggested the word 'glide' for the quality of surface indicated. 'Surface' is more comprehensive, and includes the crusts and liability to sink in them. From this point of view the surface is distinctly bad. The ponies plough deep all the time, and the men most of the time.

Thursday 30 November 1911

Camp 26. A very pleasant day for marching, but a very tiring march for the poor animals, which, with the exception of Nobby, are showing signs of failure all round. We were slower by half an hour or more than yesterday. Except that the loads are light now and there are still eight animals left, things don't look too pleasant, but we should be less than 60 miles from our first point of aim. The surface was much *worse today, the ponies sinking to their knees very often. There were a few harder patches towards the end of the march.*

Friday 8 December 1911

Our case is growing desperate. Evans and his man-haulers tried to pull a load this afternoon. They managed to move a sledge with four people on it, pulling in ski. Pulling on foot they sank to the knees. The snow all about us is terribly deep. We tried Nobby and he plunged to his belly in it. Wilson thinks the ponies finished but Oates thinks they will get another march in spite of the surface. If it comes tomorrow, if it should not, we must kill the ponies tomorrow and get on as best we can with the men on ski and the dogs. But one wonders what the dogs can do on such a surface. I much fear they also will prove inadequate.

Saturday 9 December 1911

The ponies were quite done, one and all. They came on painfully slowly, a few hundred yards at a time. By this time I was hauling ahead a ridiculously light load, and yet finding the pulling heavy enough. We camped and the ponies have been shot. Poor beasts! They have done wonderfully well considering the terrible circumstances under which they worked, but yet it is hard to kill them so early.

Scott's Musings Before Settling into Cape Evans

Monday 17 April 1911

In choosing the site of the hut on our Home Beach I had thought of the possibility of northerly winds bringing a swell, but had argued, firstly, that no heavy northerly swell had ever been recorded in the Sound; secondly, that a strong northerly wind was bound to bring pack that would damp the swell; thirdly, that the locality was excellently protected by the Barne Glacier; and finally, that the beach itself showed no signs of having been swept by the sea, the rock fragments composing it being completely angular.

When the hut was erected and I found that its foundation was only 11 feet above the level of the sea ice, I had a slight misgiving, but reassured myself again by reconsidering the circumstances that afforded shelter to the beach.

The fact that such question had been considered makes it easier to understand the attitude of mind that re-admitted doubt in the face of phenomenal conditions.

The event has justified my original arguments, but I must confess a sense of having assumed security without sufficient proof in a case where an error of judgment might have had dire consequences.

It was not until I found all safe at the Home Station that I realised how anxious I had been concerning it. In a normal season no thought of its having been in danger would have occurred to me, but since the loss of the ponies and the breaking of the Glacier Tongue I could not rid myself of the fear that misfortune was in the air and that some abnormal swell had swept the beach; gloomy thoughts of the havoc that might have been wrought by such an event would arise in spite of the sound reasons that had originally led me to choose the site of the hut as a safe one.

The late freezing of the sea, the terrible continuance of wind and the abnormalities to which I have referred had gradually strengthened the profound distrust with which I had been forced to regard our mysterious Antarctic climate until my imagination conjured up many forms of disaster as possibly falling on those from whom I had parted for so long.

We marched towards Cape Evans under the usually miserable conditions that attend the breaking of camp in a cold wind after a heavy blizzard. The outlook was dreary in the grey light of early morning, our clothes were frozen stiff and our fingers, wet and cold in the tent, had been frostbitten in packing the sledges.

A few comforting signs of life appeared as we approached the Cape; some old footprints in the snow, a long silk thread from the meteorologist's balloon; but we saw nothing more as we neared the rocks of the promontory and the many grounded bergs that were scattered off it.

To my surprise the fast ice extended past the Cape and we were able to round it into the North Bay. Here we saw the weather screen on Wind Vane Hill, and a moment later turned a small headland and brought the hut in full view. It was intact – stables, outhouses and all; evidently the sea had left it undisturbed. I breathed a huge sigh of relief. We watched two figures at work near the stables and wondered when they would see us. In a moment or two they did so, and fled inside the hut to carry the news of our arrival. Three minutes later all nine occupants were streaming over the floe towards us with shouts of welcome. There were eager inquiries as to mutual welfare and it took but a minute to learn the most important events of the quiet station life that had been led since our departure. These under the circumstances might well be considered the deaths of one pony and one dog. The pony was that which had been nicknamed Hackenschmidt from his vicious habit of using both fore and hind legs in attacking those who came near him. He had been obviously of different breed from the other ponies, being of lighter and handsomer shape, suggestive of a strain of Arab blood. From no cause that could be discovered either by the symptoms of his illness or the post-mortem held by Nelson could a reason be found for his death. In spite of the best feeding and every care he had gradually sickened until he was too weak to stand, and in this condition there had been no option but to put him out of misery. Anton considers the death of Hackenschmidt to have been an act of 'cussedness' – the result of a determination to do no work for the Expedition! Although the loss is serious I remember doubts that I had as to whether this animal could be anything but a source of trouble to us.

He had been most difficult to handle all through, showing a vicious, intractable temper. I had foreseen great difficulties with him, especially during the early part of any journey on which he was taken, and this consideration softened the news of his death. The dog had been left behind in a very sick condition, and this loss was not a great surprise.

These items were the worst of the small budget of news that awaited me; for the rest, the hut arrangements had worked out in the most satisfactory manner possible and the scientific routine of observations was in full swing. After our primitive life at Cape Armitage it was wonderful to enter the precincts of our warm, dry Cape Evans home. The interior space seemed palatial, the light resplendent, and the comfort luxurious. It was very good to eat in civilised fashion, to enjoy the first bath for three months, and have contact with clean, dry clothing. Such fleeting hours of comfort (for custom soon banished their delight) are the treasured remembrance of every polar traveller. They throw into sharpest contrast the hardships of the past and the comforts of the present, and for the time he revels in the unaccustomed physical contentment that results.

I was not many hours or even minutes in the hut before I was hailed round to observe in detail the transformation that had taken place during my absence, and in which a very proper pride was taken by those who had wrought it.

Simpson's Corner was the first visited. Here the eye travelled over numerous shelves laden with a profusion of self-recording instruments, electric batteries and switchboards, whilst the ear caught the ticking of many clocks, the gentle whir of a motor and occasionally the trembling note of an electric bell. But such sights and sounds conveyed only an impression of the delicate methodical means by which the daily and hourly variations of our weather conditions were being recorded – a mere glimpse of the intricate arrangements of a first-class meteorological station – the one and only station of that order that has been established in polar regions. It took me days and even months to realise fully the aims of our meteorologist and the scientific accuracy with which he was achieving them. When I did so to an adequate extent I wrote some description of his work, which will be found in the following pages of this volume. The first impression that I am here describing was more confused; I appreciated only that by going to Simpson's Corner one could ascertain at a glance how hard the wind was blowing and had been blowing, how the barometer was varying, to what degree of cold the thermometer had descended; if one were still more inquisitive he could further inform himself as to the electrical tension of the atmosphere and other matters of like import. That such knowledge could be gleaned without a visit to the open air was an obvious advantage to those who were clothing themselves to face it, whilst the ability to study the variation of a storm without exposure savoured of no light victory of mind over matter.

The dark room stands next to the parasitologist's side of the bench, which flanks Sunny Jim's Corner – an involved sentence. To be more exact, the physicists adjust their instruments and write up books at a bench that projects at right angles to the end wall of the hut; the opposite side of this bench is allotted to Atkinson, who is to write with his back to the dark room. Atkinson being still absent his corner was unfurnished, and my attention was next claimed by the occupant of the dark room beyond Atkinson's limit. The art of photography has never been so well housed within the polar regions and rarely without them. Such a palatial chamber for the development of negatives and prints can only be justified by the quality of the work produced in it, and is only justified in our case by the possession of such an artist as Ponting. He was eager to show me the results of his summer work, and meanwhile my eye took in the neat shelves with their array of cameras, etc, the porcelain sink and automatic water tap, the two acetylene gas burners with their shading screens, and the general obviousness of all conveniences of the photographic art. Here, indeed, was encouragement for the best results, and to the photographer be all praise, for it is mainly his hand that has executed the designs that his brain conceived. In this may be clearly seen the advantage of a traveller's experience. Ponting has had to fend for himself under primitive conditions in a new land; the result is a 'handy man' with every form of tool and in any circumstances. Thus, when building operations were to the fore and mechanical labour scarce, Ponting returned to the shell of his apartment with only the raw material for completing it. In the shortest possible space of time shelves and tanks were erected, doors hung and windows framed, and all in a workmanlike manner commanding the admiration of all beholders. It was well that speed could be commanded for such work, since the fleeting hours of the summer season had been altogether too few to be spared from the immediate service of photography. Ponting's nervous temperament allowed no waste of time − for him fine weather meant no sleep; he decided that lost opportunities should be as rare as circumstances would permit.

This attitude was now manifested in the many yards of cinematograph film remaining on hand and yet greater number recorded as having been sent back in the ship, in the boxes of negatives lying on the shelves and a well-filled album of prints.

Of the many admirable points in this work perhaps the most notable are Ponting's eye for a picture and the mastery he has acquired of ice subjects; the composition of most of his pictures is extraordinarily good, he seems to know by instinct the exact value of foreground and middle distance and of the introduction of 'life', whilst with more technical skill in the manipulation of screens and exposures he emphasises the subtle shadows of the snow and reproduces its wondrously transparent texture. He is an artist in love with his work, and it was good to hear his enthusiasm for results of the past and plans of the future.

Long before I could gaze my fill at the contents of the dark room I was led to the biologists' cubicle; Nelson and Day had from the first decided to camp together, each having a habit of methodical neatness; both were greatly relieved when the arrangement was approved, and they were freed from the chance of an untidy companion. No attempt had been made to furnish this cubicle before our departure on the autumn journey, but now on my return I found it an example of the best utilisation of space. The prevailing note was neatness; the biologist's microscope stood on a neat bench surrounded by enamel dishes, vessels, and books neatly arranged; behind him, when seated, rose two neat bunks with neat, closely curtained drawers for clothing and neat reflecting sconces for candles; overhead was a neat arrangement for drying socks with several nets, neatly bestowed. The carpentering to produce this effect had been of quite a high order, and was in very marked contrast with that exhibited for the hasty erections in other cubicles. The pillars and boarding of the bunks had carefully finished edges and were stained to mahogany brown. Nelson's bench is situated very conveniently under the largest of the hut windows, and had also an acetylene lamp, so that both in summer and winter he has all conveniences for his indoor work.

Day appeared to have been unceasingly busy during my absence. Everyone paid tribute to his mechanical skill and expressed gratitude for the help he had given in adjusting instruments and generally helping forward the scientific work. He was entirely responsible for the heating, lighting, and ventilating arrangements, and as all these appear satisfactory he deserved much praise. Particulars concerning these arrangements I shall give later; as a first impression it is sufficient to note that the warmth and lighting of the hut seemed as good as could be desired, whilst for our comfort the air seemed fresh and pure. Day had also to report some progress with the motor sledges, but this matter also I leave for future consideration.

My attention was very naturally turned from the heating arrangements to the cooking stove and its custodian, Clissold. I had already heard much of the surpassingly satisfactory meals that his art had produced, and had indeed already a first experience of them. Now I was introduced to the cook's corner with its range and ovens, its pots and pans, its side tables and well-covered shelves. Much was to be gathered there from, although a good meal by no means depends only on kitchen conveniences. It was gratifying to learn that the stove had proved itself economical and the patent fuel blocks a most convenient and efficient substitute for coal. Save for the thickness of the furnace cheeks and the size of the oven, Clissold declared himself wholly satisfied. He feared that the oven would prove too small to keep up a constant supply of bread for all hands; nevertheless he introduced me to this oven with an air of pride that I soon found to be fully justified. For connected therewith was a contrivance for which he was entirely responsible, and which in its ingenuity rivalled any of which the hut could boast. The interior of the oven was so arranged that the 'rising' of the bread completed an electric circuit, thereby ringing a bell and switching on a red lamp. Clissold had realised that the continuous ringing of the bell would not be soothing to the nerves of our party, nor the continuous burning of the lamp calculated to prolong its life, and he had therefore added the clockwork mechanism that automatically broke the circuit after a short interval of time; further, this clockwork mechanism could be made to control the emersion of the same warning signals at intervals of time varied according to the desire of the operator – thus because, when in bed, he would desire a signal at short periods, but if absent from the hut he would wish to know at a glance what had happened when he returned. Judged by any standard it was a remarkably pretty little device, but when I learnt that it had been made from odds and ends, such as a cog-wheel or spring here and a cell or magnet there, begged from other departments, I began to realise that we had a very exceptional cook. Later when I found that Clissold was called in to consult on the ailments of Simpson's motor and that he was capable of constructing a dog sledge out of packing cases, I was less surprised, because I knew by this time that he had had considerable training in mechanical work before he turned his attention to pots and pans.

My first impressions include matters to which I was naturally eager to give an early half-hour, namely the housing of our animals. I found here-in that praise was as justly due to our Russian boys as to my fellow Englishmen.

Anton with Lashly's help had completed the furnishing of the stables. Neat stalls occupied the whole length of the lean to, the sides so boarded that sprawling legs could not be entangled beneath and the front well covered with tin sheet to defeat the 'cribbers'. I could but sigh again to think of the stalls that must now remain empty, whilst appreciating that there was ample room for the safe harbourage of the ten beasts that remain, be the winter never so cold or the winds so wild.

Later we have been able to give double space to all but two or three of our animals, in which they can lie down if they are so inclined.

The ponies look fairly fit considering the low diet on which they have been kept; their coats were surprisingly long and woolly in contrast with those of the animals I had left at Hut Point. At this time they were being exercised by Lashly, Anton, Demetri, Hooper and Clissold, and as a rule were ridden, the sea having only recently frozen. The exercise ground had lain on the boulder-strewn sand of the Home Beach and extending towards the Skua Lake; and across these stretches I soon saw barebacked figures dashing at speed, and not a few amusing incidents in which horse and rider parted with abrupt lack of ceremony. I didn't think this quite the most desirable form of exercise for the beasts, but decided to leave matters as they were till our pony manager returned.

Demetri had only five or six dogs left in charge, but these looked fairly fit, all things considered, and it was evident the boy was bent on taking every care of them, for he had not only provided shelters, but had built a small lean to which would serve as a hospital for any animal whose stomach or coat needed nursing.

Such were in broad outline the impressions I received on my first return to our Home Station; they were almost wholly pleasant and, as I have shown, in happy contrast with the fears that had assailed me on the homeward route. As the days went by I was able to fill in the detail in equally pleasant fashion, to watch the development of fresh arrangements and the improvement of old ones. Finally, in this way I was brought to realise what an extensive and intricate but eminently satisfactory organisation I had made myself responsible for.

Chapter 8

The Long Winter

The sun set for the winter months on 23 April 1911 and the party settled into Cape Evans. Scott maintained a 'rank' approach from his naval days. Everyone had their task and the scientific work continued, with observations and measurements carried out, equipment kept up to standard and the dogs and remaining ponies taken out for daily exercise. It was obviously important for the men to keep up a physical fitness regime too and they played football with Scott noting: 'Atkinson is by far the best player, but Hooper. PO Evans and Crean are also quite good.' One diversion for the men was to re-launch the *South Polar Times*, which Shackleton had started during the *Discovery* expedition. Its editor was Cherry-Garrard. Scott spent a lot of time calculating sledging rations and weights for the forthcoming polar march. The pre-planning included regular lectures on a wide range of subjects with Ponting talking about Japan, Wilson about sketching, Oates on horse management and geologist Frank Debenham about volcanoes. Levick studied birds and marine life and Priestley focussed on geology. As far as Scott was concerned, this part of the expedition was proceeding well:

Sunday 14 May 1911

Grey and dull in the morning.

Exercised the ponies and held the usual service. This morning I gave Wright some notes containing speculations on the amount of ice on the Antarctic continent and on the effects of winter movements in the sea ice. I want to get into his head the larger bearing of the problems that our physical investigations involve. He needs two years here to fully realise these things, and with all his intelligence and energy will produce little unless he has that extended experience.

The sky cleared at noon, and this afternoon I walked over the North Bay to the ice cliffs – such a very beautiful afternoon and evening – the scene bathed in moonlight, so bright and pure as to be almost golden, a very wonderful scene. At such times the Bay seems strangely homely, especially when the eye rests on our camp with the hut and lighted windows.

I am very much impressed with the extraordinary and general cordiality of the relations that exist amongst our people. I do not suppose that a statement of the real truth, namely, that there is no friction at all, will be credited – it is so generally thought that the many rubs of such a life as this are quietly and purposely sunk in oblivion. With me there is no need to draw a veil; there is nothing to cover. There are no strained relations in this hut, and nothing more emphatically evident than the universally amicable spirit that is shown on all occasions.

Such a state of affairs would be delightfully surprising under any conditions, but it is much more so when one remembers the diverse assortment of our company.

It was Scott's 43rd birthday on 6 June and a 'feast' was held to celebrate. Scott recorded of that day:

It is my birthday, a fact I might easily have forgotten, but my kind people did not. At lunch an immense birthday cake made its appearance and we were photographed assembled about it. Clissold had decorated its sugared top with various devices in chocolate and crystallised fruit, flags and photographs of myself.

After my walk I discovered that great preparations were in progress for a special dinner, and when the hour for that meal arrived we sat down to a sumptuous spread with our sledge banners hung about us. Clissold's especially excellent seal soup, roast mutton and red currant jelly, fruit salad, asparagus and chocolate – such was our menu. For drink we had cider cup, a mystery not yet fathomed, some sherry and a liqueur.

After this luxurious meal everyone was very festive and amiably argumentative. As I write there is a group in the dark room discussing political progress with discussions – another at one corner of the dinner table airing its views on the origin of matter and the probability of its ultimate discovery, and yet another debating military problems. The scraps that reach me from the various groups sometimes piece together in ludicrous fashion. Perhaps these arguments are practically unprofitable, but they give a great deal of pleasure to the participants. It's delightful to hear the ring of triumph in some voice when the owner imagines he has delivered himself of a well-rounded period or a clinching statement concerning the point under discussion. They are boys, all of them, but such excellent good-natured ones; there has been no sign of sharpness or anger, no jarring note, in all these wordy contests! All end with a laugh.

Nelson has offered Taylor a pair of socks to teach him some geology! This lulls me to sleep!

There was another celebration on 22 June to mark Midwinter Day, the Antarctic equivalent of Christmas

Thursday 22 June 1911

The sun reached its maximum depression at about 2.30pm on the 22nd, Greenwich Mean Time: this is 2.30am on the 23rd according to the local time of the 180th meridian, which we are keeping. Dinner tonight is therefore the meal that is nearest the sun's critical change of course, and has been observed with all the festivity customary at Xmas at home.

At tea we broached an enormous Buzzard cake, with much gratitude to its provider, Cherry-Garrard. In preparation for the evening our 'Union Jacks' and sledge flags were hung about the large table, which itself was laid with glass and a plentiful supply of champagne bottles instead of the customary mugs and enamel lime juice jugs. At seven o'clock we sat down to an extravagant bill of fare as compared with our usual simple diet.

Beginning on seal soup, by common consent the best decoction that our cook produces, we went on to roast beef with Yorkshire pudding, fried potatoes and Brussels sprouts. Then followed a flaming plum-pudding and excellent mince pies, and thereafter a dainty savoury of anchovy and cod's roe. A wondrous attractive meal even in so far as judged by our simple lights, but with its garnishments a positive feast, for withal the table was strewn with dishes of burnt almonds, crystallised fruits, chocolates and such toothsome kickshaws, whilst the unstinted supply of champagne, which accompanied the courses, was succeeded by a noble array of liqueur bottles from which choice could be made in the drinking of toasts.

I screwed myself up to a little speech, which drew attention to the nature of the celebration as a half-way mark not only in our winter but in the plans of the expedition as originally published. (I fear there are some who don't realise how rapidly time passes and who have barely begun work, which by this time ought to be in full swing.)

We had come through a summer season and half a winter, and had before us half a winter and a second summer. We ought to know how we stood in every respect; we did know how we stood in regard to stores and transport, and I especially thanked the officer in charge of stores and the custodians of the animals. I said that as regards the future, chance must play a part, but that experience showed me that it would have been impossible to have chosen people more fitted to support me in the enterprise to the south than those who were to start in that direction in the spring. I thanked them all for having put their shoulders to the wheel and given me this confidence. We drank to the Success of the Expedition.

Then everyone was called on to speak, starting on my left and working round the table; the result was very characteristic of the various individuals – one seemed to know so well the style of utterance to which each would commit himself.

Needless to say, all were entirely modest and brief; unexpectedly, all had exceedingly kind things to say of me – in fact I was obliged to request the omission of compliments at an early stage. Nevertheless it was gratifying to have a really genuine recognition of my attitude towards the scientific workers of the expedition, and I felt very warmly towards all these kind, good fellows for expressing it.

If good will and happy fellowship count towards success, very surely shall we deserve to succeed. It was matter for comment, much applauded, that there had not been a single disagreement between any two members of our party from the beginning. By the end of dinner a very cheerful spirit prevailed, and the room was cleared for Ponting and his lantern, whilst the gramophone gave forth its most lively airs.

When the table was upended, its legs removed, and chairs arranged in rows, we had quite a roomy lecture hall. Ponting had cleverly chosen this opportunity to display a series of slides made from his own local negatives. I have never so fully realised his work as on seeing these beautiful pictures; they so easily outclass anything of their kind previously taken in these regions. Our audience cheered vociferously.

After this show the table was restored for snapdragon, and a brew of milk punch was prepared in which we drank the health of Campbell's party and of our good friends in the Terra Nova. *Then the table was again removed and a set of lancers formed.*

By this time the effect of stimulating liquid refreshment on men so long accustomed to a simple life became apparent. Our biologist had retired to bed, the silent Soldier bubbled with humour and insisted on dancing with Anton. Evans, PO, was imparting confidences in heavy whispers. Pat Keohane had grown intensely Irish and desirous of political argument, whilst Clissold sat with a constant expansive smile and punctuated the babble of conversation with an occasional 'Whoop' of delight or disjointed witticism. Other bright-eyed individuals merely reached the capacity to enjoy that which under ordinary circumstances might have passed without evoking a smile.

In the midst of the revelry Bowers suddenly appeared, followed by some satellites bearing an enormous Christmas Tree whose branches bore flaming candles, gaudy crackers, and little presents for all. The presents, I learnt, had been prepared with kindly thought by Miss Souper [Mrs Wilson's sister] and the tree had been made by Bowers of pieces of stick and string with coloured paper to clothe its branches; the whole erection was remarkably creditable and the distribution of the presents caused much amusement.

Whilst revelry was the order of the day within our hut, the elements without seemed desirous of celebrating the occasion with equal emphasis and greater decorum. The eastern sky was massed with swaying auroral light, the most vivid and beautiful display that I had ever seen — fold on fold the arches and curtains of vibrating luminosity rose and spread across the sky, to slowly fade and yet again spring to glowing life.

The brighter light seemed to flow, now to mass itself in wreathing folds in one quarter, from which lustrous streamers shot upward, and anon to run in waves through the system of some dimmer figure as if to infuse new life within it.

It is impossible to witness such a beautiful phenomenon without a sense of awe, and yet this sentiment is not inspired by its brilliancy but rather by its delicacy in light and colour, its transparency, and above all by its tremulous evanescence of form. There is no glittering splendour to dazzle the eye, as has been too often described; rather the appeal is to the imagination by the suggestion of something wholly spiritual, something instinct with a fluttering ethereal life, serenely confident yet restlessly mobile.

One wonders why history does not tell us of 'aurora' worshippers, so easily could the phenomenon be considered the manifestation of 'god' or 'demon'. To the little silent group that stood at gaze before such enchantment it seemed profane to return to the mental and physical atmosphere of our house. Finally, when I stepped within, I was glad to find that there had been a general movement bedwards, and in the next half-hour the last of the roysterers had succumbed to slumber.

Thus, except for a few bad heads in the morning, ended the High Festival of Midwinter.

There is little to be said for the artificial uplifting of animal spirits, yet few could take great exception to so rare an outburst in a long run of quiet days.

After all we celebrated the birth of a season which, for weal or woe, must be numbered amongst the greatest in our lives.

Dr Edward Wilson had come up with the idea of a scientific journey to obtain Emperor Penguin eggs from a rookery near Cape Crozier (he had suggested this in the *Discovery* expedition's scientific reports), with the aim of following up his earlier research. Wilson wanted to collect the eggs at their embryo stage to examine the development of the birds. All this necessitated a trip in the depths of winter to obtain eggs in at that stage. Scott at first refused the trek because of its risks across 130 miles of challenging terrain and bitterly low temperatures, but then relented and a party comprising Wilson, Bowers and Cherry-Garrard set out on 27 June 1911. But there was another aim on this journey – to experiment with food rations and equipment in advance of the coming summer's polar journey.

Meanwhile, Amundsen was sending despatches to *The Times* that were full of enthusiasm about his own endeavours:

The goal of our voyage was the bay that indents the great Antarctic ice-barrier in longitude 164deg W and latitude 78deg 30mm S. It was a long voyage that we had before us – 16,000 nautical miles from home – and it was decided to make no stop on the way, for the time was short and it was necessary to make the most of it. We should have to reach the Barrier by the middle of January if we were to get our work done…On the first day of January the first ice was sighted. That fitted well. Next day a few detached ice floes began to appear. In the evening of the 2nd we crossed the Antarctic Circle and at 10pm there lay the Antarctic drift ice before us! It did not look particularly imposing; a few strips of spring-frozen, newly-broken ice. Nothing of that kind could hinder us, and we stood straight in longitude 176deg W (about) and latitude 66deg 30min S. It took us four days and nights to get through the belt of packed ice, and on the evening of the 6th we emerged into open sea…With the exception of two small bergs, we did not see a sign of ice from the time we entered it until we sighted the Barrier in about 78deg S latitude…We sighted the mighty Barrier at 2.30pm on January 11. One would be less than human if one could behold such a sight unmoved. As far as the eye can see, from Western to Eastern horizon, this wall of ice rises perpendicularly to a height of 100ft. And yet it is only a very small part of it that one sees. What must the man have thought who first came upon this wall, and for whom all further advance seemed impossibility? […] The day after we sighted the Barrier we reached this bay, still in the same situation – about longitude 164deg W. It was so full, however, of recently broken-up bay ice that there was no question of getting in. We therefore took a little run eastwards along the edge of the Barrier to await events. The next morning (January 13) we returned, and then found that so much of the ice had floated out that there was an opportunity for us to get in…On the following day (January 14) we found a landing-place well suited for our enterprise. The long 16,000 mile voyage was safely accomplished, and we were only one day out in our calculation. We had arrived a day too early…After having safely moored the vessel to the ice, we set to find a suitable place for wintering. This did not take long. About 2h kilo-metres from the ship, at the foot of a ridge, well protected from the south-east winds, we found an ideal place; and on Monday (January 16) we began to unload our cargo. Two men at once set about the erection of the house, while the rest of the land party continued to bring up the building materials and provisions. With our 116 dogs we had draught-power enough but it was often slow work getting the heavily-laden sledges up to the site, which lies at a height of 15ft. But our dogs know how to draw. It is a pleasure to work with them. They are all picked animals from Greenland. It is three weeks since we began the building of our station, and now everything is ready. The desolate, icy landscape has undergone a great change. The silence is broken. Where formerly only a solitary penguin or the track of a seal crossed the height there now is a whole little village. Our solidly-built little house stands safe and secure, sunk 4ft down in snow as hard as rock and supported by backstays on all sides…The principal food depot is about a kilometre from the station, and contains provisions sufficient for two years. Since we came here we have lived almost entirely or seal-meat, and would not exchange seal steak for any dish in the world. There are great numbers of seals here, and we shall soon have preserved enough both for ourselves and all our dogs for the winter. In a few days the Fram will be ready to leave us. She goes north with greetings and messages, and we shall begin our journey towards the south...I can say nothing more with regard to our future prospects. We shall do what we can.

The Times – 7 June 1911

Travelling during the Antarctic winter was a new challenge for the men. Scott wrote that it was 'a bold venture, but the right men have gone to attempt it'. Cherry-Garrard later described the horrors of the nineteen days it took to travel the 60 miles to Cape Crozier, recalling one day, 5 July, when the temperature fell below minus 77°F (minus 60°C) and there was 109 degrees of frost as 'as cold as anyone would want to endure in darkness and iced up clothes'. (Cherry-Garrard was to forever remember the trip as 'the worst journey in the world' – giving the title to the book he later wrote in 1922). The men's equipment, clothes and sleeping bags were constantly iced up (having to be bent back into shape) and the daily distance travelled was often little more than a single mile.

Criticism in retrospect is easily cast at Scott. But one has to remember that his team was just one of a handful who had ever wintered on the Antarctic – there was little data to aid him with his intent. It is a fact, however, that Scott felt he had previously experienced all that the unforgiving continent could throw at him. Amundsen's lack of such experience may have actually helped with his success – for he prepared himself for an unknown nightmare. In the end, Amundsen encountered conditions that were less harsh than he had anticipated.

On 4 July Atkinson went missing after he and Gran – 'two adventurous spirits' – ventured out without Scott's knowledge. Gran returned in time for dinner but it had taken him almost an hour to cover a couple of hundred yards in the bitter weather. Atkinson was still out there somewhere in a blizzard and Scott wrote of the search party they had to organise:

Tuesday 4 July 1911

A day of blizzard and adventure.

Evans, PO, Crean and Keohane, being anxious for a walk, were sent to the north with a lantern. Whilst this desultory search proceeded the wind sprang up again from the south, but with no great force, and meanwhile the sky showed signs of clearing and the moon appeared dimly through the drifting clouds. With such a guide we momentarily looked for the return of our wanderer, and with his continued absence our anxiety grew. At 9.30 Evans, PO, and his party returned without news of him, and at last there was no denying the possibility of a serious accident. Between 9.30 and 10 proper search parties were organised, and I give the details to show the thoroughness I thought necessary to meet the gravity of the situation. I had by this time learnt that Atkinson had left with comparatively light clothing and, still worse, with leather ski boots on his feet; fortunately he had wind clothing.

PO Evans was away first with Crean, Keohane and Demetri, a light sledge, a sleeping bag, and a flask of brandy. His orders were to search the edge of the land and glacier through the sweep of the Bay to the Barne Glacier and to Cape Barne beyond, then to turn east along an open crack and follow it to Inaccessible Island. Evans (Lieut), with Nelson, Forde and Hooper, left shortly after, similarly equipped, to follow the shore of the South Bay in similar fashion, then turn out to the Razor Back and search there. Next Wright, Gran and Lashly set out for the bergs to look thoroughly about them and from thence pass round and examine Inaccessible Island. After these parties got away, Meares and Debenham started with a lantern to search to and fro over the surface of our promontory. Simpson and Oates went out in a direct line over the northern floe to the 'Archibald' thermometer, whilst Ponting and Taylor re-examined the tide crack towards the Barne Glacier. Meanwhile Day went to and fro Wind Vane Hill to light at intervals upon its crest bundles of tow well soaked in petrol. At length Clissold and I were left alone in the hut, and as the hours went by I grew ever more alarmed. It was impossible for me to conceive how an able man could have failed to return to the hut before this or by any means found shelter in such clothing in such weather. Atkinson had started for a point a little more than a mile away; at 10.30 he had been five hours away; what conclusion could be drawn? And yet I felt it most difficult to imagine an accident on open floe with no worse pitfall than a shallow crack or steep-sided snow drift. At least I could feel that every spot that was likely to be the scene of such an accident would be searched. Thus eleven o'clock came without change, then 11.30 with its 6 hours of absence. But at 11.45 I heard voices from the Cape, and presently the adventure ended to my extreme relief when Meares and Debenham led our wanderer home. He was badly frostbitten in the hand and less seriously on the face, and though a good deal confused, as men always are on such occasions, he was otherwise well.

His tale is confused, but as far as one can gather he did not go more than a quarter of a mile in the direction of the thermometer screen before he decided to turn back. He then tried to walk with the wind a little on one side on the bearing he had originally observed, and after some time stumbled on an old fish trap hole, which he knew to be 200 yards from the Cape. He made this 200 yards in the direction he supposed correct, and found nothing. In such a situation had he turned east he must have hit the land somewhere close to the hut and so found his way to it. The fact that he did not, but attempted to wander straight on, is clear evidence of the mental condition caused by that situation. There can be no doubt that in a blizzard a man has not only to safeguard the circulation in his limbs, but must struggle with a sluggishness of brain and an absence of reasoning power, which is far more likely to undo him.

In fact Atkinson has really no very clear idea of what happened to him after he missed the Cape. He seems to have wandered aimlessly up wind till he hit an island; he walked all round this; says he couldn't see a yard at this time; fell often into the tide crack; finally stopped under the lee of some rocks; here got his hand frostbitten owing to difficulty of getting frozen mit on again, finally got it on; started to dig a hole to wait in. Saw something of the moon and left the island; lost the moon and wanted to go back; could find nothing; finally stumbled on another island, perhaps the same one; waited again, again saw the moon, now clearing; shaped some sort of course by it – then saw flare on Cape and came on rapidly – says he shouted to someone on Cape quite close to him, greatly surprised not to get an answer. It is a rambling tale tonight and a half thawed brain. It is impossible to listen to such a tale without appreciating that it has been a close escape or that there would have been no escape had the blizzard continued. The thought that it would return after a short lull was amongst the worst with me during the hours of waiting.

2am – The search parties have returned and all is well again, but we must have no more of these very unnecessary escapades. Yet it is impossible not to realise that this bit of experience has done more than all the talking I could have ever accomplished to bring home to our people the dangers of a blizzard.

Monday 10 July 1911

We have had the worst gale I have ever known in these regions and have not yet done with it.

The wind started at about mid-day on Friday, and increasing in violence reached an average of 60 miles for one hour on Saturday, the gusts at this time exceeding 70 mph. This force of wind, although exceptional, has not been without parallel earlier in the year, but the extraordinary feature of this gale was the long continuance of a very cold temperature. On Friday night the thermometer registered −39°. Throughout Saturday and the greater part of Sunday it did not rise above −35°. Late yesterday it was in the minus twenties and today at length it has risen to zero.

Needless to say no one has been far from the hut. It was my turn for duty on Saturday night, and on the occasions when I had to step out of doors I was struck with the impossibility of enduring such conditions for any length of time. One seemed to be robbed of breath as they burst on one – the fine snow beat in behind the wind guard, and ten paces against the wind were sufficient to reduce one's face to the verge of frostbite. To clear the anemometer vane it is necessary to go to the other end of the hut and climb a ladder. Twice whilst engaged in this task I had literally to lean against the wind with head bent and face averted and so stagger crab-like on my course. In those two days of really terrible weather our thoughts often turned to absentees at Cape Crozier with the devout hope that they may be safely housed.

Battling against the odds, the party built an igloo at Cape Crozier with a roof made from wood they had taken along with them. The igloo shelter was later almost destroyed in a blizzard with force eleven winds that also swept away the tent, which was crucial for their return journey. Luckily this was recovered half a mile away. The team attempted to keep their spirits up by singing and there were times they feared they would never make it back. They used their igloo as their base from which to visit the penguin colony and collect five Emperor Penguin eggs – two of which were dropped by Cherry-Garrard as he stumbled. (The three that managed to survive the journey were to find their way first to London's Natural History Museum and then the University of Edinburgh. But they proved inadequate to back up any of Wilson's theories). That night as they prepared supper a drop of hot penguin blubber hit Wilson in the eye leaving him half-blind and in excruciating pain.

Sunday 30 July 1911

Two quiet days, temperature low in the minus thirties – an occasional rush of wind lasting for but a few minutes.

One of our best sledge dogs, 'Julick', has disappeared. I'm afraid he's been set on by the others at some distant spot and we shall see nothing more but his stiffened carcass when the light returns. Meares thinks the others would not have attacked him and imagines he has fallen into the water in some seal hole or crack. In either case I'm afraid we must be resigned to another loss. It's an awful nuisance.

The group finally set off for the return journey to Cape Evans, arriving there on 1 August. It was no easier trek. Cherry-Garrard's teeth split in the freezing temperatures; unable to sleep in their sleeping bags they napped as they walked, awoken only when they bumped into another team member; they yearned for a warm bed and hours of comfortable, peaceful slumber. Upon their return, their ice-encrusted sleeping bags weighed 74lbs more than when they had set off. Nevertheless, Scott was to look back on the journey as 'a very wonderful performance' and strongly believed that the resting of rations and equipment for the forthcoming polar trek was 'as near perfection as experience can direct'. But the men's faces betrayed the ordeal they had suffered and Herbert Ponting wrote: 'Their looks haunted me for days. Once before, I had seen similar expressions on men's faces – when some half-starved Russian prisoners, after the Battle of Mukden, were being taken to Japan...' Cherry-Garrard noted: 'Antarctic exploration is seldom as bad as you imagine, seldom as bad as it sounds. But this journey had beggared out language; no words could express the horror.' Scott described the trek as 'one of the most gallant stories in polar history'.

It was all far removed from the lightheartedness Ponting once portrayed in his poem *The Sleeping Bag*:

On the outside grows the furside. On the inside grows the skinside.
So the furside is the outside and the skinside is the inside.
As the skinside is the inside (and the furside is the outside)
One 'side' likes the skinside inside and the furside on the outside.
Others like the skinside outside and the furside on the inside
As the skinside is the hard side and the furside is the soft side.
If you turn the skinside outside, thinking you will side with that 'side',
Then the soft side furside's inside, which some argue is the wrong side.
If you turn the furside outside – as you say, it grows on that side,
Then your outside's next the skinside, which for comfort's not the right side.
For the skinside is the cold side and your outside's not your warm side
And the two cold sides coming side-by-side are not the right sides one 'side' decides.
If you decide to side with that 'side', turn the outside furside inside
Then the hard side, cold side, skinside's, beyond all question, inside outside.

It was on 23 August, shortly after Victor Campbell's 36th birthday, that the sun returned to the Antarctic.

Sunday 10 September 1911

A whole week since the last entry in my diary. I feel very negligent of duty, but my whole time has been occupied in making detailed plans for the southern journey. These are finished at last, I am glad to say; every figure has been checked by Bowers, who has been an enormous help to me. If the motors are successful, we shall have no difficulty in getting to the glacier, and if they fail, we shall still get there with any ordinary degree of good fortune. To work three units of four men from that point onwards requires no small provision, but with the proper provision it should take a good deal to stop the attainment of our object. I have tried to take every reasonable possibility of misfortune into consideration, and to so organise the parties as to be prepared to meet them. I fear to be too sanguine, yet taking everything into consideration I feel that our chances ought to be good. The animals are in splendid form. Day by day the ponies get fitter as their exercise increases, and the stronger, harder food toughens their muscles. They are very different animals from those we took south last year, and with another month of training I feel there is not one of them but will make light of the loads we shall ask them to draw. But we cannot spare any of the ten, and so there must always be anxiety of the disablement of one or more before their work is done.

ER Evans, Forde, and Gran left early on Saturday for Corner Camp. I hope they will have no difficulty in finding it. Meares and Demetri came back from Hut Point the same afternoon – the dogs are wonderfully fit and strong, but Meares reports no seals up in the region, and as he went to make seal pemmican, there was little object in his staying. I leave him to come and go as he pleases, merely setting out the work he has to do in the simplest form. I want him to take fourteen bags of forage (130lbs each) to Corner Camp before the end of October and to be ready to start for his supporting work soon after the pony party – a light task for his healthy teams. Of hopeful signs for the future none are more remarkable than the health and spirit of our people. It would be impossible to imagine a more vigorous community, and there does not seem to be a single weak spot in the twelve good men and true who are chosen for the southern advance. All are now experienced sledge travellers, knit together with a bond of friendship that has never been equalled under such circumstances. Thanks to these people, and more especially to Bowers and Petty Officer Evans, there is not a single detail of our equipment that is not arranged with the utmost care and in accordance with the tests of experience.

It is good to have arrived at a point where one can run over facts and figures again and again without detecting a flaw or foreseeing a difficulty.

On 15 September a team of Scott, Bowers, Simpson and Edgar Evans went on 'a remarkably pleasant and instructive little spring journey' to the western mountains.

Roald Amundsen, the Norwegian explorer who reached the South Pole just days before Scott and his team.

Captain Robert Falcon Scott in full naval regalia c.1900. Scott served on board several warships during his naval career, starting out as a midshipman on the HMS *Britannia* in 1883. Scott's signature can be seen at the bottom of the photograph.

Sir Clements Robert Markham, President of the Royal Geographical Society, c.1900.

The RRS *Discovery* moored to the ice at the start of the Terra Nova Expedition, winter 1910.

Men of the Terra Nova Expedition hauling a sled full of supplies.

Some of Scott's men are seen here digging in to the snow to seek shelter from the freezing wind.

Siberian ponies on the Terra Nova Expedition.

One of Roald Amundsen's dog sled teams taking a well earned rest, with the Norwegian flag flying proudly behind them.

Captain Lawrence Oates during the Antarctic Expedition, 1911.

Scott taking a break from pulling his sledge, c.1911

Captain Lawrence Oates tending the pack ponies on the Terra Nova Expedition, 1911, with two dogs contentedly sleeping at his feet.

Scott writing in his journal inside the Cape Evans hut, winter 1911. The Cape was originally discovered by Scott on his Discovery Expedition of 1901-04 and, on returning for the Terra Nova Expedition, the hut was built as Scott's main headquarters.

Scott and his team after reaching the South Pole, only to find that they had been beaten in the race by Amundsen's Norwegian team.

Captain Scott and his team shortly after reaching the South Pole, 18 January 1912 (top left to right: Lt Henry Bowers, Capt Robert Scott, Dr Edward Adrian Wilson; bottom left to right: PO Edgar Evans, Capt Lawrence Oates).

Scott's Hut, located at Cape Evans on Ross Island. Originally built by Scott and his team in 1911, this picture shows the hut still standing after 100 years. In 2009, almost £3.5m was raised to help preserve it.

Boxes of supplies still survive inside Scott's hut today, preserved in time by the freezing weather conditions.

Scott's Georgian townhouse as it stands today in Chelsea, London, where he lived before leading his fatally unsuccessful expedition to the South Pole.

On board the deck of RRS *Discovery*, which was lovingly restored by the Maritime Trust in the 1980s.

Scott's ship, RRS *Discovery*, as she appears today, berthed at Discovery Point, Dundee. The ship was originally built here in 1900 and, after being saved from the breakers yard by the Maritime Trust in 1979, was brought back to her place of birth in 1985.

Statue of Captain Scott, built at Waterloo Place in Westminster, 1915.

Chapter 9

The Push South

Scott first revealed his plans for the South Pole march on 13 September 1911, stating the aim was to reach it by 21 December. Teams of men would set out, using motor-sledges, ponies and dogs for the Barrier stage of the journey, which would bring them to the Beardmore Glacier. At this point the dogs would return to base and the ponies would be shot for food. Thereafter, twelve men in three groups would ascend the glacier and begin the crossing of the polar plateau, using man-hauling. Only one of these groups would carry on to the pole; the supporting groups would be sent back at specified latitudes. Scott would make his decision about who would be in the final group during the journey. (He eventually set out later than first planned to give the ponies a chance in less bitter temperatures.) He estimated a return of around 27 March, having liaised closely with meteorologist George Simpson. Simpson calculated that the average temperature then would around 20°F – unpleasant but bearable. Scott was more than aware of what the men would be facing. For during his *Discovery* expedition, he, Evans and Lashly had endured thirty-five days on the polar plateau admitting they were 'done in completely'. Now they were facing seventy-five days. In an almost-fatalistic observation, Scott said: 'I don't know whether it is possible for men to last out that time...I almost doubt it.'

On 26 October 1911, Scott included his opinions about some of his team in his diary writings. He names some, but simply gives a letter in referring to others:

Words must always fail me when I talk of Bill Wilson. I believe he really is the finest character I ever met – the closer one gets to him the more there is to admire. Every quality is so solid and dependable; cannot you imagine how that counts down here? Whatever the matter, one knows Bill will be sound, shrewdly practical, intensely loyal and quite unselfish. Add to this a wider knowledge of persons and things than is at first guessable, a quiet vein of humour and really consummate tact, and you have some idea of his values. I think he is the most popular member of the party, and that is saying much.

Bowers is all and more than I ever expected of him. He is a positive treasure, absolutely trustworthy and prodigiously energetic. He is about the hardest man amongst us, and that is saying a good deal – nothing seems to hurt his tough little body and certainly no hardship daunts his spirit. I shall have a hundred little tales to tell you of his indefatigable zeal, his unselfishness, and his inextinguishable good humour. He surprises always, for his intelligence is of quite a high order and his memory for details most exceptional. You can imagine him, as he is, an indispensable assistant to me in every detail concerning the management and organisation of our sledging work and a delightful companion on the march.

One of the greatest successes is Wright. He is very thorough and absolutely ready for anything. Like Bowers he has taken to sledging like a duck to water, and although he hasn't had such severe testing, I believe he would stand it pretty nearly as well. Nothing ever seems to worry him, and I can't imagine he ever complained of anything in his life.

I don't think I will give such long descriptions of the others, though most of them deserve equally high praise. Taken all round they are a perfectly excellent lot.

The Soldier is very popular with all – a delightfully humorous cheery old pessimist – striving with the ponies night and day and bringing woeful accounts of their small ailments into the hut.

X...has a positive passion for helping others – it is extraordinary what pains he will take to do a kind thing unobtrusively.

One sees the need of having one's heart in one's work. Results can only be got down here by a man desperately eager to get them.

Y...works hard at his own work, taking extraordinary pains with it, but with an astonishing lack of initiative he makes not the smallest effort to grasp the work of others; it is a sort of character that plants itself in a corner and will stop there.

The men are equally fine. Edgar Evans has proved a useful member of our party; he looks after our sledges and sledge equipment with a care of management and a fertility of resource that is truly astonishing – on 'trek' he is just as sound and hard as ever and has an inexhaustible store of anecdote.

Crean is perfectly happy, ready to do anything and go anywhere, the harder the work, the better. Evans and Crean are great friends. Lashly is his old self in every respect, hard working to the limit, quiet, abstemious and determined. You see altogether I have a good set of people with me, and it will go hard if we don't achieve something.

The study of individual character is a pleasant pastime in such a mixed community of thoroughly nice people, and the study of relationships and interactions is fascinating – men of the most diverse upbringings and experience are really pals with one another, and the subjects that would be delicate ground of discussion between acquaintances are just those that are most freely used for jests. For instance, the Soldier is never tired of girding at Australia, its people and institutions, and the Australians retaliate by attacking the hide-bound prejudices of the British army. I have never seen a temper lost in these discussions. So as I sit here I am very satisfied with these things. I think that it would have been difficult to better the organisation of the party – every man has his work and is especially adapted for it; there is no gap and no overlap – it is all that I desired, and the same might be said of the men selected to do the work.

That same month, Scott took the time to write to the wives of some of his team. One letter was to Lois Evans, wife of Edgar. Scott wrote: 'Although I have never met you, your husband has told me a great deal about you so that I can imagine that you and the children will be waiting to see him home again next year. He is very well indeed, very strong and in good condition.' Scott added that their planned journey might take longer than predicted, but that Lois must not be 'anxious or worried'. (The letter did not arrive until the following May, months after Edgar Evans and Scott had died.)

At the end of October that year, Scott had to break some bad news to his men; the expedition was financially severely stretched and the funds had run out. The team was asked if it was willing to stay on without pay and many agreed. Others, because of ill health or other commitments, decided to return home on the *Terra Nova*. These included Taylor, Ponting, Day, Clissold and Forde.

The problem of reaching the South Pole from a wintering station is a problem of transport. The distance to be covered, there and back, is about 1,500 miles; the time at disposal in a single season is about 150 travelling days. An average of 10 miles a day can be easily maintained by men, provided adequate transport arrangements are made. There are three means by which the traction for heavy sledge loads can be provided – viz, ponies, dogs and motors, and each must be considered, not only with regard to capacity for work, but also with respect to the changes in the nature of the track to which reference has been made. Mr Shackleton has shown the brilliant results that may be achieved by pony traction on the Barrier surface, but he has also shown their unsuitability for work on glaciers. Dogs, if not overladen, could be used for glacier work and might travel the whole distance to the Pole, if properly husbanded by being lightly laden and well fed on the lower plateau. The motor sledge is a new development, and bids fair to become the most promising means of polar transport. Profiting by Mr Shackleton's experience, which showed that a motor could be run in the lowest temperatures, but that its wheels were not sufficient to support it on the soft snow of the Barrier, a special design has been adopted, and has undergone satisfactory trials in the Norwegian snows. Mechanical transport has obvious advantages in the Antarctic regions, inasmuch as (i) it is capable of accomplishing more work for the fuel expended than either the pony or the dog; (ii) it expends no fuel when not actually in use; (iii) the motor can be constructed sufficiently long to bridge dangerous crevasses. The plan for the journey to the South Pole from King Edward VI Land includes the use of the three means of sledge traction describes. Ponies will be taken in sufficient numbers to ensure a thoroughly adequate amount of food being taken to the base of the glacier. A dog team with a relay of men will transport the loads over the glacier surface, and a picked party of men and dogs will make the final dash across the inland ice sheet. Motor sledges will, according to their proved capacity, be a main agent or useful auxiliary to the transport plan. If they reach the foot of the glacier there can be little doubt they will ascend it, and greatly simplify the difficulties of the further journey. If they fail to reach the glacier, they will at least, as far as they can be taken, relieve the ponies and dogs of weights, and increase the safety of the return journey.

The Times – 1911

Before setting off the southern party wrote to family and friends. To his wife Scott spoke of his concern about Amundsen beating him: 'I don't know what to think of Amundsen's chances. If he gets to the Pole it must be before we do, as he is bound to travel fast with dogs, and pretty certain to start early. On this I decided at a very early date to act exactly as I should have done had he not existed. Any attempt to race must have wrecked my plan, besides which it doesn't appear the sort of thing one is out for [...] You can rely on my not saying or doing anything foolish, only I'm afraid you must be prepared for finding our venture much be-littled. After all, it is the work that counts, not the applause that follows.' Scott wrote in his diary: 'The future is in the lap of the gods. I can think of nothing left undone to deserve success.'

The march south began with the motor sledges on 4 October 1911, led by Edward Evans and comprising Day, Lashly and Hooper. The main party of Scott, Wilson, Bowers, Oates, Atkinson, Cherry-Garrard, Wright, Edgar Evans, Crean and Keohane followed on 1 November 1911 – with a setback when Scott realised he had left the Union Jack flag given to him by Queen Alexandra at base. It was eventually delivered by Tryggve Gran. Cecil Meares and Dimitri Gerof followed on with the dogs. Everyone else remained at Cape Evans to carry out further exploration and research in Victoria Land. Scott assumed the *Terra Nova* would return in January bringing Victor Campbell and his northern party back to Cape Evans, whereby Campbell would take command.

There were mixed transport groups (motors, dogs, horses), with loaded sledges, travelling at different rates, all designed to support a final group of four men who would make a dash for the Pole. One motor sledge broke down after 14 miles, the other after little more than 50 miles – causing Scott to note: 'So the dream of getting help from the machines is at an end' – so the party man-hauled 740lbs of

A second geographical expedition got under way on 14 November 1911, which was to centre on the Granite Harbour, around 50 miles north of Butter Point. The party this time was made up of Taylor, Debenham, Gran and Forde. The initial stage involved arduous travel over sea ice before reaching Granite Harbour on 26 November. Headquarters were established at a site christened Geology Point where the men constructed a stone hut. The next few weeks were devoted to exploration and surveying work on the Mackay Glacier, and a range of features to the north of the glacier were identified and named.

On 18 February 1911, Campbell's party was taken to Cape Adare, some 450 miles north of Cape Evans. For nearly a year their attempts to investigate the area were blighted by the severe weather. And so it was on 8 January 1912, the *Terra Nova* dropped them 250 miles further south on a coastline called Evans Coves, which looked promising for their five-week exploration. The six-man team had enough equipment and provisions to last until the *Terra Nova* returned.

But they did not know that the ship had run into an ice pack and was forced to abandon the return trip and instead go to New Zealand for the winter. The following exploits and endurance of Campbell and his men equal any on that fateful Antarctic trek. The Antarctic summer was ending and they became prisoners in the camp they had made out of tenting attached to a cave. They could not understand why the *Terra Nova* had not come to rescue them, with Priestley writing pitifully: 'Expect her any minute now [...] Hope deferred, maketh the heart sick. We can do nothing but lie and think and try to sleep, though none of us are doing much of the latter...'

Feeling they had for some reason been forsaken, the party realised their only hope of survival was to attempt the hazardous 200 mile journey back to Cape Evans. But for this they had to wait – and do all they could to survive – until the spring. They made do with the makeshift tent which was too small for anyone to stand up in. A stove made out of blubber gave some warmth but was not pleasant in such a small, confined space. And they were forever faced with starvation, despite Frank Browning's luck on 12 March of not only shooting a seal but finding around 40 fish still undigested in its stomach. The men had no other choice but to bunk down in what George Levick described as this 'damned, dismal little hole'.

On 10 April they saw a party of men approaching them. It was not the victorious Scott but a party of his dispirited men bearing the news that his team was well overdue in their return – and their priority, above anything else, was to find them. Campbell's party could not help but feel resentful that they were not being rescued. A rescue party under the command of Edward Atkinson had set off on 17 April 1912, but was forced to turn back because of the weather. It was only later that they, and the men who walked on to look for Scott, realised just how gruelling a time Campbell and his men had had. For on the voyage home to Britain, the *Terra Nova* stopped at Evans Coves to pick up equipment the group had left there. It gave the opportunity for men to go ashore and visit the ramshackle shelter. Wrote Cherry-Garrard, who had remained on the ship: 'I wish I had seen that igloo with its black and blubber and beastliness. Those who saw it came back with faces of amazement.'

But for now, Campbell's party had to wait on and endure the icy prison they gloomily nicknamed 'Inexpressible Island'. Answering the call of nature, especially with the chronic diarrhoea they now suffered from, was an undignified affair. And of course, there was the unrelenting cold. 'Campbell got private and stern frost-bitten. Poor chap. He came in a bad way, half collapsed,' wrote Levick one night.

The men constructed makeshift latrines (one for the officers and one for the men), but these had to be sited so close to the entrance of their shelter that it made day-to-day existence almost unbearable. By this time the men's health was deteriorating greatly. Browning's hands were frostbitten up to the wrist and George Abbott had sliced through three of his fingers while trying to stab at a seal. The rancid meat they were forced to eat was causing food poisoning. Eventually, the winds that had forced them to take cover for so long also broke up the sea ice around them, heralding the chance to press on at last. On 30 September 1911, weak and hungry beyond belief, the men set off for Cape Evans. The daily distance they covered varied from 3 to 8 miles. At one point, concerned over Browning's welfare, the men considered leaving him in a tent with most of the equipment so they could make quicker progress to Cape Evans and then hopefully return to collect him. But by an amazing stroke of luck, they came across a flagpole marking supplies left by another team who had been exploring the coastline. Campbell and his men were able to feast on hoosh (pulped and bloodied seal meat), cocoa, raisins, biscuits and butter. This meal gave them the strength to finally arrive at Cape Evans on 7 November, over seven weeks after they had left Evans Coves. Despite being so weak and such a bleak return – including crossing the difficult Drygalski Ice Tongue – the men still stopped to collect specimens (later retrieved from Cape Adare and Evans Coves by *Terra Nova*).

It wasn't a joyous reunion. For there they heard of the deaths of Scott and his team. It was 26 January 1913 – exactly two years after Scott had set out from Cape Evans to embark on their bid to conquer the South Pole.

Now Campbell and his team had one final task – to leave a small depot of provisions near their former Antarctic 'home', Hut Point at Cape Evans, to benefit any others who might pass that way in the future...

supplies for the remaining 150 miles reaching their assigned latitude two weeks later. During the journey, Scott sent a series of conflicting orders back to base concerning the future use of the expedition's dogs, leaving it unclear whether they were to be returned to base camp and saved for future scientific journeys or were to assist the polar party home. This was to prove another fatal flaw in the expedition.

Early in 1912 another geological exploration of the McMurdo Sound between the McMurdo Dry Valleys and the Koettlitz Glacier was undertaken. The work was carried out by a party consisting of Griffith, Taylor, Debenham, Wright and PO Evans. They landed at Butter Point opposite Cape Evans from the Terra Nova on 26 January and four days later the men had established its main depot in the Ferrar Glacier region. They conducted explorations and survey work in the Dry Valley and Taylor Glacier areas before moving southwards to the Koettlitz Glacier for further scientific work. The party started back on 2 March taking a southerly route to Hut Point, arriving there on 14 March.

* * *

Scott's party caught up with Evans' motor party on 21 November but progress was dispiritingly slow. Ponies fell weakly to the ground and the men felt their rations were insufficient. The first pony was shot dead on 24 November. On 29 November their spirits were lifted when they realised they were passing further south than the previous *Discovery* expedition. What they did not know was that Amundsen was already south of the 80th parallel and was covering up to 25 miles a day...

Depots were laid at regular intervals of about 70 miles, each containing food and fuel for a week for the returning parties. On 3 December Scott wrote: 'Our luck in weather is preposterous [...] the conditions simply horrible.'

The party awoke to a blizzard on 5 December: 'One cannot see the next tent, let alone the land. What on earth does such weather mean at this time of the year? It is more than our share of ill-fortune, but the luck may turn yet.' The men were forced to stay in their tents for four days – 'Resignation to misfortune is the only attitude, but one not easy to adopt...it is very evil to lie here in a wet sleeping bag.' The bleak mood would have darkened even further if they knew that Amundsen was well away from the storm and now around 100 miles away from the South Pole.

The delay meant literally eating into the already depleting rations and when they resumed their trek on 9 December the outlook was no more optimistic. The ponies had to be flogged to urge them on through the soft, new-fallen snow, an action that broke the hearts of the despairing men. It was only upon reaching the entrance to the Beardmore Glacier that the ponies were finally put out of their misery. Their skins were used to make a tent. The men named the site Shambles Camp. Scott's gloom was recorded in his diary:

Saturday 9 December 1911

At 8pm the ponies were quite done, one and all. They came on painfully slowly a few hundred yards at a time. By this time I was hauling ahead, a ridiculously light load, and yet finding the pulling heavy enough. We camped, and the ponies have been shot. Poor beasts! They have done wonderfully well considering the terrible circumstances under which they worked, but yet it is hard to have to kill them so early. The dogs are going well in spite of the surface, but here again one cannot get the help one would wish. (T 19°.) I cannot load the animals heavily on such snow. The scenery is most impressive; three huge pillars of granite form the right buttress of the Gateway, and a sharp spur of Mount Hope the left. The land is much more snow-covered than when we saw it before the storm. In spite of some doubt in our outlook, everyone is very cheerful tonight and jokes are flying freely around.

All supplies for the final push had been brought to the foot of the Beardmore Glacier. But the four-day delay had cost Scott dearly.

Meares turned back with the dogs on 11 December because there was no food left for them. Scott was later to realise that the animals would have greatly aided their ascent of the glacier. Reliant only on their own strength, the men now each had to haul more than 200 pounds of equipment and rations up the 100 miles of the 10,000ft high glacier. Despite the freezing conditions, such exertion saw the team sweating and Scott upped food allocations to help them keep up their strength. This depleted the vital rations even more.

On 13 December – the day before Amundsen reached the South Pole – the party had taken nine hours to cover less than 4 miles. Scott wrote: 'I had pinned my faith on getting better conditions as we rose, but it looks as though matters are getting worse instead of better.' Bowers wrote that he had 'never pulled so hard, or so nearly crushed my inside into my backbone by the everlasting jerking with all my strength on the canvas band round my unfortunate tummy'. Scott, nevertheless, was still optimistic:

Sunday 17 December 1911

Camp 39. Soon after starting we found ourselves in rather a mess; bad pressure ahead and long waves between us and the land. Blue ice showed on the crests of the waves; very soft snow lay in the hollows. We had to cross the waves in places 30 feet from crest to hollow, and we did it by sitting on the sledge and letting her go. Thus we went down with a rush and our impetus carried us some way up the other side; then followed a fearfully tough drag to rise the next crest. After two hours of this I saw a larger wave, the crest of which continued hard ice up the glacier; we reached this and got excellent travelling for 2 miles on it, then rose on a steep gradient, and so topped the pressure ridge. The smooth ice is again lost and we have patches of hard and soft snow with ice peeping out in places, cracks in all directions, and legs very frequently down. We have done very nearly 5 miles…In spite of the hard work everyone is very fit and very cheerful, feeling well fed and eager for more toil. Eyes are much better except poor Wilson's; he has caught a very bad attack. Remembering his trouble on our last Southern journey, I fear he is in for a very bad time.

We got fearfully hot this morning and marched in singlets, which became wringing wet; thus uncovered the sun gets at one's skin, and then the wind, which makes it horribly uncomfortable.

Our lips are very sore. We cover them with the soft silk plaster, which seems about the best thing for the purpose.

I'm inclined to think that the summit trouble will be mostly due to the chill falling on sunburned skins. Even now one feels the cold strike directly one stops. We get fearfully thirsty and chip up ice on the march, as well as drinking a great deal of water on halting. Our fuel only just does it, but that is all we want, and we have a bit in hand for the summit.

The pulling this afternoon was fairly pleasant; at first over hard snow, and then on to pretty rough ice with surface snowfield cracks, bad for sledges, but ours promised to come through well. We have worn our crampons all day and are delighted with them. P.O. Evans, the inventor of both crampons and ski shoes, is greatly pleased, and certainly we owe him much. The weather is beginning to look dirty again, snow clouds rolling in from the east as usual. I believe it will be overcast tomorrow…

Scott had no idea when he ordered the four weakest members of the party – Cherry-Garrard, Wright, Keohane and Atkinson – to head north on 20 December with Atkinson instructed to bring the dog teams south to meet the returning polar party, that Amundsen was already at the South Pole. The Norwegian had achieved the feat on 14 December with relative ease compared to Scott's endeavours and his team had even managed to get sixteen hours sleep a day. It would add further anguish to Scott when he later discovered Amundsen had enjoyed leisurely skiing on the Transantarctic Mountains after his victory.

The next day Scott's party set up camp on Upper Glacier. The conquest of the Beardmore Glacier lifted their spirits. They were making good progress, averaging 14 to 17 miles a day compared to the 10 that Scott had anticipated. He wrote: 'To me for the first time our goal seems really in sight.' But Evans' party of Bowers, Lashly and Crean was struggling – something that irritated Scott: 'I have told them plainly that they must wrestle with the trouble and get it right for themselves. There is no possible reason why they should not get along as easily as we do.'

By now, the men were using up 6,000 calories a day but consuming only 4,500 – equating to starvation. The freezing temperatures sapped their strength to such an extent that melting ice and snow for the precious water they needed to drink was too much.

Christmas Day 1911 was spent struggling against a strong wind and achieving 17½ miles. The men's Christmas meal comprised slushy mixtures of pony meat, an improvised chocolate drink, sugar, crumbled biscuit and raisins thickened with arrowroot, a tiny piece of 'plum duff', crystallised ginger and caramels. To them it was a feast of which Scott wrote: 'It was difficult to move. Wilson and I couldn't finish out share of plum-pudding. We have all slept splendidly and feel thoroughly warm – such is the effect of full feeding.' It was the last meal they were to truly enjoy.

Decision That Dogged Scott

The issue of instructions regarding the dogs has always been confused and controversial. Atkinson had to interpret and carry out Scott's changing instructions about how the dogs were to be employed after their return from the Barrier stage of the polar trek. Scott's original orders, which were 'never changed', were that the dogs were to be saved for scientific journeys in the following year and were 'not to be risked' otherwise. However, in orders to George Simpson and Cecil Meares immediately before his departure south, Scott ordered that after their return from the polar journey the dogs should be used to transport 'rations [...] and as much dog food as they can carry to One Ton Camp by 12 January 1912. The only obvious reason in requesting a dog food depot to be in place at One Ton by January 1912 would be to allow the dogs to travel further south later and assist the returning polar travellers. Unfortunately, Scott did not make this clear, even though it is likely he believed the dogs might be needed for a safe return. In the end, although the rations were left, for some reason the dog food wasn't. The significance of this was clear later when it meant that any future movement of the dogs south of One Ton for any reason would be difficult.

Historians say that Scott also complicated the situation by taking the dogs much further on the polar journey than had been originally planned, so that they were not back at base until 5 January. But fears that he might need the assistance of the dogs were evident in Scott's order to Atkinson on 22 December that he should 'come as far as you can'. Again Scott did not give a full explanation and again, his orders were not questioned. Atkinson, now suffering problems with his eyes and general poor health, was still complying with the orders that the dogs should not be risked and stayed where he was. Did Atkinson realise Scott was foreseeing a difficult return? After dispatching Cherry-Garrard and the dogs to One Ton on 26 February, Atkinson, who was by now aware that there was no dog food at One Ton wrote: 'It cannot be too firmly emphasised that the dog teams were meant merely to hasten the return of the southern party and by no means as a relief expedition.' But Scott's party was not yet overdue and according to Cherry-Garrard, Atkinson had instructed him to 'use his judgement' in the event of his not meeting Scott at the One Ton depot. His choices were to wait, or to proceed further south by killing dogs for dog meat – he had no other option in the absence of the dog food depot.

On 31 December, New Year's Eve, the team stopped for several hours to cut the sledges down from 12ft long to 10ft. During this, Edgar Evans injured his hand. That same day Scott ordered Edward Evans and his party to store their skis at a depot and continue on foot. On reflection, this was a strange decision to make. Was abandoning the heavy skis, boots and bindings to save weight? Or did Scott want to compare progress of foot and skis? Whatever, he wrote in his diary: 'Only 170 miles to the Pole and plenty of food.'

On 31 December, Scott's diary entries read:

New Year's Eve. 20.17. Height about 9126. T –10°. Camp 53. Corrected Aneroid. The second party depoted its ski and some other weights equivalent to about 100lbs. I sent them off first; they marched, but not very fast. We followed and did not catch them before they camped by direction at 1.30. By this time we had covered exactly 7 miles, and we must have risen a good deal. We rose on a steep incline at the beginning of the march, and topped another at the end, showing a distance of about 5 miles between the wretched slopes that give us the hardest pulling, but as a matter of fact, we have been rising all day.

We had a good full brew of tea and then set to work stripping the sledges. That didn't take long, but the process of building up the 10ft sledges now in operation in the other tent is a long job. Evans (PO) and Crean are tackling it, and it is a very remarkable piece of work. Certainly PO. Evans is the most invaluable asset to our party. To build a sledge under these conditions is a fact for special record. Evans (Lieut) has just found the latitude – 86° 56' S., so that we are pretty near the 87th parallel aimed at for tonight. We lose half a day, but I hope to make that up by going forward at much better speed.

This is to be called the '3 Degree Depot', and it holds a week's provisions for both units.

There is extraordinarily little mirage up here and the refraction is very small. Except for the seamen we are all sitting in a double tent – the first time we have put up the inner lining to the tent; it seems to make us much snugger.

10pm – The job of re-building is taking longer than I expected, but is now almost done. The 10ft sledges look very handy. We had an extra drink of tea and are now turned into our bags in the double tent (five of us) as warm as toast, and just enough light to write or work with. Did not get to bed till 2am.

But things started to go wrong. The cut on Evans' hand did not heal, probably because of vitamin deficiencies; Oates' feet were getting worse (he was also probably suffering the early signs of scurvy). On foot without skis, Bowers found it hard to keep up.

By 4 January 1912, the last two four-man groups had reached 87°34′ S – and Scott announced his decision; five men and not four as originally planned – he,

Edward Wilson, Lawrence Oates, Edgar Evans and the last-minute choice of Henry Bowers – would go forward; the other three (Teddy Evans, William Lashly and Tom Crean) would return with Evans being told to instruct Meares to bring the dog teams out in mid-February to meet the returning party. Back in June Scott had made notes on what he expected from the men who would accompany him on his final push:

> *I took the opportunity to note hurriedly the few points to which I want attention especially directed. No doubt others will occur to me presently. I think I now understand very well how and why the old surveyors (like Belcher) failed in the early Arctic work.*

> 1. *Every officer who takes part in the southern journey ought to have in his memory the approximate variation of the compass at various stages of the journey and to know how to apply it to obtain a true course from the compass. The variation changes very slowly so that no great effort of memory is required.*
> 2. *He ought to know what the true course is to reach one depôt from another.*
> 3. *He should be able to take an observation with the theodolite.*
> 4. *He should be able to work out a meridian altitude observation.*
> 5. *He could advantageously add to his knowledge the ability to work out a longitude observation or an ex-meridian altitude.*
> 6. *He should know how to read the sledgemeter.*
> 7. *He should note and remember the error of the watch he carries and the rate it is ascertained for it from time to time.*
> 8. *He should assist the surveyor by noting the coincidences of objects, the opening out of valleys, the observation of new peaks, &c.*

Teddy Evans was bitter about being sent back but while a useful member on board a ship, he was a hindrance on land. Wrote Wilson: 'I never thought for a moment he would be in the final party.' Added Bowers: 'Poor Teddy…I am sure it was for his wife's sake he wanted to go. He gave me a little silk flag she had given him to fly at the Pole.' It was an emotional farewell for all with Lashly and Crean in tears. The enlarged party of five tested the available rations. It was yet another foolhardy and fatal decision, for cooking for an extra man used up more fuel, took more time, and made an already cramped tent uncomfortable. Also, Bowers, not expecting to join the South Pole push, had left his skis behind at the foot of the glacier and had to make the trek on foot. But there seemed enough rations for everyone and the Pole seemed so near.

On 9 January the team passed Shackleton's furthest southern point and believed they were making expedition records but it was desperately hard, as Scott wrote:

Tuesday 9 January 1912

I never had such pulling; all the time the sledge rasps and creaks. We have covered 6 miles, but at fearful cost to ourselves...Another hard grind in the afternoon and 5 miles added. About 74 miles from the Pole – can we keep this up for seven days? It takes it out of us like anything. None of us ever had such hard work before...Our chance still holds good if we can put the work in, but it's a terribly trying time...It is an effort to keep up the double figures, but if we can do another four marches we ought to get through. It is going to be a close thing...

Thursday 11 January 1912

Lunch. Height 10,540. T –15° 8'. It was heavy pulling from the beginning today, but for the first two and a half hours we could keep the sledge moving; then the sun came out (it had been overcast and snowing with light south-easterly breeze) and the rest of the forenoon was agonising. I never had such pulling; all the time the sledge rasps and creaks. We have covered 6 miles, but at fearful cost to ourselves.

Night camp 63. Height 10,530. T –16.3°. Minimum –25.8°. Cloud has been coming and going overhead all day, drifting from the SE, but continually altering shape. Snow crystals falling all the time; a very light S breeze at start soon dying away. The sun so bright and warm tonight that it is almost impossible to imagine a minus temperature. The snow seems to get softer as we advance; the sastrugi [eroded snow], though sometimes high and undercut, are not hard – no crusts, except yesterday the surface subsided once, as on the Barrier. It seems pretty certain there is no steady wind here. Our chance still holds good if we can put the work in, but it's a terribly trying time.

Saturday 13 January 1912

Lunch. Height 10,390. Barometer low? Lat. 89° 3' 18". Started on some soft snow, very heavy dragging and went slow. We could have supposed nothing but that such conditions would last from now onward, but to our surprise, after two hours we came on a sea of sastrugi, all lying from S to E, predominant ESE. Have had a cold little wind from SE and SSE, where the sky is overcast. Have done 5.6 miles and are now over the 89th parallel.

Night camp 65 – Height 10,270. T – 22.5°, Minimum –23.5°. Lat. 89° 9' S. very nearly. We started very well in the afternoon. Thought we were going to make a real good march, but after the first two hours surface crystals became as sandy as ever. Still we did 5.6 miles, giving over 11 for the day. Well, another day with double figures and a bit over. The chance holds.

It looks as though we were descending slightly; sastrugi remain as in forenoon. It is wearisome work this tugging and straining to advance a light sledge. Still, we get along. I did manage to get my thoughts off the work for a time today, which is very restful. We should be in a poor way without our ski, though Bowers manages to struggle through the soft snow without tiring his short legs.

Only 51 miles from the Pole tonight. If we don't get to it we shall be d——d close. There is a little southerly breeze tonight; I devoutly hope it may increase in force. The alternation of soft snow and sastrugi seem to suggest that the coastal mountains are not so very far away.

The weather, however, was against them. At one point Scott told the men to abandon their skis when they became clogged with soft snow and then told them to retrace their steps and retrieve them when the going got easier. This wasted valuable time.

Monday 15 January 1912

It is wonderful to see that two long marches will land us at the Pole...it ought to be a certain thing now, and the only appalling possibility is the sight of the Norwegian flag forestalling ours.

But on 16 January 1912, in the distance that 'appalling possibility' became reality. Diary entries showed his despair:

We started off in high spirits in the afternoon, feeling that tomorrow would see us at our destination. About the second hour of that march, Bowers' sharp eyes detected what he thought was a cairn...half an hour later he detected a black speck...we marched on and found that it was a black flag tied to a sledge bearer; nearby the remains of a camp...this told us the whole story. The Norwegians have forestalled us and are first at the Pole. It is a terrible disappointment for me and I am very sorry for my loyal companions.

Wednesday 17 January 1912

Camp 69. T. −22° at start. Night −21°. The Pole. Yes, but under very different circumstances from those expected. We have had a horrible day − add to our disappointment a head wind 4 to 5, with a temperature −22°, and companions labouring on with cold feet and hands.

We started at 7.30, none of us having slept much after the shock of our discovery. We followed the Norwegian sledge tracks for some way; as far as we can make out there are only two men. In about 3 miles we passed two small cairns. Then the weather overcast, and the tracks being increasingly drifted up and obviously going too far to the West, we decided to make straight for the Pole according to our calculations. At 12.30 Evans had such cold hands we camped for lunch – an excellent 'weekend one.'...Tonight little Bowers is laying himself out to get sights in terrible difficult circumstances; the wind is blowing hard, T – 21 degrees, and there is that curious damp, cold feeling in the air which chills one to the bone in no time. We have been descending again, I think, but there looks to be a rise ahead; otherwise there is very little that is different from the awful monotony of past days.

Thursday morning, 18 January 1912

We have just arrived at this tent, 2 miles from our camp, therefore about 1½ miles from the Pole. In the tent we find a record of five Norwegians having been here... We carried the Union Jack about ¾ of a mile north with us and left it on a piece of stick as near as we could fix it...Well, we have turned our back now on the goal of our ambition and must face our 800 miles of solid dragging – and goodbye to most of the daydreams!

It was a bitterly disheartened group of men who, after a sleepless night, made their way to the Pole the following day. There they found Amundsen's tent in which he had left a note for Scott and a letter for King Haakon, which he asked Scott to deliver. There was also a record of the names of the Norwegian party: Roald Amundsen, Olav Olavason Bjaaland, Hilmar Hanssen, Sverre H. Hassel and Oscar Wisting. Scott's anguish is indicated in his diary with words that would go down in history: 'The worst has happened [...] All the daydreams must go [...] Great God! This is an awful place [...] Now for the run home and a desperate struggle. I wonder if we can do it?' The sight of dog tracks compounded Scott's agony – why had he not retained his faithful and resilient dog teams?

Spirits at an all time low, the party spent the rest of the day sketching, photographing and making notes – and taking dispirited pictures of themselves standing by the Union Jack they had stuck in the ground.

Amundsen had beaten them by five weeks.

Chapter 10
A Testing and Tragic Trek

The party then set off on the 800-mile return trek, aiming to call in at the depots laid along the way in a bid to beat the ever-worsening weather and cold. But the men became thinner, hungrier and their health deteriorated. Scott's diary entries recorded their gloom:

Wednesday 24 January 1912

Lunch T −8°. Things beginning to look a little serious. A strong wind at the start has developed into a full blizzard at lunch, and we have had to get into our sleeping bags. It was a bad march, but we covered 7 miles. At first Evans, and then Wilson went ahead to scout for tracks. Bowers guided the sledge alone for the first hour, then both Oates and he remained alongside it; they had a fearful time trying to make the pace between the soft patches. At 12.30 the sun coming ahead made it impossible to see the tracks further, and we had to stop. By this time the gale was at its height and we had the dickens of a time getting up the tent, cold fingers all round. We are only 7 miles from our depot, but I made sure we should be there tonight. This is the second full gale since we left the Pole. I don't like the look of it. Is the weather breaking up? If so, God help us, with the tremendous summit journey and scant food. Wilson and Bowers are my standby. I don't like the easy way in which Oates and Evans get frostbitten.

As Scott's team suffered, Amundsen's had arrived back at the Bay of Whales on 26 January, ten days ahead of schedule, having successfully covered an average of 23 miles a day and with such a supply of rations that both men and dogs enjoyed extra helpings and plenty of chocolate. The team had got back with all its members healthy in 99 days – 'The whole thing went like a dream' recorded Amundsen. Meanwhile, Scott's writings reflected his despair:

Sunday 4 February 1912

The temperature is 20° lower than when we were here before; the party is not improving in condition, especially Evans, who is becoming rather dull and incapable. Thank the Lord we have good food at each meal, but we get hungrier in spite of it.

So how did Amundsen succeed and with a team of men never wanting for food on their perilous trek, his beasts of burden fulfilling his demands and with so few flaws encountered? Mistakes were certainly made in the initial planning of Scott's expedition. He believed he could emulate Shackleton's success with pony teams. But Shackleton had fallen 100 miles short of his attempt to reach the South Pole, beaten back by bad weather, thereby not testing his ponies' endurance to the full. Scott's ponies could not endure the extreme Antarctic conditions and were unable to handle the going in soft snowfall. Further, they were taken to a terrain barren of vital fodder necessitating a greater load aboard the *Terra Nova* (with Oates having to resort to loading more than he and Scott had agreed), and with no chance of any other nourishment. And, unlike carnivore dogs, a pony death cannot be utilised to feed their fellow animals. Amundsen only took dog teams. Scott had researched into the usefulness of dogs, discovering that two dogs could haul on food rations equating that of rations required by one man. So why were his dog teams not larger? As the dogs perished, more manpower was required to haul; manpower hugely weakened by the bitter cold, shortage of rations and diminished physical strength. The vast majority of Scott's men were not accomplished skiers, while Amundsen only took those who were (including skiing champion Olav Bjaaland). Amundsen's sledges were lighter than Scott's; his clothing more protective. Scott's expedition team was large – more than sixty men manning the ship and twenty-five making up the shore party – compared to Amundsen's methodically-chosen group of nineteen. Amundsen worked out exactly who would join him on the final South Pole push and only nine men wintered at their ice-shelf hut *Framheim*. Scott delayed choosing his shore party, keeping the final selection to himself until he was 150 miles from the Pole. And then he decided upon a five-man party instead of four, putting further deprivation and hardship their way.

Lack of the proper nutrition needed by Scott's team has also been criticised. Before setting off for the final push, the men were suffering nutritional deficiencies, living off overcooked fish, penguin and seal meat destroying any vitamin C – a vital vitamin that would have prevented the scurvy they eventually suffered from. Amundsen's team ate fresh seal and penguin, a diet they had gleaned from the indigenous people of the Arctic regions. Other differences in the diets were that the biscuits eaten by the British team were made with white flour and sodium bicarbonate; the Norwegian biscuits were made of oatmeal and yeast, which provided essential vitamin B to keep the nervous system healthy.

It would take Scott 140 days to cover the same distance and his men were suffering. Evans was depressed and quiet, his injured hand filling with pus, his toes and fingers badly frostbitten. It is believed he also had head injuries after falling on the ice. 'He is absolutely changed from his normal self-reliant self,' wrote Scott. Oates' toes were turning black. Mentally, all the men were defeated. They had not accounted for the fact that at such a high altitude the demand for greater oxygen increased heart and respiration rates, and the body needed more calorie intake. So it is hard to understand why, on 7 February, as they began their descent, the team stopped for the day to collect more geological samples – 35lbs in all, which were added to the sledges. Scott noted some of their collection:

Thursday 8 February 1912

Steered in for Mt Darwin to visit rock. Sent Bowers on, on ski, as Wilson can't wear his at present. He obtained several specimens, all of much the same type, a close-grained granite rock, which weathers red. Hence the pink limestone…The moraine was obviously so interesting that when we had advanced some miles and got out of the wind, I decided to camp and spend the rest of the day geologising. It has been extremely interesting. We found ourselves under perpendicular cliffs of Beacon sandstone, weathering rapidly and carrying veritable coal seams. From the last Wilson, with his sharp eyes, has picked several plant impressions, the last a piece of coal with beautifully traced leaves in layers, also some excellently preserved impressions of thick stems, showing cellular structure. In one place we saw the cast of small waves on the sand. Tonight Bill has got a specimen of limestone with archeo-cyathus – the trouble is one cannot imagine where the stone comes from; it is evidently rare, as few specimens occur in the moraine. There is a good deal of pure white quartz.

On 11 February the men got lost and took 12 hours to escape from a maze of pressure ridges. Wrote Scott:

Sunday 11 February 1912

R. 25. Lunch T –6.5°; Supper –3.5°. The worst day we have had during the trip and greatly owing to our own fault. We started on a wretched surface with light SW wind, sail set, and pulling on ski – horrible light, which made everything look fantastic. As we went on light got worse, and suddenly we found ourselves in pressure. Then came the fatal decision to steer east. We went on for 6 hours, hoping to do a good distance, which in fact I suppose we did, but for the last hour or two we pressed on into a regular trap. Getting on to a good surface we did not reduce our lunch meal, and thought all going well, but half an hour after lunch we got into the worst ice mess I have ever been in. For three hours we plunged on ski, first thinking we were too much to the right, then too much to the left; meanwhile the disturbance got worse and my spirits received a very rude shock. There were times when it seemed almost impossible to find a way out of the awful turmoil in which we found ourselves. At length, arguing that there must be a way on our left, we plunged in that direction. It got worse, harder, more icy and crevassed. We could not manage our ski and pulled on foot, falling into crevasses every minute – most luckily no bad accident. At length we saw a smoother slope towards the land, pushed for it, but knew it was a woefully long way from us. The turmoil changed in character, irregular crevassed surface giving way to huge chasms, closely packed and most difficult to cross. It was very heavy work, but we had grown desperate. We won through at 10pm and I write after 12 hours on the march. I think we are on or about the right track now, but we are still a good number of miles from the depôt, so we reduced rations tonight. We had three pemmican meals left and decided to make them into four. Tomorrow's lunch must serve for two if we do not make big progress. It was a test of our endurance on the march and our fitness with small supper. We have come through well. A good wind has come down the glacier which is clearing the sky and surface. Pray God the wind holds tomorrow. Short sleep tonight and off first thing, I hope.

A snowstorm hindered progress a couple of days later and so it was a great relief to finally reach a depot. That was to be short-lived. Rations still had to be reduced, they were 30 miles away from the next depot at Lower Glacier, covering only 6 miles a day, and Edgar Evans was giving great cause for concern. There was now only one meal left for each man. On 17 February Evans kept dropping out of the team, at one point found by Scott in a state of exhaustion: 'He was on his knees with clothing disarranged, hands uncovered and frostbitten and a wild look in his eyes.' Evans lapsed into a coma and died quietly that night. It solved a dilemma – whether to try to plod on carrying a sick man or abandon him…There was still 430 miles to go.

Saturday 17 February

A very terrible day. Evans looked a little better after a good sleep, and declared, as he always did, that he was quite well. He started in his place on the traces, but half an hour later worked his ski shoes adrift, and had to leave the sledge. The surface was awful, the soft recently fallen snow clogging the ski and runners at every step, the sledge groaning, the sky overcast, and the land hazy. We stopped after about one hour, and Evans came up again, but very slowly. Half an hour later he dropped out again on the same plea. He asked Bowers to lend him a piece of string. I cautioned him to come on as quickly as he could, and he answered cheerfully as I thought. We had to push on, and the remainder of us were forced to pull very hard, sweating heavily. Abreast the Monument Rock we stopped, and seeing Evans a long way astern, I camped for lunch. There was no alarm at first, and we prepared tea and our own meal, consuming the latter.

After lunch, and Evans still not appearing, we looked out to see him still afar off. By this time we were alarmed, and all four started back on skis. I was first to reach the poor man and was shocked at his appearance; he was on his knees with clothing disarranged, hands uncovered and frostbitten, and a wild look in his eyes. Asked what was the matter, he replied with a slow speech that he didn't know, but thought he must have fainted. We got him on his feet, but after two or three steps he sank down again. He showed every sign of complete collapse. Wilson, Bowers and I went back for the sledge, whilst Oates remained with him. When we returned he was practically unconscious, and when we got him into the tent quite comatose. He died quietly at 12.30am. On discussing the symptoms we think he began to get weaker just before we reached the Pole, and that his downward path was accelerated first by the shock of his frostbitten fingers, and later by falls during rough travelling on the glacier, further by his loss of all confidence in himself. Wilson thinks it certain he must have injured his brain by a fall.

It is a terrible thing to lose a companion in this way, but calm reflection shows that there could not have been a better ending to the terrible anxieties of the past week. Discussion of the situation at lunch yesterday shows us what a desperate pass we were in with a sick man on our hands at such a distance from home.

Finally reaching Shambles Camp, the men feasted on meat from the ponies they had slaughtered at what now seemed a lifetime ago. They needed all the food they could get as there was still 400 miles of difficult terrain ahead of them on the Barrier and the Antarctic summer was drawing to a close.

Sunday 1 March 1912

Cold, very cold…we are in a very queer street since there is do doubt we cannot do the extras marches and feel the cold horribly…amongst ourselves we are unendingly cheerful, but what each man feels in his heart I can only guess.

By this time Wilson and Oates had given up their writings.

On 6 March, Oates with his gangrenous toes was a 'poor soldier nearly done'. Scott instructed doses of up to thirty Opium tablets to be given to any man who requested them. Distances of only 6 miles a day were being covered; they would run out of food 13 miles before One Ton Camp. Arriving at the Middle Barrier Depot on 2 March, Scott found their oil supplies had evaporated leaving them short and noted: 'With the most rigid economy it can scarce carry us to the next depot 71 miles away.' The team found an oil shortage at the next depot on 9 March too and, because of the confusion, no dogs to help them on the journey, which would, Scott wrote 'have been our salvation'. Daily marches were now down to less than 5 miles, and the party was desperately short of food and fuel.

Diet Downfall
The rations carried by all the sledging parties on the expedition were based on nutritional science as understood in 1910, before knowledge of Vitamin C and its prevention of scurvy (from which is understood some of Scott's party suffered). Emphasis was given to high protein content with the intent of replacing calories burned during the heavy work of sledging, especially man-hauling. In fact, the caloric values of the rations were greatly over-estimated, although this was not apparent until many years later. The staple daily ration per man was 16 ounces (450g) biscuit, 12 ounces (340g) pemmican, 3 ounces (85g) sugar, 2 ounces (57g) butter, 0.7 ounces (20g) tea and 0.57 ounces (16g cocoa. The men's diet was supplemented on the southern journey by the meat from the ponies they had slaughtered – but this still would not have made up for any nutritional deficit.

Having made camp, the men awoke to a temperature of –37°F on 13 March; the next day this dropped to –43 degrees. On 16 March Oates was done for. He requested that the men go on without him and leave him to his fate inside his sleeping bag, but the team stuck with him another day. If fate had been kinder to Oates he would have died in his sleep that night. Instead, he awoke and uttered the immortal words that one will forever associate with the tragic expedition. 'I am just going outside and may be some time.' Oates' actions sealed the grim inevitability for them all.

Friday 16 March or Saturday 17 March 1912

Lost track of dates, but think the last correct. Tragedy all along the line. At lunch, the day before yesterday, poor Titus Oates said he couldn't go on; he proposed we should leave him in his sleeping bag. That we could not do, and we induced him to come on, on the afternoon march. In spite of its awful nature for him he struggled on and we made a few miles. At night he was worse and we knew the end had come.

Should this be found I want these facts recorded. Oates' last thoughts were of his mother, but immediately before he took pride in thinking that his regiment would be pleased with the bold way in which he met his death. We can testify to his bravery. He has borne intense suffering for weeks without complaint, and to the very last was able and willing to discuss outside subjects. He did not – would not – give up hope till the very end. He was a brave soul. This was the end. He slept through the night before last, hoping not to wake; but he woke in the morning – yesterday. It was blowing a blizzard. He said, 'I am just going outside and may be some time.'

He went out into the blizzard and we have not seen him since…we knew that poor Oates was walking to his death, but though we tried to dissuade him, we knew it was the act of a brave man and an English gentleman. We all hope to meet the end with a similar spirit, and assuredly the end is not far.

While Scott had such fine words to say about Oates, Oates' intense loathing of Scott had prompted him to secretly heap praise on Amundsen, the man who had reached the Pole a month before them. Oates concluded that Amundsen 'must have had his head screwed on right' to use dog teams to pull his sledges. It was 'very different to our wretched man-hauling' of sledges, he observed. Oates was horrified at the 'greatest lot of crocks I have ever seen' and said: 'Scott's ignorance about marching with animals is colossal.'

Here it is worthwhile looking at Scott's relationship with his men. It is a challenge to understand the real Robert Scott because his team had such contrasting opinions of him. Oates disliked him greatly and some of his team members also expressed negative feelings. Others adored Scott. It is often as if we are hearing about two different expeditions entirely. It is unfair to criticise Scott for personal failings and difficult traits because they are present in us all. But at the same time his desire to reach such an historic goal was sometimes marred by stubbornness and poor judgement. A good leader of men is also a good listener of men and this was not always the case with Scott. He did not take kindly to having his orders challenged even if, such as in the case of Oates' greater experience and knowledge of ponies, the challenge was a fair one. The approach to leadership by Scott and Amundsen was the most telling difference. Scott's leadership was honed by his training as an English naval officer, a training that saw him seeing the correct way to oversee his team being the division of 'officers' and 'men'. Amundsen has been described as a more 'innovative individualist – a professional explorer with a genuine passion for snow and ice' whose 'competitive focus and drive was unparalleled.'

On 19 March the sad and broken group of three struggled on, still 11 miles from One Ton Depot and 24 miles beyond the original intended location of the depot. On 21 March, a fierce blizzard hit. The three men were forced to make camp. One can only wonder at their thoughts, knowing that crucial food supplies were so close. The end was now very near. Scott's right foot was so badly frostbitten he could go no further and he contemplated amputation. 'But will the trouble spread? That is the serious question.'

Wednesday 21 March 1912

Got within 11 miles of depot Monday night; had to lay up all yesterday in severe blizzard. Today forlorn hope, Wilson and Bowers going to depot for fuel.

Thursday 22 March and Friday 23 March 1912

Blizzard bad as ever – Wilson and Bowers unable to start – tomorrow last chance – no fuel and only one or two of food left – must be near the end. Have decided it shall be natural – we shall march for the depot with or without our effects and die in our tracks.

The men knew they were going to die. Wilson wrote to his parents: 'Looking forward to the day when we shall all meet together in the hereafter. I have had a very happy life and I look forward to a very happy life hereafter when we shall all be together again. God knows I have no fear of meeting Him – for He will be merciful to all of us. My poor Ory [his wife] may or may not have long to wait.'

Knowing he had little time, Scott used what strength he had to write the last letters of his life. Incredibly, he somehow managed to write twelve, including one each to his wife Kathleen and sister Hannah. To Kathleen he wrote of his hopes for young son Peter, his desire that she should re-marry and his heartfelt thoughts on the expedition:

To my widow,

Dearest Darling – we are in a very tight corner and I have doubts of pulling through – In our short lunch hours I take advantage of a very small measure of warmth to write letters preparatory to a possible end – the first is naturally to you on whom my thoughts mostly dwell waking or sleeping – if anything happens to me I shall like you to know how much you have meant to me and that pleasant recollections are with me as I depart.

I should like you to take what comfort you can from these facts also – I shall not have suffered any pain but leave the world fresh from harness and full of good health and vigour – this is dictated already, when provisions come to an end we simply stop where we are within easy distance of another depot.

Therefore you must not imagine a great tragedy – we are very anxious of course and have been for weeks but in splendid physical condition and our appetites compensate for all discomfort. The cold is biting and sometimes angering but here again the hot food which drives it forth is so wonderfully enjoyable that we would scarcely be without it.

We have gone downhill a good deal since I wrote the above. Poor Titus Oates has gone – he was in a bad state – the rest of us keep going and imagine we have a chance to get through but the cold weather doesn't let up at all – we are now only 20 miles from a depot but we have very little food or fuel.

Well dear heart I want you to take the whole thing very sensibly as I am sure you will – the boy will be your comfort. I had looked forward to helping you to bring him up but it is a satisfaction to feel that he is safe with you. I think both he and you ought to be specially looked after by the country for which after all we have given our lives with something of spirit which makes for example – I am writing letters on this point in the end of this book after this. Will you send them to their various destinations?

I must write a little letter for the boy if time can be found to be read when he grows up – dearest that you know I cherish no sentimental rubbish about re-marriage – when the right man comes to help you in life you ought to be your happy self again.

I hope I shall be a good memory certainly the end is nothing for you to be ashamed of and I like to think that the boy will have a good start in parentage of which he may be proud. Dear it is not easy to write because of the cold – 70 degrees below zero and nothing but the shelter of our tent.

You know I have loved you, you know my thoughts must have constantly dwelt on you and oh dear me you must know that quite the worst aspect of this situation is the thought that I shall not see you again. The inevitable must be faced – you urged me to be leader of this party and I know you felt it would be dangerous – I've taken my place throughout, haven't I?

God bless you my own darling I shall try and write more later – I go on across the back pages. Since writing the above we have got to within 11 miles of our depot with one hot meal and two days' cold food and we should have got through but have been held for four days by a frightful storm – I think the best chance has gone. We have decided not to kill ourselves but to fight it to the last for that depot but in the fighting there is a painless end so don't worry.

I have written letters on odd pages of this book – will you manage to get them sent? You see I am anxious for you and the boy's future – make the boy interested in natural history if you can, it is better than games – they encourage it at some schools – I know you will keep him out in the open air – try and make him believe in a God, it is comforting.

Oh my dear my dear what dreams I have had of his future and yet oh my girl I know you will face it stoically – your portrait and the boy's will be found in my breast and the one in the little red Morocco case given by Lady Baxter. There is a piece of the Union flag I put up at the South Pole in my private kit bag together with Amundsen's black flag and other trifles – give a small piece of the Union flag to the King and a small piece to Queen Alexandra and keep the rest a poor trophy for you!

What lots and lots I could tell you of this journey. How much better it has been than lounging in comfort at home – what tales you would have for the boy but oh what a price to pay – to forfeit the sight of your dear face.

Dear you will be good to the old mother. I write her a little line in this book. Also keep in with Ettie and the others – oh but you'll put on a strong face for the world

– only don't be too proud to accept help for the boy's sake – he ought to have a fine career and do something in the world.

I haven't time to write to Sir Clements – tell him I thought much of him and never regretted him putting me in command of the Discovery.

Scott also wrote to his naval comrades Sir Francis Bridgeman – 'After all we are setting a good example to our countrymen, if not by getting into a tight place, by facing it like men when we were there', and Sir George Egerton, Reginald Smith and Sir James Barrie – 'I may not have proved a great explorer but we have done the greatest march ever made and come very near to great success,' and to his brother-in-law, William Bruce.

Scott wrote too to the mothers of Oates and Bowers, to Wilson's wife, to J.J. Kinsey in New Zealand and to Sir Edgar Speyer – '…but we have been to the Pole and we shall die like gentlemen…' He felt he had to defend his management of the expedition, saying: 'Every detail of our food supplies, clothing and depots…worked out to perfection…We have missed getting through by a narrow margin which was justifiably within the risk of such a journey.'

Finally, Scott wrote a 'Message to the Public' in which he tried to explain and defend the expedition's trials and tribulations:

For my own sake I do not regret this journey which has shown that Englishmen can endure hardships, help one another and meet death with as great a fortitude as ever in the past. We took risks, we knew we took them; things have come out against us, and therefore we have no cause for complaint, but bow to the will of Providence, determined still to do our best to the last…Had we lived, I should have had a tale to tell of the hardihood, endurance and courage of my companions, which would have stirred the heart of every Englishman. These rough notes and our dead bodies must tell the tale, but surely, surely a great rich country like ours will see that those who are dependent on us are properly provided for.

Scott's son, aged just two, sent two notes to his father as he and his mother awaited his return in 1912. One said: 'Dear Daddy I am going to be a drummer.' The other simply said: 'I love you.' They never reached him.

Scott is presumed to have died on 29 March 1912 – possibly a day later. His last diary entry was dated 29 March and read: 'Every day we have been ready to start for our depot 11 miles away, but outside the door of the tent it remains a scene of whirling drift. I do not think we can hope for any better things now. We shall stick it out to the end, but we are getting weaker, of course, and the end cannot be far. It seems a pity but I do not think I can write more. R Scott. For God's sake look after our people.'

Chapter 11

An Icy Grave

The Terra Nova, *the vessel of the British Antarctic expedition, was sighted off this port early this morning and anchored shortly after daybreak. Contrary to expectation, she does not bring back with her Captain Scott and his Antarctic party. Her commander was entrusted with the following brief message from Captain Scott, which he had sent back to the base of the expedition before the* Terra Nova *left. 'I am remaining in the Antarctic for another winter in order to continue and complete my work.' The latest news sent back by Captain Scott to the base at McMurdo Sound showed that on January 3 he had reached a point 150 miles from the South Pole and was still advancing. It was clear that had Captain Scott delayed notifying his progress until he had actually reached the Pole, news from him could not have reached the* Terra Nova *before she was compelled to leave owing to the setting in of the winter and the freezing of the Ross Sea. Captain Scott's own full message will follow.*

The Times – 1 April 1912

Cherry-Garrard left Hut Point with Dimitri and two dog teams on 26 February, arriving at One Ton Depot on 4 March and depositing the extra rations. Scott was not there. With supplies for themselves and the dogs for twenty-four days, they had about eight days waiting time before having to return to Hut Point. The alternative to waiting was moving southwards, and in the absence of the dog food depot this would mean killing dogs for dog food as they went along, thus breaching Scott's 'not to be risked' order (but within Cherry-Garrard's brief from Atkinson to 'judge what to do'). However, Cherry-Garrard decided to wait for Scott. On 10 March, in worsening weather, with his own supplies dwindling and unaware that Scott's team was fighting for their lives less than 70 miles away, Cherry-Garrard turned for home. He would later sum up the fatal expedition as a 'business that simply bristles with ifs: an accumulation of decisions and circumstances that might have fallen differently ultimately led to catastrophe…but we were as wise as anyone can be before the event'. Atkinson would later write, 'I am satisfied that no other officer of the expedition could have done better', but Cherry-Garrard was troubled for the rest of his life by thoughts that he might have taken other actions that could have saved the polar party.

After Cherry-Garrard's return from One Ton Depot without news of Scott, there was great concern. Atkinson, now in charge at Cape Evans as the senior naval officer present decided to make an attempt to reach the polar party, and on 26 March set out with Keohane, man-hauling a sledge containing eighteen days' worth of provisions. In very low temperatures ($-40°F$, $-40°C$) they reached Corner Camp by 30 March when, in Atkinson's view, the weather, the cold and the time of year made further progress south impossible. Atkinson recorded, 'In my own mind I was morally certain that the [polar] party had perished.'

On 29 October 1912, an eleven-man polar search party led by Atkinson and including Lashly, Wright, Gran, Williamson, Nelson, Hooper, Keohane and Cherry-Garrard set out to find Scott and his team. They were accompanied by teams of mules that had been dropped off by the *Terra Nova* during one of her supply visits.

On 12 November the three-man party of Gran, Williamson and Nelson found the tent containing the frozen bodies of Scott, Wilson and Bowers in their sleeping bags. Wilson was on the left with his hands crossed on his chest, Bowers was on the right and Scott was lying half out of his sleeping bag with one arm stretched towards Wilson. Wrote Gran of the pitiful scene: 'It was a horrid sight. It was clear he had had a very hard last few minutes. His skin was yellow, frostbites all over' but he added: 'They died having done something great – how hard must not death be having done nothing…'. In a bag lying near the bodies were the 35lbs of Beardmore rocks the men had carried with them to the end.

Atkinson read the last entries in Scott's diaries and the men's last gruelling trek and their suffering became clear:

The causes of this disaster are not due to faulty organisation, but to misfortune in all risks which had to be undertaken. 1. The loss of pony transport in March, 1911 obliged me to start later than I had intended and obliged the limits of stuff transported to be narrowed. 2. The weather throughout the outward journey, and especially the long gale in 83 degree South, stopped us. 3. The soft snow in the lower reaches of the glacier again reduced the pace. We fought these untoward events with a will and conquered but it ate into our provisions reserve. Every detail of our food supplies, clothing, and depots made on the interior ice sheet and on that long stretch of 700 miles to the Pole and back worked out to perfection. The advance party would have returned to the glacier in fine form and with a surplus of food but for the astonishing failure of the man whom we had least expected to fail. Seaman Edgar Evans was thought the strong man of the party, and the Beardmore Glacier is not difficult in fine weather. But on our return we did not get a single completely fine day. This, with a sick companion, enormously increased our anxieties. I have said elsewhere we got into frightfully rough ice, and Edgar Evans received concussion of the brain. He died a natural death, but left us a shaken party, with the season unduly advanced. But all the facts above enumerated were as nothing to the surprise that awaited us on the Barrier. I maintain that our arrangements for returning were quite adequate and that no one in the world would have expected the temperature and surface that we encountered at this time of the year. On the summit in Lat 8 deg to Lat 86deg we had minus 20 to minus 30. On the Barrier in Lat. 82deg, 10,000ft. Lower, we had minus 30 in the day and minus 47 at night pretty regularly, with a continuous head wind during our day marches. It is clear that these circumstances came on very suddenly, and our problems are certainly due to this sudden advent of severe weather, which does not seem to have any satisfactory cause. I do not think human beings ever came through such a month as we have come through, and we should have got through in spite of the weather but for the sickening of a second companion, Captain Oates, and a shortage of fuel in our depots for which I cannot account, and, finally, but for the storm which has fallen on us within 11 miles of this depot at which we hoped to secure the final supplies. Surely misfortune could scarcely have exceeded this last blow. We arrived within 11 miles of our old One Ton Camp with fuel for one hot meal and food for two days. For four days we have been unable to leave the tent, a gale blowing about us. We are weak, writing is difficult; but for my own sake I do not, regret this journey, which has shown that Englishmen can endure hardship, help one another, and meet death with as great fortitude as ever in the past. We took risks. We know we took them. Things have come out against us, and therefore we have no cause for complaint, but bow to the will of Providence, determined still to do our best to the last. But if we have been willing to give our lives to this enterprise, which is for the honour of our country, I appeal to our countrymen to see that those who depend on us are properly cared for. Had we lived I should have had a tale to tell of the hardship, endurance, and courage of my companions that would have stirred the heart of every Englishman. These rough notes and our dead bodies must tell the tale, but surely, surely a great, rich country like ours will see that those who are dependent upon us are properly provided for. [Signed] R. Scott, 25th March 1912.

The party gathered up personal effects and then collapsed the tent over the bodies. A cairn of snow was erected topped by a cross created from Gran's skis. Three days later they found Oates' sleeping bag but not his body. The bag had been cut open along most of its length to enable him to get into it with his severely frostbitten feet. Another cairn was made and a note left – 'Hereabouts died a very gallant gentleman...'

On 25 November the party returned to Hut Point to hear that the northern party had safely returned to base.

The *Terra Nova* arrived to take the remaining expedition members home on 18 January. Before they left they put up a cross to the memory of:

Lieutenant H.R. Bowers
Petty Officer Edgar 'Taff' Evans
Captain L.E.G. Oates
Captain R.F. Scott
Dr. E.A. Wilson

It bore the quotation from Tennyson's *Ulysses*: 'To strive, to seek, to find, and not to yield'

It was indeed a tragic failure by the team. But there were times when it seemed Scott was so hellbent on achieving such enduring acclaim for himself that had it been humanely possible he would have done so alone. His constant diary references to having his expedition blighted by bad luck and abnormally extreme weather do not contain any suggestion that he could have planned it all so much better. It was his choice to push on in harsh conditions; he set the dates for each trek and made the decisions. And what he and his team endured equalled that experienced by Amundsen, but he and his men succeeded in their quest – and with comparable ease.

On 24 January 1913, William Bruce penned a letter called *Homeward Bound* in which he described his anxiety at having to break the tragic news to Kathleen, his sister and Scott's wife: 'I am in terror as to how my sister will take the news.' He added: 'We all rather wonder why the Norwegians should have been granted every facility, while our people met worse weather and hardships than any human beings have ever been able to talk about.'

Chapter 12
Amundsen's South Pole Success

Captain Amundsen's Achievement. From the telegrams now received there is little room for doubt that Captain Amundsen has reached the South Pole. From the English point of view he may not have 'played the game'. we cannot forget the secrecy under which for months he shrouded his intention to steal a march on the man who had for years been making his preparations to attain the coveted goal. This was all the more unnecessary, for no one would have welcomed co-operation in the work of South Polar exploration more than Captain Scott. Unfortunately Captain Amundsen notified the latter of his intention too late for Captain Scott to get into communication with him. Still, no one who knows Captain Amundsen can have any doubt of his integrity, and since he states he has reached the Pole we are bound to believe him. For the present we have only the bare fact that he has done so; whether during his journey there and back he made any discoveries of importance we can only learn on the publication of his narrative. One thing we know – he had nothing else in view save a 'dash for the Pole'. He had no intention of carrying out scientific investigations; he was unhampered with the heavy equipment required for this purpose; he had nothing too think of but his dogs, his sledges, his provisions and clothing. As soon as he landed at Whale Bight, 400 miles east of Scott's quarters, he could start across the Great Ice Barrier and lay down his depots for the final dash as soon as the light of the following spring permitted. This he would seem to have done, and must have started much earlier than Scott in order to be able to get out so soon as he has done...It may be that Captain Amundsen and the full story of his dash will make a substantial contribution to our knowledge of Antarctic conditions. From the brief summary that has been furnished by the Daily Chronicle we learn that after the final start it took Amundsen and his companions about two months to reach the Pole. After they got on to the plateau on which the Pole is situated, it seems to have been easy going...At all events, we may be sure that when Scott has the opportunity to tell us of what he and his well-trained staff have accomplished, it will be seen that science has reaped a rich harvest and that a substantial addition has been made to our existing knowledge of the Antarctic continent. Now that the South Pole has been reached, geographers will be free to carry on their investigation of this huge continent without any unpleasant element of rivalry, such as has existed hitherto in both ends of the earth.

The Times – 9 March 1912

It seemed that right from the moment Roald Amundsen set his heart on being the first man to reach the South Pole he was destined to succeed.

Born near Oslo on 16 July 1872 into a family of seaman and ship-owners (though his father died when Amundsen was only fourteen), Amundsen was a more straightforward man than Scott and had become fascinated by the world's icy and undiscovered plains as a boy. Long before Scott seriously considered Antarctic explorations Amundsen was making preparations – he even slept with his windows open to toughen himself up. Amundsen gave up his medical studies at twenty-one to set about fulfilling his dreams of becoming an explorer, serving first as a seaman in 1894 on board an Arctic merchant vessel and then in 1897 as first mate on the *Belgica*, the first ship to winter at the Antarctic. Its party went on to study the South Magnetic Pole. All this was giving Amundsen great insight into what would be needed for the future. On his return, Amundsen bought the 27ft ship *Gjoa* and in just under two years made his way through the North-west Passage. His team spent two winters on King William's Island carrying out scientific work and befriending Eskimos, whose expertise at living in such bitter conditions was to prove invaluable. The party spent another winter off the mouth of the Mackenzie River, returning in 1906.

After this he set himself another goal – the North Pole – only to have this dream dashed when American Naval officer Robert Peary did just that in 1909. So in 1910 Amundsen sailed on the *Fram* for Madeira with only two of his crew – his brother Leon and the ship's commander Lieutenant Nilsen – being told of his plans. The rest of the men assumed they would be on their way to Buenos Aires and then northwards to the Arctic. They were finally told the true intentions when they anchored.

Amundsen recorded: 'It was with a clear conscience that I decided to postpone my original plan for a year or two and to try to solve the last great problem...the South Pole...Although I have never seen this part of the Antarctic regions, I was not long in forming an opinion diametrically opposed to that of Shackleton and Scott, for the conditions both of going and surface were precisely what one would desire for sledging with Eskimo dogs, to judge from the descriptions of these explorers. If Peary could make a record trip on the Arctic ice with dogs, one ought, surely, with equally good tackle, to beat Peary's record on the splendidly even surface of the Barrier.'

Amundsen was also heavily in debt and knew that the only way to recoup money was by way of such a notable achievement.

So we come to the debate of character between the two men who embarked on the push to the South Pole. Amundsen was ruthless, deceitful and arrogant. He thought little of honour when it came to the historic race, forsaking any gentlemanly agreement in his quest and knowingly turning the trek into a race and rivalry. He may have felt uncomfortable over the slaughter of his dogs purely for food but he saw it as a necessary part of the expedition. But at the onset he had done all he could to ensure the animals' comfort while hauling. His initial planning and preparation, and his ability to endure were all faultless. His single-minded approach to being victorious is what won him the ultimate prize. Scott was undoubtedly more honourable, honest and courageous. He was also more admirable in his wish to harvest the Antarctic of some of its secrets. One could not imagine Amundsen even considering wasting valuable expedition time on gathering icy plain mementoes and allowing them to become an extra burden, both in a practical and a mindful way, no matter how scientifically treasured they would be. Scott fought his demons when it came to overruling his love of animals and their necessary slaughter – feeling it cruel to make the dogs endure unnecessary suffering when hauling and only killing them as a last resort. One can only imagine how his spirit was broken upon hearing that Amundsen had created a South Pole race and his despair at arriving at his goal after Amundsen. Scott battled on with his quest – he had no other choice – but even then, he still kept his expedition a combination of ultimate exploration and distracting research. The latter was carried out with some of the greatest risks, most challenging weather and biggest calamities. All took their toll on a group of men whose capability and copability should have been at a premium for the real task in hand.

Scott and Amundsen would never meet – Amundsen did not keep to his agreement to see Scott when he visited Oslo (then Christiana) in 1910.

It was with much bitterness that Scott heard how Amundsen switched plans to reach Cape Horn and the Pacific gateway to the Arctic Ocean to head for the South Pole. Amundsen sent a telegram to Scott saying: 'Beg leave to inform you proceeding Antarctica.' Amundsen had decided to sail directly for the Ross Sea so the telegram had been left in Madeira with instructions that it was not to be sent until the *Fram* sailed.

From then, the race was on.

But Amundsen's passage was always so much easier – and he had no intention of detracting from his mission with any scientific stop-offs. His vessel the *Fram* coped admirably with all she encountered and Scott's party soon learned that Amundsen was 60 miles nearer the pole that they were. They had also established several depots. Amundsen's itinerary was to take the *Fram* into the Pacific then south into the Bay of Wales. There the shore party would disembark on the Ross Ice Barrier and the *Fram* would go to Buenos Aires for the winter.

The *Fram* set the men down in January 1911. They were 788 miles away from the South Pole. Some have latterly said that the Ross Ice Barrier, the largest floating ice shelf in the world and dismissed by Shackleton as a suitable base, was not a wise choice by Amundsen. But he had faith:

> *I knew that this plan of wintering on the Barrier itself would be exposed to severe criticism as recklessness, foolhardiness, and so forth…I had devoted special study to this particular formation of the Barrier. For seventy years, this formation – with the exception of the pieces that had broke away – had persisted in the same place. I therefore concluded that it could be no accidental formation…I therefore had no misgivings in placing our station on this part of the Barrier.' He kept to his plan: 'to get everything – equipment and provisions – conveyed far enough into the Barrier to secure us against the unpleasant possibility of drifting out into the Pacific in case the Barrier should be inclined to halve. I had therefore fixed upon 10 miles as a suitable distance from the edge of the Barrier. But even our first impression of the conditions seemed to show that we should be spared a great part of this long troublesome transport.*

Amundsen's instincts were right – but he may also have been the subject of extreme good luck. His base camp could easily have crumpled beneath him – a disaster that would have certainly meant a different outcome to the one he eventually found in polar history. However, they suffered no incidents after erecting their prefabricated hut *Framheim*, which had been created by Jorgen Stubberud, twenty-eight, the party's youngest member. The hut was to be the base from where the men would organise stores and lay depots. The depots were sited 60 miles apart: the first containing seal meat, pemmican for the dogs, biscuits, butter, milk powders, chocolate, matches and paraffin; the second, a huge store of pemmican for the dogs; and the third containing further ample supplies. Amundsen attached great importance to not only having enough food but the right kind too, as he knew scurvy was a great threat. Hence, stores comprised a variety of fresh vegetables together with salted meat and bacon, supplies of tea, coffee and sugar, as well as a large range of wines and spirits donated by an Oslo store. The cook was Adolf Henrik Lindstrom, forty-six, who had accompanied Amundsen on the trip to the north-west Passage. His expertise at creating fine dishes was praised by South Pole member Helmut Hanssen who said: 'To the end of my days I shall see before me Lindstrom standing at the end of the table, comfortable and round, while the four of us at each side of the table sat expectant like hungry young birds in a nest, waiting for the hot cakes he dealt to each from the tower in front of him.'

It all made the trek to the South Pole sound like a jolly adventure rather than an expedition to unchartered territory. But then, Amundsen's team was meticulously prepared. Later observers were to note that unlike Scott, Amundsen had chosen to wear loose-fitting fur clothes like the Eskimos. Scott's team wore heavy woollen clothes, which were difficult to keep dry. Also, Amundsen's choice of sturdy, thick-coated dogs – delivered to Norway by the Royal Greenland Trading Company – and light sledges enabled his party to cover many more miles a day. Scott's decision to make his expedition multi-purpose is also open to criticism. Amundsen succeeded because he had one aim; to reach the South Pole. He neither wished nor allowed this singular focus to be blurred by combining it with any other. While Scott was overseeing scientific projects and data-collecting, Amundsen was simply ploughing on to achieve his goal. Scott should have made his expedition with the same singular determination, thus ensuring a far greater chance of success. Nothing should have got in the way of such an historic and momentous exploration. Having achieved it, Scott could have returned to the Antarctic on later occasions to carry out scientific work as a separate, significantly less highly-charged expedition.

It was on 3 February that the *Terra Nova* sailed into the Bay of Whales after being unable to go ashore on King Edward VII Island. There, the crew came across the *Fram* with Amundsen and his men on board. Campbell, Levick and Pennell enjoyed breakfast with them and Amundsen offered to give Scott's team some dogs. Pennell in turn offered to take the *Fram's* mail to New Zealand. There was more bonhomie between these two unlikely groups, with Amundsen driving his dogs up to the *Terra Nova* when he went for lunch. Priestley, in particular, was impressed by the way Amundsen controlled his dogs – just one whistle and they all lay down quietly. Scott's men also noticed how a false deck had been built on the *Fram* to protect the dogs from storms. There was also an awning to protect them from the sun and a carefully thought-out dog diet of dried fish, pemmican and lard.

Historians state that the Bay of Whales was the best starting point for an attempt on the Pole. Amundsen knew that the bay, chartered by Ross in 1841, was still in the same position as when Borchgrevink landed there in 1900 and when Shackleton sailed by in 1908 and gave it the name Bay of Whales. The Bay was 60 miles closer to the Pole than the McMurdo Sound. Hearing of Amundsen's meticulously worked-out itinerary with every thought given to every aspect of his expedition, Scott remarked: 'There is no doubt that Amundsen's plan is a very serious menace to ours.' His party wanted to confront Amundsen and their feelings were summed up when Cherry-Garrard noted: 'We had just paid the first instalment of making a path to the Pole, and we felt, however unreasonably, that we had earned the first right of way.'

Writing in her book, *Antarctic Destinies*, Stephanie Barczewski said: 'Amundsen might have seen his base camp crumble beneath him if the unstable ice rimming the Bay of Whales had calved from the Barrier edge at the wrong time. He might not have found another glacier in addition to the Beardmore to prove a route up the Tran Antarctic Mountains. If either of these things had happened, which they easily could have, polar history, and Amundsen's reputation would have been very different.'

Then followed a winter of six months of darkness. The time was used wisely by Amundsen and his team, calculating how to lessen loads, how to keep comfortable and even inventing new ideas such as improving sleeping bags with reindeer skin.

On 27 August the party was ready to start off on those last 788 miles, but there were to be setbacks. The drastic temperatures hindered them. They set off on 7 September only to be driven back to *Framheim* seven days later. The men were disillusioned, the dogs suffering – and Amundsen feared Scott was ahead of the game. Doubts set in amongst the party, especially from one, forty-four-year-old army captain Frederick Hjalmar Johansen, who with another man, thirty-year-old Kristian Prestrud, a lieutenant in the navy (who had been given the responsibility of drawing up charts and making astronomical readings and calculations), felt he had been left to struggle along behind the returning group while Amundsen was well ahead. After voicing his concerns he was dispatched with Prestrud to King Edward VII Land to carry out small scale scientific research. It was a devastating blow but the two men stood alone against Amundsen. Just over a year after returning home to Norway, Johansen killed himself.

Amundsen finally set off on 19 October 1911, with four other men and four sledges each drawn by twelve Siberian Huskies (and carrying reduced weight). Amundsen reached their southernmost supply depot on 5 November. He had picked his team with great care. Helmut Hanssen, forty-one, had been at sea since he was eleven. He was a Master Mariner and had accompanied Amundsen on the North-west Passage expedition. Amundsen had been impressed by his handling of dogs and Hanssen was made chief dog man. Sverre Hassel, thirty-five, had also been at sea since he was a boy and was also a Master Mariner. He was put in charge of the expedition's fuel supplies. Oskar Wisting, forty, was a trained navigator. Olav Olavson Bjaaland, thirty-eight, was a skilled carpenter and ski-maker.

The party was besieged by falling temperatures and blinded by snow. But at last, by 1 November, the men passed the last of the crevasses and began to make good progress. By 12 November the central Antarctic plateau came into view. Amundsen decided to make a depot and leave a month's supplies for their return. After two days rest at the depot, Amundsen carried on – at one point enjoying being pulled on skis by a rope tied to a sledge. On 17 November, Amundsen's party started on the final leg, passing mountains rising to 15,000ft. They enjoyed good weather until a blizzard forced them to stop. On 20 November they made camp – bleakly later to be called 'Butchers' by Amundsen, for this was where twenty-four of the weakest dogs were slaughtered.

By the middle of November his party was 270 miles away from the South Pole. But things did not always go his way. Unable to find an expansive through route he had to climb a narrow strip of ice where he was repeatedly forced to turn back as the dogs lost their footing. Another route was barred by giant blocks of ice. But on 4 December they reached the final plateau and on 7 December they got to what had been Ernest Shackleton's farthest point south in 1909. To celebrate this Amundsen ordered that a Norwegian flag should be hoisted above one of the sledges. He wrote:

All the sledges had stopped and from the foremost of them the Norwegian flag was flying. It shook itself out, waved and flapped so that the silk rustled. It looked wonderfully well in the pure, clear air and the shining white surroundings...no other moment in the whole trip affected me like this. The tears forced their way to my eyes; by no effort of will could I keep them back. Luckily I was some way in advance of the others so that I had time to pull myself together and master my feelings before reaching my comrades.

On 13 December Amundsen's party were camping just 15 miles away from the South Pole. Anticipation that night was high, with Amundsen recording that he had 'the same feeling that I can remember as a little boy on the night before Christmas Eve – an intense expectation of what was going to happen'. The next day – which dawned clear and crisp – they were there. Amundsen's joy is shown in this description from his book *An Account of the Norwegian Antarctic Expedition in the 'Fram' 1910–1912:* 'Up to this moment the observations and our reckoning had shown a surprising agreement. We reckoned that we should be at the Pole on 14 December. On the afternoon of that day we had brilliant weather – a light wind from the south-east with a temperature of –10° F. The sledges were going very well. The day passed without any occurrence worth mentioning, and at three o'clock in the afternoon we halted, as according to our reckoning we had reached our goal.'

Another Norwegian flag was erected; this time on top of the tent they planned to leave at the Pole. Recorded Amundsen: 'Five roughened frostbitten fists it was gripped the post, lifted the fluttering flag on high and planted it together as the very first at the Geographical South Pole.'

To ensure they were actually at this magical point, the men carried out distance tests around the camp using sextants and then celebrated with extra rations. They had beaten Scott to the South Pole by thirty-five days.

Amundsen named the site King Haakon VII's plateau after their Norwegian king and penned a note he knew Scott's party would eventually come across:

As you probably are the first to reach this area after us, I will ask you kindly to forward this letter to King Haakon VII. If you can use any of the articles left in the tent please do not hesitate to do so. With kind regards I wish you a safe return. Yours truly, Roald Amundsen.

Amongst the items left were a spare sextant and a pair of mittens.

In short, Amundsen's success was due to his choice of dogs (though he was later criticised by animal-lovers for slaying over half of them to feed the others and the men), his single-minded determination, experience, thorough planning and management. Their journey there and back took ninety-nine days at an average daily speed of 19 miles a day – nearly 1,900 miles in some of the world's most hostile areas. Although suffering some frostbite, the party returned home without sickness or injury. Amundsen's dream had been so easily fulfilled while Scott's became a tortuous and tragic nightmare. Nevertheless, Amundsen's achievement was overshadowed by Scott's failure when the world took the British hero to their hearts. When Amundsen was invited by RGS President Leonard Darwin to dine with the Society, Sir Clements Markham resigned his council seat in protest.

All this hurt Amundsen bitterly for he saw it as a slight not only on himself but on the men who had accompanied him. He wrote: 'Honour where honour is due. Honour to my faithful comrades who, by their patience, perseverance and experience, brought out equipment to the limit of perfection, and thereby rendered our victory possible.' Amundsen returned to Norway in 1913 after a stay in South America. He wrote *An account of the Norwegian Antarctic Expedition in the 'Fram' 1910–1912* with the dedication: 'To my Comrades, the Brave Little Band that Promised In Funchal Roads to Stand by Me in the Struggle for the South Pole. I Dedicate this Book. Roald Amundsen, Uranienborg, August 15, 1912.' [*sic*]

Commentators have compared the achievements of Scott and Amundsen and most are in agreement that Amundsen's skills with ski and dogs, and his general familiarity with ice conditions, gave him considerable advantages in the race for the Pole. They note that Scott's own view on the tragic expedition comprised mainly of a series of misfortunes rather than mismanagement.

With the funds he received from his expedition – as well as from his writings and lecture tours – Amundsen established a shipping business. His plans for an expedition to the North Pole were thwarted by World War I, but he attempted the trek again in 1918. It was not successful and he was beaten by the unpredictable currents as he sailed across the Pole from the North Siberian islands. His next ambition was to achieve another 'first' – this time flying over the North Pole. He flew within 170 miles in 1925 but was beaten by aviator Richard Byrd. A few days later Amundsen went over in an airship from Spitsbergen to Alaska with Italian aeronautical engineer and Arctic explorer General Umberto Nobile. The two were later to fall out but, despite this, Amundsen set off to join an international search for Nobile when he was lost on another flight in 1928. He set off from Bergen on 17 June but his seaplane crashed in the polar seas and Amundsen was never seen again. This great explorer had come to rest in the part of the world he had become as one with.

Chapter 13

A Nation Mourns

Captain R.F. Scott, the famous Antarctic explorer, and four other members of the British South Polar expedition have died amidst the southern ice. The five men were the whole Southern party. They had reached the Pole on 18 January 1912, just over a month after Captain Amundsen, the Norwegian, and had struggled far back towards safety when they were overcome. Captain Scott and his last two companions died, it is believed, on the 29 March 1912. They had descended the glacier from the great inland plateau on which is the Pole. From its foot they had marched northward to within a few miles of a stock of provisions at a place named by them One Ton Depot. There, almost in reach of succour, the struggle ended. Presumably, the bodies were found by a search party sent out from the base on McMurdo Sound, for Lieutenant Evans, of the Terra Nova, *Scott's ship, who reports the disaster, gives details which must have been learnt from the dead men's records. One is that the explorers found at the Pole a Norwegian tent and so knew that Amundsen had been there before them. Death was due to exposure and want. On the journey southward, the party left One Ton Depot on November 17; on January 18 they were at the Pole; on March 29 the last survivors died near One Ton Depot. Thus sixty-two days were spent on the march south and seventy-one at the Pole and on the way back. Those few day's delay, due very likely to bad weather, were perhaps the cause of the final disaster. It should be noted that even in the sixty-two days are included five days delays, due to a storm encountered during the ascent in December of the Beadmon glacier.*

Mrs Scott, the wife of the explorer, is now on her way to New Zealand. Her plan was to meet her husband there on his return from the Antarctic. She left San Francisco for Auckland a few days ago, and is now out of reach of news. She will not hear of the disaster until the steamer on which she is travelling establishes wireless telegraphic communication with New Zealand. The names of the men who reached the Pole and perished are:- Captain Scott, Royal Navy. Dr Wilson, chief of the scientific staff. Captain Oates, Inniskilling Dragoons (in charge of ponies and mules). Lieutenant Bowers, Royal Indian Marine (commissariat officer). Petty Officer Evans, RN (in charge of sledges and equipment).

The Times – 11 Feb 1913

The expedition was expected back in New Zealand early in April 1913. In January, Kathleen set out via America to meet her husband and his men. After a few days of camping with cowboys in New Mexico, she set out from San Francisco aboard RMS *Aorangi*. While sailing between Tahiti and Raratonga Kathleen was summoned to the captain's cabin. His hands were visibly shaking as he handed her a message received by wireless. It read simply: 'Captain Scott and five others perished in a blizzard after reaching the South Pole January 18th.'

Kathleen went into shock, and unable to fully comprehend the news of her husband's death spent the rest of the day seemingly carrying out normal activities such as playing cards, discussing American politics with fellow passengers and even taking a Spanish lesson. Her brother Wilfred, together with Edward Wilson's wife Ory, Edward Atkinson and Teddy Evans who had taken the *Terra Nova* down to McMurdo Sound to embark Scott's party and the rest of the expedition, met her in Wellington. Atkinson handed Kathleen her husband's diary (as Scott had requested) and last letter. She was later herself to write: 'There never was a man with such a responsibility and duty, and the agony of leaving his job undone, losing the other lives and leaving me uncared for must have been unspeakable.'

The world was informed of the tragedy when *Terra Nova* reached Oamaru, New Zealand, on 10 February 1913. Within days Scott became a national icon. A fierce nationalistic spirit was aroused; the *London Evening News* called for the story to be read to schoolchildren throughout the land to coincide with the memorial service at St Paul's Cathedral on 14 February.

Of high courage and endurance, he had proved himself a first rate organiser and a born leader of men. He was a man of wide culture and extensive reading, interested in everything that concerns humanity. He was a man of genuine modesty, warm-hearted, with troops of friends in all ranks of life, and bright and entertaining as a companion, firm in his friendship and chivalrous in his conduct. In appearance he was thick-set, sturdily built, with a strong, clean-shaven face, tight determined lips and keen blue eyes. His manner at first acquaintance gave little indication of the geniality, the keen enthusiasm and the strenuous personal force, which were traits of his character, and made him extremely popular among all with whom he came in contact...Captain Scott's one son was born before he left England on his last expedition and pictures of the little boy when two years old were sent as a Christmas card by his mother to reach the explorer.

The Times – 11 February 1913

The news of Scott's death reached Sir Clements while he was staying in Estoril, Spain. He returned to England and was later to assist with the preparation of Scott's diaries for publication.

Scott's diaries were to play an in important role in revelations of the reality of polar exploration. *Scott's Last Expedition*, edited by Leonard Huxley, appeared in 1913 and the account was popularised – not least to raise funds for the expedition, which was in debt. A facsimile of the diaries produced in 1968 included an introduction by Scott's son Peter, who drew parallels between his father's endeavours and modern space exploration. Even today, Scott's articulate, detailed and often deeply-moving entries still inspire.

The Times reported on the glowing tributes paid to Scott in the New York press, which claimed that both Amundsen and Shackleton were 'amazed to hear that such a disaster could overtake a well-organised expedition'. On learning the details of Scott's death Amundsen was reported as saying, 'I would gladly forgo any honour or money if thereby I could have saved Scott his terrible death.'

Mr T.V. Hodgson, Curator of the Plymouth Municipal Museum, who was one of the scientific members of Captain Scott's South Polar expedition in 1901–4, says of his former leader: He was an admirable leader, a man of sound judgment, keen observation, and ripe experience and these characteristics inspired confidence in all his men. Our New York correspondent telegraphs that the news of the fate of Captain Scott and his four companions has greatly shocked the community there and throughout the country and that the deepest sympathy is expressed everywhere. All the afternoon newspapers in New York devoted columns to such details of the catastrophe as were available and extended accounts of the expedition and Captain Scott's career. The editorial comments pay glowing tributes to Captain Scott and his party, and express the hope that the valuable scientific data they must have accumulated have not been lost.

The publication of Scott's diary and farewell letters made him a national hero. A wave of grief swept the nation. Reviewing the diary in *Punch*, *Winnie-the-Pooh* author A.A. Milne wrote:

I have never met a more beautiful character than that which is revealed unconsciously in these journals. His humanity, his courage, his faith, his steadfastness, above all, his simplicity, mark him out as a man among men...It is a wonderful tale of manliness that these two volumes tell us...I have been for a few days in the company of the brave...and every hour with them has made me more proud for those that died and more humble for myself.

An eleven-year-old girl, Mary Steel wrote a poem, which ended:

Though naught but a simple cross
Now marks those heroes' grave,
Their names will live forever!
Oh England, Land of the Brave!

The survivors of the expedition were suitably honoured on their return, with polar medals and promotions for the naval personnel. In place of the knighthood that might have been her husband's had he survived, Kathleen Scott was granted the rank becoming Lady Scott and precedence of a widow of a Commander of the Order of the Bath.

Kathleen faced a tremendous debt from the expedition but ironically, with the death of its leader and her husband came funding that paid all outstanding debts and provided grants to all dependants. For the response to Scott's final plea on behalf of the dead men's families was enormous by the standards of the day. The Mansion House Scott Memorial Fund closed at £75,000 (equal to over £3.5m today). Kathleen, her son, mother and sisters received a total of £18,000. Wilson's widow got £8,500 and Bowers' mother £4,500. Edgar Evans' widow, children and mother received £1,500 between them. (Many felt the families should have received more.)

This still left £12,000, which was handed over to Cambridge University and used towards the foundation of the Scott Polar Research Institute. (Officially constituted in 1926 and of which Frank Debenham became the first director.)

Although many of the crew shared Kathleen Scott's belief that photographer Herbert Ponting had made a fortune from the Antarctic, his claim that he lost money on the expedition is supported by the record of his wealth at death, which amounted to only £815.

Together with Kathleen and the family, there was another who felt the grief deeply – Sir Clements Markham. In 1913 he wrote an accolade to Scott:

Fourteen years ago Robert Falcon Scott was a rising naval officer, able, accomplished, popular, highly thought of by his superiors, and devoted to his noble profession. It was a serious responsibility to induce him to take up the work of an explorer; yet no man living could be found who was so well fitted to command a great Antarctic expedition. The undertaking was new and unprecedented. The object was to explore the unknown Antarctic continent by land. Captain Scott entered upon the enterprise with enthusiasm tempered by prudence and sound sense. All had to be learnt by a thorough study of the history of Arctic travelling, combined with experience of different conditions in the Antarctic regions. Scott was the initiator and founder of Antarctic sledge travelling.

His discoveries were of great importance. The survey and soundings along the barrier cliffs, the discovery of King Edward VII Land, the discovery of Ross Island and the other volcanic islets, the examination of the Barrier surface, the discovery of the Victoria Mountains – a range of great height and many hundreds of miles in length, which had only before been seen from a distance out at sea – and above all the discovery of the great ice cap on which the South Pole is situated, by one of the most remarkable polar journeys on record. His small but excellent scientific staff worked hard and with trained intelligence, their results being recorded in twelve large quarto volumes.

The great discoverer had no intention of losing touch with his beloved profession though resolved to complete his Antarctic work. The exigencies of the naval service called him to the command of battleships and to confidential work of the Admiralty; so that five years elapsed before he could resume his Antarctic labours.

The object of Captain Scott's second expedition was mainly scientific, to complete and extend his former work in all branches of science. It was his ambition that in his ship there should be the most completely equipped expedition for scientific purposes connected with the polar regions, both as regards men and material that ever left these shores. In this he succeeded. He had on board a fuller complement of geologists, one of them especially trained for the study of physiography, biologists, physicists and surveyors than ever before composed the staff of a polar expedition. Thus Captain Scott's objects were strictly scientific, including the completion and extension of his former discoveries. The results will be explained in the second volume of this work. They will be found to be extensive and important. Never before, in the polar regions, have meteorological, magnetic and tidal observations been taken, in one locality, during five years. It was also part of Captain Scott's plan to reach the South Pole by a long and most arduous journey, but here again his intention was, if possible, to achieve scientific results on the way, especially hoping to discover fossils, which would throw light on the former history of the great range of mountains that he had made known to science.

The principal aim of this great man, for he rightly has his niche among the polar Dii Majores, was the advancement of knowledge. From all aspects Scott was among the most remarkable men of our time, and the vast number of readers of his journal will be deeply impressed with the beauty of his character. The chief traits which shone forth through his life were conspicuous in the hour of death. There are few events in history to be compared, for grandeur and pathos, with the last closing scene in that silent wilderness of snow. The great leader, with the bodies of his dearest friends beside him, wrote and wrote until the pencil dropped from his dying grasp. There was no thought of himself, only the earnest desire to give comfort and consolation to others in their sorrow. His very last lines were written lest he who induced him to enter upon Antarctic work should now feel regret for what he had done.

'If I cannot write to Sir Clements, tell him I thought much of him, and never regretted his putting me in command of the Discovery.'

CLEMENTS R. MARKHAM.
September 1913.

Markham was awarded honorary degrees from the Universities of Cambridge and Leeds – the latter at which he was described as 'a veteran in the service of mankind', and 'for sixty years the inspiration of English geographical science'. Markham read his last paper – *The History of the Gradual Development of the Groundwork of Geographical Science* – for the RGS in 1915, the same year he attended a service at St

Peter's Church, Binton, near Stratford-upon-Avon where a window was dedicated to Scott and his men, and assisted at the unveiling of the Royal Navy's statue of Scott. Scott's death hit Markham hard but he continued to lead a busy life writing and travelling despite being plagued by gout. He too was to die tragically – when reading in bed by candlelight. The bedclothes caught fire and although his butler rushed in to help and put out the fire, the shock was too great and Markham died, unconscious, in January 1916. His last diary entry talked of a visit by Scott's son Peter.

Kathleen carried on her work as a sculptor, creating statues of many high profile figures of the day such as kings, prime ministers, writers and adventurers – including Nansen, who asked her to marry him. Kathleen turned down his proposal but kept him as a friend.

In 1915, accepting a commission by the then Commanding Officer of HMS *Vernon*, Kathleen lovingly sculpted a bronze statue of her husband with one of his faithful dogs. The statue was paid for by all the ship's officers. It went to Portsmouth, first to the naval base along the Parade, then to a site called Storehouse 11 (now the National Museum of the Royal Navy), and finally to a site between the Mary Rose Museum and Porter's Lodge, allowing public access to it. The listed statue is inscribed with one of Scott's most moving diary entries: '...the gale is howling about us, we are weak, writing is difficult but for my own sake I do not regret this journey, which has shown that Englishmen can endure hardships, help one another and meet death with as great a fortitude as ever in the past. We took risks, we knew we took them. Things have come out against us and therefore we have no cause for complaint but bow to the will of providence determined to do our best to the end.'

In 1922 Kathleen married Edward Hilton Young, a politician who later became Lord Kennet of the Dene, and she took the title Baroness Kennet. Kathleen had another son, Wayland Hilton Young, in 1923 who became writer and politician. Kathleen died of leukemia in 1947 and her son in 2009.

Oates also went to his death not realising that he was a father. A little girl, who was born at an unknown location in Ireland, was taken from her young mother – rumoured to be only twelve years old – and sent to an orphanage in the south of England and grew up not knowing her father's identity. Oates was unaware of the child, and the dark secret remained untold for about a hundred years.

The *Terra Nova* had its figure head removed in 1913. This was taken to the Museum of Wales in 2009. The vessel itself returned to its former life as a whaling and sealing ship, finally being sunk by ice off Greenland in 1943.

Amundsen's ship the *Fram* is a visitor attraction in Oslo. But it bears a chilling tale – and not just that of the Antarctic. In 1936, a year after the *Fram* was brought onto dry land, one of Amundsen's closest friends and fellow expedition member, Oscar Wisting, asked to spend a night on the ship for old times sake. He was found dead in his cabin that next morning.

Scott's diaries were bequeathed to the nation by his family and are housed at the British Library. They have appeared in many forms since their first publication in 1913.

Chapter 14

Hero or Fool?

The loss of Scott and his party put Britain in mourning – even overshadowing Amundsen's feat in being first at the Pole. For many years Scott was viewed as a tragic hero who did not deserve criticism and any feelings of those linked to the expedition or relatives of those who died were not voiced publicly. And Scott was undoubtedly capable of commanding great personal loyalty. 'He wouldn't ask you to do anything he wasn't prepared to do himself,' said *Terra Nova* stoker William Burton. Tom Crean, the Irishman who accompanied Scott on both the *Discovery* and *Terra Nova* expeditions, was particularly fond of Scott saying: 'loved every hair of his head.' Further, it was clear that the dislike Oates had had for Scott was not shared by Henry Bowers and Edward Wilson, the two men who had died alongside him. Bowers had written: 'He is one of the best and best-behaved up to our best traditions at a time when his own outlook must have been the blackness of darkness.' Wilson said: 'There is nothing I would not do for him. He is a really good man.'

Apsley Cherry-Garrard's 1922 book, *The Worst Journey in the World*, said mistakes were made and that Scott was 'weak' and 'peevish', but said Scott was 'the last of the great geographical explorers'. In 1927, amateur historian John Gordon Hayes concluded in his book, *Antarctica: A Treatise on the Southern Continent*, that it was the transport arrangements that let the expedition down.

Scott's reputation survived after World War II and into the 50th anniversary of the disaster in 1962, fiercely protected by his widow. He was portrayed very much as a hero in a well-known 1948 film, *Scott of the Antarctic*, with John Mills in the title role.

Reginald Pound was the first biographer given access to Scott's original sledging journal in 1966. He revealed personal failings that cast a new light on Scott but Pound continued to praise his heroism, writing of 'a splendid sanity that would not be subdued'. There was no real change in public perceptions until the 1970s, by which time nearly all those directly concerned with the expedition were dead.

More books appeared, each of which to some degree challenged the positive public perception. The most critical of these was David Thomson's *Scott's Men* in

1977. In Thomson's view Scott was not a great man, 'at least, not until near the end' describing his planning as 'haphazard' and 'flawed' and his leadership characterised by lack of foresight.

Controversy was further ignited with the publication of Roland Huntford's book, *Scott and Amundsen* in 1979, which was re-published and televised in 1985 as *The Last Place on Earth* (the title the book would take when later re-printed). Both caused an uproar with the film having Scott's wife Kathleen committing adultery in Berlin with Amundsen at the very time Scott was just a few days from death, furthering Huntford's suggestion of infidelity. Huntford was critical of Scott's supposedly authoritarian leadership style and of his poor judgment of men, and blamed him for a series of organisational failures that led to the death of everyone in the polar party. Huntford accused Scott of being autocratic and bullying. He described Scott as an 'heroic bungler' and 'recklessly incompetent'. Huntford, the *Observer*'s Scandinavian correspondent, wrote the book after interviewing Tryggve Gran for the newspaper in 1974. He later said that the editor telephoned him: 'to say there might be a book in it. I agreed with him and was astonished to find that when the piece was published, he had added a footnote saying I was working on a new biography of Scott and Amundsen. So that sort of settled things.'

When other books were brought out defending Scott, Huntford stood his ground. 'Scott and his men should have been better prepared for extreme Antarctic conditions. When Amundsen went south, he planned on the worst case scenario, whereas Scott assumed the best possible conditions. Scott's party had six years of experience between the five of them, whereas Amundsen's group had a century of skiing between them,' he said. 'Amundsen was a professional who wrote, "Victory awaits him who has everything in order. Defeat is certain to him who has neglected to take the necessary precautions." In contrast, Scott was a gentleman amateur, and believed that pluck, spirit and improvisation were more important than careful planning. He once said, 'Gentlemen don't practice.' He noted that Amundsen also refused to travel any later than mid-February, before the colder March temperatures that Scott was to travel in.

The main criticisms from by Huntford and others unsure of the worth of Scott's endeavours, include:

- His general character faults such as being aloof, self-absorbed, over-sentimental, inflexible and obtuse.
- Erroneous judgment of character such as his 'favouritism' of Edgar Evans and harshness towards Shackleton.
- Failing to organise effective transport, which ended in a mix of sledges, ponies and dogs with the importance of dogs not heeded.
- Deciding to turn the final four-man team into five, thereby putting pressure on rations.

- Not paying enough attention to depot laying, resulting in the placement of One Ton Depot too far to the north – and meaning it was beyond their grasp in that tragic trek back to base.
- Insisting on stopping to collect the 35lbs of geological samples when time – and the temperature – was so against them.
- Giving inconsistent and contradictory instructions about the use of dogs in connection with the returning polar party.
- Did Scott do it right? The answer of course is 'no', otherwise the glory of being first to the South Pole would have been his. Instead, he is the kind of hero the British hold the most affection for – one who *almost* claimed victory, missing it only because of misfortune and the dishonourable actions of a foreign rival.

In 1996 in *I May Be Some Time*, English author Francis Spufford described the fated expedition as a 'devastating evidence of bungling', adding that Scott doomed his companions, then covered his tracks with rhetoric. Travel writer Paul Theroux called Scott 'confused and demoralised…an enigma to his men, unprepared and a bungler'.

In her book, *Antarctic Destinies*, Stephanie Barczewski wrote: 'There is no denying that Scott, as all polar explorers do, made mistakes. There were small ones, such as forgetting the Union Jack as he set off for the Pole, and big ones, such as the problem of fuel evaporating from the tins as they lay in the supply depots. Did these accumulate in such a way that disaster became inevitable? If so, nearly every polar expedition would end in disaster…his most egregious error related to transport, for by the time that he set forth for the Pole on the *Terra Nova* expedition, he had plenty of evidence that the ponies were not capable of accomplishing what he required. The superiority of dogs dawned on him too late.'

In summing up, Barczewski says: 'Whether all of Scott's mistakes, taken in sum, added up first to the loss of the race to the Pole and then to the deaths of five men, is an open question. And even if they did, it is equally unclear that he made an inordinate number of errors. It must be remembered that his and Amundsen's expeditions were only the third and fourth ever to winter on the Antarctic continent; there was simply not enough data available for Scott to have prepared for every eventuality. His great experience of Antarctica, in fact, may have worked against him. Scott cut his margin for error closer than did Amundsen because he felt secure in doing so based on his *Discovery* experience. Amundsen, lacking first-hand knowledge, assumed the conditions would be much worse than they were.'

Sir Clements Markham, Scott's 'mentor', came in for criticism too. Hugh Robert Mill, Ernest Shackleton's first biographer and RSG librarian, said Markham had run the Society in a dictatorial manner and some of his published papers were questioned over their accuracy. Frank Debenham, the geologist who had worked alongside Shackleton and Scott, called Markham 'a dangerous old man'. William Bruce, Scott's bother-in-law and fellow team member, wrote of Markham's 'malicious opposition to the Scottish Antarctic expedition'. He said he always felt that Scott was Markham's protégé and that Markham 'felt it necessary, in order to uphold Scott, that I should be obliterated'. Despite this, Bruce and Scott remained friends. Bruce's colleague, Robert-Rudmose-Brown, referred to Markham as 'that old fool and humbug'.

But Markham received tributes from King George V, acknowledging his life and work; from the RGS and other learned bodies with which he had been associated; from the Naval Commander-in-Chief at Devonport; and from Norwegian Explorer Fridtjof Nansen, as well as goodwill messages from around the world..

Sadly for a man so undeserving of such a tarnished reputation, Scott's name was further blighted in 2002 when a nationwide poll in Britain to discover 100 Great Britain's put Scott at number fifty-four while his nemesis, Shackleton, was at number eleven.

'There is no doubt that Scott made mistakes,' said Nigel Watson, executive director of New Zealand's Antarctic Heritage Trust. Watson accepts the expedition was also plagued by that great defeater of all challenges – bad luck. He adds of Scott: 'He's certainly a character that has been subject to revisionist history over the last hundred years and that will continue [...] I think what ultimately has captured people, particularly in the Western world, is that heroic failure.'

There have, of course, been those who are quite rightly determined to defend Scott. These have included travel writer Diana Preston, author of *First Rate Tragedy: Robert Falcon Scott and the Race to the South* Pole in 1998. She summarised: 'The point is not that they ultimately failed but that they so very nearly succeeded.' This was followed by meteorologist Susan Solomon who, in her 2001 book, *The Coldest March*, argued that although Scott fully understood the challenge of Antarctic conditions and was adequately prepared, the temperatures in March 1912 were abnormally low. She wrote: 'That posed tremendous problems for them: frostbite; a lack of wind to fill the sails they were counting on, because when it gets cold it's quite calm; and the snow became quite sandpapery under these conditions. It was a triple whammy that made it impossible for them to make the 15–20 miles a day they needed to do to survive [...] instead, they were making only 5–8 miles a day and dealing with a sledge that felt like lead [...] it was absolutely devastating.' This book prompted gratitude from Scott's grandson Falcon who said at the time: 'We're very pleased about this. We always knew that the weather was bad – that was in all his diaries – but we don't know how unusually bad it was [...] this new book goes some way towards putting the record straight.' Huntford, however, said his opinion of Scott remained unchanged: 'I stand by everything I wrote. The reality is that Scott and his followers, with the exception of Meares the dog-driver, were totally and utterly unsuited to the conditions in which they were trying to work. What kind of explorer is it who is taken by surprise?' For good measure he threw in the information that Oates had had no faith in Scott's leadership and had written to his mother saying: 'I dislike Scott intensely and would chuck the whole thing in if it were not that we are a British expedition and must beat the Norwegians.'

Latter-day explorer Sir Ranulph Fiennes wrote a biography in 2003, which was a strong and positive look at Scott's goals and achievements. In an obvious determination to uphold Scott's memory, he dedicated the book to the 'Families of the Defamed dead'. He said Huntford's criticism were based on ignorance of the Antarctic, saying for example that Huntford's suggestion the party should have worn furs rather than their woollen clothing was misplaced as 'man haulers would be unable to move in furs [...] they would perspire too much [...] furs are only correct for dog drivers [...]' Fiennes also hit out at Huntford's dismissal of Scott's scientific aims and his carrying of rocks – 'a pathetic gesture to salvage something from defeat at the Pole' – saying that the 35lbs of rocks collected would reveal 'the key to the origin of Antarctica'. It has been suggested that the rocks Scott and his team hauled back with them could have contributed to the fatal conclusion of their South Pole venture. All the scientific samples gathered and data recorded cannot be undermined as this proved vital in gaining knowledge of an hitherto unexplored corner of the world – knowledge that was boundary breaking in Scott's time, proved crucial to future expeditions and that has formed the basis of research papers that are considered finite, valuable and unquestionable today. Contemporary scientists still use the climate data collated by Scott to track global warming.

Fiennes was criticised for personal attacks on Huntford and by those who said that his own experiences as a polar explorer did not give him licence as an authority on the subject. (Incidentally, while some have made comparisons between Scott and Fiennes, he himself has said he identifies more with Lawrence Oates.)

In 2005 David Crane published another Scott biography, *Scott of the Antarctic: A Life of Courage and Tragedy in the Extreme South*. Crane said it was a changing world that had detracted from Scott's achievements: 'It is not that we see him differently from the way they [his contemporaries] did, but that we see him the same, and instinctively do not like it.' But of Scott's decision to take five men and not four on the final South Pole push, he said: 'There was nothing whimsical, nothing sentimental about the inclusion of a fifth man [...] when the time came to confirm that final party, everything from Evans' interests and the safety of the returning team to the convenience, comfort, tent-craft and logistical "tidiness" of his own team were scarified to the ruthless determination to bag the Pole.' Reviewing the book in the *Guardian*, Kevin Rushby wrote: 'Crane is undoubtedly correct to say that Scott was neither a great explorer like Amundsen, nor a charismatic leader like Shackleton, but what comes through clearly in the description of those last few days is what a good death he had. Forget all the discussion of dogs versus ponies, of the calorie requirements and the motorised sledges – all the myriad little ways in which Scott got it wrong. At the end, in that final personal apocalypse, he got something right that we can all admire, even envy. David Crane has written a fine biography of that Scott, the flawed but timeless hero [...]'

In 2006, explorer Bruce Parry tried to recreate Scott's trek in the BBC2 series *Blizzard*. Parry lost so much weight living off rations equating to those taken by Scott and his party that he had to abandon the project. He said: 'History has treated Scott fairly shabbily. It's very in vogue these days to diss our Victorian and Georgian explorers with their stiff upper-lip approach and, for the last few decades, Scott has borne the brunt of that [...] to me he's a national hero.' Scott himself said: 'I may not have proved a great explorer but we have done the greatest march ever made and come very near to great success.'

Chapter 15

Words on Scott's Tragic Endeavours

Perhaps when on my printed page you look,
Your fancies by the fireside may go homing
To that lone land where bravely you endured.
And if perchance you hear the silence calling.
The frozen music of star-yearning heights,
Or, dreaming, see the seines of silver trawling
Across the ships abyss on vasty nights,
You may recall that sweep of savage splendor,
That land that measures each man at his worth,
And feel in memory, half fierce, half tender,
The brotherhood of men that know the South.

By Sir Douglas Mawson, found in a book from the John King Davis Collection at the Australian Antarctic Division Library.

A POEM
By CHAS MOSS
EAST RETFORD, NOTTS
5TH APRIL, 1913

Reprinted from the *Retford Gainsborough and Worksop Times.*

COMMANDER SCOTT, RN, AT THE SOUTH POLE

Britannia mourned her son
Whose work was done;
And would have burst her mighty heart in song
Of triumph, chivalry, and pride of race,
But ere the words which trembled on her tongue
Could find in music their appointed place,
The melody was broken,
In sorrow felt and spoken;
And all the joys which waited on the years
Dissolved, unuttered, in the nation's tears.

These tender chords
Too sad for words
Which mark the music lives of men provide,
Swept o'er the sea to foreign strands,
Awoke regret in other lands,
And in the King's dominions far and wide.

While here, beneath St Paul's familiar dome
Where Englishmen, in unity, rejoice,
And where in that one universal home,
A common sorrow finds a common voice,
His Majesty the King
Met with his people there,
To join with all who sing
Or breathe a word of prayer:
He heard the strains appealing roll,
In "Jesu, Lover of my soul;"
The voices like the plangent sea,
In "Rock of Ages cleft for me;"
The March whose tones would haunt awhile
The shades of each sequestered aisle;
The funeral drums, and final call
In solemn note which rounded all.

And he whose memory was thus revered,
With all who shared his lamentable fate—
That manly soul to every heart endeared,
Was one of those who make the country great;

Who gloried in our Island Home,
The open sea, the tossing foam;
Endowed with English pluck and pride,
Who struggled, won the prize, and died;
And not a single soul who met
To mourn his loss, would there forget
That far away
His lifeless clay
Was lying shrouded in its deep repose,
Beneath the mantle of eternal snows.

The ship, Terra Nova, *with modern equipment,*
Had left for the voyage with Scott in command,
Its object The Pole in the frozen Antarctic,
And wintered alongside that desolate land.

The winter was over, the summer approaching,
And all things were ready in view of the day;
The depots established, the route to be followed,
And now it was time to be up and away.

Away from the ship in its icy enclosure,
Away from the island where Erebus flamed,
Away with provisions in several sledges,
To store in the depots allotted and named

Away to the south o'er the limitless Barrier,
Where chasms and yawning crevasses abound,
Half hid or agape on surface uncharted—
A plateau afloat, of a thickness profound.

This plateau in places was thinly encrusted,
And broke to the tread like the sound of a gun;
In others 'twas furrowed, or covered with crystals,
All angles and colours which flashed in the sun.

Anon its [sic] was bordered with foothills and glaciers,
Beyond were the mountains in summer aglow
Victoria Land of a beauty appalling,
Eternally clad in its vesture of snow.

Supporters departed, and Scott and his comrades
Unfaltering, plunged in the solitude vast;
Provisioned with fuel and food for the journey—
That perilous journey the longest and last.

They plodded along in this death-dealing climate,
Where life is unknown and where silence prevails;
Yet on, ever on as they tugged at the harness,
Encumbered by drifts and the buffeting gales.

At night they encamped, and they measured the rations;
They reckoned the distance, position reviewed;
They saw they were near to the end of the journey,
And started at daylight with courage renewed.

In spite of the hardships they won through in triumph,
Determined in will, with an eye on the goal;
Heroic in suffering, strong in endeavour,
As, shoulder to shoulder, they swung to The Pole.

Exulting, they hoisted the Flag of the Homeland,
And round it they stood as it sang in the breeze;
Aloft at the zenith in regions Antarctic—
This land of the snows and the ice-covered seas.
They left it floating there
Tossed in the frigid air,
Where friends come not nor enemies attack—
The proof of duty done,
The sign of victory won,
And turned their footsteps on the homeward track.

Day after day, night after night,
League upon league they fought the fight;
In frost too keen for us to understand,
Or dream of in this highly-favoured land;
In blizzards oft which whirled and raced
Across the broad and snowy waste;
Amid the winds' persistent beat,
And ice which cumbered sledge and feet.

'Twas rough,
But not enough
To daunt this band of fearless men
Already nearing home again;
Or hinder them from pulling through,
Though food was short, and fuel too.

But sickness, and the dire delays
Which sickness brings in various ways,
Hung o'er them like a funeral pall
As black as night, which darkened all.
The seaman, Evans, known and fully-tried,
On rough ice fell, and shortly after died;
And there below
His cloak of snow,
Sleeps on at peace through storms in fury rave,
Where comrades laid him in his lonely grave.

But further trouble lay in wait
Impossible to over-rate,
And which exceeded human skill,
When Captain Oates was taken ill;
Who grew still worse in fighting on
Through snow and ice till strength was gone;
And soon, alas, the truth was clear—
His work was done, and death was near.

His friends he knew
Were staunch and true,
Who could not, would not him forsake,
Their tacit resolution break—
Whate'er befal
Die one die all!
But saw that in his death their safety lay,
And staggered forth to die—the only way.

"I'm going out," said he,
"And for some time maybe."
Some time?
Sublime!
All time for him was at an end,

Except the time to save his friends—
His loyal friends, and set them free
By one last act of chivalry.

In mortal sickness, weak and pale,
He bent before the Polar gale—
The blizzard awful, cold and dense,
The furrows, and the void immense;
Till stricken down, and covered o'er
With whirling flakes, he rose no more;
And in a drift,
Or icy rift,
Or chasm we may never scan,
There lies an English gentleman—
A stainless knight of high degree
In honour and integrity.

The three companions who alone were left,
Provisions done, exhausted and bereft,
Defied the blizzard once again
Which swept across the rugged plain;
And struggled on with steady tramp
To reach the Hut at One Ton Camp;
Where all they wanted there awaited,
These very needs anticipated,
But fate perverse that saving help denied.
And, when eleven miles away, they died.

We know "the world's a stage," and human kind
Are players all. Each fills the part assigned;
And when the role is played, whate'er it be,
The player exits to eternity.
But such an exit, such a scene
In such a place had never been—
The "exit" from a narrow tent,
Where light and shadow strangely blent;
The "scene" a trackless waste and drear,
Where ice and drifted snow appear,
A deadly silence brooding o'er
Except when storm and tempest roar;
Where life is not—a scene indued

With weird and ghastly solitude;
The "place" a country far removed
From England, home, and friends beloved—
That fair sweet home across the sea,
Enshrined anew in memory.

And in that well-fought struggle at the close,
These actors 'prisioned by relentless foes,
Their work well done throughout the stirring play
With fortitude and courage passed away.
In Dr Wilson science lost a sage,
Whose art and learning oft adorned the age;
Enthusiastic, patient, sure,
His perseverance made secure
The specimens which still remain—
To knowledge strength, to science gain.
And in Lieutenant Bowers, he who passed
Through all with all and bravely died at last,
The army lost a trusty sword,
A gallant office deplored,
Whose grit and spirit showed again
The daring of his countrymen.

And in that tent so cold and chill,
Wherein they lay for ever still,
Commander Scott sat writing, writing there
A few last words, official, writ with care;
At point of death,
With laboured breath;
Sat writing there, with drooping head
And fingers numb, among the dead;
Still writing, with the end in view,
His vision clear, his moments few;
Still writing, when his pen relaxed,
The strength which held it overtaxed;
Until the pulse which fluttered, stood,
Compelled by lack of warmth and food;
And then to Providence resigned,
He slowly quietly reclined;
Triumphant, though defeated, all alone,
And joined his comrades in the Great Unknown.

Long after on that sacred ground
The document he wrote was found—
A touching story, true and plain,
Wherein the dead men live again—
A brief review of late events;
The fight against the elements;
The deaths, delays, and cold intense
Beyond all human prescience—
A chronicle, in which we see
The finish of the tragedy;
The fortitude in face of doom,
Starvation in a living tomb,
Farewells across the tossing foam
With bursting hearts in letters home;
As one by one they fall asleep,
And lights go out in shadows deep—
A record with a last appeal
To men with hearts, to men who feel—
A plea from those who nevermore
Would land upon their native shore,
For loved ones left and sore bereaved,
Of whom they thought, for whom they grieved—
A great and solemn trust committed there,
To England's honour and to England's care.

Ay! Toll the bell at old St. Paul's,
And meet within its hallowed walls
To mourn the nation's loss in tears—
A hero whom the world reveres,
And wish he might have laid at rest
On Motherlands beloved breast—
The man who won and winning died,
And could no more whate'er betide.

Then ring a glad triumphant peal,
Till steeples rock and towers reel;
Let music play and colours fly;
Fling out the Union Jack on high;
Bedeck and crown the British Isles
With floral wreaths, and songs, and smiles—

Because a Briton true and bold,
A sea-dog like the men of old,
Went sailing blithely o'er the foam—
His hunting-ground, a second home—
Who wrought a great and mighty deed,
The pride of all of English breed;
And left enrooted in his honoured name,
The fragrant flower of immortal fame.

The poem below appeared in the *Bournemouth Graphic* on 14 February 1913.

THE HEROIC FIVE

January 18th, 1912. – Captain Scott reached the South Pole.
February 17th, 1912. – Petty-Officer Evans died.
March 17th 1912. – Captain Oates died.
March 29th, 1912. – Captain Scott, Dr Wilson and Lieutenant Bowers died.
All honor to those who died

For England's fame and glory;
From their own lips we ne'er shall hear
Their brave, heroic story.
A few rough notes to us remain
To tell us of these heroes;
Written, when death was near; the end
To misery in the land of snows.
Petty-Officer Evans, the strongest man
Was the first to meet his doom,
And the great ice plateau, his last resting place,
Was the gallant, heroic man's tomb.
See the brave self-sacrifice of Captain Oates,
For of his own will he went
Out into the blizzard, to try and save
Those lives, that were so near spent.

The blizzard then became so fierce,
That the three brave men had to stay;
With food and safety, only just
A few short miles away.

For four long days the blizzard raged;
When they were starved and worn
These men then laid them down to rest;
With hopes for a brighter dawn.

All glory be to those who died,
It is the nation's duty and lot
To honour, the names we've learned to love,
Bowers, Wilson, Oates, Evans and Scott.

'GRANT'
Parkstone, February 12th, 1913.

Chapter 16

Fortunes of the Survivors

Many of the main crew from the *Terra Nova* expedition went on to forge distinguished careers in their particular fields of expertise. Most were awarded Polar Medals by King George V. Undoubtedly, what they had learned and experienced during that fateful journey moulded their future lives.

Edward Evans suffered badly from scurvy on the Antarctic journey back to base and would have died but for the gallant efforts of William Lashly and Thomas Crean to sledge him back. He was invalided home in 1929 but returned in 1913 to take charge of the last few weeks of the expedition. Evans went on to enjoy a successful naval career and at the start of World War I became a commander, distinguishing himself greatly in action against six German destroyers in 1917, which earned him the rank of Captain and the Lloyd's Gold medal for saving life at sea. He wrote a book about his experience called *Keeping the Seas*. (He also wrote a book called *South with Scott* in 1921.) More promotions and titles followed during his service, the last one as Admiral. Evans was made a baron, Lord Mountevans of the *Broke* (the name of the vessel on which he had first shown such bravery), in 1945. He died in 1957 aged seventy-five. His expedition exploits are commemorated by Mount Evans in Victoria Land and Cape Evans on Ross Island.

Edward Atkinson worked for a short while at the London School of Tropical Medicine before going on a medical expedition to China to investigate a parasitic flatworm that was affecting the health of British seamen. During the war Atkinson contracted pleurisy and was hospitalised when he was sent to Gallipoli to investigate fly-borne diseases. He served on the Western Front and fought at the Somme, earning himself the DSO. Atkinson showed incredible heroism during an explosion aboard HMS *Glatton* at Dover when, despite being burned and blinded, he saved the lives of several men. For this he received the Albert Medal. After the war, Atkinson revealed research he had done that showed the rations the *Terra Nova* team had had to survive on were greatly insufficient for what they had to endure and equalled virtual starvation. Atkinson suffered a breakdown after the death of his wife in 1928 but went on to re-marry. He died suddenly on board ship on 20 February 1929, aged forty-seven. His friend Cherry-Garrard paid this tribute: 'His voice has been with me often since those days – that gruffish deep affectionate monosyllabic way he used to talk to you [...] he could not help the tenderness poking through. I am glad to have this opportunity to witness something of what we owe him.' Atkinson's memorial is the Atkinson Cliffs on Victoria Land.

George Simpson went back to his old job in Simla at the Indian Meteorological Services. He also used some time there to compile notes he had made on the expedition. He was drafted for service during World War I and was the meteorological adviser to the British Expeditionary Force in Mesopotamia. He was later Assistant Secretary to the Board of Munitions. In 1920 Simpson was appointed Director of London's Meteorological Office where he researched atmospheric electricity, ionization, radioactivity and solar radiation. He also carried out research into the causes of lightning and established the Simpson Wind Force Scale, a modified version of the Beaufort Wind Force Scale. Simpson was knighted in 1935, came out of retirement for World War II to take charge of the Kew Observatory, and continued his research into thunderstorms until 1947. Dr George Simpson died aged eighty-seven in 1965. Simpson is commemorated by the Simpson Glacier, the Simpson Glacier Tongue and Simpson Peak in the Scott Mountains.

Thomas G Taylor had left Antarctica in March 1912 unaware of the fate that had befallen Scott's party. In 1913 he was awarded the King's Polar Medal and made a fellow of the RGS. He wrote an account of the expedition in *With Scott: The Silver Lining* in 1915. In 1916 he earned a doctorate at the University of Sydney for his physiographical and geomorphical Antarctic research and was made Associate Professor of Geography in 1921. A book he wrote arguing against the Australian government's policy limiting immigrants to whites only was banned from schools. He went on to write numerous books about the effects of the environment in shaping race. However, in 1927 Taylor was made the first president of the Geographical Society of New South Wales. Two years later he accepted a post of Senior Professor of Geography at the University of Chicago and in 1936 founded the Geography department of the University of Toronto. In 1940 he was elected president of the Association of American Geographers, the first non-American to be elected to the post. He returned to Sydney in 1951 and in 1954 was elected to the Australian Academy of Science, the only geographer to receive this distinction. He published his autobiography *Journeyman Taylor* in 1958 and in 1959 was named the first president of the Institute of Australian Geographers. Taylor died on 5 November 1963, aged eighty-two. In 1976 his head appeared on an Australian postage stamp. Another stamp in 2001 commemorated him and fellow explorer Douglas Mawson. Taylor's Antarctic legacy are the Taylor Glaciers and the Taylor Valley.

Edward Nelson worked as a Senior Naturalist at the Plymouth Laboratory then saw active service with the British 63rd (Royal Naval) Division in the Gallipoli campaign and in the French trenches. After the war he was scientific superintendent of the Fisheries Board for Scotland and wrote a paper on the manufacture of drift bottles, which were used in tracking the movement of waters in the North Sea. Nelson died in 1923, aged just thirty-nine. He is commemorated by the Nelson Cliff on the west side of the Simpson Glacier.

Frank Debenham served in World War I as a lieutenant with the 7th Battalion, Oxfordshire and Buckinghamshire Light Infantry, serving in France and Salonika. He was badly wounded in 1916 and was awarded an OBE a year later. Debenham became a fellow of Gonville and Caius College, Cambridge, where he lectured in cartography. With money left over from the public donations made after Scott's death, Debenham fulfilled a personal dream of an Antarctic learning centre and founded the Scott Polar Research Institute with Raymond Priestley. He was unpaid director 1920 to 1946. In 1931 Debenham was appointed Professor of Geography at Cambridge University. During World War II he trained service cadets, lectured to Royal Air Force navigators and devised relief-model techniques for briefing commandos. He was vice-president of the RGS from 1951 to 1953 and was awarded their Victoria Medal in 1948. A prolific author, his works included *In the Antarctic: Stories of Scott's Last Expedition 1952* and *Antarctica – The story of a Continent*. Frank Debenham died in Cambridge in 1965, aged eighty-one. He is commemorated by the Debenham Glacier, the Debenham Islands and the Debenham Peak.

Charles Wright enjoyed a distinguished career in the First World War, during which he gained the Military Cross and OBE. He became in turn director of the Admiralty Research Laboratory and director of scientific research at the Admiralty. With the formation of the Royal Naval Scientific Service in 1946 he was appointed first chief of the service. He then returned to North America to continue his own research, working at the Scripps Institute of Oceanography, the Defence Research Board of Canada's Pacific Naval Laboratory and the University of British Columbia. He retired on Satspring Island, near Vancouver, British Columbia. His report on the glaciological work of the *Terra Nova* expedition, written jointly with Sir Raymond Priestley and published in 1922, became a classic in its field. Like his fellow Antarctic scientist Thomas Griffith Taylor, he was married to a sister of Raymond Priestley. He was knighted in 1946 and died in 1975. Sir Charles Wright is commemorated with Mount Wright, Wright Bay, Wright Lower Glacier, Wright Upper Glacier and the Wright Valley.

Raymond Priestley served as adjutant at the Wireless Training Centre from 1914 to 1917 and then with the 46th (North Midland) Divisional Signal Company in France. He was involved in the taking of the Riqueval Bridge, part of the Hindenberg Line and was awarded the Military Cross. Priestley became a Major after the war and was seconded to the War Office to write a history of the signal service. His research and papers on glaciers in the Antarctic earned him a BA at Cambridge in 1920, the same year he co-founded the Scott Polar Institute with Frank Debenham. Priestley was elected fellow of Clare College in 1922 and two years later joined the university's administration staff. He went on to hold a number of academic and government administrative posts in Australia (including vice-chancellor of the University of Melbourne and England (including chancellor of the University of Birmingham, and was knighted in 1949. Priestley retired in 1952 but served as chairman of the Royal Commission of the Civil Service, deputy director of the former Falkland Islands Dependencies Survey (later called the British Antarctic Survey), president of the British Association for the Advancement of Science, and president of the RGS. Priestley made a return journey to the Antarctic in 1956. He was eighty-seven when he died in Cheltenham in 1974. Mount Priestley, the Priestley Glacier and Priestley Peak are all named after him.

Cherry-Garrard was deeply affected at the discovery of the polar party bodies, especially those of Wilson and Bowers with whom he had made the journey to Cape Crozier. He developed clinical depression upon his return home and attempted to 'cure' himself by writing about his experiences – constantly dwelling on what could have been done to avoid the tragic outcome. His 1922 book *The Worst Journey in the World* – a piece of work encouraged by friend and neighbour George Bernard Shaw – became a classic, hailed as one of the greatest true adventure stories ever written. It was obvious Cherry-Garrard admired Scott but he also wrote: 'England knows Scott as a hero; she has little idea of him as a man [...] he was sensitive, femininely sensitive, to a degree which might be considered a fault [...] he had moods that might last for weeks....he cried more easily than any man I have ever known [...] he was peevish, highly-strung, irritable, depressed and moody [...]'

A television drama-documentary of the same name showed the site of the igloo Cherry-Garrard and his two team members created near the penguin breeding ground. Some of the original equipment was still there. (The igloo had been discovered by the Fuchs-Hillary Trans-Antarctic expedition of 1957.) Cherry-Gerrard also published an obituary of expedition photographer Herbert Ponting. He died in 1959. The three intact penguin eggs that he, Wilson and Bowers brought back from Cape Crozier are in London's Natural History Museum. He is commemorated with Mount Cherry-Garrard on the Victoria Land and Cherry Icefall in the Queen Alexandra Range.

Herbert Ponting's dream of bringing the magic and the mystery of the Antarctic to an enthralled nation via moving images ended the moment the bodies of Scott and the others were found. It also meant there was no money to be made – money that was sorely needed to 'pay back' the cost of the expedition (in the end public donations went some way towards this). Ponting was frustrated and felt all his achievements were redundant. In 1921 his photographic book, *The Great White*

South, was published and was successful enough to enable him to fund a short film in 1933 called *Ninety Degrees South*. He also gave lectures on the Antarctic. But none of this compensated for the reward and recognition he had once believed would be his. Ponting died in London in 1935. The Scott Polar Research Institute purchased the Ponting Collection in 2004 for £533,000 and in 2009, with publisher Salto Ulbeek, published a selection of the collection. One of Ponting's photographic darkrooms was reconstructed in the collections of the Ferrymead Heritage Park in Christchurch, New Zealand. Ponting is commemorated with Ponting Cliff in northern Victoria.

Tryggve Gran was awarded the Polar Medal by George V. He developed an interest in aviation and on 30 July 1914 became the first pilot to cross the North Sea. At the outbreak of war he was a First Lieutenant in the Norwegian Army Air Service but was rejected from service because of Norway's neutrality. He got in after assuming the identity of 'Captain Teddy Grant' of Canada and served in 1916 with No. 39 Squadron on Home Defence, flying the Sopwith Camel on the Western Front with No. 70 Squadron during 1917, and later commanding various RAF units in Arkhangelsk and North Russia during the Allied intervention in 1919 (the same year he was the first man to fly from London to Stockholm). Gran was promoted to major and awarded the Military Cross for distinguished war service. After the war he lectured on aviation and his journeys to the polar areas. In 1928 Gran led the search party to find Roald Amundsen, lost flying while trying to discover the fate of Umberto Nobile's North Pole expedition. During World War II, Gran was reportedly a member of NS, Viking Quisling's Nationalist Party Ansonia Sampling – 'National Gathering'. (During World War II, from 1942 to 1945 Quisling served as Minister-President of the collaborationist Norwegian government, after being appointed by the German authorities. After the war he was tried for high treason and executed by firing squad at Akers Oslo Fortress. Today in Norway and other parts of the world, 'quisling' is a synonym for traitor.) It was speculated that Gran feared reprisals from the pro-German nationalist party because of his commitment to the Royal Air Force in World War I and that his friendship with Goring and his bitterness over not being offered a full-time job in the Norwegian Army Air Service may have been reasons for his support of the NS during the Nazi occupation of Norway. After a trial in 1948, Gran was found guilty of treason and sentenced to prison for eighteen months. He died at his home in Norway on 8 January 1980, aged ninety. Mount Gran on the north side of the Mackay Glacier is named after him.

Thomas Crean was a member of the eleven-man search party who searched for the bodies of the four explorers. He and Lashly were awarded the Albert Medal, 2nd Class for saving Evans's life. Crean was promoted to the rank of Chief Petty Officer. He was also one man who would make a third expedition to the Antarctic when asked on board by Ernest Shackleton, who knew him from the *Discovery* expedition and who was also impressed by his feats on the fated *Terra Nova* expedition. Crean joined Shackleton's Imperial Tran Antarctic expedition on the *Endurance* on 25 May 1914, as Second Officer. He was in charge of one of the dog-handling teams. But he took control when the team was at one point forced to take to lifeboats. After returning to Britain in November 1916, Crean resumed naval duties. He was promoted to the rank of Warrant Officer in recognition of his service on the *Endurance* and was awarded his third Polar Medal. For the rest of the First World War he served at the Chatham barracks, and then on HMS *Colleen*. In 1920 he was approached by Shackleton to accompany him on another Antarctic expedition (the Shackleton-Rowett expedition), but turned down the offer because he was married with a family and wanted to go into business after retiring from service. However, on his last naval assignment, with HMS *Hecla*, Crean suffered a bad fall that left him with impaired vision and he was retired on medical grounds in 1920. He and his wife opened a public house in Annascaul called the South Pole Inn. In 1938 Crean suffered a burst appendix and was taken to hospital but as no surgeon was available there he was transferred to *Cork*. The delay resulted in an infection and Crean died in hospital on 27 July 1938 aged sixty-one. His name lives on in Mount Crean in Victoria Land and the Crean Glacier on South Georgia. A one-man play, Tom Crean – *Antarctic Explorer*, was written by Aidan Dooley and one performance took place at the South Pole Inn, attended by Crean's two daughters Mary and Eileen (then in their eighties) who described their father as 'a very humble man.'

William Lashly, together with Thomas Crean, was awarded the Albert Medal, 2nd class for saving Edward Evans' life. He retired from the Royal Navy but later joined the reserves and served in the First World War in HMS *Irresistible* and HMS *Amethyst*. After the war he became a customs officer in Cardiff. After retiring in 1932 Lashly returned to his home town of Hambledon. He called his house 'Minna Bluff' after one of the landmarks *en route* to the South Pole. Lashly died on 12 June 1940. His diaries, *Under Scott's Command – Lashly's Antarctic Diaries*, were edited and published by Commander A.R. Ellis in 1969. They provided an illuminating insight into both the *Discovery* and the *Terra Nova* expeditions from a more ordinary team member rather an officer. He is commemorated with the Lashly Glacier and the Lashly Mountains.

Robert Forde's involvement with the expedition led to him being promoted to Chief Petty Officer on the HMS *Vivid* on which he served during World War I. After leaving the navy he retired to Ireland and died there in March 1959. Forde's name lives on with the naming of Mount Forde at the head of the Hunt Glacier. On the 50th anniversary of his death in 2009, two memorial bronze plaques were unveiled – one at Cork Harbour depicting Forde with a sled and another at his home.

Patrick Keohane served as the district officer of coastguards for the Isle of Man. He later rejoined the Royal Navy and served in World War II. Keohane died in Plymouth in 1950 at the age of seventy-one.

Anton Omelchenko fought in World War I, then joined the Red Army and was later involved in setting up a kolkhoz (collective farm) at Bat'ki. He was killed by a stroke of lightning in 1932.

Victor Campbell was promoted to Commander and during World War I fought in the Dardanelles. He was awarded the DSO and OBE. Campbell emigrated to Newfoundland in 1922. He died there in 1956. The Campbell Glacier and the Campbell Tongue in Antarctica's Terra Nova Bay are named after him.

Demetri Gerof settled first in England and then New Zealand before returning to Nikolayevsk where he worked in the gold mines. He died in 1932.

George Levick founded the British Schools Exploring Society in 1932 and became its president. He died in 1956. Mount Levick is named after him.

Bernard Day returned home after the first year of the *Terra Nova* expedition. He settled in Australia. He applied to join the Ross Sea Relief Expedition 1916–1917.

Cecil Meares joined the Royal Flying Corps during World War I and reached the rank of Lieutenant-Colonel. He later went to live in Canada. He died in 1937 aged sixty.

Harry Pennell was appointed commander of HMS *Queen Mary* in 1914. He died on 31 May 1916 in the Battle of Jutland, when it was sunk by German ships.

Thomas Williamson is commemorated by Williamson Head and Williamson Ridge.

Frederick Hooper died in 1955 and is commemorated with Hooper's Shoulder.

George Abbott has Mount Abbott and Abbott Peak named after him.

Harry Dickason is commemorated by Mount Dickason.

Walter Archer started a catering business in London. He is commemorated with Cape Archer.

Thomas Clissold emigrated to New Zealand after World War I and became a vehicle inspector in Napier.

Scott's son, Sir Peter Markham Scott, found it no chore or challenge to follow his father's wishes and take an interest in natural history. He was the founder and first chairman of the World Wildlife Fund, founded many local and national bodies including the Gloucestershire Trust for Nature Conservation, Wildfowl and Wetlands trust, and Falkland Conservation. He was also the originator of the Red Data Books listing endangered species, as well as more than thirty other illustrated books. In short, Peter – global traveller, war hero and champion sportsman – was a living tribute to his father. He was described as probably one of the most influential conservationists of the twentieth century – and the first to be knighted. He died in 1989.

A Diary of Hope and Tragedy

1910
15 June 1910: The *Terra Nova* sets sail from Cardiff, Wales. (Scott joins the ship later in South Africa and stays on it until it reaches Melbourne, Australia, where he leaves it again to continue fundraising.) He receives a telegram from Roald Amundsen informing him that he too is 'proceeding south'.
The *Terra Nova* heads to New Zealand.
29 November 1910: The *Terra Nova* leaves Port Chalmers, New Zealand. Scott is once again on board – together with thirty-four dogs, nineteen Siberian ponies and three motorised sledges.
10 December 1910: The *Terra Nova* hits the southern pack ice and is forced to stop for twenty days before being able to continue south.

1911
4 January 1911: The *Terra Nova* arrives off Ross Island and looks for possible landing sites – eventually proceeding to the 'Skuary' (which the team renames Cape Evans) about 15 miles north of Scott's 1902 *Discovery* Expedition base. The shore parties disembark with the ponies, dogs, motorised sledges and the bulk of the party's supplies.
18 January 1911: A prefabricated accommodation hut is erected
26 January 1911: Griffith Taylor, Debenham, Wright and P.O. Evans land from *Terra Nova* at Butter Point for a geological exploration of the west coast of McMurdo Sound.
   A party under Campbell heads east but fails to land on King Edward VII Land shore. Campbell sails north-west to Victoria Land instead. On the return, the *Terra Nova* encounters Amundsen's expedition camped in the Bay of Whales.
27 January 1911: Depot-laying begins on the Barrier for the polar party push.
30 January 1911: The western party establishes its main depot in the Ferrar Glacier Region and conducts explorations and survey work in the Dry Valley, Taylor Glacier and Koettlitz Glacier areas.
4 February 1911: Corner Camp is established 40 miles from Hut Point by the depot-laying party. (The team later lay One Ton Depot at 79° 29' S, more than 30 miles north of its original intended location.)
9 February 1911: Victor Campbell's eastern party sets sail and becomes the northern party.
17 February 1911: The northern party arrives at Robertson Bay and builds a hut for the 1911 winter close to the old headquarters of Norwegian explorer Carstens Borchgrevink.
2 March 1911: The western party starts for home taking a southerly route.
14 March 1911: The western party arrives back at Hut Point.

6 June 1911: Scott's 43rd birthday and the party celebrate with a 'feast'.

21 June 1911: Midwinter Day, the Antarctic equivalent of Christmas, and cause for another celebration.

27 June 1911: Wilson, Bowers and Cherry-Garrard set out on a scientific trip – the 'Winter Journey' – to Cape Crozier to collect Emperor penguin eggs. The journey is also used as an experiment with food rations and equipment in advance of the trek to the Pole.

4 July 1911: Atkinson goes missing after he and Gran – 'two adventurous spirits' – venture out without Scott's knowledge. He later turns up having fallen asleep in a 'snow bed'.

16 July 1911: The Winter Journey party arrives in Cape Crozier. It has taken the men nineteen days to travel just 60 miles in temperatures at times as low as 77°F (–60°C). Their equipment, clothes and sleeping bags are constantly iced up.

1 August 1911: The Winter Journey party returns to Cape Evans with three penguin eggs.

13 September 1911: Scott reveals his plans for the South Pole march. He says sixteen men will set out for the Beardmore Glacier with motor-sledges, ponies and dogs. The dogs will then return to base and the ponies will be shot for food. Then twelve men will ascend the glacier in three groups and begin the crossing of the polar plateau, using man-hauling. Only one of these groups will carry on to the Pole. The supporting groups will be sent back at specified latitudes. Scott says he will decide upon the final polar group during the journey.

24 October 1911: The Motor Party (Lt Evans, Day, Lashly and Hooper) start off from Cape Evans with two motor sledges. They aim to haul loads to latitude 80°30′S and then wait for the others. The dog and pony parties follow on behind.

1 November 1911: Both motor sledges break down, forcing Lt Evans, Day, Lashly and Hooper to man haul the supplies for the remaining 150 miles. It takes them two weeks with temperatures never rising above zero.

14 November 1911: Griffith Taylor, Debenham, Gran and Forde start a separate journey over sea ice to Granite Harbour, 50 miles away from Butter Point, to explore and conduct survey work on the Mackay Glacier

15 November: Fighting constant snowfalls, the team reach One Ton Camp.

24 November: The first pony is killed.

4 December 1911: The polar party reaches the Gateway to the Beardmore Glacier. A blizzard strikes, forcing the men to camp until 9 December. This means breaking into rations intended for the Glacier journey. The ponies have to be beaten as they flounder in the deep snow. The remaining exhausted ponies are shot when the blizzard subsides.

11 December 1911: Meares and Dimitri turn back with the dogs because there is no food for them and the polar party begins the ascent of the Beardmore Glacier

12 December 1911: The party of twelve is divided into groups and set out to man haul the sledges up the glacier towards the summit 10,000ft above. The men are now hauling over 200 pounds, sinking into the soft snow and suffering snow-blindness.

13 December 1911: Scott's party has travelled less than 4 miles in nine hours.

14 December 1911: Norwegian Amundsen reaches the South Pole.

20 December 1911: The polar party reaches the Polar Plateau and lays the Upper Glacier Depot.

22 December 1911: Atkinson, Cherry-Garrard, Wright and Keohane are sent back by Scott with instructions for the dogs to be brought out to meet and assist the polar party on its return journey the following March. The remaining eight men continue south.

25 December 1911: The party has a Christmas 'feast' including plum-duff. It is the last proper meal they will enjoy. The team advances 17½ miles.

31 December 1911: The team stops for several hours to cut the sledges down from 12ft long to 10ft.

1912

3 January 1912: Scott decides to take five men forward to the Pole (Scott, Wilson, Oates, Bowers and Edgar Evans). This change of plan involves the re-calculation of weights and rations to take the unscheduled extra man into consideration. Lt Evans, Lashly and Crean return to base. Evans is given more orders about the dogs being brought south to meet the polar party but he becomes seriously ill with scurvy and has to be carried on a sledge from One Ton Depot to a point 35 miles south of Hut Point.

4 January 1912: The *Terra Nova* returns from New Zealand and transfers the northern party to the Evans Coves area to conduct more geological work.

6 January 1912: The team crosses the line of latitude where Shackleton turned back and are further south than they believe any man has been before.

15 January 1912: The northern party is due to be picked up by the *Terra Nova* but the ship is unable to reach them.

16 January 1912: Just 15 miles from their goal, the polar party spots Amundsen's black flag in the distance.

17 January 1912: They reach the Pole and discover that Amundsen has beaten them.

18 January 1912: After confirming their position and planting their flag, Scott's disheartened party turns homewards. The team initially make good progress, although Scott begins to worry about their physical state – particularly that of Evans and Oates.

26 January 1912: Amundsen's teams arrives back at the Bay of Whales, ten days ahead of schedule, having successfully covered an average of 23 miles a day and with such a supply of rations that both men and dogs enjoyed extra helpings and plenty of chocolate.

5 February 1912: The Granite Harbour geological party begins to trek southward.

7 February 1912: The polar party begins its descent of the Beardmore Glacier but have difficulty locating their depots. Evans is now suffering from a hand injury, severe frostbite and a head injury following several falls on the ice.

11 February 1912: The men get lost and take 12 hours to escape from a maze of pressure ridges.

17 February 1912: Evans collapses at the bottom of the Beardmore Glacier. He dies that night. The surviving team marches on battling against some of the most extreme weather conditions ever recorded in the region.

18 February 1912: The northern party's pick up fails due to heavy pack ice, which prevents the *Terra Nova* being able to reach them. The Granite Harbour geological party is rescued from the ice. Crean, one of the three men returning from the polar party, leaves Lashly with an ill Lt Evans and walks on alone to Hut Point. Atkinson and Dimitri are there with the dog teams and a rescue party is formed.

22 February 1912: Lt Evans is brought to Hut Point, barely alive and, in the confusion, Scott's latest orders about the deployment of the dogs are overlooked.

26 February 1912: Cherry-Garrard leaves Hut Point with Dimitri and two dog teams to re-supply One Ton Depot. They decide to wait for the polar party to return.

2 March 1912: The polar party reaches the Middle Barrier Depot. There is little oil left.

9 March 1912: The polar party reaches the next depot but there is no sign of the dogs they were expecting to help them.

10 March 1912: With the weather getting even worse, Cherry-Garrard turns for home. He is unaware that the polar party is fighting for their lives about 70 miles away. When he returns with no news, there is concern for Scott and his men.

17 March 1912: Oates steps outside the polar party's tent and to certain death saying, by Scott's account, 'I am just going outside and I may be some time.'

20 March 1912: Scott, Wilson and Bowers struggle on to a point 11 miles south of One Ton Depot but are halted by a fierce blizzard. They make daily attempts to journey on but a combination of weakness, hunger, frostbite and the unforgiving weather hinders them. Supplies eventually run out.

26 March 1912: Atkinson and Keohane set out from Hut Point on a search party, man-hauling a sledge containing provisions for eighteen days.

29 March 1912: Scott's final, poignant diary entry. It is presumed he died on this day, together with Bowers and Wilson.

30 March 1912: Atkinson and Keohane reach Corner Camp but decide not to progress any further due to the extremely low temperatures.

17 April 1912: A party under Edward Atkinson sets out from Cape Evans to relieve the northern party but is beaten back by the weather. The northern party is forced to spend the 1912 winter in a snow cave battling meagre rations, frostbite, hunger and dysentery.

April to September 1912: The remaining expedition members winter at Cape Evans continuing their scientific work.

30 September 1912: The northern party starts out for Hut Point some 200 miles down the coast.

29 October 1912: A polar search party sets out to find Scott and his men. It is accompanied by a team of mules that had been landed from *Terra Nova* during a re-supply visit.

7 November 1912: Incredibly, against all odds, the northern party reaches Cape Evans after a perilous journey across the Drygalski Ice Tongue.

12 November 1912: The polar search party finds the tent containing the frozen bodies of Scott, Wilson and Bowers.

15 November 1912: The polar search party finds Oates' sleeping bag but fail to find his body.

25 November 1912: The polar search party returns to Hut Point and learn that the northern party has returned safely to base.

1913

18 January 1913: The *Terra Nova* arrives to take the remaining expedition members home. A large wooden cross is erected on the slopes of Observation Hill, overlooking Hut Point, inscribed with the names of the five dead men and a quotation from Tennyson's *Ulysses*: 'To strive, to seek, to find, and not to yield.'

10 February 1913: The *Terra Nova* reaches New Zealand, and the world is informed of the tragedy.

14 February 1913: A memorial service is held at St Paul's Cathedral, London.

The Rise and Fall of Robert Falcon Scott

1868: 6 June: Robert Falcon 'Con' Scott is born in Devonport.

1881: Scott joins the Naval ship HMS *Boadicea* as a midshipman. (He is later transferred to other ships over the years to complete his training.)

1883: Scott passes his exams, coming seventh out of a class of twenty-seven and emerges from HMS *Britannia* as a midshipman.

1886: As a midshipman aboard HMS *Rover* he takes part in a race between four English cutters in St Kitts in the West Indies. Scott's boat wins and he is invited aboard HMS *Active* to dine with the Commodore. Present at this dinner is the cousin of the Commodore, Clements Markham, who is so impressed with Scott that he writes that he is 'the destined man to command the Antarctic expedition'. Scott continues serving in ships of the Royal Navy until 1901.

1888: Scott passes his exams for Sub-Lieutenant and is awarded four out of a possible five First Class certificates in pilotage, torpedoes and gunnery, coming in with the highest marks in his class in his year.

1889: Scott's career progresses smoothly, with service on various ships and he is promoted to Lieutenant.

1891: After a long spell in foreign waters, Scott applies for the two-year torpedo training course on the depot ship HMS *Vernon*, marking an important career move. He graduates with First Class certificates in both the theory and practical examinations.

1894: While still serving as Torpedo Officer on the *Vulcan* Scott learns of the financial disaster that has befallen his family.

1897: Scott hears of his father's death of heart disease aged sixty-six while serving as torpedo lieutenant on the Channel squadron flagship HMS *Majestic*.

1899: When home on leave from HMS *Majestic*, Scott encounters Clements Markham who informs him there is an imminent Antarctic expedition.

1900: Scott receives his letter of appointment as leader of the *Discovery* expedition. He and Markham go to Christiania in Norway (later to become Oslo) for discussions with Fridtjof Nansen, a scientist who had undertaken a scientific and exploratory trip to the Arctic in the *Fram*, which had served as an oceanographic-meteorological-biological laboratory.

1901: The *Discovery* arrives in Cape Town. The expedition, under Scott's command, goes on to explore the Ross Sea area and King Edward Seventh Land, venturing further south than any other ship thus far.

1904: Scott returns to Britain on the *Discovery* with the team being hailed as heroes – especially Scott of whom Markham declares: 'Never has any polar expedition returned with so great a harvest of scientific results.' Scott is promoted to Captain.

1905: Scott's book *Voyage of the Discovery* is published on 2 October and is described by the *Times Literary Supplement* as 'a masterly work'.

1906: With public praise being heaped upon him and now often mixing in Royal circles, Scott returns to a full-time naval career in January. First as assistant to the Director of Naval Intelligence at the Admiralty and then as Flag-Captain to rear-Admiral Sir George Egerton on HMS *Victorious*. Both are welcome promotions, not just for the kudos but for the financial reward as Scott was still supporting his mother. Scott approaches the RGS about the funding of a second Antarctic expedition.

1908: 2 September: Scott marries sculptress Kathleen Bruce at the Chapel Royal, Hampton Court Palace.

1909: 14 September: The couple's only child, Peter Markham Scott, is born. Scott takes up the London-based post of Naval Assistant to the Second Sea Lord but he is not to remain there for long. By December he is released on half pay to take over command of the 1910 British Antarctic expedition – later to be known as the *Terra Nova* expedition.

1910: The *Terra Nova* reaches Melbourne *en route* for the Antarctic. Scott continues is fund raising in South Africa, New Zealand and Australia.

1912: The end of a fated expedition. Scott and his team reach the South Pole but only after Norwegian Roald Amundsen. They die on the return journey. Their bodies and incisive diaries are found by a search party eight months later. Scott is knighted posthumously because of his heroism. Despite their failure to arrive at the South Pole first, much important scientific findings had been made during the expeditions.

Chapter 17

The Mystique and Magic of the South Pole Expedition Lives On

The legend that was the South Pole Expedition goes on with no sign that the interest will wane or that memories will not continue to be resurrected. Every country that Scott and his men had connections with has commemorated the fatal trip in some way.

In the dozen years following the disaster, more than thirty monuments and memorials were set up in Britain alone – including those lovingly created by Scott's widow, the talented sculptor Kathleen Scott. The statue of him in Waterloo Place, London, bears a plaque on which are written some of his last plaintive words:

> 'Had we lived I should have had a tale to tell
> of the hardihood endurance and courage
> of my companions which would have stirred
> the heart of every Englishman
> but these rough notes and
> our dead bodies must tell the tale.'

In 1925, at Mount Wise, Devonport, a memorial was unveiled by Scott's fellow expedition member Charles Royds. The memorial represents 'Courage', supported by 'Devotion' and crowned by 'Immortality'. 'Fear', 'Death' and 'Despair' are trampled underfoot. The bronze medallion contains the portraits of Scott and his fellow fated explorers, Oates, Wilson, Bowers and Evans. Memorials to Scott are also in Emmanuel Church, Exeter, Devon, and in London's St Paul's Cathedral in a stained-glass window depicting an angel holding a globe showing Antarctica, a penguin and a submarine. There are the words 'Death swallowed up in Victory' and the names of the men who perished. One of Cardiff's most familiar landmarks is a clock tower in the form of a lighthouse, which was erected at the south end of Roath Park Lake in 1915, and which is surmounted by a model of the *Terra Nova*. Also in the city is a snow-white abstract Scott memorial commemorating the centenary anniversary of the 'Age of Antarctic Discovery' and depicting Scott man hauling south with the faces of his companions ice-bound. Also in Cardiff, the Royal Horticultural Society created a special centenary garden at Cardiff Bay 'to epitomise the spirit of endeavour and ambition prevalent in Cardiff today'.

The Union Jack flag carried to the South Pole by Scott's party was safely brought back to Britain and is now kept at Sandringham. Sledge flags used by the pole party are kept at Exeter Cathedral. Many more items relating to the expedition are on view at the Scott Polar Institute in Cambridge, the Oates Museum in Hampshire, Cheltenham Museum and at the *Discovery* in Dundee. At Eton College there is a plaque commemorating former pupil Lawrence Oates and a medallion in the library section of the Memorial Buildings. Oates also has a gold memorial plaque in the church in the village of Gestingthorpe, Essex, where he grew up. (His mother used to cross the road every day to polish it.) Another memorial to Oates is a display dedicated to him at the Royal Dragoon Guards Museum in York. The Oates Museum at Gilbert White's House, Selborne, Hampshire, focuses on his life and that of his uncle.

The foundation of the Scott Polar Research Institute at Cambridge was the expedition's most tangible legacy with its promotion of Antarctic science. Twenty-five volumes of findings had been published by 1925. And, largely thanks to Debenham's efforts, the remaining balance of the Scott memorial fund set up in 1913 was directed to establish the Institute in 1920, with a new memorial building opened in 1934 (at Gonville and Caius College in Cambridge, the fireplace in the rooms used by Edward Wilson has an inscription of his name). Edward Wilson is also remembered with a full-length figure in sledging gear at the Promenade, Cheltenham, Gloucestershire. The statue is by Scott's widow Kathleen and bears the words of Scott about him: 'He died as he lived a brave/true man. The best of comrades and staunchest of friends.' Henry Bowers has a memorial in St Ninian's Church, Rothesay, Argyll and Bute Scotland and there is one to Reginald Skelton in the Church of St Mary the Virgin, in Aldingbourne, West Sussex, given by his three children. Amongst many others, there is also a memorial window to Scott in Binton Church, Warwickshire.

As director of the institute, Debenham – together with Priestley, a fellow of Clare College and university administrator, and one of Shackleton's Endurance scientists, James Wordie, a fellow of St John's College – made Cambridge the centre of polar research in Britain.

Many more were established in other parts of the world. The American scientific base at the South Pole, founded in 1957, is called the Amundsen–Scott South Pole Station, to honour the memories of both polar conquerors. Bearing testimony to the sharing of a long and rich history between Antarctica and New Zealand, the latter has numerous memorials and memorial sites to Scott and his team. (New

Zealanders took part in Antarctic exploration from the mid nineteenth century in international teams.) And of course, Scott used New Zealand as a base for both of his expeditions and it was the country from which the sad news that he had died was transmitted to the world in February 1913. The first memorial in the country is believed to have been a marble plaque unveiled at a boys school in Oamaru, overlooking the harbour, in 1913. This was followed by a memorial oak tree. The people of Oamaru launched an annual memorial essay-writing competition, which then became the Robert Falcon Memorial Speech Competition in 2001. Other memorials in New Zealand are at Queenstown, which was unveiled in December 1913, at Port Chalmers in 1914, and one by Kathleen Scott at Christchurch, which was unveiled in 1917. In 1957, Scott Base, New Zealand's permanent Antarctic research station was opened. The base was originally established to support the privately-run Commonwealth trans-Antarctic expedition of 1955–1958, whose New Zealand team was the first to winter there.

In December 1999 two blocks of butter from the 1912 expedition were found in stables attached to the hut at Cape Evans. They were discovered by the Antarctic Heritage Trust, which had decided to launch a preservation venture amidst fears that despite the extreme cold, remnants of the expedition may be deteriorating. Lizzie Meek from the Trust said the butter was a 'treasure find' adding: 'It's quite amazing how strong the smell is after nearly a hundred years…I'm not sure I'd want it on my toast.'

In December 2004 it was announced that over a thousand original plate-glass negatives of photographs taken by Herbert Ponting on Scott's expedition were to be housed at the Scott Polar Research Institute at Cambridge University. The negatives were bought with a £500,000 Heritage Lottery Fund grant, saving them from the risk of going abroad or to a private collector.

In May 2010, objects from the South Pole expedition were sold at auction for £75,000. They had been found in Derby in the attic of a woman called Jackie Church whose father was Edward McKenzie, one of Scott's crew. The items included a compass, photographs, letters and a journal. Interest was shown from as far away as New Zealand and South Africa – both countries visited by Scott in the run-up to the expedition. Highlighting desire for the objects, a watercolour of the *Terra Nova* painted by McKenzie, which was estimated to sell for £200, went for £8,350; a journal by McKenzie recording Scott's death sold for £7,500; the compass for £4,350 and a wooden carving of the *Terra Nova* for £4,600. Alan Judd from Bamfords Auctioneers said: 'It was a unique collection. I've never had a reaction like it, and as an auctioneer it was the most enjoyable auction of my career.'

But it was the 100th anniversary in 2012 of Scott's last expedition that brought his name well and truly back into the limelight again.

An International Scott Centenary expedition, organised by the Scott Polar Research Institute, set off to recreate the arduous journey to Scott's final resting place. Relatives of the five men who perished flew in to hold a memorial service. The institute said the aim of the venture was also to provide an: 'inspiring focus to our education and outreach programme. The programme will involve people from a multitude of backgrounds and ages, so inspiring the community at large and the leaders of tomorrow.'

A centenary exhibition, the result of partnership between London's Natural History Museum, the Antarctic Heritage Trust (New Zealand) and the Canterbury Museum in New Zealand, was held first in Australia, then London and finally New Zealand. The exhibitions brought together for the first time rare scientific specimens collected on the expedition with real artefacts collected by Scott and his team.

A host of events were organised throughout the country, including lectures, dinners, plays, conferences and visits. The International Scott Centenary Expedition Ltd commemorated the centenary with Polar Fun Days throughout Plymouth. These included science demonstrations such as the glacier melting process and re-enactments of experiments from Scott's expedition.

A major schools event was the nationwide fund raising by teenagers for their own Scott Centenary Scholarships. These are for expeditions run by the British Schools Exploring Society, founded in 1932 by northern party member Murray Levick.

The National Museum of the Royal Navy in Portsmouth organised a special centenary display of an original sledge used by Thomas Williamson when he was a member of the search party, and, pair of skis.

The Rutherford Foundation supported Antarctica New Zealand and the Cambridge Commonwealth Trust to establish a PhD scholarship at the Scott Polar Research Institute.

British Nautical Heritage company Quba & Co launched a Centenary range that included 'Scott's Centenary Trapper Hat', Centenary mint cake and Centenary Scott Parka.

In June 2010, the anniversary month of Scott's departure for Antarctica, the Polar Museum at Cambridge re-opened with new galleries showing the history of Arctic and Antarctic explorations. A special Scott room displayed his clothing, food, transport and scientific equipment as well as Captain Oates' abandoned sleeping bag (selected as one of the top 100 items in a BBC *A History of the World* project).

Sadly, those wishing to make a pilgrimage to see Scott's tomb would find it far beyond their reach. The cairn has been swept over by decades of storms and snow, encased in the Ross Ice Shelf as it inches towards the Ross Sea. In 2001 glaciologist Charles Bentley estimated that the tent with the bodies was at that time under about 75ft of ice and about 30 miles from the point where they died.

In about 275 years the bodies will reach the Ross Sea, and float away inside an iceberg that has broken off from the shelf.

* * *

Scott's diaries were given to the nation by his family and are held in the British Library. The journals have appeared in numerous editions since their first publication in 1913, including:

Robert Falcon Scott, (1954*) Scott's last expedition; The Personal journals of Captain R.F. Scott on his journey to the South Pole*
Tylers Green University Microfilms, (1968) *The Diaries of Captain Robert Scott, a Record of the Second Antarctic Expedition, 1910 –* 12 Vols. 1–6
University Microfilms, (1968) *The Diaries of Captain Robert Scott: a Record of the Second Antarctic Expedition, 1910–1912.* Vols. 1–6.
Scott Polar RI, E. Wilson, edited by H.G.R. King (1972) *Diary of the Terra Nova expedition to the Antarctic, 1910–1912*
Elspeth Huxley, (1977) *Scott of the Antarctic*
Peter King, editor (1999) *Scott's Last Journey.* Duckworth
R. F. Scott, (2003*) Scott's Last Expedition: The Journals of Captain R.F. Scott*
Max Jones, (2003) *The Last Great Quest: Captain Scott's Antarctic sacrifice The Voyage of the Discovery.* John Murray, London
Oxford University Press, (2005) *Journals: Captain Scott's Last Expedition*
Folio Society, (2009) *Scott's Last Expedition: The Journals of Captain R.F. Scott*

Bibliography
Apsley Cherry-Garrard, *The Worst Journey in the World: With Scott in Antarctica 1910–1913*
Robert Falcon Scott, *The Voyage of the Discovery*
Frank Debenham, *Antarctica; the Story of a Continent*
Louis Bernacchi; Jim Pipe, *To the South Polar Regions*
G. Hattersley-Smith, *Scott of the Antarctic*
Elspeth Huxley, *The Norwegian with Scott: The Antarctic Diary of Tryggve Gran, 1910–13*
Griffith Taylor, *With Scott: The Silver Lining*
Susan Solomon, *The Coldest March*
W H Smith, *Great Explorers*
Stephanie Barczewski, *Antarctic Destinies*
Ann Savours, *The Voyages of the Discovery*
Sir Ranulph Fiennes, *Captain Scott*
Roland Huntford, *Race for the South Pole: The Expedition Diaries of Scott and Amundsen*
Thayer Willis, *The Frozen World*
Desmond Wilcox, *Explorers*
BBC History
archive.timesonline.co.uk

The Scott Polar Research Institute
The Scott Antarctic Expedition 2011–12. www.scottantarctic.com
NMM Learning team. Nmm.ac.uk
EyeWitness to History.com
raceforthepole.com/journals/scott
Polar Publishing.lineone.net
Oxford Dictionary of National Biography. www.oxforddnb.com
www.coolantarctica.com
www.south-pole.com

PAWNS
OF THE
PROPHET

KIRANIS
BOOK 2

RONALD A. GEOBEY

Temple Dark Books

Thanks for your support, Bez.

Also by the Author

Kiranis
Gods of Kiranis

Kiranis Book 2: Pawns of The Prophet
First (Absolute) Edition
Copyright © Ronald A. Geobey 2022

Cover art (The Shield) by Eugen Baitinger
www.ebaitinger.de

Cover design & Typesetting by Temple Dark Books
Temple Dark Publications Ltd.
www.templedarkbooks.com

The Author asserts the moral right to
be identified as the author of this work

ISBN (E-Book): 978-1-8382594-7-1
ISBN (Paperback): 978-1-8382594-6-4

For *Abigale* and *Hannah*.
No matter what life may throw at you, you must continue to dream.
Because it is only through our dreams that our future can find us.

To fear death, my friends, is only to think ourselves wise, without being wise: for it is to think that we know what we do not know. For anything that men can tell, death may be the greatest good that can happen to them: but they fear it as if they knew quite well that it was the greatest of evils. And what is this but that shameful ignorance of thinking that we know what we do not know?

Socrates, 469-399 BCE

Hear, my child, your father's instruction, and do not reject your mother's teaching; for they are a fair garland for your head, and pendants for your neck. My child, if sinners entice you, do not consent. If they say, "Come with us, let us lie in wait for blood; let us wantonly ambush the innocent; like Sheol let us swallow them alive and whole, like those who go down to the Pit. We shall find all kinds of costly things; we shall fill our houses with booty. Throw in your lot among us; we will all have one purse" – my child, do not walk in their way, keep your foot from their paths; for their feet run to evil, and they hurry to shed blood. For in vain is the net baited while the bird is looking on; yet they lie in wait – to kill themselves! and set an ambush – for their own lives! Such are the ways of all who are greedy for gain; it takes away the life of its possessors.

Proverbs 1:8-19, Anonymous, Approx. 4th Century BCE

PROLOGUE

Senate Buildings, Tokyo, 330 NE[1]

Samuel Vawter was fully aware that he was a narcissist. And he was ultimately proud of it. A man of intellect and imagination, he was ambitious and resolute, tenacious and talented, the perfect combination of traits for his line of work. Of course, without the legacy into which Samuel had been born, such traits may well have been overlooked. Less than a century earlier, during the fallout from the Cage event, his grandfather had capitalised on the inevitable political and economic chaos. He had used his then considerable financial weight to bribe, scare and promise all the right people in all the right places into using his company like a safety deposit box. He then set about reminding all the wrong people in all the wrong places that his company was a manufacturer and purveyor of some of the most advanced weapons systems on the planet, thus ensuring that bad people bought his product line and contributed to the security of the funds submitted by the good people. Of course, all of that depended upon the subjective nature of right and wrong or good and bad, but old Grandfather Vawter had cared little for such...flexible

---

[1] NE = New Era – retrospective dating fixed the Move (2150 CE) to Year 0. The Cage event in 2380 CE was newly dated to 230 NE. Note that the NE calendar is now also defunct, given what was learned of the Move in the 6th century NE.

1

designations. Times had always changed, but money was power, and when that money bought and sold weapons, it was the most powerful kind. Old Grandfather Vawter was moved to action by the words of a certain John Harrogate, the man who had revealed, in his posthumous address to the world, the subterfuge and betrayal of a covert organisation overseen by Anev Tesckyn.

It was Tesckyn's people who had, in a fool's deal made with the Kwaios Council, arranged for the abduction of millions of people by way of the Cage. Tesckyn had believed that he could use the Cage to return Earth to the universe to which it belonged. This had been implied by the Kwaios as part of the deal, but they had failed to mention that they were not in control of the Cage. The abductees had been taken to the planet known as Kiranis and they had suffered a terrible fate. Not death, but not life either, for they had found themselves subsumed physically and psychologically within the form of monstrous creatures born out of the primordial chaos of the forming planet. And when the Cage had finished its work at Kiranis, it had vanished from sight, taking the planet with it. Kiranis was never seen again, and the people of Earth were infuriated by the incident. Tesckyn's people were hunted down and killed, an operation which took decades but had a strangely unifying effect upon a population haunted by the reasons. But as their proverbial backs were turned and hopes for world peace filled the airwaves, something else was going on, for the legacy of Anev Tesckyn would not be so easily obliterated.

In the aftermath of his terrible error and the return of the mighty Kwaios Council to this part of the galaxy, Tesckyn had seen fit to involve in the affairs of Earth a species called the Illeri. They had offered to construct the Shield around Earth. It was an enormous undertaking and Tesckyn knew that he would not see it completed in his lifetime. And that was without considering the assassin's bullet which passed through his brain twelve years later. Unfortunately, it was too late to stop the Illeri. The construction work was undertaken by automated machinery, highly advanced and seemingly impervious to the weapons of the day. Numerous attempts were made by autonomous militant groups and people calling themselves freedom fighters, but it seemed that the more the people of Earth tried to obstruct the work, the harder and faster the Illeri automatons worked. More of them arrived as the years went on, dropped off in Earth orbit like migrant workers. The closest things came to a work stoppage was short of forty years into the project, when a Kwaios vessel raced into the Sol system, destroying ships and outposts in an attempt to get to the Shield. When it reached Earth, weaponry and defensive systems of which the people had not even been aware were activated around the perimeter of the Shield, and the Kwaios ship was crippled. The Illeri robots towed it away, leaving the dying ship at a position just inside lunar orbit. The Kwaios never came again. This incident made it clear that construction of the Shield would not and should not be stopped, and the people of Earth became resigned to its shadowy presence.

As the decades went on, the progress of the work was akin to someone gradually blocking up every window in the house, but it soon became clear that the windows could be opened as the Shield came closer to full functionality, and politicians swiftly found the rhetoric of optimism leading to their taking control of a panicked people. For the first time in human history, one single entity, the Senate, ruled Earth. At least, that was how it appeared. In truth, what had always been known remained so: the rich ruled Earth. They controlled the resources, the food and, most importantly, the weapons. And Samuel Vawter stepped up to take control of what his father and grandfather before him had long known would become the most powerful corporation on the planet. Each of them had often been asked the question, 'So, what's your secret? What have you got that your competitors don't?' but they would simply smile and change the subject. Because there was something else of which old Grandfather Vawter had taken control.

As part of the deal Tesckyn had made with the Kwaios Council, his organisation had come into possession of Kwaios technology. When Tesckyn had retreated from the furious response of the people to Harrogate's call to arms, he had taken the secrets of Kwaios tech with him, guarding them as a dragon's treasure. But the backlash of hatred against his operatives not only saw them hunted down and killed; it also saw their finances frozen or appropriated and the organisation financially crippled. Grandfather Vawter just happened to knock on Tesckyn's secret door at exactly the right time with an offer he could not refuse. The fact that the old man walked out of the secret lair of the most wanted man on the planet with Kwaios technology minutes before a bullet went through Tesckyn's brain was surely a coincidence. As was the beginning of the end for Vawter's competitors.

It is a powerful truism that the enemy of one's enemy is one's friend. As humankind looked out into the dangerous stars around them, the Shield became a more comforting prospect, and the legacy of Grandfather Vawter found itself attached to government interests. By the time Samuel Vawter took over the company, the days of operating behind the scenes like a black-op contractor had passed, and he was very much in bed with the Senate. It was a comfortable bed, but Samuel thought it wise on occasion to keep the covers on and sleep near the edge. Exposure equalled vulnerability, and Samuel had no intention of becoming vulnerable. He saw the Illeri as a threat to the security of Earth, a theory only strengthened by the relentless progression of the Shield and the complete lack of communication from the Illeri since construction began. Samuel was baffled by the Senate's refusal to send a fleet to the Illeri home world to get answers, which was why he had sent someone himself. Because of the nature of the operation, the mercenary he had sent had been ordered to keep off all communication channels until he reached his destination. Two years had now passed, and there had been no word from the mercenary. The Illeri remained a mystery, a situation which would not last much longer, for the Illeri were on their way to Earth.

As he stood in the darkness, he tried to push all other concerns from his mind as he focused on the most important operation of his life. For the briefest of moments, he wondered what his grandfather would think if he could see his progeny now. The irony had the potential to bring laughter as much as it did tears. Wearing one of his favoured grey suits, Samuel stood in a darkness of his own design. He had deactivated all lighting in the room, and he waited with growing impatience as the minutes dragged on. There was silence but for his even, sometimes protracted breathing as he held the cold black cube in his hands. They had told him to come here so the communication would not be detected. These conspirators were more powerful than any of his other business associates, but this was a business of mutual benefit to both parties. Even if he did not understand their gain, still he appreciated their payment.

The cold box grew gradually warmer in his hands, but he knew this was due to his sweating palms. Then the room changed,

4

stretching outwards in every direction, a virtual sensation that challenged his perspective and his senses. The ceiling rose, great columns of blue and the shimmering metal of hybritech lifting it high beyond his ability to focus upon it. Flashing lights, integrated bio-technical cabling and alien console systems surrounded him. But he was not alone.

Tall, so tall that he felt the need to step back to comprehend its enormity, a figure of shimmering silver, black and blue stood facing him. 'You are not required to speak,' the Kwaios told him, the words first coming in that dreadful language that hurt human ears, before it was translated by the device in his hands and transmitted to his brain. He nodded dumbly, respecting their requirements. Any businessman knows that there are compromises to be made during negotiation. The Kwaios continued: 'Our work is advancing to a further stage. We require an increase in supply. You will ensure that the influx is increased by a factor of ten.'

Samuel was about to argue, but the image of the huge Kwaios moved closer towards him. 'This is not open to negotiation,' it reminded him. 'You will increase our supply, and we will provide you with the payment you seek.' Samuel smiled as the Kwaios clarified, 'You will live forever.'

With the conversation ended, Samuel came out of the small antechamber and looked around the larger room in which it was situated. Giant windows overlooked a great city, and sunlight bounced off the surface of a massive glass table. Samuel stared into the reflected light for a moment, allowing his eyes to lose focus as he revelled in the temporary escape from reality. From the door through which he had left the antechamber, another figure appeared, a man in a black cloak of dragons. Naveen looked solemn, focused and driven. 'Are you ready?' he asked.

Samuel nodded as he turned, his eyes readjusting to the unnatural light of the room and his resolve strengthened by the presence of this enigmatic figure. 'They won't know what hit them, will they?'

Naveen grinned as he replied, 'That's the general idea, yes.'

PART 1
EARTH

The Sentience could be known, it could be felt in the heart and in the mind, yet still our people turned from its guidance. And so, the Sentience brought the Cage, and with it a plague to make us slaves to mediocrity so that the unworthy might be judged. But Mannix Relland had prepared the way, and those of pure heart were Chosen for Renewal. Now the Sentinels oversee those who have yet to Ascend, guiding our children and keeping our ways. As the Sentience is righteous, so shall Ascension set us free.

Extract from the so-called 'Monologues of Ascension' (author unknown), restored from corrupted Psy-cells discovered in 709 NE in the ruins of the Great 'Si' Library in Berlin. The 'Monologues' are copies of earlier texts thought to be composed by a Presbyter of the Church of the New Elect c. 320-370 NE. They are now housed in the Millennium Temple on Kiranis. It is unclear as to whether 'Ascension' in this extract indicates a retrospective on the events of the year 330, or it was an ambiguous theological concept pre-dating those events; a concept to be later legitimated by them.

THE MEC SYSTEM

MEC Station Gamma-48, Sector Π6

The Argo ploughed the darkness in which stars would grow. It was a thing of beauty, this black-shredding ship. Sleek and fast, its rows of proximity beacons were like strings of pearls embedded in the shimmering skin of an obsidian predator searing through the waterless depths. And a predator indeed, because like many things of beauty, the Argo was lethal, a trickster of seductive destruction. Small windows along its hide emitted pinpoints of light belittled by the proximity beacons. But through these pinpoints one could see life. As the Argo was nearing a gigantic station living in the shadows of a nearby star, Captain Abigale Saranne was enjoying the silence as she traversed one of the outer corridors. There was no activity in this area of the ship, and she trusted that there was none anywhere else. Well…almost anywhere else. As she reached an elevator door, she tapped the control panel and said, 'Medical.' After a few seconds, the face of a man in his early forties appeared on a small screen. Green-eyed and handsome, his light brown hair was retreating from an encroaching forehead and losing the battle on two fronts, as invading grey also assaulted on the left and right flanks. *'We're ready, Captain,'* he reported. *'Just you and me to go.'*

'Good,' Abigale replied. 'I want the bridge crew as soon as we're through.'

The man furrowed his eyebrows. *'I'm not a big fan of flouting protocol.'*

'You'll have to trust me on this one, Doc,' Abigale assured him. 'I just can't tell you why.'

On matters such as this, the conflict of authority between Command and Medical usually ended in stalemate, serving nobody's interests. The doctor conceded, aware that there was little time to argue. *'I'll skip straight to Engineering after the bridge then…to get back on track.'*

Abigale gave a little laugh. 'I can't imagine you skipping anywhere.'

The doctor smiled. *'You'd be surprised what I get up to when you're all out!'*

9

'I really don't wanna know.'

'*Call me from the bridge*,' the doctor said, as a warning sounded from his console. '*We're within scanning range*.'

'Will do.' Abigale tapped the panel and, as the screen went blank, the elevator door opened. She stepped in.

The dark station came to life as the Argo continued towards it. It was seen to be cylindrical as thousands of points of light burned the shadows, but it opened with an internal spiralling section separating its two operating units in anticipation of its latest client. The station was a portal to the MEC network.

Abigale looked at her reflection in the mirrored wall at the rear of the elevator. She was tired, and it showed. Loath to wear much make-up, the darkness around her eyes was rescued from over-exposure by her sallow skin. Yet still she could see it; she knew it was there. Her blue eyes saw an older woman than the one to whom it had become accustomed. And her long brown hair framed a face which had seen too much. She was looking forward to getting home. As she began to tie up her hair to transform herself into Practical Mode, she said, 'Bridge,' and two things happened: the elevator began its ascent, and the mirrored wall became almost fully transparent. Abigale could still see her reflection, enough to aid in fixing her hair, but she could also see something wonderful.

The self-perpetuating engine of the Argo represented a considerable evolution of even the most trusted and economical quantum intake conversion drives which had become the norm in the past century, but its mechanics were a secret fiercely protected by the Vawter Corporation. Whereas a standard QUIC engine collected its fuel on a quantum level as the vessel moved through space – its hordes of bots processing a theoretically endless supply of energy – the pulsing and swirling sphere of multi-coloured lights in the centre of the Argo was the effect of the undulating waves of mirror-cased bots obscuring the true heart of the operation. It was suicide to investigate closer, a determination not unfounded. As captain, however, Abigale was necessarily privy to its secrets. She knew that the engine of the Argo was one of a kind, but it was not the only thing on view as the elevator rose higher, allowing Abigale to look down upon it.

10

The internal walls of the inner corridor-run of every deck could be seen, as well as the scores of elevator cars and lines. Hundreds of robotic automatons with various duties moved around the weightless interior, their mag-drive propulsion systems humming amidst the glow and pulse of the engine. Abigale loved this sight, the inner workings of the ship. It reminded her of the doll she once took apart as a child, much to the frustration of her father. As she sat in her room amidst the pieces, she had looked up at him sweetly and explained, 'I wanted to see how she cried.'

Flickers of blue light could be seen in the space between the two ends of the cylinder as the great MEC station prepared for the arrival of the Argo. Like an enormous glowing mouth waiting to swallow the vessel, the spiralling centre had been opened according to the dimensions of the ship, allowing for its passage through this giant metal portal. The interior of the portal activated then, crackling blue energy igniting to create a sheet of bright blue light.

The elevator stopped and, rather than having to turn around and exit the way she had entered, as on most other decks, Abigale watched the glass descend to open the elevator onto the short corridor leading to the bridge. It was also transparent, and Abigale walked a curving path until she reached the bridge, feeling a familiar shiver run through her as she stepped into the deathly, but occupied, silence. It welcomed her with a whispering, *'Remember me?'*. Seventeen of her crew were here, unconscious at their stations, laying comfortably in reclining chairs designed for this specific, haunting purpose. Abigale went swiftly to her own chair and settled in, pressing the button to recline with her left hand. Tapping the panel with her right, she said again, 'Medical.'

A holo-image of the doctor projected from the ceiling. *'Comfy?'* he asked.

'And if I say no?' Abigale quipped.

'Not my problem. Close your eyes and relax.'

'Ooh, I bet you say that to all the girls!' Abigale closed her eyes and tried to relax as she heard the soft hum of the hypo-spray moving into position at her neck. On the end of a short arm attached to the chair, the hypo-spray was ready to administer the sedative which would render her unconscious. It reached her

11

neck, and with a short, sharp hiss, its pressurised delivery system shot the sedative through her pores and directly into her bloodstream. She was quickly out. Down in Medical, the doctor followed suit, until the Argo was like a ghost ship, its unique engine shutting down until it set as a solid reflective sphere. Power was systematically cut off in a pre-determined hierarchy of systems, until only the string-of-pearls proximity beacons were active. Then they, too, were shut down, until – all lights out, all life out – the Argo was drawn like a black moth into the sheet of blue energy inside the automated station. The prow of the ship pushed into the energy wall, but it was not destroyed. Instead, once the entire ship was devoured, the spiral reversed and closed the station, before an aperture opened on its dark surface and a ball of bright blue light shot out across the galaxy. Travelling at immense speed, it vanished into the darkness.

Ω

Many light years away, a very different ship was approaching Earth. A majestic vessel, it was beautiful like the Argo but larger and more powerful, the killer whale to the Argo's great white shark. It appeared to cause ripples in the fabric of space as it came closer to the planet around which similar technology was being brought to fruition. For here, finally, were the Illeri, a species whose reputation preceded them only insofar as their mysterious nature had become synonymous with the Shield. Only slightly larger than the C-1 Battle Cruisers of Earth's military, the Illeri ship boasted no lighting of any kind, no indication of windows or the flashing, coloured strips of a proximity detection system. There was no visual evidence of life on board; but appearances could indeed deceive.

Star Marshal Rami Marush had heard little about these people, these strange new friends whom he observed from the command centre of the lunar station. A life form known only to humans as a Type-4 Sentient, this classification identified the Illeri as a primarily aquatic life form, and as such it was likely that they were loath to spend too much time away from their natural habitat. Marush tried to imagine them interacting with the Senate representatives, grinning as he pictured someone throwing the bureaucrats into a gigantic tank to swim with the Illeri ambassador.

'Could do with a joke, sir,' a familiar voice cut in. Marush did not particularly like the man, but he chuckled softly as he turned to see Commander Collenson, his direct subordinate for this operation, walking up the ramp towards him and saying, 'Been a long day.'

'Just thinking about this meeting,' Marush explained. 'How they're gonna do it without drowning.'

Collenson nodded, stony-faced as always. 'Should be interesting,' he agreed, missing the joke, 'although we won't see any of it 'til we get home. There's something interfering with civilian broadcasting.' He handed a light-key to the star marshal, who put it on his right palm and activated it. The projection jumped up from his hand, displaying approach vectors for the visiting ship as Collenson explained, 'They're clear for entry. Far as we can tell, the Shield itself is guiding them in.'

'Probably what's blocking the broadcast,' Marush noted.

'As long as it's nothing more than that. I don't like knowing nothing about these guys.'

Marush nodded in agreement. 'Well, that's what this is all about. Fifteen planets and seven different species under their watch, all of them out farther than we're willing to go without a MEC station in tow. It'd be nice to find out how they managed to get all that power without antagonising the Kwaios. Either they've nothing the Council wants, or something they just can't take.'

'Dunno which is better.'

'I know what you mean,' agreed Marush. As the sleek monster passed the moon and reduced to minimal speed, an escort of seven battle cruisers attached themselves. On the lunar station, an alarm suddenly sounded and shouts were heard across the command centre: 'We got incoming! Multiple targets!'

They had clearly been monitoring the approach of the Illeri, these predators. With terrible speed and ferocity, scores of ships arrived from different directions, assorted in size and strength. With some risking being torn apart by the sudden drop in velocity, this was apparently a concerted attack. Marush ordered fighters launched from the lunar station to engage them, but it quickly became clear that these were diversionary tactics on the part of the attackers. Larger vessels materialised in the space between the Shield and the escorted Illeri ship, Garran battleships opening fire on Earth's cruisers without delay. Marush could see only the flashing bursts of explosions in the distance and Earth itself was just a dark sphere looming in the background, but his screen magnified the scene just in time for him to witness something magnificent. In the shadow of the Shield, the Illeri vessel came alive, thousands of lights illuminating its surface, countless weapons pummelling the Garran ships and tearing them to pieces. Another alarm sounded and Marush shouted, 'Report!'

'A vortex, sir! Above the North Pole!'

The darkness beyond the zenith of the Shield rippled as if a stone had disturbed a pool of black, and three ships birthed from the darkness. The outer hulls of the warships of the Jaevisk Society were now composed of a shimmering network of black and reflective metal, and they were deadlier than ever, from Marush's viewpoint appearing to descend upon their Illeri target like ravenous birds. The battle cruisers from Earth were severely damaged and would not last much longer, but even the Garran found themselves in the line of fire as the three Jaevisk ships opened fire on everything in their path. This was not a concerted attack at all. It was a moment of opportunistic chaos brought on by the Illeri arrival. Although the final guest at the party was fashionably late, it swiftly made its presence felt. The Argo roared into the fray like an angry beast.

Countless weapons, some never before seen by the attackers, disabled and destroyed everything that came up against it, and the Jaevisk found its lead ship with a gaping hole in its belly as strange missiles burst from this unique vessel to blow it wide open. The Jaevisk realised too late that the tide had turned as this new horror maintained a collision course with the weakened section of the lead warship, ripping it in two as the Argo burst through the explosion and the wreckage. Stunned by these tactics, the Jaevisk fled, waiting until they had reached a safe distance before opening a vortex and returning to the sanctuary of their space, leaving behind the burning debris of a warship. It was not long before the Garran and the other unidentified attackers followed suit, with Earth's military vessels snapping at their heels. In the aftermath, it appeared that the Illeri had suffered little damage, and they made no attempt to contact anyone to express any form of gratitude. Their lights went out again. And they resumed their course to Earth.

The Shield constructed around the blue planet deactivated its defence systems. Electromagnetic fields of protection went down, surface-to-orbit guns switched off and thousands of apertures opened to reveal the patchwork of metal encompassing the Earth. The metal world opened, allowing the Illeri vessel to enter its domain. Marush watched it passing through the Shield and he felt a shiver run through him as he observed, 'It's like it recognises them.'

Ω

The Shield was not exactly connected to Earth, but it was clear that some form of symbiosis had been engineered. Reaching down through the clouds from the interior panels were hundreds of metal columns, making contact with Earth at major bodies of water. Some of those descending into oceans were less than a hundred kilometres apart. They maintained their positions by way of the synchronous orbit of the Shield from which they protruded, and there was a constant hum of activity from these giant 'Fingers of God', as the people called them. It was known that water was regularly sucked up through these columns, and that cloud cover and precipitation were now intricately connected to the mechanics of the Shield. But apart from government rhetoric about regulating planetary temperature, further details were not forthcoming. The Illeri vessel docked on the interior of the Shield, and a comparatively tiny shuttle launched from it, following one of these great columns as it descended towards Japan.

Tokyo had long been a bustling hub of people, money, technology and power. Now it was the seat of the Senate, the centre of political control and the hope for the future of humankind. The fact that it occupied a precarious position on the planet, from a tectonic point of view, spoke either of the relentless determination of the Senate or its resignation to the temporary nature of government. Kai Tzedek was of the former school of thought, because of and despite the obvious power of his mysterious guests. Senator Tzedek was a tall man, dark-haired and dark-skinned. In these days of human exposure to so many other species of potential enmity, it was tempting to imagine that something so seemingly irrelevant as skin colour no longer mattered within human society. But then human society had always been prone to tendencies of segregation. It was an integral aspect of self-identity. If everyone were considered the same, the individuality so important to materialistic humanity would be compromised. Tzedek certainly valued his individuality, as he did his materialistic fulfilment. Money and power were everything to him, and he savoured what the two brought into his life.

His wife had been attracted to him primarily because of his obvious potential to climb the political ladder. She saw where he was going in life, and so she attached herself to him with such parasitic tenacity that he swiftly came to resent her. She may have seen where he was going in the long term, but she certainly had no idea where he had been going during the day or with whom he spent his time. At least, until a jealous secretary informed her. Tzedek had reacted as one might expect of any powerful man whose individuality was threatened. It cost a lot less than he had at first been quoted to get rid of the two women. But then Tzedek was a man who liked to shop around to get the best deal. The messy part was tidying up after his wife and secretary had been found dead, because he could allow neither the man who took the job nor the ones whose quotes he had rejected to survive. For that, he invented a story and asked a close and powerful friend of his to remove the assassins from the picture. Then he bought himself something nice, invited a young woman around to his home and opened an expensive bottle of wine. Now that he thought of it, he could not remember the colour of her skin. *Maybe it really doesn't matter*, he thought, grinning as the shimmering black Illeri shuttle touched down on the lower roof of the block-spanning Senate building.

Tzedek stood with his colleagues, men who thought of themselves as his equals – and here his grin faded – on the upper roof, two storeys above the landing surface. They were flanked by an armed escort of twenty men and women. The morning fog hung lazily above them all, wondering whether it belonged to this scene of diplomatic uncertainty. Tzedek glanced up to remind it that it did not.

Depressurisation systems hissed and vapour escaped from the shuttle while a ramp extended from the side. The ramp was formed by two black extrusions reaching out to the surface like probing claws. Once they had made contact with the roof, a sheet of energy connected them, forming a pathway down from the bulkhead door which had not been noticed until it opened. It was not so much a door as it was a vanishing trick. The portal in the outer bulkhead was simply no longer there.

While the members of the armed escort were dressed in navy and red, and the Senate representatives were clothed in many different styles and colours of ceremonial attire – Tzedek himself wearing a dark blue robe over a white suit with gold lining – the Illeri delegation had apparently decided not to dress up for the occasion. Tzedek's robe rippled in the breeze as two dark figures filled the wide portal in the black shuttle. They emerged slowly into the light, not walking but rather hovering, levitating a little more than an inch above the energy surface of the ramp, and their appearance unsettled everyone gathered to welcome them. For unless the Illeri were mechanical creatures, it was clear that they were not willing to show their true form. Encased from head to whatever passed as their feet in polished black metal, they resembled ancient knights from Earth in their intricate suits of overlapping armour. The layers of metal were fused in such a way that it was impossible to determine a beginning or end to the pattern, and there were no visible joints or points of vulnerability. The parts which may have protected arms were drawn back at the shoulders, where they flared up and out, almost as if wings were hidden inside. What was visible, however, and what drew the attention of the armed escort, was the array of integrated weapons in the armoured suit. The armed escort of the Senate was looking upon its counterpart.

Senator Mohammed Al-Rais leaned into Tzedek, saying quietly, 'You better be right about this, Kai,' to which Tzedek side-eyed him with sufficient condescension to remind him that he was as much a party to these proceedings as any of those standing with him. A third figure emerged into the light at the top of the Illeri ramp. This one was over two metres in height, slightly taller than the first two and distinguished from them by no other visible means. As it descended the ramp, however, the two guards stepped aside in obvious deference, waiting until it had passed them. Once it had, they returned to the ramp and, to the surprise of everyone watching, they went back into the shuttle and the door closed behind them, the bulkhead reappearing as if sealing a breach. The Illeri dignitary was left alone.

Tzedek led the others down the steps from the upper roof, his arms outstretched as if he might embrace the alien. Which of

17

course he would have done if required. Graciously, there were no feet to be kissed, but... 'On behalf of the Senate,' he beamed, 'I welcome you to Earth...Ambassador. It is our pleasure to finally –'

The voice which dismembered Tzedek's fawning was metallic and chilling, sufficient to detract from the mystery of an Illeri speaking English. 'We will see...Echad,' it demanded, pronouncing the '*ch*' like a '*k*' rather than the guttural sound required of a name derived from an ancient Semitic tongue. The ensuing silence was enough to suggest to the fog that it could descend ever so slightly on the proceedings, just to add some atmosphere. The Senate representatives were close enough now to look up into the eyes of the armoured suit, but Tzedek could see only his reflection in those black globes. A chill ran through him which had nothing to do with the morning wind picking up at this altitude. 'I think I understand,' he replied finally. 'Our initial contact with your species happened during a tumultuous time for our people, and yes...a man named Echad played a prominent role in the events, but...that was quite some time ago. That man is long dead.' Tzedek managed a little laugh, before adding, 'We humans do not live very long.'

The cold stare of the Illeri suit was almost suggestive as the ambassador replied, 'We know.' The huge suit turned towards the doorway on the roof, and it began to float towards it. 'Echad had a son,' the ambassador continued as the Senate party quickened its pace to keep up. 'We will see Echad.' The senators began to whisper amongst themselves, but Tzedek's glare warned them to silence.

Inside the welcoming warmth of the top floor of the Senate building, where towering ceilings were the result of merging two levels, giant windows welcomed the morning light, enticing it in with open arms before taking it captive. A long, elliptical table with a blue and white stretched Earth across a surface of polished glass adorned the centre of the vast room. On a day like this, the Shield was painfully absent from the representation of the planet. At the place where Senator Tzedek would normally sit, the Illeri ambassador had toppled the chair and stood patiently for the humans to join it. They moved to their designated positions as Tzedek was forced to concede his own, moving instead to the opposite end of the table. He had long hated sitting with his back to the door, and many of the others took pleasure in his discomfort, barely able to conceal their spiteful smirks. Tzedek ignored them, concentrating instead on the big picture so he could maintain a modicum of respect for this powerful species. Illusions of deference were important in these times of transition. 'The Shield is complete,' said the Illeri as soon as everyone was settled and silent.

Tzedek felt a slight jarring sensation in his head with every word the Illeri spoke, as if someone was scraping a fork across the dinner plate of his brain. 'That's excellent news, Ambassador. I'm sure you can imagine how difficult it's been for our people to live so long amidst its construction.'

The ambassador was silent. Either it could not imagine or it did not care. Tzedek pressed on, desperate to strip away the tension. 'I wonder if I might ask some questions concerning the capabilities and function of the Shield.'

'Questions are permitted.' The Illeri voice was grating and seemed to scrape the windows around them all before it went into their ears. Tzedek found himself grinding his teeth before continuing. 'As I'm sure you're aware, the main reason for our…government at the time requesting the Shield…' he began, ignoring the heads turning towards him (there was no point getting into the specifics of authority from a century earlier), '…was to set up an advanced defence system designed to protect us from the Kwaios Council. But they haven't been seen anywhere near us in decades, so…maybe they're no longer concerned with us.'

'The Kwaios are…deceptive,' said the ambassador. 'You should remain protected. The Shield will protect your world in many ways. Planetary temperature is regulated through the hydro pillars and the operative cycle of the apertures.'

Tzedek nodded. So, what the people of Earth called the Fingers of God were called hydro pillars. It made sense, and while this was clearly a deflection on the part of the ambassador, Tzedek was nonetheless intrigued by the technology. 'Yes, we've noticed that,' he replied. 'The dispersion cycle has proved remarkable in combating global warming, although of course the Shield itself is responsible for the great majority of heat being trapped. But due to the overall decrease in temperature, we've had considerably less precipitation. We're beginning to experience some serious droughts and associated agricultural problems. It's also been noticed that the…hydro pillars are drawing greater volumes of

19

water up into the Shield than the levels of vapour released into the upper atmosphere would suggest. Perhaps you could explain the…imbalance.'

For a moment there was silence and the ambassador stood motionless. The gathered senators found themselves searching for answers within the lifeless black eyes of the armoured suit. Then the ambassador spoke: 'Your sea levels have been rising for centuries, claiming large areas of otherwise habitable land. Initially, the Shield contributed to this problem, but the activation of the hydro pillars now provides a remedy. The Shield stores significant amounts of water, and you can control the balance between water extraction and vapour release. Apertures can be opened over specific areas to focus the light of your star on areas of unwanted freezing, as they can be closed on other areas to encourage freezing. Because the combined mass of the Shield and your planet would have resulted in orbital instability if polar ice had remained as it was when construction began, planetary mass has been altered to compensate for the synchronous movement of both bodies. If there is too much water on your planet, it can be stored in the Shield, and if the combined mass of the planet and the Shield threatens orbital stability, water may be released into space. This is the full functionality of the dispersion cycle.'

Everyone at the table was stunned. The symbiosis occurring here was far beyond anything they had imagined, and Tzedek was first to voice his concerns. 'It sounds like Earth is completely dependent upon the Shield, Ambassador. This isn't the message we want to deliver to our people.'

It was impossible to tell whether the ambassador was concerned by this reaction. 'The Shield is a complex machine,' it replied. 'We will instruct you thoroughly. Never have you been in complete control of your planet. There will be no more drought because you will regulate precipitation. Food will grow where you decide, and you can now reclaim land lost through centuries of flooding. Harmful radiation from your star will decrease and you will oversee your climate on a global scale.'

Kai Tzedek sat back in his chair and glanced at Al-Rais. The man was nodding slowly with wide eyes and a smile of wonder, and Tzedek shared his enthusiasm. This was an unprecedented step forward and it was a concept simply oozing power like nothing before. Whoever controlled the Shield literally controlled the world. Not just its money and resources, but its weather, its food production and ultimately where people could live. The Senate had struck gold, for the Shield was the ultimate fortress, protecting Earth from the outside while defining it from the inside. There were some narrowed eyes of distrust, and Tzedek grinned at the short-sightedness of the disbelievers. He rose from his chair and began to clap, that age-old human custom of displaying satisfaction at the show. Mohammed Al-Rais did the same, and the others gradually joined him and Tzedek. The Illeri ambassador offered no indication that he appreciated or even cared that they were happy. Once the clapping had died down to an uncomfortable state of uncertainty, the Illeri spoke again, saying, 'We will see Echad.'

Tzedek shook his head with a smile, still caught up by the excitement. 'Echad is dead,' he reminded the alien pleasantly. 'I assure you, he died out at Kiranis and he had no children.'

'He had a son,' the Illeri argued.

Tzedek chuckled with good humour. 'If he did, he didn't tell anyone,' he quipped. The joke was lost on the alien, and it moved away from the table, floating back the way it had come, passing Tzedek on its way to the doors opening out to the roof. 'Ah...' Tzedek began, to which the alien stopped and waited. 'Perhaps you'd like to see some of our world. I mean...now that you've helped us to change it. I assure you, we have some impressive landscapes and geological phenomena.'

The ambassador turned and the black orbs stared into Tzedek's soul. 'No,' it replied eventually. 'We will see Echad. This is our price for the Shield.' The Illeri turned back to the doors and continued out to the roof. As the senators hurried to the doors, they watched the Illeri ambassador ascend the ramp to the shuttle. It passed through the vanishing portal in the bulkhead, which closed behind it. But the shuttle did not leave. For a short while, Tzedek and the others watched it in silence as the wind picked up again, and Al-Rais came up beside him, leaning in close. 'So where *is* he?' he asked quietly, the words almost lost to the wind.

'I'm not sure,' Tzedek replied. 'Deep in Garran territory last time I checked. Most likely headed for Omneri.'

'Omneri?' Al-Rais nodded. 'So, he's still looking for them.'

'I don't think he'll ever stop.' Tzedek looked up towards the shadows cast by the Shield, saying, 'We should never have told him.'

'Well, he's clearly not the only one who knows,' said Al-Rais, nodding towards the Illeri shuttle. 'What are we gonna do about this?'

Tzedek turned to his colleague. 'Whatever's going on, the Jaevisk and the Garran clearly aren't overjoyed by the Illeri being here,' he noted. 'So, our priority is to figure out exactly *why* they're here, cos if this is Illeri PR, they need to work on their people skills.' He put a hand on Al-Rais' shoulder. 'Does that sound like something you'd be interested in overseeing, Mohammed?'

Al-Rais nodded and said, 'Absolutely,' completely taken in by the unexpected camaraderie and sense of inclusion. Tzedek was known to consider himself superior to the rest of the Senate. Of course, what Al-Rais could not have known was that the attack on the Illeri ship had come as no surprise to Tzedek. And as to the reason for the Illeri being at Earth, Tzedek was happy to have Al-Rais conduct some wild goose chase for answers of which he was already in possession. He just hoped that the captain of the Argo had not complicated matters with her recklessness. Not now that the clock was well and truly ticking.

He looked towards the heavily protected annex room situated next to the doors through which the alien had left, drawing in a controlling breath.

THE CAPTAIN

Military Dry Dock, West Pacific Sync Orbit

Abigale scratched her head for the third time in less than two minutes, running her hands through her long hair. She could not explain the sensation, but there was a feeling that something was not right. 'I think that damned machine got my hair wrong,' she complained as Carenna Moreno, her second-in-command and one of the few people she considered a friend, came up beside her. Carenna smiled and looked at her reflection in the window, beyond which they could see the ongoing repairs to their ship in the dock. 'I think mine looks *better*,' she remarked, flicking it out playfully from both sides of her neck. 'More…bounce.' Abigale laughed as they watched the small maintenance vessels buzzing around the Argo. The prow of the ship and ten decks around it were crushed from smashing through the Jaevisk Warship, and it was for this reason alone that Abigale was standing here. She had been denied landfall until she received the inevitable reprimand for what must surely have seemed to others a maniacal course of action. And she could hear the footsteps of consequence approaching.

Carenna and Abigale turned as five men came up the ramp towards them, none of them showing concern as to what was happening beyond the window to their left. 'Tell them you were drunk,' Carenna joked under her breath.

'Again?' Abigale replied from the side of her mouth, maintaining her composure as Carenna turned her head away, covering her mouth and pretending to clear her throat before looking back at the military officials. 'Something amusing, Commander Moreno?' she was asked by one of them.

'No, sir,' she replied as she straightened with military decorum. 'I am never amused, sir.'

A reprimand for sarcasm was cut off as the man on the far right of the group, dressed in civilian clothing of grey practicality, raised his hand. Abigale was surprised to see her superiors lapsing to silence as the civilian addressed her cordially. 'Captain Saranne,' he said, smiling pleasantly, 'my name is Samuel Vawter. I am –'

'I know who you are, Mister Vawter,' Abigale interrupted him. 'I know my ship is privately commissioned.'

23

Samuel's smile was a few degrees colder as he replied, 'The Argo is *my* ship, Captain. On loan to the military. And I can take control of it whenever I see fit. You'd do well to remember that.'

'I'll keep it in mind,' said Abigale. 'Of course, I hope we can hold on to her for a while. She's a beauty.'

He laughed wryly, stepping close enough to whisper to her, 'Are you patronising me, Captain? Because I'm sure you don't want to make an enemy of me.'

Knowing her friend and captain only too well, Carenna had stepped wisely to one side, wincing as Vawter spoke. Abigale replied, 'Are you *threatening* me, Mister Vawter? Cos right now, I'm not sure what I want to make of you.'

Samuel appeared to enjoy this turn in the conversation, and he could not help but grin as he moved back and asked, 'Why did you ram the warship?'

Abigale was not an idiot. Despite Vawter's light-hearted demeanour, she understood what was at stake here. 'I knew they wouldn't anticipate it.'

Samuel appeared to like the answer. 'So, you were going for the…unexpected?'

'Exactly. They're unsettled by what they can't predict.'

'You understand the Jaevisk?'

'No,' Abigale admitted, 'but I understand men with power.' There really was no disguising the venom in the conversation now as Samuel replied, 'Really? I do hope you're not comparing the men of the Senate with the Jaevisk, Captain.'

Before Carenna could stop her, Abigale replied, 'I wasn't talking about the Senate.'

Samuel took a deep breath to calm himself, because he knew that time taken to maintain one's composure was time well spent. 'The Argo is the most advanced ship available to the military, Captain,' he reminded her. 'The damage you did today will cost billions, and yet these men…' he gestured to the four behind him, 'have convinced me to leave you in command of one of my prized possessions. I trust you won't be so reckless with her again.'

Abigale brushed imaginary debris from her right shoulder and breast, a gesture which did not fail to attract the attention of every man gathered, Vawter most definitely included. 'Your concern for my crew is touching, Mister Vawter,' she replied. 'Now, if that's all,

I'd like to get back to *my* prized possession. She's waiting for her mother to come home.'

Samuel's eyes had lifted to meet her steely gaze once again, and he felt a rush of excitement course through him. Not because she had aroused him – at least not only so – but because she had walked into his trap. 'It's interesting you should mention your crew,' he remarked, stepping back from her. Now she could see the concern on the faces of the military men as he continued: 'Because something else happened which I believe you'd call...unexpected.'

She glanced at the others, asking, 'What's he talking about? What's going on?' Carenna stepped up protectively as Samuel told her with a poisonous grin, 'You killed twelve of your crew when you rammed the warship, Captain. Not my concern, I know, but...I thought you should hear it from me. Now, if you'll excuse me...I have a flight to catch.' He winked provocatively before turning to leave, pushing past the four men. They watched him go before they turned back to Abigale and Carenna. Abigale was stunned and Carenna asked, 'Is he serious? We lost people out there?'

One of the men, middle-aged, tall and plump with ruddy features, nodded. 'I'm afraid so. These men are here to investigate.' Carenna and Abigale hardly glanced at the other three, and Abigale said, 'I don't understand. There were no fatalities reported.'

The man shook his head. 'You presumed everyone was pulled back from the forward sections, right?'

Abigale nodded, noting that the other men were listening intently and taking notes. 'As per my orders,' she replied. 'I gave them before we entered the MEC station.'

'Why?'

'I...' Abigale glanced at the battered ship in dry dock. 'I was warned about the attack.'

'By who?'

'An Axcebian trader,' Carenna put in. 'Out in 184.'

The red-faced man glanced at Carenna, nodding slowly. 'Okay...so a trader heard some rumours,' he said. 'Was that all?'

'What do you mean?' asked Abigale.

'Well, you didn't just rush here, did you? You ignored MEC protocol not only by jumping the network queues but by having yourself and your bridge crew revived before vital systems were manned. And it looks like you knew before you even entered the MEC that you needed your forward sections evacuated! What are we supposed to think here, Captain?'

Abigale looked at the ship again, and then back at her inquisitor. 'You're *supposed* to think that we saved a lot of lives today!'

'That's not gonna work,' the man replied, shaking his head. 'How did you know to protect the prow?'

'Protect...?' Abigale looked at Carenna, saying, 'That's exactly what *he* said!'

Carenna nodded as the man demanded, 'Who...the trader?'

'Yeah,' Abigale replied. 'He said I'd need to protect the prow. When we got here and saw the warship...our trajectory...' she shrugged. 'It just...made sense. It was like...'

'Like he knew what was going to happen?'

Both women nodded and the man stepped closer, the others stepping up also to continue with their impeccable notetaking as he said, 'You need to tell us everything you remember about this trader, Captain. *Everything*. It's imperative that no one intercepted your conversation with him.'

Carenna and Abigale exchanged glances, before Abigale admitted, 'I think someone might have. There was a burst of interference and...' she nodded, 'he cut us off quickly after that.'

'What's going on?' asked Carenna. 'Who *was* he?'

'That's not your concern,' the man told them. 'We'll examine your com data. But we still need to know why those people were in the forward sections despite your order to pull back.'

'I've no idea,' said Abigale, 'but if you give me their names...that might help.'

'You can leave the investigating to us, Captain. For now, enjoy your shore leave. Once our intel locates this trader of yours, you're going straight back out to get him. We need him here by the end of the week.'

'What? Why? He's just a debt collector.'

'So when you find him,' said the tall man, 'tell him we owe him.'

$$\Omega$$

Walking across to the transport hubs on the outer fringes of the gigantic space-dock, Abigale waved farewell to Carenna as she headed to the Gamma-Route station, while she herself headed to Delta. If the words of their superiors were anything to go by, they would be seeing each other again very soon. Carenna lived in Russia, and the shuttles on the Gamma-Route went that way every hour. Delta-Route covered the countries of western Europe, and Abigale lived in Ireland, the last stop on Delta. The next shuttle left in ten minutes, meaning Abigale would be home in less than three hours, allowing for any delays caused by casual observers of the Illeri ship. Since their arrival, scores of civilian craft had taken people up to see the vessel docked inside the Shield. Most of these tour operators acquired clearance from the military to cross their flight paths, but some private craft did not.

Abigale's journey was made in silent contemplation, piecing together the events of the day. She stared out the window into the busy and occupied darkness, making a mental reminder to speak to the Argo's doctor when she returned to the ship. Perhaps he had made some error during the revival process. But that should have had no bearing on their position on the ship, so she could be wrong. Given the time between the emergence of the ship from the MEC in Earth territory and the fight with the Jaevisk, all Abigale could think was that those twelve people had been revived before anyone else, and that something had led them to the forward sections of the ship. What Abigale needed to know was who they were and in which sections they had been. Pushing it to the back of her mind, she thought of her ten-year-old daughter, Hannah. Abigale had promised her a trip by MEC to an archaeological dig on one of the planets orbiting the star Gliese 581, discovered in the early twenty-first century, long before the Move. It was impossible to say whether archaeological excavations in the Home Universe would have found anything even remotely interesting, but the dig on this 581g was proving fruitful, having uncovered ruins of cities built before the first dinosaur had walked on Earth, in either Universe. 581g was certainly in the so-called 'Goldilocks' zone, which had drawn attention to it, but Goldilocks had long ago left the woods. Although Abigale felt like doing little more than soaking in a hot bath on her balcony, she was not one to break promises to Hannah, who saw her mother so infrequently these days. With a smile of contentment and Hannah's face in her mind, she slept for a while, but when she woke, tears were drying on her face and she felt a terrible emptiness. It was often this way when she came home, for memories of her husband were inevitably stirred. He had been such a gentle soul, loving and caring beyond measure, but at the same time fiercely protective of both ladies in his life. Hannah was only five when he had died, and since the moment he had first taken his baby girl in his arms, his life had greater purpose than ever before. Abigale still recalled the tears of joy she and Daniel had shared in the delivery room, but that memory had been later tainted by the tears she had shared with Hannah when Daniel was gone. And it inevitably led to recalling Hannah's words as the coffin was lowered into the dark, cold earth. Squeezing her mother's hand, she had said, 'Don't worry, Mom. We'll see him again one day.'

But such comforts were for the innocent and the faithful, and Abigale was too far beyond either to find a way back. She looked out the window to see the ruddy sunset burning through the grill of the Shield over Ireland. 'Coming down over Derry now, Captain,' one of the stewards told her as she passed her seat. Conscious of her drying tears, Abigale wiped her cheeks with both hands and forced a smile. 'It's good to be home,' she replied absently, blissfully unaware that nothing would ever be the same again.

Ω

As she walked up the path, she knew instinctively that something was wrong. The last time Abigale had returned home, Hannah had set out a banner to welcome her. Under the watchful eye of Karolina, her Nanny, she had even tried her luck in the kitchen, preparing what had been – for all the wrong reasons – an unforgettable meal. Today, however, there was silence in the house as Abigale closed the door behind her, and there was every sign that the place had recently been cleaned and tidied. Karolina had certainly been doing what she was hired for, but she was also a friend, and it was unusual for her to miss Abigale's homecoming. 'Hello?' Abigale called. 'You here, sweetheart?' Silence remained, and Abigale made her way across the living room to the large black console on the wall. It lit up as she approached, activating and welcoming her in its friendly female voice. 'Hi, Maria,' Abigale replied. 'Any messages?'

'*Hannah went to Gliese 581g this morning,*' the computer informed her. '*She is due home at midnight.*'

Noting that Karolina was not mentioned, Abigale felt a shiver run through her. 'Who did she go with?'

There was a moment of silence, as the computer seemed to struggle with the answer, before responding, '*That information is unavailable.*'

'Unavailable?' Abigale was not convinced. 'Are you telling me that not one of your twenty-two on-site cameras saw the person she went with?' If the computer had seen this person, they would have been identified instantaneously by way of the Global Mainframe to which every security system available to the military forces was connected. '*That is correct,*' the computer replied.

'Oh, come on, Maria. At a stretch, I'll buy that you couldn't identify the person, but…what…you didn't even *see* them?'

'*That is correct.*'

Abigale stared at the console for a moment, trying to make sense of this. 'Show me security recordings for their time of departure,' she ordered.

'*That information is unavailable,*' the computer repeated. The screen went blank. Now Abigale's suspicions were raised, and she offered her palm to be scanned by the Network activation grid, the military equivalent of the CivilNet. 'Access today's transport itinerary for MEC station Alpha-3, Mars orbit,' she requested. The information was displayed and she said, 'Locate Traveller Saranne, H.'

Scrolling through the list of thousands of people, her daughter's name and destination was displayed and highlighted. A second Traveller was highlighted beneath Hannah's name, but it said simply, "Companion". This was highly unusual, and Abigale tapped the word. The computer buzzed and a monotone voice a lot less pleasant than Maria stated, '*Access to this Traveller denied.*'

'Explain,' she demanded.

'*Level 1 clearance required.*'

'Military?' she mused aloud. The computer buzzed again: '*Access to this Traveller denied.*'

Abigale knew there was only one way to do this. 'Display return itinerary for Traveller Saranne, H.' The information was shown. Whoever this Companion was, they were due to return to station Alpha-3 tonight. With Hannah. Abigale looked at the word "Companion", the chill of fear replaced by the thrill of anger.

29

'Whoever you are,' she told the screen, 'I'll see you at the station. You still there, Maria?'

'*Yes, Abigale. I'm here.*'

'What time did Karolina leave?'

'*She has not left.*'

Abigale's stomach almost turned. She could have simply looked around the house, but instead she said, 'Locate her.'

'*Karolina is in her bedroom.*'

Abigale knew then. She knew what had happened, and for some time she could not bring herself to go upstairs. She knew she should call the police, but there was a chance they would take Hannah into care or Abigale would be forced to resign her command. They would also take over the investigation and Abigale wanted to look this person who had taken her daughter in the eyes before making them pay. Her mind reeling, she climbed the stairs and, passing Hannah's room with heart-wrenching reluctance, she saw Karolina's feet on the bed through the next open door. The girl was only twenty, and she would often stay here when Abigale was on deep space runs. As Abigale pushed back the door, she saw that Karolina was lying face up on the bed, still and silent. There was no sign of struggle or injury, and Abigale toyed with the idea that perhaps she had simply fallen asleep. As furious as she would be with the notion that Karolina had slept through the abduction of her daughter, Abigale still preferred that to…the alternative. Yet neither was the case, for Karolina groaned as Abigale approached the bed. Her voice was little more than a pained whisper as she explained: 'They…took her.'

'Karolina!' Abigale was on the bed and it was clear that the girl had been drugged, paralysed in some way. *They?* Her child was snatched by a team and brought to the MEC station! Could it have been that terrorist group, out to get military personnel? 'Who took her?'

'Don't know,' she whimpered. 'So…fast.' She started to cry, and Abigale stroked her hair soothingly: 'It's okay, Karolina. I'll find her.'

'Please…call…a doctor.'

Abigale stood up from the bed. 'I can't do that. I'm not losing her.' Karolina made a sound indicating that she did not understand, and Abigale explained, 'If I report this, they'll take Hannah. If these people wanted you dead, you would be.'

'But they…drugged me.' She started sobbing.

30

'I know. I'm sorry.' Abigale walked out of the room and closed the door behind her, her heart breaking.

Ω

She was waiting in the Arrivals area of the feeder post serving the Mars MEC station. A shuttle had taken her up through the Shield, where she discreetly boarded an interplanetary freighter with her military clearance and headed for Mars. The civilian vessels emerging from the MEC station would take their passengers – *Travellers*, as they were known in the MEC system – to the closest feeder post, where they would be processed to resume their journey by whatever means they had arranged. The itinerary for Hannah and her mysterious escort failed to mention the intended means of her ongoing journey, but Abigale intended to take her home with her on the next military transport.

The feeder post was relatively quiet, and cleaning bots roamed the floors somewhat aimlessly, as if anticipating the end of their shifts. That or their batteries were running low. Intelligent Marketing targeted Abigale's little corner of the world, the holograms buzzing around her head like ghostly moths of commercialism. The good thing about IM was that one could literally swat them aside; gently to browse the adverts, forcefully to end the show. As soon as Abigale saw Hannah, she was decidedly forceful. The IM ended as she called, 'Hey, Glitterbug!' and headed to intercept her. For the briefest moment, she was sure that Hannah did not recognise her, appearing somewhat disoriented. Then light returned to her eyes and she smiled and shouted, 'Mom!' as she dropped her souvenirs and ran to Abigale. Captain Saranne had her daughter in her arms and the world was immediately better. Beyond Hannah, back at the Arrivals gate, was a morbid scene, four black-garbed men wheeling a covered body on a trolley. Someone must have died somewhere along the route. Then Abigale remembered her reason for coming here and she got to her feet, looking around desperately for what she presumed would be some shady figure. There was no one else in sight, apart from the dark scene of death.

'Hannah...' Abigale asked softly, staring at the passing trolley, 'who took you to Gliese?' Hannah did not reply, and Abigale stared

31

at the covered body suspiciously before asking the men, 'Hey…what happened?'

The response was short and sweet. Well…not sweet: 'Some old bag's heart gave out soon as she stepped out this end.'

Abigale stared at the one who had spoken, a sallow-skinned, unkempt brute whose appearance echoed his vulgarity. 'That *old bag* could be someone's wife…or *mother*!' she snapped as they moved away.

The men laughed as one, and Abigale got the distinct impression that she was outside the joke. A chill ran through her, and she turned back to Hannah, who was gathering her fallen items. 'Who took you, Hannah?' she asked her daughter, more forcefully this time. 'Why did you come back on your own?'

What happened next would long haunt her, and Abigale felt a churning in her stomach as her daughter ignored her and stepped back pointedly. Yet it was not because of the anger in her mother's voice. This was something else entirely. With a smile of ghostly contentment on her face, Hannah stepped back in and took her mother's hand, leading her away from the Arrivals area. Abigale could find no words.

In the distance, next to a military vehicle parked in a restricted area, one of the black-garbed men looked back a final time as they loaded the body into the truck.

THE DOCTOR

GenLab-3 Health Facility, Berlin

The world-renowned geneticist Doctor Ian Romis stood over the body on the table before him as two of his clinical staff prepared to hold it down. Despite the head being securely fixed to the operating table and the body strapped at each appendage, the extra staff knew they would still be required. Romis was ready to operate a laser implement designed to create cavities in the skull, and a tiny white box was on a small shelf protruding from the laser housing. The nurse next to him operated the vacuum, preparing to lift the bone flap which would be secured through suction. Romis flicked a switch on the laser-cutter, and it hummed lightly as the illuminated targeting system was activated and the energy grew in preparation. The crosshairs projected on the shaved skull narrowed as Romis moved the device closer, preferring to do so manually rather than relying on the electronic alternative. The laser emitter descended into position and he fired the invisible beam, filling the room within seconds with the smell of burning ozone. The skull was breached, and the nurse lifted the bone flap, deactivating the vacuum as she transferred it with tongs to a saline-filled dish. As Romis moved the laser housing aside, he used a simple scalpel to cut through the final layer of protection, a filmy membrane clinging to the brain itself. Before he continued, he looked up to the control room, and one of the observing team gave him the confirmation he was looking for over the intercom, *'The field is active, Doctor. The room's secure.'* Romis nodded, then pressed a release catch on the side of the white box. The lid popped open, and the two orderlies strained their necks to see what was inside as the doctor reached in with finger and thumb. He withdrew a minuscule object – a metal disc, black and silver. As he brought it closer to the open skull, he tapped a button on a console beside him. Scores of threadlike tendrils erupted from the disc, immediately shooting towards the heat of the subject brain. The body convulsed with neural shock and the orderlies struggled to hold down the flailing limbs. But the apparent agony of the unconscious subject swiftly subsided, and the probing tendrils of the disc could be seen inside the head, resting into place and connecting with their relative organic positions.

Romis was impressed with himself, and it showed. He looked up at the control room. 'Any reaction out there?' he asked. A woman in a blue suit shook her head. '*Not than I can see,*' she replied over the intercom. '*But if the Kwaios know we have this, they'll find a way of tracing it.*' Romis nodded and returned his focus to the activity of the Jaevisk marker device, before he was interrupted again. '*How's our girl?*' asked a different voice from the control room; a familiar and, at this stage, unwelcome voice. Romis indicated that the subject be turned over before looking up again to see Samuel Vawter: '*She holding up okay, Doctor?*' the man asked. The doctor nodded, glancing back to the vital readings as the orderlies turned the woman onto her back. He leaned over her, seeing her eyeballs moving beneath the lids, REM sleep the only activity they could allow for now. 'She's dreaming, as usual,' Romis reported, unable to keep a thin smile from his face as he looked up again at Vawter and added, 'It's all Cassandra can do these days.'

'*Best way to keep her out of trouble, I'd imagine,*' Vawter agreed.

Ω

Doctor Romis hung his white coat in his locker and closed the door. He took a glass of water from the table in the centre of the room and drained it before collapsing into the welcoming chair. He was tired, hungry, and quite preoccupied when the man in the grey suit entered the room. 'Doctor, it's good to finally meet you face to face,' he said, his hand outstretched towards Romis, who looked up in surprise.

'Sorry, I didn't hear you come in,' Romis replied, shaking the offered hand and feeling something akin to an insect bite as he got slowly to his feet. A rush of blood caused him to sway a bit as he added, 'Ah, Mister...Vawter, isn't it?'

Everyone knew who Samuel Vawter was, and he nodded and smiled knowingly, recognising the need of a narcissist to maintain his own sense of superiority. 'That's right,' he replied. 'I'm one of the chief benefactors of this institution.'

Romis' smile was warm and practiced. 'Of course, yes,' he said. 'I've heard a lot about you.' Romis did not trust these people,

34

throwing their money at situations they hoped would change the world. What was their angle? Of course, his own deviation from medical ethics left him with little ground for self-righteousness. 'I understand there was an accident with one of your vessels,' he continued.

'The *military* consider it an accident, Doctor,' Samuel declared. 'I consider it recklessness. But then who am I to argue with the military?'

'You're the guy who pays their wages.' The words had escaped before Romis had even tasted them in his mouth. To his surprise, Vawter seemed to find this amusing. 'Indeed I am,' he agreed. 'Perhaps workers' rights have finally gone too far.'

'Oh, I think that happened a long time ago, Mister Vawter.' The doctor poured himself another glass of water and offered the same to his visitor, who declined, saying, 'Call me Samuel, please,' as he sat on the low table. With his back to Romis, he continued: 'So, Doctor...did you hear anything else about this...accident?'

Romis returned gratefully to the chair and swallowed the water, his nostrils flaring as he tried to detect in the air any traces of impending danger. 'I heard there were some...fatalities,' he replied carefully, 'but then that's to be expected when you ram a Jaevisk warship, I suppose.' He chuckled ironically. 'An impressive tactic, I thought.'

Samuel did not agree: 'When it comes to my property, Doctor, I prefer to have it treated with a bit more respect.'

'Well, with all *due* respect...Samuel...perhaps you're in the wrong business?' Romis took a black overcoat from the wall and put it on, turning to face his visitor.

'Oh, I don't think so,' Samuel replied, ignoring the attitude as he stood up. 'I'm in the most lucrative business there is – war.'

'Is that why I'm doing all this? Some obscure military goal?'

'Come now, Doctor, you know as well as I do that advancement begins on the battlefield. With the right mind, all of our technology can essentially be used for battle.'

'Were you always such a cynic, Samuel?' Romis pushed past him and walked out of the room, but he stopped when he heard Vawter call to him: 'We're celebrating the tenth anniversary of the first MEC route tomorrow, Doctor. I'd like you to be there.'

Romis turned, but the man had not even followed him. Still in the locker room, he was waiting for an answer, his arrogance total.

Romis had met his match. 'Why would you want *me* there?' he called back.

'Two reasons,' came the reply. 'You're highly respected in your field. The people know this, and they'll listen to you.'

'*Listen* to me?' Romis swallowed his pride and returned to the door, nodding: 'So...reason number two...what do you want me to say to them?'

'I want you to remind them how safe MEC is,' Samuel told him, smiling. 'I want the people of Earth to be assured of a safe journey, whether they're exploring, or vacationing, or...whatever. Young men and women even need to be convinced of the safety of MEC before they'll sign for military service these days.'

Romis could find nothing immediately wrong with this, which made it all the more frustrating. 'Well, I've...never travelled by MEC myself,' he replied, 'but I'm fully aware of its safety record. I can explain that much, but little else.'

Samuel nodded gratefully, knowing full well that this man had not been through MEC. 'Thank you, Doctor,' he said. 'That might just do. If you don't mind me asking, why have you never travelled yourself?'

'Hypocritical terror,' he explained with a grin. 'I'm in the system, like most people, but...I guess it defies my profession. After all, I like to keep people in one piece!'

Samuel found the answer amusing, but not for obvious reasons. 'You should try it sometime. It's quite...' he shrugged, 'extraordinary.'

'That's what worries me.' Romis turned to leave, asking, 'When and where tomorrow?'

'Senate Buildings, about eleven. And there's one more thing, Doctor.'

'Yes?'

'The victims of Captain Saranne's recklessness will be brought here. I want you to attend to them personally. Your findings are to be brought only to me. Is that understood?'

'I'm sure it doesn't need to be...Mister Vawter,' Romis replied. 'Now, if you'll excuse me, I'm going home.' He stalked away and Samuel opened his right hand, reading the display on the dermascreen he had equipped with a nanoneedler. The screen read: *Traveller ID: Ian Romis. MEC Journeys: 0. Mnemonic Profile: Updated.* Looking up to see Romis pushing through a door at the end of the corridor, he sighed in resignation. And perhaps something darker.

Ω

The Shield was fully open for the first time in months, allowing the sun to shine on more than just a selected area of the world. Although the coverage was not, of course, total – with the projection of the open Shield sections blanketing the world in a patchwork of shadow and sun – it was still a welcome change to the prolonged periods of darkness. There was still a lot of opposition to the Shield, and rightly so. The infamous actions of Anev Tesckyn a century ago were sufficient evidence against trusting an alien race with the welfare of humankind. Opposition parties maintained that a giant error in judgement such as the Shield would see the downfall of the Senate, possibly worse. Unfortunately, the opposition parties had no leverage, nothing to convince the people of Earth that life would be better without the Senate. They did not have MEC, the political incentive that had reinvigorated the waning power of the Senate. And it was a truly amazing incentive.

Doctor Ian Romis, highly respected geneticist and covert Senate puppet, tried to estimate the size of the crowd gathered in the main square at the fore of the Senate buildings. It was a futile enterprise. Word had spread across the world of his presence here today, and he found that slightly unnerving. There were plenty of other dignitaries around the world who would have been just as effective in declaring the safety of MEC. Hundreds of millions of people who had travelled by MEC were in perfect health, true testament to its reliability. Doctor Romis was a solitary man – or tried his best to be – and there was something about all this that set his mind racing.

Standing on the balcony of the seventh floor, from where he would make his speech, Romis felt a tsunami of anxiety as an idea struck him. Opposition leaders would not want this. With the arrival of the ultimately disturbing Illeri delegation and their ominously powerful vessel docked inside the Shield, the promises of the Senate were doing little to sway the suspicions of the populous. It was an opportune time for the opposition to incite ideas of political revolution. However, it was not political revolution that worried

37

Romis, for right now he was sure that the heat he felt was the result of a laser-sighted weapon trained on his chest. He then shivered, and there was a tingling in his forehead. He thought he might vomit. Would they want to kill him? There were more than mere suspicions being brought to the fore these days. Rumours of the Senate employing mercenaries for secret missions had reached the ears of the military, and Romis had been unfortunate enough to overhear this distasteful tale. He realised that he wanted no part of all this, and he should never have agreed to make this speech. He simply wanted to do his job, to remain a silent player. The problem, of course, was that he was playing a game that would one day be far from silent. And he feared that he would find himself rolled out of play long before he reached Home.

'Ah, Doctor!' Romis heard the voice but felt compelled to ignore it. Admittedly, he was so preoccupied with imaginings of imminent assassination that he could not tear his gaze from the many vantage points of which a sniper might avail. So many vantage points. Samuel Vawter stepped up beside him and, as the Senate Members filed out onto the long balcony amidst the cheers of the swarm of people below, he whispered to Romis, 'Kindly wake up, Doctor. The Senate will look favourably upon anyone who strengthens their hold on the world.' And there it was, the reason he was here, served with Vawter's derision and a dash of political corruption.

Senator Kai Tzedek approached, offering his hand in a perfunctory gesture of welcome. 'I finally get to meet you face to face, Doctor Romis,' he said, as the handshake dragged Romis across the metaphorical line. There was no going back now. He glanced at Vawter as he noted the similarity in greeting, like some well-honed mantra, appropriate for just such an occasion. Romis felt as if the wolves had been circling for a long time, and that they had just closed in around him, a wall of important people, a select circle of which he was now an honorary member. 'I've been a great admirer of the Senate for a long time,' he lied, sliding into the expectant role with ease and a smile. 'Not everyone in my field gets to meet their ultimate employer.'

'Not everyone is as good at their job as you, Doctor,' Tzedek replied, the compliment dripping venom, its implications beyond measure. 'And...ultimately...everyone in every field works for the Senate. Even those who don't want to...' he winked conspiratorially, 'and some who don't even realise it.' He fixed the doctor with a glare that spoke volumes, as Vawter took the front of the balcony and addressed the masses, his words simultaneously broadcast around the world.

'I realise it,' Romis declared, disturbed by Tzedek's glare.

'And you don't want to.'

'Are you asking me or telling me?' Romis heard it in his own voice, the absence of pretence. He could no longer disguise his feelings, and it was as if this man had found them deep inside him and dragged them out.

'Your personal opinions are irrelevant for as long as you wish them to be, Doctor.'

'Which means?'

'Simple. Keep them to yourself. Do your job. We want the device ready by Saturday.'

'What? What's the rush?'

Tzedek smiled the smile of all conspirators and turned to join his fellow Senators. 'Make us proud, Doctor,' he called back as he heard Vawter announce him to the crowd. A great roar went up, for Vawter had prepared them well, promising a month of free space-travel across the entire MEC network. And here was the man who would assure them of just how great a deal this was: Doctor Ian Romis, highly respected geneticist, and covert Senate puppet. Romis took a deep breath as he added political conspiracy to his repertoire, stepping forward to tell his lies.

Ω

Obscured from the Senate's snipers on a much higher balcony outside their field of cover, Abigale watched through her binoculars and listened as the infamous Doctor Romis began to speak about the safety record of the MEC network. Abigale found herself listening intently despite her reason for being there, for now more than ever she needed to understand fully how this system worked. Too long she had allowed herself to remain in ignorance about MEC, like the rest of the beguiled sheep of planet Earth. Abigale recalled being both fascinated and terrified when she learned that the system required the breaking down of one's body into countless millions of molecules before being transformed into a ball of energy and fired across the galaxy, only to be put back

39

together by the station at the other end of one's journey – and somehow with your clothes still on! Ten years later, the safety record of the system spoke for itself. Not one person had died from MEC travel. Still, there were some three billion people on Earth who had yet to use it. These were either the people who were afraid of it, or simply could not afford it. Being in the military, Abigale had no choice but to use it for operational purposes, and the matter of cost never entered the equation. Even her off-duty travel was free. Vawter's offer of a month's free MEC use was about to change everything.

The audio system enhanced Romis' voice to great effect, but Abigale had stopped listening, for something else had caught her eye through the high-powered lenses. On the balcony where Romis and the Senate stood, the owner of the Argo, Samuel Vawter, appeared to whisper something in the ear of Senator Kai Tzedek. Tzedek nodded and the two men began to step back inside the building. Abigale saw that Senator Al-Rais had also seen this, but he was too late to react. There was a high-pitched 'zip' sound as the projectile tore through the air from far beyond Abigale's position and way outside the Senate's field of protective cover. Half a second later, the balcony on which the Senate were standing exploded. In the main square below, the crowd erupted in terror. Someone had just attacked the Senate. Their beloved leaders might all be dead. The only way the people would ever recover from this traumatic event was by taking a free trip on the MEC system to remind themselves that the galaxy was a wonderful place.

Ω

Romis opened his eyes, looking up at the harsh lights above him. Momentarily disoriented, he lay where he was until the ringing in his ears ceased and his eyes focused on the ceiling. Bile rose in his throat and he felt the onset of nausea as he forced himself to sit up on the table. He dropped his legs over the side to his left and sat there, looking around. He was in his lab, alone in the silence and sterility of familiar surroundings. 'How did I get here?' he whispered, glancing up to see that no one watched him from the room above.

The beeping of a computer console on the wall startled him, and he hesitated a moment before walking across to it, settling his nerves and steadying his breathing. There was a message waiting to be seen. 'Display message,' he told the computer. The black screen lit up, and the smiling face of Senator Kai Tzedek greeted him as it explained: *'Sorry to leave you alone, Doctor, but we're close to finding the people who tried to kill you. I trust you remember what happened. If not, well...maybe that's for the best. As long as you're well and fit to resume work. You should probably remain in the lab for a few days.'* Tzedek's smile dropped as he warned, *'Don't talk to anyone, Doctor. We're not sure who you should trust.'* The screen went blank.

For a moment akin to hypnosis, Romis stood there staring at the dead monitor. And it stared back. He realised he had no memories that fit with this man's description of events. The last thing he remembered was meeting Samuel Vawter at the end of a long day at work; he remembered shaking hands with him. Someone had tried to *kill* him? But when? Had he still been here? Or on his way home? There were times in one's life when knowing the truth was not necessarily the best option. Romis, however, was a man whose entire life revolved around pushing the boundaries of knowledge and, as such, truth was a temporary and flexible construct. Today's truth was often tomorrow's lie, and Romis needed the truth of what happened today. He just hoped it would remain so tomorrow, because he did not think his nerves could take it. Tapping the screen, he said, 'Access CCI footage for Laboratory A.' The closed-circuit imaging files were displayed in hourly increments and Romis breezed over the timestamps, realising that he had no idea which hourly slot he needed to see. 'Display live feed and reverse at double-time,' he told the computer.

He saw himself standing at the screen, and he turned around to see the camera mounted on the wall behind him. When he looked back, the screen showed him returning to the table upon which he had woken. He watched himself lying there, motionless, and he became impatient. 'Increase speed,' he said. At four times the speed of normal play, the footage raced in reverse, and Romis watched the minutes go by. Still too slow. 'Increase speed,' he said again. And again. And again. The minutes raced by at thirty-two times normal speed, and it took more than five agonising minutes until Romis saw something different. Three hours ago, as he was

41

lying unconscious, someone suddenly appeared next to him and lifted him off the table, the speed of the footage distorting the continuity. 'Pause!' he shouted. On the screen, he saw himself in the arms of two men dressed entirely in black, their faces covered like counter-terrorist operatives. 'Play at normal speed!'

The men carried Romis to the table and set him down, one of them pressing an injector to his neck. His immediate thoughts were for the drug coursing through his veins at that moment, something which had taken three hours to bring him around to full consciousness. 'What did you give me?' he whispered. The men could be seen leaving the room, and Romis wanted to see if they were otherwise alone, if for no other reason than to figure out who 'we' was in the conspiracy to which Tzedek had alluded. 'Access footage for camera...' He looked around the room, locating the one with the best view of the door. 'Number five,' he said. Five looked directly at the door, but when Romis told the computer to resume playback from the same timeframe through that camera, it appeared unwilling to comply. '*File corrupted*,' was as close as it came to an apology. He set about checking the footage from the other cameras, hoping that the men's departure had been picked up by one of them. It was a waste of time, and he ended up finding the nearest chair and sitting down, trying to make sense of things. He pushed the sleeve up on his right arm, and then the left, noticing that there was not a mark upon him. Not a scratch, or any sign of recent surgery. Hadn't he just survived some sort of attempt on his life? Tzedek had said in the recording that someone had tried to kill him. *Him! Doctor Ian Romis!* The thought of it made him vomit, and he hung from his chair as he decorated the once sterile laboratory floor with what should have been the contents of his last meal. Instead, there was only bile and saliva, and he retched until his chest ached, feeling more alone than he had ever been.

This place no longer felt like his workspace. Waking here stunned and confused was bad enough, but then he had been reintroduced to reality by a man he had never before met but who spoke as if they were compatriots in some grand scheme. No, this place now felt like his tomb, and he felt a chill run through him as he thought about going out again into the world. He walked back to the table and climbed up on it, settling into a foetal position to sleep this nightmare away. Hopefully, he would learn the truth by tomorrow, and that he would not be doomed by today's lie.

THE VICTIMS

Senate Buildings, Tokyo

Kai Tzedek was sitting alone at the large table, which looked considerably larger now that there was no one else to occupy the seats. People all over the world were in mourning for the Senate members who had been killed by some evil assassin intent on destroying the democratically supported unity and peace of humankind. Tzedek smiled. It would be some time before elections replaced the dead senators, so there was enough time for Tzedek to do what was required. He had less than a week before it all kicked off, but things were moving along smoothly. When they wrote in the history books the aftermath of what was to happen here, the truth would be somewhat obscured, but Tzedek was confident that his actions would be vindicated. Of course, he was probably going to be the one to dictate to the writers of said history his version of the truth. And that would be sufficient to preserve the legacy he desired.

A wonderful breakfast was laid out in front of him, and Tzedek savoured the fact that this was the first time he had been able to eat such a spread at the Senate table in relative silence. Some peaceful music performed by a little-known orchestra washed over him like a mental massage, and he lost himself to this brief solace as he gazed out of the giant window to his left and bit into a juicy red grape. But like all such times, they were fleeting.

The door opened on the opposite side of the room and his personal secretary entered. She was too old now to arouse him as once she had, but she was excellent at her job, and so he chose not to let her go. Beautiful young women were plentiful in Tzedek's world, but women of elegance and intellect were more difficult to find. 'I specifically asked not to be disturbed, Rachel,' he complained as she approached him. 'Good news or bad, I really wanted some peace this morning.'

Rachel ignored him, well accustomed to his moods and proclivities. As she reached the table, she placed an unusual communication device in the centre, setting it down in the middle of Europe on the enormous map of the world. 'This most definitely couldn't wait, Kai,' she explained.

He loved the way she said his name, but he resented that she felt comfortable enough to use it. Of course, that was his own fault. 'What is it?'

'This is an intra-stellar com receiver,' she told him. 'There's someone asking to speak to Samuel Vawter, but I figured you'd want to intercept the communication...considering...'

He leaned forward, wiping grape juice from his lips with his sleeve. 'You figured right,' he commended her. 'Who is it?'

'It's Kallon Raesa.' She watched his eyebrows raise and she nodded, saying, 'Exactly. The mercenary Vawter sent out to Illeri two years ago.'

'Okay,' said Tzedek, gesturing to the device. 'Let's see what he's been doing out there all this time.'

Rachel nodded and tapped a key on the device. Although a holographic projection was activated, there was no clear visual display, and static interference, both visible and audible, crackled over the speaker for a moment. Rachel gestured for Tzedek to speak, and he did so: 'This is Senator Kai Tzedek. To whom am I speaking?'

'*My name's Kallon Raesa,*' came the crackly reply, with a head taking shape in the light above the device. '*I need to speak with Samuel Vawter. This channel was supposed to be monitored only by Vawter. What's going on?*'

Tzedek smiled and chuckled softly. 'There's no cause for concern, Mister Raesa,' he explained. 'Samuel Vawter and I have an...understanding. I believe you and he agreed upon a certain word to guarantee security.' The mercenary did not reply and Tzedek said, 'Vengeance.'

There was another short silence, until the mercenary was heard again, saying, '*I remember telling him it wasn't the most imaginative code word, but he assured me that –*'

'That it was the most appropriate, yes,' Tzedek interrupted. 'Decidedly Vawter.'

'*Absolutely. So, I guess things are changing quickly back home? I mean, I've only just got here and I can tell you the game's changed big time!*'

Tzedek looked at Rachel and whispered, 'Just *got* here?'

She was equally confused: 'He should at least be on the way *back* by now.'

Tzedek nodded. 'Unless Vawter told him to take the scenic route to avoid detection. He didn't exactly explain himself to me at the time.' He returned his attention to the wavering head in the hologram, and thought for a moment before saying, 'Well, the game is certainly changing rapidly, Mister Raesa, as I'm sure you can imagine. Samuel and I are being…kept on our toes, you might say. He'll be delighted to hear you've been in contact, especially in light of our visit from the Illeri ambassador.'

The head of light was silent for a moment, and Tzedek wondered if the connection had been lost. 'Are you still there, Mister Raesa?' he asked.

'*I'm still here*,' Raesa replied, '*but I'm confused. You say the Illeri ambassador has been at Earth?*'

'Well…yes,' said Tzedek, detecting the concern even amidst the poor quality of the conversation. 'As a matter of fact, he…or it, we're not sure…' he laughed a little, before adding, 'Well, they're still here. They're docked up on the Shield.'

'*Is there some way I could see the ambassador? A recording of his arrival or something like that?*'

It was a strange request, but Tzedek realised instantly that it was a necessary step. 'Of course,' he replied. 'One moment.' He turned to Rachel, asking her, 'What can you get me?'

'There's footage of the ambassador standing right where you are now,' she told him, taking a pocket-sized light pad from her jacket. Tapping some keys, she brought up the recording and set about sending it through the communication device. She nodded to Tzedek, and he said aloud, 'You should be receiving some footage now, Mister Raesa. You'll have to run a decryption.'

The time it took for the file to be received, decrypted and viewed by the mercenary out at the distant planet was agonising for Tzedek, and he absently resumed eating his fresh fruit as he waited, keeping his eyes fixed on the unidentifiable head in the hologram. It seemed that by the time Kallon Raesa eventually watched the footage, he instantly replied, '*I'm pretty sure that's not the Illeri ambassador.*'

Tzedek dropped a blackberry, feeling it hitting his lap but unconcerned as to its onward journey. 'What do you mean? I mean…how do you know? If you just got there…how could you know what their ambassador looks like?'

'You're kidding, right?' said Raesa. *'It's in a biosuit. I'm not exactly looking for a handlebar moustache! Anyway...I wouldn't need to know what their ambassador looks like to know that's not him...or it...or whatever.'*

Tzedek leaned over his breakfast, frustrated by both this guy's attitude and being out of the loop. 'What are you talking about?' he snapped. 'Of course you'd need to know, if you're being asked to identify him!'

'Look...I'm not happy to be telling you this, Senator, considering I'm the one stuck out here and I haven't managed to find a real, live Illeri yet...'

'What? Well, what *have* you found?'

'I'm not exactly sure, but I'll let you know when I am. All I can tell you is that the only Illeri I've seen so far were dead, stuck in what looked like an escape pod, but if they were to wear biosuits, they'd be way smaller than whatever that guy had. The Illeri are only about the size of a big dog...without its legs! So, whatever was in that recording wasn't Illeri, never mind an ambassador. I'd get someone up to that ship pretty quick if I were you. Might be time to scrape some bugs off the Shield!'

Tzedek did not finish his breakfast that morning. It was such a shame because he was really looking forward to the loganberries. At times like these, one needed to keep one's strength up.

Ω

Doctor Romis, on the other hand, had no problem keeping his strength up or keeping his food down, for he felt like a new man today. Which was good, considering what he had to face. Twelve bodies from the Argo incident awaited his ministrations, and his laboratory had been rearranged to accommodate them, laid out as they were in a circular configuration, cold and pale on the tables and posing questions he was now feeling reluctant to ask. 'I don't understand why they want me to look at them first,' he complained as he stood over the closest cadaver. 'The autopsies should have been done before I weighed in.'

Standing on the opposite side of the body, a young man in surgical garb shrugged: 'It's probably just cos they died on one of Vawter's ships. Maybe he's hiding something and he knows we'll keep it under our hats.'

47

Romis looked up from the body, catching the attention of his assistant. 'I'm sure it's nothing like that, Tom,' he stated, pointedly frowning and surreptitiously shaking his head to warn the orderly from making any further statements of a similar nature. Tom looked up at the control room – every room in this facility could be observed in the same way – to see only two female staff busy at their stations. He looked questioningly at the doctor, whose thoughts were tumultuous as he replayed Tzedek's words in his mind: *We're not sure who we can trust.* 'Let's just get on with our work,' Romis told him, forcing a smile. 'I think I remember how to do this.' He took the scalpel from Tom's hand, who got the hint and nodded, saying, 'What exactly are we looking for? I mean, didn't they die when the Argo rammed the Jaevisk ship? It seems so…straightforward to me.'

'You know, Tom…' Romis lowered his voice, 'I'm not exactly sure what we're looking for. On the other hand, I'm *absolutely* sure that it won't be straightforward when we find it!'

Ω

Abigale's hitherto unrestricted movement through the private hospital was being blocked by a woman who might politely be described as…larger than life. 'I'm sorry, Miss,' the Staff Nurse was saying haughtily, 'but Doctor Romis is extremely busy and doesn't exactly see *walk-ins*. You do realise he's not a public physician?'

Abigale glared at the woman. 'I know exactly what he is. And I don't just mean a man who miraculously survived an assassination attempt! Do you know who *I* am?'

The Staff Nurse looked Abigale up and down and shrugged indifferently. 'You're Captain of the Argo. But that hardly means –'

'Actually, it does,' Abigale argued, pushing past the woman and calling back, 'If you don't tell me which room he's in, I'll just start checking every one of them.'

'I'll have you removed before you have a chance!' the large lady promised as she chased after her. 'You don't have clearance for this *building*, never mind a personal consultation with Doctor Romis. He simply *won't* see you!'

Abigale turned back to approach the nurse, taking a breath to calm herself before coming face to face with her. When she spoke, her tone was cold and relentless: 'Doctor Romis is the only person who can help me, and if you don't get him, I'll be forced to…cause trouble.' She gestured downwards and the nurse followed her gaze, seeing the bulge of a gun beneath Abigale's jacket. 'Do you understand?'

There was the sound of someone running towards them and Abigale looked beyond the nurse. 'Got here as soon as I could,' Carenna explained, the dark red waves of her hair still showing signs of a recent wash. She smiled. 'I fired my hairdresser.'

Despite the situation, Abigale could not keep the smile from her face. 'I need you to wait here and watch for anyone taking an interest in me.'

'You got it.' Carenna was also armed, and she opened her jacket to make the weapon more accessible as she gestured with her head towards the nurse: 'She taking you to Romis?'

The nurse turned back from looking at Carenna and she nodded to Abigale with an ironic smile, gesturing down the corridor as she said, 'Right this way, Captain.'

Ω

Tom checked the readings again, shaking his head with confusion as he said, 'It's definitely gone, Doctor. There's no other explanation.'

'That's not possible,' Romis argued. 'Unless he was misdiagnosed.' Romis looked up at the control room, and one of the women acknowledged him as he called out, 'Get me Doctor Sullivan from the European College of Medicine.' He then turned back to Tom. 'Any of the others showing anything like this?'

Tom shook his head. 'Everything else squares with the records. Even the slightest conditions these people had before they went through MEC were still there when the ship came out.'

'Which is exactly how it's supposed to happen,' remarked Romis. 'Put us back the way we were.' He looked up when the woman in the control room called him over the intercom. 'I'll be right up,' he told her. 'Keep an eye on the readings on this one, Tom. Run another full scan. I know you're convinced, but…we might have missed something.'

'Suppose it's possible,' agreed Tom, 'but do you really think the computer would miss something like that? It's pretty significant.'

'Don't put all your faith in computers.' Romis snapped his gloves off and dropped them to the trolley next to the dead man. 'This shouldn't take long.'

Tom watched the doctor ascending the stairs to the control room, and then he looked back at the corpse. 'Where's your tumour gone?' he asked it, activating the scan. The bed rose slightly, and then moved slowly back under the MRI arm, which lit up the bed as it began to study the body. A door burst open on the far side of the room, and Tom turned to see the Staff Nurse from B-Block escorted at gunpoint by a brown-haired woman wearing what appeared to be military clothing. 'This is Captain Saranne of the Argo,' the Staff Nurse explained, with more disdain than fear. 'She wants to see Doctor Romis.'

Tom glanced up to the control room, where Romis and the two women appeared to be engaged in debate. 'I'm sure he'll see you in a minute, Captain,' Tom replied evenly, as the nurse swiftly left the room. 'You're not going to need a gun in here.' He gestured towards the bodies around the room as he shrewdly, perhaps cruelly, declared, 'These people are already at your mercy.'

Abigale locked the door behind her, lowering her gun as she approached the closest body and then drew back the sheet covering it. She gasped with shock, recognising the pallid face. 'These are my crew,' she said softly, before turning to Tom and snapping, 'Why are they here? This is a genetic facility, not a morgue!'

'There's no need to be overly concerned, Captain,' Romis answered as he descended the metal stairs. 'Anyone whose death relates to MEC operations has to be examined at a genetic level.'

Tom looked up at Romis, confused by his change in attitude. Only minutes ago, they had wondered the same thing, and with no one having ever died from MEC, protocol was something of a mystery to medical professionals. Romis flicked him a glance of further warning, and Tom felt a chill engulf him as he looked back at the intruder, asking her, 'Is that why you're here? You're looking for an explanation?'

Abigale raised her gun, feeling her emotions getting the better of her. 'Don't try me, kid,' she warned the young man. 'I had no idea the bodies had been brought here.' She turned to Romis as he reached the floor, and she said, 'I'm here to see *you*, Doctor.'

Romis grinned strangely as he replied, 'You only had to ask, Captain. After all, I do *work* for the military establishment.'

'Oh, right…you're at my disposal, is that it?'

'Something like that.' He found himself confused by her attitude, almost as if she saw him as the enemy.

'It's nothing like that, Doctor, and you know it.' She stared at him for a moment, before realising that the two women in the control room above were contacting someone for help. She fired three shots up at the glass, and the two women screamed, protecting their heads as the glass exploded and fell crashing to the laboratory floor.

Romis lunged instinctively at Abigale, surprising himself as much as her by grabbing her arm and shouting, 'What are you *doing*?'

She could have fought him off. She could easily have escaped his grip, but she saw something in his eyes that made her hesitate. He appeared…haunted, confused. She had seen that look very recently. 'I'm…I'm sorry,' she said. 'I didn't know who else to turn to.'

Tom watched on as Romis calmly lowered her shooting arm and said, 'I don't understand, Captain. Apart from the recently deceased here, I'm not aware of any connection between us.'

She held his troubled gaze for a moment before saying, 'MEC, Doctor. MEC and Samuel Vawter.'

'What's going on, Doc?' Tom asked him. 'What's she talking about?'

Romis said nothing, and Abigale continued: 'I saw what happened to you yesterday. Hell knows how you survived! I was watching when the balcony exploded.'

'So was the rest of the world,' Tom put in. 'What makes your perspective so special?'

Abigale was finding it difficult to ignore the young assistant, but she remained fixed on Romis. She could see his concern, his fear; and she read in his eyes a considerable lack of perspective on yesterday's events. 'What did you see?' he asked her. 'What happened?'

Abigale looked around the room. The women in the control room had not moved from their huddled fear, and apart from Tom, there was no one else to hear what she had to say. And yet the cameras high on the walls still rolled as she said, 'I saw them stepping back, Doctor. Tzedek and Vawter.' She looked at Tom and said, 'They invited him up there...and they stepped back.'

Tom was finally silent, and he stared with his mouth open at Abigale and then at Romis, calculating the implications of the conversation. Romis looked around the room, and despite his confusion and the growing fear, he took greater notice of the cameras than Abigale had. 'Not here,' he told her, imagining he could hear booted feet running through the hospital corridors. 'We need to go.'

'I'm not going *anywhere* with you,' Abigale argued, stepping back and raising her gun again. 'You...*stood* up there and defended that system! You've no idea what it's capable of.'

Romis valiantly raised his hand, saying, 'Look, I don't know what happened, okay? I don't even remember being there! But if you don't get to the point soon, you'll be discussing it with Vawter.'

'What happened to you?' Tom asked Abigale. 'That's why you're here, right?'

Abigale nodded, tears coming as she explained: 'My daughter went through MEC without me. We had a trip scheduled, but...someone else took her. The network wouldn't identify the person, but...there was someone else. And when she came back...'

Tom and Romis were hanging on every word, and they had little to say as she finished, 'She didn't know who I was.' She stared at them, desperate for an answer. Anything. 'She didn't *recognise* me,' she pressed. 'It was like she was in a trance until I spoke to her. I...can't explain it, but...it scared me. And now she seems...different, like...like she's not really my little girl.'

The MRI arm had just finished its scan of the dead man, almost on cue. Tom and Romis exchanged glances of concern, conscious not to glance across at the silent corpse now looming in the background like a signpost. Abigale could see that they knew something, but any further discussion was interrupted by banging on the door as someone shouted, 'Open this door immediately!'

Romis glanced up at the two women in the control room, noting that they had remained huddled since the explosion of glass and they had probably not been paying attention to anything which had been said. At least, he hoped not. Abigale stepped up to him and offered her gun, saying, 'Please help me figure this out, Doctor.'

52

He looked into her eyes, seeing there the same frustration he had felt since waking yesterday in this very room. 'I'll do what I can,' he promised, gesturing to Tom as he said, 'Get up there and delete the records for patient twelve. And any evidence of my conversation with his doctor.'

Tom nodded and set about erasing the evidence, unsure as to why but sufficiently engrossed by the intrigue to comply. The door burst in, and Hospital Security swiftly escorted Abigale from the laboratory, grabbing her gun from Romis. Outside the room, she saw Carenna struggling in the grip of two uniformed security guards, but it was not Carenna who caught her attention the most. It was Samuel Vawter, standing to one side, observing everything. Their eyes met, and a thin smile lifted the corners of his mouth. But as Abigale was dragged past him, she thought she saw in his eyes a haunted look which had only recently become familiar.

THE WARLORD

It's late at night when I think of death; in the darkness, the silence...when I can hear my breath. To sleep's embrace, perchance then to die, yet through my fears have wandered I. And seeing there the carriage-worn path of that poet's journey in her musings' wrath, I spied the flicker of life's weak flame as it struggled 'gainst the bellows of mortality's reign. Beyond the hallowed ground of despair, the absence of senses awaited me there. But I laughed in disdain and delivered my scorn, for I had set face to a life reborn. So, pour out the fuel running dry 'pon the ground. No use I for light in this new dark I've found.

Extract from Samuel Vawter's diary

GenLab-3 Health Facility, Berlin

After watching Captain Saranne being taken away, Vawter decided to make a quick detour to the laboratory annex. He would speak with both Romis and Saranne in due course, but he did not want to pass up this opportunity to see the clone without being disturbed. He closed the door behind him and stood inside the small room, simply staring. The clinical environment was silently hallowed, the harsh white light illuminating the body akin to a ray of sunlight permitted to pass through the protecting embrace of the Shield. To look upon her was fairy-tale, but to touch her was something different. And Vawter had yet to do so.

In life she must have been beautiful indeed. But this was not life. Here she lay, eyes open but unseeing, her chest rising and falling as the machine allowed, her very being determined by his technology. Vawter dared himself to touch her face as he imagined how the original Cassandra must have looked when she smiled. Feeling the chill of her pallid flesh, he snapped his hand back as that same chill crept through him, instantly regretting the contact. The chill was that of death, of nothingness, a terror chill that oftentimes enveloped Vawter, dragging him down with the lethargy of fear and hopelessness. His heart pounded, and he hated his awareness of its ephemeral nature. For one day he would feel it beat its last...before feeling nothing ever again.

Death Anxiety, they called it. Knowing it had a name gave it power, and life, validating it as something distinct from his paranoia; at the same time as its independence relieved him of any accountability to introspection. Knowing that others must suffer with it also did little to alleviate its hold on him. As a boy, conditioned by stories of a higher power observing all and sundry, such thoughts, ideas and terrors evoked by an inevitable end had never even occurred to him. They had never crept into his unsuspecting mind, eating away at his love of life, no matter how unfair or lacking in promise that life may have seemed. For it was life that he enjoyed and cherished more than anything else. This was a statement that to most seemed so obvious as to be unworthy of analysis, as people continued with their daily chores and routines, seemingly oblivious to the fact that one day it would all end. And they would know nothing about it.

Recently – although he would have been unable to pinpoint how recently, if asked – Vawter found himself more and more despising people like that, for surely they took life for granted, running around like ants at society's whim, while people like him spent their time breathing the fresh air, taking in their surroundings, appreciating the world. Of course, his wealth and power allowed him such indulgence. Perhaps, though – and this was where the irony was paramount – he was jealous of those ignorant of death, of those who turned to whichever concept of a higher power was prevalent and popular in their cultural context. These were the people who lived life that little bit more, happily ignorant of the end, loath to dwell on its implications; for they were safe in the belief of an afterlife. While Vawter spent his time in quiet rooms or even amidst breathtaking landscapes thinking one day that he would never again experience such a thing – anything – he mused that he was achieving less than he should have been amidst his self-inflicted depression than those who did not think like him. Even the smallest pleasures were tainted by the ever-present mockery of fleeting contentment.

He rarely socialised. He took little pleasure from listening to the idle chatter of those he thought of as inferior, because deep down, in a place so heavily guarded by his misplaced superiority and his towering, all-consuming ambition, his fear laughed at him. This was a secret place within his soul – another contradiction, another lie – where he was taunted by his own lack of confidence, his own sense of discomfort. In short, but perhaps not so short, Vawter felt that he did not belong. Not just with those whose existence seemed to mock his dreams and goals, but to the world itself, to this time. He had long felt like an outsider – and imagined he must have always felt this way – as if he could not find his peers; as if they had not yet been born. In his dreams, he belonged to tomorrow, always looking to the future. And here, in all its madness and glory, the future mocked him, because he would die there. He would never see it, for the future was always out of reach.

Looking into the open, frozen eyes of the clone on the table, his reflection there was like a sign, an omen. Here was the secret. Here was the future. Here was the end to all his fears. He was so close that he could feel the spectre of Death looking over his shoulder, taunting him with premature departure. For He would not be happy about this. A beeping in his ear interrupted him, but Vawter did not flinch. Tapping the cartilage, he said quietly, 'What is it?'

'We intercepted a communication a few hours ago. Tzedek seems to have been talking to someone out at Illeri.'

'A few *hours* ago?' Vawter noted pointedly.

'Sorry, but it took some time to trace the source. The signal was patched directly through the Illeri star.'

'Sounds like someone knows what they're doing.'

'Exactly. Usually multiplies the return signal and bounces it all over the place. But once the link was made, this was strong and precise.'

'You think Tzedek sent someone out there?'

'If he does, they don't get in touch very often. We've never seen anything like this.'

'So, what are you thinking?'

'The sender might have waited for a specific stellar alignment allowing him to do this, which could imply a schedule of sorts.'

'Far from coincidence, then, considering what's going on.'

'In the extreme, yes.'

'I suppose it's too much to hope you were listening in?'

'Afraid so. It was a selective bi-channel encryption.'

Vawter had to admire the effort. 'Clever,' he commented. 'You recorded it, I trust.'

'We did,' the caller replied. *'You want us to pull it apart? Might be able to reconstruct the conversation, but it'll take time.'*

'What do *you* think?' Vawter replied sarcastically. 'When I meet Tzedek, I want a full sweep of the Senate buildings.'

'I'll put it in place.'

Vawter tapped the earpiece and stared at the clone, until there was a polite knock on the door and a man was heard calling, 'You wanted to speak to Doctor Romis, Mister Vawter?'

'I still do,' he replied. 'Bring him in.'

The door opened behind him and he stepped back from the body, turning to see Romis approaching with two soldiers. Vawter indicated that they should leave as he said, 'You're proving to be more trouble than you're worth, Doctor.'

Romis shook his head and said, 'Oh, I think I'm worth the trouble,' as he passed the table on which the clone lay and he sat on a chair against the wall.

Vawter chuckled. 'Maybe you are,' he agreed, 'but not to everyone.'

'What's that supposed to mean?'

'Let's just take a moment, Doctor, to imagine that you don't know everything. You know…a wild assumption.'

'Point taken,' Romis conceded, secretly trembling with the possibilities implied by what Abigale had said of the incident on the balcony. He wanted desperately to confront Senator Tzedek about what he had seen on the CCI footage, and he was sure Vawter would know the truth, but Romis was more afraid of the truth than he was of the lie. He stood up on uncertain legs and came to the table, standing opposite Vawter as he said, 'But let's also imagine that I know more than I'm comfortable with. I'm not a fool, and I'd like the opportunity to make my own decisions regarding my work.'

'I'm not so sure that's a good idea, Doctor.'

'Why…because you think I'll say no?'

'The thought had crossed my mind.'

Romis reached out and closed the eyes of the clone. 'A hundred years ago,' he said, 'the choices this woman made led to the abduction of millions. Everything changed because of her. We've no idea what was going on in her head, but we're tampering with it nonetheless. I think it's the wrong call.'

Vawter nodded, acknowledging without caring: 'We still don't know exactly what happened, Doctor. And we don't really know that she was responsible.'

'So, you need me to figure it out?'

'We need to know what she was capable of. The Jaevisk implant was said to have been the cause of psychic abilities, although we've no idea what Cassandra could actually do. After

57

those people were taken by the Cage, the Church fell apart and they couldn't find anyone left who had one of those things in their head. They had no connection left to what happened.'

'Except for Echad's son,' Romis reminded him, 'who disappeared amidst some Garran-filled conspiracy theories.'

'I heard the stories,' Vawter replied, keeping his gaze fixed on the clone. 'But now this…thing…is our only way of discovering the truth. This is the key.'

Romis was not particularly fond of the language being used. 'The way I understand it,' he said, 'this…*thing*…is as much a human being as you and me.'

'Then I suggest you alter your understanding,' Vawter corrected him. He pointed at Cassandra's clone, saying, 'This is a tool…a means to an end. We need answers, and this is the way to find them. Only now with the Senate in control have we the freedom to work with clones.' He grinned, looking across to Romis, and adding, 'Not that that would have stopped us, of course, but…anyway, yes, Doctor…you are worth a little trouble. I've no problem admitting that. As a matter of fact, you have my word that you can have anything you want once this project is completed.'

'Now why does that sound like a bribe?'

'Because that's exactly what it is. If it makes you more comfortable, Doctor, you could treat this as a personal favour.'

Romis laughed, practically sneering: 'That's supposed to make me feel *more* comfortable?'

'Set your personal feelings aside, Doctor.' His tone changed as he moved around closer to Romis, adding, 'And stop digging. You're not being paid to investigate military protocol or patient records.' Romis considered lying, but it was pointless and Vawter smiled. 'You didn't really think that just deleting from this end would hide what you were doing?'

'I suppose not,' said Romis. 'But with the captain of the Argo snooping around, things are getting complicated fast. She knew nothing about her people being brought here.'

'And she'll be back out of the picture once the Argo is seaworthy again. Don't worry about her. Anyway, I've heard she's had a little trouble of her own and I'm going to deal with it personally.'

'I'm sure you are.'

'Your blunt scalpel approach is refreshing, Doctor. I'm sick of people pussyfooting around me. Say what's on your mind before you explode.'

Romis decided he would. Some of it, anyway: 'Patient twelve had a tumour removed by the MEC system!'

Vawter stared at him for a moment. 'That's impossible. And ridiculous.'

'Not according to Doctor Sullivan's records.'

'So that's why you contacted him,' Vawter said, nodding.

'Yes. That man had a cancerous tumour going into MEC. Now, whether he didn't want to get tied up in the relentless bureaucracy of health insurance or he just didn't have time to report it, his record hadn't been updated, so the system wouldn't have been aware of it.'

'But that's no reason for it not to put it back in the right place.' Vawter had to remain focused on the lie to get to the truth. 'I presume you were going with Doctor Sullivan's pre-MEC diagnosis…which you rechecked?'

Romis nodded. 'And I ran another MRI. It's gone.'

'And what was the…prognosis?'

The doctor shrugged. 'It was malign, if that's what you mean. Look, there's no point clutching at straws. It didn't just heal itself. He went in with a tumour and came out without it.'

'Ironic that he had to die anyway,' Vawter remarked. 'Any insight about their position on the ship?'

'I thought I wasn't to interfere in military procedures.'

'You answer questions, Doctor. Leave the speculation to me.'

'Sure.' Romis walked across to a monitor on the wall and tapped in his access codes as he explained: 'In most cases, we can tell where people were before the ship entered the MEC.'

Vawter joined him at the screen. 'Radiation signatures,' he said.

'That's one way, yes.' He pointed to the screen, where statistics and anatomy charts were displayed, saying, 'And three people who died in the forward sections of the Argo are lying in my lab with signatures consistent with the engine room.'

'How's that possible?' asked Vawter. He thought for a moment, before saying, 'Saranne said she ordered everyone back from the forward sections. She was adamant that no one had been at the prow of the ship. Any possibility that radiation from the engine would retain these levels if engine room staff just went up front last minute?'

Romis shrugged. 'I suppose it's possible, which brings us to sedation protocols being overlooked. There's no trace of the sedative in their bloodstream. There's always residual evidence, and in very precise quantities.'

Vawter nodded. 'Captain's orders are always submitted to the MEC system, along with rosters, assignments. It knows where everyone should be, and it's supposed to return them exactly as it found them.'

'Well...where they should be and where they actually are...' said Romis, 'may be very different things if sedation protocols are ignored.'

'Ignored...or avoided?' Vawter wondered.

Romis stared at the monitor for a moment, before turning to Vawter. 'You think they did it on purpose? Thrill-seekers skipping the hypo just to figure out what happens if they stay awake?'

'Why not? Either that or the Argo's medical staff can't do their jobs properly.'

'But you're not buying that one,' Romis noted.

Vawter shook his head. 'There's something strange about this. Are you positive that the radiation signatures place them on different parts of the ship?'

'Your theory of running up front's worth considering, but...'

'But you're not buying that one.'

Romis grinned. 'No, I'm not. But you won't like what I'm thinking, especially after your *free travel* speech the other day.' His expression changed as he launched his first probe: 'Which nearly got me killed!'

Vawter held his gaze, nothing to add on the matter. 'Nearly,' he agreed. 'Go on.'

Romis stared, and seeing there was nothing coming, he changed course: 'I think the MEC system gathered them up...*because* they were awake!'

Vawter laughed. 'Gathered them *up*? You make it sound like it's *alive*!'

Romis was not impressed by the response, and his anger forced him onwards. 'I just answer the questions, remember? *You're* the one who speculates!'

'I'm not enjoying your tone right now, Romis.' Vawter's voice was cold.

'That's *Doctor* Romis…*Mister* Vawter. Now, whether you like it or not, the evidence shows that those people were awake…in their prescribed stations…going into the MEC system. And, for some reason, they materialised in exactly the place that Captain Saranne had ordered to be evacuated.'

Vawter ignored the attitude now, and just focused on the information, more than a little disturbed by the possibility. A person going into MEC and never coming out was not exactly Marketing Gold. But this…this was something different. Something worse. 'What you're suggesting is…dangerous, Doctor, to say the least. That the system deliberately put them in harm's way? Why would it do that?'

'Who wrote the sedation protocols?' Romis countered.

Vawter felt a tightening in his chest, as if the meddlesome doctor had reached in and gripped his heart. Not something a hypochondriac enjoyed. Romis noticed the change in Vawter's expression, the reddening of his cheeks, and Vawter noticed him noticing. Despite the lightness in his head, he stepped up to the doctor, whose courage rapidly waned. 'Now, you listen to me,' Vawter hissed. 'You work for us, and the extent of your value has been made very clear. I wouldn't want to taint it by measuring it against your expendability. So, your speculation ends here, as does any further discussion on this matter. I'll arrange a temporary shutdown on all civilian transit through MEC. The military will, of course, need to continue using it, so…' He shrugged and stepped back, looking at Romis, then the monitor, and then the clone, before turning to head for the door.

'So they'll have to take their chances,' Romis finished for him, shaken but not completely unmanned.

'Get back to work, Doctor,' Vawter called back. 'And no more conspiring.' Vawter closed the door behind him and stood in the corridor for a short time, looking around and gathering himself, his head spinning. MEC was the success story of the century and, coupled with the Shield, it was the linchpin of Tzedek and Vawter's control of Earth. If people began thinking that the system was taking on a life of its own, the senator would be furious. In light of what he had just done to take power for himself, that fury was not to be underestimated. Vawter, however, was no ordinary man and was in possession of no ordinary resources. As a result, he cared little for what Senator Tzedek thought. What bothered him was that Romis' suspicions were dancing around the truth, and the only way Vawter could find out what caused them would be to speak with his associates. But what would he say to them? *Sorry, but I'm not happy with the service you're providing.* He shook his head. *I think your technology just killed some people.* They would not even flinch. If he could identify their laughter amidst the noise of their language, his ears would probably bleed. Of course, there were other things to deal with before he rushed off to call the Customer Complaints department.

The corridor was still busy with its traffic of humanity. Returned now to the civilian area of the facility, Vawter wondered what he was about to hear. Captain Saranne was reputed to be a level-headed member of the military, so her recent behaviour suggested that something had very much disturbed her. Either Romis had ignored what she had to say or he had decided to keep it to himself, and his staff were covering for him – Vawter would find out. The two soldiers guarding the door did not salute him, nor would he expect them to. All he did was fund their weapons research, and he had little inclination to risk his life fighting alongside them. As he walked past them, he could feel their side-stares and sense their hostility. It was something he was accustomed to, a part of his life that had been written in stone since he made his first profit from a military enterprise. It was both the definition and the bane of his vocation.

The private room was silent but for the breath-like humming of the machinery next to the bed on which lay Abigale Saranne. Her head to one side, she was facing away from her visitor, gazing dreamily out the window. 'Captain?' he gently called to her. 'How are you feeling?'

The effort of turning her head to him suggested that it was made of lead, and her left cheek sunk into the pillow as she saw him there. 'What have you done to me?' she breathed, exhausted and full of grief. Tears escaped onto the white linen.

'You've just been mildly sedated, Captain, that's all,' he replied. 'It's for your own protection. I understand that you're upset about the losses on your ship, but –'

'That's not...it,' she interrupted. 'My...daughter.' Her eyes closed as fatigue swamped her. Vawter watched her for a moment, noticing for the first time how attractive she was, how peaceful and heavenly her sleeping face appeared. Something reached up to him from inside, a memory of passion, of love…of loss. He forced it back into its cage, throwing the key far into the icy past, where it belonged. His head began to ache. Pressing a button on the wall next to the bed, he waited until one of the soldiers stepped into the room. 'Bring Captain Saranne's daughter here,' he told him. 'Empty the room next to this one and have it disconnected from the Grid.' The man looked at Vawter, and then beyond him to Abigale, his feelings clear. This woman was one of their own. 'Don't send soldiers to pick her up,' Vawter continued. 'We don't want to frighten her. Tell her she's going to see her mother, that she's been sick…and she's gonna be fine.'

The soldier nodded, his expression softening. 'I'll arrange for a friend of the family to bring them,' he replied.

Vawter gave a brief smile and turned away. Remembering something, always thinking ahead, he turned back before the door was closed. 'Wait!' he called. 'Contact the Argo's doctor. The girl should know him. She'll be comfortable with him.'

If the soldier had known of an ulterior motive, he would not have smiled and nodded again. The door closed and Vawter looked back at the patient, before saying, 'And so will you.'

Ω

Hannah was subdued as the Argo's doctor, Kyle Ganna, led her down the corridor. She was an inverted reflection of his mood, however, as his mind raced and his heart pounded as he struggled to make sense of the situation. The last time he had spoken with Captain Saranne, the crew of the Argo were preparing for MEC transport. He should have spoken to her since then, but everything went downhill very quickly after that. Twelve people had died during the fight with the Jaevisk, and now the captain had apparently gone mad, blaming the military institution and its medical subsidiaries for that terrible loss.

Ganna had no explanation as to why the crew members were in the forward sections of the ship, and had not been permitted access to the post-mortem investigation. What cheered him somewhat was the fact that Abigale's madness had resulted in her waving a gun in the face of Ian Romis. Ganna had never liked the

63

man. Far too interested in the outer realms of medicine for Ganna's taste, Romis had done everything in his questionable power to acquire the post of Chief Geneticist under the covert guise of military operations. He was a man obsessed with the future of medicine, all too prepared to sacrifice the ethics of the present. Ganna, on the other hand, wished for nothing more than to save lives and follow the codes and oaths he held dear. Which was why the deaths on the Argo left him feeling decidedly disturbed.

Outside the guarded room, a tall man in a suit of dark grey smiled warmly as Ganna approached. 'Doctor, thank you so much for taking the time,' he said, as Ganna's hand was taken and shaken without his permission. 'I know you're all on shore leave and enjoying the fresh air, but...' he shrugged.

Ganna forced a smile, knowing who this man was and what he represented. As he spoke, he could see in Vawter's eyes that his resentment had registered. More than that, though, he realised that he had been brought here for more than the welfare of the girl. 'I'm happy to do whatever I can for Captain Saranne, Mister Vawter,' he declared. 'Anyway, whenever I come home, I'm berated at length for staying away so long, which tends to take away from the whole "Welcome Home" experience.'

'I imagine it would,' remarked Vawter, thinking only of how ungrateful this man must be to dismiss the comfort of having someone to come home to. 'So, you've heard what happened?' His head gestured towards the private room.

'I heard she blames your organisation for the dead crewmen.'

'You flatter me, Doctor,' said Vawter, grinning ironically. '*My* organisation?' He laughed, playing with the man. 'I'm no more than a piece of the puzzle, a wheel in the machine. Still, I've chosen to take control of this matter personally, so I'm sure that makes you feel a lot more comfortable.' Ganna found himself nodding, and Vawter took his smile down to Hannah to speak to her. But the smile faded as he found the girl staring at him with a strange expression of familiarity. He felt a shiver run through him as she remained silent with eyes fixed upon him. Then she blinked, and Ganna was convinced that she had just snapped out of some kind of hypnosis as she looked up from Vawter to him and asked, 'Can I see her now?'

He nodded, his suspicious gaze fixing on Vawter as the grey-clad man rose to stand again and said, with no little unease, 'Ah...yes...of course you can,' as he opened the door. The doctor was about to accompany the girl as they stepped forward, but the guards blocked Ganna's way. Hannah, who did not even notice this exchange, ran to her mother's side, while Ganna asked Vawter, 'I take it you need to speak with me?'

'You learn fast, Doctor.' Vawter turned, and the soldiers escorted Ganna behind him. As they entered the adjacent room, someone crossed the corridor behind them, slipping stealthily into Abigale's room and closing the door quietly behind him. Inside the room, Hannah turned, expecting Ganna. 'Who are you?' she asked. 'Where's the doctor gone?'

'I'm a doctor, too,' Romis told her. 'I'm here to help your mother.'

'To get better?'

'No,' he replied, shaking his head. 'To get out of here.'

Ω

Abigale was still affected by the sedative, and she could only keep her eyes open for a short time before drifting back towards her dreadful slumber. The guards had not yet been replaced, a convenient and, Romis thought, suspicious oversight on Vawter's part. Hannah struggled to hold her mother upright in the wheelchair with one hand as she pushed it with the other while Romis led the way, heroically keeping an eye out for observers. Medical staff passed them, throwing cursory glances for the most part as they continued their routine activities. Those who did show any significant interest were persuaded by the presence of the eminent Doctor Romis and the smiling girl that all was well, and so subsequently ignored them, logging the scene in the back of their memory for future and likely third-party scrutiny.

'What's happening?' Abigale groaned as she woke again.

Romis turned back to her as they hurried out of the building. 'I'm getting you out of here. I think there's someone that can help. But I need to get you somewhere where I can examine Hannah first.'

'Why?' Her lethargy practically evaporated. 'What's wrong with her?'

'I can't be sure yet, but one thing I do know…there's something wrong with *me*.'

'What do you mean?' asked Abigale. 'Are you sick?'

'No…but that's the problem.' A large white vehicle was waiting for them, and Tom was inside, beckoning for them to hurry. He opened the rear doors and extended a ramp for the wheelchair. Romis pushed it up the ramp, and they could hear shouting from behind them. Without turning to look back, because he was better not knowing that a score of soldiers had been mobilised to stop them, Romis bundled Hannah into the back of the ambulance with her mother and shouted, 'Secure the chair,' before running around to the front to get in. Tom started the engine and manoeuvred the ambulance to the maglev concourse as a hail of bullets struck the armoured exterior. The on-board computer requested a route number and Tom replied, 'Eight,' directing the concourse systems to select the maglev track which would take them out of the city and connect the vehicle's EM link to the correct frequency. The invisible 'routes' ran underneath the superstructure of the maglev network, and these concourses were like way-stations placed at major city destinations. The driver selected a route initially based on major thoroughfares, but the frequency could be readjusted along the way to reach specific destinations. As the bullets continued to hit the vehicle, which was well equipped for urban operations, Romis was sure that he had never felt more alive. Which was ironic.

$$\Omega$$

Ganna was seated in the centre of the empty room. 'I can't imagine what you hope to achieve from this…interrogation, if that's what it is.'

Vawter shook his head, walking around the doctor, who refused pointedly to concede to the intimidation tactic. 'Call it a meeting of minds, Doctor,' said Vawter. 'There are questions to be answered, mysteries to be solved. Life is all about the pursuit of truth and the discovery of lies.'

'I thought for people like you, life was about power,' Ganna argued. 'You thrive on war and death. You design it.'

'No, I simply fund it. Would you leave the welfare of humanity to politicians and...*senators*,' he hissed the word, 'when all *they* see of war and death are the after-action stats?'

'The welfare of humanity is in the hands of people like Captain Saranne, decent people who would gladly die for this world.'

Vawter was silent for a moment, and he moved slowly around to stand in front of the man, hunkering down as if conversing with a child. 'Would *you* die for this world, Doctor?'

Ganna thought for a moment, his thoughts twisting and turning like a knotted lace of information. Where was this going? 'Yes, I would,' he declared, sitting up straight and proud, 'but I would rather save lives than sacrifice them.'

Vawter leaned closer, resting his hands on Ganna's knees, an intimate gesture that served to erode his resolve as he leaned back with distaste. 'You know, Doctor,' Vawter whispered, his face so close that Ganna could smell his musk, 'I envy you.' He rose then, leaving a bewildered man in his chair. 'What?' asked Ganna.

'I do...truly,' Vawter replied. His tone was genuine, the words full of sentiment. 'I envy you your courage that you'd give your life to preserve the freedom and the power of humanity. And as such I envy that of Abigale Saranne.'

'But you have her sedated in there, guarded by your soldiers.'

'Things are not always what they seem, Doctor. For one, they're not my soldiers. I don't have soldiers, only people who seek to share a world I'm destined to control.'

'Forgive my candour, Mister Vawter, but now you sound a little insane.'

Vawter grinned and shrugged, saying, 'The bane of the ambitious. What would you say if I told you that something unbelievable is going to happen very soon? That here...on this planet...nothing will ever be the same again?'

'I'll stick with insanity if you don't mind.'

'It must be a requirement in your profession, this lack of foresight for the consequences of being so blunt. My new friend Romis has already been warned to keep his thoughts in check.'

'Romis is a pompous fool.'

'You know him?'

'We graduated together. He was a friend...for a while.'

'Until his ambitions made you part company?'

'Something like that.'

'Ambition will do that.' Vawter went to the door and opened it slightly, clearly curious as to the cause of the noise outside. There was shouting, and Ganna was certain he could hear distant gunshots. The door was closed again and Vawter said, 'It's all about to change, Doctor. Now, tell me one thing. When you oversee the sedation process on the Argo, would you know if someone didn't get their hypo?'

Ganna shrugged. 'I don't personally monitor every single hypo,' he explained. 'I oversee the process, yes, but the duties are passed to the MEC Officer in each section. And on top of that, as well you know…the Argo has a lot of auto-delivery systems.'

Vawter nodded. 'Okay…but with the right friends amongst the medical staff…the crew could be left to their own devices with the hypo? They could choose not to take it?'

'Why would they do something like that? There's no telling what could happen to them. It's potentially lethal!'

'Oh, it *was* lethal, Doctor, but it was exactly because there's no telling what could happen that they did it.'

Ganna shook his head. 'I don't believe that. I knew some of them well. They were level-headed people, not some thrill-seeking adolescents.'

'Perhaps they were merely curious. Haven't you ever wondered what happens out there…how MEC works?'

'Of course, but I wouldn't risk my life to find out.'

'Really? You'd gladly give your life to protect the planet, but when this mysterious technology promises to take you apart and put you back together…you leave it all to chance?'

'It's not threatening to kill me.'

'That may not be the case anymore, Doctor. I want you to help Romis discover the truth. They'll be leaving soon.'

'*They*?'

'Your shipmates, Doctor. I've had a change of heart.' He opened the door and stepped aside.

Ganna looked at him for a moment, clearly confused. 'Whose side are you on?'

'*Side*?' Vawter smiled. 'I'm on *my* side, Doctor. And considering you serve on *my* ship, that also puts you on my side.'

'I guess things really aren't what they seem,' remarked Ganna as he went for the door. Soldiers were running towards the room, and they ignored Ganna as he left, pushing past him to get to

Vawter. He looked back in, seeing and hearing Vawter issuing them with orders. These were not even his men, and he caught Ganna's eyes as they hurried back out of the room to do his bidding. There was a sparkle of amusement and mischief there, and Vawter gave the slightest grin to strengthen Ganna's suspicions. And to confuse him even more.

Ω

There was no time to find a private location. He needed some answers before proceeding any further. As the soldiers left the room, Vawter kicked the door shut, and turned to lean back against it. He took the black cube out of his pocket and stood with it in his right hand. It grew cold in his grip, and he felt his head lighten, a breeze of ethereal release lifting the tension from his mind, easing his throbbing veins and caressing his temples. His vision blurred, and the hospital room became as insubstantial as a melting oil-painting, its definition dissolving, leaking away to drown him in its vanishing colours and lines. From behind, beneath and inside this dying reality, the Kwaios communication room emerged, coming into focus as if it had always been there, waiting for someone to glimpse clues of its existence behind the real world.

'Your request for communication is ahead of schedule,' a monstrous voice accused him.

Vawter flinched, gritting his teeth as he said, 'I realise that.' He struggled to keep the anger and sarcasm from his voice, for he could ill afford to anger them at this stage of the proceedings. 'But I have a problem.'

'We are not interested in your misgivings or ineptitude. We have guaranteed our part of the deal. You must do the same or face the consequences.'

He did not want to dwell on the specifics of the consequences. 'Well, someone is interfering in my part. And I think there may be a problem with the MEC system.'

'The system is flawless. Any undesired consequence on your part should not be considered accidental. Tell us of this interference.'

Vawter's mind reeled. 'One thing at a time,' he argued. 'Twelve people are dead. They were placed in the wrong area of their vessel, and a collision with a Jaevisk ship killed them. The MEC system put them in danger, against the specific orders and schedules of the ship's manifest. I would consider that a flaw, wouldn't you?'

There was a moment of silence, and the huge figures in the virtual distance were in clear discussion of the matter. Finally, the voice confirmed Vawter's darkest suspicions: 'The incident was not a flaw. Protocol was ignored. This is unacceptable.'

He was stunned. Romis was right. 'You had them killed for staying *awake*?' Vawter shouted.

'This communication must be terminated. Your volatile nature is a liability. You did not choose a private –' The Kwaios stopped talking, and Vawter felt a chill run through him. Something that disturbed the Kwaios was disturbing indeed. 'What's wrong?' he demanded. 'What's happening?'

'We are in danger of being monitored. Explain the interference you spoke of.'

'Someone took the daughter of a military officer through the MEC without authorisation. Now there's something wrong with her, and the officer's beginning to ask questions. There are others who threaten the operation as a result. I need your help in discovering the identity of the people responsible.'

'If you had contacted us from a MEC station, that would have been possible. But now this other party will take extra measures to conceal themselves.'

'I don't understand. Why would they do that?'

'Because they just heard every word you said!' The image vanished, snapping Vawter back to reality as if he had been slapped in the face. He tapped the com device on his ear, and said, 'I want a com sweep of this entire facility. I want to know who's monitoring outgoing and incoming signals.'

'*Already got it*,' came the reply, '*and you're not gonna like it.*'

'Get to the point.'

'*The com on an abandoned construction station inside the Shield just lit up and focused everything on your position.*' Vawter swore, looking at the black cube in his other hand, running through possibilities in his head. 'How close to the Illeri ship is this station?'

'*Too close. You could walk there if you were suited up.*'

'I'm gonna see Tzedek. Call ahead, but not a word about this.'

'*Sure. Do you want anything done about the Illeri ship?*'

'Not yet. Any luck with the message from Illeri?'

'*Not fully, but we think we've identified the caller.*'

'And?'

'*We're pretty sure it's Kallon Raesa.*'

'Who?' Vawter felt a disturbing pain at the peak of his head, as if an acupuncturist had sneaked up behind him and jabbed his crown. There was a short silence, until his contact replied, '*The…mercenary you sent out to Illeri. I know it's been…two years, but…here he is.*'

Vawter felt his head spinning as the words sank in, and there was now a throbbing in his right temple. He had no recollection of sending anyone to Illeri, but his own people clearly thought he had. Tzedek's deception was clearly running far deeper than he had imagined, and Vawter was familiar with the 'work' of Kallon Raesa.

'*Are you still there, sir?*'

'Yes,' he replied, 'I am. I'd…completely forgotten about Raesa. Let me know what else you get from the conversation. I need to know what he told Tzedek.'

'*Sure. And in the meantime?*'

'I've work to do. I want you to put everyone on alert.'

'*Everyone? Is that a good idea?*'

'None of this is a good idea. But we're not turning back now. Tzedek may have already played his hand. It's time I played mine. Oh, and one more thing…'

'*Yes?*'

'Help Romis. He hasn't got a chance without us.'

Ω

Tom looked in the driver side mirror. Three military vehicles were in pursuit, standard crowd-control transports, gaining fast. Luckily, they couldn't risk using their EM-pulse weapons within the maglev system. The consequences would be exponentially disastrous. The maglev system had an upper speed limit for civilian vehicles, but the ambulance was equipped with a protocol override. Unfortunately, it was designed for a trained driver capable of navigating the transitions between the frequencies of the subsurface routes, and Tom was not such a driver. He was beginning to curse his dependence on AutoDrive as the transports bore down on them. The enhanced VR of the mirror gleefully zoomed in on a soldier in the lead vehicle reaching out with an

71

automatic weapon, before a burst of gunfire removed the mirror. Armoured the ambulance may have been, but it would not hold up very long against a sustained assault. If the military managed to bring them to a halt, Romis and Tom would have to surrender rather than risk their deaths and those of Saranne and her daughter.

The maglev surface up ahead opened into a killing zone as the high-rises on either side seemed to step back to allow the authorities do their job, but a dark shadow fell upon the ambulance as they cleared the last pair of flanking buildings, and Romis looked up. 'What the hell is that?' shouted Tom.

'They must have called for help,' said Romis. The ambulance was pummelled by intense weapons' fire from the three chasing vehicles as they spread out in an inverted arrowhead and prepared to flank them with increased speed, and somehow a wayward shot screamed through the vehicle right between Tom and Romis, missing everyone inside as it pierced back and front windows. 'I thought these things were bulletproof!' Romis screamed in panic as Tom struggled with the controls. 'I dunno what's *wrong*!' shouted Tom. 'It must have knocked out the AutoDrive!'

'Then disengage it!' Romis snapped as he looked up at the dark shape descending from above. The system must have been struggling to regain control of itself, but Tom's conflicting attempts to guide the ambulance were making it impossible. 'I can't drive manual!' he said, evidently so as the ambulance swerved wildly again, this time impacting heavily with the left-flanking vehicle and sending it wide of the pursuit. In the back, Hannah screamed as the wheelchair toppled over and Abigale was thrown from it. It was a sleek, shimmering blue craft that bore down upon them from the clouds, and Romis could clearly see the hull weapons turning towards them…and beyond them. It opened fire, powerful cannons blasting gaping holes in the pursuing vehicles. Within seconds, the three military vehicles were incapacitated and burning, and a grappling arm was descending from the vessel. It grabbed the ambulance with an ominous 'clunk' and took it up, returning from where it came.

THE SENATOR

Senate Buildings, Tokyo

Senator Tzedek sat quietly in his chair at the head of the table. Only one other person occupied the room, the only one with whom he could openly communicate. His enigmatic conspirator – his presence here reminding Tzedek of how far over his head things had gone – stood with his back to the table, hands clasped behind him as he looked out over the city. It was almost as if he could see what was happening so far away, where Tzedek's plan appeared to be falling apart despite coming ever more into fruition through the crusade of a reluctantly resurrected geneticist. Tzedek's fellow conspirator wore a black cloak, falling mere millimetres short of the polished floor in which no reflection ensued. He also wore a smile as he turned around and approached the table, and Tzedek watched him with deeply ingrained suspicion, not unlike a new king struggling to accept that his deceased father stood before him, taunting him with his return from the dead, teasing him with the annulment of his control. For control was ever in the hands of this man, hands in which Tzedek was a mere puppet.

The senator watched the shimmering patterns on the black cloak, a dragon on either side, one of gold and one of silver, as the Prophet stopped moving and the cloak did not. The dragons were slithering and clawing, their essence trapped within the silken garb, their motion as subtle and beautiful as Tzedek had once thought this plan to be. But the subtlety was eroding as swiftly and unpredictably as a serpent's strike or the disembowelling swipe of a dragon's talon. 'Look, are you sure this is –'

'How many *times*, Tzedek?' the man snapped, as the dragons snarled. 'If you deviate from my instructions, everything will blow up in your face and you'll be knee deep in the ash. You understand?'

'I'm not comfortable having others make decisions for me.'

'Everyone makes their own decisions, Tzedek. You, Vawter, the Kwaios…everyone.'

'And if those decisions go against your plan…whatever that is…what then?'

Naveen smiled. 'I'm sure you put a jigsaw together when you were a child.'

'Don't *patronise* me! I understand the complexities of a major offensive.'

'Really? Then perhaps a little mental extrapolation is called for, because even if you had to determine the collective futures of everyone on this planet, it would take countless lifetimes for you to prepare for every possible outcome and contingency. For me, it's been considerably easier, but this is about more than just one planet. The galaxy will be affected by what I'm doing.'

Tzedek stared at him for a moment. 'There's not much of a comeback to that, is there?'

Naveen smiled sympathetically. 'I suppose not. But while I can tell you that I've the fate of humanity in my hands, you should rest assured that these hands are very capable. In saying that, don't allow yourself to feel belittled. You need to see that you're an integral part in all this, someone who's truly valuable to the evolution of your species.' He gestured towards the giant windows with one of his very capable hands. 'Out there, billions of people don't know what's happening. They think their day-to-day actions are irrelevant, that their lives are pointless. But you and I know that's not the case. We know that everyone and everything matters when we not only have the box the jigsaw came in – we made it.'

'You're aware that kids stopped playing with jigsaws a long time ago, right?'

Naveen laughed: 'The analogy still works.'

Tzedek nodded. 'So, we're all a means to an end?'

'If you like. But you're still important and I need to know you'll stay the course. I know this thing with Vawter is difficult for you.'

'It feels like I'm deceiving a friend, yes. But if you're as powerful as you say, why do you need any of us to do anything?'

'A good question,' Naveen commended him, 'if a little short-sighted. As far as you're concerned, there are only a few days before all this comes to a conclusion. But this is just another stage, another new beginning. Learn what you can from all this, Tzedek, because there is a great journey happening and all of you on this world are merely passengers. When the journey ends, and this world ceases to be, you won't be here.'

'We'll be wiped out?' Tzedek felt his heart pounding against the edge of the table as he realised he had leaned forward to listen carefully to Naveen. His heart taunted him with mortality.

Naveen shook his head, the slightest of grins bringing a sinister light to his eyes. 'You'll be...*we'll* be...elsewhere,' he replied. There was a knock on the door and Tzedek jumped back as Naveen vanished. He felt the tickling sweat of revelation run down his forehead, and he wiped it away. 'Yes?' he called.

Rachel opened the door and came in, looking around for a moment to locate the man with whom Tzedek had been speaking. 'Vawter is ah...demanding a meeting,' she informed him, her eyes still darting round the room. 'He's on his way.'

'A bit presumptuous, isn't it?' Tzedek regained his composure and rose from his chair, walking up to the centre of the table.

'His people said it was urgent.'

'Did they now?' Tzedek filled a glass with water from the jug on the table and drained it as the secretary waited. 'I'm going to need these...*people* of his located. Then get the Guard to evaluate their defensive capabilities.'

'Yes, sir. Can I get you anything?'

'No.' He rose and glanced at the spot where Naveen had stood, before saying, 'I'm going home to spend some time with my family.'

'But...Vawter...'

'Can wait, Rachel.' As he passed her on his way out, he had a thought and smiled as he said, 'Actually, have the new kitchen girl bring him a meal and a nice bottle of wine. He needs to relax more.'

'The *new* girl? But isn't she...?'

He silently held her gaze and Rachel grinned. 'Good to see the wheels are still turning, Senator,' she remarked. But he ignored her and opened the door, noting with considerable melancholy that her admiration did not excite him as once it had. He was also preoccupied by the realisation that Vawter was on his way here and the opportunity had just arisen to introduce a new asset to the equation. Tzedek's head was spinning with the intricacies of it all. For Naveen must surely have known.

Ω

Vawter patted his mouth with the napkin as the empty plate was lifted from the table. 'More wine, sir?'

He looked up at the young woman, who smiled at him as he nodded. She proceeded to fill the glass as he watched her, his eyes flicking downwards to admire her legs. 'Did you enjoy your meal, sir?' She had caught him studying her body, but she appeared undisturbed.

'Yes…I did. Thank you.' He was slightly embarrassed. 'Will the senator be much longer?'

'I really couldn't say, sir. I'm just a waitress.' She smiled again, with less enthusiasm, and turned to leave. He watched her go, enjoying the view, but her words stuck in his mind. 'Wait!' he called to her. She stopped and turned. 'Why would you say that?' he asked her. 'That you're *just* a waitress?'

She shrugged, saying, 'I…was just being honest, sir,' as she grinned nervously. 'I didn't mean to –'

'Stop calling me "sir",' he interrupted her. 'What would you like to do with your life? A waitress is what you do, not what you *are*…or *who* you are.'

'My family couldn't afford to send me to college,' she explained. 'I wanted to be an architect, or a ship designer.' She smiled nervously again, but this time there was more warmth, perhaps genuine. 'I always dreamed of working for you, actually.'

Vawter smiled, gesturing for her to come close again. She did so, and he relieved her of the bottle of wine as he indicated that she sit next to him. As she did so, he passed his glass to her and took another for himself from the centre of the table, having earlier wondered why a second one was necessary. His mouth was dry, his stomach churning, his heart pounding. He felt both elated and terrified at the same time, a tumultuous conflict, for he could not recall the last time he had spoken to a woman in such a setting. He watched her sip the wine from where his lips had been, and he could see that she was as nervous as he. This settled him somewhat, and he laughed. 'I don't bite,' he assured her.

'That's not what I heard,' she replied, her dark brown eyes sparkling in the light. Outside, the sun was setting beyond the partly open Shield, its distorted disc of burning orange like a fire behind a grate. Such beauty was secondary now as Vawter looked into this young woman's eyes, watching the edges of her soft, subtly coated lips rising with a smile that offered a reprieve from the threatening darkness of night. 'To be honest, I was a little worried about serving you this evening,' she said.

'Is my reputation that bad?'

Feigning fear of rebuke, she nodded, her smile once more lifting his heart. Such was the intensity of this sensation that he felt the need to avert his eyes. Such hope for Vawter was inevitably associated with the expectation of its demise, bolstered by memories of the same. He blinked as he turned away and he asked with his head slightly lowered, 'So...do you have any designs I might be interested in?'

She hesitated, sensing a subtle shift in his mood. Setting down the glass, she pushed the chair back and stood up. 'I'm sorry, I really should be getting back to the kitchen.' When he looked back to her, she saw the hint of moisture in his eyes and realised she had misread the situation: 'Maybe we could...discuss this some other time, Mister Vawter.'

He nodded. 'Perhaps you'd like to see some of the newest ships in my fleet. They're quite impressive.'

'I'm sure they are.' She bit softly on the corner of her bottom lip, a half-smile playing on her features as the sunset illuminated her dark, lustrous hair. 'I better go.'

'What's your name?'

She laughed, realising that this most important piece of information had been overlooked. 'It's...Amara,' she told him, watching his eyes carefully. 'You can get me here any time.'

Vawter felt a sudden stab of pain behind his eyes, accompanied by an electric shock of memory. A chill went through him as he pictured the icy tunnel collapsing all around him...and her. The waitress noticed his discomfort, but he rebounded swiftly: 'If you tell me your surname, I can get you...anywhere.'

'I...I'm usually here.'

He nodded. She wanted him to contact her there. 'I'll get you here, then,' he promised, thinking little of it.

She walked away, to be grabbed outside the door by a figure waiting in the shadows: 'Well played,' Tzedek congratulated her in a harsh whisper.

She struggled, but without conviction. 'I don't know what you're talking about.'

'Game's up, Jena. You hardly thought you could hide out in the Senate buildings without catching my eye, did you?'

The waitress weighed up her options, and then played her hand: 'I can get access to his ships. The new ones.'

Now it was Tzedek's turn to call her bluff. 'Why would I want that?' Luckily, she could not hear his heart pounding as everything teetered on the brink of exposure.

'Because it's obvious you two aren't getting along these days.'

Tzedek's relief was held in check. 'I'll find a place for you to stay so I can keep an eye on you,' he told her. 'And I *will* keep an eye on you.'

'I'm sure you will.'

'Now run along to the kitchen, there's a good girl.'

She held his arrogant gaze with a threatening glare of her own, but she conceded and walked away without another word. As Tzedek stepped through the door, Vawter looked up. 'Nice of you to keep your appointment,' he noted sarcastically, his anger tempered by the buzzing in his head. Something was not right, and his body knew it. Who was that girl? Did she know about *his* Amara? Or was it just coincidence?

'I had other things to deal with,' Tzedek replied, making his way to his chair. 'Did you know that Saranne escaped? And she wasn't alone.'

'Romis helped her…yes, I know.'

'And someone helped *him*. Care to explain?'

'Not right now, no. You and I have some things to discuss.'

'Do we?'

Inside the ambulance, Romis shouted at Hannah to find oxygen masks as the mystery vessel continued upwards and darkness awaited. Tom closed the ventilation system as Romis scrambled across the seats into the back of the swaying vehicle, to help the children and to find another oxygen cylinder to take into the front. There were four cylinders on a rack, and he took one down, handing it to Hannah. 'Plug the tube from that machine…' he shouted, pointing beyond Abigale, 'into this, and press the green button. When you draw a breath from the mask, the oxygen will feed through.' He took another cylinder down and grabbed a mask offered to him by Hannah. 'Wait until you feel the air running out,' he warned her. 'I really don't know how long we'll be up here, or where we're going.'

'Will my Mom be okay?' Hannah called over the wind. Romis nodded and smiled, looking back to Abigale. *'Just take turns with the air. Slow, deep breaths, and try to keep calm. If you need me, try to make a noise without wasting oxygen!'*

He returned to the front, where Tom was straining his neck to look up at the still rising craft. He turned when Romis sat back down and he shouted, *'No sign of stopping this side of the Shield!'*

'They might not let us through the Shield,' Romis replied, connecting the tube he had pulled through from the back to the oxygen cylinder. He handed a mask to Tom, who nodded gratefully and took it. *'Any ideas yet?'* he asked the doctor.

'I can't take it all in,' Romis declared, looking down through his window at the diminishing world. *'This could be Vawter's way of showing me that I shouldn't mess with him, but the soldiers down there weren't his, which means they were the Senate's.'*

'But if that's true, then the Senate's turned against Vawter.'

'Or the other way around,' Romis agreed. *'If we can't get through the Shield in the next few minutes, Tzedek's won.'* There was a creaking sound as the outside pressure dropped and the sporadic cloud beneath them dropped away. The air was thin, and Tom held the mask to his face as Romis pressed the button on the cylinder. *'Okay, Hannah,'* he called back. *'You need to start the oxygen now. Don't worry about the noises. Don't be scared.'* He took the mask from Tom and took a breath himself, slowly and purposefully inhaling as the glass around them began to crack, spider-webbing outwards from the bullet hole. *'Easy for you to say,'* remarked Tom, as Romis reached forward with a piece of surgical tape in a desperate attempt to seal the lethal breach.

'For a start, you can tell me about the communication you intercepted from Illeri.'

Tzedek held his gaze for a moment, wondering how much Vawter knew, before saying, 'Ah...that.'

'Yes...that, Tzedek. What are you keeping from me? And why haven't you investigated the Illeri ship?'

'Investigate it? Why would I do that?'

'It's been sitting up there for three days now, and there hasn't been a word from them since you met their ambassador.'

Tzedek's eyes betrayed him, but he deflected swiftly, hoping to avoid the sticky circumstance of Kallon Raesa and his troubling observation. 'Their ambassador asked to see Echad.'

'Well, that's not gonna happen any time soon, is it?' Vawter countered. 'But that's not it. There's something else going on, and you're determined to keep me in the dark. I don't respond well to that, Kai.'

'What? Why would I do that? You're my most trusted ally! My *only* ally, for God's sake!'

'Really?' Vawter rose and walked across to the window. 'Then perhaps you could explain why you're keeping such a close eye. An old Shield station intercepting my off-world communications, for example.'

Tzedek was genuinely taken aback, but Vawter was too busy watching the clouds to witness his expression as he said, 'Samuel, this is news to me, I assure you.'

'You *assure*?' Vawter spun round in anger. 'You don't assure me of *anything* anymore! I've got that fuckin' Romis asking questions about what we have him doing, and because you had everyone else of his calibre murdered, there's no one to replace him! We're *days* from our deadline, and someone up there is spying on me. Don't tell me you know nothing about it. You met with the Illeri, for fuck's sake. The dock you gave them is practically next door to that station! I thought you'd at least be more subtle.'

Tzedek was trying to put all this together. It was imperative he maintained this alliance at such a late stage, but he was already considering the consequences of its erosion. 'You have to believe me, Sam. I know nothing about this intercept. I mean, they may not even –' He stopped, pressing the first two fingers of his right hand against his forehead as he gritted his teeth angrily. He was committed now, cursing himself under his breath.

'May not even *what*?'

Tzedek took a deep breath, inhaling the warm air rising from the hole he was digging. 'A…confidential informant…' he reluctantly lied, 'has suggested that whoever's up on that ship…isn't Illeri.'

'Isn't –' Vawter laughed. 'And you *believed* this…confidential informant?' Vawter realised this was the secret communication his people had intercepted. *Was this coming from the mercenary*

80

Raesa? His head ached again, his brain sounding a muffled scream. It was like a part of him was trying to get out.

'I...had no reason not to.' For a terrible moment, Tzedek realised that Raesa could have lied, but he shrugged off the idea. 'Look, it was a plausible explanation. This person has seen the Illeri on their home world. The only one who *has*. He said they're about dog-sized and wouldn't need such a massive biosuit!'

'And he's qualified to judge their requirements for operating in our environment, is he? Your...mercenary errand boy.'

Tzedek blinked as Vawter glared at him, his expression saying, *Yes...I know.* Tzedek shook his head, setting aside the potential implications of Vawter gaining knowledge of...certain things. One problem at a time. 'He was adamant, Sam. Sounded like there was more, but...he cut me off...or he was cut off. I don't know. Look, whoever these...things are...they know about Arrien.'

Vawter went cold. 'That's not possible.'

The Senator shrugged. 'I don't see why not. If they're not Illeri, then...it could be anyone who's been watching since the Cage was here.'

'The *Illeri* have been watching since the Cage was here, Kai. They weren't quick to come to our rescue, but they conveniently wanted to be our saviours afterwards. Why have we ignored their self-interest for so long? Just because Tesckyn was so quick to see altruism doesn't mean we should be so naïve!'

'Look, if these people know about Arrien, and they've gone to the trouble of stealing an Illeri ship to get their hands on him, then Kallon will find out. And if he got *one* message out...'

'Well, let's hope he does. Cos if it took two years for him to get in touch, he's not exactly a likely candidate for getting to the church on time, is he? And speaking of his message...' Vawter had to go all in now: 'I don't appreciate you intercepting it.'

What is this? Does he actually think he sent Raesa? Is he calling my bluff? 'You're being paranoid, Sam. There was no way of knowing a signal like that was for you. There was a bi-channel encryption, and if I'd waited for you to stop playing your little games and get here, it would have decayed completely and we'd have nothing.'

Vawter nodded reluctantly, unsure about his own argument as the pain in his head got worse. He knew he had not sent Raesa, but his people thought he did and now he was pretending he did!

Did Raesa think the same? If the mercenary died out there, he would never find out. The confusing part was that Tzedek was talking as if he also thought Vawter had sent Raesa to Illeri. Vawter felt his temple throbbing again and there was a sensory blade behind his right eye.

'I think we should get back to the timetable,' Tzedek suggested. 'Why don't you tell me what you're doing with Romis and Saranne? Romis should be working on the clone, not rescuing damsels in distress and deranged children.'

The small, sleek ship emerged into the space between the outer atmosphere and the Shield, its unorthodox cargo swinging aimlessly and beginning to spin. Illuminating the stark, metallic omnipresence of the Shield were thousands of red lights, proximity beacons around the apertures. The apertures were made of hundreds of overlapping metal sheets, and they would crush any ship trying to enter or exit if the Shield started to close. Power to the engines of the mystery craft increased, a thrumming pulse that caused it to accelerate towards the Shield, towards the relative safety of outer space.

Inside the ambulance, the consumption of oxygen was relative to the heightened state of panic in which everyone found themselves. The metal panels and doors of the vehicle were beginning to buckle as the vacuum of space took even deeper breaths, threatening to rip the vehicle open as it inhaled through the makeshift seal at the bullet hole, now looking like the most desperate and uneducated surgical attempt to stop the pulse of arterial blood. None of them would survive if it gave way. Romis, eyes wide with terror, looked back to see Hannah holding tight to her mother, cowering together as they shared the oxygen mask. Somehow, the glass of the front window had not yet broken, but it was so badly cracked that he could not even see out. He was not sure he wanted to.

Vawter smiled thinly as he tried to think things through and ignore the pain. Tzedek must have been aware that he was bluffing about Raesa, and yet he avoided the matter. But he found himself more readily disturbed by the remark about Saranne's daughter, because her reaction to him had been unsettling. And what did Tzedek know about it, anyway? 'You should leave this one to me,' he told him. 'I'll get Romis back on schedule. That's all you have to worry about.'

'I'm…afraid I can't tolerate anyone losing their way right now, Sam,' Tzedek declared. 'Especially you.'

'Which means…?'

The door opened and six soldiers entered, their rifles levelled. 'Which means,' Tzedek explained, 'that you'll be escorted to your nearest vessel, where you'll remain under guard until I'm convinced you can be trusted. You'll return Romis and Saranne to my custody, and I'll examine their indiscretions personally.'

Vawter shook his head with mock regret as he said, 'That's…not gonna happen, Kai.' He stepped back, retreating to the large windows. In the distance, a dark shape could be seen moving through the darkening clouds of evening. It was moving fast, and it was big. Tzedek watched as if in a dream, waking only in time to turn and run as – at the same time as the soldiers prepared to open fire on Vawter – the dark shape shimmered to become a large gunship filling the sky next to the Senate building. Its weapons were immediately active, expertly trained on those inside. Bullets scythed through the windows with such speed that the panes remained momentarily intact. The soldiers were buffeted and torn by the barrage of burning projectiles as the glass collapsed from the frames, and Vawter simply turned as the firing stopped, jumping out through the empty window frames to land on a platform extending from the hovering vessel. An airlock opened and he disappeared inside as Tzedek stepped back into the room. He shook his head as he regarded the dead soldiers and the retreating ship. Naveen appeared at the shattered windows as if passing through an invisible curtain. 'You really should have known better,' he commented, looking around and below him at the shards of glass on which he stood…yet did not stand. 'The man funds your weapons programs, Tzedek. Did you think he was going to come unprepared?'

'What am I supposed to do now? He knows about *Raesa*. And that was the most confusing conversation I've ever had! I lost track of *my* side of things, never mind *his*!'

'Yes, you did,' the Prophet agreed, as if consoling a child. 'But he was told about Raesa and he was quick to play along, that's all. He doesn't have time to go to Illeri. Just enough to get the Argo on track, though. You did well. And Romis will push Vawter just as we need him.'

Tzedek inhaled deeply and nodded: 'It's just...confusing, keeping this up. And what the hell is going on with the Illeri? Who's up on that ship?'

Naveen smiled. 'The future,' he replied, before vanishing as someone entered the room. It was the young woman to whom Tzedek had recently spoken, and she stared momentarily at the place where the Prophet had been. Swift to store this valuable information for another time, she smiled at Tzedek as he turned to her. 'You find this amusing?' he dared her.

'I find it educational,' Jena explained, 'considering I'm the one going up against this guy.'

'He was ahead of me. But you'll have him eating out of your hands, I'm sure.'

'Just my hands, Tzedek?' she jeered. 'I think I can do better than that.'

'Don't try my patience,' the senator warned. 'I can always have you locked up and get someone else for the job.'

'On such short notice?' She shook her head. 'You don't have the time or the opportunity to get someone new close to him. I'm all you've got.'

He stepped swiftly forward and grabbed her by the neck, hauling her to the tips of her toes. 'And I wouldn't recommend you overestimate the value of that,' he hissed. 'You are *not* in control here. Got it?'

Jena had neither flinched nor struggled, and she sneered as she warned him, 'Control...is a matter of perspective.' Her eyes gestured downwards, and Tzedek realised without looking that she held a knife to his groin. His grip tightened slightly, causing her to gasp, but she responded by pressing the knife harder against him as she managed to say, 'I wouldn't...advise it.'

He released her and stepped back from the deadly blade. 'Sometimes I wonder if you people realise who's in charge,' he commented, turning to regard the damage once more. 'You all live for money, but you forget it comes from the Senate. You *answer* to the Senate.'

'The Senate no longer exists, Tzedek,' she reminded him, grinning devilishly. 'I made sure of that.'

Tzedek's eyes widened. '*You*...? I didn't hire *you*!'

'No...you didn't. But the other guy was...clumsy. Fell out of a window, apparently.'

Tzedek nodded and smiled, admiring the way she had positioned herself. But a personal vendetta was the last thing he needed. 'You put yourself here,' he realised. 'To get to Vawter?'

'Don't concern yourself with my reasons,' Jena assured him. 'I'll do what you need me to do.'

'You've no idea what that is yet.'

She shrugged: 'Whatever. I'm here now.'

'Fair enough. So, you clearly didn't tell Vawter your real name.'

'No. I told him it was Amara.'

Tzedek was not sure how to take that, considering the danger it posed. Memories did not die easily. 'That was a mistake.'

'I don't think so. I gained his trust, didn't I?'

'I wouldn't be so sure about that,' the Senator warned her. 'Don't get complacent.'

'I don't even know the meaning of the word.'

'Just keep your wits about you. Samuel Vawter isn't someone you play games with.'

'I can see that,' she laughed as she walked towards the empty window frames. The wind whipped in and caught her hair as she turned back to Tzedek: 'I guess by now you don't trust anyone, do you?'

'Trust amounts to submission, Jena.' He moved to the table. 'And I never submit.' He tapped a button on a com panel. 'Close the Shield,' he ordered. 'Don't let Vawter escape. If he does, we may have to initiate Protocol B.'

Ω

The blue craft raced upwards, returning fire to the Shield that now sought to cease its passage with closure and mounted weapons. Other vessels arrived to join the attack on the Shield guns, aiding Romis' mystery rescuers. Five ships eventually passed through the closing aperture, one of them still carrying the ambulance as it was slammed against the closing metal. Tom was thrown forward, his head smashing against the fractured window, which could take no further punishment. It exploded outwards, and they felt the air being sucked from their lungs, their veins pulsing and expanding. But almost as swiftly as this torture began, it ended. A huge ship waited immediately beyond the Shield and it closed its cargo doors with all five vessels safely inside, the battered ambulance crashing onto its side on the deck. Hannah cried, Romis cried, Tom was insensate, and Abigale was regaining consciousness as oxygen spirited in. 'Good to see you again, Captain,' a familiar voice welcomed as hands reached for her. 'Can't say the same for you, Romis, but…every cloud, eh?'

Ian Romis, slightly disoriented and not sure whether he was dead or alive, looked up through teary eyes at the man offering his hand. 'I never thought I'd be happy to see you, Ganna.'

'I've a feeling you're gonna have to get used to that,' replied the Argo's doctor, helping Romis from the ruined vehicle. 'Once we get you checked out, we've a lotta work to do.'

As Romis regained his footing and his composure, he looked around the massive cargo bay to see that five military craft of varying design were unburdening themselves of scores of men and women, most of them dressed in combat clothing and carrying weapons. He recognised only one of these people, a tall man in a grey suit, an expression of grim determination on his face as he approached. 'Glad you could make it, Doctor,' said Vawter. 'Welcome to the Argo.'

THE ARGO

Mars Geostat-2

Romis lay back gratefully on the bed in Ganna's sick bay with his head pounding and his eyes closed. He felt Ganna's presence next to him. 'What's going on?' he whispered. 'What am I doing here?'

Ganna was equally conspiratorial. 'You know, I was hoping you could tell me. That Vawter guy gives me the creeps. Did you know he interrogated me while you were heroically rescuing the captain?'

Romis opened his eyes to a squint and grinned. 'Still don't know what I was thinking,' he admitted, 'but I'm glad I got her outta there. She was important to them for some reason. Or her story was.'

'Her story...oh, right, Hannah.' Ganna tapped some buttons on a console over Romis' head. 'She was pretty freaked out by the whole thing.'

'Have you examined the girl yet?'

'Hannah? Why?'

Romis pushed himself up and looked at him. 'Are you *serious*? There's something *wrong* with her, and I'm willing to bet it's the same as...' His head screamed at him, and he settled back down.

'The same as *what*?' Ganna leaned over him. 'I know you're hiding something.' Their eyes met and Romis nodded, refusing to divulge anything yet: 'I need your help.'

Ganna chuckled derisively. 'The great Ian Romis needs the help of a lowly sick-bay doctor?'

'They were never my words, and you know it,' Romis argued. 'You chose your own path. The offer was there.'

'Yeah, but the ethics weren't.' Ganna sighed. 'Look, I'm not doing this again. What do you want me to do?'

'While there's still time, get my medical records uploaded. I need you to examine me.'

'For what?'

'A few weeks ago, I had an associate diagnose me with prostate cancer.'

'I'm...sorry to hear that,' said Ganna genuinely. 'You want me to see if there's still time to get rid of it?'

'No,' Romis replied. 'I want you to check if it's already gone.'

Ω

Abigale watched as the other ships arrived, joining the now treasonous fleet close to Mars. The Pegasus, the Minotaur, and the Medusa were all built to the visual specifications of the Argo, but they lacked its superior firepower and manoeuvrability. The smaller vessels, numbering fifteen so far, ranged in size and strength, from a two-person Delta-class fighter to a long-range destroyer with a crew of sixty-three. It was by no means an invincible group considering how much of Vawter's technology was in the hands of the Senate, but Tzedek would think twice before attacking Vawter – and the Argo – and that was enough of an advantage for now.

He entered the room using his personal access codes that – on a ship he owned – would override any security measure. There was no doubt she heard him come in, but still she failed to turn from the window. 'Marvellous, isn't it?' he commented quietly, his voice sending unexpected shivers through her. 'All my children together in one place.'

'That's really how you see them?' she wondered, refusing to face him. 'These weapons?'

'They're my creations,' he replied. 'My only creations.'

'You'd think differently if you had *real* children.'

'That'll never happen.' He was standing behind her now, and she could feel his presence, his power, his arrogance. She conceded, turning from the scene as shuttles launched and docked around the vessels of war. 'Never?' she asked, surprised to hear in her voice a sympathy for which she cursed herself.

'Even if I had a chance to father a child, I can't see the point. Bringing forth a life just so it can die isn't my idea of achievement.'

She was stunned by his words, at the same time sickened and saddened by his morose philosophy. 'That's a dreadful way to live your life,' she accused him, thinking of Hannah, wondering what she would do without her. What she would have done if she had not walked back out at the feeder post.

'It's the only way I know,' he confessed, his steely manner absent. He managed a smile. 'But I'll find another one.' He revealed no more, stepping past her to touch the window with outstretched palms. He leaned forward, looking down from the fifteenth deck with childlike wonder. 'Soon,' he whispered.

'What do you mean?' She felt suddenly cold, as if a breeze had passed through her bones.

Reclaiming his demeanour, he pushed back from the window and turned round. 'I'm so close,' he told her, asking himself in the deep wells of his soul why he was telling her any of this. 'I'll change everything.'

Abigale managed a nervous laugh. 'What do you mean...everything? For who?' She held his piercing gaze, shivered as he smiled, the flashing lights of a passing shuttle casting animated shadows across the room. 'For me,' he whispered, '...first,' brushing past her as he made to leave the room. She felt a tremor run through her, different to the chills of anxiety. And she realised his touch had aroused her. 'You don't have to go,' she called to him before she could stop herself.

He hesitated, turning his head slightly so she could see the side of his face. 'After what I've done to you? How could you possibly want my company?'

'I think you need company,' she dared, torn between an almost intolerable and inexplicable sympathy and the need to get the truth about what happened to Hannah. 'I think you want someone to talk to.' She stepped closer. 'There's nothing wrong with that.'

'I think...' he turned fully and she stopped as he said, 'that you think too much, Captain.'

'Abigale,' she reminded him, realising that he was discomfited by the threat of intimacy. His arrogant façade was deteriorating, yet for her part she knew that she was being drawn into something beyond her control. It both scared and excited her. Either way, she could use it.

He nodded. 'Abigale,' he said softly, 'we don't have time for...talking. Tzedek won't wait much longer before making a move. I need to get to Phobos.' Despite the conviction in his voice, she could feel his anxiety, the urgency of his plans. He spoke as if the moon were light-years away.

'I'm a good listener,' she offered. 'Sometimes, that's all a person needs.'

'I know exactly what I need!' he argued. 'And it's not platitudes and sympathy. They alleviate nothing.'

'If your fears are getting the better of you, you should face them,' she suggested. 'They can seem quite irrational once you fight back.'

He shook his head. 'Mine is the most rational fear of all. No one can fight it.' He turned away from her, opening the door. 'We all lose,' he said, before stepping out into the bright corridor. Abigale stepped out after him, watching him walk away, realising that, in this light, he was not the threatening figure they all imagined him to be. He was just another man, cloaked in power by the terror of failure and weakness. He was hiding from the world like some child under the covers, where nothing existed beyond that protective layer until the lights were on. If she had respected him in the past, she would have lost that respect now. But she had not, and so now she merely pitied him. His melancholic soul had infected her.

Abigale made to step back inside, hearing as she did so an officer approaching Vawter. 'There's a small civilian craft approaching,' she heard the man report. 'A woman is requesting to come aboard to talk with you. I don't know how she got out here unnoticed.'

'Her name?' Abigale heard him ask, an edge of anticipation in his voice. 'Amara,' the man replied. Vawter turned his head to look back down the corridor, but Abigale was swift to move in out of sight. 'Tell her I'll see her in a few minutes,' she heard him reply.

Abigale made her way across her quarters to the com panel on the wall. 'Commander Carenna Moreno,' she requested. A few moments later, Carenna was looking back at her from where she stood on the bridge: *'How are you feeling?'* she asked.

'Much better. I heard we've you to thank for that suicide flight.'

'The grappling hook wasn't my idea, okay?' Carenna assured her, laughing. *'Vawter said it was the quickest way, cos Tzedek was bound to close the Shield.'*

'I don't understand all this. Why weren't you taken into custody?'

Carenna shrugged. *'I was held for about an hour. Then Vawter's men relieved the soldiers, and I was blindfolded and taken to a hangar. Couldn't tell you where, but that ship and a crew were waiting, and I was told to pick you up. Wasn't gonna argue with that.'*

Abigale took a deep breath, thinking quickly. 'I want you to do something for me.'

'*Sure…what is it?*'

'There's a woman coming aboard called Amara. She asked to meet Vawter personally.'

'*I'll find out who she is.*'

'Okay. Something's not right.'

'*That's an understatement. I'll keep you posted.*' Abigale nodded and turned away from the monitor as it went blank. Outside, she could see that modifications were being made to the engines of the gathered vessels. 'What are they doing out there?' she asked aloud, looking to the aft starboard engines of the Argo, where the same work was taking place. In the distance, she could see the flash from the closest MEC station as a ship exited into Mars orbit and headed for the feeder post. Then she looked back at the engines of the surrounding ships, and the pieces fell into place. 'You're not using MEC anymore!' she gasped. 'What the hell's going on?'

Ω

Tom, his head bandaged and a stupid smile on his still-dazed face, looked down at Romis as he lay face-down on the table, covered with a sheet. 'Isn't this good news?' he asked.

'Not necessarily,' Romis declared. 'Sure, it's great the cancer's gone, regardless of whether or not I could have cured it myself, but…why is it gone?'

'Like that guy and his tumour.'

'Exactly.'

'What's that?' asked Ganna, returning to the table. 'What guy?'

'One of the crewmen of this ship who died a few days ago.'

'Oh, right.' Ganna was immediately contrite: 'It seems that may have been my fault.'

'I don't think it was,' Romis assured him. 'One of the victims came out from the MEC system without a tumour he was supposed to have.'

'Supposed to?'

'His doctor hadn't updated his records, so the MEC system wasn't aware of it.'

'Well, neither was I,' said Ganna. 'Why wouldn't he tell me about it?'

'How much service time would he have lost getting that treated under your recommendations? No offence, but private treatment was his best option. He was due to get started once the Argo got back.'

Ganna sighed regretfully. 'And you're saying the tumour wasn't there when you checked the...bodies?'

'The MEC system wasn't aware of it,' Romis repeated, as if this answered everything, 'just like with me.'

'I thought you'd never travelled by MEC,' Tom argued. 'You never trusted it.'

'I never travelled *voluntarily*.'

'What are you saying...?' Ganna shook his head and laughed the words: 'Someone put you through the system and took away your cancer? A bit fanciful, isn't it?'

Romis exhaled with barely concealed anger. 'Everything you can't understand is fanciful, Ganna. That's why...' He stopped himself.

'Why I work in a sick bay?'

'NO! Look...that's not what I mean. But just for once, think outside the box, will you? What if there's some reason Vawter or Tzedek would want as many people as possible to travel by MEC? What if some sort of information is being gathered about us all? Or some sort of tests? Or maybe it's not information they're taking?'

'You mean genetic samples?' Ganna offered, at once horrified and fascinated by the idea.

'Now you're getting it,' Romis congratulated him, turning around on the table, holding the sheet in place to protect his dignity. 'What if something's extracted from us when we pass through?'

'They could be building a database of genetic information,' Tom suggested.

Ganna shook his head. 'They could do that without all that trouble and expense. For heaven's sake, blood samples are all they need for that!'

'What if it's not all they need? Who knows what they're planning? They've got this clone...' Romis was swiftly realising that he had a dangerous habit of saying too much. He could almost taste his foot.

'A clone?' Ganna glared at Romis, swallowing his distaste for this unethical practice. 'Of who?'

92

Romis sighed. 'Cassandra Messina,' he confessed, realising that it was too late to hold back. He needed to get to the bottom of whatever was going on, and everything seemed relevant.

'*The* Cassandra Messina?' Ganna looked at Tom, who shook his head, saying, 'I don't know anything about it.' Ganna returned his attention to Romis, who had swung his legs down from the table. Tom handed his clothes to him and, wrapping the sheet around him, he walked to a screen, behind which he dressed. 'Are you telling me,' Ganna resumed, 'that you've cloned the woman responsible for the abduction of millions of people from Earth?'

'She wasn't responsible,' Romis argued wearily. 'Anyway, she doesn't realise who she is or what she can do. That's why the experiments are...'

'Experiments!' Ganna was disgusted. 'I should have known.'

'Do you ever *listen* to yourself?'

'I listen to my *conscience*. Now get back to your clone not knowing who she is.'

'She's not *my* clone.' Romis fixed his shirt and walked out from behind the screen. 'There's a carefully controlled protein imbalance in her brain preventing her from getting a fix on her identity and memories.'

Ganna thought about this for a moment. 'So, she's like a...*blank*...or something?' It was the way he stared at Romis that set the train of thought in motion. It was the disgust he felt that allowed the terror of Romis' own paranoia to take control and begin to put it all together. But it was Tom who hit the metaphorical nail on the head. It was Tom who realised that this was a far larger concern than a missing tumour or cured cancer. It was Tom whose voice pierced the silence as he quietly voiced the awful words of revelation. 'Just like the captain's daughter,' he said. 'For a second, she didn't know who she *was*. She didn't remember who she'd travelled with. Oh, God...' he felt sick, the horror of it all eating away at him. 'She's a clone,' he stated, and there was no argument, no challenge.

Romis looked at the image on the wall, the backlit scan of his body, the enormity of this simple examination striking him in the heart with a fist of iron. 'I'm a clone,' he said quietly. He was trembling now, tears rolling down his cheeks as he looked imploringly at Ganna and Tom, before saying, 'I died!'

Ω

Jena smiled as Vawter came towards her, every inch the man of power and influence. Here, in view of those who served him, this was the act required of him. But she had seen something else within him and, combined with what she had learned about him, she was sure she could accomplish her mission. 'Now, I'm sure you shouldn't be up here,' he welcomed her, taking her hand as she descended the last few steps of her boarding ramp. 'How did you get out before the Shield closed?'

'I was already out,' she said. 'Tzedek sent me on an errand.' Vawter's expression darkened as he heard that name. 'Don't worry,' she said, 'he doesn't know I'm here, and I'm sure he won't be lost without his lunar spices.'

Delighting in some respite from his dissent, Vawter smiled. 'I'm sure he'll be lost without *you*.'

'Well, he'll have to get used to it, because I'm not going back.' She walked past him, heading for the closest door to leave the docking bay.

'Why?' asked Vawter, his instincts roaring threats as he simultaneously fought them back. 'Where will you go?' He hoped she would stay.

She did not look back. 'Have you room for me here?'

'Of course I do, but just...tell me...' he grabbed her arm gently and she turned to face him, 'why have you left?'

'Because I heard he tried to kill you,' she replied, 'and I...well, I was worried about you.'

Vawter smiled. 'Really?'

She nodded, linking her arm with his as the door closed behind them. 'Why don't you show me where I can stay?'

He took the chance, ostensibly the risk every man will take when presented with the opportunity. 'Well, you could stay with me until we find something suitable for you.'

'That sounds perfect,' she replied, smiling as they walked down the corridor. Vawter was smiling too. But both smiles were a lie.

Ω

'Well?' Abigale arrived on the bridge and Carenna turned, heading swiftly towards her. 'What have you got?'

Carenna shook her head in astonishment. 'I can't believe he didn't have her checked out.'

'He wasn't looking at her with his brain,' remarked Abigale, immediately shocked by her tone. Carenna thought she detected jealousy, but she wisely ignored it as she explained, 'I had her face scanned as she walked out of her ship...which, by the way, is no civilian vessel. It's got a dampening field, an EM flux, so I figured it was hiding something nasty.'

'You found a way around it?'

'Still working on it. I can tell you that what we can see is just an exoskeleton over something not in our database, but the problem's more about its software. I can't close the framelink.'

Abigale nodded: 'Making it the only thing on board that our systems can't interface with.'

'Exactly. I'll let you know as soon as we crack it.'

'Sure, but...like you said, why didn't Vawter check her out? Or her ship? It's one thing to let the little guy do the thinking for you, but not in the middle of a situation like this.'

'Oh, you'd be amazed how stupid men can be, no matter what's going on.' Carenna flashed a devious smile and Abigale laughed, saying, 'I'll take your word for it. So, what are we gonna do? Cos I could really go for kicking that thing out the back door if it's not hooked to the frame, you know?'

'Yeah, of course. But we need to find out more about this girl, cos the face rec got zip. She's probably a mercenary, so finding out exactly who she works for will help us figure out what she's up to. If it's Tzedek, he might have a mothership out here waiting to get its shuttle back. If she's working for someone else, or...some*thing* else, this could get messy fast.'

Abigale shook her head: 'I've had enough surprises for one day,' she said. 'I'm gonna talk to this sneaky little bitch.'

Ω

Ganna took a deep breath before pressing the access panel. He found himself counting under that long and relaxing exhalation, enabling calm and control. A welcome illusion. Reaching ten, he made to press the panel again, but the door opened and Vawter stood there, his expression a silent but insistent glare. 'I'm...sorry to bother you,' Ganna genuinely stated, 'but it's important.'

Vawter's eyes narrowed as he looked at the doctor for a short, debilitating moment, in which Ganna felt that all air was being drained from the corridor in which he stood. A flicker of movement behind the man in the doorway, and Ganna saw a young woman reach out from her chair to raise a glass from a table. 'I have company,' Vawter explained, the necessity to do so lost to him even as he said it. 'How important is it?'

Ganna felt the need to step closer, knowing that the information he and Romis had gathered in the last few hours should not be shared with everyone in earshot. He whispered as Vawter instinctively leaned closer in unison. 'More important than you can imagine,' he dared dramatically, hoping against hope that their information was not old news to this man. If this were the case...Ganna shuddered to think.

Vawter got the message, though, and he turned back to the woman in his quarters. 'Make yourself at home,' he told her, his uncharacteristic tone and smile setting Ganna's nerves on edge. 'I'll be back soon.'

'I'll be waiting,' she replied. Ganna found himself straining to get a better look at this woman, taunted only by her bare legs and the arm that returned the glass of what appeared to be wine to the table. Then he found himself looking up at the raised eyebrows and questioning glare of Vawter. 'Sorry.'

'Lead the way, Doctor,' the tall man replied impatiently. 'As you can imagine, I'm quite eager to get back.'

Ganna decided to remain silent, nodding and walking away as Vawter followed him. In a few minutes time, they would reveal their findings to him. And then they would be closer to knowing who was behind this terror.

Ω

As Ganna opened the door to Medical, Vawter received a call. 'Go ahead,' he said aloud. Ganna thought he had spoken to him and he entered the sick bay as Vawter delayed outside, listening to the report: *'There's an annex room in the main Senate chambers, right next to where you were.'*

'I saw it, yes,' Vawter replied. 'What's in it?'

'Well, that's the problem. We can't tell. Whatever Tzedek's hiding in there, it's heavily shielded. It's not a large room, though.'

Vawter looked around to confirm there was no one in earshot. 'So, there could be someone in there?'

'*A person? I suppose so. We didn't consider that.*'

'I think you should. I want you to go through everything that was reported about the Cage incident. The Nostradamus...the guy who called himself a prophet...everything.'

'*I'm not following.*'

'Then try to keep up. The guy who got onto the Nostradamus claimed to know the future. And so did this...prophet. What if they really were from the future? Or there was someone somehow communicating from the future?'

'*You mean...from now? Our time?*'

'And Tzedek's protecting them. Pretty valuable assets, wouldn't you say?'

'*We'll go through everything.*'

'Good. And the other matter?'

'*I'll, ah...send you the file. Interesting reading.*'

'Always is.' Vawter closed the channel and took a moment to think before he opened the sick bay door. 'So, what was so important, Romis?' he snapped as the door closed behind him. Tom and Romis occupied the sick bay, and Abigale's daughter lay on one of the beds, either asleep or unconscious. Vawter could not tell and did not care.

Romis turned from a console. 'You're not going to like this,' he began. 'As a matter of fact, if this gets out, no one on Earth is going to like it. But what we want to know is whether you knew about it in the first place.'

Vawter stared at him for a moment, before breathing a derisive laugh, shaking his head, and turning to Tom. 'Perhaps *you'd* make more sense,' he suggested, 'because I don't have a clue what your mentor here is talking about.' Tom glanced at Romis, who sighed and nodded, gesturing that he take over.

'You should really stop asking permission to speak!' Vawter mocked, prompting Tom to blurt out, 'We know what the MEC system does!'

'Congratulations,' Vawter joked, nonplussed. 'Now, if that's all...' He turned to leave.

'It's a cloning system,' continued Romis, stopping him in his tracks. The silence then was like the aftermath of an explosion, the ears of the observers ringing while their minds reeled with the consequences. Vawter kept his back to them, so there was no opportunity to judge his reaction. 'What do you mean?' he asked quietly.

Romis cleared his throat as his heart hammered. 'The vanishing tumour...Captain Saranne's daughter...even I had a minor cancer removed. I know what you did to me, Vawter. You had me killed and cloned somehow. But your foolproof system didn't put me back the way I was because my cancer wasn't in the system.'

Vawter turned. 'Maybe the cancer wasn't as serious as you thought,' he suggested, with little conviction. Then he shook his head with frustration: 'You realise you're complaining about the system fixing an imperfection? And as for having you killed and cloned...that's ridiculous!'

'I saw the CCI footage!' Romis roared. 'I saw your people bringing me back to my lab and Tzedek left me some bizarre message! And Captain Saranne saw me being blown to bits while you and Tzedek walked away without a scratch! What the hell am I *supposed* to think?'

'MEC's not *supposed* to fix imperfections,' Ganna interjected. 'If that were the case, everyone with a disease would be using it like some miracle cure.'

Vawter refused to be drawn into an argument as a sharpness teased the back of his eyes. He was convinced that his secret dealings with the Kwaios still needed to be protected above all else, but the proximity of these men to the truth disturbed him, let alone what Romis was saying about Tzedek. 'This is nonsense,' he declared. 'MEC is exactly what it stands for...matter energy conversion. It works.'

'How?' asked Tom, the simple question luring Silence back into the room, an entity which thrived in this atmosphere. They all stared at Vawter, who remained as expressionless as possible. But Tom was not giving up. 'Who invented the technology?' he pressed. 'Who endorsed it? Do *you* know...or do we have to put it to *Tzedek*?'

'MEC is *mine*,' Vawter argued. 'It's the culmination of a century of my family's hard work and determination.'

'But your family didn't *invent* it,' Ganna argued. 'You inherited your father's company, but MEC came out of *nowhere*. As I recall, you refused to answer any questions about it. You wouldn't explain how it worked back then, and you're just as evasive *now*.'

'You don't *know*,' Romis accused him. 'You haven't the faintest idea how it works!'

'Again…that's ridiculous!' As he made to leave the room once more, Hannah was waking. Unlike the last time she had seen him, there was no vague recognition. This time it was sure, it was strong. She let out a high-pitched gasp and pointed accusingly, crying, 'Get him away from me! He's a bad man!'

Vawter stepped back, knocking medical instruments off a trolley. He looked around the room at them all, wondering whether this was a nightmare. He had no idea how this girl knew him, let alone why she should harbour any fear of him. Romis caught his terrified glare, bewildered as to the extent of Vawter's knowledge on MEC. But what he could not have known was the real reason for Vawter's terror. As it all became blindingly clear.

Ω

Abigale pressed the key on the panel and waited, her impatience evident. 'Come on,' she muttered, 'come on.' She pressed the key twice more, only to find herself face to face with the mystery woman as the door opened. She was wearing a loose-fitting gown of rich crimson, tied at the waist. It did not reach beyond her knees. 'Oh, hi,' said Jena pleasantly, 'are you looking for Sam?'

'I'm looking for *Mister* Vawter,' Abigale replied. 'Is he here?'

'It must be annoying for you to have to answer to a man,' the girl challenged her with mock sympathy. '*I* answer to no one.'

'That's not what I heard,' said Abigale, smiling sweetly. 'But then there's always so much talk on a ship like this. Maybe I've got it wrong?'

The girl looked at her for a moment, considering, planning, calculating. 'Why don't you come in and wait for him?' she offered. 'I'm sure he won't be long.'

'Are you?' Abigale pushed past her, and the girl laughed under her breath, her perfect teeth forming an animal grin of primitive warning. She stepped back into the room and the door closed behind her. 'Am I missing something here, Captain?'

Abigale poured herself a glass of wine and looked around the quarters. 'You know, that's the thing I can't get used to about this job,' she said as she sipped her wine. 'Even kitchen staff in the Senate buildings recognise me.'

'It must be great to be famous,' remarked the young woman as she returned to her chair, taking a route around the furniture which ensured that her back was never exposed to the captain, 'but personally I'd prefer to be rich and in love.' She sat down and watched Abigale carefully, reading her. 'Are you in love, Captain?'

'Don't tell me *you* are...sorry...I didn't catch your name?'

'It's Amara.'

Abigale gave a little laugh. 'Of course it is,' she said, setting her glass down and withdrawing a gun from the back of her belt. 'Now let's drop the act,' she suggested, sitting opposite the girl with the gun pointed at her. 'I know who you are, and I know what you intend to do.'

Jena smiled, unflinching. 'I seriously doubt that, Captain,' she argued, 'but perhaps what you *do* know is enough for you to take such a risk.'

'A risk?' Abigale leaned forward, the glass table the only thing keeping her from scratching those pretty eyes out. 'In case you hadn't noticed, I'm the one holding the gun.'

Jena laughed. 'Do you honestly believe I've survived so long in my profession by allowing people like you to get the upper hand?'

Her demeanour was one of such confidence that Abigale felt hers draining away. Her hand began to tremble as apprehension coursed through her, but she took a deep breath and steadied herself. 'There's no way you could move out of the way fast enough.'

'Oh, I'm going nowhere, Captain.' She laughed, leaning back in the soft chair. 'And it's you who won't move fast enough.'

'You're bluffing.'

'Am I?' Her eyes sparkled, her amusement evident. 'There's a device under the cushion you're sitting on, a tiny mine that will erupt within a fraction of a second if you move that cute ass of yours.' She grinned. 'So do sit still.'

'I don't believe you. You could hardly have known I was *coming*, never mind sit right *here*.'

Jena shrugged. 'Makes no difference to me, Captain, but it's the last thing you'll ever get wrong.' She winked. 'And you'll never see your beloved...*Mister* Vawter again.'

'Who are you?'

'I thought you knew.'

'I know you're a mercenary assassin, and that your ship isn't what it appears to be.'

'I'm sure you won't believe me, but you don't need to concern yourself with that.'

'Really?'

'Yes, really. The Argo is out here because you've got bigger fish to fry.' She smiled and raised her eyebrows mysteriously.

'You're a twisted little thing, aren't you?'

'Oh, you have to be in this game, Captain. You know, you may as well let go of the gun. The extra weight on your hand will have you trembling all over in no time.'

Abigale conceded that this might be a good course of action, and she allowed Jena to take it from her. The gun was laid on the table, and Jena laughed. 'Now the odds are even,' she said. 'Whoever gets to the gun first wins.'

'I should have known.'

'I wouldn't dare make a mess of such lovely furniture,' she joked…before her expression changed. 'Now we can talk, because you need to listen carefully. You, your ship, and this fleet may be all we can count on to survive.'

'What are you talking about?'

'In the next few days, every space-going species with so much as a pea-shooter is going to be heading for the Kiranis system.'

'The Kiranis system? Why?'

She grinned: 'Because the fifth planet is about to make a dramatic comeback.'

Abigale's eyes widened. 'What?' she breathed. 'How do you know that?'

Jena pouted with feigned disappointment. 'And I thought you'd done your homework,' she teased. 'Don't you know I hang out in all the right places?'

'You're working for Tzedek.'

Jena shrugged. 'For…*with*…it doesn't matter. Vawter, on the other hand, *was* working with him…up until very recently. Don't ask me what happened, but there's been a breakdown of trust. So, while Tzedek has me up here keeping an eye on his ex-conspirator, he's pushing ahead with the plan, anyway.'

'Which is?'

'Kiranis. It's *all* about Kiranis, sweetheart. I mean…I'm just going with what I've…*overheard*…' she grinned again, 'but apparently, they found a way to get onto the planet once it reappears. Tzedek's got further plans, though, and if it all works out, the Jaevisk are gonna think Christmas has come. Or whatever their equivalent is. But with everything that's going on back home, I think we're the only ones left to follow through.'

'I don't buy it,' Abigale argued, shaking her head. 'How's our little fleet supposed to get through the Jaevisk blockade?'

'No, no, that's not what I mean. They've got some mysterious stealth craft for getting through the Cage.'

Abigale laughed derisively. 'Sounds like nonsense to me.'

Jena shrugged, satisfied so much with her misdirection. 'Whatever. But from what I can figure out…once Kiranis is back, we've all the time in the world to get on to it.'

'What do you mean?'

'They're gonna make sure it doesn't disappear again.'

Ω

Vawter could not get out of Medical fast enough. He ran down the corridor, Romis and the others watching him flee. He thought of returning to his quarters, but the girl would be there, and he could not face her just now. The revelation with which he was dealing was eating away at him, firing his stomach with dread, and he had no idea that Abigale and the waitress had been looking for him until he literally bumped into them. Jena was knocked from her feet as Vawter rounded the junction with such haste that he almost passed them. 'What's going on?' Abigale shouted.

He stopped and turned, his features haunted and terrified. Then he walked swiftly up to her and tried to speak, his lips trembling, tears in his eyes. She took his hands and asked him gently, 'What's wrong? What's happened?'

'Am I alive?' he whispered, his voice breaking. 'Am I…real?'

'What do you mean? Of course you are.' Abigale glanced back at Jena as she got to her feet and asked, 'Why would you say that?'

'Something's happened,' he explained, transfixed by Abigale's unexpected compassion and finding himself compelled to truth. 'Your…daughter. She…' He hesitated, before saying as if someone had told him, 'It was *me*.'

She released his hands, and he was instantly crestfallen, as if a life-giving tube had been dragged from his body. 'What do you mean?' she demanded, stepping back from him. '*What* was you?'

'I need to check the records for station Alpha-3,' he told her, turning away from her. But she grabbed his arm, spinning him back to face her. 'What have you *done*?' she shouted at him. 'What did you do to her?'

'No...' he pleaded. 'It wasn't...really me.'

'I'd get to the point if I were you,' Jena suggested.

He nodded, staring into Abigale's angry glare. 'I think I've been...used,' he said. It was such an understatement that he found himself laughing desperately as he left the two women behind. This time, when he walked away, Abigale did not follow, and as he quickened his pace and his mind, he struggled with it all. His people thought he knew about Kallon Raesa, and Tzedek went along with his bluff to that effect. Abigale's daughter, who had been taken through MEC and came back...different, recognised him. Tzedek must have murdered and then sanctioned a clone of his closest ally so he could further manipulate the situation and take power for himself. It was the only explanation, and on top of that, Tzedek somehow and for some reason cloned Romis. Probably to ensure complete control over the doctor's work. But the agreement with the Kwaios had been clear on one thing: if the truth were about to come out, the evidence had to be eradicated. Luckily for Vawter, it was all in one room.

Ω

Vawter's frantic exit was not forgotten, but Ganna had other things on his mind, and he was moving around Romis like a visitor in a zoo. 'How is this possible?' he said.

'What?' asked Romis. 'That I was brought back to life?'

'Cloning is hardly the same, Romis,' Ganna argued, 'which you know quite well. The consciousness isn't transferred. Memories are wiped.'

'You sound like you don't believe that,' noted Tom.

Ganna shrugged. 'I...I know I don't *want* to, but what kind of technology has to be involved to do something like that? So quick, so perfect...and to retain your identity...?' He shook his head. 'It's a scary thought, but…if it's true, you must realise what you're suggesting. That it's not our technology.'

'The thought had crossed my mind,' Romis admitted. 'The work I'm doing with the Messina clone is decades away from this sort of thing…at least. But how you find that more amazing than matter-energy conversion, I don't know!'

'But what about Vawter?' asked Tom. 'You think he knows?'

'When I saw his reaction to Hannah, I was tempted to dismiss it, but…I can't be sure. What if there's a Vawter clone out there doing whatever it wants? Pretending to be him and using his resources?'

'What if the one we just *spoke* to is a clone?' Ganna suggested. 'How the hell would we *know*? And anyway, what's Vawter's clone doing taking children on sight-seeing trips by MEC?'

Tom made a growling sound and looked as if he might pull out his hair: 'This is all way over my head!'

'Well, you're not alone on that, Tom, trust me,' said Romis. 'I've no idea what we're supposed to…' The lights went off in the room and the door closed, locking with an audible clunk of doom. All the equipment around them deactivated and there was the faintest hissing sound from above. 'What's that smell?' asked Ganna.

Ω

Abigale and Jena reached the door of the sick bay just as it closed and locked. They stepped back in surprise and pressed the keys of the access panel. But the panel went blank and nothing happened. Then, from inside the door, they could hear shouting and pounding against the metal portal. 'Doctor!' Abigale shouted, hammering her fist in response. 'What's happening?'

'Stop Vawter!' came the muffled response. 'He's…' There was the noise of coughing and gasping for breath. Then there was silence.

Abigale and Jena exchanged glances of shock. 'He's *what*?' Abigale called desperately. Then they heard what sounded like something falling to the floor. 'Oh, my god, where's *Hannah*?' Abigale screamed, once again banging the door in vain. '*Hannah*!'

The sounds from inside had ceased and Silence called to Abigale, telling her all she needed to know. Slumped to her knees before the door, she sobbed and called for the girl who was the centre of her universe. Jena watched her and momentarily

104

considered consoling her, but Vawter was on the move, and she had a mission to complete. Leaving the captain to her despair, Jena hurried to intercept her mark.

Ω

When Jena came into the docking bay, Vawter was walking towards a small shuttle – her shuttle. He saw her and she stopped, taking in his appearance. Dressed entirely in black, he looked more like a mercenary soldier than a playboy weapons' salesman. He carried guns, knives and gadgets, and all traces of his recent emotional breakdown had evaporated. 'I have work to do,' he called to her as she walked across the vast floor towards him.

'Maybe I can help,' she suggested. He looked at her for a moment, his expression advising her in its silence to cease her progress. She stood and waited as he looked her up and down, this time uninterested in her body and noticing only now the clothes she had been wearing in the corridor. As well as the black leather jacket and grey fatigues into which she had changed, she had even dared in her desperation to carry a gun in her belt. 'A little out of character for a waitress,' he noted, his lips stretching into a thin smile of what may have been admiration. She moved gradually closer, aware of the proximity of his sidearm to his free hand. 'When you work in the Senate buildings, you have to be prepared for anything.' She took his soft chuckle to be one of genuine amusement, which in a sense it was, but it was a mistake not to consider it further. 'I suppose you do,' he agreed. 'Maybe you *can* help me.' He gestured towards the shuttle, an invitation she accepted without sufficient analysis, convinced she was still on track. After all, she still controlled the bomb.

Ω

Carenna was on the bridge when the Argo received the communication request. Through the starboard window, she could see the shuttle on which the mercenary girl had arrived moving away. 'Lock weapons and put it up,' ordered the commander. The viewer activated, a network of holographic projectors that seemed to close the physical gap between both vessels as Vawter and Jena appeared to sit amongst the crew of the Argo. Carenna took in the still confusing alliance of Vawter and the mercenary girl seated next to him. 'It's time for me to leave,' he said simply, absently working the console in front of him. 'And you're wasting your time with a weapons' lock…' He looked up: 'Just as you were in trying to seal the bay.'

Carenna's glance to her weapons officer confirmed it as he shook his head. Vawter's control of the situation was complete, and he capitalised on the momentum: 'Tell Captain Saranne to go to my quarters if she wants answers.'

'*Answers*?' Carenna roared. 'You've just *murdered* her *child*! What could you *possibly* say to her?'

'You've no idea what's going on here, Commander,' he replied. 'But with my *personal* goals in jeopardy, I've even less consideration than usual for other…situations. In saying that, I had no part in hurting the *real* Hannah Saranne. Head for the Sieltor system, find a ship called the Styx…and its captain will take you where you need to go. Use only the upgraded FTLs. Stay away from MEC. Your friend out there will be doing the same.'

'There's no *way* I'm turning my back on you,' Carenna snapped, stalking up to the holographic Vawter. 'You *sit* there…you arrogant son of a *bitch*…and dictate to *me*? After what you've *done*?'

'Just accept that you don't get it, Commander,' Jena interjected. 'Things'll go a lot easier that way.'

'For who? *You*?' She turned to Vawter: 'You *do* know who she is, don't you? Cos I find it very hard to believe you fell for her crap!'

Vawter grinned and Jena realised. She reached for a gun but he was already there, pointing it at her head. 'Oh, *I* know,' he said. 'I just wanted to see how this played out.' He winked at Carenna and the viewer deactivated, returning her perception of the bridge to normal. All they could do was watch the shuttle moving farther away. Heading for Phobos.

Ω

Within minutes, Abigale sat silently in the half-light of Vawter's room. Carenna had warned her not to do this, but she desperately needed answers. Despite the horror of Vawter's confession – if that was what it was – he was undoubtedly the only one who could provide clarity amidst this nightmare. Waiting on the table in front of her was a small black cube, no more than two inches square. She had heard of these devices; she knew they were a communication gateway to the most fearsome species in the galaxy. Her fear, warranted as it surely was, was in no way a match for her curiosity, and she reached out to take the cube in both hands. It was cold, and she shivered as she closed her eyes and took a deep breath. When she opened them again, everything had changed. Shimmering columns of blue and silver rose high into the darkness above her, crystalline tubes twinkling and pulsing with lights and energy. The floor was polished black, reflecting the apparent infinity of the virtual structure. As she gazed in wonder at the mirrored floor, she saw the upturned image of a man approaching. She looked up swiftly and saw him there. 'Don't be afraid,' Vawter gently warned her.

'What is this?'

'It's a recording of sorts. Think of this as a...chat room on the global net.'

Abigale's laughter was no more than a mocking exhalation. 'This is no global net. You're using the Kwaios communication network to leave me a message.' She shook her head. 'How are you responding so freely?'

'The interface is intelligent, designed to use my image to answer your questions. It adapts accordingly.'

Abigale found that she was able to stand up, as well as wondering if she was really still standing in Vawter's quarters. 'Would it adapt if I kicked you in the balls, do you think?'

'I don't understand the question,' the image replied casually, immediately losing its realism for Abigale.

'Get to the point!' she snapped. There was a pause, as the image presumably prepared to launch into Vawter's recorded message. It flickered and was suddenly dressed differently. The clothes appeared casual and unpretentious, so unlike the man she thought she knew; and yet so like the man of whom she had dared to catch a glimpse. 'I have very little time,' he began, 'but I need you to appreciate the enormity of what I'm about to tell you. I felt that I could open up to you...in a way I haven't done since my Amara died...'

Abigale had heard the stories about Antarctica and she was intrigued, but flashing imaginings of Hannah's fate tempered what sympathy she might have dared to experience as he continued.

'Since then, I've struggled with an intense fear of death, an obsession with the knowledge…the *knowledge*,' he strained, 'that one day my life will stop. I realised that the only way I can defeat this…death anxiety…is to –' The image buzzed and crackled, and Abigale felt a chill run through her as it moved closer, replaced by a Samuel Vawter dressed in more functional, military-like clothing. His expression was set, determined, his voice more urgent: 'I'm a clone,' he announced coldly, all traces of his earlier panic evaporated. 'Just like your daughter was.'

Abigale was horrified. '*What*?' Her stomach turned: 'How's that *possible*?'

'We made a deal with the Kwaios. They gave us the technology to move freely around the galaxy and we gave them…us.'

Abigale's head was spinning. 'I don't understand,' she said. 'Why would the Kwaios want human clones?'

The image buzzed, and Abigale realised there were limits to how much this projection of Vawter would give away. It was sticking to a script: 'There was a plan,' it continued. 'To get Kiranis back.'

'How?'

'We have a special ship for the mission. A small prototype craft that's centuries beyond us. And centuries beyond the Kwaios.' The projection smiled: 'They'll be distracted by their own agenda.'

'Which is?'

The buzz again. Then: 'I've decided to abort the mission. I have something else in mind. Something more…personal. I've turned on Tzedek and he'll want to punish me…and anyone with me. The only person who can protect you is Arrien Echad, the great-grandson of the Captain of the Nostradamus. He knows everything. He's out at Sieltor Promies.'

'What about my daughter?' Abigale's anger was muted and controlled, her loss and confusion weakening her. 'Where is she?'

'Arrien will find her.'

The words lifted her beyond measure, and the tears came: 'What do you mean? *How*?'

But the image faded, and she was left standing alone for a moment until the Kwaios communication room also disappeared. She was lost, and felt helpless for the first time since her husband died. But if this Arrien could find her Hannah…the *real* Hannah…then she would set the galaxy alight to find him.

Ω

As soon as Abigale stepped on to the bridge, Carenna came up to her and cut her off before she could order the course for Sieltor. 'We cracked it,' she said. 'It's a key! A trigger!'

'What do you mean?' asked Abigale, still reeling from the conversation with the projection. 'A key for what?'

Carenna was clearly excited. She loved this stuff: 'Her shuttle is the catalyst for a catastrophic systems overload...for one specific vessel. It took a while to find it. An old flame working in Vawter's R and D division was...*painfully* eager to help out.'

Abigale was intrigued. 'The stupidity of men, right?'

'You got it!' She took the captain by the arm and led her to the monitor showing the craft. It was not unlike the Argo, but many times smaller. 'May I present to you the latest prototype stealth craft from Vawter Inc!'

Abigale gasped, feeling like an idiot: 'This is it!' she said. 'The one they're gonna use to bring Kiranis back!'

Carenna's eyes widened: 'Ah...*what*?'

'I'll explain later.' Abigale looked out the forward window. 'If she destroys it, she'll change everything. She couldn't be working for Tzedek. She might not even be working for anyone on *Earth*.'

Carenna was beyond taking it all in. 'So, what do we do?'

There was a clear choice: save Samuel Vawter from the mercenary and potentially change the course of human history; or take the Argo into Garran territory and face a terrible onslaught to find the one man who could find her daughter. She saw Hannah's blank face again at the MEC feeder post. Then she saw her – her *clone*, goddammit! – choking to death in Medical. 'Get us to the Sieltor system,' she ordered. 'Vawter's on his own.'

Ω

The small shuttle brought Jena and Vawter to Phobos, the innermost moon of Mars. 'Are you going to explain why you took my ship?' she asked him. He had secured her to her seat, and she had remained silent as they made the trip, revising, recalculating. There was more than one way she could activate the systems overload, and it was all about timing now.

Vawter simply smiled and pointed as something came into view. It was at the same time black and non-existent, its outer hull apparently merging with the blackness of space around it. 'The stealth ship,' she realised, exhaling dramatically. 'Why is it out here? I hope it's as good as it looks.'

'It's called the Redeemer,' Vawter told her, 'and it's out here because I had it moved out here.' He looked at her pointedly: 'And nothing's as good as it looks.' He sent a signal to the Redeemer, which was not large enough to contain the shuttle within, but instead had an interfaced airlock designed to treat attached craft as part of the greater whole. This Jena knew.

Vawter docked the shuttle with relative ease, and he took a deep breath to calm himself. 'I'm coming for you,' he whispered. Jena presumed he meant Tzedek, and said nothing, preparing herself. Her heart was pounding as she realised that she would have to die with him.

'How well can you fight?' he asked her. 'I mean *really* fight. Cos where we're going is heavily guarded and Tzedek will expect it. I don't plan on getting off the Redeemer once we're aboard, but...just in case.'

Her curiosity got the better of her. 'I can fight,' she said coldly. 'But I fight better for a reason.'

Vawter nodded. 'I get that. You know, when you said your name was Amara...' he chuckled ironically, 'I knew you had to be part of this. You had to come with me.'

'Oh, really?' Jena was sickened, her anger rising.

'I mean...I knew you were lying and used the name to mess with my head, but...' He moved to her and began releasing her from her bonds.

'Did the name bother you that much?'

He looked at her and their eyes met. She saw the tears there and was momentarily thrown off course as he said, 'More than you could possibly know. She was everything to me. My life.' He moved away and headed towards the airlock. Tapping the access panel, he was focused on accessing the Redeemer as Jena used the console before her to activate the program as she said with a broken voice, 'She was my life, too.'

'What?' Vawter turned to her. 'You *knew* her? I thought you were just another gun for hire.'

She nodded: 'It's ironic, really. Your company erased my identity a long time ago. Before you even met her. I'd been hired to infiltrate the New Elect.'

'So…how did you know Amara?'

Jena stalked up to him, her mask completely gone, her teeth bared: 'You left her to DIE!' she roared. 'They pulled you out and you never went back in!'

Vawter backed into the airlock: '*What*? No…that's not what happened!'

'Well, that's what they told me…when they *finally* told me. I had no idea where she was…' She was openly crying now, years of pain and rage pouring out as she found herself in the moment she had fantasised about for years. 'She was…all I had.'

Vawter remembered a fleeting conversation with the woman he had loved. He recalled how proud Amara had been, of the only member of her family who had never hurt her. 'You're her *sister*!'

'Yes,' she sobbed. 'And I've nothing left. No one.'

'But that was *years* ago!' Vawter pointlessly argued, as Jena stepped into the airlock and closed the door behind her. 'Why didn't you come to me back then? Why wait all this time?'

'I waited…and watched. I wanted to see you grow in power and get close to what you wanted. Before taking it all away. Before ending it all.'

The fear gripped him, turned his stomach as he realised she meant to kill him. 'What have you done?'

'The moment we board the Redeemer, a systems overload will begin. It'll destroy it.'

'What? *No*! I *need* it!' He was surprised that he did not prioritise his own life at that crucial moment: 'I have to *save* her. I have to get her *back*!'

Jena could feel her blood running cold and her head was light: 'What are you talking about?'

He held his head with panic as he replied, 'The Redeemer follows the *Lines*. I can get back to Antarctica…back to when it happened.' He roared in anguish, and lashed out at Jena, pinning her by the neck to the airlock door behind her. 'I have to *save* her!'

Jena's mind was reeling, and she could not find the will to fight him. But just as she reached up to grab his hand, something happened. It was as if something had struck the shuttle, or the Redeemer, or both. 'What was that?' Vawter demanded of her. But

111

she did not know. And, stuck in an airlock lest the Redeemer explode, neither of them could have known that a Kwaios ship was dragging it into its giant belly.

THE BODIES

Senate Buildings, Tokyo

The Shield had remained closed throughout the Central night, and Tzedek had monitored the activities of the renegade fleet carefully, witnessing the departure of a shuttle carrying two people from the Argo to Phobos. Then he had been informed – very quietly – of the materialisation out there of a Kwaios ship, and he had breathed a sigh of relief, confident now that things were back on track. He was sure now that Naveen had anticipated it all, but still it was better to see these things come to fruition than to simply accept them on faith. And he knew, since Kallon Raesa's warning about the Illeri, that Naveen was keeping a lot from him. *Oh, to know the bigger picture.*

A meeting was arranged in the Senate chambers, and the table was occupied by interim representatives of global constituencies, people Tzedek could trust to abide by his reasoning; for he himself had appointed them. They sat and waited as he stared out of the window, watching the re-opening of the Shield. The morning sun poured in as if the walls of a dam had crumbled before a torrent, and Tzedek squinted with the pleasure. The Argo was gone, and with it the bothersome fleet, undoubtedly under the command of Captain Saranne. And these people had no concept of the great scheme unfolding around them.

'What happens now?' someone asked. Tzedek chose not to turn around as he replied, 'We examine our findings and proceed accordingly. I take it there are findings to examine, considering my orders.'

'The Illeri vessel is under close observation as we speak,' another voice explained, 'but we've found little of interest. The Illeri are still refusing to explain their silence, ignoring every communication request.'

Tzedek stretched his neck, moving his head around in a circular motion, looking upward and exhaling noisily. 'I ordered the ship boarded, did I not?'

A short silence. 'We thought it would be prudent to determine their intentions and capabilities before such action –'

Tzedek spun around. 'Listen to yourself, Pritchard,' he snapped, 'babbling on like some politician in the media lights! I ordered the ship *boarded*! Simple as that. I also wanted the nearby station raided. Why wasn't that done?'

A military figurehead at the opposite end of the table stood and said, 'I refused, sir.'

Tzedek was dumbfounded, shaking his head and closing his eyes lest they fall out of his head. 'You...*refused*?'

Pritchard chose his ally. 'General Tellin is the most experienced military man in this room, Senator Tzedek,' he defended him, 'if not on the planet.'

Tzedek nodded. 'Now that Vawter is gone, perhaps,' he conceded, 'but that doesn't give him the power to rescind my orders. I'm sure you have an explanation, General.'

Tellin nodded. 'We all witnessed the arrival of the Illeri ship, and the subsequent attack. It's quite obvious...with all due respect, sir...that the only weapons capable of combating them are on vessels belonging to Vawter. And of all ships, the Argo is gone!'

'Are you suggesting, General...that I give our old friend a call and ask him to lend us a hand? Hmm?' Tzedek walked the length of the table, heads turning to regard him. 'Come back, all is forgiven...is that what you're saying?'

Someone cleared their throat. 'Yes?' Tzedek enquired, looking in the direction of the sound. 'Ah, Mister Adler...you have a question?'

Adler hesitated, but his curiosity found his courage: 'May we ask...Senator...exactly what Vawter did that you *can't* forgive?'

'No, you may not. Suffice to say that there are things none of you need to know. Bear in mind that you are not the new Senate, and I might warn you not to get too comfortable in those chairs. You're here to assist me and to maintain order in your constituencies. Is that understood?'

There was a general murmuring of assent. 'Is that *understood*?' Tzedek shouted. The assent was considerably more vocal, and Tzedek looked at the general again. 'Now, will you carry out my orders,' he looked across the room, where armed guards stood...waiting, 'or should they carry out theirs?'

The general did not need to see what was being suggested. He took a com unit from his pocket: 'Red Squad, move to board hostile vessel. Blue Squad, enter monitoring station Gamma-5. Authorisation code Alpha 8-1-2.'

'*Acknowledged*,' each team replied. General Tellin fixed his eyes on Tzedek: 'It's done.'

'Now, that wasn't so difficult, was it?' said Tzedek. 'Sit down.' He began to journey around the table to the right of the general, his hands clasped behind his back. He was silent until a discreet beeping sound alerted the gathering to an incoming message. Tzedek removed a small device from his pocket and a hologram activated in the centre of the table. In transparent blue, a woman stood and introduced herself. '*Apologies for the disturbance, sir*,' she began. '*I'm in charge of the clean-up crew after the recent Garran incursion.*'

'The Jaevisk showed up too, if I recall,' Tzedek reminded her dryly.

'*Of course, sir, yes. There's been a development amongst the debris that I believe is…significant. Am I free to speak?*'

Tzedek considered that for a moment, but he anticipated little trouble in the conversation: 'Go ahead.' As he spoke, the general slammed his fist on the table and shouted, 'Damn it!'

'What?' Pritchard jumped to his feet and everyone looked to the general. The holographic woman was speaking, but no one was listening. 'They've been wiped out,' Tellin explained. 'The Illeri ship opened fire before they got anywhere near it!'

Tzedek took a deep breath, sensing the diminishing faith of his interim government. 'What about the station?'

'Empty, except for four Illeri biosuits.' The general rose from his chair, adding, 'Whoever or whatever was in that station has somehow escaped.'

'Somehow isn't good enough, General. Tell your men to keep looking. If something got out, they need to find how and where.'

'And the Illeri ship?'

Tzedek hesitated, feeling their eyes upon him. '*Sir…I need to know how to proceed. Can you hear me?*' The hologram was still talking, and Tzedek returned his attention to the miniature woman: 'You'll have to repeat that.'

'*The MEC fuel ship, sir*,' she explained. '*What should I do about it?*'

'Why should I care what you do about a fuel ship?' he asked.

'*There must be a bad connection, sir.*' The girl hesitated. '*I was talking about what we found inside the fuel ship. Human bodies, sir. Lots of them.*' Everyone heard her that time, and now their eyes were boring holes in Tzedek's head.

Kai Tzedek had always been a consummate liar, ever since he was a child. He had not thought of his mother for quite some time, but just then he could picture her condescending smile and hear her voice in his head as she said, 'Can't wait to hear you talk your way outta this one, Kai.' But just as he was about to try, everyone heard the sound of the door of the annex room unlocking. They may even have heard Tzedek's heart pounding as he rushed to intercept the emerging enigma.

INTERVAL 1
FOUNDATION

If we do not commemorate, and re-enact, and revisit in our minds the deeds and words of our ancestors, we will forget not only what they have done, but the world they created for us. Indeed, if we forget the past, the future is lost, for it is founded upon the world of today.

From the 'Musings of Marcellus Echad' (c. 440 NE), discovered in pseudo-Kwaios data-nodes in the wreckage of the Omega Orbiter. Ironically, little is known of this Echad patriarch, but his legend ensured the longevity of the family ideology, which remained firmly planted in stories of a bygone Earth and an ancestor murdered by their sworn enemy. Only after the 7th Century decimation of their legacy did the remnants of the Echad family actively seek to ingratiate themselves to posterity. Of course, considering the Millennium Event, it is likely much investigation into their past would inevitably have been undertaken.

Kwaios Wreck, High Earth Orbit, 298 NE

Nine-year-old Samuel could not stop smiling, so much that he had a pain in his jaw. His father held his hand, looking down every now and then to make sure that the rest of his son was still attached. Elias Vawter was a burly man, towering over his stringy little boy, but the demeanour he displayed to the rest of the world was completely alien to Samuel. He had never before experienced it and Elias had no intention of ever allowing such a thing to happen. Grandfather Vawter had been a tough son of a bitch and Elias had never felt close to him. He did not want the same for his relationship with Samuel. Of course, there was also the danger of being too soft on the boy, but there was time for change. He was only nine, after all. Elias smiled down at Samuel, and the boy smiled back, his eyes wide with excitement and anticipation. Whereas the rest of the world might have interpreted the smile as that of a wolf before feeding, Samuel knew that it was a smile of love and warmth and the promise of safety.

The two Vawters stood in the airlock as the hissing of depressurisation filled their ears. 'No one's ever been up here, Sammy,' Elias told his son for the hundredth time, proud that he had arranged this visit. 'Imagine that…they just left it alone.'

Samuel nodded, looking back at the mercenaries behind them. Twelve armed men and women accompanied them on their little trip, and Samuel did not understand why. His eyes fixed on one of the automatic rifles in his line of sight. 'Don't worry, kid,' the closest man told him. 'We're not gonna need these.' Samuel nodded again, and looked back up at his father, who smiled again. Everything was fine.

'You double-check those readings, Jack?' Elias asked in his deep voice.

'Yep,' Jack replied, flicking the safety switch on the rifle at which Samuel had been looking, as the outer airlock began to open. 'Nothing doing, Boss.'

Elias glanced down at the safety switch, raising his eyebrows as Jack shrugged and said, 'Force of habit. Don't worry about it.'

'I don't worry,' Elias reminded him.

The wall of air which hit them as the seal was broken on the other vessel was stagnant, but the smell was more metallic than organic. Elias was reminded of the smell of his antique coins in his sweaty palm and was surprised to find that he did not like it. 'Well…' he said by way of ceremony as he took a step forward, 'let's see what the Kwaios left us.'

Twenty-eight years had passed since the Kwaios attack on the Shield. The wreckage of their vessel, small by Kwaios standards but still dwarfing battleships at Earth, hung in the sky in the way of the moon. At certain times of the year, people could see its strange, broken form overshadowed by the celestial satellite. Unsure as to whether the Kwaios crew had died from the Illeri defence or whether they would take some time to die, no one had bothered to send anyone up to investigate. There was enough happening on Earth to keep security forces and the military occupied, and Grandfather Vawter figured he had enough Kwaios technology to keep him going. That and the risk involved in boarding a Kwaios ship kept him and everyone else away. Elias Vawter, however, was different. He ate risk for breakfast, hoping he might choke on it a bit just so he could feel how close to death he could take himself before coughing it up. Elias Vawter looked up at the moon one day, saw the Kwaios ship grinning down at him and knew that he had just been dared to come visit. So, he hired the right people, and brought his son along with him, intending to show the world just what sort of risks he was willing to take, and what sort of risks humankind should be taking to make themselves kings of their own castle once more.

They crossed the threshold and Samuel suddenly felt different. With that single step, everything changed. This was not fun, nor exciting. The ghostly chill in the air inside the alien ship had just whipped away any warmth he might have imagined was emanating from his father or his protective hand. 'Dad,' he said meekly, 'I don't like it here.'

For Samuel Vawter, the Universe changed in that moment, for as his father turned to look down at him, all Samuel saw was a demonised version, thrown into shadow by the cold blue lights of the still active hybritech as he replied, 'Grow up, boy. This is the day you become a man!'

The mercenaries pushed past them, spreading out and beginning their recon. Dragging Samuel with him, who had now started to whimper with tears on his cheeks, Elias decided to wander around without the team. The ceilings were incredibly high, and Samuel nearly fell backwards as he tried walking and looking up to the shadowy heights amidst the Kwaios pillars. There were no corridors in the ship at all. Instead, an immense open plan deck was suspended amidst the great pillars of flickering blue and silver, and there were circular gaps around the tops and bottoms of each pillar so that one could see the decks above and below. The Kwaios could not have fit through those gaps, but Samuel knew that he would, and he began to think that he would trip and fall down one of those holes and become lost in the basement of this monstrous place. Or perhaps fall forever. 'Please, Dad,' he begged, 'can we go home?'

Elias twisted him violently as he got to his knees before the boy. 'Listen, Sam!' he snapped. 'I want you to remember everything you see here. Look around you and remember everything!'

Samuel sniffed and asked, 'Why?'

'Because this is a Kwaios ship,' Elias reminded him. 'And they hate humans. They hate you, and they hate your mom. Whatever you're told in school or by anyone else, we have no friends out there in the galaxy. All of them hate us, and the sooner you realise that the better.' He stood up and gestured expansively to indicate their surroundings. 'And the Kwaios hate us most of all, you can be sure of that.'

'But why...why does everyone hate us?'

'Cos we don't belong here, Sam. Don't they teach you kids anything in school?'

Samuel shook his head. Apparently not. 'But why do I have to remember everything?' he pressed. There was shouting from their left and Elias grabbed Samuel, lifting him in his arms and carrying him. The boy almost went headfirst over his father's shoulder as Elias ran, but his father continued to speak to him. 'One day...' he panted, 'you'll be...as powerful as me. More even. You need to learn...everything about them. Then you'll be ready.' They came upon two of the recon team, Jack and a younger man, standing before a vast array of consoles and equipment. 'What is it?' Elias demanded. 'What did you find?'

Jack pointed at one of the upright consoles, confused by what he had discovered. 'You should probably check it out yourself,' he replied. 'I can't read their damned language.' Elias let Samuel down to the floor and took his hand again, dragging him over to the console and glancing cautiously at Jack as he passed him. He could see the man was edgy, and he could sense the tension in the air. Elias unzipped the front of his jacket as he came to the console, his back to Jack and his comrade. Elias had learned a considerable amount of the Kwaios text, considering that his father's financial success had been built on Kwaios technology. 'What does it say?' Jack asked gruffly. 'How did it get here?'

The question was too shrewd to have been incidental, and Elias realised that Jack was not as uneducated as he had hoped. 'I'm guessing you've figured it out for yourself,' Elias replied.

'What's he talking 'bout, Jay?' asked Jack's partner. 'You can read that shit?'

Jack had one hand on his rifle, keeping it low but ready as he continued with Elias: 'You knew about this?'

Elias shook his head, refusing to turn around. 'It was a theory, that's all.'

'A theory? Sure...I get it. The powers that be didn't want anyone finding out the truth, so they didn't even bother investigating.' Jack chuckled darkly. 'No wonder there's been no life-signs up here for so long.'

'We have to be careful what we say from here on, Jack,' Elias told him. 'There was no truth to be found until this moment, alright? No one else knows.'

The younger man stepped closer. 'Someone gonna tell me what the hell's goin' on?'

Samuel jumped in fright and stepped closer to his father as Jack spun on his partner and shouted, 'There are no *bodies*, you idiot! There never were!'

The guy looked from Jack to Elias to Samuel and then back to Jack before asking, 'What do you mean...there never were? Someone took them?'

'There was no crew on this ship,' Elias explained, still looking up at the console. 'I told them to check. Again and again, I told them. It made no sense. This thing's been sitting here for nearly thirty years and the Kwaios never came to claim their dead or even destroy the ship to stop us getting our hands on it.' He shook his head. 'We should have seen it coming. After what they did with the Cage...'

'I don't get it,' the young mercenary admitted. 'No crew? Like it's a...'

'A drone, yeah,' snapped Jack. 'They sent it here to attack the Shield.'

'But not to test our defences,' Elias added.

'No.' Jack suddenly stepped in and pushed Elias aside, failing to take note of how the big man responded as he slapped his hand on the console and explained to his young comrade: 'They did it so we'd keep building the damned thing! The Illeri defences took them out and we all threw our hats in the air and said, "Hey guys, you wanna hand?"' He shook his head and added, 'It was all a trick. The Kwaios saw us coming before we saw them.'

'So...' the young guy was still catching up, 'the Kwaios are helping the Illeri?'

'Give that boy a badge!' Jack spun round to face Elias, only to find himself looking down the barrel of a gun as Elias said, 'I'm sorry, Jack.'

'The hell you *are*!' Jack shouted as he raised his own gun. But it was too late. Elias shot him in the throat and then turned the gun on Jack's partner, who was too stunned to react. 'Well, you sure aren't value for money,' said Elias as he pulled the trigger. Samuel had bundled himself in under the consoles and his father simply reached down and grabbed him out. 'Time to go, Sam,' he told him. 'They'll come looking for them and they won't be happy.' He dragged Samuel by the hand again, saying, 'Two I can handle. Ten...that's a different story.'

Samuel could hear shouting from behind them and Elias gathered his son up in his arms again, hurrying back to the shuttle. As he stepped through the airlock, he took a brick of explosives from an overhead bin, activated the attached trigger and hurled it back into the Kwaios ship. He sealed the airlock just in time to keep their pursuers out, and the mercenaries hammered soundlessly at the glass, screaming and cursing Vawter. The shuttle moved away, and the outer airlock closed, separating Samuel and his father from the horror of the Kwaios ship.

Samuel certainly did remember everything about that day. He remembered everything about that ship and about how much the Kwaios hated him and his mother. His mission had started that day. His life as he knew it had begun that day. But what Samuel remembered most was the revelation of his father's true nature. In the shuttle on the way back to Earth, the boy looked up to him and took his hand – the one which had fired the shots. 'You said I'd be ready, Dad,' Samuel reminded him. 'Ready for what?'

Elias smiled down at him, and this time Samuel saw the wolf as his father replied, 'Ready for the war, Sam. Ready for vengeance.'

That was a strange thing to say, and Samuel had not understood it then. He fell asleep on the way home, not waking even as the shockwave from the explosion which obliterated the Kwaios ship rocked the shuttle. He learned a lot as the years went on, but nothing was as important as what he had learned that day – that nothing and no one was ever what or whom they seemed. Everyone was capable of great subterfuge. His father had hidden his true nature from Samuel until that day, but it was through the revealing of Elias Vawter that the true nature of the Kwaios had ultimately been revealed. Years later, when Elias Vawter lay dying, Samuel took his hand and looked at him. They had not spoken for a long time, and Elias had but one question for his adult son: 'Are you ready, Sam?'

Samuel leaned close and whispered his answer, and Elias died with a smile on his face. The smile of a wolf.

PART 2
SIELTOR

After a long time, the Slavemaster died. Our Brothers and Sisters cried out in their anguish, praying to the Sentience to grant them peace. For they had been bred for war. But the Sentience remembered its children and took notice of them. Their cry was brought to the Breath of Ascension, and with him came hope, and life. He was the First, born of an age of endings.

In the *Lamentations of Omneri*, the author takes some liberties in reconstructing the history of our people held captive in the Sieltor System. The allusion to the events of 330 NE is more concrete here, but we can move our *terminus post quem* to a much later date, knowing that the eclectic works of the Si Monks – to which the Lamentations belong – was not begun until after the Reunification of the 7th century NE. Note especially the reference to Carak Tae Ahn in decidedly derogatory terms. This demonisation of the Garran Elder inherently overlooks the role he played in protecting the Echad line.

THE SLAVEMASTER

Khas City, Sieltor Prime, 330 NE[2]

The old Garran looked out over Khas city, a metropolis embracing the horizon in every direction. It was a decidedly ugly place these days, he thought, with its choked levels of transit and a hundred and twenty million Garran doing everything they could to survive it, endure it, get out of it. But Carak was not one for flight. He had faced Sori, Cquaston, Jaevisk and human enemies in his time. And, of course, the Kwaios. He had looked into the eyes of evil incarnate, a burning face of malevolence that he hoped never to comprehend, let alone see again. Some of the things he had done were justified by his own sense of right and wrong. Some were not. And others still were justified by an outside party – a wolf in sheep's clothing, as the humans would say. This outside party had visited him on numerous occasions over the many years since his encounter with the mysterious time-travelling Garran he had known as Malik Ki Jen. He had later learned of Malik's true name, but it had been too late by then. When you were from the future, looking back at the concrete nature of the past, genealogies did not lie. They laughed, chipping away at your conviction that things could be changed, while you choked on the dust. The outside party to whom all things were justified had a habit of laughing at his pawns. For they knew not what they did.

As the sun pressed down on Merchant's Peak, an enormous structure bearing witness and worship to the paradoxical success of the unnecessary, Carak knew that he was no longer alone in his reverie. Without turning around, he said, 'I find the futility of it all quite humbling.'

Naveen respected the use of the Garran language, mainly because he admired its uniformity across all Sieltor worlds, an achievement unmatched by humans with only one world. And so, he replied in Garran: 'It's often beneficial to be humbled.'

Carak grinned, turning as the Prophet approached without disturbing the dusty surface on the high rooftop. '*You*?' he

---

127

chuckled, changing to English. '*Humbled*? When exactly did this monumental event occur?'

'Well…that's a matter of perspective, I suppose.'

The old Garran nodded. 'Good to know it'll happen someday.' The sun burst upon the peak, flowing down its flanks as it sank farther below the constructed horizon. They watched its descent in silence, until Naveen asked in the new darkness, 'So, did it help? Being introduced to the bigger picture?'

Carak shivered, for various reasons. 'That was decades ago, Naveen. And when Anya died in my arms, the last thing I was thinking about was the bigger picture.'

'One death is all it takes, Carak. Each is as significant as another.'

'I find that hard to take…from you.'

'You think I don't value them?'

Carak heard the ice in his tone and regarded him briefly. 'I no longer know what to think. Knowing that the World Killer is going to turn up in my family one day fills me with greater humility and helplessness than I had ever thought possible.'

'Would it help to know that he didn't choose his path?'

'Not in the slightest. Not considering that you'll put him on it.'

'You presume too much. Chaerakh won't be born for another few hundred years. A lot can happen.'

Carak sighed. 'I'm too old and tired for all this. What do you want, Naveen?'

Naveen laughed genuinely: 'You *live* for all this, Carak. I'm surprised you get out of bed without an elaborate conspiracy theory as to how you got there!'

The Garran chuckled softly. 'You could be right. This morning I found myself wondering about the supply chain behind my mattress. By lunch, my desk was full of the manufacturer's financial records.'

'My point exactly. You're obsessed with deception. You see it everywhere.'

'Because it *is* everywhere. Now tell me what you want and leave me in peace. Tell me what you want and promise me I'll never see you again.'

'Now *that*…I can promise.'

Carak turned to him, knowing that this was it. The last task. After this, no one would be able to ask anything of Carak Tae Ahn. 'Will I have time to see my family?'

'I'm not going to kill you, Carak.'

'But someone will.'

Naveen nodded. 'You'll have some visitors from Earth soon. Things will get…complicated, and your work will finally be revealed to the humans.'

'I'm almost relieved by that. But please tell me I won't be killed by some idiot human with a grudge.'

'No. They're coming to support a mutual acquaintance. *You*, on the other hand, will have to answer to someone with whom you've long shared the details of your experiments.'

Carak's heart skipped: 'The Kwaios? They're coming for me?'

Naveen gave a thin smile: 'I need you to ensure your visitors get to Heragon.'

'Are you *insane*? You want me to reveal where the Kwaios hold countless *millions* of humans?'

'That's exactly what I want you to do. A ship called the Argo is coming this way. It's extremely important that it gets to Heragon, and that will only happen if you lead the way. You'll recognise the bait when it gets here.'

'Cryptic to the end.'

'Indulge me, Carak. The Argo has to get to Heragon, and you need to arrange a little…adjustment to its architecture. This is your chance to do something that will restore the balance of power. You did help the Kwaios tip it in their favour, after all.'

'I don't need reminding!' snapped Carak. 'But directing the humans to Heragon will *infuriate* the Kwaios. They'll wipe us *out*. It's not only me you're endangering here.'

'It's only you, Carak. You have my word.'

'Well, that's incredibly comforting! Give me *something* to work with.'

'Abigale Saranne is the Captain of the Argo,' Naveen explained, 'a ship powered by a one-of-a-kind quantum intake engine.' Carak held his gaze as his mind raced with the implications, before the Prophet added, 'Oh, and she's coming for Arrien Echad.' He vanished as the city was coming alive with artificial light and the sounds of evening. Carak stood wide-eyed for a moment. The Echad boy was coming here. A boy no more, of course, but still…finally…it was coming to an end. And the Argo had a QUIC engine! He shivered again, the immensity of Naveen's scheme reminding him of his mortality. If anyone had stood with him, he would have explained that the moisture in his old eyes was caused by the wind coming in from the west. But that would have been a lie.

THE ECHAD CHILD

Ptah, Second Moon of Sieltor Omneri

It was not merely at Earth that the consequences of the Cage event still resonated. For the great-grandson of Adam Echad, the consequences were personal, for he believed that through them he might understand who he was. He suffered from nightmares, erratic and inconsistent occurrences the rarity of which was offset by their intensity, and he was not ashamed to admit that they scared the hell out of him. At least to himself. He was also fully aware that they had begun only once the truth had been revealed to him. Senator Kai Tzedek had explained it all to him, and sometimes Arrien wished that he had not:

Following the return to Earth of the Nostradamus and the burial of the murdered Adam Echad, his partner, Anya, had been spirited away to an undisclosed location to await the birth of her son, fearful of what she described as a demon stalking her. Her family never saw her again, and it was never learned whether she had survived or even if her child had been born. It was a secret kept from the public domain. But the child had been born, the line continued, and evidence of genetic mutation quickly came to light. This was the secret kept from the Jaevisk, the reason the Echad legacy was so significant; for the rumours about the stowaway on the Nostradamus, the man who had claimed to be from the future and in possession of strange psychic powers, began to resound with a ring of truth. Anev Tesckyn tried to locate Anya, but despite his resources, he could not. Rumours abounded that the newly appointed governor of Sieltor Prime, Carak Tae Ahn, had a hand in protecting Anya from exposure. But back then, the world was full of rumours and speculation as the chaotic aftermath of the Cage event reshaped Earth forever. Another popular theory roused the attention of Tesckyn, as he made allegations against a civilian weapons' contractor named Gilbert Vawter, accusing him of hiding Anya and her child and endangering humanity by not offering the child to the Kwaios Council; but the allegations were never confirmed. After Tesckyn's assassination and Vawter's rise to the forefront of Earth's weapons production and his newfound association with the government, people stopped asking.

131

No one on Earth knew that Arrien existed, because interest in the story diminished amidst the changing tides of power. Decades later, there were only a handful of people on Earth who might have considered it important that a descendant of Adam Echad was still around. What Arrien could not know, of course, was that someone visiting Earth was asking for him. For now, he embraced the anonymity to which he was so accustomed, using the freedom it brought to do what he must. He vowed to find the people he called The Exiles, descendants of those taken from Earth by the Cage and then handed over to Carak like an unwanted present so he could do with them as he wished. It was ironic that the descendant of a child said to have been protected by Carak would find himself committed to infiltrating Garran territory and exposing what he believed to be the greatest atrocity suffered by humans at the hands of those occupying the Sieltor worlds. As he sat fixated on the drone feeds, a tiny internal voice reminded him to question why that infiltration was only now proving successful. For the Garran had protected this secret for a hundred years.

Arrien had trained with the best, but only he had succeeded in piloting multiple microdrones at once. Holographic projections floated before him, permitting control of three simultaneous drone flights, and the trick was to use one's peripheral vision so that the eyes never needed to move. Arrien had honed his peripheral vision with the aid of meditative viewing, a skill he had developed under the tutelage of a Sori blood priest whose fascination with human physiology had facilitated a proverbial meeting of minds; not to mention Arrien's unbridled access to the Sori home world, Senkara. Despite visibly antagonising every Sori with whom Arrien came into contact, the patronage of a blood priest was sufficient to guarantee his safety. After learning some everyday phrases in the dominant dialect amongst their complex primary language, Arrien gradually found some of them warming to him. They were at least tolerant of his presence, and that was a start. It all changed with the study of human victims of a Sori raid, when the blood priest compared them with what he had learned of Arrien's physiology. The priest accused Arrien of deceiving him and things went rapidly downhill. The escape from Senkara had upset Arrien on numerous levels, mainly because the closest any human had come to peaceful relations with the Sori had been disrupted by the fact that Arrien was not the same as the rest of his species. In truth, this event served to crystallise his resolve for finding the people held on the Sieltor worlds, because more than ever before he saw them as *his* people. They had been different amongst the people of Earth, and they remained different to this day. There were other possibilities on Earth for contact, of course, but the Church of the New Elect had remained so well hidden over the past century that Arrien decided against seeking them out. The last thing he wanted was to expose them again to the prejudices of society for the sake of his own personal mission. Anyway, it was clear that someone very powerful was protecting the Church. Tzedek and Vawter had been looking for them for years, and they had apparently incomparable resources at hand. Of course, their ultimate goal was finding the descendants of the people taken to Kiranis, but Arrien knew that one had to accept one's limitations. At least Sieltor Omneri was still in this universe.

'How's the mesh holding up?' Arrien asked, from a flight chair suspended from the ceiling of the drone deck on his ship, the Styx. Beneath and around him, everyone else was engaged in cyber defence, maintaining the geo-mesh routing network allowing Arrien to pilot the drones on an alien world. The use of drones for warfare and surveillance had reached its peak on Earth in the late twenty-first century, with UAVs and MAVs operating almost self-sufficiently around the planet. Advancements in artificial intelligence meant they had become semi-autonomous extensions of security organisations, acting independently upon information gathered from surveillance networks. Ironically, the obvious dangers of these advancements were not the reasons for the eventual decline in drone warfare. Instead, the vulnerabilities of the control signals were exposed as cyber-terrorists devoted themselves to disrupting the ever-expanding networks created by the drones as they covered more and more territory. The drones responded by cycling their transmission frequencies amidst real-time firewall redactions, counter-attack coding, and redundant deflection signals, but it became clear that control should be transferred to more secure laser-based orbital networks. The prototype geo-mesh was born, a network of thousands of control nodes around the planet through which the activities of the drones were maintained. Each relatively tiny node needed a propulsion system, maintaining a geosynchronous orbit relative to a surface position corresponding to the original terrestrial network. Decades of surface networking was extrapolated and transferred to the new orbital network, and live viewing mapped the world without having to wait for obsolete military satellites to reach optimal positions. The cost was immense, financially and ethically. Robots watched the world, everywhere and all the time, acting on their own mechanical initiatives. The geo-mesh looked like it was there to stay, until the events of 2150.[3] Following the Move, when everything orbiting Earth vanished and the people encountered the Garran for the first time, it was clear that guarding one's immediate territory was no longer a priority.

'It's holding,' someone called from below. 'The AI is starting to notice something's not right, but it'll think for a while that it could be a firewall glitch or a bunch of sensor echoes. It won't sound the alarm until it detects our firewall.'

'Less than six minutes 'til deterioration curve,' another voice called out in the marginally illuminated room. Arrien was the only person to redevelop the geo-mesh system. Travelling through space on vessels large enough to carry hundreds or even thousands of people was one thing; infiltrating alien worlds undetected was something else entirely. Drones were vital to surveillance operations in enemy territory, but Arrien doubted his strategy would have worked any farther into the Sieltor system, or even on a larger body. Ptah, the second moon of Omneri, was a very small celestial object, a mere one thousand kilometres from pole to pole, but like its parent, it was heavily industrialised. Information gathered by Arrien's diverse intelligence network had led him here, and initial sweeps of the moon appeared promising. In three major population centres, there were anomalous life-form readings amongst the Garran. Granted, there might have been Axcebian merchants or even Sori slave traders down there, but not in these numbers. No, finding hundreds of non-Garran on the moon of a world known for advanced technological and biological experimentation aligned perfectly with the information Arrien had received. He was positive that this was the place, that he was finally in sight of his objective, and three days ago he ordered the construction of the geo-mesh around Ptah.

---

[3] As per n.1, 2150 CE was retrospectively designated 'Year 0' of the NE (New Era) calendar.

The nodes were nanoscopic in Arrien's design, necessarily so to avoid detection during the deployment and construction phase of the mesh. The covert nature of the construction made for an agonisingly slow affair, and the crew had been stretched to their psychological limits amidst the fear of discovery. Three days of nerve-jarring work was then immediately followed by this surveillance operation, which could only last eleven minutes. The problem with Arrien's geo-mesh was ironically reminiscent of the now centuries-old terrestrial drone network. It was ultimately detectable, and it would eventually lead those who discovered it back to the operator. That was why Arrien had equipped the nodes with a deactivation protocol, designed to collapse the mesh and render the nodes inoperable within a given timeframe. Following the operational peak, the deterioration curve monitored the gradual top-down deactivation of hierarchical systems within the nodes. The rapid decrease in control, which would take less than ninety seconds, meant that everything needed to be done before the peak was reached. In other words, Arrien had less than six minutes to find The Exiles.

The microdrones were visible once attention was drawn to them, so it was imperative to keep their flight obscured until engagement with the target was absolutely necessary. The flight of the three drones could have been delegated to others in the crew, but Arrien knew that he needed to take full responsibility here. Any mistakes would be his alone. Of course, success would also be his alone, and that was more important. The drones were each within a kilometre of their respective target buildings, as Arrien had planned their rate of approach so their arrival coincided. From the command deck, a report came to his earpiece concerning the fleet of cruisers orbiting the moon: 'Arrien...cruiser twelve just powered up manoeuvring engines.'

'Probably just stretching their legs,' he replied calmly. 'Let me know if they break formation. 'Til then...zip it!' Arrien took a deep breath and regained focus. Fifteen powerful star cruisers were in orbit only a thousand kilometres outside the outer reaches of the geo-mesh. If they detected it...Arrien pushed the thought back into the darkness where it belonged. The drones were within visual range of their target buildings and there was no room for distraction. Around him, the men and women staffing the drone deck quit their chatter as they continued their counter-detection measures.

Drone One entered its target through a ventilation duct high in the east wall, Drone Two flew without constraint underneath a damaged door, but Three was not so lucky. The third target building was part of an old tectoplasmic refinery sitting atop a vent which, Arrien had been informed, was sealed. The drone, its heat shields deteriorated from passing through the atmosphere, could not handle the heat from the vent. A different route could have been calculated had Arrien been given the correct information. He neither visibly nor audibly reacted as he saw the drone drop from his control, but he swore to himself that someone was in for a bloody nose within the next ten minutes. And they could almost feel it. What they could not have known was that the loss of Drone Three was only the beginning.

Drone Two rose to the ceiling of a long corridor that opened into a large circular chamber. The drone rotated and mapped the room so that Arrien could ascertain its dimensions and make a decision. Three staircases led to three mezzanine levels, and there were four rusted doors in various states of disrepair, one of them looking like someone had tried to break out from behind it. 'Gimme a direction, you stupid robot!' he snapped. 'Follow the life-signs!' He reached up to remove Three from the holo-imagery and spread One and Two across his field of vision. Drone One was still negotiating the ventilation system in what they presumed was an enormous manufacturing plant, but it also seemed to have lost its way. 'They've stopped tracking,' he whispered, before demanding of the crew in general, 'Why've they stopped *tracking*? I'm not showing any guidance errors.'

'Four and a half minutes!' came the report of the imminent operational peak.

'Answer the damn question!' Arrien shouted. In the corner of his left eye, he could see a monitor flashing red. 'What's going on?'

'The AI's on to us. But it's emitting sensor ghosts rather than attacking the drones.'

A computer playing with them: that was almost an insult. Arrien felt a momentary taunt of insignificance as he imagined that no real live Garran would even know he had infiltrated their facilities if the AI got the upper hand. With the drones unsure as to their destination, Arrien would have to take complete control. 'Kel,' he called calmly, 'warm up the engines. Quietly.' Less than four minutes until the mesh started deactivating and more real live Garran than they could handle would be all over them. 'On it, Boss,' came the reply over the com from his favourite voice amongst the crew. Arrien found himself relishing the potential engagement, because the Garran would not expect his exit strategy.

Ω

Shrouded in a darkness concealing their boredom, the Elders listened as the master aide brought the news: 'We have yet to locate the control ship, but the AI at Ptah has detected a robotic infiltration.'

'A *robotic infiltration*?' one of the old Garran mocked. 'I believe the humans call them "drones".'

'Why presume there are humans out there?' another countered. 'The aide is simply bringing us facts devoid of speculation.'

'Who else would –'

Heavy leather shifted in the shadows as a deeper voice interrupted: 'Silluc is right. Speculation leads only to misjudging the situation.'

'And how…exactly,' asked the first voice, 'would *you* judge the situation, Carak?'

The eldest of the Garran Elders laughed but chose not to waste time on childish argument. Instead, he addressed the aide: 'Order the Omneri Guard to open fire on their patrol.'

The first Garran audibly choked. '*What*?' he snapped. 'Are you *insane*?'

'Quite the contrary, Menalis. I simply know how to deal with a prowling wolf.'

'What are you talking about?'

'I'm going to kill some sheep.' He stepped down from his seat on the raised platform in what had once been the Hall of Governors and he leaned in to whisper something to the aide as he reached him.

'What are you telling him, Carak?' Menalis demanded. 'We've all had enough of your secrets!'

Carak ignored him as Master Aide Halek bowed and dismissed himself. In the time since the overthrow of Ben-Hadad, the

137

administrative and political structures of the Sieltor worlds had been altered by the swift and violent ascendancy of the Tae Ahn family. Carak had both risen into and redefined the ancient role of the Elders, but his continued dealings with humans and his past dealings with the Kwaios – as well as the mystery of what had happened to him out at Kiranis – meant that some of his political counterparts maintained a measure of usually cloaked suspicion. Clearly, that cloak had been thrown to the floor; but today, Carak was quite happy to wipe his feet on it. 'They are *our* secrets, Menalis,' he replied, after a moment of silence sufficient to remind the other of the pecking order. Apparently, it was a wasted moment.

'Really?' Menalis countered. 'How is it, then, that only *you* are aware of the details?'

Carak grinned. 'I'm merely protecting you, old man. This way you can remain unaccountable.'

'*Old man*?' Menalis' laughter was almost genuine. '*You* are the eldest here, Carak!'

Carak held his angry glare as the proverbial penny dropped, before saying quietly, 'Precisely. Eldest amongst Elders. If that means nothing, then *we*...mean nothing.'

'We are supposed to be a collective,' Silluc argued. 'That should mean something, Carak. We serve our *people*, not ourselves.'

Carak looked to the fourth Elder, who remained silent as he smiled softly and nodded. And Carak knew then what he could do for these aged servants. 'Menalis, Silluc...Geram...' he looked at each in turn, 'I know you all wonder and whisper...and I've kept you in the dark about a lot of my activities. But I allowed myself to be drawn into something far greater than myself...or our people. I can't tell you what's coming, but I can tell you this: get away while there's still time. Spend your darkening years somewhere far from this system...and far from *me*.' He focused then on Menalis: 'Because it won't be long before you're thanking my ghost for keeping *my* secrets...to myself.'

He made to leave, and Geram asked, 'Is there nothing we can do?' But Carak made no reply, continuing to walk away as he heard Menalis snap, 'Don't be such a *sycophant*, Geram! All he wants is for us to keep our noses out of his business!' He shouted after Carak: 'I won't be manipulated, Carak! Do you hear me? I'm not afraid of you and your spies!'

Carak ignored him, walking out of the dusty irrelevance of the Hall of Elders and feeling neither sadness, nor regret. Instead, the unmistakable warmth of excitement was coursing through his veins as he set out on a path that would change everything. Reaching sunlight, he drew himself up, inhaling deeply and thinking about Naveen's portentous words. Yet as he released his breath, he smiled and shivered with delight, feeling more alive than he had ever thought possible. If Death were coming for him, Carak would make the beast work for his soul.

$$\Omega$$

'Just reached OP!'

The deliciously comforting hum of the ship's engines kept Arrien focused, and as a cold blue light pulsed around the drone deck to indicate they were now operating within the deterioration curve, he felt a great calm descend upon him. It was disrupted as someone shouted, 'Missiles launched from the surface! They're targeting their own fleet!'

That was unexpected. Someone with at least as much guile as Arrien must have been calling the shots, but Arrien read this course of action as a sign of desperation. 'They're here,' he whispered. 'I found them.' Every second was crucial now, but the last ten minutes had proven fruitless. With the tracking failure, it had taken almost half that time to manually correlate the drone travel with the overlaid maps marked with destination points. When Arrien had eventually flown the two remaining drones to those respective coordinates, he found two empty sites and cloned signal emitters. With only four minutes remaining, the drone crew found another set of life-signs, and Arrien had chosen to take the risk of flying the drones to a second destination. The actions of the Omneri Guard on the moon below convinced him that the risk had been worthwhile.

One of the star cruisers was hit by a volley of missiles, and it broke apart spectacularly, thousands of soldiers murdered by their own. There was no effect on the Styx, and the last two drones still raced towards the reacquired life-signs amidst warnings of dying fuel cells. 'Another round!' The ops officer was panicking now. 'They're on to us, Arrien!'

Arrien realised that both drones were heading towards similar terrain despite their positions in different regions of the moon. The topographical projections showed only flat wasteland along their trajectory, but there were other, more unsettling, readings. 'Massive levels of radiation, Arrien,' he heard a quiet female voice report. 'Probably testing grounds.'

Her tone was sufficient to make Arrien's heart sink. 'It's a trap,' he realised. 'They're distracting us up here!' Another star cruiser was blown apart, and Arrien was shaken in the suspended chair by the proximity of the blast. 'You missed a surface launch, Alex!' he snapped. 'Find it!'

'I...' Alex checked his monitors. And he found it. 'They must have hidden them in the first volley. Arrien, they're almost on top of you.'

Arrien flinched as a missile overtook each of his drones, but the fuel cells lasted long enough to see where they were headed. To see something he would never forget. Filling two impact craters and stretching as far as the camera on each drone could see were piles of human bodies. The images were seen by every member of the crew on both the drone and command decks, but only for a second. Still, it was long enough to see their broken, naked bodies before the feed was lost amidst an intense flash of light from which everyone averted their eyes. Arrien did not, could not, hesitate: 'Full weapons! Thrust six!'

The Styx erupted from inside a hollowed-out star cruiser, in the middle of a fleet being attacked from its own command centre. Were it not for the ensuing debris field and the chaos and confusion, twelve star cruisers would have torn them apart. Still, the Garran recovered quicker than expected, and the intruders took a battering. They only managed to limp away because of some clever manoeuvring and, as Arrien would later learn, the Garran continued taking fire from the moon. To say that this was unexpected was a gross underestimation of the circumstances, although it made sense in light of the final horror he and his crew would see before leaving Omneri; for the field of floating bodies in Garran military uniforms through which they made their escape were not Garran at all. They were human.

Ω

Menalis was infuriated by Carak's dismissive attitude. Who did the man think he was to ignore a descendant of Sensata Hag Mar, the Hero of The Lacettin Arc? Of course, considering that the man had only moments ago ordered the deaths of thousands of Garran soldiers, Menalis' damaged pride could wait. He gestured to his personal guard, and the four heavily armed men and women stood close to him as the remaining Elders emerged from the hall with their own protective detail. 'Geram. Silluc,' Menalis addressed them as they stepped out of the shadows, catching them by surprise.

'Menalis?' Geram raised a hand to assure his and Silluc's guard that all was well. Still, the tension was palpable as Silluc asked, 'Why are you waiting out here?'

'I like to speak in the open,' Menalis replied. 'Unlike the...eldest amongst Elders who has you so enthralled.'

'Carak has always put the good of our people first, Menalis,' Geram argued. 'Granted, he may not include us –'

'The *good* of our *people*?' Menalis spat. 'He wiped out the entire San Setta family and marginalised any others capable of challenging his own! How was that for the good of our people?'

'If that were true,' said Silluc, although without much conviction, 'then it resulted in much needed stability.'

'Stability?' Menalis looked at Geram. 'Do you think his *latest* move will result in stability?'

They exchanged glances, remaining silent until Silluc asked, 'What do you intend to do?'

'You mean...because you're both afraid to take action?' Menalis acknowledged their silence: 'I'll go to Omneri and find out what's going on out there.'

'The planet's likely to have been locked down, Menalis,' Geram warned him. 'You won't get close enough to launch a lander.'

Menalis smiled. 'Well, it's a good thing your whore-runners have long had no problem evading the Omneri Guard, Geram. Of course, that's probably because the Guard sample the merchandise before sending it down to the miners.'

As Geram stammered pointlessly, Silluc made a good show of looking disgusted, but Menalis had gathered enough information over the years pertaining to the vices of both men to know that neither could even see the moral high ground. 'Menalis,' Silluc put in, 'I think you should know that the entire fleet was destroyed out there. The Guard continued to fire even after the humans escaped.'

Menalis was stunned. '*Why*?' he gasped. 'Why would he give such an order?' His shock quickly turned to anger. 'And HOW…could you *possibly* support such a murderer?'

Geram shook his head. 'Menalis, you know Carak's allies are more powerful than any force we could gather against him. Do you really want to risk bringing the *Kwaios* to our door?'

'What I want to *risk*…is regaining control of our *destiny*! If we do *nothing*…then we really are as worthless as Carak suggested.' He glared at Silluc, but a flick of his right hand mobilised his guard and they raised their charged weapons. 'Are you with me on this?'

Silluc knew that his and Geram's protective detail would not be fast enough to save either themselves or their wards. 'No more Garran need die today.'

'They don't usually die on *my* orders,' Menalis reminded him. 'Where is your fleet?'

'The majority of it protects Teuvas.'

'The Jaevisk have long stopped caring about Teuvas. Get your ships together. I'll transmit coordinates to rendezvous at Omneri. Both of you will liaise with your contacts out there and get us through the blockade.'

'How?' Geram demanded. 'They won't want government ships poking around.'

'Follow the lead of your illustrious Elder,' Menalis suggested. 'Lie!'

Ω

Arrien was back on the command deck, considerably less confident of his trajectory than when he had left it. The rest of the crew were silent, processing what had happened while allowing their commander do the same. After a while spent staring into the distant blackness between the lifeless asteroid to which they had anchored themselves and their death-filled memories of the encounter at Omneri, Arrien rose from his seat, shook his head, and said, 'I'm sorry.' No one responded, and he continued: 'I shouldn't have brought you out here. I mean…I knew it would be bad. How could it *not* be, right?'

'It's not like we're on a draft, Arrien,' Kel reminded him. 'We all volunteered for this.'

'I know,' he replied. 'But what we just saw…' He exhaled heavily and walked towards the forward window. And the melancholy was infectious. A tall, burly man approached him and whispered in his ear, 'I didn't volunteer.'

Arrien turned to Jaime with an incredulous expression: 'What?'

With a matter-of-fact tone that only this giant of a man could get away with, Jaime nodded and said aloud, 'Yeah, man, I'm in it for the money.'

Arrien stared at him, and the room was deathly silent. 'What's the problem, Jaime? You're worried I'm backing down?'

Jaime raised his hands defensively. 'Hey, I just wanna get paid. Money when the curtain falls, right?'

'And not before.'

'Well…curtain's still up. Quit standing round and let's do what we do.' Jaime returned to his station and Arrien looked around at the crew before asking, 'Which is…*what*…exactly?'

'See this thing through,' said Jaime. 'You think we got those people killed, right?'

'Don't *you*?'

Jaime shook his head and grinned. 'See, now I *know* you're not on form. I'm thinking all we saw out there was a commercial.'

Arrien held his gaze and then nodded. 'They knew we were there all along.'

'And they put on a show.' He pointed at Arrien: 'For you.'

The crew were enthralled. '*Me*? What makes you say that?'

'You've always said the Garran would be experimenting on the descendants of the New Elect. But we haven't heard anything back home about the Church for a hundred years!'

'The Garran would have to breed them,' Kel put in.

'And control their numbers,' Arrien realised. 'Carefully.'

'So, they wouldn't just wipe out thousands without at least planning ahead for replacements.'

'So, there are more. Maybe a lot more.'

'What if…' Kel paused. 'What if they were already dead?'

Arrien puffed his cheeks and blew out: 'You mean…the star cruisers were drone ships?'

'Why not?' Kel looked out into the darkness as if she might see the floating bodies around the Omneri moon. 'If it was a show, for *you*, then all they wanted you to see with *your* drones was death. Make you think the trail's gone cold.'

'It's incredibly complex to drone something as large as a star cruiser, Kel. I mean, we saw what they were using for the attack on Earth. Why use something so small when they could have used our people as cannon fodder in much more powerful ships?'

'But if they could...' Jaime pressed, 'what would that mean?'

'A number of things.' Arrien lowered his head and stroked his eyebrows with a forefinger and thumb. 'First of all...that Omneri was a trap. A distraction while they moved their base of operation. Second...that someone knew we were hiding inside that star cruiser. Considering how long we planned for that, that concerns me. But the third...the third is much more worrying.'

'Why?' asked Kel. 'What is it?'

'Sam Vawter told me a story once about a drone ship. A big one.'

'Let me guess,' Jaime quipped. 'You can't tell us about it?'

'Not right now. But if whoever is over the program we just saw being shut down back there...has the technology to drone a star cruiser, I'd be willing to bet they're not working alone.'

'Oh,' said Kel, 'I see where you're going. The Kwaios.'

'I think it's worth keeping in mind...even if you're wrong, Kel. It was the Kwaios who delivered these people to the Garran, after all. Stands to reason they'd keep an eye on their investment.'

'So...what you're saying...' said Jaime, suppressing all irony, 'is that if I wanna get paid...we're gonna need some backup.'

Arrien grinned. 'Considerably more,' he agreed, although his grin died as he saw Jaime's expression. 'Don't worry, big man,' he assured him. 'I've still got friends back home.'

Jaime nodded. 'Okay, but we're out *here*...and the Kwaios like playing games.'

Arrien could think of no response. Because Jaime was probably right. The problem was that only Arrien knew the implications of a possible Kwaios involvement, considering the games they were already playing back home.

Ω

Halek had been Master Aide to the Elders for as long as he cared to remember. And he did care. His father had served in the court of Ben-Hadad, and Halek had watched the man lose all faith in the system. Halek had felt the thrill of revolution course through his veins when the San Setta and Tae Ahn killed the fat governor and set about restructuring the socio-political world of the Garran, but it was swiftly bled of its potency by the systematic murder of those perceived to have supported the old regime. When Carak had then orchestrated the annihilation of the San Setta, Halek realised that nothing had changed. As expected, Carak had called Halek to his service, explaining that while he would ostensibly be Master Aide to the Elders as a single political entity, his loyalties lay ultimately with Carak himself. Halek had accepted, knowing that his father would have been proud. 'Remember, Halek...' the old man had whispered as he lay dying and Halek held desperately to his hand, 'that no matter who is in power...there is nothing more important than loyalty to one's family.' Halek remembered.

He watched the dropships arriving, certain that no one would be monitoring the activity of a few trading vessels weighing anchor at this abandoned refuelling depot on Crith, the barren third moon of Sieltor Promies. The Sori lander dug its claws into the dusty ground and spewed its depressurisation, while the representatives of the Axcebian and Vesstal interests were approaching from their respective craft. The Cquaston had not yet landed. The eight-foot Axcebian reached Halek first and inclined its great head, speaking through a translator embedded in its skull: 'You have called us here earlier than expected. Where is Elder Carak?'

Halek smiled amiably. 'Carak has directed me to begin the demonstrations and accelerate the process. The merchandise is ready, and he wants the sales to move swiftly once he reveals his purpose to our people. These are...delicate times.'

The Vesstal was female, shrewd and suspicious: 'We had been assured that Carak alone would oversee the proceedings. We are taking huge risks trafficking in humans.'

'As are we,' Halek reminded her. 'You may leave now, if you wish, but the bidding will begin without you.' The Vesstal acquiesced, and Halek saw that behind them, the Sori Slaver had not come alone as instructed. 'Why have you brought a blood priest?' Halek demanded.

The crimson-skinned alien seemed to gurgle and cough, a language which the Sori refused to transmit to others for creating an interpretative database. Halek's translator detected the language and made an attempt: 'He interest of human physical body. Confirm difference to blood read.'

Halek thought a moment, while in the distance, the huge form of the Cquaston Trader was lumbering towards the secret gathering, creating a dust-cloud in its wake. 'If I understand you correctly,' the master aide replied, 'your priest wants to check that these humans are different to normal ones.'

The Sori Slaver turned to the blood priest, who gestured that this was correct. And Halek realised that the priest understood Garran without a translator. He addressed him directly: 'These humans have been bred from those taken from Earth by the Kwaios Council. They are considerably different.'

The priest responded in Sori, for speaking the Garran language was not in his repertoire: 'Different, yes,' the translator chipped in. 'Considerably...' The priest stared at Halek for a moment, before adding, 'I confirm.'

If they knew that Halek had an arsenal of automated weapons trained on them, they would not be so bold. But he knew that his status as an underling had to be maintained for a little while longer. The days of serving Carak Tae Ahn and his ilk were about to end abruptly. The coup of the San Setta and Tae Ahn a century ago had changed Halek's world, and he had positioned himself knowing that Carak would choose to console the son with an occupation worthy of his family name. But that was decades ago, and the wait had been long and frustrating. Halek now walked the tightrope between the tempting impetuosity born from being so close to his goal, and the regard for patience now that his decades of observation and intelligence were about to pay off. As the great bulk of the Cquaston Trader reached the group, Halek smiled and turned to gesture towards the huge door behind him as it began to swing open: 'I assure you all that you are about to be rewarded for your patience. Once you take possession of the merchandise, you'll come to realise why Elder Carak had to keep his work secret for so long. And whatever the Kwaios are up to out at the Kiranis system, you'll be one step ahead if they ever mount an attack.'

Halek did not need to hear the translator's attempts at interpreting their excitement as they made their way past him. But nothing could match his excitement. For he was about to change Carak's world in a way the Elder would not possibly anticipate. Because there was nothing more important than loyalty to one's family.

Ω

There was no blockade. As his fleet came up on Ptah, Menalis pointed to the swathes of sweeper bots orbiting the Omneri moon at high speed. 'What are they doing?'

'They're gathering up the dead nodes from the drone control grid,' the commander explained. 'The humans left them behind.'

'I imagine they had little time to collect them,' said Menalis dryly. 'Has there been any response from the Omneri Guard? I want to understand why they fired on their own troops.'

'You mean apart from Elder Carak's orders?'

Menalis turned sharply. 'That's *precisely* what I mean, Commander!'

The commander was silent, and Menalis understood why as he caught a number of glances from the intrigued bridge crew. 'You think I'm at risk of creating a precedent here?' he asked the man.

'I do, sir. If you were to give such an order right now...you would want it carried out. And I would at the very least lose my command if it were not.'

The old, but not oldest, Elder sighed and nodded. 'It's a difficult situation, Commander. And this is a conversation we will take up again after we know what happened here. Now, has there been any response?'

'Nothing, sir. But we're picking up residual radiation from a number of surface locations. It looks like there have been five nuclear detonations...very recently.'

'Put us in orbit of the closest location. Distribute the coordinates across the fleet and disperse our ships accordingly. Contact Elder Silluc's command ship and have them head directly to the debris field. I want them to see –' There was a silent, shadowy impact against the starboard window, and everyone looked to see what had caused it. There was nothing to be seen at first, although sensors began picking up incoming objects. Menalis walked towards the window, seeing a slowly spinning object getting larger

147

and larger as it approached the ship. 'What is that?' he demanded, pointing. 'Are we under attack?'

'It's too slow to be a missile,' said the commander. He looked to his officers: 'Well?'

'It's a body, Commander,' came the report. 'Must be from the Omneri fleet.'

'What?' He came up beside Menalis and watched the military-uniformed corpse spinning towards them. Then he saw the rest of them. 'Look!'

The ships of the Elders were still outside the standard parking orbit for Ptah, and it was that alone which spared them the bombardment. Thousands of bodies had fallen into that orbital path, as had the debris from the ships they had recently manned, and all of this rushed around from the other side of the moon as if in a race. It was a chaotic, horrific scene, the spinning and slamming together and breaking in pieces of bodies and metal kept in check only by the order of gravity. Like a nightmarish asteroid field, some of the bodies were knocked out of the orbital path by internal collisions. And it was these poor souls which were colliding intermittently with the ships of the incoming fleet. 'Commander! Elder!'

They both turned as one of the officers called them to her station. 'What is it?' asked Menalis.

'I'm…not sure what this means,' she said, as they came up to her and she pointed at her monitor, 'but those bodies out there are not Garran!'

In silence, Menalis and the commander stared at the readings, and the rest of the bridge crew were mesmerised as Menalis confirmed, 'They're all human!'

The commander felt an immense relief, but kept his emotions in check. At least now it mattered a lot less that the Omneri Guard had destroyed their own ships. 'How do you wish to proceed, sir?' he asked Menalis. 'The Omneri Guard will clean this up.'

Menalis turned to the man with disgust. 'Clean this *up*?' he snapped. 'You think that because they were human, they're now just floating *garbage*?'

The commander restrained from responding as he indeed believed, opting to wait until Menalis walked away to the forward window and issued his orders: 'Disperse the fleet and get teams down to every one of those detonation sites. I want to know what else happened here.' He turned back to the commander: 'I suggest you begin by wondering why thousands of humans were manning our star cruisers. Because whatever the Omneri Guard just helped Elder Carak to cover up...whatever he's got planned...he clearly doesn't need any of his own species to carry it out!'

Ω

Arrien was getting tired of looking out at the rock surrounding them, but the crater into which the Styx had been moved kept them surrounded by sufficient metallic elements to confuse Garran sensors. Kwaios sensors were another matter, of course, but the relative proximity of the scores of battleships and star cruisers which had just arrived at Ptah kept the Garran top of the watchlist. Once they turned their attention to finding Arrien and expanding their search grids, the asteroid field lying between the orbital paths of Omneri and Promies would be an obvious focal point. According to the ghost probes Arrien had ordered launched into their wake, the newcomers were currently more concerned with what had happened on the surface than anything else. It was with that information that Arrien realised that what they had witnessed was not necessarily the obliteration of a concerted Garran program to infiltrate Earth. Instead, it was much more likely that a rogue element in the Garran leadership was running the Omneri show. And that sounded all too familiar to Arrien.

Relations with the Garran had deteriorated over the past century to such a degree that even their political structure was now an unknown entity, but Arrien could read the writing on the wall: Carak Tae Ahn was still the Belshazzar to Arrien's pious prophet. In fact, with lifespans exceeding those of the human average by sixty or seventy years, Carak could have played any number of Babylonian kings while imagined saviours came and went. The great irony was that while Carak was surely approaching his end, Arrien knew that his own life had yet to truly begin. So, in the same way that Babylon had provided the foundation for a new way of seeing not only the past but ultimately the future, this alien place in which Arrien now found himself would define him. He simply had no idea how.

Kel's voice interrupted his thoughts. 'Make it good news,' he pleaded as he turned to her.

'I think we found another facility,' Kel reported. 'Closer to Promies. We'll have to skirt the belt to get there, but there's been a lot of activity coinciding with our visit to Omneri.'

'So, Jaime was right. We're being led by the nose.'

'Could just as easily be the Garran on their own,' Jaime offered. 'Looks like they cleared the Omneri facility just before we got there.'

'I don't think they're alone in this,' Arrien disagreed. 'Someone told them we were coming.'

'You wanna keep going?' asked Kel. 'I'm still trying to get Raesa, and we could really use that stealth ship right now.'

'He should have been back from Illeri by now,' Arrien mused. 'The Redeemer's one of Vawter's...*prized possessions*, as he'd say. Fastest thing he ever made. Try cycling the frequencies and keep on it, but...we can't wait any longer. The hounds'll be on us before we know it. Plot our course and get us moving.'

Ω

Halek knew there was something wrong. The Sori Slaver and his accompanying blood priest had moved away from the others – and from Halek's translator – and their discussion sounded excited, heated. Without understanding their language, Halek interpreted the priest's expressions as evidence of his frustration. Behind Halek, the other representatives were each examining the physiology of one of the four comatose human drones, and from what he could gather, they were impressed, and the respective deals would soon be closed. So, what was the problem with the Sori?

'How have you determined that they are fully adaptable to our needs?' the Vesstal female enquired. It was a perfectly valid question, but Halek ignored her, moving towards the Sori. The others were instantly alert to the change in atmosphere, and they watched as the Sori turned to face Halek. The slaver unclipped a weapon at his waist, and Halek pressed a button hidden in his right palm. Silently, the automated guns concealed above and around them rotated and chose their respective targets. 'I gather there's something that concerns you,' said Halek. 'Whatever it is, I'm quite sure it can be remedied.'

150

The blood priest spoke, and Halek's translator picked it up: 'These humans...different. Not considerably. Not enough.'

'Not...*enough*?' Halek wondered. 'I don't understand.' Neither did the others, but their suspicions grew and they edged closer. The Sori Slaver explained: 'Priest see human considerably different. Human stay. Human learn. Human false. Priest seek now.'

Halek stared for a moment. *What are they talking about?* 'Are you talking about a specific human?' he asked. *Is this the only reason they're here?* 'It would not be one of ours, I assure you. They are all coded and contained.'

'What do you mean...human false?' the Vesstal asked. Halek was really starting to dislike this one.

'I study human,' said the blood priest. 'Teach see many at one time. Earth human not able. These humans...' he pointed to the drones, 'not able. Considerably different human able. Considerably different human...false.'

Halek felt a chill run through him. *Could he actually be talking about Carak's pet project? This could work out a lot better than I had expected.* 'This human...' he said, feeling the eyes of the others on him. 'You're saying he was different from his species *and* from these...' The next word hung on to his tongue for a moment, teasing him as he realised the irony of the conversation. 'Drones,' he breathed.

'This I say,' the blood priest replied. It stepped closer to Halek and stared into his soul, saying, 'You know false human. Where?'

Halek could not seem to lie as those black hole eyes drew him in. 'You said you taught him how to concentrate on multiple things at once...many at one time? He just flew three drones around the second moon of Omneri. But he escaped.' *No,* Halek realised, *Carak orchestrated his escape with the order to fire on the Omneri fleet.*

The blood priest turned away and Halek's head dropped as if fingers had been withdrawn from beneath his chin. He frowned as the Sori made their way towards the exit, but perked up as he realised they had left their payment behind. 'Where are you going?' he called. But they did not answer, and Halek turned back to the others with nothing left to say.

The Cquaston Trader rumbled in his language and Halek's translator beeped: 'I will take their share of humans.'

Halek looked up and nodded. Who was he to argue with someone so large?

Ω

Lately, Arrien was spending more and more time reading ancient books, the sacred works of Earth's religions. He loved the Bhagavad Gita and had recently enjoyed the Book of Mormon, that literary project of the Latter-day Saints that sought to supplement and redefine the authority of Christianity. Yet his spare time recently – and there had been more of late, prior to the chaos of the Sieltor worlds – had been taken up by the Holy Qur'an of Islam and that amalgamation of Jewish and early Christian cultural memory, the Holy Bible. In their stories of prophets mediating the words of the divine, they resonated with him in a way which both humbled him and spoke to him of his own self-indulgent fantasies. They taught him that he would have to be patient if he wanted to achieve his true potential, and that there would always be those who wished him harm. Here, amidst an interplanetary conspiracy which was increasingly appearing to be centred on him, the ancient writings so central to Muslim and Jewish identity in a reality increasingly diminishing their significance brought him peace and guidance. He could see why so many people had been intrigued by the Church of the New Elect in their appropriation – some would say misappropriation – of these texts, even while so many others were suspicious of their ideologies. When he got back to Earth, he decided, he was going to sit down with their leaders – if he could find them – and learn as much as he could about them. Sitting back with the open Qur'an on his lap, he closed his eyes and tried not to think of the suspicion his particular circumstance provoked in those around him. A knock on the door disrupted the closest he had been to drifting off to sleep in two days. There was only so much stimulant one could take before the body began rejecting it. 'Come in,' he called.

Kel poked her head through a half-opened door: 'Hey…can I talk to you?'

'Of course.' Arrien felt a shiver of intrigue and arousal as she came in and closed the door behind her. 'Everything okay?' He chuckled as he said the words. 'Well…of course everything's not okay, but…you know what I mean.'

152

'Yeah, I know what you mean.' She sat opposite him and forced a smile, before saying, 'I'm worried. Maybe even a little scared.'

'*You*?' Arrien smiled softly. '*Scared*?'

She raised her hands defensively, joking, 'Hey, I said "a little"!'

'That you did. What's going on? This isn't just about what's up ahead.'

'No...' she sighed, 'it's not. Look, ever since you had us warn the Argo about the attack on Earth, the crew have been a bit...weird. Edgy, you know?'

He nodded, leaning back on the couch. 'I can understand that. And I appreciate the heads-up. How are you feeling about it?'

She gave a little laugh. 'Weird,' she said. 'Edgy.'

'You're still okay with me, though, right?'

'Yeah.' Her voice lacked conviction. 'Maybe. I just...I mean, you *predicted* it, Arrien. You saw the future. It's a bit...'

'Scary?' he finished for her. She nodded, and he stood up to get himself a drink: 'Look, it's not like I'm some kind of doomsday prophet or anything. I just have these...dreams from time to time.'

'And how do you know they're not just dreams? I mean...when you get them. Obviously, the last one panned out, but...there was a possibility it was just a dream.'

'I guess so.' He sipped the drink and brought one for her as he returned to the couch. Handing it to her, he said, 'It's hard to explain, but sometimes...I just know the difference. Dreams are dreams. These are...' he shook his head, clearly holding back, 'something else.'

'But you risked exposing yourself...exposing all of us.' Kel sighed. 'I think that's the main concern.'

'Sure. I can see that.' He moved to the edge of the couch: 'Did I ever tell you what happened to my parents?'

Kel met his eyes. 'You said they were murdered,' she replied quietly. 'In front of you.'

Arrien nodded. 'It was my fault.'

'That can't be true.'

'It is. Just like you said...I risk exposing myself with every dream I reveal. I told my parents that something terrible was going to happen. They believed me. I didn't know why, and I never thought to ask. But they did...and they warned everyone. Millions of lives were saved, but...someone was watching. Someone realised what happened.'

'And they came for you?'

'No.' Arrien shifted back into the chair, clearly uncomfortable. 'A single Garran...the strangest one I've ever seen...wild red hair, looked a bit crazy, to be honest, but these are a kid's memories...he was waiting in our house a few days later. I think he wanted to kill me, but...someone was directing him. It was like he was talking to himself, but I could...*feel*...that someone else was there. Whoever it was only wanted my parents dead. They needed me alive, but...they needed me to feel the pain of losing them.'

'I don't understand,' said Kel. 'Why would anyone do that to a child?'

'To ensure that the child grew up along the right path. Running. Hiding. Searching.'

'So, you think someone...what...*created* your destiny?'

'You're not buying it?'

Kel exhaled and shook her head. 'I dunno, Arrien. I mean...you told only a few of us who you were. And I get that being the great-grandson of Adam Echad must be a bit of a burden...'

'You have no idea,' he assured her, more curtly than intended.

'Okay,' said Kel sharply, 'so I've no idea. But you're carrying it round like a noose. And it *will* be the death of you if you keep convincing yourself you're some kind of messiah who can't escape whatever fate you've imagined. I've seen you with your head in those religious books...but here's something for you to think about. That part where a prophet is judged only after his predictions come true? Which I'm all for, by the way. What if it also means that we should stop fixating on what we think is going to happen or what others say will happen, and that we should just get on with our lives until whatever happens...happens?'

Arrien held her glare, sensing her checked anger. 'I wish I could, Kel. I really do. But you asked me how I know they're not just dreams, and all I can say is this: when they come to me, I don't just see them like an observer, or even play in them like an actor. Someone...some...*thing* picks me out of my body and puts me there. To watch. I'm not just seeing something that's *going to happen* in the future. I'm *in* the future watching it happen!'

'That's not possible.'

He shrugged. 'Everything's impossible until it's possible.'

'Well, that's a great explanation!'

'Look, this isn't just about me, Kel. You know what happened back home.'

'You mean with that *church*? We've been over this, Arrien. No one's seen them!'

'No, and Vawter and Tzedek have been looking...but whether they're still around or not, they were different from everyone else. And they knew that. It was the very reason they thought they were special.'

'Which in this case means "better", right?'

'They thought so, yes.'

'Well, don't *you*? I mean, this is where you're going. You've taken this mission upon yourself because no one can find the New Elect at home and you think their descendants are out *here*!'

'Adam Echad should have been with the Church, Kel,' Arrien reminded her calmly. 'His personal logs recount strange dreams...not unlike mine. And there's all that stuff about the guy from the future...who's supposed to be descended from *me*! You expect me to ignore all that?'

'No.' Kel shook her head sadly. 'I expect you won't.'

'Would *you*?'

She grinned sheepishly. 'I suppose not. But then I'm not the Second Coming.'

Arrien laughed genuinely. 'There have been so many claims to that title that we've either long passed it or it's never gonna happen.' He reached over and took her hands, surprising her. 'Listen, I get that people can get a bit freaked out around me. I've had long enough to learn *that*. But there's something going on that I know I'm a big part of, and I have to see it through. If nothing else, finding out what part I'm supposed to play might actually help me sleep better!'

'Without your crazy dreams.'

'Preferably.' He leaned back and looked at a monitor on the wall which was displaying their trajectory. 'How much longer?'

Kel rose and went to the monitor. 'Less than an hour.'

Arrien threw back his drink and joined her. This time the arousal was felt by her as he touched her waist and whispered, 'Thanks for listening.'

She turned and looked up into his eyes, saying, 'Someone has to,' before stepping away from him and heading for the door. 'Can't have you going nuts on us.'

Arrien chuckled as she left the room, feeling the emptiness return as he thought, *Too late*.

Ω

As Carak stepped out of the vehicle at the end of the long walkway and looked around at the tell-tale signs that this small house at the edge of Khas City would soon be consumed by the ugliness of progress, he felt old. Very old. Naveen had made it clear that he did not have much time left, which was why he had ordered Halek to accelerate his dangerous game. He just hoped that the Kwaios were watching him and not Halek, although with representatives from other species arriving, their attention would most certainly be piqued. His recent conversation with the Kwaios was as much about keeping them distracted as anything else, but it had convinced him that he had been right to speed things up:

'Samuel Vawter has arranged for an increase in supply,' they informed him. 'We are close to our goal.'

'Really?' Carak was intrigued. 'If you asked Vawter for an increase, something must have changed.'

They did not respond, and Carak pressed, fearing the worst: 'Are you not going to tell me?'

'Did you think we would not discover what you were doing with your facility at Sieltor Promies?'

Carak's heart felt like it might jump out of his chest, but he grinned, needing to redirect them: 'A little insurance policy, that's all. Anyway, how I use my private supply is my business.'

'Not if it is bait for the Echad child.'

'He's hardly a child,' Carak argued, relieved that they had misunderstood the purpose of his facility. 'And seeing as you want him so much, surely bait is a good idea?'

'You have protected his line, Carak. Why would we trust what you say?'

'Have you any idea what I've been protecting them from?' he snapped. *'You may think you're the almighty Kwaios, but this...thing, whatever it is...is like nothing I've ever encountered!'*

'It is a god,' the Kwaios stated.

That shook Carak somewhat. 'How...'

'It is not from this galaxy. It has been watching since Kiranis returned.'

'I don't understand. A god? What does it want?'

'It wants the Prophet, the one you call Naveen.'

'Why?'

'That is not relevant now. But the god will come to this galaxy. And it will not come alone. We need the Echad child.'

'To stop it? To...protect us?'

There was no response, and Carak nodded knowingly. 'I didn't think so,' he said. 'If you want him, come and get him.'

Now it was their turn to be lost for words. Was this Garran really goading them? After a silence designed to intimidate him, their response was chilling: 'We will.'

Disconnecting from a lifetime of bowing to their superiority, Carak felt a freedom unlike anything he had imagined. The ramifications were terrifying, but his optimism knew no bounds now that his fate was certain. As the humans would say, "It couldn't get any worse". One way or the other, everything would change within hours, but there was something more personal with which Carak wished to deal. He lifted the latch on the gate and made his way towards the house, memories of deceit and heartache interwoven with unrequited love and immeasurable adoration.

She was waiting for him at the ornate double doors, standing amidst a veritable aura of bright flowers and rich, lustrous plants. Vella was advanced in years now, but she was still slightly younger than Carak, and he looked at her as he would a young Garran woman back when he was a frustrated adolescent. The fact that she still maintained her loyalty to a long-dead thorn in Carak's side did nothing to temper his feelings. 'You always know when I'm coming,' he quipped. 'Are you sure you're not psychic?'

Despite the playful glimmer in her eyes, there was ice in her tone as she replied, 'If I was, I'd be locked away somewhere with the rest of your experiments!' She turned on her heel and disappeared back into the house. But the doors were left open. Carak hesitated, looking around again. His driver was young and would have no memory of the events which had transpired at this house, when a camouflaged Kwaios dropship had tried to take the mysterious Malik from right under the nose of the Jaevisk. Despite coming here from time to time to see Vella, the place still unnerved Carak. For there were still many unanswered questions.

'Close the door if you're not coming in, old man,' she called. 'But I'd rather not drink this wine alone.'

He grinned. Stepping into the house was like stepping back in time, and the memories flooded back of him coming here to tell her of Malik's death. The fact that he did not believe his own words had not made the task any easier. Vella was staring at him, reading him. 'I hope you're not here to open old wounds,' she warned, offering a glass of liquid sunset.

'I'm still waiting for mine to close, Vella,' he replied, accepting the Goruset wine. It was incredibly expensive, and she should not have been able to afford it. She did not seem to care that Carak was unlikely to overlook that fact.

'Malik used to say that we punish ourselves the greatest.'

There were so many levels of irony in those words that Carak chose not to respond. This she noted, smiling softly as if achieving a tiny victory. Carak sat down and took a mouthful of wine. He let it rest in his mouth for a moment, savouring it. Knowing that it would soon be tainted by the conversation to come.

'Why are you here, Carak?' Vella asked. 'Why today? There was a massacre out at Omneri and you're sitting here drinking plasmaberry wine. I'm sure our usual debate about what's best for our children could have waited for another day.'

Carak slowly swallowed the wine, feeling the kick of the unique berry heating his throat. 'Perhaps the circumstances demand a shift in priorities.'

Vella regarded him for a moment, intrigued. 'Is that your way of saying that your daughter is more important than the lives of Garran soldiers? You certainly have my attention, if that's the case.'

'It's not that simple,' Carak told her. 'Things are…complicated. And there's…not much time.'

'What do you mean?'

Carak considered lying, but there was no point. This would likely be the last time he saw her. 'I spoke to the Prophet.'

'And?' Vella had met the human called Naveen, and she did not trust him. 'What did he say this time to get you all worked up? What mysterious task has he laid upon you that he can't do for himself?'

Carak loved this woman. She was afraid of nothing and no one. He hated Malik, or Chaerakh, or whatever his name was, for his memory still kept her at arm's length. 'The task is irrelevant,' he explained quietly. 'I'm here because of how it will end.'

His tone said it all, and she set her glass down. 'How...' she struggled with the words, feeling tears building but willing them away. 'He could be wrong.'

'Have you ever known him to be wrong?' Carak smiled. 'You and I have grown old, me despite what I've done and who I've tormented...but everything he said about my daughter and your son...and their son. He appears out of nowhere and looks the same as he did back when the Cage came to Earth. That crazy woman who killed Echad might have been right to call him a god.' With the word came an unexpected chill, and Vella once again read his discomfort.

'What else happened?' she asked. 'Are the children going to be okay?'

He took some wine and nodded vehemently. 'Oh, yes. Yes, don't worry...this isn't about them. Although I would like to see Laen today. Do you think he'd come to see me?'

'I'm not sure. You said some wicked things last time you spoke. He thinks you resent the birth of their son.'

'You know that's not true.'

'It's not me you need to convince. You ordered my son not to have a child with Kera. Since Jerrach was born, you have seen him once. What would Senneya have said?'

Carak felt a chill again, but it was not at the sound of his dead wife's name. It was the other one. Jerrach. So similar. Kera had explained that it was a dialectic variant on his own, but Carak was still looking to the future in a present sullied by the past. As he looked in Vella's eyes and saw the pain there, his emotions raged. Family had been everything to Carak, but his grandson, so small, so helpless, so innocent of all Carak had imagined for him...he was a reminder of the temporal chains with which Carak's life had been bound. How could he tell Vella that the only time he had seen the child was to take a blood sample and pray that the DNA would not mark him as related to the man who had called himself Malik? A sample of Malik's DNA, or at least from the charred remains left in his quarters before they had handed them over to the Jaevisk, had been kept in a cryo-vault for decades, and Carak's stomach had churned as the tests were run. Oh, how he had prayed. 'He doesn't deserve this,' he replied finally, with tears in his eyes. 'None of them do.' He rose from his seat: 'I'm sorry.'

'*This*?' Vella countered. 'There is nothing but what you've created in your head, Carak. You need to live now...*here*...with your family.'

'Perhaps,' he conceded, without conviction. After a moment's silence, he looked around and said, 'Do you ever wonder why we bother with anything other than just living?'

'No, I don't, Carak,' she replied gently. 'It's all I've been doing. You, on the other hand, have spent too long trying to outwit the Universe. But then men are always more concerned with their legacy than they are with...just living.' She reached out and took his hand. 'Go and see Kera. Now. Take your grandson...who is now a walking, talking citizen of the world you created...take him in your arms. Kiss his cheek. Hold your daughter. That's the legacy *she* would want.'

He choked back his tears as he nodded. 'Will you send Laen to me? I have something for him.'

Vella stood, still holding his hand. 'Are you sure this is it? It's not another one of his tricks?'

Carak shook his head. 'He said the Kwaios would kill me. I have to direct the humans to Heragon.'

'So, it's finally coming?'

'After all these years,' he confirmed. 'All my work protecting the Echad line is about to pay off.'

Despite her tears, Vella smiled. 'You must be excited.'

'I suppose I am,' he agreed. 'But the price is high.'

'The highest.' She reached up and kissed his cheek. 'You're a better man than you allow yourself to believe.'

He nodded slowly. 'That would be nice.' Breaking away from her, he turned to leave, saying, 'You know I have long loved you?'

'I know,' she replied. 'In another time-line, perhaps.'

Carak chuckled at their old joke as he opened the door. 'I'll see you there,' he said, before disappearing out of Vella's life forever. She watched him through the window as he straightened himself outside and his driver opened the door. She knew he would shake off the conversation and the emotions in light of what was to come. He needed to focus.

Vella sighed, feeling a presence in the room. 'I have to send Laen to see him,' she said. 'Naveen said it was the only way. And I don't want to imagine a life in which you never existed.' She watched Carak get into the vehicle. 'I have always felt sorry for him, my love,' she said. 'But the Universe took hold of Carak Tae Ahn and refused to let go. You of all people know what that's like.'

Ω

Arrien ordered the Styx to a stop at a point as close as possible to the autonomous facility while still providing the relative protection of the asteroid field. Long-range scopes provided them with images of a convoy of nondescript transport vessels manoeuvring into docking positions. 'They must have cleaned out the Omneri operations and left just before we got there,' said Kel. 'You think they'll be ready for us?'

'I think we should presume so, yes,' said Arrien. 'Still no contact with Raesa?'

Kel shook her head. 'I sent an encrypted com check, but...nothing.'

Jaime called out as he pointed at one of the communications monitors: 'Any chance this Raesa guy ended up in another galaxy? There's a message on the beta channel, but the source coordinates don't correspond to anything I've seen before! I don't wanna risk a systems breach.'

Kel and Arrien went to his station and stared at the readings, and Arrien shook his head in confusion. 'I've no idea,' he admitted. 'The Kwaios sometimes use stars to amplify their communications, but our systems aren't compatible. This is different, though.' He pointed to a string of coordinates. 'Can we plot that?'

Jaime nodded. 'Running it now.' It did not take long, and he puffed and shook his head as he said, 'It's a singularity near the galactic centre. There's no way someone's routing a signal from *that* far away in anything *near* real-time!'

'Wait...' Kel was watching the coordinates. 'It just changed.'

They ran the numbers again. 'Another black hole,' said Arrien. 'What the hell *is* this?'

'If our systems are identifying it as a message...' said Kel, 'and it's from someone who knew enough to ride the beta channel...'

'Then we should listen to it,' Arrien agreed.

Jaime did not. 'I don't think that's –'

'Do it, Jaime.'

A few moments later, there was a crackling over the com and Arrien heard Kallon Raesa, an old mercenary friend, speaking as if from the bottom of a well: *'I hope the right person gets this, because it's only for him. Anyway, I'm at Illeri...well, I was at Illeri...and everything's just gone to hell...literally, I think. I don't trust anyone right now, but I'll say this – MEC is a lie. Vawter lied to us all. I get it now. And I get why you avoided it. Whatever you do, stay away...from MEC, from Earth...especially from Earth! Just stay away. As for me...'* There was a short laugh followed by a long breath: *'I'm not left with many choices.'* There was a bit more crackling, and the message ended.

'What the hell was that about?' asked Jaime. 'MEC is a *lie*? Stay away from *Earth*? I mean...what the *fuck*?'

Arrien ignored him. 'Looks like we're going in on our own. I want an approach vector in five minutes. Use the convoy as cover.' He walked off the command deck, leaving his crew more confused than ever.

Ω

The World Killer. That was what both the Kwaios and the Jaevisk had called him. Carak had known him first as Malik, but that was nothing more than an alias designed to infiltrate Carak's command structure and to continue about whatever business he had planned. Time travel made Carak's head spin, and Naveen was not the only one who had more than once turned up in front of the ageing Garran looking just as he had when Kiranis had first been reborn and Carak's alliance with the Kwaios had changed everything for the people of Earth. The last time, he had come to Carak for one reason alone:

'I'm here to talk about my son,' Chaerakh had said.

'What about him?' Carak had snapped. *'He's no concern of mine.'*

'Well, I...need him to be.'

The humility Carak detected evinced a side to Chaerakh that the other had not imagined. But then he never really knew the man. 'I don't understand. What are you saying?'

'I have to go,' Chaerakh explained. 'I know I'll be back. I've…seen myself older. But I'm not sure how long it will take.'

'Surely your owner can tell you?' Carak sneered. It had been years since he had seen Naveen, and at this stage he had hoped never to see him again.

'Whatever you do…please don't blame Laen for my sins. He's only a child.'

'Your sins? You mean your crimes.'

Chaerakh held his hateful glare but kept his anger in check. This was of the utmost importance, for many reasons. 'All I need to know is that you will visit Vella and my boy from time to time. Keep them safe.'

Carak fought the temptation to revel in the man's desperation. Chaerakh's humility was genuine, and they both shared a common cause for the paths of their fate. 'Kera has been asking to spend more time with me lately,' said Carak finally. 'I'll take her out of the city and introduce her to Vella. If nothing else, she needs a good female role model in her life.'

'Thank you,' Chaerakh breathed. 'I'll find a way to repay you one day.'

The repayment, which Chaerakh must surely have known, was the gradual bonding of both of their children until they were practically inseparable. Now both old men, if Chaerakh were still alive out there somewhere – and Carak had seen no evidence to the contrary – shared a grandson, and the Universe probably laughed.

There was no time to get weighed down by old mistakes, when there was still enough time to make new ones. Carak called out to his driver: 'Has there been any update from the Promies facility?'

'No, sir. The humans are at the edge of the asteroid field. They could be waiting for something.'

'I'm sure they've called for help, at least,' Carak agreed. 'Put me through to the facility. They should be scanning for drones. According to Halek, there's a very talented pilot out there.'

'I'm connecting you now, sir.'

'Good. Where are the fleets of the other Elders?'

'Menalis appears to be staying at Ptah, but Silluc and Geram have been sent after the humans.'

Carak frowned. 'I had hoped Menalis might go with them,' he said. 'Arrien Echad is going to need all the cannon fodder I can find when the Kwaios show up.'

The driver smiled. 'Well, at least Menalis took the bait.'

'I suppose two fleets are better than none,' Carak agreed. 'I was hoping all those star cruisers wouldn't be destroyed for nothing.'

Ω

Arrien was troubled by the message from Kallon Raesa. Not because of the warnings to stay away from either the MEC system or Earth – he was aware of very good reasons to avoid both. Instead, Arrien was reacting to a more personal appreciation of doom, for he had sensed – from the sound of Kallon's very first word – that the man was in grave danger. Rushing back to his quarters, Arrien knew that a line had to be crossed. It was a huge risk, but he figured that if the Kwaios were already watching, then using one of their devices would make little difference to their attempts at locating him. Particularly not in the way he intended to use it.

His heart was pounding as he closed the door behind him. It was hidden, and had been since Samuel Vawter had first given it to him, yet still he could sense its ethereal grasping, seeking him out. It was longing for him to come to it, to hold it, to use it, like some sentient toy of personal arousal. There was no way Vawter intended for Arrien to use it as he was about to, for Arrien had designed the means and Arrien was one of the very few people capable. Taking first the metal case from beneath the bed, he opened it out completely and tapped the operational panel covering the join at the centre hinge. It came to life, emitting blue light and humming softly. Then, from each corner, red light shot out from tiny crystals, disappearing beneath the centre panel. Taking and releasing a deep breath, Arrien moved to a locked cabinet next to the bed. Inside it was a locked safe, and inside that was a Kwaios communication device, a black cube four inches around that made even the most powerful men shiver with apprehension. Arrien, however, was not going to communicate with anyone.

He set the cube atop the operational panel and pressed gently. The mechanism was comprised of Jaevisk and Kwaios

164

components, the latter obtained without question from Vawter's corporation, the former with considerable delicacy and not too little subterfuge. The Kwaios did not like people knowing how to open their devices, but the Jaevisk advocated its necessity, for they wanted only what was inside.

The black cube clicked open, revealing a red crystal considerably larger than its counterparts at the corners of the open case. As soon as it opened, the red lines connected with the centre crystal, and a beam of red light shot upwards and disappeared through the ceiling of Arrien's quarters. Although the configuration was the same as the Jaevisk Slave-to-Reaper power transfer, the Kwaios communication device did not contain a Reaper. It was only a Slave, as was the one from which the corner fragments had been taken. For what Arrien was about to attempt, for the very first time, it was all he needed. He could feel perspiration on his forehead as he closed his eyes and leaned over the device. He gritted his teeth in anticipation of what he thought would be pain, but when his head was over the centre crystal and the red beam of light no longer continued upwards, he felt an immeasurable sense of calm. Unfortunately, it lasted only for as long as he forgot what he was supposed to be doing.

As soon as he thought of Kallon Raesa, he felt as if his head had been put in a vice on the end of a retractable leash. His consciousness was whipped out of his quarters, out of the ship, and he was speeding away from the Sieltor system before he knew what was happening. This was like the dreams he had tried explaining to Kel, but in being awake when the journey began, it was ultimately more terrifying. He roared in pain as heat seemed to build in his brain, but he knew somehow that his real body sat in silent stillness, his head hung over the red beam that penetrated his mind. As if he might breathe through lungs which were still in his quarters, he fought to calm himself, desperately trying to control what was happening. He shouted, 'STOP!'

And he stopped.

With the vice-like grip released from his mind, he could feel his body, like a ghostly association with corporeality that he did not need out here in the vacuum of space. His arms were not there, but he imagined himself with phantom limbs pointing at the closest celestial body. The vice took him again and he raced towards a rogue comet, hurtling silent and alone through the blackness. The vice released him, and he hung there next to it, mesmerised by its beautiful icy tail. It was only when he turned away from it, and the lingering glow faded, that he saw the red lines. Everywhere. Countless. They crisscrossed and collided, merged and refracted. And he realised what they were. 'Kallon Raesa,' he said aloud, yet not aloud. One line amidst thousands pulsed gently, continuing until the others around it relented to make it more visible. It drifted towards Arrien, and with a hand that was merely the idea of a hand, he grabbed it. The vice gripped again, and Arrien raced off towards what he presumed was the planet Illeri. It was not long, however, before he realised that Illeri would never be reached. The red line he was following began to appear more fragmented, brittle and unsure of itself. At least, this was until Arrien realised that the red line was gradually being consumed by a black one. When it was all black, Arrien felt a chill rush through him, and the Universe started to slow down.

The black line began to spiral, and Arrien's consciousness spun with it as he twisted towards something he knew he should not be approaching. The black line, only visible intermittently against the backdrop of stars, was leading him towards a phenomenon of similar composition: he could only see this absence of space because of the stars which should have been visible beyond it. It was not a black hole, because nothing tangible was being drawn towards it. This was a void belonging to a very different layer of reality.

A hand slammed against Arrien's imagined chest and he stopped dead. A man occupied the darkness between him and the otherworldly vacuum. Had he been standing, he would have been tall, and the cloak he wore, undulating despite the lack of gravity, was decorated with images of dragons – one gold, the other silver – which seemed not so much to occupy the fabric as live upon it. The man was perhaps in his early forties, with a strong jaw outlined by stubble carefully shaped to simulate the shadows of bestial fangs. 'That's as far as you go, Arrien,' he said, with a commanding but understanding tone. 'These portals aren't for you.'

Arrien stared at him, wondering where to start. With the old favourite, perhaps: 'Who are you?'

'My name's Naveen. Most people just call me the Prophet.'

'I've heard of you,' said Arrien. 'Sam Vawter spoke about you with a mixture of resentment and fascination.'

166

Naveen grinned. 'Well, a man of his particular concerns would be somewhat resentful, I'd imagine.'

'What do you mean?'

The Prophet waved it away. 'Doesn't matter. What are you doing out here?'

'I'm looking for someone called Kallon Raesa. He was sent to Illeri, but –'

'He's not there anymore.'

'You know where he is?'

'You won't be able to find him, Arrien. You need to go back…now.'

Arrien looked beyond Naveen to the black portal, realising that Kallon must have passed through. This is where his line ended. 'How are you out here?' he asked. 'Did you use a Kwaios crystal?'

'A Kwaios crystal? Interesting description. No, I didn't. I have my own way of getting around.'

'So, where are you? Your body, I mean.'

The Prophet laughed, in a place where there should not have been a sound. 'My body? If you knew the answer to that question, you'd be the most hunted man in the Universe. Next to me, of course.'

Arrien looked around. The red lines were hazy, unclear and indistinct, but there were still just as many. He pointed back to the portal: 'What is it? Why did Kallon go through? How did he *get* through when he can't see what we can see?'

'I think you know the answer to that. Now get back to your ship.'

Arrien knew he was in over his head. But he also knew…that he had to know. Just not today. As he turned his body around, Naveen warned him, 'Be careful out here. Whoever or…*whatever* you meet next time might not be so…amicable. There are greater dangers than the Kwaios, you know.'

He left the Prophet behind, rushing back to the Styx with thoughts of the impending Kwaios arrival intermingled with confusion over what had happened to Kallon. He vowed to find a way to pass through one of those black portals, but he knew that right now…there were more important things to deal with.

Ω

167

The facility was enormous, the ever-increasing proximity of the Styx crediting the sprawl of thousands of interconnected modules with a size that the long-range scopes could not have emulated. Jaime whistled appreciatively. 'Now this looks more like it,' he said.

'Glad you're impressed,' Arrien quipped as he returned to command. 'When you're finished admiring it, find me a reasonably safe place to kick down a door, will you?'

Jaime grinned. 'On it.' As he worked on reducing the impact of their intended excursion, Kel came up to Arrien: 'You okay?'

He shook his head. 'No. Something's happened to Kallon. Something…well, something bad. I'm not sure. It's weird, but, despite being so close to all this, I feel like I should just drop it all and go help him.'

'That's not weird,' Kel assured him, touching his arm. 'Priorities change when someone you care about is in trouble. Doesn't mean we can't set course for Illeri once we're done.'

'Without MEC, there's no point,' Arrien disagreed. 'We'll either be too late to help him, or he'll be back home with his feet up and we'll have wasted our time going all the way out there.' He pointed out the bow window: 'Let's just get this over with.'

Kel nodded, but she looked at him for a moment as he walked towards the window. Something had changed in him, and she just hoped that his apparent loss of passion for this mission would not see them all dead.

Ω

Carak was home. Or at least, he was outside the building within which both his dreams and nightmares resided. If, as the humans would say, home was where the heart was, then he would find home only in the next world. With Senneya. It was not that Kera was no longer loved; instead, she was a reminder of the pain of losing her mother. And that pain was intensified by the insult of her attachment to Chaerakh's son. The fact that Carak had facilitated it, manipulated or not, did little to temper his resentment of the situation. Still, there was the future to protect, no matter how twisted it had become; and despite believing that Naveen did indeed hold all the cards, perhaps there was a period along the timeline within which Carak's family could find peace. It was worth a try.

Laen was waiting for his father-in-law at the steps, flanked by two armed men in uniforms unfamiliar to Carak. 'I don't appreciate being summoned like some sycophantic underling, Uncle,' he declared stiffly.

Carak eyed the younger man's protective detail. 'There are so many things wrong with that complaint, Laen,' he replied, turning to his son-in-law and smiling. 'For one, a sycophantic underling wouldn't need to be summoned.' Carak entered the house, calling back, 'And I've told you to call me Father.'

'You can keep your distance inside,' Laen quietly assured his bodyguards as he followed the Elder. 'I can barely recall the last time I *saw* you, Uncle,' he replied, 'never mind what you told me!'

It was a well-founded attack, and Carak winced. 'It's been too long,' he agreed. 'I hope to see Kera and...' he couldn't bring himself to say the name, 'my grandson later.'

The omission was not lost on Laen, and he swung back: 'Jerrach...' he said pointedly, 'would be happy to see you, I'm sure.' That was a lie, but Laen had his limits. 'Although I'm not sure when he'll be back from training.'

Carak stopped in his tracks. 'Training,' he whispered. 'Have I missed so much?'

Despite himself, Laen laid a hand on Carak's shoulder, saying, 'Too much. But there is still time.'

Carak averted his eyes and nodded, his emotions reeling. *No*, he wanted to say, *there isn't*. He steeled himself, concealing both his sadness and his apprehension as he led his son-in-law deeper into a house he had long known was unnecessary large. Laen could well refuse the proposal to come. 'Is the protection really necessary?' Carak asked him, looking back to the armed guards maintaining about a ten-pace distance as they approached a heavy wooden door keeping the corridor in perpetual darkness.

'I've been promoted,' Laen explained, realising only now that he had never been in this part of the house. 'They came with the ridiculous salary. Apparently, I'm important now.'

Carak reached the door and pressed his palm against it. A green glow emanated from the outline of his hand and a dull clunk could be heard from within the room. Carak chuckled with genuine humour. 'What you're about to see might change your perspective on that,' he said, turning to Laen. 'But you come in alone or you don't come in at all.'

Laen locked eyes with his father-in-law for a moment. He had heard tales and rumours all his adult life of the activities of Overseer and then Elder Carak. The man was an enigma, a hero to as many as he was a villain. It was said that he might still be in some kind of political or economic alliance with the Kwaios, and Laen had long imagined a time when his familial connection to the man might facilitate some clarity on the matter. Carak cocked his head: 'Well?'

Laen nodded slowly and then turned to his bodyguards. 'Wait out here.'

'Sir,' one of them argued, 'we were ordered to watch you at all times.'

'I'm perfectly safe here,' Laen told them. 'This man is my family.'

That made Carak smile. The guards knew who this man was, and they knew that he was not to be trusted. But Laen was insistent: 'Wait here or find another job!'

They reluctantly conceded, and Laen gestured for Carak to proceed. 'Let's see what's behind the magic door,' he mocked.

Carak ignored the sarcasm, knowing that what Laen was about to see would be sufficient to stop his wagging tongue. As he stepped into the room, he moved aside to allow Laen to take it in. And as the door closed and locked behind them, Carak was grinning from ear to ear like a child showing off his latest toy. While Laen appeared to have lost control of his jaw.

Ω

The approach was proving much less eventful than Arrien had anticipated. Jaime certainly was not about to let that go unnoticed: 'We're heading straight into another trap here.' He was surprised when Arrien nodded and replied, 'Probably.'

'So, what do you wanna do?' asked Kel. 'Cos if the show back at Omneri was for you…'

'Then the trap's for me,' he finished. 'I know.' He pointed at what was most likely a docking port in the nearest arrangement of modules. 'Match rotation and bring us in,' he ordered.

The pilots did so as Kel looked at Jaime, her expression urging him to say something. He shrugged and shook his head, before asking, 'You bringing the rangers?'

Arrien nodded. 'You don't honestly think I'd get all sacrificial now, do you?'

'Be a nice change,' Jaime quipped. And Arrien laughed. 'Just keep the engine warm, Jaime,' he told him. 'I'm gonna get suited up. Garran atmosphere doesn't agree with me.' He left command and made his way to the evac area. The mercenaries who called themselves rangers were already gathered, distributing weapons and supplies and joking amongst themselves. They quietened when Arrien entered, but not necessarily out of respect. Their commander stepped up: 'You sure a single point of entry is the way t'go?'

'I'm not really sure of anything,' Arrien admitted. 'But this is the least used access point right now. And I'd rather have us all stick together.'

'Or die together,' someone muttered. The commander turned on the woman: 'Keep it shut, Katie! Or stay here!' He turned back to Arrien. 'Look, I get it. The centre of this place is crazy with dropships and bots. But it's a long way t'go to get there. And you know we're gonna have to get there.'

'Yeah, I know,' Arrien agreed. 'With that much activity, it's bound to be where they're keeping them.' He smiled and laid a hand on the commander's shoulder. 'But hey...the bots are outside, right? That's gotta be a good thing.'

The commander did not look convinced, but he grinned at Arrien's confidence. Someone had to kick up the morale. Hundreds of floating human bodies back at Omneri had sullied it somewhat. 'What happens if we find them?'

'*When*...we find them,' said Arrien, and now everyone was listening, 'we have a choice to make. And it could depend on any number of things, not the least of which is how many there are.'

'Ship's been stripped to the bone like you ordered,' the commander reminded him, 'but we're only talking...what...twelve, thirteen hundred max? If Omneri was anything to go by, there could be hundreds of thousands here.'

'Hopefully, we're not gonna be alone for very long,' Arrien assured them, 'but I don't know who's coming and what sort of capacity they're bringing. Which is why...' he looked pointedly at the weapons and explosives laid out for the team, 'we'll be putting any we can't take with us...out of their misery.' He walked away from the team to get himself suited and prepped for entry to the

171

facility. The silence of the team was broken by two things: first, the sound of the docking clamps connecting to the Garran structure; and second, a voice over the com as Kel could be heard warning them, 'We've got incoming! Two of the fleets we saw back at Omneri.'

It was ridiculous, of course, to think that they could have done this without rousing attention, but then the Omneri job was supposed to be the end of it. This was completely nuts. Arrien closed his eyes and tapped the inner airlock release, praying silently for his backup to arrive. Although he had no idea how they could help against probably a hundred star cruisers and battleships. As the team followed him into the airlock, they were decidedly vocal. And as the door closed behind them, the pressure equalisation began, sounding considerably more sibilant than usual.

Ω

Halek looked at the monitors as his guests kept their distance both from him and each other. This was unexpected, to say the least. An unidentified ship had just docked at the Promies facility, where the entire stock of merchandise were now stored. On top of that, scores of warships were on their way and their transponders identified them as fleets belonging to the Elders Silluc and Geram. Were they coming for him? Had Carak thrown him to the wolves? Out here on this otherwise insignificant rock spinning around Promies, Halek felt quite cut off from the rest of Garran civilisation. Still, he would rather be completely alone than have these parasites blame this mess on him. 'I think you should all leave,' he told them. 'Whatever is going on, it won't look good that you're here...in such proximity to the main facility. Our Elders do not necessarily agree with everything Carak does, as you might imagine.'

Although they glared at him as if they might stay and rip his arms off, they eventually conceded that perhaps their absence would be for the greater good. Halek was happy to see them go, but he soon became transfixed by something else displayed before him. For it appeared that the Sori ship was closing in on the facility. And it would get there long before the Garran fleets. A shiver of reality disturbed made him turn around, to see a human

172

male standing looking at him. His black cloak moved unnaturally, and Halek blinked to assure himself that the monstrous shapes upon it were not moving. 'Who are you?' he asked.

Naveen smiled. 'I'm surprised Carak didn't tell you all about me,' he replied in English.

Halek's nose wrinkled when he heard the language, but he spoke it: 'I hate human languages.'

'All of them?'

'All of them. You must be the human from the Kiranis system. The Prophet.'

'I suppose I must,' Naveen agreed. 'You must be angry.'

Halek found himself scowling. 'Carak always knows what's coming...' he growled, 'which I suppose is down to you.' He stepped closer, certain that the creatures on the cloak were staring at him hungrily. 'So, he knew I'd be stuck out here!'

'*He* didn't,' Naveen clarified. 'But *I* did.'

That tripped him somewhat. 'What do you mean? Why would you care where I was or what I was doing? I thought you manipulated leaders and armies and entire planets!'

'Armies are comprised of individuals, Halek. And planets are populated by them.' He moved closer to Halek so that the gap was almost completely closed, and Halek was sure that the shadows were being dragged behind him. Then he spoke the words which sent something akin to an electric shock through the vengeful underling: 'And some individuals are merely leaders-in-waiting.'

Halek met his eyes and held fast for longer than intended. The man's stare was hypnotic. 'What do you want me to do?' he asked.

'Your plans for bringing Carak's program into disrepute...and more...' Naveen reminded him, 'are dead. You won't make it out of here once the Elders' ships start scouring the area.'

The wind passed through Halek's torn sails. But Naveen's presence suggested they could be stitched. 'You're not here to watch me die,' he declared.

Naveen nodded and looked around. 'All your years serving Carak, and you never asked yourself how he moved around the system and conducted his affairs without his rivals noticing.'

Halek shook his head. 'He had me conduct counter-intelligence operations,' he argued. 'I created distractions.'

Naveen grinned. 'They were for *you*, Halek. He knew you could never be trusted after what happened to your father. That's exactly why he brought you into his service. He had to keep you close.'

'But...' Halek was stunned. *Carak had known all along?* 'So how...I mean...what are you talking about?'

'While Carak is even less than a secondary concern for the Kwaios, they still observe and facilitate his work. They provided him with the means to move freely around this system. Only this system, but...it's sufficient. The technology required to do so is incredibly complex and uses massive amounts of energy.'

'What is it? How does it work?'

'Well, Carak has what you might call a key, but...there is another way. You see, this facility is *here*, on this moon...but it's also everywhere in the system. At least, everywhere it's connected to.'

'I don't understand.'

'I'll put it this way, Halek.' Naveen looked around again and then stared right back into Halek's eyes: 'If you want to put an end to Carak once and for all...you'll have to destroy this place.' He pointed to the automated weapons: 'Bring it down around you and stand on the spot where you first saw me.'

Halek laughed. 'You must think I'm a fool!'

Naveen shook his head. 'This is your only way, Halek. You'll see how it works when you pull back the curtain.' He chuckled. 'Then you can kill the wizard.' He stepped back into the shadows and vanished.

Halek followed him and felt something under his feet. Then he saw them, four small squares arranged in a large square of sufficient size for him to stand within. His feet started tingling, and he knew instinctively that it was not a lie. Somehow, this was how Carak had always come to this place. But where had he come from? Where would Halek go?

Palming the control unit for the weapons system as he checked the monitors again and saw them displaying the converging variables which would ultimately see him dead, he knew there was only one way to find out. And, taking a deep breath, he activated the guns.

Ω

174

'This room is here,' Carak was saying, as Laen stepped in and turned around to see that there was no door and the room stretched away as far in that direction as it did in every other. 'But it's also out there.'

'What do you mean?' Laen gasped, afraid to take another step forward upon the transparent floor through which he could see the sparsely occupied vastness of space. He felt slightly nauseous, and his head swam as he took in the distant points of light embracing a familiar scene of planets and moons. Yet this was no viewscreen. It was as if they stood floating in the middle of the Sieltor system, and Laen had no sense whatsoever of a floor beneath his feet. It had to be there, and so he stamped one foot. It went farther down than it should, and he almost lost his balance.

'It's Kwaios tech,' Carak replied, righting his son-in-law with a reassuring hand on his shoulder and a self-satisfied grin. 'At least, it started as Kwaios tech. I paid some Jaevisk acquaintances to duplicate the original system. They called it cross-dimensional observation, and they were decidedly unimpressed, if I read them correctly.' Carak dismissed the staggering technology with a wave of his hand, unwilling to go further into its implications. 'The point is that from here I can keep an eye on my operations around the system.'

Laen pointed to a relatively large floating planet in the centre of the scene. 'Is that Promies?' he asked, as the planet approached him and the scale shifted.

Carak nodded. 'You've just activated the viewer on its third moon. Do you see anything else?'

Laen stepped closer, and once again, as if the scene recognised his needs, the autonomous facility housing Carak's life's work came gradually into view. It was like the planet had pushed it towards him before traversing the same space to fill the universe behind. He reached out with wonder, but Carak shouted, 'NO!' He grabbed Laen's arm, warning him, 'You'll bring us too close!'

'Too *close*?' Laen was shocked. 'Isn't this just an image?' He looked back. 'A projection?'

Carak shook his head. 'No...neither. We're not just here, Laen. Think of this as a...viewing platform, but one that simulates *our* movement, rather than moving what you're watching. But it's not

175

only the perspective that's different. If you draw us too close, the result could be catastrophic.'

'But that makes no sense.' He looked around at the stars in the darkness. 'We wouldn't be able to *breathe*, for a start!'

Carak laughed. 'Don't try to understand it,' he advised. 'I still don't. All I know is that it's not just about observation. We can step through to the storage facility at Crith...where this viewer is located. We can step through to any one of the viewers.' He withdrew a black cube from his pocket. 'But I would need this. Without it, there's no telling where I'd come out.'

'I've heard about those things, Carak,' Laen said accusingly. 'None of it was good.'

Again, Carak offered a dismissive wave. 'In my experience, Laen, only the weak think of those with more power as the enemy.' He offered the cube to the younger man. 'But you and I, Laen, have the perspective to see opportunity in powerful enemies. As the humans say, you can judge the power of a man by the enemies he keeps.'

Laen eyed the cube cautiously, reluctant to take it. 'You *keep* the Kwaios, Carak? That sounds more than audacious.'

'Of course it is. But it's no less wise for being so. If we cower before the Kwaios, we'll end up like the humans.' The cube was proffered again, and left wanting again.

'The humans?' Laen turned back to the Promies facility, noticing only now the ship which had docked with it. 'What's happening here, Carak?' he asked as he pointed at the alien ship. 'Did you lure them to this place?'

'In a way, yes.' Carak put the cube down on an unseen table, and it floated amidst the stars. 'But they didn't need much coaxing. Their commander is Arrien Echad, great-grandson of the captain of the Nostradamus.'

'What?' Laen felt he might be on the verge of grasping the significance of the scene. This was more than a novelty display to impress him or gain his trust.

'He's here to find his people.'

Laen stared at the ship, as if he might see through its hull. 'So it's true,' he breathed.

'Most of it,' Carak conceded. He exhaled heavily, and Laen felt for the first time that he was seeing a tired old man. 'I have a lot to tell you, Laen. And...if you're willing...a lot to offer.'

Laen realised what he was suggesting. 'Carak, I…' He took in the scene again, noticing another ship approaching the facility at Promies. 'Is that a Sori ship?' He stepped back, and the planet and the facility retreated, both shrinking until the latter was almost indistinguishable in the wake of the world. Were it not for the tiny light of the Sori ship moving towards it, he could have pretended it did not exist. He already wished that it did not. 'I don't think I want this, Carak. Whatever…*this* is.'

'This is your destiny, Laen. This is everything I've worked towards, everything I've engineered to ensure that our family retains its influence in the wake of our political failings.'

'What do you mean?'

'It's only fear that keeps the other Elders in check. Fear that usurping me might bring the Kwaios down upon them.'

'Would it?'

'I honestly don't know. But something is about to happen here that will either crystallise or destroy Garran relations with the Kwaios. I've put them in a compromising position, giving them no choice but to show themselves. I'm tired of their games.'

Laen laughed ironically, and Carak smirked as the younger man said, 'I've heard everything now. Although I'm not sure I'd judge your decision wise.'

'Recklessness and wisdom are fickle lovers,' he joked. 'Anyway, what do you think? Are you willing to be my successor in this? Are you at least intrigued?'

Laen looked back at Promies, seeing something else approaching the planet. Something farther out, and larger. 'Of course I'm intrigued,' he said, as he pointed at the object and it was brought to him until he could see that it was a fleet. Although he had heard about the terrible events at Omneri, he could not have known that this fleet had just completed its translight journey from that planet.

'Silluc's fleet,' Carak explained. He pointed to the left and the view moved to find a second fleet not far behind. 'And Geram's. I made sure they knew not to accompany their fleets beyond the asteroid belt. Hopefully, they're safe on Omneri, but that will depend on whether or not Menalis figures out what I've done.'

Laen looked at his father-in-law. 'Which is what, exactly?'

177

Carak was about to explain when the room began to tremble, vibrations pulsing through it, increasing in intensity with each pulse.

'What's *happening*?' Laen shouted as objects began to fall off shelves gradually coming back into view as the universe which surrounded them began to crumble. The problem was that the viewed reality was still connected to the one in which they stood, and as it appeared to move away, it seemed to be taking this one with it. But then there was a great pulse, and one single stellar object was distinguishable before them, growing in size and clarity. Laen screamed furiously, helplessly, as a dark and desolate moon just kept coming. 'It's Crith!' roared Carak, desperately looking around for the Kwaios cube. 'I have to shut it *down*!'

Ω

The screaming automated weapons continued their destruction of everything in sight, and as supporting structures deteriorated and the hangar in which he stood began to crack and crumble, Halek was trembling with terror. He wanted to run, to find a safe place to hide from this madness, but he stood rooted to the spot upon which the Prophet had told him to stand, desperately trying to convince himself that it was the only truly safe place in the facility. The walls collapsed inwards, and the floors began to twist and warp, before shunting towards him as if he held a giant vacuum. He let out a shout as pieces of the floor snapped up into the air, joined quickly and all around him by everything else making up the scene before him. Before he knew what was happening, everything began merging in a great floating, spinning circle, pieces of stone and metal and synthetic building material fusing with the human clones until nothing was whole or distinct. Halek was left standing on the square platform, surrounded by the surface of Crith and a circle of everything which had made up the secret facility. 'What's happening?' he roared.

Below him, the square illuminated red, the four squares activating the greater square within which they sat. And Halek felt a force grip him, rooting him beyond his control. He was terrified. 'No!' he screamed, as he tried to lift his feet. The spinning circle changed shape, its interior now bending down to the surface of the moon. No, not down to the surface, Halek realised. Bending inwards, towards the square. Towards him. It kept spinning, but it was now being stretched, creating a funnel which pushed the thin, sharp inner circle closer and closer to the only living thing left on Crith. He screamed.

But before the funnel could slice him, Halek was sucked out of reality. When he returned, he was as shocked to see his company as they were to see him.

Ω

It was a dead air that filled the corridor as the airlock on the Garran side of the Promies facility closed behind Arrien and the Rangers. It may have been all down to their imaginations, but the air seemed to cling to body hair before travelling down through the pores to cool the blood vessels beneath. As a result, hearts were pounding and the adrenal gland was working overtime. The air whispered its unwelcome, for they were a foreign entity in this place. True, they were looking for other humans, but not humans like them. Arrien knew that the ones they would find were engineered descendants of those taken from Earth; engineered to deal with the environments of Garran-seeded worlds. Which was why the air was breathable, but not necessarily good for them. Arrien felt as if he could taste it, and he wrinkled his nose as he turned to the commander: 'Let's get this done fast, Lee.'

'Damn right,' the commander replied. 'Seen enough lately to make me homesick.' Lee split the unit, sending one group ahead of he and Arrien, keeping the other behind. The corridor was strange, with smooth, black square panels separated by semi-cylindrical conduits on the floor, ceiling and walls, making a cubic enclosure demarcating the interior of each module. These ridge-lined bumps and pillars were icy cold to the touch, but that same cold did not emanate from them. Arrien snapped his hand back as the Forward Team moved on, stepping over the first conduit. 'Wouldn't wanna be doing this with the lights out,' Katie muttered as she led the way, keeping her rifle-light fixed on the floor.

'Fraid you'll get lost, Kitty?' one of the men teased.

'I'd just follow your stink, Ped,' she replied, focused on the way forward.

Arrien was looking around, trying to follow everything illuminated by all the moving flashlights. He had a headache, but

179

he attributed it to anxiety as he tried to figure out where to go. There was no sign of a junction, but this adhered to the exterior schematics, so this was not a concern. Instead, an electrical scratching inside his brain was warning him that not all was as it seemed. And even though he had expected as much, the proximity of the trap into which he and the others were surely walking bore heavily upon him. 'Stop,' he said quietly, extending an arm so the commander walked into it. 'Something's not right.'

'We can't stop here, Arrien,' Lee argued. 'We're only on the edge of this place.'

'I'm not so sure about that.'

Lee's flashlight illuminated the still proceeding Forward Team: 'What do you mean?'

They did not have to wait long to find out. Completely in unison and without warning, the black panels forming the floors, ceiling and walls shrunk in size, snapping inward to form smaller square versions of themselves so that they were disconnected from the partition pillars. They were all jolted where they stood, but Katie shouted out as she stumbled between a panel and a conduit, whereby all realised that the conduits were tubes heading off in every direction. Katie's rifle saved her, and it was jammed between the edge of the floor panel and the tube as she hung from the sling strap. But as those closest to her moved swiftly to her aid and grabbed her arms to haul her up, something grabbed her from beneath. The gun slipped…and she was gone.

Then Arrien saw it, all around them. The panels were still dark, but they could now be seen through, and scores…no, hundreds of people were beneath, above and on either side of them. The skin of these humans appeared blue-grey, but it was difficult to be sure in the low light and through the panels. They stood, staring vacantly, but there was something in their eyes that indicated awareness on some level. 'They're drones,' said Arrien. 'They're waiting for orders.'

'I don't think so,' Lee disagreed. 'Giving an order to pull Katie down to them would be a waste of time.'

'So, you think they know what they're doing?' Arrien moved closer to one of the walls, careful not to get too close to the edge. He stared into the eyes of one of the motionless people, and it stared back at him. Before giving him a dark grin. Too late to stop it, Lee watched in horror as hands came through the wall panel and took Arrien, who was too stunned to react. When the commander opened fire on them, his bullets hit the solid panel and ricocheted. Two of his team were hit, one of them in the head. The panels turned opaque again, and Lee roared in fury. But then, as panels appeared in front of and behind them, sealing them within the cubic module, everything changed.

Ω

With the Kwaios cube now in his hands and even as the room continued to shake, Carak stared at Halek. And Halek stared back. Laen raised a gun, wobbling on his feet: 'Who are you? How did you get here?'

'This is Halek, my master aide,' said Carak warily. He did not suggest that the gun be lowered. 'And that's a good question.' As he was talking, he twisted a corner of the cube, and the room completely reverted to reality. The looming moon, Crith, was gone, and the shaking subsided. 'How did you get here, Halek?'

Halek stared at the Kwaios cube, knowing it was the key about which Naveen had spoken. 'Crith came under attack,' he lied easily. He had years of experience behind him. 'I don't know who it was, but the Sori were acting strangely and the Vesstal female was too inquisitive for my liking. The Sori left and before I knew what was happening, the whole place was collapsing around me.'

'Yet you escaped,' Carak noted, stepping towards him. 'Completely unharmed.'

'Miraculous,' Laen commented, lowering the gun. Carak turned to him and nodded: 'A singularly astonishing outcome, indeed.'

Why is the boy here? Halek thought. Then he eyed the Kwaios cube in Carak's hands. And a thought struck him. A plan. 'I was just...stepping back,' he explained. 'Trying to get as far back from the hangar entrance as possible. I thought perhaps there was another way out.'

'And you found it,' said Carak.

'Yes. I was...lucky.'

Carak turned and walked away from him, saying, 'We'll return to this mystery, Halek. But for now, there's something I need to see.' He turned back with the cube raised and twisted it from the centre. Blue light lit its frame and the wall behind Halek vanished, before the void of space that replaced it began to flow into the room,

181

replacing everything around them. Halek was somewhat less impressed than Carak knew he should have been, but as he pointed towards Sieltor Promies and brought it forward, the unfolding scene within which they now stood was sufficient to distract from Halek's unexpected materialisation. Because the massive facility in high orbit above Promies was changing.

Ω

The modules of Elder Carak's storage facility were to the naked eye and even to those inside it connected by the web of metal conduits, but even these were composite pieces, and they began to split along their length into quadrants marking the six sides of each cubic module. Cables now connected the modules as they moved apart from each other in every direction, their position determined by spherical units scattered throughout the structure which acted as feeder and retractor mechanisms through which the cables ran. There seemed to be no central or control node. On the command bridge, the crew of the Styx were watching this chaos unfold, and the danger was painfully apparent. 'We've lost their transponders!' Jaime reported anxiously.

'You still following the last module they were in?' asked Kel.

He nodded: 'Yeah, but there was a blackout before everything went to shit. They could have been split up!'

'Then track the surrounding modules as well!' Kel snapped back as she moved closer to the forward window. The madness continued before her eyes as she heard Jaime gathering people to help. 'Where the hell are you, Arrien?' she whispered. Then she was warned that the Garran fleets were within weapons range, and the VR brought up the small Sori craft disappearing into the milieu of modules. The Styx was larger, and not as manoeuvrable, but there was no choice. 'Take us in,' she ordered.

Ω

Arrien had no idea where he was. But the people who took him did not intend to hurt him, of that he was sure. They held him firmly as they saw an approaching module through the transparent panels. 'Stay with us,' he was warned sternly as they stepped up closer to the panel. He needed no explanation to appreciate that this was the best course of action. As the module struck the one they were in, they took him through the panels, and he was in awe of the technology allowing this to happen. 'Why are we running?' he asked. 'Are you escaping?'

'No,' replied the huge man currently holding his arm. 'You are.' They turned right and headed down the corridor, at least twenty of them remaining in this group. They were all splitting up. 'We need to keep moving.'

'What are you talking about?' Arrien argued. 'I'm here to rescue you. I've searched for years…for all of you!'

'Maybe. But the Kwaios have been looking for *you* a lot longer.' He stopped and turned to Arrien, saying, 'And we can hear them coming.' He flashed a mysterious grin as they reached another panel. The configuration of the modules was strange, and it was difficult to tell if they were passing through internal or external partitions. Passing through this next one, Arrien found himself in a massive circular room, and as he looked up and around at the storage compartments lining the walls, within which he could see people presumably in stasis, he realised that something was wrong. 'This isn't in the facility,' he stated, causing the others to stop their onward journey. 'This is too big to have been inside one of those modules.'

'There's no time to explain, Arrien,' a woman called back. 'The facility is more than you can see from the outside.'

'And it's not just about what you see,' the big man added. 'Carak learned a lot since dealing with the Kwaios and the Cage.' He gestured for Arrien to keep up as they resumed.

'You know about the Cage?' Arrien was surprised. 'That was a hundred years ago.'

'We're not the mindless drones you expected, are we?'

Arrien shook his head. 'Obviously far from it.' They were almost at the opposite end of the storage chamber. 'But I've seen them used.'

'Every batch has its rejects,' said another man. 'They've no self-awareness.'

'Sounds like you're okay with all this,' Arrien noted suspiciously. He looked back around at the bodies in the storage units just before they reached an exit panel. Beyond it, another module could be seen moving towards them across the emptiness.

'*Okay* with it?' quipped the giant. 'We helped *design* it!'

Arrien was grabbed again and dragged through the panels. But this time the module came under attack, and his captors appeared shocked. Arrien needed no psychic powers to know what they were thinking: how did this assailant find them in the midst of the chaos and with their constant movement? Of course, unlike Arrien, they had never before encountered a Sori blood priest.

Ω

The Styx was moving slowly on minimal thrusters, now that Kel had taken them fully into the lion's den. The module and cable system was intricate and seemed to be able to change its composition, meaning that tracking specific modules as they moved progressively farther from each other was a task that did not fit the three-dimensional expanding grid Jaime had hoped to plot. But the problem was more complex than that, as Jaime observed: 'It's like there's something else in here. Something we can't see.'

'What do you mean?' asked Kel, turning back to him.

'Sensor ghosts all over the place,' he explained. 'And some of the modules phase in and out on the grid as if something was getting in the way.'

Kel thought for a moment, realising she was in one of those moments in which Arrien would have known what to do. Arrien always thought outside the box, but it was more than that. Arrien liked to reshape the box to his own ends. She nodded as if hearing his voice inside her head, when it was just her own inner dialogue providing her with a solution. 'Start mapping them,' she ordered excitedly, making her way up to Jaime's station. 'Don't ignore them.'

Jaime's eyes narrowed before he nodded with a grin and said, 'They're not ghosts.'

'No, I don't think so. But we shoulda known Carak's trap would be a helluva lot more intricate than some mix 'n' match puzzle.' Kel pointed at some recent scans that were moving on to a peripheral monitor. 'Whatever these shapes are, they're part of it...somehow.'

'We've been painted!' came a snap report. 'Garran missiles incoming!'

'Roll out the spinners!' Kel ordered immediately. 'But keep them on a tight leash in here.'

As Jaime was compiling a virtual image of the facility now incorporating the ghost readings, the spinners shot out from all round the ship's perimeter. These spherical bots were self-aware EMP weapons, designed to locate and disable the guidance systems of incoming projectiles with a highly focused pulse. They moved out in every direction from the Styx, but the uncertainty about their surroundings meant that the spinners would read their environment differently with every rotation of the main sensor. So Jaime's constant re-mapping was now intricately connected with their defence. And with the spinners maintaining a close orbit of the Styx, knocking out guidance systems might not be enough to stop a missile strike.

'Here they come!'

The Garran had been thorough, moving out around the facility to cover as many potential escape routes as possible. Majestically orchestrated, the two fleets launched their salvos simultaneously, meaning that hundreds of missiles were hunting the Styx. Almost immediately, the outer modules were exploding. The Garran began clearing the way towards the Styx, and Kel knew there was no way out: 'Tell me something, Jaime. Tell me something good.'

Jaime looked at her, eyes wide as he shook his head. 'I don't get it,' he told her. 'I'm not sure we're even in a vacuum right now.'

'What are you talking about?'

'Brace! Brace!'

As the missiles, scores of them, bore down on them, the spinners came alive, locking on and emitting their focused EM charges. But these charges caused something unexpected to happen. Something weird. Some of the missiles exploded as if impacting with something, some of the spinners exploded for the same reason, some of the missiles went straight through the spinners as if they were not even there...and then some of those missiles went straight through the Styx to blow nearby modules apart. Others, however, did exactly what they were supposed to do. With the tight orbit of the spinners, even those missiles whose guidance systems were fried by the EMP continued under their own momentum. They slammed into the hull of their target, and the Styx took too much damage to escape the fight.

The world became very different then for Kel and Jaime and the rest of Arrien's crew, and internal bulkheads started sealing areas of the ship deemed salvageable by autonomous evac systems.

They were about to be set adrift amidst a Garran trap, and there was no sign of rescue.

Ω

Abigale stared as the VR cleared up the image after the Argo dropped from its self-propelling slipstream. She was overwhelmed, unsure of where to start. The Garran fleets were bombarding the strange station orbiting Sieltor Promies, but it would not be long before they turned their attention to this ship from Earth, whose crew had bypassed their own systems' protocols and cut a route through the Sieltor system to get to an inner planet. Every space-faring race knew the hazards of maintaining FTL velocity within the boundaries of a star system. 'Damage report!' she ordered.

'Hard to believe we're still in one piece,' said Carenna as she came up beside her and handed her a techsheet. 'But I can't fault the nav team.'

Abigale nodded: 'They anticipated the asteroid belt. We wouldn't be having this conversation if they hadn't.'

'They did more than anticipate it. They liaised with the drive room and calculated the rate of deceleration necessary to get us through one of only three potential entry points.'

'They did their jobs, Commander.'

Carenna baulked but kept quiet.

Abigale inhaled and calmed herself. She had been on edge all the way here, desperately trying to come to terms not only with the loss of the clone of her daughter, but also with the knowledge that her real daughter was out here somewhere and the only person who could find her was smack in the middle of the madness coming into view before them. 'Sorry, Carenna. Just…bear with me on this.'

Carenna laid a hand on her shoulder. 'We'll find her. Okay?'

Abigale forced a smile: 'Okay.' She again took in the scene, before turning to the crew: 'The rest of Vawter's ships are now a few hours out because their commanders wouldn't take the same risks you took for me.' She looked at Carenna and said, 'For that, I'm grateful to all of you. But now we're amongst the wolves and we have to fight like a lion.' She turned back to the forward screen and pointed: 'Somewhere out there is a man…*one* man…who knows where my little girl is. But there's much more going on than that. The guy we're looking for is the great-grandson of Adam Echad, and seeing as he's not even supposed to exist, you might begin to understand why he's so valuable.' The bridge crew were stunned, but they regained focus as gravitational disturbances registered on the ship's sensors and crackling blue lines could be seen around the Promies facility. All around it.

Ω

The Sori blood priest was in a trance as his pilot followed his instructions. Protruding from the priest's right ear was a data node, which was sending a signal to the navigation interface. The pilot had been well trained in interpreting the apparently garbled and meaningless information, and his travelling companion was a master of meditative viewing. Unlike Arrien, who had trained under him, the priest could see telepathically, and he could follow up to five paths of progression once his mind had fixed on an origin point for each. Unlike Arrien, the priest did not need monitors or screens of any kind, but the priest realised now that Arrien would soon figure out precisely how to do all of this...and more. Because Arrien, like the Sori blood priest from Senkara, could see the Lines.

The priest, whose name was Tankalana Reyta, had seen Arrien taken by the clones, the first point of Arrien's Fate Line at which Reyta made a sound connection. With each change in Arrien's location within the altering facility as the modules moved around, the blood priest followed the reformulating Fate Line – no easy task. Because the Promies facility was not wholly here and not entirely visible – Reyta recognised the use of Kwaios cross-dimensional positioning – he had to allow for the nature of a Fate Line being altered by the games played by Arrien's captors. The fact that Arrien was moving from module to module across an ever-changing playing field moving in and out of existence meant that his Fate was constantly being re-written. The priest had to keep up with these changes and he could not be immediately confident that he was following the right Line.

The Lines did not lie, although they could temporarily deceive. They were not bound by visual or cross-dimensional tricks, and they could penetrate the fabric of spacetime and follow their designated quarry anywhere, and to any time it might go. With

187

each change in location, the hypothetical Fate Lines dissolved behind a reformulated origin point, and the resuming Line snapped backwards to reconnect with the earlier point, correcting Arrien's personal timeline. The priest was barely aware of this occurring, or at least did not need to concern himself with it, focused as he was on the ever-correcting forward journey of his prey. Wherever his telepathic peripheral vision envisaged the disintegration of a Line, he would abandon it and focus on another one. This went on for some time as the Sori craft moved cautiously around the ever-changing facility, the pilot aided by the navigational instructions fed by the priest's understanding of the strongest Fate Line. But eventually the priest was able to anticipate Arrien's movement and he found him. He opened his eyes as the pilot brought them to within close weapons range: 'Attack!'

Ω

From out of the crackling blue sphere now forming all around the facility, hundreds of egg-shaped objects emerged, and even while the Garran star cruisers refocused their weapons to attack this new arrival, beams of white energy shot out from the eggs and pierced everything in their path to meet at a central point. From here, a burst of light blasted outwards and deactivated the cross-dimensional filter hidden in the centre of Carak's chaotic conundrum. This was the Kwaios answer to the problem, revealing every module and chamber by rendering their own technology useless. The Garran ships were not affected, but the Kwaios eggs began drifting aimlessly, and Abigale knew their owners would not be long in picking them up. 'We have to get in there,' she ordered as she kept her eyes on the viewer. 'They'll be...' She stopped as something caught her eye in the centre of the facility, and the crew watched as she tapped a bracelet on each wrist before gesturing towards the huge viewer and magnifying the image, dragging it outwards with both arms. Then she tapped with her right index finger on the object in the centre, and a yellow square appeared around it. 'Can't be,' she said, magnifying only this image as it was dragged out of the surrounding scene.

'Is that what I think it is?' asked Carenna. 'A *MEC station* in the middle of a *Garran outpost*?'

'Yes, it is.' Abigale turned and looked at the crew. 'And as soon as we get Arrien Echad…that's our ticket outta here.' That restored morale somewhat as the Argo moved in. But this new light they foresaw at the end of the tunnel was not what it appeared to be. For a start, it was a one-way ticket.

Ω

The Sori craft docked with the module in which Arrien was now being surrounded by clones attempting to shield him from harm. The module kept moving, of course, but the Sori no longer cared. The blood priest needed to understand the capabilities of this human. Having the Kwaios and the Jaevisk aware of the Lines meant that Sori strength was limited in this part of the galaxy. But if humans were changing…evolving before their eyes…

As with all blood priests, a message would be sent home when Reyta died here, and his sacrifice would ensure his immortality when the Day came. Reyta also knew that if the Prophet was engineering all of this, his choices had been foreseen, but still…he had to know. The Prophet knew his pawns well. They cleared the airlock, the pilot and the priest, armed with nothing the humans would have recognised as a weapon. And the clones were waiting.

It registered with Reyta that these humans were physically stronger than they should have been, but even a Sori blood priest taken by surprise was more agile and bred to kill. Thrown through the air and slammed against a wall upon entry to the module, Reyta was unfazed as he got to his feet. He let them come to him as his pilot shot at the second wave of clones with bio-naut spikes ejected from beneath the flesh of his forearms. These living projectiles never missed, because even if anticipated and avoided, their tendrils snapped out to hook their targets, shredding skin and searing bone with biochemical heat. Following this, the spikes were drawn to their targets to begin drilling. The corridor was quickly filled with screaming and the smell of burning.

Arrien watched from the far end of the corridor as the blood priest who had trained him in peripheral viewing closed his eyes and waited like a spider amongst flies, shrugging off his black body-wrap which fell softly to the ground like a veil of shadow. Reyta was also equipped with organic weaponry, but his were not launched. Instead, his spikes erupted from his now naked body so that he was entirely protected by razor-sharp armour as he launched himself in amongst the group of five clones. Blood sprayed and gushed as he twisted and stabbed and sliced, dancing around them as they fought with fists, elbows, knees and feet, delivering blows against him which damaged his spikes while at the same time cutting and burning as they became dislodged in attacking limbs. It was not long before the two Sori stood in the midst of dead clones, covered in blood barely noticeable upon their red skin as they fixed their attention upon Arrien. And the single clone protecting him.

He was enormous, this human, and Reyta knew that his strength would be prodigious. But that was not what concerned him, for he could feel that this one was different. Reyta flinched as something inside him, and yet not exactly inside him, was tugged. This human could access the Sentience! He could not see the Lines, as could Reyta and Arrien, but he could use those who could. And right now, both Arrien and Reyta were conduits to his salvation. As the giant human closed his eyes and appeared to embrace serenity, Arrien let out an increasingly higher-pitched roar of pain before falling to his knees. Reyta realised too late what the clone was doing as he felt another, more tangible tug at his chest, and his heart stung. He gritted his yellow teeth, but he arrogantly restrained his pilot from firing at the clone as one of his feet shifted towards the humans. He needed to learn as much as possible before his Fate Message was delivered to Senkara. He had thought he was here to learn about Arrien, but Arrien was only part of what was happening here.

Reyta glared at the imposing figure, his focus waning as another sharp tug at his chest drew him closer. The clone opened his eyes and pointed back at Arrien, writhing on the floor behind him. 'You followed the Lines to find him,' he said to the Sori. 'Your curiosity brought you here.'

Reyta realised that his curiosity had indeed been used against him. Yet it was impossible to know whether the clone was aware of the extent of his own manipulation, for surely the Prophet was using these perversions of nature for his own ultimate end. The blood priests of Senkara were possibly the only people in the galaxy to whom Naveen had revealed his great scheme. And they had been horrified. Many had abandoned their faith, stopped reading the Lines. But Reyta conceded to the inevitability of the

Prophet's timeline. And chose instead to learn all he could for the sake of future generations of Sori who would survive the coming terror.

He gestured to his pilot and the two Sori moved apart to prepare to flank the giant clone. Arrien roared again and Reyta lost his balance as the connection was completed. In his mind, he saw that both his and Arrien's Fate Lines had been fused, and his terror was absolute as the clone said, 'Now follow *this*!'

He turned and kicked Arrien so hard that he rolled towards and through the permeable panel. Reyta let out a bellow of fury as his pilot launched a barrage of spikes at the clone, who went down silently and died with a cold grin on his face. Reyta had no choice. He was dragged rapidly by an unseen force, face-down along the floor until he could see the dark wall at the end of the module. Although his pilot tried to catch him, he was too late. And Reyta passed through. What he saw astonished him.

Ω

Laen kept a watchful eye on Halek, even as he tried to take in everything they were seeing. The modules of the Promies facility had been fading in and out of existence while the missiles of Garran star cruisers sought and destroyed the vessel which had fled from Omneri and was commanded by Arrien Echad. But Echad had escaped into the facility, or more likely, had been led by the nose. The Sori tried to reach him, their intentions unknown. Halek had filled them in on that part. Surprisingly, the mothership from which the blood priest had launched had remained hidden out at one of Omneri's moons and had not even tried to rescue their doomed compatriots as the facility came alive, the Garran attacked, and the Kwaios disrupted the entire illusion. But then the Sori had always been a mystery.

Carak was careful not to point overtly at the MEC station for fear of closing the gap between them, but he gestured towards it: 'Arrien is about to meet his destiny.' He turned away and poured himself a drink. 'I was a young man when I started all this.' He knocked it back and took a deep breath, his back still to both men. 'I've lied and deceived, manipulated and...' He lowered his head and sighed.

191

'And killed,' Halek finished for him as he moved into position beside Laen. Laen could feel that there was something wrong, a tension building, but he was so caught up in the majesty of what was unfolding out at Promies and what he was hearing from his father-in-law that he was unprepared for what came next.

Carak turned around, steely eyed now as he realised the predicament he was in. Naveen had made it clear that he would die soon, that someone close to him would pull the trigger. And here was that someone. 'Move away from him, Laen.' The younger Garran did so, but it was too late. Halek had taken Laen's gun, and he gestured with it for Laen to keep moving.

'They were complicated times, Halek,' Carak told him. 'Your father was…losing his way.'

'You mean losing *your* way, Carak,' the aide sneered. 'He had been naïve enough to think you could change the heart of Sieltor…and I remember *despising* him for that!' Halek wept with guilt. 'In classrooms of my peers, they mocked my father for supporting you, and while we prayed for yet another revolution, my father tried to convince me that you were the answer to stability.'

'I *was*!' Carak replied defiantly. 'Children in their safe little schools have no concept of what it takes to bring peace to a divided people.'

'But my father did. He learned the hard way. And when he confronted you about the murders and treachery, you decided it was time for him to go.'

Laen was slowly and cautiously working on removing a knife concealed in the back of his jacket, but he would have to throw it or lunge at Halek. And he found himself wondering if risking his life for Carak was something he truly wanted. The uncertainty shamed him. And yet it was unavoidable. 'We have had stability for a long time, Halek,' Carak was saying. 'I can't change the past.'

'No,' Halek agreed. 'You simply take it upon yourself to shape everyone's future.' He shook his head, saying, 'Well…no more,' as he raised the gun. Laen moved forward without thinking, and yet still he was too late. It might even have been his movement that shocked Halek into pulling the trigger. The bullet went through Carak's throat, and Halek ducked aside as Laen lunged at him with the knife. As Laen stumbled forward, Halek rushed to Carak's failing form and snapped up the Kwaios cube, twisting it desperately with no idea what he was doing. He moved swiftly, throwing the gun at Laen as he grimaced and prayed and stepped forward into whatever space was being offered. Some might have said there were worse places he could have ended up. Some would be wrong.

Ω

Abigale had been somewhat over-confident of their ability to make it through the madness and reach the MEC station, never mind having little time to adhere to sedation protocols. Finding Arrien Echad was a task inexorably moving beyond the realms of possibility, and scores of Garran star cruisers had been gradually positioning themselves to envelop the entire Promies facility until the Argo was left with no option but to fight its way through to the centre. The modules were still moving, which made following a fixed course difficult even as they provided opportunities for cover and defence. Many times the Argo narrowly avoided destruction as salvos of Garran missiles sought them out and blew a section of the station apart instead. The reverse also applied, however, as manoeuvring so rapidly within the constraints of an ever-changing obstacle course while avoiding projectiles led to many collisions. One way or the other, the Argo was being battered.

The probes sent out to find Arrien Echad were searching for a needle in a haystack. In squads of five, they zipped around the facility at lightning speeds, stopping intermittently to form up with a central probe surrounded by four to scan their immediate proximity and send the readings back to the bridge. They had been homing in on human life readings, with all six squads spiralling towards the centre. Towards the MEC station. Then came the words Abigale had been waiting for: 'Got him.'

'What?' She bolted to the workstation of the officer handling squads 3 and 4. 'How do you know?'

He swiped the readings up to the mid-floor imager, and the picture was decrypted. It was clear. Amidst a nightmare scene of human bodies floating towards the MEC station, only one was clothed. They saw a red-skinned Sori as an explosion flashed beyond the probes, but it was tumbling aimlessly and was likely dead. 'My God...' Carenna exclaimed, 'how do we get him before he goes through?'

'Shortest distance,' said Abigale, moving towards the forward viewer. 'All guns forward!' she ordered. 'And pick up the pace. Anything gets in our way…we're going through!'

It was nuts. The crew knew it. The captain must have known it. Carenna sure as hell knew it: 'You're gonna give us a reputation,' she quipped, recalling the Jaevisk ship back at Earth.

Abigale was in a dark mood, picturing little Hannah in undefined darkness.

Carenna inclined her head and smiled, but the two women shared a look of apprehension. This would be the ultimate test, not only of the crew's resolve but of the ship itself. What likely scratched at the back of everyone's head was the absence of the Kwaios. They had disrupted the station's ability to conceal its components, but they had not yet come to claim their prize. They had not attacked at all, and Carak's plan to use the fleets of the Elders as cannon fodder in much the same way Naveen had positioned the Garran armada at Kiranis a century ago had proven futile. But then Carak should have known such a thing. For Carak had been one of the few people – Garran or human, at least – who knew how MEC worked. One of the few who knew that the Kwaios were always close. As the Argo maintained its course to smash through everything until the MEC station was in their sights, and still under fire from the Garran, the nav team punched in destination requests. But the MEC station was unaccommodating. 'Captain,' one of them shouted, 'it's only got one pre-programmed destination!'

'Where?' Abigale demanded.

'The Kiranis system. The Kwaios world.'

There was no response. What could she say? They had gone so far down the rabbit hole that to turn back now would rip them to shreds. Not the ultimate test, then. That was still to come.

Ω

Halek had time to catch his breath. That was a relief, at least. But then he realised where he was, and his heart was in his throat. One of the modules of the Promies facility, empty and cold. There was a humming sound vibrating through his bones, and he immediately set about finding its source. It grew louder as he walked the silent corridors, until he came to what appeared to be a power generator situated in what was likely the centre of the module. He went to it and, finding a control panel, he activated a holographic projection of what was going on here. The module was part of a network keeping the vacuum of space outside an area at the heart of the Promies facility, and one of the stations used by the humans to transport themselves across the stars waited within. Perhaps Halek should have found a way to interrogate Carak before killing him. But of course his hand had been forced and there had been little time for a clever plan. He looked at the projection again and realised that he should be able to see the MEC station from an adjacent corridor.

He made his way quickly to the narrow passageway, finding himself staring into space through one of the window panels. There it was, the enigmatic MEC station hanging in the intermittently illuminated distance. It did not belong here, any more than Halek did. A sudden missile impact shook the module, and Naveen appeared behind Halek as the generator stopped working and power was lost. Halek turned and blinked, clearly confused. 'How do I get out of here?' he asked desperately. A shadow was growing behind Naveen, quickly throwing the conversation into darkness.

'You don't, Halek,' the Prophet replied coldly. 'Ever.'

'*What*?' Halek was incensed. 'But you said I was a leader-in-*waiting*!'

'I say a lot of things. You killed Carak, and he was one of the few people I'd call a friend.'

'You...you *told* me to!'

'Obedient to the end. Your father would be proud.' He vanished, leaving Halek staring at the panel before him. He moved closer, and tears came unbidden. For the shadow closing in upon the module was the prow of a ship. In that moment, a moment which seemed to wait for Halek to appreciate its splendour, the aide to Elder Carak found himself thinking of his father. Thinking of how his father had belittled him, compelled him into a world of political intrigue and self-interested power play. Halek had been an artist when younger, a creator of beauty, of expressions of life and passion. His father had convinced him to set all that aside in favour of emulating him, even as he surely knew that Halek had never found his desires truly fulfilled by his position. Why had he done all this in memory of such a man? Why had he not thought of his own future...of the consequences of his actions? Why had he not looked to life, rather than allowing thoughts of death to map his destiny?

As the ship bore down upon the module, Halek mused that it was perhaps a thing of beauty, and that he would have liked to sculpt a replica from fesaro resin and nonna bark. That would have been beautiful indeed. And, with his father long dead, he would have cared little for what the old bastard might have thought.

Ω

Human bodies floated everywhere, and Reyta realised he was amongst them. He had no idea how he could breathe because this should have been a vacuum. In this huge expanse marked out by a sphere of disconnected modules, he could see Arrien moving inexorably towards one of the massive stations that the humans had set up all over their territory, the ones they foolishly believed broke them down and fired them across the stars. He had no idea how or why this station was in the middle of this Garran-engineered chaos, but it certainly did not bode well. Considering who really operated them.

There was a flash below him and he saw an explosive force causing ripples upon the invisible surface keeping the vacuum of space out of here. Then he noticed another to his left, and another. Garran missiles, launched from the many star cruisers surrounding the facility, were taking potshots at anything perceived as hostile. In this madness, there were many targets to be found, and Reyta thanked the Lines that he had stumbled into this twisted haven, even as his onward journey took him closer to the MEC station. In the corner of his eye, he registered the approach of a floating human body, but he could not control his movement, and it was soon upon him, its flailing limbs making it seem as if he were under a terribly uncoordinated attack by its horrific nakedness. Without gravity through which he might build resistance, he could do little more than the comatose human as he, too, rolled and tumbled aimlessly. Eventually, he pushed the body away, and he realised that he had been moving closer to the strange MEC station all along. Extended for the entry of ships, its glowing blue arm seemed more like the mouth of a Treskan feeder plant, and he the hapless, hypnotised zessbird. The glow made it impossible to

196

distinguish between the tumbling body of Arrien Echad and those of the other humans, but Reyta was sure that Arrien must have passed through by now. He would have been panicked, of course, but not as much as Reyta. For the blood priest knew what came next.

There was a rule. And breaking that rule had consequences. If a Sori took their own life, their Fate Message would be lost to the Black Lines, left between realities for the rest of time. Their lives, their memories, their legacy…all would be lost. Reyta thought he had accepted this. He thought that such an idea would never cross his mind. But then he had never expected to be floating helplessly towards such a fate.

As he tumbled ever closer to the MEC station, something new caught his eye, far out at one edge of the sphere of modules. It was a ship, a beautiful ship, approaching at collision speed. He read all this, he felt it, as if his Fate Line had been tugged again. And a great weight was lifted from him. He would not have to decide whether to embrace the terror of the MEC system or cut his own throat. As he spun, the Argo moved out of his line of sight. But he knew it was there, and all was well. For as it slammed into one of the modules of the Promies Facility, the protective shield keeping out the vacuum of space was broken.

The MEC station appeared to react violently, consciously, as countless metal tentacles snapped out to collect the humans who would otherwise die as the oxygen was lost. It was with this desperate reaction that Reyta realised what was happening here. He understood why the Prophet had allowed Elder Carak to continue his research, and to hide this place from the Kwaios. For the humans being taken here were not the prey of the Kwaios. They were ammunition set against them, and this hidden MEC station was the chamber of a gun. Reyta closed his eyes, willing himself to relax as all air was sucked from his lungs and he embraced Enlightenment. He felt his Fate Message leaving, pulsing outwards across the Lines to return to Senkara, but it was intercepted by the most unexpected of things – another Sori. In a painful heartbeat, Reyta's Line search located this brother, finding him trapped in a glass container filled with viscous fluid. This Sori struggled in his bonds, but Reyta knew that he had been cloned, and this was in a part of the facility left intact amidst the madness. Reyta had no time to do anything, but the terror amidst which he died defined his Fate Message as it was relayed home. Had he been alive long enough to witness the extremely short visit of a Kwaios scout ship, materialising with one purpose alone, he would have had valuable information for the Sori. Information which would have saved many lives.

Ω

As the Argo broke through, the probes raced ahead, and as she saw the Kwaios scout ship taking Arrien, Abigale's heart sank. But Carenna voiced the obvious: 'If they're taking him to the Kiranis system…that's where we'll find him.'

Abigale nodded. 'Punch it in. Follow him,' she ordered. 'Launch the repair nets and seal any breaches!'

'Captain, we can't do it,' Carenna argued. 'We'll be sitting ducks if we have to sedate everyone!'

'We're not sedating anyone,' the captain replied. 'We're going through as we are.'

'Are you *serious*?' snapped Carenna. 'After what happened back *home*?'

Abigale turned on her: 'Watch your *mouth*, Commander! If you can't follow orders, then sit it out!'

'You'll see us all dead for her, is that it?'

'I'd see the *world* dead for her,' the captain hissed. 'But you wouldn't understand that!'

Carenna's eyes welled up, and with trembling lips she breathed, 'How dare you!'

Abigale glared at her, but her heart was breaking. She had gone too far, yet still there were stars to be crossed. 'Punch it in,' she called out again. 'Stay the course. Let's see what this MEC system really is.' The Garran onslaught continued as the automatons of the repair nets worked on the collision damage and the arm of the MEC station was adjusting for the dimensions of the Argo, but they were suddenly hammered by so many missiles that their manoeuvring thrusters were disabled, and they had to rely solely on their forward momentum to get them through. As Garran ships moved in around them, another attack took out their life support systems and the bridge went dark. 'NO!' Abigale screamed, wasting vital oxygen as a star cruiser blocked their path to the station. It took considerable damage in doing so, absorbing the impact of their momentum, but while the crew were collapsing to the floor and drifting into oblivion, the Argo came to a stop with a Garran star cruiser as a fender.

Ω

Arrien had been awake as they took him. Somehow, despite being kicked out of the module into space and floating across what should have been a vacuum, he had not only avoided losing consciousness; his journey had been far from aimless. He had taken in as much as possible, some of it requiring his reading the Lines: the attacking Garran; the knowledge that the Styx had been lost; the blood priest latched to his Fate Line; the Argo on approach, then breaking through the protective field; the blood priest dying as oxygen was lost. And then, of all horrors, the Kwaios arriving to take him. The speed at which he was dragged into their vessel rattled him to such an extent that he passed out...

As Arrien saw his Fate Line crackling and splintering around him, a cacophony of sibilant voices circled his head like a sonic cloud. 'Weee...seeee...youuu,' they whispered. 'Youuu...arrr...ussss.' He recalled passing into the MEC system and figured that he was now at the mercy of the Kwaios. Yet there was no sign of the blue light of their technology, the deceptively calming hum of their hybritech. Instead, there was merely darkness, and Arrien was lying on a surface of dust and stone, black and grey and white mixed together like the cooled and broken aftermath of a pyroclastic holocaust. He pushed himself to his feet, and his right hand went through the blackness beneath as if he had rested upon charred meringue. There was no fiery flow beneath the dried surface, although his instinct was to snap his hand back as if it might be incinerated before his eyes. 'Weee...seeee...youuu,' the voices hissed again, as the depression he had made began to break open, cracks spiderwebbing outwards as he in turn backed away. 'Youuu...arrr...ussss.'

Beneath the dried surface a great horror was revealed to Arrien, for as he tried to escape the tectonic obliteration threatening to envelope him, closing in and spreading out in every direction, he saw the true source of the dust, and knew that none of what he stood upon was stone or dried volcanic residue. Burned

199

and broken flesh was the topsoil, and bones and skulls were the earth beneath. 'Weee...seeee...youuu.' He imagined that the absent dead were whispering from their mass graves. Arrien spun round, trying to locate the source of the voices, but knowing that they were everywhere. 'Who are you?' he shouted out. 'What do you want from me?'

The ground gave way beneath him and he dropped into the terror of a thousand hells. The dust of cremation filled his mouth and nostrils and he choked as he continued to fall. He flailed helplessly, grabbing for skeletal fingers and arms and legs which were attached to nought and simply came with him as he descended. As if time had slowed sufficiently for him to acknowledge what he was seeing, he was able to identify that the bones down here were not human. Kwaios skulls glared at him accusingly through hollowed eye sockets. Then he struck ground, the wind knocked out of him as he lay on his back, looking up now at the clouds of dusty dead Kwaios above him. He groaned and rolled to one side, seeing someone a short distance away in the same position as him. With some effort, he got to his feet again, watching as the man in the distance did the same. Arrien regarded him for a moment, the suspicious glare returned with equal force by his unidentified companion. Deciding he had had enough of this, Arrien began to stalk towards the man, seeing that the man was doing the same. And not just him. There, to his left, a man was walking parallel to Arrien. And there...another...to his right. Sensing a presence behind him, Arrien spun round to see yet another man, facing him and staring as he did precisely the same.

'Who are you?' Arrien and all the men shouted simultaneously. 'Weee...seeee...youuu,' the countless voices hissed through the air. There were suddenly hundreds of figures around him, and Arrien saw then that they were all reflections of him, like walking, talking mirrors. It had been these reflections of him calling out all along, not the dead of the clouds. 'Youuu...arrr...ussss,' they said again.

'What do you mean?' Arrien roared. 'I don't know what you mean!'

The reflections all turned to face him at once and they shot towards him as if catapulted forwards, enveloping him in a crowd of his own likeness. 'Youuu...arrr...ussss!' they hissed angrily, the words filling his brain and causing him to scream aloud. And then *there was just one voice, his voice, and it came from the reflection of himself which stood directly before him. It almost pressed against his face as it said gently, calmly, 'We are all you, Arrien. And you are all of us.' Without warning, this reflection of him punched its right arm painlessly into Arrien's chest, before pushing its hand up and into Arrien's own right arm as if fitting into a sleeve. As the reflection twisted its body to step into Arrien as if putting on an overcoat, and he saw the back of his own head coming towards his face, his right arm rose of its own volition...*

Arrien awoke with a shout, sweating and trying to catch his breath as he felt a cold floor beneath him. A communication cube tumbled towards him, stopping just short of his head, and he took it. 'You have not been cloned, Arrien Echad,' said a Kwaios voice from a body he could not see. 'But your distinctiveness will no longer be your own.' Arrien's head swam. And he returned to black.

Ω

Menalis rose from the floor and the unconscious female, regarding her through the visor of his boarding suit. As far as humans went, at least the way he understood it, she was likely to have been considered handsome. But then humans were fickle and shallow, so there was no way of judging the consistency of such opinions. 'This is the captain?' he asked with distaste, over the open com. 'They seem to have lowered their standards.'

'This is the ship that came to the aid of the Illeri at Earth,' a respected senior officer interjected. 'This one is more than she appears.'

Menalis was impressed, but he declined to show it. 'Anyone who sets a collision course for a Jaevisk Warship should have their head examined,' he said, looking around the bridge at the comatose crew of the Argo. 'Without their repair nets, they'd be dealing with irreversible hull breaches after breaking up Carak's pet project, never mind the battering we just inflicted.'

'What do you want to do with them?'

Menalis took a deep breath, hating the smell inside these outfits, and looked up at an officer who had pushed aside a human slumped over his workstation to make sense of the readings. The officer felt his glare and reported: 'I think they were going to the Kiranis system. To the third planet.'

'Why would anyone choose to go to the Kwaios home world?' Menalis mused.

The senior officer was running a hand absently through Carenna's hair: 'Who can fathom the mind of a human?'

Menalis laughed. He had known this Garran since the Firarra campaigns, and neither were disposed to formality. The genocides of Firarra had been the ultimate leveller. 'So, what do you suggest, Villon? Even with an armada behind me, I'm not willing to sacrifice thousands of our soldiers to satisfy my curiosity.'

Villon let go of the commander's locks and looked around, the eyes of the boarding crew upon him. He pointed to one of them, saying, 'Generate an interior schematic of the ship and deliver it to me. Then arrange to have the ship pushed through their beloved network.' Villon shared a smile with Menalis as the Elder asked, 'What comes next?'

Villon switched channels and raised three fingers. Menalis switched, but still Villon waited until he had moved closer before speaking privately: 'Do you remember the fallout from Ben-Hadad's exchange of energy with the Jaevisk?'

Menalis nodded, but his eyes narrowed suspiciously. 'I seem to recall Carak taking control of the new program.'

'That's true,' said Villon, looking around the bridge. 'But he never had the entire supply.'

The Elder was fascinated, if a little concerned he had been kept out of the loop: 'Those...red stones?'

'Some of my...connections have protected a stockpile since the uprising,' Villon explained carefully. 'And they're not stones.'

Menalis stared at him for a moment. 'We'll get back to your...*connections* later,' he stated coldly. 'What do you mean, they're not stones?'

The tension was palpable, but these men were professional enough to stay on point. 'It's organic material, Menalis,' said Villon. 'Crystallised blood and tissue.'

'*What*? From what species?'

'We're going to put one of them into the engine housing, Menalis. This ship isn't what it seems. It uses a standard QUIC engine, as the humans call them, harvesting and processing quantum energy, but it has a Jaevisk life engine at its core!'

202

Menalis was stunned. 'I didn't think the humans used them.'

'They don't. But our experiments since the Jaevisk gave one to Ben-Hadad have shown that these engines draw from what Carak called a para-quantum source. You need to appreciate the enormity of what might happen, because if we put this...*stone* in the engine, its purpose will be altered.'

'I'll ask once more...what *species*, Villon?'

Villon took a long breath before replying, 'Kwaios.'

And Menalis, knowing what he knew, what had been learned from infiltrating Carak's operation over the decades, appreciated the enormity. Just as Carak had said he would.

Ω

Arrien supposed he must have passed out again, but he could not be sure. He was now standing, with no memory of even getting to his feet. He stood in a corridor with a glass wall on the side he faced, a larger version perhaps of the transparent and permeable panels of the Promies facility, and he steeled himself to take a few steps forward to learn of his whereabouts. The floor was polished ebony, the ceiling – stretching high, so high, above him – was blue, with threads of silver and gold wires. His mind screamed answers and suggestions at him, but he was too stunned to interpret its mania. And the glass wall beckoned.

He dared not look until he was close enough, a subconscious thrill-seeking creature inside him longing for a shock, forcing him to take in everything in sight in one grand gesture of overwhelming terror. So he closed his eyes, keeping his head down and his arms out before him, moving slowly forward until his palms touched the warm transparent surface. He took some deep breaths, slowing the pounding of his heart. And then he opened his eyes...

It was a great factory, stretching into the distance and dropping down as far as he could see, with levels and fields of machinery, all working on one product. Human bodies, encased in tubes and viscous liquids, being moved around, passing from machine to machine, various degrees of work accredited to each level of the terrible place. They were not alive, not aware, not yet complete, and he could even make out the horrific lack of detail in blank, featureless faces. 'Clones,' he whispered to himself, as the pieces

203

started falling into place even as they still obscured the bigger picture.

He heard them coming, heard their semi-metal footsteps, their painful dialogue. He looked down to see the black box, and he waited for them as he picked it up, seeing their shadows lengthen and terrify. Four great Kwaios, each twice his height, rounded the bend of the alien corridor as the grisly work continued beyond the glass wall. 'Welcome, Arrien Echad,' he heard the voice in his head translate, amidst the nagging pain of their language. 'The first and the last.'

They were mocking him, and he steeled himself again, looked at each of them defiantly, finding within himself a completely unjustifiable courage. 'You won't win this,' he declared.

They exchanged glances and a terrible sound made his knees buckle. They may have laughed. He almost dropped to the floor, but he kept his balance and waited. 'You are unaware of what this is,' he was told. 'You are the future of humankind, and as such you will be their doom.'

'What…what are you going to do with me?'

'You will bring us to Ascension. The Kwaios Council will once again be lords of the galaxy, and we will face the coming gods.'

'I'll die before I help you!' Arrien roared at them.

'Many times,' they agreed. There was a faint sound, and a feeling, as if an airtight container had been opened. 'We have arrived at Heragon,' they told him. 'Now you will see the truth, the fate wrought upon your people by one selfish human.' They turned, expecting him to follow. Which he did, as he whispered the name of that selfish human: 'Vawter!'

Ω

The backup was late, but not fashionably so. And there was no grand entrance to be made, because there was nothing they could do against such an overwhelming force. The crews of the Pegasus, the Minotaur, and the Medusa watched as their sister ship was shunted towards the glowing arm of the unusual MEC station by a Garran carrier. The Argo was consumed by the station, and it vanished. Captain Gerard Hill of the Pegasus oversaw the renegade fleet, for all that designation was now worth. 'Where did they send them?'

'There's no destination menu,' came the reply. 'I'm working on it, but I've never seen a station with this configuration.'

'Why help an enemy ship through its own transport network?' Hill asked rhetorically. 'And why the hell is there a station here in the first place?' He thought for a moment, staring out at the Garran star cruisers as they began obliterating the modules of the Promies facility. Some gathered up the egg-shaped weapons of the Kwaios, but what caught Hill's eye was a tiny red flash in the upper left corner of the VR. He activated his gloves and zoomed in, moving forward to see the distant beacon of an escape pod. Then he saw another, and the crew were audibly concerned. 'Paint that area and get me an ID,' ordered Hill. 'I want to know who else was out here.'

It took a few minutes for the transponder readings to come back, and an officer reported: 'Power's nearly gone on the pods, but they're from a ship called the Styx. Only three confirming life, but there could be more. No validation code, but it's one of ours.'

Hill nodded. 'Move us in. All of us.' They were scanned, and a few star cruisers targeted the larger ships without following through. They made their superiority known, but for some reason the Garran allowed them to pick up the pods and leave. Sometimes it paid to be insignificant.

'I've identified the destination, sir,' the nav officer reported. 'It's the Kwaios world in the Kiranis system, the third planet.'

Now Hill was understandably concerned, for it was starting to look like the Garran were working with the Kwaios, as had been presumed of Elder Carak for many years. He recalled well what had happened to the crews of various ships sent out to the Kiranis system on suicidal goose chases, and he responded as any sane person would. 'We're going home,' he declared. 'I've had enough of Samuel Vawter's games. Collect the survivors and get us out of here.'

Ω

The forensic dismantling of Carak Tae Ahn's strange facility out near Sieltor Promies was well underway, and Elder Menalis was overseeing many related operations when a report came back from a team investigating one of the few groups of integrated modules unaffected by recent events. A holographic rendering of their surroundings was activated in the centre of the huge command floor set up in a cargo hold, and Menalis and senior officers watched as the team moved into a fully functional cloning division. Either unaware of or unconcerned with what had transpired across the enormous facility, Garran scientists and doctors were going about their work when the team came upon them. They raised their hands and claimed that they had simply been following orders, the usual defence of unethical underlings, and Menalis ordered them taken for questioning. For his eyes had already glimpsed what was up ahead in this gradually unfolding representation of the truth. The team pushed on, and giant containers came into view, each of them containing a single clone. But these clones were not human. In fact, they were not all simply one species, and Menalis could see at least a Sori, an Axcebian and a Cquaston. 'What *is* this?' Menalis breathed. He turned to seek out Villon amongst the gathered officers, but his old friend was already on his way, with a strange expression on his face. He glanced at the holographic aliens in stasis and gestured for Menalis to come to him.

'There's been a development,' Villon whispered urgently. 'And I'm not sure what it means.'

'Enlighten me,' the Elder demanded. 'It can't be much more unsettling than *this*!'

'Carak has been *murdered*,' Villon reported, 'by his *son-in-law*!'

Menalis looked at Villon for a moment, and was surprised to feel sorrow touch him, for Carak had long been a formidable man, an inspiration to millions of Garran, and the aggravated death of an Elder was always a shock amongst Garran society. 'I stand corrected,' he said.

INTERVAL 2
PURIFICATION

Some would say that Love and Death are polarised in the lives and works of Man. Despite both enduring great scrutiny and inspiring every measure of art and philosophy, Love eludes precise definition while Death is more tangible than we would wish it to be. Love is an experience, while Death is not; instead, it is the unburdening of experience, while Love is the experience of unburdening. Yet it is upon the mystery of love that we can rest our faith, lay out our sins and free ourselves from pain. And it is in this sense that I would see Love and Death as having much in common.

From the *Sage Thoughts of Gaelius*, Third Mage of New Antioch, c. 542 NE

Ross Ice Shelf, West Antarctica, 318 NE

Vawter's corporation had long ago taken control of the polar regions and their once hidden resources, but the construction of the Shield meant that the destruction of the ice had to be reversed. The gravitational and electromagnetic stability of the planet was soon to become part of the symbiotic processes of the Illeri structure and, while the Shield would soon be capable of adjusting to compensate for the mass of the ice sheets, the consistency of the polar mass would make things considerably less complicated. The complexities of the Shield and the effects it would have on Earth's mass were yet to be clarified to any degree of satisfaction as far as Vawter was concerned, but an advance message from the Illeri home world had instructed him to act. And so here he was, freezing his unmentionables in the nether regions of the world. Luckily, he had invited Amara along, and not just to deal with the problem. He hated being apart from her these days and he found any excuse to turn work into a vacation for them both. She clapped her gloved hands together and scowled at him playfully. 'Things are getting cold that shouldn't be cold, Sam!' she called to him, her blue eyes glistening amidst the frosty whiteness around her. Her nose was red.

'I told you to wear the thermals, Snow White,' Samuel reminded her. 'If you hadn't been so concerned about the layers making you look fat...' He winked and grinned and turned to one of the contractors as the man approached with the data for the operation.

Amara chuckled and pulled her mask up over her nose. She secretly loved it here and loved what Samuel's people were doing. Reclaiming ice fields was not easy, but the Illeri Shield would help. The south polar sections would be in place within days, and they would keep the sun out for years to come. The same was happening at the North Pole, but Amara had not gone to see that. She said she wanted to wait to see penguins, but Samuel told her it was unlikely. Their numbers had plummeted dramatically over the centuries and, like much of the wildlife of Earth, their behavioural patterns and life cycles had been severely disrupted by the Cage event.

Amara walked away from the forty-strong team of technicians, engineers, and conservationists. Samuel had been mistaken for a philanthropist for his agreement to fund this operation, and Amara

209

had laughed at his apparent discomfort, while he secretly savoured her admiration. Certainly, this was all about power, but the collateral damage was quite acceptable. The Ross Shelf had deteriorated considerably over the centuries, and while the Cage had contributed to this destruction, the resource investigations had not helped. But temperature change had played its part, and Ross was one of the shelves tempering glacial melt, so it needed reinforcing. Ironically, the process which would begin here would involve drilling platforms penetrating the expanse of ice west of the Transantarctic Mountains so that cryo-blasting machines could be installed hundreds of metres below the surface. When activated, these powerful devices would begin freezing processes to draw the underlying water up and into the shelf, expanding the ice from beneath and within while reducing the volume of water.

Amara looked to the northeast, where the Queen Alexandra and Elizabeth ranges were visible. Mount Kirkpatrick rose majestically into the freezing air, shaking off the ice like a triumphant troll surveying the spine of Antarctica. Mesmerized by the beauty of the place, Amara was oblivious to Samuel's approach, yet when a hand was placed gently on her shoulder, she knew it was him. 'I love it here,' she confessed.

'I know you do,' he said.

'Can we come here again?'

'Sure. I'll be keeping an eye on the work anyway, so…'

She grinned. 'Any log cabins around? You know…with a roaring fire and a ridiculously ostentatious hot tub? Oh…and lots of wine.'

Samuel laughed. 'I'll have someone build us one, will I?'

She turned to him. 'I'm sure you could.'

'Well, it's true that nothing is beyond me, my dear,' he quipped, kissing her red nose. 'Which reminds me…'

'What?'

'I've something to show you.' He pointed to a waiting helicopter. 'Something…special.'

'Hmm. How special?'

'Put it this way – I'm not exactly allowed to show you. Or anyone, for that matter.'

She smiled, but there was something in his eyes that bothered her. 'I'm…intrigued,' she replied nervously. 'You sure you wanna show me?'

He shrugged. 'Well, I was gonna bring my other woman, but...'

She chuckled, but she recognised that forced grin. He wanted to share something with her. Something important. And she found that her heart was racing as they made their way to the helicopter and the propellers began rotating. 'Where are we going?' she asked over the com as they strapped themselves in. Samuel closed the door and pointed towards the mountains: 'The other side.'

Her eyes widened. East Antarctica had been declared a no-go zone since the Cage. It was said that a massive area around the South Pole had been irradiated when the Cage activated and Earth had vanished, and that even now, a century later, thermonuclear radiation lingered in the freezing air and clung to the packed ice. But in a flash of certainty, Amara realised that a lot of things were said about the events of 230, and they were all lies. She should have known that Samuel would be in possession of truths contrary to popular belief, but she had never pressed him about the secrets he held. They were simply part of his job.

The helicopter rose swiftly into the air and Amara was soon looking out across the mountain range as they headed for the South Pole. The giant troll looked decidedly less menacing from up here, and yet Amara would not allow herself to feel masterful as men were wont to do. Humility was necessary in this part of the world. It kept you alive. The helicopter passed over Kirkpatrick and she saw it ahead. She saw the void. She saw the emptiness. Where the pole should be. 'What the hell...?' she gasped.

'Something else, right?' said Samuel.

Amara heard the awe in his voice and it made her feel even more moved. Humility was one thing, but awe...that was truly something else. 'Yeah,' she found herself saying. 'Something else.' For a hundred kilometres and more centred on the South Pole, an abyss had been opened in the world, an inverted cone of icy deterioration. A smaller aperture of black was at the deep centre, with sloped walls of ice desperately trying to survive the warmth emanating from deep inside the Earth. 'This is the reason,' Amara realised. 'This is why we're here.'

'Yep. One hundred years of melting since the Cage blasted a hole in the world. We have to do something about the loss of ice mass, but we can't stop *this* thing.'

'And no one knows about this?'

'Best they don't. The Shield is being built to protect us from the Kwaios, and that's the song we're gonna sing. There was violent opposition against its construction until the Kwaios attack back in sixty-eight. Can you imagine if people knew we were building another cage to fix the damage from the first one?'

The helicopter hit some turbulence and the pilot headed southeast. 'I'll get us down somewhere safe,' he reported. 'Crosswinds are a bitch round this thing.'

Samuel nodded and Amara gripped his arm, saying, 'I'm not sure I wanna go down there, Sam. I've seen enough…really.' He smiled softly: 'Trust me, honey…you ain't seen nothing yet.'

Fear rushed through her belly, but Amara nodded as he took her hand, and she forced a smile. The helicopter set them down only about thirty kilometres from the perimeter of the ice slopes, and Amara was surprised to see what looked like a small research station. A selection of vehicles was outside, but there was no sign of activity. 'It'll be warm inside, I promise,' said Samuel, as he opened the door of the helicopter with his left hand, his right intent on keeping her with him. 'Some consolation, I suppose,' she joked nervously as she removed the com and allowed him to help her out onto the snow. He recognised her concern and held her arms. 'We're perfectly safe here,' he assured her. 'Okay?'

She smiled and nodded, taking a deep breath to calm herself: 'Okay.'

What Amara thought was a station was nothing more than the entrance to an elevator shaft, and she held tightly to Samuel as they descended into Antarctica, through the ice cap and down into the continent proper. 'What is this place?'

'Without being dramatic?'

'Please.'

'The answer to everything.'

She stared at him and he laughed: 'Okay, so maybe that was…*slightly* dramatic.'

'You think?'

The elevator came to a stop and Samuel waited at the open door, suddenly unsure of himself. 'What's wrong?' asked Amara. 'Don't make me any more freaked out!'

'Sorry. It's just that this…changes things. You won't see the world the same.'

'But you…want me to see this…right?'

He nodded. 'I'd like you to understand, that's all.'

'Understand what? *You*?'

'What I'm doing.'

'Okay.' She gestured towards the open door. 'Lead the way.'

He bore a wide and excited grin, like a child showing a friend his favourite toys. The corridor into which he led her was sterile, a cold blue colour broken intermittently by grey doors on either side, leading into offices and laboratories situated behind frosted glass. There were many other corridors leading away from this central one, but Samuel did not deviate, keeping them headed to what she knew instinctively was the hole in the world. They soon came to large glass doors guarded by four armed men. 'Mister Vawter,' they greeted him. 'Good to see you again, sir.'

'You too,' Samuel replied, oblivious to the man's name. 'We're heading to the observation module.' The guards looked at each other and Samuel stepped up to them: 'Is there a problem?'

'We're waiting for the results of a stability sweep. We wouldn't want you and...' They looked at Amara and she introduced herself. 'We wouldn't want anything to happen.'

Amara leaned in and whispered, 'Maybe we should do this another time.'

'No,' Samuel argued, with enough force to assert his authority over the men and cause concern for Amara. He turned to her: 'I brought you here to see this. The sweeps are routine. I wrote the protocols myself.'

The guards said nothing. They had said all that was necessary, and no one could blame them. The cameras were recording the conversation and they were covered. Samuel waited until one of them relented and opened the glass doors. Amara felt the warmth immediately, a rush of metallic air that made her tremble with pleasure and shiver with apprehension, and she followed Samuel as he walked on. She realised that he had stopped holding her hand just before the guards came into view. A few minutes later, with the guards forgotten and the doors keeping this world from the next – or was it the other way round? – they came to a vehicle on their left which marked the start of a track running off into the distant darkness. Samuel stepped into it and offered Amara his hand, smiling again. She hesitated, but in this mysterious place, Curiosity was a strong opponent and difficult to master. There was no closing hatch and no doors, and only rudimentary seatbelts assured her of safety. 'I've done this many times, Amara,' Samuel told her, somewhat impatiently as she stepped in and fastened the belt. 'It's perfectly safe.' He grinned again. 'And completely worth it.'

She nodded quietly, angry at herself for conceding to him. She did not want to do this, whatever it was. She wanted to know, but from a safe distance. He activated the track vehicle, and it jolted into movement inside what was essentially a transparent tube set into the tunnel cut into the rock. The ride was smooth as the track took them ever closer to the abyss they had seen from above, and the temperature was steadily increasing until Amara felt like she might pass out. She unzipped her outdoor gear, but Samuel had not done the same. Perhaps she was imagining the heat, or perhaps she was feeling something else. 'How much longer?' she asked.

'A few minutes. Relax.'

There was no more conversation, and the heat increased until Amara could see up ahead an opening, a light of hope that offered air as soon as she had seen it. She found herself lifting from her seat to get a better view as the track along which they had been travelling ended in the most magnificent of places, a glass dome suspended from the end of the tube and hanging out over the abyss. Amara's face was alive with wonder as Samuel helped her from the vehicle and she looked around at the circle of meltwater cascading down around them from the inverted cone of ice above. Bright lights beamed out from the observation module in every direction, illuminating this chthonic wonder as Amara felt tears in her eyes. But she had not seen it all yet. 'Come back,' Samuel called to her, holding out his hand. 'You need to stand here.'

A circular platform in front of the stationary vehicle was at the exact centre of the dome floor. A holo-console appeared and Amara joined him there, hypnotised by the sight around her. Samuel took her hands and looked into her eyes. She could sense his passion, his excitement, and his desire to share with her a wonder beyond anything he could have given her in any other place. 'What is it?' she asked quietly. 'What am I seeing?'

'Not yet,' he replied, pausing for a moment to adore her. 'When the Cage was activated, thousands of red lines were seen penetrating the planet. The reports from the surface at that time say that an impact could be felt...everywhere at once. Before we factored that in, it was presumed that the core had been blasted by the energy from the south pole of the Cage passing through the planet, but…that's not what happened. The core had just been used like…an engine, whipping all that power around until there was enough energy built up.'

'Built up for what? To make the planet…disappear?'

Samuel shook his head. 'It didn't disappear, Amara. It was…moved.'

'What? To where?'

'Well, that we don't know. Another…dimension? Another universe?' He shrugged. 'We're not sure. But we think we understand how it happened.' He tapped some keys on the console and every light went out. Amara gasped in fright, and he grabbed her hand. 'It's okay,' he whispered. 'Look.'

Following his gaze, she saw that the water flowing down from the ice cap was being illuminated by flashes of red. Here, in the darkness with the man she loved, this magical sight was the most intimate moment she had ever known, and her skin tingled as her heart pounded in her chest. Samuel's voice was soft and sure, and she leaned into him as he explained: 'This place…this hole in the world…wasn't created by the Cage blasting into the planet. It was created by the core blasting the energy of the Cage out, so that it could do what it was supposed to do, and the ice has just been deteriorating around ground zero since then. It looks like the energy pulse that obliterated the South Pole was part of a process designed to open a wormhole. And because the Cage was the machine that created the wormhole, it took Earth with it.' Amara had no words, and Samuel tapped some more keys on the console. 'Thing is…we're not dealing with any sort of energy we understand.' There was the sound of numerous panels being released around the platform upon which they stood, and they withdrew as the floor of the dome gradually retracted to reveal a glass floor open to the depths below. 'This is what the Cage left behind,' said Samuel.

Amara saw then the source of the mysterious illumination, and she put it all together. Snapping red lines of silent energy were launching themselves up from the darkness like dancing electrical snakes. Where they struck the cascading falls, they sparked as the water was momentarily electrified and Amara turned around and around to take it all in, laughing aloud. 'Oh, Sam!' she cried. 'This is...amazing!' She laughed again and asked, 'What is it?'

Now it was Samuel's turn to laugh, but there was a bitterness to it and Amara stopped as he said, 'There's no way I can say this without being dramatic.'

'I think we're well past that,' she said, grinning uncertainly.

He nodded. 'I guess so. You've heard of the Church of the New Elect?'

'Sure. They're all gone now, right?'

'Maybe. We're...still working on that. But if they're not...this would be the most important place in the world for them.'

'Really? Why?'

'It's complicated, but...the Cage was powered by...something strange. According to the Garran, there were some sort of...stones or crystals or something, and...this is the energy they emit.'

'I don't understand. What does that have to do with that church?'

'Well, that's the weird part. This...energy...facilitated the movement of Earth. Which is...unsettling if the Church are right about it. See...they believe it's...conscious...sentient.'

Amara looked down at the snapping lines again, this time seeing them differently. They looked hungry, malevolent. 'They think this...*these*...are *alive*?'

Samuel hesitated and shrugged one shoulder before replying, 'They think it's...God, Amara.'

Amara had not looked up, entranced as she was by the energy and by Samuel's words. 'God?' she wondered, moving towards the edge of the platform. 'NO!' Samuel grabbed her and hauled her back. 'You can't do that.'

The red lines were suddenly more numerous, and they began reaching higher, snapping against the glass floor of the dome. It began to tremble and the water around them began to crackle, vapour shooting out from the falls as the electricity flailed wildly and aggressively. 'What's happening?' Amara screamed. 'What did I do?'

'I don't know!' Samuel shouted, holding her as he tried to close the aperture. The console was not responding. 'I've never seen this before.'

'It knows I'm here,' said a voice from behind them. 'I tend to upset it.' They turned to see a man standing on the glass, out near the edge. He wore a long black cloak with creatures of gold and silver moving around on it. They snapped at the lines, which had now redirected their attention to the newcomer, viciously attacking the glass beneath him. Illuminated by the flashing red energy, the man's face could be seen only intermittently, his stubble-lined face appearing in the half-light to mimic the shadows of wicked incisors running along his jaw. He started walking towards the pair, and Samuel drew a gun: 'That's close enough!'

'I'm not here for you, Samuel,' the stranger said, his voice booming around the subterranean chamber. 'I'm here for *her*.'

'Like *Hell* you are!' Samuel fired repeatedly at the man, but the bullets passed through him to the distant waterfall.

'No,' said the stranger as he continued to approach, 'I'm not.'

'Who are you?' Amara shouted. 'What do you want?'

'Who am *I*?' The man laughed. 'I'm *God*, Amara.' The red lines were pummelling the glass beneath him and cracks began to show in the surface. 'And you might consider this…divine intervention!'

'We have to get out of here!' said Samuel, leading Amara back along the track.

The man gestured towards the vehicle and it was flung across to the edge of the dome, smashing the glass there. Now the structure started to tremble violently, and the glass was cracking everywhere. Samuel and Amara began to follow the track on foot, and Samuel looked back to see the red lines finally breaking through the glass and enveloping the black-cloaked man as the module disintegrated around him. But he did not appear to be affected, and he smiled as he shouted, 'See you soon, Sam!'

Alarms were blaring, but lockdown protocols would see the area closed off until stability was regained. With the module destroyed, it would be a long time before anyone came down here, and the journey back to the guard post would take hours by foot. But Samuel and Amara never made it that far, for the destruction of the module reverberated through the rock. And before they were even a hundred metres into the tube, it was crushed under the weight of the collapsing tunnel and huge sections rained down upon them, pinning them to the tracks. Two days passed before a rescue team found them. Two long days, with Samuel slipping into and out of unconsciousness. Two eternities, not knowing whether Amara was even within his reach, never mind alive. Two lives, where he took her down here and she died, and yet did not. Two lives.

PART 3
ILLERI

Segregation is, sadly, endemic to the human condition. The fallacy of distinction is almost always extrapolated from social constructs pertaining to the realms of politics, religion, and other manifestations of culture, so that we might articulate a 'counter-culture' derived from the uncomfortable proximity of another constructed in precisely the same manner; and with precisely the same motivations. One of the most potent and yet ridiculous fallacies of distinction in the history of humankind was constructed around the colour of the skin. This fallacy convinced the human species that they were not, in fact, one single entity.

In these latest days of madness, a distinction has emerged which once again threatens to divide us in the same way. It is not a particularly new one, for people have long used constructed genealogies and notions of genetic purity to elevate themselves. The idea that blood can somehow be 'pure' or 'true' and that one man might be judged better than another by this criterion is the height of idiocy. And yet it is this distinction which has in our days come to the fore.

The only difference this time is that the distinction is real; and the well-nourished illusion of equality has been destroyed by the truth of supremacy.

From the eponymous *Concessions of Evegutt* (c. 358 NE), an eclectic collection of writings from a self-styled philosopher surgeon who was part of the earliest programs of Sensitive identification. His resentment of our ancestors is abundantly clear.

THE FIRST SENTINEL

London, England, Earth, 328 NE

They were hunting again, a team of six in insulated suits splashing through the long-abandoned underground tunnels of London, shocking the water intermittently with just enough current to lay insensate whoever might be unfortunate enough to be in their way. Down here languished the forgotten of the world – the losers, the hopeless, the miserable – and yet none of these everyday creatures were the prey of these specialised hunters. For also down here was the Remnant of the Church of the New Elect. They lived mostly underground these days, in hiding all around the world. It was said that the Kwaios had once attempted to come for them, almost sixty years ago, but the Illeri Shield had crippled the Kwaios ship and left it to rot. Now, the descendants of those who had escaped the abduction of the Church were less than pariahs, consigned to non-existence. They mingled with the normal homeless communities all over Earth, but they were far from normal.

Despite the absence of the Jaevisk implant in these later generations of the Church, echoes of psychic development remained. Yet they were merely echoes – fleeting hints of abilities of which they might have one day been in possession had they been allowed the luxury, the time, the technology. Many had tried to hone these skills so briefly alluded to by strange dreams, hallucinations, and other not so ethereal manifestations. Some struggled to focus on the thoughts of others, cacophonous ramblings racing through their minds as people sat with them. Others tried to move objects with their minds, confused initially by things which seemed to wobble or shake or even levitate when they thought about them. There were stories of many different personal and even group experiments, but there were as many stories of people suffering breakdowns or going insane as a result. Most of the descendants of the Church of the New Elect chose to cease their attempts at harnessing whatever it was lying dormant in their minds, until children born into the exiled community dismissed the dream-like hints of their abilities as nothing but the products of their imagination. Maintaining their identity ultimately and ironically meant that the descendants of the Church had to obscure their distinctiveness. The one thing which still had the potential to reveal them, however, was their blood. Rubidium levels had fallen towards the norm for as long as the Jaevisk implant was in place, but the refusal amongst many living in the wake of the Cage incident to have the devices replicated for their children resulted in a resurgence of the Church's distinction by blood. The descent into concealment began, and it was in these disused tunnels in the ancient city of London that one of the largest Church communities resided.

'There!' one of the hunters shouted over the com, pointing to a fallen child twitching face down in the filthy water. Two of them stopped at the body as the others rushed on, and a boy of no more than ten years was hauled roughly out of the water and twisted around. But they cared little for the innocent face, for the truth was in the heart. A device was activated, and a needle jabbed into the upper chest. Both men looked at the reading – normal rubidium levels. They threw the body back into the water and hurried on.

Stifling a gasp of anguish as tears filled her eyes, Harriet remained in the shadows, gripping her jacket with desperation. Designed to conceal her from the heat-sweeps of the hunters, the jacket had been a gift from her father when she had turned sixteen. She took one last look at the dead boy before easing her way back into the duct and finding a different route home. She knew these tunnels well, because she was born down here, attended to by a doctor from the surface who had been paid to keep his mouth shut after helping baby Harriet through her first weeks. She was born weak and struggling for breath, not unusual for Church babies brought to term underground, but Harriet's circumstances had been sufficiently complicated to require outside help. Still, the decision to involve an outsider was not taken lightly. Had Harriet been born into a different family, she may well have been allowed to die. But she was a Messina, and the extended family of the infamous councillor killed a century earlier had been hunted down around the world, some managing to escape the backlash against Cassandra's demonisation.

Now twenty years old, Harriet's infant health was a distant memory for the community, although there were still nights when she woke coughing with tears in her eyes from a nightmare of claustrophobia, as if her subconscious wished her to recall with vivid terror the proximity of death. Today, however, death was all too proximate, and not just because of the boy in the tunnels. Finding her way back to where she had lived most of her life, she returned to her father's bed and gripped his weakening hand. Harriet's mother stood behind her with her hand on Harriet's shoulder, feeling her daughter trembling beneath the jacket. 'Hunters?'

Harriet nodded, and her mother squeezed her shoulder. These two Messina women were the last to openly carry their name, and without Harriet's father to protect them, it was possible that the Church would see them banished or worse. They certainly would not give them up to the surface authorities, for to do so would reveal the survival of the Church, but like predatory animals kept at bay by a dying campfire, those who still harboured enmity for the Messinas would not be long in making their move as Harriet's father breathed his last.

His fingers twitched and Harriet raised her head. 'Dad...?' she asked hopefully. 'Can you hear me?'

He groaned and her voice broke as she sobbed, 'I'm here, Dad. Me and Mom.'

'I...saw you...' he whispered, his vacant eyes staring at the corbelled ceiling. Harriet's mother gripped her shoulder tighter and leaned closer to hear him. 'What's he saying?' she asked.

'Harriet...' His voice was raw and distant, and Harriet moved up on the bed. 'Yes, Dad,' she replied. 'What is it?'

He was silent for a moment. Then: 'I saw it, Harriet. I saw it die.'

'Saw what, Dad?' she humoured him. 'What did you see?'

'The whole planet,' he said dreamily, horrified. 'I saw it die!'

There was something about his tone that made Harriet turn to her mother and ask, 'Is he...is this *real*?'

'I've no idea. It could be the medication –'

Harriet gasped as her father gripped her hand forcefully and turned to glare at her: 'This is our time, Harriet! We have to take our *place*!'

Tears streamed down her cheeks and both women thought him delusional. But then he said something they would never forget, for the Church community had always kept abreast of the politics of the surface world. Thomas Messina died soon after that. His eyes closed and he drifted off into the most peaceful slumber without ever speaking another word. For all that needed to be said had been said in those final moments of lucidity: 'Find Samuel Vawter! The Illeri world is going to die!'

Ω

Half a day later, on the opposite side of the world, Samuel Vawter was lost in thoughts of thoughts ending, in futile imaginings of the cessation of imagination. How to define nothingness? He could not remember what triggered these thoughts, but once the concept of death entered his head, it was difficult to compartmentalise it to any welcoming degree. He understood that for as long as humankind had existed, and possibly even amongst its antecedent species, the fear of death had defined internal musing and external action to such a degree that socio-cultural constructs devoted to imagined divinity – responsible for the greatest divisions in society – had arisen to consume our fears and mutate them into others more insidious. If it were true that so many acts of aggression were sustained by a triumvirate of wealth accumulation, self-righteousness, and the scapegoating of the illusory, then it was equally true that behind all these justifications lurked the correcting force of mortality.

Amidst his rapturous musings on death, Samuel Vawter imagined himself receiving a burst of inspiration from a power in which he did not believe. And it told him that what he was experiencing – the stomach-churning terror of inevitable demise tempering every chance he had of being happy – was akin to the most primitive ecstasy of all. For the fear of death was the purest and most honest of all terror. It needed no priests or shamans, nor any kind of manipulative mediator. It called for no offerings, no place of worship, nor any ritual to keep its relevance contemporary. Death was everywhere, always and forever, attached not to any past event or person or perceived revelation; but to every single one of us throughout all time then, now, and still to come. No one needed to be convinced that it was the most important thing in which to believe, or that any form of it was more genuine than another.

Descending ever deeper into the darkness, Samuel knew that Death was the only true god. He may have seen the infuriated tentacles of the Sentience clawing for recognition in the depths of the Earth, but a god knows true power only with knowledge of its presence. One of the central tenets of his alliance with Kai Tzedek was that the truth of the Sentience be kept from the people of Earth at all costs. And one of the determining factors maintaining that secret was the voluntary concealment of the Church of the New Elect. Rumours of their survival endured amongst the general population, but while Tzedek oversaw the search and Samuel provided the equipment to keep it going, they were getting nowhere insofar as a leadership structure was concerned. Only careless underlings and naïve children were found in various and increasingly ingenious rat-holes around the world. The latter knew nothing of value, while the former continued to surprise with their ability to defend against interrogation procedures.

Samuel swung his legs off the relaxer couch and shook off the dark malaise. Thoughts of the Church ironically overwhelmed his thoughts of death, offering as they always did the distraction of a purposeful day. When had he checked the search logs last? He commanded the building's AI to open the blinds, and the sun began to flood the room. He was about to call his personal assistant when the young man knocked on the door and opened it without invitation: 'Mister Vawter, there's…someone here to see you,' he said, ending with an inflection that left Samuel wondering if there really was someone there.

'You don't sound so sure, Paul.'

Paul smiled, realising how he had sounded. 'Sorry, I…I can't remember her name. It's like…it was there, and…' He shook his head. 'Must have had more to drink last night than I thought.'

'I'll pretend I didn't hear that.' Samuel stood up and straightened his clothes. 'Show her in.' The interruption was welcome, but in hindsight he would muse that this interruption was something more than coincidence. A young woman only slightly shorter than Samuel was ushered in and he found himself staring for longer than was polite, before gesturing for Paul to leave. The woman was beautiful, but then Samuel had seen so many beautiful women that he suffered from a disconcerting mix of sexual frustration and indifference, each liaison tempered by the fantasy of the next.

'Thank you for seeing me,' his visitor smiled politely.

Samuel was looking at the sun bouncing off the waves in her long blonde hair. 'Ah…yes, of course. What can I do for you?'

Her smile now was no more than perfunctory. 'I have a message for you,' she explained; and Samuel thought he could see tears in her eyes. Perhaps it was just the light. 'It's from my father.'

'Your father.' Samuel nodded, sensing that something was wrong. What was it Paul had said...*he couldn't remember her name?* 'And who exactly are *you*?' he asked.

Harriet smiled thinly. 'I think you already know that,' she replied. 'At least, in a general sense.'

'The Church,' Samuel realised. 'You've done well to hide so long.'

'Better than you've done to find us.'

'I'm always open to suggestions.'

'I'm not the enemy. I want to establish that right here and now.'

'That remains to be seen. 'Til then, I'll keep an...open mind.'

'You should do more than that. You should start thinking of me...of the Church...as...' she shrugged, '*guardians*. Sentinels.'

Samuel refrained from replying that he would indeed be thinking of her: 'Really? And what are you watching for, exactly?'

'Well, the Kwaios, for a start.'

'Okay.' Samuel's eyebrows raised: 'You have my attention.'

'Well, it's about time. You and Kai Tzedek have some plans, I believe.'

He stared at her for a moment, this time with completely different intent. He grinned and laughed gently, turning away as if breaking a spell. 'Let's get back to my initial question.'

'Who *am* I?'

'I find that knowing someone is of the utmost importance during a conversation, don't you?'

She shrugged: 'Let's just say I'm the last of an infamous line.'

Samuel realised immediately what she meant, and he laughed more genuinely. 'But I thought she was...' He shook his head. 'The universe certainly likes its jokes, doesn't it?'

'The *Sentience*...doesn't joke, Mister Vawter. It guides us all. Oversees everything.'

'Sounds familiar.'

Harriet shook her head. 'If you mean this...*prophet*...he's nothing compared to the Sentience. It's the very essence of existence, connecting and defining everything.'

'Actually, I was thinking of the theologies you guys rounded up to legitimate yourselves, but…seeing as you brought him up…'

'You're working for him?' Harriet looked disappointed in him, and Samuel felt as if he were being scolded by a parent. '*With* him,' he argued, 'not *for* him.'

'You think you can get on to Kiranis so easily?' she laughed. 'A stealth ship racing across the galaxy and passing through the Cage?'

'How…' He stepped back from her. 'Are you reading my mind?'

'Now how would I do that?' she teased. Revealing that they had within the last few hours captured a high-level engineer working for Tzedek and broken him just in time for this meeting would be a mistake. She needed to keep the upper hand. 'You need to know what you're dealing with,' she pressed. 'And you know quite well that your prophet friend plays his cards close to his chest.'

'You think he's hiding something.' Samuel was already convinced of this.

'Of course I do. But he's not the only one. We know about your facility in Antarctica. But what you saw is not the Sentience.'

'Really?' Of course, they would want to conceal the truth, and Samuel was not easily fooled. The memories of the cave-in crept around his brain, scratching painfully. 'So, what was it, then?'

'It's what you might call an echo of the Sentience, but only because the Cage tapped some of its power when it abducted our people. It drew it straight out of the fabric of the Universe, so what's left here is like…dismembered energy. It's probably best to think of it in terms of a…phantom limb. And it's looking for its body.'

Samuel chuckled. 'I think you're just being dramatic…Miss Messina.'

'No…not really.' Harriet had not been called that for a long time, and it was as if Vawter knew it did not sit well with her. 'Although what will happen will actually be the other way round. The body's going to come looking for the limb.'

'You're trying to tell me that this…universal awareness you worship is…looking for its big toe or something?'

Harriet found that genuinely amusing. 'We can work together on this, Mister Vawter. I'll say it again…I'm *not* your enemy!'

Samuel pondered the possibility for a moment. 'What exactly do you want from me?'

She held his gaze for a moment, knowing without having to read his mind that he wanted her. Badly. 'Look, this isn't going to make much sense, initially.'

He smiled at her, knowingly. 'The most rewarding things usually don't.'

Neither of them had moved towards each other, but the unseen electricity crackled between them. Harriet had to switch it off: 'The Illeri home world is going to die.'

That was a passion-killer if ever he had heard one. And the implications were myriad. The Shield was still some years from completion, and the Illeri had yet to send a delegation to Earth. 'Are they...coming here?'

Harriet shook her head. 'A refugee crisis is the least of your concerns, believe me. But there's an opportunity here. The dismembered energy trapped in the Earth's core needs to be reconnected. Earth needs to be reconnected to the Sentience.'

'And how exactly would you achieve that?'

'Earth needs to move. A relatively tiny shift in our position in the galaxy, but enough to give the planet back to the Sentience.'

Samuel laughed aloud. 'I've heard some crazy stuff in my time, but *this*...'

'I'm serious, Mister Vawter. Look, you need to understand...the Sentience isn't something separate to the Universe. It *is* the Universe. It's in a symbiotic state with matter, energy...*gravity*...'

'*Gravity*?' Samuel's smile dropped. 'What's your point?'

'I know it's far away...*very* far away...but we won't go unaffected by the destruction of Illeri. Certain planets are integral to the networked consciousness of the Sentience. Illeri is one of them. Earth used to be, until the Cage shifted our position. Don't pretend you didn't know about that. Anyway, when the Sentience loses Illeri, we'll feel it here...because we're outside the network. We have to be ready to...' she shrugged, 'ride the wave, you might say.'

'Ride the *wave*? No, I wouldn't say that at *all*! Unless you're *insane* or lying...we'll be torn *apart*!'

Harriet smiled. 'Well, that's why...we have a *shield*...Mister Vawter.'

He felt like a child who did not understand the instructions. 'But the Illeri *designed* it! I mean...this couldn't have been part of their *plan*.' He stared at her: 'Could it?'

228

'I don't know,' Harriet lied. 'The Illeri are a species we know nothing about.'

'Well, we'll have to fix that, then. How long do we have?'

'It's difficult to say, but...from what we've learned, our best guess is about two years.'

Samuel shook his head. 'That's too tight a timeframe. The last MEC station along the way would leave even our fastest ship so far out we couldn't guarantee a round-trip in time.'

'Really?' Harriet did not sound convinced.

'You know something I don't?'

'I know something you *do*, Mister Vawter. If you really wanted to use your *fastest* ship...'

'Now I'm starting to dislike you, Miss Messina.'

'Well, I'm sorry the honeymoon's over,' she quipped, 'but your personal feelings are irrelevant. This is about the survival of our species, regardless of anyone's perception of the Sentience. So, I think you should take the risk that a round-trip isn't in the picture.'

'First of all, I'm not going to risk the Redeemer not being here and ready when Kiranis shows up. But you really expect me to send someone on a suicide mission?'

'Yes. As soon as possible. You need answers.' She stepped towards him. 'But you have to keep this between us. All of it. The truth about what's under Antarctica, the Redeemer out at Illeri...but mostly the part about moving Earth.'

'Yeah, that little detail wouldn't go down too well with the general population.'

'I'm not talking about the general population. You need to keep Tzedek in the dark.'

He regarded her suspiciously, saying, 'He'll know the Redeemer is gone. He's been drooling over it since it was built. And anyway, why would I wanna keep him out of this? We've been on the same page for years!'

She gave a little laugh of derision, and Samuel hated her for it. 'Well, we're writing a new book, Mister Vawter,' she told him. 'And this is your chance to make the credits.' She offered her hand: 'So...are *we* on the same page? Because there's a lot you need to know.'

THE MERCENARY

Illeri, 329 NE

Kallon Raesa had been looking forward to a change of scenery, but he had not expected this. More than six months ago he had left the outer limits of human-controlled space, in the form of a MEC station so rarely used he had imagined it full of spiders clambering over each other in a desperate bid to find the transfer area and hitch a ride on whatever vessel was unlucky enough to punch in the wrong coordinates. There had been times he thought they might have come along with him, and dreams of spiders crawling into open orifices were not conducive to a good night's sleep. On more than one sleepless night, he had to talk himself out of duct-taping his own mouth shut. But if the spiders could see him now, they would have no problem getting in.

He had cut the main engine approaching the Illeri home world, wisely choosing to come in quietly and see what was what. Skirting one of its six moons, he had found an escape pod drifting lifelessly and had drawn it in to inspect it. The Redeemer was a small craft, built for speed and evasion more than anything else, and because it was mostly engine, there was little room for a rescue mission. It had a fully prepped medical bay, strange for a single-occupant craft, but Kallon was no doctor and was far from the nursing kind, so the set-up was wasted on him. For whatever reason the Redeemer was built, it was not equipped for pulling aliens out of a self-inflicted coffin. Nonetheless, Kallon was a curious soul, and he had been sent out here for answers. Samuel Vawter had failed to supply him with a list of correlating questions, so it was convenient that they had been presented to him in this manner.

Finally, a century since the people of Earth had heard of them, a human was about to see an Illeri. Anev Tesckyn's naïve acceptance of their offer to protect the planet against the Kwaios had proven a novelty with a short lifespan, but the work could not be stopped and a Kwaios attack had been foiled by the Shield. The void of uncertainty had been filled with concrete fear, always a potent foundation for recklessness. That same recklessness led Kallon to suit up and step out the airlock to the tethered pod, but what he found was so unlike the revelation he had been expecting that he wondered if this whole trip had been worthwhile. Of course, that opened the floor to new and considerably more disturbing questions, but they could wait.

Opening the hatch of the pod, he had realised that his suit would not allow him to fit through the airlock, and so he began looking for a window to get a glimpse of the aliens. There were no windows. Frustrated, Kallon retrieved a plasma cutter and set about widening the hatch. When he did, he was relieved to find that the inner airlock aperture was larger than the outer. He was able to make it through, and immediately he wished he had not. Two…things…lay unmoving inside transparent tubes. His flashlight revealed that there were almost certainly eyes on these things, or what he hoped were eyes, but they ran a line along a form that looked like the sort of creature one might find at the bottom of a dark lake or in a deep-sea cave. There were no visible limbs, although appendages might have retracted into the holes he had initially presumed to be eye sockets. There was just no way of knowing, without taking one of these things out and bringing it back to examine it. Even had Kallon been willing and able to do such a thing, the alarm in his helmet warned him that something was approaching his position. He activated the retractor line and made his way back to the Redeemer. As he moved away from the pod, he witnessed its destruction. What looked like an automated weapons system blew it apart and then appeared to scan for life signs. What happened next gave Kallon reason to question the wisdom of continuing this mission, for while the attacking object clearly scanned the Redeemer, it had simply turned away and left the mercenary sitting there with a pounding heart.

As Kallon's heart had slowed down, however, he realised the risk he was taking by sitting there. He had been scanned, which meant that data pertinent to his whereabouts and his mode of transport would be transmitted to whomever had sent the weaponised probe. He had no choice but to follow it. While it had been a fast little bugger, the Redeemer was faster, and he caught it along the path of the second moon and blew it to pieces. But Kallon's wisdom had once again been scrutinised as he reached the first moon of Illeri, for there were signs of activity on its surface which had promised a welcome at the planet for which he was thoroughly unprepared. The ruins of a massive weapons and monitoring facility scarred the reddish moon, and his own readings informed him that the destruction was about a century old. A century in human terms, that was, which immediately piqued his interest, considering the Illeri automatons had turned up at Earth around then.

Yet it was not until he moved away from the moon towards the planet proper that he beheld the sight that invited spiders to nest in his open mouth. It was not merely that hundreds of vessels of varying shapes and sizes orbited and oversaw operations on the planet, their dropships and attendant craft swarming in every direction; nor that debris littered the space between Kallon and this scene as if a cleaning crew had pushed it into a higher orbit; nor that intermittent weapons fire blasted the surface below as if mopping up a spill. Instead, it was the disturbing realisation that, beyond all this, a planet which was supposed to be dominated by highly intelligent aquatic life was black and lifeless, as if every drop of water had been ejected into space.

Ω

At the same time as Kallon was staring at the war-blasted alien planet and deciding what the hell he should do next, a heavy-set Garran with a shock of red hair was elbows deep in a huge machine of his own design – as his favourite ones were – and waist deep in a subterranean pool of what little water was left on Illeri. 'How do I always end up in some end-of-the-world cave?' he shouted. 'This could have been set up anywhere on the planet.'

A voice so soft and soothing it might have been his own mother's – if he had ever heard it – replied, 'We would have been discovered anywhere else, Chaerakh. You know that. And this is the place to where the Sentience has retreated.'

Chaerakh looked around, not seeing the Illeri who had spoken to him. They were hidden in the water, their only comfort left now that the occupation was reaching its climax. 'I've seen what the Sentience can do,' he argued. 'And it doesn't...*retreat* anywhere!'

'You have seen more than any should see,' the hidden Illeri agreed. 'But you know that the Sentience sees the bigger picture. It *is* the bigger picture. A time of revelation is upon us.'

'That would make a nice change. Naveen isn't one for revelation. Just more lies and manipulation until you feel like your head will explode.'

Another Illeri voice, slightly raspier than the first, said, 'Naveen has a path which must be followed. He is a future which must be fulfilled. What he does is what he must –'

'Give it a rest, will you?' Chaerakh snapped. 'I'm tired of all the mystical gibberish!'

There was a splash in the water, and Chaerakh saw one of them move away. 'I think you upset him,' the first Illeri quipped.

Chaerakh laughed: 'And I think he'd tear my head off if you didn't need me to make this happen.'

'Most likely. You should know that the human has arrived. He destroyed one of your probes.'

'Do you think he's seen your guests yet?'

'I would imagine so.'

Chaerakh stood and straightened his back with a groan: 'Well…let's hope he doesn't turn tail and run, or all this will be for nothing!' He held his right arm out and yawned as he regarded the various control icons set into the time-worn gauntlet. 'Are you ready?' he asked, tapping the relevant key without waiting for an answer.

Ω

Samuel Vawter had instructed him to make contact as soon as he discovered something of significance. This certainly ticked the box, and Kallon knew that if he did not send a message back to Earth now, he might never get another chance. As humbling as that was, he was not one to baulk at the first sign of danger, no matter the scale. In this, Vawter seemed to him a kindred spirit, and for the same singular reason.

Kallon activated the com, which had been dark since the Redeemer had left Earth orbit. After a few moments in which he worked to isolate the frequency Vawter had provided, a terrible lament filled the cabin, and Kallon was rocked by what he was sure was a woman groaning and sobbing in anguish. The past flashed, but he kicked it back with a growl as the crying died out, and he gathered himself as the speakers crackled and whined. He said nothing as he opened the channel, as Vawter had instructed, waiting instead until someone picked up at the other end. A familiar voice whispered his name and a shiver ran through him as he muttered, 'What the hell's going on?'

233

'*This is Senator Kai Tzedek.*' Kallon jumped as the strong voice eventually sounded: '*To whom am I speaking?*'

'My name's Kallon Raesa. I need to speak with Samuel Vawter. This channel was supposed to be monitored only by Vawter. What's going on?'

He could hear Tzedek release a gentle laugh, before saying, '*There's no cause for concern, Mister Raesa. Samuel Vawter and I have an...understanding. I believe you and he agreed upon a certain word to guarantee security.*'

Kallon opted to test the man, and waited until he heard, '*Vengeance.*' But now he was confused. If Tzedek was supposed to be in the dark about Vawter's plans, how did he know the word? He might have tortured Vawter for it, of course. And that meant that Vawter might even have been killed in the interim. Kallon kept his cool: 'I remember telling him it wasn't the most imaginative code word, but he assured me that –'

'*That it was the most appropriate, yes,*' Tzedek interrupted. '*Decidedly Vawter.*'

'Absolutely.' Was that venom in the Senator's voice? 'So, I guess things are changing quickly back home? I mean, I've only just got here and I can tell you the game's changed big time!'

Kallon struggled to hear a whispered conversation, but the interference was masking it and his instruments could not clean it up. Tzedek was eventually heard again: '*Well, the game is certainly changing rapidly, Mister Raesa, as I'm sure you can imagine. Samuel and I are being...kept on our toes, you might say. He'll be delighted to hear you've been in contact, especially in light of our visit from the Illeri ambassador.*'

All kinds of darkness began dancing around Kallon's head at that. What the hell was going on? He looked back out at the armada of vessels, reassessing the scene. Maybe this was an evacuation, rather than an invasion. That might explain the escape pod, but then the strange scanner probe had destroyed that. Perhaps the Illeri intended to leave no trace of ever having inhabited this world. But then...where were they going?

'*Are you still there, Mister Raesa?*' he heard Tzedek ask.

'I'm still here,' answered Kallon, 'but I'm confused. You say the Illeri ambassador has been at Earth?'

'*Well...yes. As a matter of fact, he...or it, we're not sure...*' Kallon heard him laugh again, and felt like punching the man in the

234

face. There was nothing funny about this: *'Well, they're still here,'* Tzedek went on. *'They're docked up on the Shield.'*

It could have been the beginning of a mass asylum request, Kallon supposed, but it made little sense. 'Is there some way I could see the ambassador?' he asked, realising that he was the only person who could match what was here with what was there. 'A recording of his arrival or something like that?'

'Of course,' Tzedek agreed. *'One moment.'* Kallon waited, staring out at the alien ships with a knot in his stomach. It was as if they were glaring at him. *'You should be receiving some footage now, Mister Raesa. You'll have to run a decryption.'*

The monitor showed the partitioned file being compiled at this end and Kallon began the decryption process, standard protocol for dealing with information so far from home, and particularly on such a sensitive mission. Before the file was ready to view, another signal was received, this one from a distress beacon. 'The hell is *this*?' Kallon muttered as he located its source deep in the planet below. 'Is this why you sent me here, Vawter? Some crazy rescue mission?'

Tzedek's video footage began to run and Kallon was transfixed. A huge figure encased in a black biosuit towered over the human delegates in the Senate buildings, and Kallon scanned the image, hoping…praying…that he would find signs on the exterior of the suit of some sort of filtration device, perhaps one designed to take water molecules from humid air. Unless it was very well hidden, it simply was not there. 'I'm pretty sure that's not the Illeri ambassador,' he said as he reset the com.

'What do you mean?' Tzedek was understandably perturbed. *'I mean…how do you know? If you just got there…how could you know what their ambassador looks like?'*

'You're kidding, right?' said Raesa. 'It's in a biosuit. I'm not exactly looking for a handlebar moustache! Anyway…I wouldn't need to know what their ambassador looks like to know that's not him…or it…or whatever.'

'What are you talking about?' Tzedek snapped. *'Of course you'd need to know if you're being asked to identify him!'*

'Look…I'm not happy to be telling you this, Senator, considering I'm the one stuck out here and I haven't managed to find a real, live Illeri yet…'

'What? Well, what have *you found?'*

'I'm not exactly sure, but I'll let you know when I am.' Maybe the rest was only for Vawter's ears. 'All I can tell you is that the only Illeri I've seen so far were dead, stuck in what looked like an escape pod, but if they were to wear biosuits, they'd be way smaller than whatever that guy had. The Illeri are only about the size of a big dog...without its legs! So, whatever was in that recording wasn't Illeri, never mind an ambassador. I'd get someone up to that ship pretty quick if I were you. Might be time to scrape some bugs off the Shield!'

He cut the link there, knowing that things were monumentally wrong and that he was about to find himself swimming in an ocean of deceit. At least, he would if there was any water down on Illeri. He weighed up his options, eyeing the flashing light of the silenced beacon before looking again at the enigmatic armada blocking his path. Taking a deep breath, he exhaled heavily before saying, 'Let's see what this thing can do.'

$$\Omega$$

'He's just locked on to the signal,' Chaerakh told his Illeri collaborators. 'He's taken the bait.'

'Good,' said the soft-voiced alien in the water. 'Then this is it, Chaerakh. You may activate.'

Chaerakh nodded. 'If you don't mind, I'm going to watch from quite a distance away.' He laughed as he began entering activation codes into the machine. 'A couple decades, maybe.'

'Yours is a charmed existence, World Killer,' the raspy voice mocked. 'To step in and out of time must be a blessing beyond measure.'

'It's far from it,' Chaerakh replied darkly, stepping back as the machine started emitting a high-pitched hum. Beyond it, the wall of the cave began to crack, stone falling into the water, creating ripples and forcing the Illeri to move back to the rock shelves around the pool. 'But I suppose it might be if I was in control,' Chaerakh continued, as translucent tentacles shot out from the water to probe these natural pathways. With strength which belied their composition, the tentacles pulled the Illeri bodies out of the water as the sound of the machine lowered in the spectrum and every wall around the pool began to rumble as the vibrations spread. The water level around Chaerakh began to drop as he

236

turned his back to the machine and watched the strange aliens rising from their natural, and preferred, environment. They were silvery blue in colour, fleshy cylindrical tubes that seemed to rebel against holding a singular shape, and the line of tentacles running along what was not necessarily their underbodies performed an array of duties ranging from mobility to senses. Four of them functioned now as legs as the bizarre Illeri stood and swayed with water dripping onto the rock. Chaerakh supposed they might have been looking at him. There was no way of knowing, but the truth was that it did not really matter. They 'saw' you no matter what.

Larger breaks began to appear in the rock walls around them, and Chaerakh calmly walked towards the entrance to the cave. 'How long?' the soft-voiced one asked him. He stopped and looked back, giving a little shrug: 'Hopefully, long enough for me to get your little chess piece here. You sure you're going to survive the exposure?'

'The Sentience will keep us safe.'

Chaerakh was unconvinced. 'I don't want to risk my neck for nothing,' he reminded them, pointing to the cave mouth. 'Not exactly my best friends out there, you know.'

'Nor ours, World Killer,' Raspy reminded him. 'We have our part, and you have yours. This will work.'

'It better,' Chaerakh told them. 'There's a lot more riding on this than saving your species!'

Ω

Kallon was pleasantly surprised and suitably impressed. The Redeemer began cycling through and then matching not only the transponder codes of vessel groups through which it had to pass, but also their metallurgical compounds and their chemical emissions. In short, the stealth craft could mimic whatever new and unusual vessel it encountered, even to the point of moving past larger ships while giving their equipment the impression that it was part of their outlying defence support or maintenance grid. Still, his progress towards the surface was an unnerving journey. 'Can't be that easy,' he whispered, almost as if he might be heard by their scanners. Which perhaps he might. An alarm sounded, and he saw what was coming. Whipping around the planet was a debris cloud – dust from the burned and parched surface. He braced himself for this blessing in disguise, for this was his way in. He re-checked the coordinates of the beacon and began furiously re-calculating his descent vector so he could drop out of the cloud in time.

The Redeemer entered the cloud and Kallon cut the engines immediately, adjusting the craft to allow it to ride the dust around the world. He sealed the intakes and burned out the exhausts, giving him a little push but resulting in the fateful mistake of igniting just enough of whatever was in the cloud and causing it to flare for just long enough that all the stealth measures in the Universe could not sustain his invisibility. Undetected by his equipment, a ship launched from one of the largest vessels high above his position. It maintained its distance, locking into a synchronous orbit as the Redeemer raced around in the dust cloud, and it plummeted towards the cloud only as Kallon was preparing to drop out of it. Intensely focused upon getting the manoeuvre correct and overwhelmed by the cacophony of proximity warnings – all of which he mistakenly attributed to the debris around him – he failed to recognise the projectiles fired from the pursuing craft. A salvo of missiles engulfed the Redeemer, some hitting gaseous rocks which exploded to create impacting waves that rocked the stealth craft, others slamming directly into the hull and blasting protective layers from its complex hide. Bruised and battered but still in one piece, the Redeemer overshot its exit point and Kallon was forced to readjust for the chaotic trajectory it now assumed. His voice commands roared at the computer to return fire, and the Redeemer took on its much larger pursuer with an array of weapons that belied its size and composition. On the mothership from which the pursuing craft had launched, dark, alien eyes observed with heightened curiosity.

The attacker broke off its pursuit, and Kallon strapped in for a bumpy landing. With nothing but scorched rock comprising all measure of the topographical nightmare laid out before it, the Redeemer informed Kallon of the high probability that it would pass through most obstacles. It was the remaining percentage of obstacles with which he was most concerned, but nothing prepared him for what happened. Instead of anything slowing his descent to any great degree, and there were numerous attempts on the part of the planet to do so, he eventually slammed right through a desiccated hillside – which might once have been a low-lying island peak – to find himself hurtling into the tectonic mystery beneath. While still travelling fast, the sight beneath and around him grabbed his attention as if viewed in slow motion. There was a great industrial enterprise here, a complex operation set into this hollowed core of the world. And he recognised two of the species involved. One was Kwaios, the other...*no, they couldn't be...*

The Redeemer finally hit hard, and Kallon was whiplashed into insensibility. He came round a few times, each episode offering something different. The first was a flashing blue automaton just beyond the forward viewscreen. The second was a Kwaios in strange, protective gear, looking in through that screen. The third was the most unexpected of all: a Garran with what looked in the half-light like burning hair, shooting the Kwaios before turning to look at him. Kallon's mind decided it had had enough for the moment.

He felt a tug on his arm and looked down to see a red line wrapped around his wrist. 'Kallon,' the familiar female voice called to him from the distance as he stood in a blackness without end. 'Just a little farther, Kallon. You're almost home. You're almost –'

'...out of here.'

Kallon caught some sounds, but they were at the same time muffled and deafening. 'Huh?' he managed.

He got a slap in the face for his effort, and his ears rang before he heard the voice shouting, '...to get OUT OF HERE!' He was lifted to his feet and the voice asked, 'You with me?'

'Yeah,' Kallon groaned. 'I think so.'

'Thinking's a good start,' said the Garran, who had thrown Kallon's arm over his shoulder and was dragging him away from the Redeemer. Kallon looked back to see the airlock closing and he groaned again: 'Where are you taking me?'

'The end of the world,' his rescuer replied. There came the sound of an engine to their right and Kallon was dropped to the ground as a spherical vessel with the identity of its crew obscured behind dark glass rose from the depths beyond the clifftop upon which he was only now realising he had crashed. In one fluid motion, the equally unidentified Garran rolled away from Kallon, somehow managed to withdraw and activate some kind of grenade launcher and fired at the sphere. A burst of rounds erupted from the vessel, but the grenade blew it apart. Kallon managed to drag his recovering body out of harm's way as debris rained down upon the clifftop, and the Garran got him to his feet as another two of the spheres rose through the fire from their counterpart. This was a dangerous place to be fighting with heavy weapons, and their attackers jumped out instead. That was when Kallon corrected his earlier disbelief and realised that their attackers were human. 'What the Hell's going *on*?' he shouted as they ran from small weapons fire. 'Who are these people? What are they *doing* out here?'

'They're not people!' the Garran shouted as he returned fire. 'And are those things for decoration?'

He was pointing to Kallon's holstered guns, and the mercenary realised that the adrenaline had slapped him back to his old self as he drew them and turned on the enemy. Dropping to one knee, he held his ground, taking out two of the black-clothed humans while the Garran killed three others before a huge Kwaios stepped out of the shadows behind them. It was encased in body armour, and Kallon knew the game had changed. Yet as the Kwaios levelled a large, double-handed blaster in their direction, the Garran pushed Kallon to the ground and shouted, 'Get down!' as two of the strangest creatures he had ever seen seemed to catapult themselves into the fight. The holes along the bodies of the dead Illeri he had seen in the escape pod were most certainly not for eyes. Tentacles lashed out from them as legs, arms, even weapons; but even that was not the astonishing part, for a bright orange glow emanating from deep inside them appeared to be the source of an energy weapon, and it pulsed out along the tentacles to be released as bolts of light that burned holes right through the Kwaios. 'Time to go,' the Garran ordered Kallon, who needed no further instruction.

As they ran, descending into the darkness and moving away from the vast industrialised area into what appeared to be a cave network, Kallon glanced back to see if the Illeri were following. 'Don't worry about them,' the Garran told him, activating a chain of light around his neck. 'They're just getting what you brought.'

'What I *brought*? What are you talking about?'

'The Redeemer, Raesa.' Kallon heard the words as if he were being punched in the ears with them: 'You brought the Redeemer.'

Ω

240

The strange ships in orbit were nothing like Kwaios vessels, and yet they were. Specifically designed for this operation, they simply had to be different from anything the people of Earth had seen before. In one of the larger vessels, this monumental operation was overseen by a regional observer, a relatively high-ranking Kwaios in the grand scheme of things. He was currently listening to reports of the unexpected activity down on the planet's surface:

'Ground forces have confirmed that the intruder's craft is comprised of material stolen from our mines on Ennorenda. But its pilot was human, and no humans have penetrated that far into the galactic heart.'

The observer leaned forward. 'But we know who *has* visited us on Ennorenda.'

'Of course, Observer,' the keen-eyed Kwaios operative replied. 'The World Killer.'

'Why would he have them bring such a craft?' the observer mused. 'This is not the same one we have seen him use.'

'Is it possible he is working with Samuel Vawter?'

'More than possible,' the larger Kwaios agreed, rising from his seat to tower over the others. 'We are monitoring Vawter's activity. Who did the pilot send a message to?'

'It was an open com link. Received by Senator Kai Tzedek.'

'Did you distort the time-link?'

'Yes, Observer. We diverted the communication through the Illeri star. His warning will be too late.'

'Humans know *nothing* of stars,' the observer hissed scornfully. 'Kill this intruder and take his craft. If you kill the World Killer, you will command the first wave when we reach Earth.'

Ω

'What do you mean, I *brought* it?' Kallon snapped as Chaerakh eventually stopped running and they caught their breath. He reached out to grab the Garran, but his hand was swiftly twisted away and he was looking down the barrel of a gun. Chaerakh's bright green eyes blazed in the light thrown up from the chain around his neck. 'Never touch me, human!' he warned through gritted teeth.

Kallon held his wild glare and grinned. 'I own a gun, too,' he reminded him calmly. Chaerakh looked down as he felt the weapon touch his stomach, his anger swiftly replaced by admiration. 'In another life, we could have been friends, Kallon,' he said.

Kallon stepped back and holstered his gun. 'Start with how you know my name.'

'You wouldn't believe me if I told you.'

'Try me.'

Chaerakh picked up the pace again and as Kallon followed, the Garran called back, 'Ever hear of the Prophet?'

'Any particular one? Where I come from, they're a dime a dozen!'

'Look...it doesn't matter. Why you were sent here is more important.'

'Vawter wanted some answers about the Illeri before the Shield was finished,' Kallon explained as they loped through the tunnels. There was a faint light ahead in the distance, and Kallon could feel something pulsing in the ground beneath them. 'They were due to visit Earth soon.' He looked back as if he might see the two Illeri: 'Guess that's not happening now.'

'Not the way you expect.' Chaerakh stopped and turned to him, saying, 'I think a little detour is in order.' He pointed to Kallon's left: 'That's if you really want the full picture.'

'Why wouldn't I?'

Chaerakh shrugged. 'In my experience, enlightenment is less comforting than ignorance.'

'Well, I didn't come all the way out here for comfort. Could have found that at home!'

Chaerakh was surprised to see the man's lip trembling and he knew he was lying. There was an immense sadness there, but Kallon suppressed it habitually, replacing it with righteous anger. 'If I was sent on a wild goose chase, I wanna know why!'

Of course, Chaerakh could not help but empathise, and he nodded as he gestured again towards a subsidiary tunnel: 'After you. Just don't make any noise...despite what you're gonna see.'

Kallon glanced back at that but kept going. The vibrations he had felt in the ground dissipated the farther they moved from what he had come to think of as a sort of central thoroughfare, and when Chaerakh turned off his neck-chain they were plummeted into darkness. 'Not a sound from here,' the Garran whispered. He seemed to be able to see much better than Kallon, and he took the lead just as the tunnel was beginning to be illuminated by tiny red lines threaded through the rock. Apparently, he liked to break his own rules, and he whispered again, 'All of this used to be below the ocean floor. The Illeri thrived down here, millions of them living in these tunnels.'

'What happened?'

'The Kwaios invaded. There was no time to mount a defence, but a lot of them got away as the occupation began.'

'Why are they here?'

'The Kwaios?' Chaerakh took Kallon towards him in a conspiratorial embrace, one arm over his shoulder as the other directed Kallon's view into a dark expanse from which a stale breeze emanated. 'They're here for this.'

It took a while for the immense scene to come into focus, but as it did, and more and more of it rolled out before Kallon's eyes, his breath grew short and his heart pounded. 'What...' he gasped, as he bore witness to the massive operation laid out before him. Hundreds of thousands of strange biosuits stood in militarised rows towards the left side of the dark and drained ocean floor. From the right, thousands of Kwaios soldiers were herding massive numbers of humans into what looked like pens for farm animals as they were led out of dropships descending from the darkness above. 'What is this?'

Chaerakh pointed to the lines of people between the pens and the biosuits. '*This*...is what's going to Earth, Kallon. This is the end of their supply line.' The humans were getting into the biosuits, with only a small contingent of Kwaios overseeing the process.

'This is what Tzedek said was at Earth!' said Kallon. 'And he said they were there *already*! Is this an invasion? Using our people against us?'

'I told you earlier, Kallon...they're not people. They're Kwaios. And as for them being there already...that's just not possible.'

'What do you mean? And what do you mean, they're not *people*?'

'After they took some of your people from the Cage, the Kwaios figured out a way to be whatever physical species they wanted. The humans you see down there are just bodies...vessels.'

243

Kallon was horrified. *Where did they get all these people?* 'You said this was the end,' he said. 'Where does it start?'

'Come on...you know the answer to *that*, Kallon,' said Chaerakh, as he turned and headed back the way they had come. 'It starts with your friend...Samuel Vawter,' he called back. 'With MEC. You know...the one-way cloning system?'

'*What*?' Kallon took another look before turning to catch up. 'Why would he create something like that? Why would he allow this to happen?'

'Ever hear the term...speculate to accumulate?'

'Are you *seriously* suggesting that Vawter's sacrificing millions of people to the Kwaios for...for what...some kind of *investment plan*?'

'The most ruthless I've ever seen, yes.' He glanced down at his right arm. 'And that's saying something. Come on, we need to move.'

'I wanna know what's –'

'NOW!' Chaerakh grabbed his arm and they narrowly escaped death as the tunnel exploded behind them, the walls caving in as dust chased them. Blasts of both energy and solid projectile weapons tore the air around them, and Chaerakh roared as a bullet sliced his right shoulder and the sound of its passing stung his ear. Both he and Kallon returned fire as they ran, shooting aimlessly behind them while struggling to keep their footing. The world around them began shaking violently, and they cut left at the previous junction just before a drilling machine broke through from above. The drill, however, was not the source of the shaking, and as Kallon saw the light ahead grow brighter, he realised he could see part of the Redeemer. As their pursuers regrouped and Chaerakh and Kallon increased the distance between them, more of the stealth ship came into view. It was hovering above a pool of water, enveloped in some kind of energy shield and hooked to a huge machine on the other side. Two Illeri – whom he presumed were those he had seen earlier – moved into view in the cave entrance, and their bodies lit up again in preparation for defence. Chaerakh and Kallon turned and fired their weapons back into the dust-filled tunnel, hearing the sounds of wounded humans and Kwaios.

The Illeri had not yet attacked, and they appeared to be waiting for the dust to clear. Chaerakh was already splashing through the water towards his machine, but Kallon stood between the two Illeri, peering into a darkness illuminated intermittently by flashes of blue from Kwaios hybritech or the searching points of energy weapons. But these dissipated as the pursuers moved back and the dust cleared...to reveal a number of obsidian-black biosuits floating slowly towards them. Like the one worn by what Tzedek had thought to be an Illeri ambassador, it had the appearance of an armoured man with wings. Concealed weapons emerged from apertures and activated, but the Illeri launched their attack first, moving forward to lash out with their tendrils and their blasts of energy, gripping and climbing the tunnel walls and ceiling to confound the armoured hybrids, whose suits alternated between absorbing and deflecting the Illeri bioweapons as they, too, fought with an array of projectile and energy weapons, the latter slashing out like blades.

Kallon watched transfixed until Chaerakh shouted, 'Get out of there, you idiot!' He turned to see the Garran checking the cables connecting the Redeemer to the strange machine, which was shaking like it might fall apart at any moment. 'What's that thing supposed to do?' he asked as he splashed towards Chaerakh, avoiding the pulsing energy shield under the exaggerated prow of the stealth craft.

'Get you home!' Chaerakh's eyes were wild now. He was fascinated by what was about to happen, but he knew the two Illeri could not possibly hold off a concerted attack from the Kwaios, whom he knew were more concerned with getting to him than anything else. Kallon stared at him for a moment, baffled: 'Then why the hell was I sent here in the first place?'

'It's about the journey,' Chaerakh replied, pushing Kallon aside as he fired at a Kwaios who was raising a large weapon at the Redeemer. 'The Illeri are down!' the Garran shouted. 'Get on board!' He dropped the gun he was using and reached down into the water to withdraw an enormous weapon the likes of which Kallon had never seen. When he fired it at the incoming Kwaios and hybrids, it screamed as if its plasma bolts caused it pain. Kallon needed no further instruction. He ducked under the shield and moved through the water beneath the Redeemer to see that the underside hatch was open. 'I'll cover you from the bridge!' he roared above the noise, realising only when the Kwaios shots were being aimed at him that he was inside the protective shield. He jumped up to grab the rails outside the hatch and then raised himself to grab an inner bar before hauling himself into the vessel. Something hot sliced his left foot and he cried out as he rolled onto his back inside the Redeemer. A bullet must have passed through the shield, which meant that it was losing power. Which, of course, it would, if the Illeri were dead.

Even with the huge plasma gun, Chaerakh was struggling to hold off the influx of Kwaios soldiers. As two more armoured hybrids came into the cave, he passed through the fluctuating shield and gave a last roar of fury and a round of plasma bolts before he, too, jumped up to the Redeemer's hatch. Just as he did, Kallon was pressing the trigger on the forward cannons and beginning to rotate the ship. The Kwaios went down and the hybrids were thrown back against the cave walls, but the impact caused the place to begin to crumble. The ceiling began to rain down upon them, but worse than that, the water level drained quickly as the bottom fell out of the cave. Chaerakh's machine went with it, and with that…the Redeemer. It listed to starboard and followed the machine into the depths of the planet, with what seemed like the planet in pursuit.

'You didn't disconnect the *cables*?' Kallon was incredulous as he struggled to maintain control of the craft. The Illeri shield was gone, and the Redeemer's hull was being pounded by falling rock and it was slamming into whatever formations happened to be in the way as the deep and complex Illeri tunnel network was systematically destroyed. 'How the hell are we supposed to get *outta* here?'

Chaerakh strapped himself in next to Kallon: 'Look…I'm just following orders! Do your best to keep us in one piece!'

It felt as if the world were devouring the Redeemer, and Kallon's head was slammed against the control panel in front of him. 'There's nowhere to go!' he snapped.

'Just keep going down,' said a calm voice from behind Kallon, in the wake of a distortion in reality that felt as if someone had momentarily squeezed his head. He managed to turn to see a tall, bearded man in a bizarre black cloak standing steadily on the floor as if the circumstances were a mere inconvenience. 'Fire the engines, Kallon. Take us as far down as you can go.'

Amidst the insanity, Kallon simply did as he was told, hearing the man ask the Garran, 'Are the cables securely connected to the light-drive?'

'Best I could get them in all *that*! Why didn't you warn me about the attack?'

'I knew you were looking forward to using the plasma cannon,' Naveen replied calmly.

Chaerakh made a sound somewhere between disgust and concession: 'When do I fire it?'

'Soon,' said Naveen. 'Very soon.'

'Fire *what*?' Kallon shouted madly as he struggled to maintain his trajectory towards what was likely the planet's core. The temperature was certainly increasing: 'What's going *on*?'

'We're going to destroy the planet, Kallon,' the cloaked man told him plainly. 'You're sitting next to the World Killer, after all. He loves this sort of thing.'

The world had gone mad and taken Kallon along for the ride. That had to be it. Maybe he was still out cold on the crashed Redeemer. Maybe he was stuck back on the last MEC station. Or maybe he had never even left Earth, and all his nightmares were simply that. Maybe she was still next to him, and he would wake soon to touch her face and see her smile.

'Now, Chaerakh,' said Naveen.

Or maybe not.

The World Killer tapped a button on his arm-panel, and the machine, which had been lighting the way for the Redeemer's perilous journey towards the core of Illeri as the cables dragged the craft with it...exploded. Kallon shielded his eyes but there was no danger to them. An enormous blast of red light shot downwards into the planet, and Kallon saw something amazing. He was instantly reminded of the threads of red he had seen in one of the tunnels, but the red lines which were illuminated by this destructive event were pulsing, undulating...alive. They were everywhere, and more and more of them appeared like stars coming into view the more one stared into the night. 'What is this?' he breathed.

'This...' the cloaked man told him as he stepped closer, 'is God, Kallon.'

'And you're taking it with you,' said Chaerakh, as the Redeemer slowed its descent and came to an unbelievable floating stop in the centre of the world. The Garran released himself from the chair and stretched his back and cracked his neck from side to side.

'What do you mean?' Kallon looked out to see nothing but blackness filled with red lines of energy.

'We arranged for the implosion of the planet,' the Garran explained. 'The Illeri wanted to ensure that if they couldn't have their own planet, then the Kwaios wouldn't either. And this way they get to kill millions of the bastards along the way.'

Kallon was overwhelmed by the scale of what was happening. He was so out of his depth that he felt he might drown in helplessness. Or hopelessness. 'How are we going to survive this?' he implored them. 'How can we possibly get out?'

'Well, *we* have a way out, Kallon,' said Chaerakh. 'You're not so much getting out as…going in.' The cloaked man glanced at the Garran as if to berate him. But he looked to Kallon again and said, 'This craft was specifically designed to go somewhere from which there's no return. But your sacrifice will ensure that what we did here wasn't in vain.'

'But what was the *point*?' Kallon argued. 'The entire Illeri race is gone!'

Chaerakh chuckled and Naveen smiled. 'No, Kallon,' he explained. 'Most certainly not. Those that escaped have been hiding since the invasion.'

'Oh…okay?' Kallon nodded. 'Where?'

Naveen said nothing, and Chaerakh leaned in and put his hand on Kallon's shoulder. 'Somewhere there's a lotta water,' he told him. 'Now, we have to go.' He stepped back and checked that he had everything he needed. Naveen nodded, before looking sympathetically at Kallon, and saying, 'I want you to know that every life means something to me. That I believe everyone should find their way home.'

'I…don't know what you're talking about.'

'You will.' He put his hand on Chaerakh's shoulder and, accompanied by that same head-squeezing distortion, they both vanished, leaving Kallon alone in a stealth craft that apparently needed no such capabilities. 'Where the hell am I *going*?' he shouted, his voice going nowhere in the emptiness. As he looked out again to see the red lines beginning to form into a tunnel and the engines of the Redeemer pushed him into it – and he then looked at his instruments to see that they may as well have been inanimate images – he began to realise that he was somewhere completely outside the natural order of things.

As the planet Illeri collapsed in upon itself, consuming everything still on and below the distorted surface, the Kwaios invasion fleet moved as many of its ships away from the destruction as possible. But the core of this planet was different to others. It held tight to the manifestations of the Sentience, and as the Redeemer pierced the fabric between space and...somewhere else...the result was like slowly piercing a balloon. An unseen shockwave burst from the event horizon, and everything in the system was obliterated. Although the destructive force of this shockwave would dissipate over time, it travelled far beyond the system. Far beyond.

Ω

The present is always defined by the past, and not only when it is built upon it. People frequently disassociate themselves from their past to sculpt a new present and aim for a new future. Kallon had done such a thing, and the past from which he had fled had not come to mind for what seemed like an age. In truth, it was only three years ago, but the suppression of great trauma requires great commitment. There were structures of memory to be adhered to, strict guidelines for what could be dealt with and what had to be ignored even in the embryonic stages of recall. It was like stopping a bush fire before the first leaf was even aflame. No one said it was healthy, but then neither was the pain. And while fire was often purgative, so much occupied the forest of memory that Kallon was not willing to set it alight.

Here, in a ship racing through an indefinable nothingness, Kallon's commitment was being challenged, his defences in danger of breaking down. He had lost track of time, but he knew he was somewhat older than when he had escaped Illeri. Supplies were gone, and it was only a matter of time. He felt a great sadness engulf him as he made his way to the medical bay, where he often slept now, and the loneliness he felt was accentuated by the emptiness of this place. Her face flashed into his mind, and he flinched with a fear which had become his only companion since the strange Garran in the dark tunnels of Illeri. And the fear reminded him.

She had been so unwell, descending deeper into a depression that took her physical vitality as relentlessly as it took her motivation for life. She had suffered a terrible loss, one that no man could truly understand. Despite his best efforts at consoling her, at comforting her and holding her and whispering words of hope and adoration, the doors of her future had closed, throwing her present into a terrible shadow from which she could not escape. She told him once that it was comforting to relent, to feel the bittersweet embrace of emptiness, for it meant that she did not have to think, to plan, to lift herself up and make mind-numbing efforts at pretence. When no one was around, she would stare at the walls, the ceiling, sometimes the floor, her head hanging as if her neck could not bear its terrible weight. Kallon cried with her many times, rocking her in his strong arms and stroking her hair. She had always loved that, would fall asleep with a smile of contentment in the knowledge that she was loved. And he had always loved how much she clung to him for comfort.

He had begun to feel useless, a man of no strength, no power, no meaning. If he could not convince the woman he loved to stand and fight for her very soul, how could he justify his motivational talks when the army called him to address the troops? He had been a hero of another age, a short but brutal conflict from which he had emerged psychologically damaged but physically stronger and determined to protect those he loved. Those memories flooded him now, of bodies broken and torn apart, of young soldiers crying for their parents as they lay dying. It was a pointless conflict in the end, for neither side had gained a thing. But Kallon had met his wife in the closing days, and he had vowed to care for her as long as he drew breath.

When he had found her, when he had returned home from another delivery of empty words of inspiration, the first thing he had noticed...the thing that brought his first tears and his soul-deep cry of anguish...was her smile of contentment. Ignoring the blood, he had gone to her, lifting her from the bath and carrying her to the bed. Lying next to her, he held her close and sobbed, stroking her hair until he, too, fell asleep.

Kallon sat up and shook his head as if the motion would relinquish the grip of the past. His breath was short and panicked and his fingers touched moisture on his cheeks as he gathered himself. He heard a voice, but it was as if it were coming from a great distance and reaching him only when he was tuned in: 'Pain is a necessary aspect of human development. It should not be ignored.'

'*Really*?' Kallon snapped, infuriated by the intrusion into his deepest thoughts. 'That's your expert opinion, is it?' There was no response, and Kallon released a primal roar of anguish, before shouting, 'SHOW YOURSELF!'

'You have observed me since your first breath, Kallon Raesa,' the undulating voice replied. 'I have surrounded you as you grew…as you lived…as your love died…and as you came to this place between places.'

Kallon looked around the medical bay, seeing no one: 'What are you talking about? Who are you?'

'I am everyone. I am everything. I am everywhere. I am the Universe.'

Kallon chuckled darkly, nodding knowingly. 'Ah, I get it.' He laughed aloud now, hooting with relief. 'I've been here so long I've gone insane!'

'Humans have always resisted revelation.' The voice was almost accusatory.

Kallon smiled, continuing his denial as he lowered himself to the cold floor and reached for his boots: 'We're a stubborn lot, I suppose.'

'And yet you appropriate my guidance for your own ends, consistently adapting it to accommodate your baser instincts. This is not because you are stubborn. It is because you are incapable of transcending the societal modes of your primitive antecedents.'

'That's a bit harsh.' Kallon was unsteady as he stepped away from the trolley. 'Sure, it took a long time to iron out the paradoxes of equality and democracy, but…we're far removed from apes, my imaginary friend. *Far* removed!'

'You crave leadership,' the voice argued. 'You resort to hierarchies constructed upon your subconscious need for an inexplicable imbalance of domination and subordination. You may treat certain members of your species better than their ape equivalents…and that took many thousands of years to materialise…but given the circumstances, you require powerful individuals to descend from their watchtower trees and enforce submission of the weak. Rather than lift the weak to your heights and teach them how to look *across* the world instead of down

251

upon it, you perpetuate the systemic submission of the many by the dominant few. And this despite knowing that the more of you that are powerful, the more powerful you could be together.'

Kallon stopped before he opened the door and looked around again, angered by what he had thought to be his own imagination; something he was now questioning: 'And what about you...*I am the Universe*? You say you're everywhere and *everyone*? That's the ramblings of the most *insidious* megalomaniac where I come from!'

'It is my inescapable nature to be all-encompassing. I don't crave power or dominance. I simply exist. The Illeri have long been amongst the few species with whom I enjoy a mutually respectful relationship. This is because they have no leaders, no constructs of status. If one is weak, it is because they are all weak, and they will attend to that problem in unison. When they are strong, every one of them is strong.'

Most people are aware of the limits of their imaginations, and if not, they are certainly aware of the characteristics of its conceptualisation. This did not sound like Kallon's. 'What are you, exactly?' he asked.

'I told you. I am the Universe. Some of your people call me the Sentience.'

'You're talking about the New Elect? Weren't they all taken away?'

'Not all. Many are still in hiding.'

'Why?'

'Because the circumstances of their domination have not yet arisen.'

'I'm not sure I like the sound of that.'

'On that we agree, Kallon Raesa. But you will be instrumental in facilitating it.'

'What the *hell* is that supposed to mean?'

'When you die...and that will be soon...you will leave this place. So, too, will this vessel that most certainly does not belong in a place of mind and soul.'

The fear gripped him again. 'I don't want to die. Seriously. If you're so powerful, why not get me outta here? Believe me, I don't wanna be here either. And I sure don't wanna be stuck on this ship any longer!'

'Only death can move someone in or out of this place. It is the natural order of things.'

Kallon's spirit lifted at that. 'You mean...someone who dies ends up here? Is...' he couldn't bear to say her name, and his voice broke: 'Is she here?'

'No one is reunited in this place, Kallon. This is a place between places. This is where the lost remain unfound.'

He sobbed and hung his head. 'I can't take any more. Please...make it stop.'

'Lay down again, Kallon. Your time has come. It is why you can hear me. It is why you dreamed of her.'

His body at first trembling with fear and the anticipation of nothing, Kallon then felt a great tiredness engulf him. It was incredibly soothing, and he smiled as his eyes closed. 'You are a hero, my love,' he heard her say. 'You're about to save us all.' Tears rolled down his cheeks as his breathing slowed. With a final exhalation of life, Kallon Raesa moved on.

He did not get to see the wonder of what happened next, for the red lines dissipated to reveal a bright light ahead. A blinding blue-white sky at the end of a frozen tunnel as the Redeemer exited the portal into reality. Along the way, as the Sentience was threaded from the core of one world to another, a reconnection occurred, one which would change the course of human development. But first, the Earth would have to stop rumbling.

INTERVAL 3
IMPLEMENTATION

Who are you? Do you know? Do you ever ask yourself? When you hide behind your deeds as if they might define you, do you wonder if one change in the past, one alteration in the course of your life might rewrite your present self? If it were possible to travel back and change one decision, would you do it? Would you risk not recognising yourself upon your return? Would you risk going insane from inner conflict? Or would you even remember that you made the decision to go back in the first place...only to find yourself less impressed with this new person you have created, with no idea that it was all your fault? But then, had this not already been the case?

Transcripts from the 3-hour long deliberations opening the 783 NE trial of Dr. Julius Varen, former Director of Psychology for the Institute of Advancements in Memory & Identity in the Hanno Western Protectorate, Telena.

Elias Vawter Medical Institute, South Africa, 318 NE

The comforting blanket of denial was being slowly withdrawn from Samuel's soul as voices intruded upon his heaven. Had Amara been there? Perhaps not. He had reached for her. But perhaps he had never even known her. 'Samuel?' she called. They called.

'Amara?'

'Yes,' she replied. But in a man's voice, she asked, 'Samuel, can you hear me?'

He groaned and waited for this new world to shed the old. Waited for it to make sense. Unaware that this would never again be the case. 'Samuel?'

The previous reality gradually relinquished its grip until he knew that it had been nothing more than a sweet dream. Still, he would have it back if given the choice. 'Who are you?' he asked the man leaning over him and shining a light in his eyes. 'I'm Doctor Maxwell,' the man replied. 'Do you know where you are?'

'I've only just come round. How the hell would I know where I am?'

'He sounds fine to me,' someone else cut in. 'And he prefers to be addressed as *Mister* Vawter!' The man stepped up to the opposite side of the bed. 'I'm glad to see you're okay.'

'And *you* are...?'

'I'm Kai Tzedek.' Samuel's hand was taken and gripped firmly. 'They say I'm an up-and-coming figure in interplanetary politics.'

'Politics? Look...where's Amara?' Samuel lifted his head and tried to see beyond the two men. The room was small, too small for a ward, even the private ones to which he had become accustomed. 'Is she here? What hospital is this?'

'This isn't exactly a hospital, Mister Vawter,' Maxwell explained. 'You're in one of your Foundation institutes.'

'What? Why?'

'There have been certain...developments,' Tzedek put in. 'We need your help to ensure that they...continue to develop.'

Samuel stared at him, reading a world of deception in those eyes, and recalling how he had reached for Amara in his dreams. He grabbed the man's arm and squeezed, demanding through gritted teeth, 'You tell me now. Where...is...Amara?'

257

'Mister Vawter…' the doctor began. Samuel turned to him, releasing Tzedek as he saw the expression and connected the tone. 'No,' he gasped. 'No…please…'

'I'm…sorry,' Maxwell continued. 'We did everything…but…'

'She didn't make it, Samuel,' Tzedek told him. 'There was just too much damage.'

Samuel had not turned from the doctor. He appeared fixated on the stethoscope. And he started counting the little metal buttons on the white coat. Then he read Maxwell's name tag. The coat was clean, bright white. Angelic. Heavenly. 'Amara…'

Unaware of an exchange between the two men, Samuel did not anticipate the injection. At first it was like a fire inside his head, but then it made him groggy. It was partly because the needle went straight into his brain, but mostly because of what they took out of him that he felt suddenly weak. As he returned to heaven, Tzedek and Maxwell left the room and headed down the corridor. Entering another room three doors down, Tzedek said, 'I don't think that could have gone any better, do you?'

Maxwell nodded. 'I imagine we caught the exact moment of realisation,' he agreed. 'Of course, these things can take a while to set in, and it's impossible to predict how anyone will react given time, but our guy can extrapolate from the real emotion and that's invaluable.' This room was ten times larger, with scores of people working on various experiments, some of which were isolated by transparent curtains. The two men walked towards the back of the room, where their eyes were simultaneously scanned before the double doors unlocked and swung open. In the centre of this domed, high-ceilinged chamber was a massive tube filled with fluid supporting and protecting a man inside. There were considerably less people working here, but one of them stood out. Not just because he was taller, or broader, or more menacing looking than his colleagues. But because he was Garran. A Garran with a shock of red hair running along his cranial ridge. He turned to the two men: 'You extracted in time?'

'As soon as we told him she was dead,' said Tzedek, resenting working with this lunatic.

'Good.' The Garran directed Maxwell towards the staff, who took the injector and began extracting its contents, while Tzedek stared at the man in the tube: 'How much longer until we activate him?'

258

The Garran laughed. 'You know, if I were this impatient, I'd be dead a long time ago.'

Tzedek looked back: 'That's not an answer, Chaerakh.'

'No, it's not. But cloning is a complex procedure calling for patience and precision. Especially if you're going to convince not only the Kwaios but the clone himself that he's the real Samuel Vawter. Layers of memory that we need to complete the character over the next year or so could crumble if he's faced with conflicting information. And remember, once the Kwaios have their transport network activated, they'll be able to monitor specific people on Earth.'

'So, we'll need to ensure that specific people never use the system.'

'Exactly.'

'So…how long?'

Chaerakh shook his head. 'Why don't you go back to your new best friend and tell him the woman he loves isn't really dead?'

Tzedek took a deep breath. In the huge tube, the clone turned until Tzedek was once again looking at Samuel Vawter. 'How am I supposed to tell *him* the Kwaios have her? That it was either that or mass abductions that would make the Cage event seem like a summer vacation? We didn't even give him a choice.'

'You have nearly two years to figure it out, Tzedek,' Chaerakh reminded him, 'but Naveen doesn't give you choices. He gives you power and you give him what he wants. You'll be a senator and Vawter will be your right-hand man. And once MEC is up and running, you better pray Naveen wants you to win. Now go back and tell your friend the truth. He needs to get his head in the game as soon as possible.'

PART 4
KIRANIS

How is it that you don't see the wonder of the stars and the magnificent glory of the Universe? Why would you simplify it with absurdities? The dead don't go to the stars, unless to be consumed by fire, and no mystical realm awaits your soul when your heart stops beating. Don't be caught up in this fantasy of a power binding us all together and mapping our fate across the Universe. The only power is the Universe itself, and while we should be in awe of it, it does not have a mind to oversee our existence and guide us to a beautiful end.

From a secret recording made by early Si census-takers at an anti-Church rally, c. 395 NE. It is ironic that the man was so close to the truth, only to have his theology warped by semantics.

THE DRAGONS

Kiranis, 230 NE

The Cage was closing in around the alien world, the wireframe adjusting the lengths between the major components to adjust to the size of the planet. Thousands of sealed capsules, carrying captive Church members, plunged through roiling clouds of dark unknown as the rate of the formation process was increased. Descending towards the planet's questionable surface at terrible speed, each victim could see only the deadly promise of a sky above and imagine the searing curse of a fate below. As the last stages of the planet's creation reached their climax, small and wayward pieces of matter slammed against the capsules, causing some of them to spin uncontrollably. Other tiny pieces, impacting at such speeds with some of the capsules that they breached the glass and protective casing, brought about the depressurisation of the capsules. Many people died before the final impact.

These impacts were varied, depending on the varying geological stages of creation waiting to embrace the captives. Some of the capsules crashed into mineral so hard that they exploded, others passed through permeable surfaces so that their occupants were caught inside the planet's crust. The balance of hydrogen and oxygen molecules which had been precipitated by the circling bands of planetary matter was altered by the energy of the Cage and water collapsed to the surface, drawn by gravity to create rivers and seas which welcomed many occupants of the capsules. Wherever the captives fell, their environment determined the form of their mutation, but not before the Garran blood had been introduced with all its accompanying agony to their midbrain.

Just as Cana's imagination had been the catalyst for the manifestation of the black dragon, that same perception of life pervaded every new introduction to this world. In dark caves and deep valleys, atop mountains and beneath oceans, the captive Church members experienced the horror of rebirth as defined by the young man sent ahead as an emissary of their terror. Waiting entities of disassociated energy sought out their respective hosts and the capsules were rent apart by expanding human bodies; whose flesh pulsed and split; whose bones grew and snapped and

263

twisted; and whose consciousness became trapped in the monstrous form of a primordial reptile. Their human consciousness was absorbed and overwhelmed by the other conscious minds which had awaited physical definition, facilitated by the re-awakening and re-prioritising of what had at one point in mankind's evolution been the brain of their reptilian ancestry. Some of the creatures spread giant wings of glory, others no more than stubs of despair. Of every colour they were, their size and characteristics defined by the geological womb of their birthing. But not all were exposed to the outer realms of the world, for some of the capsules had penetrated deep into the planet's crust.

These ones grew in protest, suffocated by the gaseous and molten heat and pressed against the rock which surrounded them. Many of them managed to escape into the upper reaches of the subterranean world, there to live a chthonic subservience to the greater beasts above. Others, however, could not escape, and still the disembodied minds were inescapably drawn to them. These creatures were misshapen, blind and furious, and their anger would ever be immense. Their curse was simply that they survived this horror.

The dragons had never been real. Formed within the re-creation milieu of Kiranis and with a helpful mixture of Garran stem-cells, the symbiotic creatures emerging from the primordial mix were substantiated only by Cana's paradoxical dream of his fate. But Cana had been consumed by the creature known as Leviathan amidst the chaos of 230 NE, and without his mental construct, many of the dragons began to mutate wildly as their respective human constituents panicked and fought for freedom. There might have been some hope of Leviathan maintaining the form of his people through the lines of the Sentience which had first implanted the concept in Cana's mind, but Naveen had seen fit to remove Leviathan, even from the extra-dimensional plane in which Kiranis now lingered. Of course, when the planet vanished and the Cage took it to nowhere, any hope of connecting to the Sentience was lost.

During a period now purposefully forgotten, a time when the nature of the planet crystallised, a new means by which these entities could once again determine their own forms arose, and human minds were again subordinated. However, some of these entities were inspired in the forms they took by a combination of resentment for Naveen's treachery, and the despair of the devotees of the Church of the New Elect who had imagined a utopian end to their abduction from Earth. These creatures were outwardly visual expressions of dark anguish and darker anger, and they began to seek each other out across the planet, banding together with their subterranean kin and a single purpose. They spent silent centuries studying the Network, the seemingly autonomous consciousness of Kiranis.

Dragons returned to the surface world, most of whom did not suffer any such soul-destroying deterioration. Some were still as majestic in form and mind as they had been on the day of their creation, perpetuated by a more amiable accommodation of the dual consciousness within. This was aided by the elevation from their ranks of a female of great power and inspiration who came to understand the Network as she had the Sentience. Asherah spent years unknown concealed with a small cadre of strong souls, honing her connection to the Network, so that, over time, many of her misshapen brothers and sisters came to her, seeking redemption through the most tangible means. She gave them new form and identity, a reason to live, and it was not long before social groups emerged from the chaos and hierarchies evolved. Grey dragons were the exception to this development, for while their forms were maintained, this was not achieved through Asherah's intervention. Somehow, there was a reverberation across the Network of Leviathan's rage, and it was like a beacon of purpose to them, defining them as the vanguard of his return. These loathsome disciples did little but harass Asherah's followers, but it was known that others who were rarely seen supported their endeavours. The centuries moved on, with no one learning the true nature of the Network.

I will be dead for the rest of time. Why would I wish to risk my life and bring such terror upon me? And yet, if I do not, I risk only existing, being. And being is only a heartbeat short of not being. Still...there is no time longer than the rest of it.

From the Third Book of the Great Mage, one of the seven taken from the Heart Crypt, the only structure known to have survived the First Dragon Purge. If we had known then what the dragons were, the galaxy would likely be very different today.

THE MEDIATOR

Gordon's Leap, Jala-bakor, Kiranis

The rider drew rein and looked down upon the town burning brightly, the afternoon breeze bearing the smell of flesh. Despite his hunger, he wrinkled his nose stubbornly and kicked the stallion on, knowing he would find only death but recognising the necessity of appreciating its purpose. He was what his kind called a Mediator, given human form for the sake of integration; but what the humans, in their ignorance, called a Guard. Completely underestimating the agonising process resulting in the production of one such as he, humans were to this Mediator akin to ungrateful children. His skin was almost black, a result of Reduction achieved by carefully controlled searing, tearing and re-constitution. His body was covered in binding lines of cauterized flesh, but the pain was naught but a memory for Haphory, who had been a Mediator for over a hundred years. Behind the mask he wore to protect humans from the self-destructive idiocies of fear and prejudice, his yellow eyes were still keen and bright, and through them he saw the treacherous truth of human-dragon integration. It was nothing but a simmering pot, beneath which powers beyond this world would soon seek to fan the flames.

The town into which Haphory rode was characteristically small for this part of Kiranis, as Jala-bakor was a loosely demarcated country in which no major territorial expansions had taken root since the inception of the Realms. In this respect, Jala-bakor was an anomaly on Kiranis, for the humans had acted true to form everywhere else on this world, conquering whenever economic gain was envisaged and moving with the rise and fall of ideologies and worldviews to motivate the polar opposites of propagation and genocide whenever and wherever they saw fit. Haphory felt the mockery of the Network at work here, though, and he knew this circumstance would not last. He knew it was so as he saw the first body. He knew even more so as he saw the butchery, the visceral but purposeful violence of those who had attended to the rest of the deaths. Everywhere he looked, men, women and children had been struck down with blunt force before having their chests ripped open. Most of them held in their death-grips their steadily blackening hearts, as if they had been handed them in remorse. Of course, the vermin and birds were always hungry, and they cared little for mourning rites. A very small amount of the others, and at this Haphory baulked, knowing what this must mean…the others were left without their hearts. And he knew that this had nothing to do with rats and crows.

He dismounted and stepped into an inn, looking around at the butchered bodies before pouring himself a drink at the bar. While guns hung at his hips, he would have no need for them here. He hunkered down and pressed his right palm on the floor, closing his eyes and concentrating. Asherah's Line was the most potent on Kiranis. Centuries of keeping herself abreast of the affairs of all its inhabitants meant that she had covered a lot of ground, both above and below the surface, but she had not been everywhere, and sometimes her Line needed to be drawn out. Haphory found it after a time, and he took a deep breath as he felt his own Line connect with hers. He exhaled only as he heard her voice in his head – her soft, seductive…deadly voice: 'Speak, Haphory. What have you found?'

'A town called Gordon's Leap,' he replied, 'in the east of Jala-bakor. Scores dead. Maybe a hundred.'

'How, my child? Who did this?'

'I don't know, Great Mother. But hearts have been taken.'

There was an understandable silence as the information was processed. 'How many?'

'I think perhaps seven. But they may have overestimated the readings.'

'Of course. I would think only two or three will suit their purposes.'

'So, it is what we feared?'

'It is what we expected, Haphory. What we have prepared for.'

'Then everything will change. Kiranis won't be safe.'

267

'Naveen never intended for us to be safe. He merely gave us the chance to grow stronger.'

With his hand still on the floor of the inn, Haphory opened his eyes and looked around: 'What will happen to the humans?'

'That's none of our concern, although the Watchers will have their own agenda now that the time is close. Go to their outpost near Laden's Folly and explain what you saw here.'

'That's not a town I enjoy frequenting, Great Mother. I have…history there.'

'I'm aware of your past, Haphory. You will do as I instruct.'

'Of course,' he conceded. 'It's been a long time since I've dealt with Watchers. Do you think they'll believe me?'

'You'll be surprised what they'll believe. Especially now that Naveen is about to bring the galaxy upon us.'

THE WATCHERS

Quis custodiet ipsos custodes?
Juvenal, *Satire 6*

Churchfield, near Laden's Folly, Jala-Bakor

The boy kicked his horse into a gallop, enjoying the rush of cool air against his face and his bare arms. The young mare beneath him seemed to fly across the stony ground, only slowing slightly as she crested the hill before racing downwards, her hooves barely clipping the surface. The young rider let out a shout of excitement which was whipped away, before leaning down to hang alongside the neck of the beast as he squinted against what was now a biting wind. The flowing golden mane snapped lightly against his face, and the way ahead became a distorted vision of hair and stone. Something large and black flashed by below him and he gasped in shock, drawing on the reins as he brought himself up in the saddle and saw the emptiness in his path. 'NO!' he shouted, dragging desperately to slow the horse as she whinnied in surprise and slowed her run as swiftly as she could. But it was too late: the ground gave way and the mare tripped and stumbled, throwing the boy over her neck as her forelegs crumpled beneath her. Letting go of the reins, he tumbled through the air, hearing nothing but the wind whip at his ears. As he descended, he expected to hit the ground without delay. Instead, his fall continued, tumbling through the emptiness of a great chasm, his screams echoing on the rocky walls. Something big and dark plummeted past him, before the leather of the mare's reins lashed his face, tearing his cheek. There was a thud below him, a sickening crack as the neck of the horse snapped, and the boy screamed anew with the fear of death. But it did not come.

He found himself suddenly suspended in mid-air, inexplicably hanging no more than a few feet from the dark stone floor at the bottom of the hellish chasm. Then he heard footsteps.

Ω

269

Deep beneath his heavily fortified Manor Home on the north-western border of Illa-sarra, Duke Jerord Dassan, Master of the Second Realm of Jala-bakor, wrinkled his nose against the smell. 'I'd sooner start seeing the necessity of all this death,' he remarked, as he watched another heart being thrown into the incinerator.

'Soon,' another man promised as he stood back from the heat. He was tall and well-built, with long white hair that made him look considerably older than the four decades weighing upon his cursed soul. 'We may be separated from the galaxy, but the Lines have their memories. And they know something is due.'

'How can memories tell the future?' Dassan turned to the white-haired man: 'And don't look at me like I'm an idiot, Balaam! This is all new to me, as you well know.'

Balaam inclined his head. 'Of course, my lord,' he replied sarcastically. 'It's simple, really. The Lines map fate, destiny, the passage of time…whatever you want to call it. They are living repositories of the past, present, and future of whoever or whatever they represent. Because they are anchored at the point of conception, the past of an individual or creature or even a planet is preserved. But because they also map out the entire future of their host, from the moment of conception, they are essentially projections of our lives. The Lines here on Kiranis which had for such a short time been connected to the Sentience still retain the memories of all their futures. But they're too faint for us to see any details.'

'I don't believe in fate, Balaam. You know that. We create our own futures.'

'I'm inclined to agree with you, Dassan. The Lines can be manipulated, twisted, shaped…and so too can the future of the host. In theory, we shouldn't be able to trace a Fate Line so easily into the future, but we think the Prophet has something to do with that.'

'Because he's from the future.'

'Precisely. Which is why he's no prophet at all. Merely a tourist in his own past.'

Dassan saw the distaste in Balaam's face, his features flickering in the light from the incinerator and the gas lamps around them. 'You resent the power that gives him,' the duke observed cautiously.

'Very much so,' Balaam admitted. 'But I think this is the way to tip the balance in our favour.'

'All of us?' asked Dassan, knowing the answer. 'Or just your kind?'

'My...*kind* are working with the fate of all of us in mind, Dassan. You'd do well to remember that.'

Dassan nodded slowly. 'If I forget again,' he said with barely disguised venom as he stepped past his guest and made for the steps to the door, 'I'm sure you'll find my Line and ensure I'm reminded.'

Balaam smiled thinly. 'What a fine alliance we have, Duke Dassan,' he remarked without turning.

'A match made in Heaven,' Dassan quipped as he closed the door behind him, the smell of burning hearts suggesting that perhaps this time he had gone too far.

Ω

In the semi-industrialised town of Laden's Folly, Turlow the smith was closing up for the night when he heard the sound of a carriage approaching. A team of four black horses pulled the dark brown carriage, and Turlow recognised the crest on the side. 'Damn that boy,' he muttered as he stepped out to greet the duke's aide.

The teamster drew the carriage to a halt and climbed down to open the door and fold out the iron two-step. 'My dear Turlow,' a jolly voice called from inside. 'Do come in...' There was a laugh. 'If you're clean enough.'

Turlow smiled. 'I've never known a blacksmith clean enough for a duke's carriage,' he replied, mounting the two-step and entering the bronze-embossed wooden contraption. He sat next to the passenger. 'It's good to see you again, Harold.'

'And you, Turlow. Tell me, why has the duke's new mare not been brought to the paddock?'

'Straight to the point, eh? That's what I like about you, Harold. No nonsense.'

'Not where the duke is concerned. And believe me, Master Smith, the disappearance of a prize mare is his concern.'

'We can't call it a prize mare 'til it's at least run a race,' Turlow pointed out.

'Perhaps. But it was running like lightning out beyond Churchfield. Then it just...' He made a gesture and said, 'Vanished.'

'And how could you know that?'

'We had someone keep track of it. Someone...special.'

Turlow turned up his nose. 'You mean one of those...mind freaks?'

'They call themselves Sensitives, Turlow, and you'd be well advised to keep your opinions to yourself.'

'I'm sure that wouldn't make any difference,' Turlow argued. 'If the rumours are true, they could tell what I thought of them without me even saying it.' He looked up and called out, 'Isn't that right?'

Harold smiled an evil little smile. 'You may mock,' he said, 'but the duke has been gathering these people to his service lately, and their leader...well, that's for another day. The horse, Turlow. I want it found. And if it's dead...'

'Yes?'

'You'll lose your forge.'

'But it's all I *have*,' snapped Turlow. 'You can't take my *livelihood* from me!'

'Racing is the livelihood of the duke and his friends, Turlow. If you've lost or killed a racing horse, you'll pay for it.' The temperature seemed to drop in the carriage. 'Consider this a light sentence for the theft of ducal property. Another man would hang.'

'I've stolen *nothing*!' roared the smith. 'How dare you accuse me –'

'Turlow!' someone called from outside. The smith looked out to see two men waiting for him, and his heart plummeted as he recognised the boy's father. 'Has Robert come back?' asked the father, a man whose brutish appearance belied his compassionate nature. 'Did he ride the mare?'

'The truth is out,' whispered Harold. 'A farm boy has stolen the horse.'

'He didn't steal it.' Turlow stepped down from the carriage and addressed the man: 'He's been gone all day, Gareth. I sent out a searcher, but there's been no sign of him. And the dragon didn't come back.'

'That's not a good sign, Turlow,' Gareth replied. 'Do you have any horses?'

272

Harold moved to the door. 'Oh, Turlow gives out horses to anyone these days,' he remarked with a grin. 'He's a charitable man.'

Turlow pointedly ignored him and nodded to the boy's father. 'Go round the back. There's a gelding and a stallion. Saddle them both.'

'That won't be necessary,' a deep voice interjected. They turned to see in the light thrown by the carriage lamps a huge, black-skinned man riding an enormous black stallion. He was sporting fine clothes, but they were road-worn and as tired as he. 'None of you will be going out there,' he continued. 'You know the rules.'

Harold stepped down from the carriage. 'And who are you to remind us of the rules?' he demanded. 'I am Aide to Duke Jerord Dassan, master of this realm.' As Harold moved closer, he saw that the man's facial features were fixed, his skin reflecting the flame. A mask.

'He's a Guard!' Turlow gasped, moving up to Harold and easing him back. 'Sir, we apologise,' said the smith, eyeing one of the pistols hanging from the man's belt. 'A boy has gone missing.' He pointed to Gareth: 'This man's son. We think he passed the markers.'

'Accidentally,' Gareth added. 'He probably couldn't control his horse.'

'*His* horse!' muttered Harold. The Guard looked at the duke's aide for a moment, before saying, 'Hurry back to your master, little man. Advise him that I'll be visiting soon. And that a stolen horse is the least of his concerns.' He turned his horse and Gareth called after him, 'Will you look for my boy? His name's Robert.'

Haphory presumed the worst, but humans thrived on hope, so he nodded: 'I'll find him.'

Ω

The carriage stopped outside the main entrance of the Manor Home and Harold wasted no time in disembarking. He reached out of the window and opened the door himself, leaping to the ground with uncharacteristic agility. The panic had set in, and he rushed past the guards as they held open the great double doors of the duke's residence, daring not to wipe his feet before trampling the

273

dirt of his travels across the carpets, and coming to his senses only as he reached the doors of the duke's study. He knocked.

'Come in, Harold,' he heard the duke call, and the door was opened for him. Seated behind the darkwood desk of the study was a man of enormous build to whom Harold was growing uncomfortably accustomed. His hair was long and white, his bright eyes glistened in the candlelight, and a smile on his crimson lips mocked the duke's aide. Harold looked around for the duke, who sat in a leather chair in the corner of the room, a goblet of wine in his right hand, profiled in a half-light of flickering flame. 'My lord.' He respectfully bowed. 'There is a...situation in the town. I'd prefer to speak with you in private.'

The duke disagreed. 'Where we spoke would make little difference to Balaam.'

Harold swallowed his distaste and inclined his head to the man, who did not respond. 'A farm boy has gone missing out at Churchfield,' Harold explained, 'along with your newest horse. The boy's father and Turlow the smith were about to search for him when a...a Guard showed up.'

Balaam rose from his chair, and Harold blinked at the height of the man. 'Describe him,' he demanded.

'Ah...it was dark, but...black skin, a black mask. His eyes looked...yellow, I think...'

'Haphory,' Balaam realised. 'A formidable Mediator to send amongst us.'

The duke left his chair and looked at Balaam: 'So they know what we're doing?'

'They may not know yet that *we're* doing it, Dassan. But yes, they must have found the bodies.'

Dassan flung his goblet across the room and roared, 'And how would they *not*? Your men left them in plain sight!'

Balaam stepped up to him until their noses were almost touching, and Harold heard a vicious whisper from the white-haired Sensitive: 'Not everyone can reach your depths, Dassan. But next time we'll see how *your* men fare!'

Dassan stood his ground and held the glare of the taller man, until Balaam backed away and returned to the chair behind the desk. 'Where did this...Guard go, Harold?' the duke asked eventually.

'He said he'd find the boy and he left. I presume he's at the outpost by now.'

'Send riders to the outpost but tell them to wait outside the markers. If they see the Guard returning, they can tell this...Haphory...that they're escorting him back to me.'

'And...the boy, my lord? If the Guard finds him?'

'You know the answer to that, Harold. But the timing will depend on whether they get an opportunity to kill him out there, under that creature's protection, or whether it should wait until he gets back here. We will see.'

Harold nodded and sighed dejectedly. 'Might I ask...for clarity, I suppose...what happens if the Watchers are revealed?'

The duke looked to Balaam, who seemed to delight in his response: 'Chaos.'

Harold felt his distaste rise again. That was not very clear at all.

Ω

Robert remembered hearing the footsteps, and he clearly recalled the onset of dread as he tried to assess the situation. Beyond that, there was nothing until he awoke where now he lay, on the most comfortable bed he had ever known. He supposed that the duke might have beds such as this in his Manor Home, but no peasant had ever set foot in that great house. Of course, that did not mean that he could not be in the house now. He had suffered a strange and terrible accident. Perhaps he had been rescued by the duke's men and brought back to the Manor Home until they had determined who he was. Then his father would be informed.

The lights in the ceiling were blinding, and as Robert took the time to focus upon the white surface above him, he realised that the source of the glowing illumination eluded him. The entire ceiling appeared to be alight, devoid of any lanterns or even the grand chandeliers said to be aloft in the Manor Home. It gradually dawned on Robert that he was somewhere completely different, and the dread returned.

He was not bound to the bed, which was a good start. Swinging his legs over the side and touching his feet to the floor, he gazed round at the light grey walls and the other beds in the room. And the silence remained. He was certainly not being watched or stalked. For some reason, this made him more uncomfortable, as

275

he imagined how alone he might be. If danger were close, it was always better to know it and appraise it than to imagine a hundred things worse.

He had been stripped of his clothes and dressed in a pure white gown, tied at the back in two places – the back of his neck and the small of his back. Naked underneath, he felt suddenly self-conscious, and he looked around the strange room again, at the bare grey walls, broken into sections by black lines that looked more like…

One of the sections began to move, confirming that the black lines were, indeed, cracks in the walls, like doors. The section directly opposite his bed pushed into the room and then moved slowly aside, revealing a way out. For a moment, the space outside the room was black and indefinable, but Robert's movement in its direction caused it to be lit up. He paused, his heart in his throat as he took another look around the room. Why were there so many beds? More importantly, why were they all empty? Curiosity took control, and Robert made his way slowly towards the door. As he moved, the lights in the room dimmed behind him, until in stages they were gone. He turned to look back into the shadows in which he had slept, and a shiver crept up his spine. He hurried out the door.

He was then in a corridor, illuminated this time by a row of tiny, round lights in the ceiling. Like eyes, they stared at the frightened boy below, guiding him to whomever had brought him. To his right, the lights were not active, forcing him to travel left. Robert was no fool, and he was not comfortable with this mystery. More than this, though, Robert did not like to be told what to do. He struggled with his decision for a while, peering into the darkness to his right while the door closed behind him, cutting off any remaining light from the room of beds. Now the near darkness threatened, and the choice was a little easier. He headed left, gathering the back of his gown as a breeze teased his nakedness. He drew the gown round to his side, holding it tight as he walked.

The walls were black, made of neither stone nor wood. With his left hand, he touched the wall beside him, feeling an icy chill run through him. This impossibly smooth surface was cold to the touch, but this chill did not seem to emanate from it. Certainly, there was a breeze, but it felt as if it were coming from an open space ahead, not from all around him. It was confusing, for cold walls should make for a cold home.

There came the sound of voices from up ahead, lowered in quiet conversation, but sufficiently loud and intrusive to halt Robert in his tracks. He was breathing heavily in apprehension, part of him anxious to discover who had brought him here and what this place was, another desperate to run and hide. He suddenly missed his parents more than anything and began to imagine that he would never see them again. It was this thought that caused him to stand his ground, once more realising that the unknown fears would unman him. He would face this mystery and deal with the consequence.

Footsteps accompanied the voices now, and Robert felt dizzy as he felt the pulsing in his neck and imagined his heart exploding with terror. He could hear words now:

'...duke only wants power,' a woman's voice was saying, 'and he knows his Sensitives can give it to him.'

'The dragons won't allow him break his word,' a man replied. 'They have to keep Naveen's laws.'

'We'll have to see what the boy can do. He might change all that.'

Robert let out a little sound of shock, before beginning a slow retreat. 'Did you hear that?' the woman asked. 'You think he got out?'

The footsteps quickened and Robert turned and ran, his bare feet slapping against the smooth floor. His pursuers burst into a run as he approached the darkness where the glowing eyes ended. Without caring what he would find or stumble upon, he plunged into the blackness. 'It's okay, kid!' the man called from behind him. 'We're not going to hurt you.'

'Illuminate Section 3-C.'

The lights came on above him, and Robert stumbled and tripped, tumbling head over heels as they caught up with him. He scrambled back to the wall, his courage dissolved as he looked up at the black-garbed figures. The woman had beautiful skin, like polished darkwood. 'Who are you?' Robert asked desperately. 'Why did you bring me here?'

The man – pale, blonde, and lightly bearded – hunkered before him. 'You remember falling off your horse?'

277

Robert nodded, still spooked. 'The ground just broke apart,' he said. 'I forgot about the markers.'

'Don't worry about that now,' the man assured him, his eyes kind and warm in the harsh light. 'You're very important to us. Which is why we made your horse come this way.' He smiled. 'You might say we called her home.'

'Home?' Robert looked around again. 'I don't understand.'

'You will,' the woman said. 'In fact, you'll soon be the only person on Kiranis to truly understand.'

'Understand what?'

'Hopefully…everything,' said the man, standing and offering his hand. As Robert took it and got to his feet, the woman asked, 'So, are you gonna tell us your name?'

'I'm Robert,' he replied politely. 'I'm from Churchfield, just outside Laden's Folly.'

'Good to meet you, Robert,' said the man, as the woman smiled. 'My name's Benjamin…and this is my wife, Celeste.'

Celeste chuckled softly: 'And I suppose you could say we're from Churchfield, too.'

Ω

Even in the darkness, Haphory could see the first circuit of marker stones. Or he could at least see the two between which he passed and thus project the circuit from there. The second circuit would have larger stones, their placement alternating with the first, and it was unlikely the boy could have passed them both without seeing any. Of course, Haphory was not human, and had considerably stronger senses, so he reserved judgement, knowing there was no way to know what had happened until and unless he found the boy. And he was reserving very little hope on that count.

As he approached the second line of stones, he could hear the growls of Grey Slaves in the darkness, those lost souls whose hunger for human flesh was a manifestation of their fury at losing Leviathan to the void. Whatever human element of their constituent selves remained, it had long been forced so far down in the warped and primitive psyche of the Greys that their ability to learn, to question, to rationalise was gone. They knew nothing but violence; and while they were mere vermin compared to their twisted, scheming brethren living in the depths of the world or on

278

ocean floors, they were numerous vermin. 'They're the least of your concerns,' a woman's voice came from ahead of him. A light shone in his direction. Not a flaming torch or a gas lamp, but something else. Something which projected out from its source and blinded its target. Haphory raised one hand, reaching for a gun with the other. 'And that'll do you no good here.'

A much stronger light, floating high above the scene, illuminated the group of men and women who stood before him. There were five of them, and normally this would give Haphory little pause, but these were Watchers, and they had weapons very different to the six-shooters at his disposal. Bulky metal rifles were aimed at him, and he raised his other hand. 'It would be a mistake to kill me,' he reminded them.

'As it would for you to continue,' said the woman. 'Don't confuse us with your usual interactions.'

'Do you know who I am?'

'No. But we know *what* you are. A Mediator for Asherah. And we're not subject to any agreements your kind have made with the people of this world.'

Haphory nodded. 'I find that ironic, considering you brokered them.'

'Keeping the people of Kiranis from finding out where they came from was, and still is, our mission.'

'And you don't ask yourselves the point of that mission?' Haphory pressed, as he boldly dismounted and walked towards them. 'You keep your ways and means hidden from them...for what reason? To feel stronger than them? Is that what your puppet master desired?'

A weapon was cocked and Haphory stopped. The woman stepped out from the group: 'We do what we were told to do, what our ancestors were brought here to do. We populated this planet with animal and plant life so these people could survive. We spread stories of their belonging to this world until eventually they believed them, so they wouldn't waste endless generations obsessed with trying to get off a world that isn't even spinning in the cosmos! And guess what...they didn't.' She stepped closer and looked up at his dark mask. 'Don't underestimate the difficulty of our work...or its purpose.'

Haphory smiled, but the gesture was lost behind his mask. 'Shame you didn't extend the same...courtesy to the descendants

279

of the Garran your owner trapped here along with the rest of us. But then I imagine there are limits to your compassion.'

The woman held a finger to her ear, and Haphory could hear a tiny voice before she replied, 'There most certainly are...Haphory. Now tell me what you're doing here.'

Haphory hunkered down, splaying the fingers of both hands on the ground and closing his eyes. The woman felt a stinging in her chest as Haphory smiled and rose again. 'We all have our tricks...Julieanna,' he reminded her, the echoes of her fate fading from his mind. He had paid little attention to anything but her identity. 'And I'm *here*...because this is the closest outpost to the massacre I discovered. A hundred or more people with their hearts ripped out.'

He allowed the stunned silence to linger, and Greys could be heard anew. Julieanna took the lead: 'Who's behind it?'

'Probably a Sensitive called Balaam. If he hasn't already discovered the truth about this world, he soon will.'

'And if he already has?'

'Then he won't delay in recruiting others and spreading fear. And then all your...work will be undone.'

Julieanna grinned knowingly. 'And you expect me to believe that you came here to warn us?' She shone her flashlight on the skin of his arms, illuminating the stitched black skin. 'You're a defector, Haphory. A relatively recent recruit to Asherah's side, I imagine.'

'Don't presume to understand me, human!' Haphory barked. 'You couldn't fathom the sacrifices I've made. And I'm here to warn you that Balaam won't be working alone. If he's gathering hearts, then he's looking for ones with power. And do you know what that means?'

Julieanna and the others clearly did not know, and he shook his head: 'For all your power over the people of this world, you still don't get what's going on.'

'Enlighten us,' said Julieanna. 'And get a move on, it's getting cold.'

'It's all in the Lines. They remember what was supposed to happen, but of course the lives of humans are too short for their Lines to be of any use. Our Lines, on the other hand, are anchored in the beginning of this world.'

Julieanna nodded, unable to maintain her façade of indifference. 'What's supposed to happen? What are we missing?'

'Your people...back on your home planet...they have a plan. To bring Kiranis back.'

'What?' Julieanna gasped, exchanging shocked expressions with her group. 'How?'

'That much wasn't clear,' Haphory lied. 'But what's most pressing for the...stability you've created...is that the Sensitives have become power hungry and they want to know more. If Kiranis is reconnected to the Sentience, they'll become the dominant power on this world, but it won't be Asherah who'll teach them.' He left it there. He was a Mediator, after all, and had merely to plant the seed. Julieanna stared at him, holding the gaze of his yellow eyes through that soulless mask until the penny dropped.

'That's not possible,' she said. 'Is it?'

'Whoever pulls their strings believes it is.'

'So, the hearts...'

Haphory nodded. 'I'll leave the rest to you.' He returned to his horse and nudged it back into the darkness. But before he was out of earshot, he called back, 'And if you haven't killed the boy for trespassing...return him safely to his father.'

The group gathered close to Julieanna, their questions coming fast: 'What did he mean?' 'What's not possible?' 'What do they want the hearts for?' She raised her hands and said, 'I'll explain everything. But we've a lotta work to do, and we need to broadcast the details of this attack to every outpost on the planet.'

They made their way back to the chasm leading to their subterranean home, and one of the men asked Julieanna, 'Do you think he knows why we have the boy?'

She shook her head: 'If he did, he'd have killed us all.'

Ω

The boy was sitting with Benjamin and Celeste, the three of them on a soft couch. They were in a room smaller than the one in which he had woken, yet still it was larger than his home. The walls were white, the furniture a shiny grey, with legs and arms made from a material not unlike that used for the finest weaponry. Benjamin must surely have known he was compounding Robert's

281

confusion when he asked, 'What do you see when you look up at night?'

Robert stared at him for a moment, then looked beyond him to search Celeste's face for any sign that the question was posed in jest. There was none. 'The...stars?' he replied carefully.

Benjamin nodded and smiled. 'I was hoping you wouldn't say dragons,' he said. 'That's a completely different conversation...and one for later. But yes, you see stars. Now what would you say if I told you they weren't real?'

The boy laughed. 'Then I wouldn't believe you,' he argued. 'Of course they're real. Everyone knows that.'

Celeste leaned in and trapped his gaze, all trace of amiability gone. 'Everyone's wrong,' she told Robert, who found himself hypnotised by her beautiful eyes. 'Everyone believes what we told them.'

'Well...' Benjamin put in, 'what our ancestors told their ancestors.'

'I don't understand.' Robert found himself retreating from them on the long couch, but he was already close to the wall, and to get up would look weak. 'Who are you people?'

Recognising Robert's discomfort, Benjamin rose from the couch and went to pour them some water. 'The people who know about us call us the Watchers,' Celeste explained. 'It's a mysterious little title we've been happy to promote.'

Benjamin handed Robert a glass of cold water and he gratefully accepted. 'There's so much we have to tell you, Robert,' the man told him. 'But there may be an easier way. We've found that those we need to teach learn better if they've seen the truth.'

'The truth about what?'

'About this planet, Robert. About the stars, the galaxy...our people.'

Celeste moved across the room to a cabinet and withdrew a strange device. It looked like a helmet, but Robert saw copper-like strings between the panels. 'Close your eyes, Robert,' she advised gently. 'This won't hurt...but you'll have to relax.'

'Wait!' He raised his hands, his courage dissolved. 'I want to go home now.'

'It's okay,' Benjamin tried to assure him. 'This is just something that'll help you see what happened. Where we came from.'

282

'Where *you* came from, Robert,' Celeste added. 'All of us.' She brought the helmet down to his head, and this time he allowed her to place it on him. He was trembling, but she took his hands once she had secured the device. 'This will only take a few seconds. I'll count to five and it'll all be done.'

He nodded gently, feeling the weight of the strange helmet. Benjamin tapped a device and Robert went into a short convulsion as the data was transferred. He could hear Celeste counting, but days passed between the numbers. He saw a planet, blue and white, and the scene was mesmerising, especially for a boy whose world had until recently stretched only as far as the boundary stones. An enormous cage appeared, surrounding the planet before closing upon it. The planet vanished and then flashed back into existence. The cage broke apart and vanished. Then Robert's vantage point sped across the stars and blackness to which he had only just been introduced, and he saw the cage again, this time around a chaotic mass of rock and flame which gradually solidified to become a planet. And he knew which one it was. He saw the pods released into the world, some of the people inside them screaming with terror as others remained unconscious.

Robert was moaning as if in a nightmare, and it built to a scream as he clawed at the helmet. Benjamin deactivated it and Celeste removed it as the boy retreated to the corner as if hunted. His breathing was laboured, his heart pounding as his wide eyes brimmed with tears. 'That can't be true!' he gasped. 'I was born here. My father and mother were born here…and theirs!'

'Yes, they were,' Benjamin agreed. 'But what you saw happened almost a thousand years ago, Robert. The device around this planet…it's still there. And it took Kiranis out of the galaxy…away from the stars.'

Celeste knelt before him and took his hands again. 'That's why they're not real, Robert,' she explained softly. 'It's a trick, an illusion.'

'Everyone has difficulty accepting it at first,' Benjamin assured him. 'But it'll make sense the more you learn.'

'You mean I'm not the only one you've taken?'

'No, Robert. Everywhere there's a Watchers' outpost on Kiranis, a child has been taken for this very purpose. A special child, yes, but there are many on Kiranis. We just have to bring them round to our way of thinking.'

'Why?'

'Because the illusion's about to be shattered. And when it does…we're gonna need protection.'

Ω

Haphory was not far from the Watchers' outpost when the duke's riders emerged from the darkness around him. 'Where's the boy?' one of them demanded gruffly as he drew rein. 'The duke wants him delivered to the Manor Home.'

Haphory's keen eyes surveyed the group. Killers all, they likely had little respect for the agreements made between their kind and his. 'I'm sure he's eager to see a farm boy safely returned to his parents,' he mocked evenly. 'Unfortunately, I couldn't find him for you.'

The lead rider grinned, enjoying the bravado. He rarely encountered men with the guts to stand up to him. 'He's probably dead, then,' he replied. 'A shame.'

'A terrible shame,' Haphory agreed, noting that the men were pretending to have skittish horses and manoeuvring into a semi-circle around him. He took firm control of his horse with his knees and lowered his hands to his guns. 'No one should have to die out here,' he cautioned them, 'or even suffer a debilitating wound. Slaves often toy with their food.'

The men looked to each other, clearly processing the possibilities. And the implications. 'We have our orders,' the leader pressed, drawing his sword. Haphory acted the instant the others did the same, shouting as he reared his horse and he opened fire. Two men were shot from their horses, a third falling from his frightened steed as Greys roared with anticipation in the distance and the others attacked Haphory. The leader slammed his horse into Haphory's before it grounded itself, and Haphory was thrown, narrowly avoiding being crushed by his mount. He rolled and came up firing, taking another rider to his right, but one of them had anticipated well and he slashed down with his sword, severing some of Haphory's fingers on his left hand. The Mediator roared in agony, coming to his knees as his hand pumped blood to the earth and the Slaves moved in with the scent of death arousing their hunger.

284

Reacting to the shift in power, the riders dismounted and came to Haphory, even as one of their fallen was dragged from the scene by a Grey Slave and his screaming chilled their blood. Like all Greys now on Kiranis, it was roughly the size of a rhinoceros, with an elongated head and a row of sharp bones running from snout to tail. It had two sets of tusks protruding from the sides of its head, one curving upwards, the other down.

Behind his mask, Haphory gritted his teeth and found his resolve, but a throwing knife slammed into his chest as he managed to take another shot with his good hand. The bullet struck a Slave as it made to take his horse, and it let out an angry howl as it backed away. 'Not so cocky now, dragon man,' the leader sneered. 'Think we should put you out of your misery.' He pushed Haphory with his foot and the Mediator fell to his left side, going down on his bloodied hand. Haphory growled, the sound not unlike that of the bullet-struck Grey, and he felt his head swimming.

He was unaware of the men closing in around him, but then something happened that changed all that. He felt the Lines, their Lines. But this was different, because his bloody fingers were feeling them pulsing through the ground, and it was as if their power was flowing back into him. As the blood continued to flow into the ground, the connection became stronger, and in his mind, Haphory felt as if his whole, undamaged hand, could grab the Lines of those around him. He did not feel in the real world the forced removal of his mask and the exposure of his mutilated face, or hear the disgusted reactions of the duke's men, lost as he was in this revelation.

The leader took Haphory's gun and shot an approaching Slave. The bullets would not kill one of these monsters, but they hurt sufficiently to make them think twice about attacking. 'Remove his head while I keep these things back!' the leader ordered. But he never got a chance to fire another bullet. Haphory, his mind focused on the plane of existence wherein the Lines could be seen and felt, manipulated…he grabbed the leader's Line and wrenched it, pulling him from his feet. He twisted as he fell on his face and the gun went off with his arm underneath him as Haphory snapped back into the world. The last two men went to him as soon as they realised he wasn't moving, and when they rolled him over they saw the wound in his chest.

Haphory took advantage of their confusion, moving swiftly to a horse and jumping to its back. Twisting the reins in his good hand, he made eye contact with a Slave moving in. It snarled at him but made no move to attack. Instead, it passed him, followed by two others. The duke's men could be heard screaming and their bones crunching before Haphory kicked the horse into a run. Before he confronted the duke, he needed to find somewhere quiet to commune with Asherah. Because as far as he knew, what he had just done had never been done before.

Ω

Balaam could sense that something significant had occurred, but he could not have explained how. Both a curse and a blessing as it was, the Gift was attuned to the twists of Fate and Time. The great majority of humankind was oblivious to the significance of everyday events, seeing merely the immediate or imagined consequences of their actions. To imagine wider, far-reaching consequences, one had at least to possess a considerable intellect. Balaam was fully aware that the duke was a man of considerable intellect, a man to watch carefully. If this had not been so, the man would have been dead long ago. And Balaam would have held the blooded knife. Sent here by his masters, one of Balaam's tasks was the appraisal of the duke's loyalties. War was coming, and it was imperative that the Masters gather trusted men and their money and people, for not all could be achieved by the same means.

Balaam had been on the floor on his belly, spreadeagled, his head to one side and his eyes closed. With his hands open and fingers apart, he had felt a tingling in his fingertips, gritting his teeth as the pain in his head began. It was always thus, lost momentarily to their power, their need to feed on the circle of life and death, drawing on his mental energy, longing to find purchase and purpose. The Lines were more than just repositories of events; they were the veins of the Network. And on Kiranis, they bled freely.

Like all Sensitives, Balaam had learned from the Masters that something had happened in this galaxy in the past, something which had altered the physical composition of the Universe and forced the galaxy from its established position in the heavens. And now, the Lines sought a way to reconnect, to become one with the Universe as they once had been. Like all Sensitives, Balaam knew that this world, Kiranis, and the other of which the Masters spoke, Earth, held the keys to this conundrum. Some Sensitives mused that this Earth was the place from which the human part of the Masters had come, but this was never a matter to be pressed during times of Commune. For the Masters' fury was potent. To quell that fury, to make it at the very least justifiable, something had to happen, something as massive and seemingly irreversible as that which had occurred in that long forgotten past, that which had severed this galaxy's link with the Universe. And, like all Sensitives, Balaam knew that the time for this event was near. Of course, what must first happen was the reconnection of Kiranis to the galaxy to which it belonged.

As a result of this grand scheme, the petty conflicts of the lesser humans on Kiranis – and even of the politics and interventions of dragons – were of little interest to the Sensitives, no more than a pastime to keep their minds busy and healthy, and their abilities honed. Still, it was a pastime in which Balaam discovered enjoyment. It sometimes had the ability to surprise him, as it had today. Balaam had allowed his mind to relax as the Lines permitted a reprieve from pain. In his mind's eye, he had followed the Line most significant to him, back from its futile probing of the skies, where he always encountered an ethereal wall keeping him in check. Travelling back along it, he had raced back down from the sky and across the world to the land in which he dwelled and even the room in which he lay. In so doing, Balaam had initiated a pulse which brought him to Introspection, allowing the Sensitive to disconnect from the Lines while still holding on to an echo of their memory.

Seeing himself rising from the floor, he had felt his inner self float upwards and outwards, until he was above the Manor Home of the duke. It was night where he lay, but day where he flew, and the boy Robert was riding out beyond Churchfield. Balaam watched him tumble from his steed, both falling into the darkness. The Watchers rescued the boy, saving him from certain death. Balaam could not see down any farther, could not discern their next course of action. It was not possible to delve into the outpost, despite being able to perceive Lines disappearing into the darkness of the chasm. The Masters had not explained why this was so, but Balaam imagined that it was down to the strange energy emanating from the marker stones surrounding the site.

So, the Watchers had found another one. They would not tell him the whole truth, of course, merely a redaction of their purpose. Maintaining the false stories of the reality of Kiranis, both past and present, was their mandate, but the reasons for its perpetuation were being kept from the Sensitives. The Masters told them only as much as they thought was necessary to achieve their ends. And now that the bloodshed had been noticed by the Great Dragons, those ends would become clear before the Masters had intended.

Balaam's ethereal self hovered over the chasm above the Watchers' outpost, and willed time forward until the Mediator, Haphory, was intercepted by the Watchers themselves. While Balaam's non-corporeal eyes were unhindered by the darkness, sound was never available from this perspective, and so he could only watch and wonder at the exchange. The Watchers brandished weapons the likes of which Balaam had never seen, but even the Mediator's pistols, undoubtedly manufactured in the heavily industrialised lands far to the east, posed a considerable threat in a land of swords and arrows. Balaam knew that reproducing those guns would tip the balance in favour of the Masters. If he could get his hands on the weapons of the Watchers…

But that was a problem for another day. The conversation was only slightly heated, by the looks of it, and the Mediator mounted his horse and left the Watchers to their deceit. It was not long before Balaam saw the duke's men intercepting the mutated dragon. There was a fight. There was always going to be a fight, and Balaam was unsurprised that the Mediator won. Certainly, it had almost swung in favour of the duke's soldiers, but Balaam witnessed a wonderful event that he knew would change everything for his kind. Haphory had used the Lines, not just for communication or travelling in any direction, but for affecting the present. For manipulating the immediate circumstances in which the owner of the Line found himself. In short, Haphory had made the leap from observation to interaction, from the ethereal to the corporeal.

Balaam watched him continue his journey, realising with a smile that he was heading to Laden's Folly. Perhaps intending to confront the duke, but no matter. Haphory, the Mediator man-dragon who had just stumbled upon a new way to use the Lines, was coming to visit. And Balaam knew that a pair of guns made in the east paled in comparison to what he had just seen.

The depths of Kiranis were like the depths of any world bearing life, its engine-like core creating a magnetic field to protect its inhabitants from being irradiated and holding them to the land like a mother desperate to keep her progeny tied to her apron strings. Gravity was the hand of the world, and great guidance was required if one somehow attained freedom from its grip and wished to survive. Thankfully, as Asherah knew, no one on Kiranis was even aware that such a thing was possible. At present, she was more like the mother of the world, trying against all odds to keep the people of Kiranis – human, Garran and dragon alike – from discovering the truth about their isolation from the Universe. In this, she was on the side of the Watchers, and she knew that those guiding the Sensitives were reckless in their planned course of action. Which was why she had to confront them.

In her dragon form, and accompanied by three ferociously loyal Reds, she came to a hole in the world, a great impact crater whose floor had been torn open by those who wished to live in the gaseous darkness to which it led. The Reds were amongst a number of dragon subspecies who could not grasp the power of the Lines, and so could not change their form at will. They alighted around Asherah's now human form, as her bare feet delicately touched the burned and barren crater floor. 'I go on alone,' she told them, to which they growled their disagreement. She smiled gently, knowing they would claw and tear their way to her if they so much as smelled a threat.

Leaving them behind, she took one last look at the sky before entering the darkness. She could smell them almost as soon as she left the surface air behind. For almost a thousand years, they had dwelt down here, and she knew that these ones were but a contingent of the Deep Dark Ones spread out across the world. They shared the same despair, the same hatred, and that made them a force to be reckoned with. Because they had not surfaced for so long, Asherah needed to know what she would be up against. For they would have learned much in such an age of isolation.

The voice that came to her as she travelled deeper, her feet now bleeding from negotiating the subterranean rock, was like a rancid breath from a throat cut by blades: 'Why is the White Bitch here?'

Asherah's keen eyes searched the rock – the floor, the walls and the ceiling channelled with masochistic force by huge bodies penetrating the world – until she saw a glimmer of intellect. A great eye, its dual-lidded protection drawn back to obscure this intruder. It was enormous, and she perceived a creature much larger than she had expected, many times her dragon size. 'I'm here to speak,' she replied defiantly. 'Your scheming on the surface has been noticed.'

The world rumbled. 'And you imagine that concerns us,' the creature replied. 'You who are the paragon of all that is right and good on Kiranis are compelled to stand in our way, is that it?'

Asherah laughed at the mockery. 'I am…*compelled*…to remind you that Naveen holds the cards. That he won't tolerate you changing the rules.'

'Then where is he?' the creature challenged, its voice reaching a threatening resonance. '*Compel* him to show himself and protect his pets!'

Asherah was silent, and now it was the creature's turn to laugh. 'I know what you fear, Asherah,' it taunted her. 'That perhaps this is the will of your new god. That perhaps Naveen will delight in your failure to maintain the illusion of order.'

She knew it was a possibility, and the creature was absolutely correct. It terrified her to think that no matter what she did, Naveen had seen it and anticipated it. And corrected it according to his needs. 'We have no future in chaos, or separation,' she pleaded. 'We may not be able to anticipate Naveen's plans for us, but surely you see that we have to stay together for whatever he has in store.'

The creature's laughter almost caused the underworld to collapse. 'You've seen the memories of the major Lines, Asherah,' it told her. 'They bear the echoes of the future for Kiranis. We already know what's in store.'

'Reconnection,' said Asherah, nodding. 'To the Universe.'

'To the Sentience!' the creature bellowed fanatically. 'And the moment of our rebirth!'

Asherah felt a terrible sense of dread, a churning feeling of uncertainty to which she had long been unaccustomed. She stumbled as her shock hit home. 'Ah, you realise now how much you've misjudged us, dragon,' the creature gloated. 'We are all over the world. In the oceans, the mountains, under the feet of your precious Watchers. But we don't belong with your kind. Because we...are HUMAN!'

She stepped to the rock and touched it, feeling Lines pulsing so close that there was no need to draw them to her. She found him almost immediately, and his past was intertwined with his present, almost as if he relived it every day. And perhaps, in his madness, he did. Perhaps it was what kept him going. She saw him in a tube, blasted down to the boiling surface of Kiranis. There was integration with one of her kind, but the red dragon which they became was shot from the sky during the Jaevisk defence of the mountain, and the human took the opportunity to fight for dominance. Retreating to a cave, the two minds struggled, until a terrible, writhing thing erupted into existence like pus from a boil. Eventually the light of the non-corporeal entity was snuffed out by the fury of the human. A powerful, obstinate narcissist, substituting his fear for endless resentment. Such was Mannix Relland, Patriarch of the Church of the New Elect.

Asherah turned and fled, unable to change her form in the confines of the cave. The Reds, breathing fire and roaring into the depths, were trying to get to her, but there were too many places through which they could not pass. When she reached them, her eyes told them all they needed to know. That the Deep Dark Ones of Kiranis were not what she had expected. And that the conflict to come would be greater than she had led them to believe.

$$\Omega$$

They had shown Robert the repopulation vaults, countless deposits of DNA samples of animal and plant life indigenous to Earth, the world from which humankind had come. They had shown him star charts and images of planets and moons, and celestial bodies and events the likes of which he had never imagined. They had demonstrated many different devices and equipment and he had misinterpreted the advanced technology as magical, before

Benjamin stopped him in his tracks by saying, 'No, Robert. We can't do magic. But you can.'

'What do you mean?' he argued. 'I don't know any magic!'

'Of all the things we've shown you…' said Celeste, smiling sympathetically as she recognised how overwhelmed he was, 'the most amazing is something that *we* can't do. But we brought you here to tell you about it before introducing you to someone who can teach you.'

'I don't understand. How could I be…special?'

Benjamin laughed gently: 'Because you're descended from the people you saw dropping from the sky. And *they* were special.'

'Our people didn't think they were,' Celeste added, 'or they didn't care about the differences.'

'What differences?'

'It started in their blood,' Benjamin explained. 'Gradually, they separated themselves from the rest of our people. Wasn't long before they started thinking of themselves as better than everyone else. Chosen for something.'

'Like what?'

'I've no idea, to be honest. Not even sure everyone else knew.'

'That's how you make people feel special,' Celeste put in. 'You keep the reason secret.'

Robert nodded: 'You mean like the Sensitives.'

Benjamin was impressed. 'Just like the Sensitives,' he replied. 'They've learned a lot about how this world works and they keep their secrets to themselves. And they're growing in numbers as they find more and more like them.' He held Robert's gaze long enough for the penny to drop, and the boy's eyes widened as he realised: 'I'm like *them*?'

'Yeah. Every human on Kiranis is descended from the people taken from Earth, but not everyone's blood is different…like the first ones. Over time, a lot of people reverted to being…' he shrugged, 'the same as us.'

'So, your ancestors,' Robert asked, 'were never…special?'

Celeste could see that Benjamin did not appreciate the question. 'Not in the way you mean, Robert,' she answered. 'They endured a terrible ordeal, abandoned on this world and charged with making it capable of sustaining life. You saw the repopulation vaults. Imagine having the fate of an entire planet in your hands.'

Robert imagined. They were clearly trying to measure him, to see what he was taking from all this. Something inside him warned him to keep his thoughts to himself, and a red flash behind his eyes made him jump and blink. 'Are you okay?' Celeste asked him gently.

'Yes,' he lied. 'I'm just...' he dismissed any further concerns with a shake of his head. 'So, what makes the Sensitives special, then? What can they do?'

'They can use what they call the Lines,' said Benjamin. 'The Sensitives claim to see them everywhere. Connected to everyone.'

'They're like a...record or map of...our lives,' said Celeste. 'None of us have ever seen one, but...the Sensitives have spent generations learning how to locate them.'

'For what?' asked Robert. 'What do they use them for?'

'To look into our past,' Celeste replied. 'And possibly our future.'

'And to communicate across vast distances,' said Benjamin. 'From one side of the planet to the other, if they want. We think they're all working together...for someone we can't find.'

'Or something,' Celeste suggested. 'Possibly a dragon.'

Robert was mesmerised: 'Why would they work for a dragon?'

'Because I told them to.'

They all turned in the vast room in which they had shown him the galaxy to see a tall man in a black cloak. Two dragons moved within the strange ethereal fabric, one of gold, the other silver. The man's face sported a beard crafted to mimic the darkness between bestial teeth, and when he smiled, the effect was horrific. 'Hello, Robert,' he said. 'You might say I've been waiting a long time to meet you.' He stepped towards them. 'I mean, it was hard for me to get here, but it doesn't actually take that long.'

'Who are you?' Robert demanded with false bravado.

Celeste and Benjamin had never seen him before, but they knew. All the Watchers knew. 'He's the Prophet,' said Benjamin. 'At least, that's what he tells people.'

'He's here to teach you everything we can't,' Celeste explained, a hint of resentment in her voice. 'He's got more secrets than anyone else on Kiranis.'

Naveen laughed. 'Why, thank you, Celeste,' he joked. 'Good of you to say.'

293

Robert pointed at the moving dragons, one of which had just gone up over the man's left shoulder: 'How are you doing that?'

'Oh, I'm not doing anything,' said Naveen, smiling. 'They move around themselves. But they're not happy to be stuck with me, I can tell you that.' He looked to Celeste and Benjamin, saying, 'We're done here. Julieanna has something she needs to tell you.'

Celeste was about to argue, but Benjamin turned to her and gently shook his head: 'Let's go.' She reluctantly left, storming out of the room like a dismissed child as Benjamin followed. He looked back at Robert and then at Naveen, who winked back at him and gestured that he continue on his way.

When they were alone, Robert stood silently while Naveen looked around the room. 'They showed you stars?' he asked with his back to the boy. 'Told you about the galaxy...the Universe...that sort of thing?'

Robert nodded, despite remaining unobserved. 'Yes. And they told me about the Sensitives and the Lines.'

Naveen turned with a nod of approval. 'Do you want to learn more?'

'Like what?'

'Like the universe they can't see. I can't show it to you the way I'd like to. Not yet. But you need to learn how to connect with the Lines and use them in a way that appreciates the bigger picture. A way that understands what they really are. You need to learn to respect them, Robert.'

'Why?'

'Let's just say that the ones on Kiranis have had too much freedom for a long time. And that's all about to change.'

Ω

Haphory needed a drink. A strong drink. His hand still bled, and he had wrapped it in the hope that there would not be a trail of Mediator blood luring Greys to Laden's Folly. That and the fact that every time blood hit the ground, he felt a shock course through him as if the Lines beneath him were leaping up to get his attention. Now crossing the outskirts of the town, he was weak and leaning to one side on his horse.

Laden's Folly was one of those towns wherein the past and the future merged where the infrastructure was concerned, with those favouring old technologies stubbornly holding on to their traditional methods while others unashamedly attempted to bolt, rivet, and weld the past out of existence. A mishmash of buildings spread out across town, owned by different people of different generations, where wood, stone, iron and glass fought for supremacy in an architectural milieu which resulted, in the end, in something beautifully unique.

The town was silent, but a mimicry of sunrise would soon bring it to life. Haphory knew that his presence would alarm the people, but he was in little mood to care as his horse's hooves clipped on the edge of the huge metal circle marking the centre of Laden's Folly. It was elaborately decorated, with swirling patterns lovingly embracing scenes from a legendary tale of foundation. One of Haphory's hands still worked, and he had reloaded his guns. A rustle of movement ahead brought him back to his senses, and he forced himself upright and alert, blinking to register four of the duke's soldiers approaching. Another four came into view up ahead to his right, but almost as if they had materialised from the half-light, the centre of town was soon populated by soldiers, some of them with crossbows, others with swords drawn...but the ones which caught Haphory's attention were the pikemen, approaching with fifteen-foot barbed spears brandished for his pleasure.

'I'm here to see the duke!' Haphory proclaimed as loud and with as much confidence as he could manage. The silence which followed was broken after a time by mocking laughter, and a tall man with long white hair – wearing a dark green robe over an otherwise functional uniform – stepped into view. 'The duke is in no need of...mediation,' this man replied.

'Balaam,' Haphory nodded. 'Choosing a name known for prophecy doesn't make you one, you know.'

'And walking and talking like a *human*,' Balaam replied without hesitation, 'doesn't make *you* one.' He smiled. 'But you're here among us this morning...to be something of a catalyst, I think.'

'A catalyst.' Haphory watched the soldiers as they closed in, and he drew a gun with his good hand. 'For what, exactly?'

'For *change*, Haphory.' Balaam chuckled. 'You don't have enough bullets. And up there on that...*wonderful* horse...for which the duke will be eternally grateful...' and at this he met Haphory's eyes as sunrise began, 'you can't touch the Lines like you did out past Churchfield.'

Haphory was taken aback, and it showed: 'You saw that?'

'You underestimate us. We've had some...education in the ways of this world.'

'From who?'

'There'll be no chance to get your messages to your *bitch* mistress!' Balaam spat. Before stepping back and giving the command with a flick of his hand. Crossbow bolts flew and bullets fired. Men fell and Haphory was struck repeatedly. But of the pikemen, he only managed to waylay two, and three of them got through his defences, piercing his sides and causing a bestial scream to escape from behind the mask. A fourth from his left made it two on each side, and Balaam wasted no time: 'Lift him!'

Haphory was removed from his horse, upwards and in terrific agony. It took some work to calm the horse, but it was led away as the pikes were bending and the Mediator's blood sprayed and poured on to the ground. The pikemen were struggling with the weight, and it was clear the weapons would soon give out. 'Okay,' the Sensitive ordered, 'bring him down!'

It was more like Haphory's body tore itself from the spearheads as he fell from their bite before the pikes were sufficiently lowered. Silent and defeated, he lay face down as Balaam shouted for the crowd's amusement, 'See how your duke's skilled defenders disabled this intruder without hitting any vital organs!' As they cheered and clapped, he leaned down to Haphory and whispered, 'Will I tell these people how your type are made? Hmm? Spoil the surprise that's coming?'

Haphory raised his head with a groan: 'How could you know that?'

'What...because the memories are stuck in the Dragon Lines?' The white-haired Sensitive laughed darkly. 'We've literally been right under your nose, dragon-man,' he mocked. Before Haphory could anticipate it, Balaam tore the mask from his face, revealing the horror beneath. Haphory stayed face down, what remained of his dignity getting the better of him. For years unmeasured he had shielded his features from humans, seeking to blame them for the envisaged consequences. In truth, of course, it was for him that the mask had been cast, for Mediators all over Kiranis displayed their face, many of them proudly, even defiantly. But Mediators all over Kiranis had not suffered a corrupted Reduction as had Haphory.

The process was complex, and in a sense grotesque. The human body from which the mutated dragon form had erupted a millennium ago was still part of that form. It was in there, albeit in its constituent pieces. Reduction was designed to draw it out, together and whole. Asherah and her most trusted disciples used the Lines in a manner kept secret from all others, working as one to recreate the human body of the person taken from Earth who still dwelt in the psychological milieu of the creature pretending to be a dragon. But that was all that was drawn out. And without fail, the human mind was lost completely, reduced to nothing. In Haphory's case, more than this had been lost, for one of the disciples working on the process had become disorientated by the journey into the past. Haphory was forever incomplete. And as Balaam ordered the duke's men to get him to his feet, the townsfolk saw what that meant.

He had no nose, merely a skeletal hole where it should have been. One of his eyes was lower than the other, and shaped badly, and he had only one ear. Again, there was an orifice where further flesh should have been and sculpting should have occurred. His black skin was split in places as if rare meat had been carved, and he had only half of a top lip. Both eyes were yellow, the consistency a small mercy amidst the chaos of his face; a face with no hair to cover the remnants of agony.

'I've never seen one as ugly as you,' Balaam remarked casually, as if seeing him through the bars of a cage. Four soldiers held him tightly, drawing his arms behind him even as his many wounds continued to bleed. 'Now that I see you without your mask, I'm inclined to think of you as all bark and no bite. And I don't say that because you're bleeding to death in the middle of town.'

The skin around Haphory's skeletal nose wrinkled with fury, his broken lip rising to reveal deadly teeth. Balaam laughed and tapped his palm against the man-dragon's charred cheek. 'All bark,' he mocked quietly, before stepping back and turning around so that the now growing crowd could hear what was being said. 'Do you know the story of this town, Mediator?' he asked aloud. 'How it got its name?'

'Do I need to?' Haphory growled. Without the mask, his voice was different. Less menacing. It sounded almost as if it hurt to speak.

'I believe so,' said Balaam confidently. 'After all, you'll be breathing your last here.' This amused many of the onlookers, but the Sensitive was concerned to note that a sizeable portion of the audience appeared to direct their hostile stares at him. He set such concerns aside, for now, and continued: 'Laden was a travelling merchant. A very wealthy one. From time to time, he was held up and robbed along the trade routes, but that's the risk travellers take on the road. Thing was…stories started to spread about how easy it was to rob the man because he *appeared* to become a target for every crook for a thousand miles around! He avoided paying duties and taxes at waystations and borders because…well, because the poor man had been *robbed*. *Again!*' Balaam chuckled. 'But Laden had only ever been robbed once. Isn't that right, folks?'

The people nodded and laughed, many enjoying the tale despite hating the storyteller. 'You see, Mediator…Laden created a sort of network of thieves. He hired men to protect him at first…after the first robbery. But then, realising the value of appearing so…*forlorn* with the odd cut and bruise and a torn shirt…and his wagon looking like a Grey had charged through it…he came up with a plan. And it only had to work once to work well. He had his protection detail stage a robbery…knock him around a bit, and they took his money away and hid it. When he reached the next border crossing or a tax-collector at a market place, he told his story and presented only the goods that the thieves were apparently not bothered taking. And you couldn't take a percentage of material goods in taxes if the people who paid your wages were waiting for those same goods to show off to their friends!

'Laden did this repeatedly along his route, but he never used the same thieves, and they operated within their own territories, so they didn't know each other. Of course, each group got a cut, and he promised them that on his way back, there would be even more. But this is where it got clever. Starting with the second group, he created a cascade effect of betrayal and murder, by telling them that back where he'd just been, a band of thieves had taken his money from the previous leg of his journey. He even told them where to find them. He was counting on the greed of thieves, of course, but who wouldn't take that bet? Each group was wiped out by the last, and gradually, over many months and at the cost of more than a few punches to the face and what have you, the stolen cash was being gathered up and following Laden along his merry way. He never had any intention of going back.

'You know, Laden's legacy made it difficult for anyone to avoid paying taxes ever again. Genuine victims of theft were no longer excused from paying up. All he had to do was hide the money himself and collect it on his way back to where he had come from, but no...he enjoyed the chaos. He enjoyed the death wrought upon those who robbed people for a living. And perhaps he envisaged a kind of justice in it all. Of course, as many would argue...it wasn't his place to dish it out.' By now, Balaam was holding Haphory's baleful glare. And Haphory knew why.

'Get to the point!' Haphory growled.

Balaam grinned. 'Oh, I will,' he threatened, before turning back to the crowd: 'So, Laden became extremely wealthy, but his scheme was discovered, and he went looking for protection amongst the only creatures on Kiranis whom he *presumed* wouldn't have any need for his hoard.' At this he raised his voice: 'Who did he go to?'

'The DRAGONS!' the crowd roared. And Balaam smiled and nodded, saying, 'Precisely. The dragons. One *particular* dragon, with whom he made a deal. He would build a town...right where they spoke...right *here*, in fact...' he pointed at the giant foundation circle before them, 'that would be a symbol of justice and order in a world Laden *knew*...was forever on the verge of chaos. The dragon, for its part, promised to always protect Laden for as long as he used his wealth only to better the lives of the unfortunate.' The Sensitive moved to one side and pointed, shouting, '*This*...dragon!'

The crowd fell silent, and Haphory felt their eyes upon him like arrowheads poised to pierce his flesh. Blood had resumed dripping from his hand, the makeshift bandage fallen to the ground, but this time the connection to the Lines brought something different. Earlier, the jolts of bio-electrical energy had been meaningless; empty refrains from the ground, chiding him for his carelessness. But that had now changed, and he realised what had been happening. An animal eye flashed in his head, and he heard an angry voice promising, 'We're coming for you, brother!'

'This dragon...' Balaam repeated, 'had seen so much more of Kiranis, and he instructed Laden as to how to amass an even greater wealth, connecting him with lines of trade no human could access. This town...*our* town...' Balaam had only been there a few months, but it worked, 'was built. But Laden didn't realise that the money and treasures coming in were the spoils of war, merely to be redistributed amongst its beneficiaries upon their arrival. And arrive...they did.' He addressed Haphory: 'Tell us what happened next, dragon.'

But Haphory did not respond. Almost in a trance now, his subconscious somewhere between Life and the Lines, he was in an involuntary state of deep communication with his incoming rescuer. What he did not expect was that Balaam had anticipated as much. 'I'll tell them, shall I?' he teased, to which the crowd laughed. 'This dragon led the various warlords...which were not all human, I might add, right here to Laden's fledgling town, where they decimated the place each time until one group tore poor Laden limb from limb when he tried to assert his right to his wealth.' He nodded, wrapping things up as his eyes scanned the crowd and he moved back to Haphory. 'I know you're calling them,' he whispered, taking renewed note of the Mediator's bleeding hand, watching as if in slow motion the crimson beads falling to the soil. With a sight beyond that of normal men, and yet not exactly something visual, Balaam discerned the leaping red of Lines engaging with the drops of blood as if catching them purposefully. 'Thank you for the lesson.'

Through the haze, Haphory picked that up, and he raised his head and groaned. But Balaam punched him hard in the face and shouted, '*Never*...make *deals*...with dragons. *That*...was Laden's Folly!'

A chill-inducing roar could be heard in the distance, and the townsfolk shouted and screamed as they saw the huge creature flying towards them. They quickly forgot all about story-time and abandoned the town square, but those who ran into the buildings to the east made a fatal error, as this was where the Green Dragon came down, smashing everything to pieces and crushing bodies beneath its great bulk. Balaam immediately issued his orders, but there was so much more in place than pikes and arrows. Gigantic, weighted nets were launched at the beast from catapults outside the town centre. The front walls of buildings all around dropped like the façades they were, revealing massive crossbows that immediately launched their bolts. The heavy, deep layers of flesh of the Green Dragon absorbed this concerted attack, but still it

300

took a heavy toll, and responded by breathing fire, lashing out with its tail and talons as it moved off the crushed buildings and came quickly at the soldiers, heading inevitably towards the metal memorial to Laden's Folly. When it reached this massive foundation plate, despite burning and clawing at men and women everywhere, everything changed.

The metal circle snapped open, taking the dragon completely by surprise to impale it on scores of barbed spikes twenty feet high. The creature howled in agony and defeat, throwing its head up and burning its anger towards the sky. The catapults around the town had been reloaded with giant boulders, and they hurtled through the air to come down upon the beast, smashing its bones and crushing its great head.

Haphory had been able to crawl back from the melee, but he could not hide from his terror and anguish. Tears flowed from his ruined face as one of his own was torn apart and crushed in such a manner. He tried to find a connection through his blood and the Lines, desperately trying to contact Asherah as he had planned to do in this place, but it was as if the death of the Green Dragon had disrupted the Network. As the dying creature was breathing its last and the men and women of the town returned to appreciate their victory, Balaam came back to taunt the Mediator further: 'Laden's Folly is what we've come to call a Dragon Killer, Haphory. It's one of many such towns and settlements dotted across this planet, all designed to keep dragons interested and then lure one to its death when the time is right. And all across Kiranis...' Balaam leaned closer, grinning hatefully before hissing, 'the time is right!'

He left Haphory there, for he considered the man-dragon inconsequential now that he had his prize. When Haphory heard the Sensitive shout the words, 'Remove its heart! Bring it to the Manor Home!', he felt the true weight of how naïve he had been. For all of this had been engineered to fulfil a single purpose. And worst of all, Asherah must not have known.

Ω

Julieanna had been dreaming of a different life when she was woken by the deafening alarm. In her dream, she lived amongst the people of Kiranis, oblivious to the delicate balance between stability and planetwide anarchy maintained by the Watchers. But

301

just before the alarm went off – or perhaps the disorienting chronology of dreams led her memory to place this before the sound rather than generated by it – she saw an alien face, a Garran. There was something familiar about him, and she fought desperately to hold on to this vanishing image as she came fully awake.

She had fallen asleep in her clothes, not even bothering to lift the bedsheets, and so she swung herself upright and pulled her shoes on. There was a loud knocking on her door. 'Come in!' she called.

Benjamin stepped in, wasting no time: 'They've killed a dragon in Laden's Folly. But it's not like any previous attacks. The Network is in shock and the crystals aren't working. I've only seen it on the monitors, but it looks like the Reaper stone is fading in and out of existence.'

'My God!' she gasped. 'If the dragons find out we've a Reaper down there, they'll come at us with everything.' She headed for the door, and he fell in behind her as she hurried to the elevator.

'We always knew that having unlimited energy would come at a price, Julieanna. The reactors were never gonna last a thousand years!'

'I know that, Benjamin.' People were running past them, getting to armouries and vehicles in preparation for the order to move out. They knew what they were supposed to do, but this was an unprecedented occurrence for which they had only ever trained. Certainly, dragons had been killed before, but this was different. It signified something larger, and required a response, if for nothing more than to prevent escalation. Julieanna and Benjamin stepped into the elevator, and Celeste was already waiting for them. 'I was coming up to get you,' she told them. 'You're not gonna like this.'

The elevator car took them down, way down, into a shielded room that even Asherah's probing of the Lines could not locate. 'You'll need to protect your ears,' Celeste warned them as the car came to a stop. When the doors opened, there was a sound that was at the same time both a high-pitched scream and a low-pitched rumble that seemed to make the inner organs vibrate. Celeste ran to a glass case on the wall to her right with her hands over her ears. The others waited at the elevator door, watching as she opened the case, the glass window shattered and fell to the floor, and she withdrew three pairs of high-powered ear protectors.

302

They put them on and turned the dial to 'Max', immediately feeling the relief from the high-pitched scream but still feeling as if their stomachs were being pressed into their spines.

Julieanna thanked Celeste with a hand on her shoulder before leading the way to the containment room at the end of the corridor. They entered through the south door, coming into the first antechamber within which was a pedestal with a faint red stone roughly twice the size of a human heart. Benjamin moved swiftly to the opposite side of it, waving his hand high in front of it in the hope of seeing something. 'There's no connection,' he gravely announced, before realising he could not be heard. Turning to look at the others, he shouted, 'It's not connecting!'

Julieanna nodded and pointed to the exit door, in which an aperture was set high to channel the red beam of light which should have been coming from the crystal. They headed towards the main chamber. When the exit door closed behind them, they immediately looked up and saw the problem. The Reaper stone was fully visible, and it had fallen before toppling off its high pedestal set in the centre of the large room. This was the point to which the four crystals should have been directing their bio-electrical energy before pulsing upwards as one to push the Reaper stone into a state of quantum flux, at which point it would collect energy from a source still unknown to the Watchers. The sound was not so harmful in the main chamber, and they removed their protection. 'What do we do?' asked Celeste.

Julieanna shook her head. 'I don't know,' she admitted. 'We've enough reserve energy for at least twenty years, but we need to know if this is happening elsewhere.'

Benjamin nodded hopefully. 'Maybe it's just us, with the dragon killed nearby.'

'That would be nice,' the older woman agreed, 'but I've a feeling there's something bigger going on. Naveen doesn't show up for the hors d'oeuvres, and I told you what that Mediator said about the plan to bring Kiranis back.'

'"Bigger" probably doesn't do it justice, then,' said Celeste. 'I'd say…monumental.'

'I'd be inclined to agree.' Julieanna took a deep breath. 'Where's Naveen now?'

Benjamin gave a little grunt of resentment. 'If he hasn't disappeared yet, he's still with the boy who just happened to fall in on top of us.'

'It's hardly the boy's fault,' Celeste reminded him. 'And you didn't have this attitude when you spoke to him.'

Benjamin raised his hands and said sarcastically, 'Oh, don't worry, I played by the rules!'

Julieanna shrugged: 'I think the time for rules is done, Ben. You can vent now if you think it'll do any good.' She headed back to the south chamber, and they followed her through it to the elevator. Naveen and the boy, Robert, were waiting for them when they came back up. 'Why aren't the Slave stones transmitting?' Julieanna demanded. 'We'll have to shut down and will probably need to replenish the whole thing!'

Naveen grinned. 'Testy as always, Julieanna. But I'm going to leave this one to my new protégé. There's somewhere else I need to be, and windows are closing fast.' He vanished, leaving them to turn to Robert for their answers. Visibly fascinated by Naveen's disappearance, Robert took a moment to notice them waiting for his explanation. He could only make educated guesses. 'He told me about the Network,' he began. 'The Fate Lines of every living creature on the planet...all interconnected, mostly indirectly.'

'Mostly *very* indirectly,' Ben said sharply. 'Look, we know what the Network is. Our people around the world have been monitoring it all our lives.'

'No, you haven't,' Robert argued. 'You've been documenting outcomes, theorising on patterns and making predictions. But none of you have seen it...or felt it.'

Julieanna and Celeste exchanged glances, for this young man was clearly more than the boy who had fallen from his horse; but Ben was not impressed. 'Well, look who's grown up in the past five minutes!' he sneered. 'You think because your blood is different to ours that you're *superior*?' Julieanna placed a hand on his arm: 'Come on, Ben. Leave it. We need to understand what's going on.'

Robert had not flinched. He felt a sense of calm unlike anything he had known. 'I know what I am,' he said. 'And I know why. I didn't ask for this.'

Celeste nodded. 'We know. We've also been looking for people like *you* all our lives. Tell us what's happening to the stones.'

'The murder of a Great Dragon shocked the Network. But it wasn't just killed. They removed its heart.'

Julieanna baulked: 'What?' The others were silent, unsure of the implications.

'Naveen told me about the other murders,' Robert continued. 'Of people whose blood is like mine. I thought it was just to stop you people from getting to us first. But it's not.'

'Energy comes from four Slave stones and one Reaper,' Julieanna said, nodding. 'There are stories of Great Dragons being killed going back centuries on Kiranis...for that very reason. It's how we have ours.'

'They thought they could use the power to get back to Earth,' Benjamin added. 'But when Naveen implemented the truce, the harvesting stopped.'

'The Sensitives have started a different kind of harvest,' Robert explained. 'Using us as Slave stones.'

'Why?' asked Celeste. 'Wherever they go, they gather enough armed men to hunt Greys. Why not use *them*?'

'I don't know yet,' the boy admitted. 'Naveen likes to keep some things to himself.'

'Oh, we know *that*!' Julieanna remarked. 'So, are you saying that Sensitives all over Kiranis are doing this?'

'Yes. Great Dragons are being killed wherever possible...in towns and settlements they call Dragon Killers. And whatever the Sensitives plan to use the dragon hearts for, they're also going to use the hearts of people like me to make it happen.'

Benjamin's eyes widened with excitement: 'This *has* to be something to do with getting us *out* of here! If that Mediator said he'd seen it in the Lines, this can't all be coincidence!'

Julieanna was slightly more cautious, and she looked to Robert, asking, 'Did he teach you to read them?'

Robert nodded: 'But I'm going to need more practice before I figure out what to do next.'

'I think it's pretty obvious what you do next,' said Celeste. 'Use the Lines, find the Sensitives, and figure out what they're up to.'

Ω

Less than an hour later, Julieanna had plugged herself into the Watchers' vast VR database, trawling through images of Garran who had been known to the people of Earth up until the time of the Cage incident. It seemed so distant and not a little irrelevant to be looking at these faces, considering they were long dead and likely forgotten back in the universe from which her ancestors had come. But her dream haunted her. She knew the face had military connotations, as she had been fascinated by the history of human-Garran conflict throughout her childhood education. Others were enthralled by the Jaevisk or the Kwaios, the Sori or Manodderi, but it was more than the similarities between Garran and human culture which drew Julieanna to her studies. Naveen had told the Watchers long ago that there were Garran on Kiranis, but the aliens remained hidden from even their advanced technology. There was no information as to how developed they were, or what sort of a threat they posed.

The VR database was not just searching through visuals without guidance. There was a memory recall option, and Julieanna was one of the few outpost operators who had chosen to have a node implanted in her cerebral cortex facilitating interface with the database. Most people considered the MR interface a waste of time, for it was hardly ever used. But Julieanna had a history of these kinds of episodes, seeing things in her dreams that bore promise for the future. She had long kept this ability a secret, for it marked her either as descended from someone who should have been part of the New Elect, or as someone whose ancestors had evolved independently on Kiranis. She was unsure which was more unsettling.

The MR held on dearly to the hazy recollection of the Garran face from her dream – for often the presumption of clarity felt upon waking faded as the day wore on – as the database continued through thousands of images. It took some time – how long she could not tell – but the MR cross-referencing came to a pause, holding one image in the virtual air above Julieanna. She could no longer feel her body, a disconnection which maintained the quality of the MR link, but suddenly she was overwhelmed by the information relating to the Garran male before her. Images from intelligence gathering over the course of his military career filled the air, and it was complemented in Julieanna's subconscious by the speculation of what had befallen him. He had died here on Kiranis, that much was certain. But no one knew how.

Now, however, Julieanna was certain that this not the case. It could not have been, for her dreams had never been wrong. They had shown her random future events and the people or creatures related to them for years now. The problem here was that this Garran was supposed to have died a thousand years ago on this world. It was impossible that he could be part of the future of it. And yet here he was, brought to Julieanna's mind by whatever strange connection she had with Kiranis and the Network to which only the Sensitives and those like Robert were supposed to have. Saying his name aloud made it real, and it sent shivers through her, for she knew that it signified a major shift in the future of humankind on this world: 'Jakari San Setta.'

Ω

While Julieanna was searching for historic Garran, Robert had set upon his own quest. Like hers, his was a quest of the mind. Unlike hers, he knew that he risked losing his altogether if he were unable to maintain his focus. Naveen had taught him how to access the Network using his own Line, but he had not had the time to explain how he would locate those of other travellers and undertake the kind of temporal interrogation required to get the Watchers the answers they needed. In the brief time he had spent with Naveen, he discerned that such an oversight was unlikely to have been incidental, and that it was more likely Robert was expected to learn how to swim before he walked where the Network was concerned.

He closed his eyes as he relaxed and leaned forward in the chair, for no other reason than presuming it was required. Initially, it was just about concentration. Naveen had told him to think about blood – its colour, its texture, its taste. While he was sure he had sucked a cut finger or two in his life, Robert could not recall its taste. But redness entered his mind, flowing in and around his consciousness like a sloshing pool, penetrating every corner of his brain until it hurt. He felt lightheaded and warm, and he reached downwards to the tiled floor, imagining his fingers stretching beyond their capacity to do so. The sensation was like something he often felt late at night when fighting his body's need for sleep. He would feel like he was floating, but there were times when his hands felt disturbingly larger than they really were. Now, however,

307

he relaxed his mind instead of struggling with the experience, and his fingers were met.

Only in his mind did he feel he could see the numerous Lines emerging to meet his probing hands. No one else would have seen them, nor understood the difficulty he had in finding his own amidst the tumult of memories and fates vying for his attention. He had not expected this, for Naveen had never given the impression that connection to the Network would be so chaotic. Unfortunately for Robert, this initial connection was only the tip of the iceberg. No sooner had he identified his own Line than he was dragged out of his body and up through the levels of the outpost. But the outpost was gone, obliterated from the sky by a metal machine the likes of which Robert had never perceived. There were more of these machines in the distance, and dragons filled the sky in every direction. But Robert felt as if something grabbed him and he shot upwards, screaming through the clouds into a darkness of illusion. Stars were here, and yet they were not stars, merely lights set into giant metal arms reaching across the world. Robert's imagined heart pounded and his breath was caught. Yet still his nightmare was not over. For he was not alone.

A white-haired giant of a man bore down upon him like a wraith, laughing maniacally before shouting, 'You don't belong here, boy!' But the man was torn apart by a swipe of a great clawed hand, and as Robert watched the echoes of his dismemberment drift away, a pair of enormous red eyes materialised in the distant blackness. A monstrous mouth opened, and Robert was engulfed in flames. He screamed anew, before a gigantic tentacle shot out of the clouds and dragged him back down to the world. 'You belong with us!' a different voice told him, as he was drawn all the way back down to the Watchers' outpost, which was once again intact and surrounded by barren wasteland beneath an empty sky. 'We are the future of Kiranis,' the voice continued, as the tentacle passed down through the levels with Robert in its grasp. But Robert was suddenly inspired to grab the tentacle, which burned away as the man screamed in pain until it was replaced by Robert's red Line. As he continued downwards, he passed himself lying on the floor next to his chair before the journey became darker and less structured. He was no longer in the Watchers' outpost but descending deep below it through compacted layers of the world, and he felt a pinching sensation begin at the back of his skull. His

Line as he entered a vast opening in this underworld became muddled, twisted and confused, and Robert realised that it was entangled with countless others. The number of Lines was mind-boggling, and Robert knew that this symbolised an immense convergence of lives and fates. But he was suddenly stopped in his journey, stuck as if in a spider's web, and he panicked. 'Keep calm,' Naveen's voice told him, as if from memory. 'You're not in danger. He just won't allow you to see anything else.'

'Who?' Robert gasped, fighting to control his breathing with imaginary lungs. What was his body experiencing back up on that cold floor? 'Who's down here?'

'The centre of the Network,' said Naveen. 'I need you to see it, Robert. With your own eyes.'

'You want me to come down here? Why?'

'Because the survival of this planet depends on it.'

$$\Omega$$

Balaam watched the heart of the huge dragon being lowered into the icy vat. A circular partition was pushed down into the barrel before more ice was poured in. Following this, four human hearts, set into the quarters of another circular partition, were added to the barrel and more ice poured in until the barrel was full. Dassan clucked his tongue. 'All that killing for four hearts,' he commented.

'Winning Kiranis back for humankind will take sacrifice,' Balaam reminded him.

'I'd prefer my martyrs to have a choice,' the duke argued. 'And I'm sure the sacrifices will always be borne by those who couldn't care less who's in control once they have enough to survive.'

Balaam looked bored by the comments: 'Don't get all moral on us now, Jerord. We're too close for you to start growing a conscience.'

'And what about the Watchers? Any thoughts on how they'll react?'

'Oh, they'll come at us very soon,' said the Sensitive. 'And very hard.'

'And are we ready?'

Balaam turned away, saying, 'I may have overused the plural.' He started down the steps towards the holding area, where the barrel was being loaded carefully on to a wagon. 'What I meant to say was they'll come at *you*.'

'*What*?' Dassan drew his sword, pointing it at the Sensitive as he followed him down the stairs. 'Where the hell are *you* going?'

'I'm going to show the Watchers the error of their ways.' Balaam turned to find the sword touching his chest, but he did not even look down. 'Don't worry, Jerord,' he assured the duke with a smile, 'you only have to hold them off until I'm ready.'

'And how will I know when you're ready?' Dassan snarled.

Balaam's smile grew: 'Oh, I imagine it'll be clear.'

Ω

Asherah may have regained her composure, but any illusion of confidence was hard-won as she stood in her human form amidst the intimidating forms taken by many of the most powerful mutations on Kiranis. The gathering of hundreds of these creatures was in a valley near the foothills of the highest peak of Kiranis, a mountain in which they had lost their first leader, but Asherah had chosen this place for another reason. The conspicuous and observable nature of the valley was the antithesis of the favoured habitats of the Deep Dark Ones, the new and formidable enemy of all who had come to hear her speak. And she was making a statement that the time for concealment had passed.

'For centuries you've had the good grace to listen to my words,' Asherah began, her voice projected across the valley as she extended her hands, palms down, manipulating the thin Lines of vegetative life so that the flora growing on every natural level around her acted like amplifiers. 'But now, I need you to HEED THEM!' Birds erupted from trees as her shouts reverberated around the site.

'We thought our greatest enemy were amongst our kind,' she continued. 'But they've been hiding because they're something else. Those we've long called the Deep Dark Ones...those we thought to be merely disinterested in our society and our concerns...' She paused for effect, chilled by the silence of so many of her kind, before shouting again, 'They are HUMAN!'

They understood. All these mutations appreciated the delicate balance of their symbiosis, but they also knew that it was the subordination of their human consciousness that kept them in their

310

current forms. They had seen Reduction and witnessed the creation of many Mediators over the centuries, but still these creations were dragons at heart. The idea that powerful mutations living across the planet might at their core be human was disturbing and dangerous. For many gathered here, this introduced a new fear to their internal psyche – that they might lose their battle against their ultimate physical host and become whatever the human wished, experiencing something they had long ago escaped: mortality. Asherah was thus unsurprised that some of the larger and more influential entities who might otherwise have brought out their human form to communicate plainly with her did not do so. They clearly now entertained the idea that they might never again change back.

'They want to reform the Church of the New Elect here on Kiranis, in anticipation of what we've all known for a thousand years: that Kiranis will return to the Universe. When it does, and the Network loses its autonomy, so too will we lose our control over Kiranis. The Jaevisk and the Kwaios will come for us. And Naveen undoubtedly has a plan for us. But more than that...we've all seen what else is coming for us...for every species in our galaxy. Naveen drew attention to us for a reason, but I still believe he's overplayed his hand. You don't provoke a god without consequence!'

One of the huge orange and brown dragons raised its head and opened its mouth, roaring in anguish before shrinking and reforming, its image vibrating as it took human form. When a huge naked man stepped out from amidst the other creatures, Asherah had one of her Mediators bring him a robe. 'Gallias,' she welcomed him. 'It's been a long time.'

'Not long enough,' the man replied. He appeared to be in his forties, but appearances were transient illusions amongst these entities. The illusion Gallias chose to present was that of vitality and strength, and even to the massive creatures around him, it was one which worked. Gallias was known to have killed dragons even in this form and was rumoured to have educated humans towards the same end. 'I had hoped never again to ally my clan with yours.' He looked up and around at some of those indicated: 'How do I assure my people that they should bleed for you? Because I'm sure that's why you called us here.'

Asherah nodded calmly, recognising that not only did Gallias speak for his own clan; his questions were representative of every leader gathered. 'You're right,' she conceded. 'We'll have to fight whatever's coming. Somehow the activity of these mutant humans and the Sensitives working for them has been hidden from us. We didn't even know about the Dragon Killer settlements. And there's only two ways that's possible – either Naveen has blocked access to an entire layer of the Network, or the Deep Dark Ones have found a way to do so.'

'Neither bodes well,' Gallias noted. 'Although Naveen is likely to have had a part either way.'

Asherah shook her head defiantly: 'We can't continue our lives believing he controls everything we do and everything we face. Our very existence will become meaningless!'

'Is that what you call this?' Gallias argued. '*Existence*?' Many dragons were heard to rumble and growl in either agreement or dissent, for Asherah was on shaky ground insofar as the meaning of their lives was concerned. 'We had achieved the pinnacle of existence before Naveen dragged us into this purgatory!'

'Which is exactly why we need to continue to defy him,' Asherah contested, 'even if he's anticipated that. If the Sensitives and their masters have discovered something we haven't, this could be a turning point for us against the Prophet. We've existed outside time, so we know that there are no absolutes to Naveen's plan. If there were, he wouldn't need to intervene.'

Gallias could not help but see the logic in her argument, and he conceded with a nod. 'Alright,' he said. 'I'll follow your lead. But with one condition.'

'Name it,' Asherah said without hesitation.

'Free us from this form. And I don't just mean dragon, or whatever version of a child's imagination the rest of us have come up with. I mean –'

'That's it!' Asherah snapped, her eyes wide as she cut him off. 'That's what we've been missing!'

Gallias did not take kindly to being interrupted, but he was sufficiently intrigued to ask, 'What?'

'Our form,' she replied, moving back from him to ensure that all could both see and hear her. 'We're dragons because we were imagined that way. I worked hard to maintain the dragon form because I...' She stumbled at that. 'I'm not sure why. But I think it's possible I never had a choice. That we're dragons because we were supposed to be.'

'Now you sound like Naveen. What are you talking about?'

Asherah looked around at her Mediators, five of them. All strong human forms, with reptilian eyes and fierce loyalty. She had overseen the Reduction process for each of them, listening to their screams and the sounds of crunching and snapping bones. Corporeal form, their curse here on this world. It was as if they were bound by it, and all Asherah had done was facilitate their complacency. 'I think the young man who was brought here at the start is still here,' she explained. 'I think he's being used to disrupt the Network, and maybe even influencing our experience of it.'

'So, how do we stop him?' asked Gallias. 'Where is he?'

Asherah's anger was mounting as she felt the weight of her naivety: 'Where Naveen told us not to look.'

Ω

Benjamin checked his rifle for the third time since leaving the outpost. The ATVs in which they travelled had not been used for many decades, and the haste with which they had been readied for this attack did little to inspire confidence. Once Laden's Folly began to expand beyond its original nucleus, the Watchers had to increasingly retract their perimeter until observation became more and more covert. By the time Benjamin was old enough to serve, daylight observation had occurred only rarely and by seasoned staff who could blend in with the locals. Vehicles had long been abandoned as a means of transport, and every active Watcher learned to ride a horse as a child. But Julieanna had ordered the ATVs fuelled and recommissioned in a hurry, and her demeanour invited no contest. It was clear that the boy, Robert, had spooked her with whatever he had told her, and she had snapped at Celeste when she had asked what was going on. All they knew was that Julieanna wanted the white-haired Sensitive removed from Laden's Folly, and that she was willing to go through the duke's personal army to do so. So, they had armed, suited up and climbed aboard six vehicles with a view to storming the town. Cannons were mounted atop some of the rollbars, RPG launchers on others, but Benjamin had never used such weapons, and he

313

imagined the same were true of all the impromptu troops around him.

'You okay?' Celeste shouted to him, squinting her eyes against the dust despite the goggles she wore. She was seated to his right and holding the bar at the back of the seat before her as they bounced over the rocky ground. Benjamin could see the outlying farmsteads of Laden's Folly up ahead, and he shook his head, replying, 'I've never killed anyone!'

Next to the driver, Lucas, a wiry dark-skinned man with a greying beard, turned back and smiled sympathetically. 'I hear ya, man,' he shouted. 'But it won't come to that. These people are gonna think we're magicians or something. They'll be too shocked to put up a fight.' Benjamin nodded and looked to Celeste, who gave a thin smile of assurance, but he wasn't convinced. He doubted Celeste was either.

They passed through the first farmstead. It was empty, no sign of activity anywhere. As they came upon more properties and occupied land, it was clear that it had all been abandoned. Or perhaps evacuated. Lucas looked back at Benjamin, but this time there was no smile, just grim concession. The people of Laden's Folly would not be shocked. And what was to come would come. Benjamin checked his rifle again.

Ω

Duke Jerord Dassan had been born into his position. It was always going to be his. His sense of entitlement had been absolute. Everything he had ever needed was at hand, while everything he wanted was only ever a few hands away before being passed into his. As a child, he had naively swallowed the old legend of Laden as if the man had been a hero, an advocate of the poor and needy, taking only the money of greedy, unscrupulous, and often violent men and women in the name of justice for those less fortunate. Jerord's mother had changed all that, beginning by revealing to him the means by which his father had acquired his wealth. The man had killed or disenfranchised any who stood in the way of his greed, and Jerord came to see his father as the opposite of their town's founder. As Laden's folly began to encroach on the territory of another minor noble and fighting inevitably began, Jerord witnessed a horrific massacre which still haunted him to this day.

Not because it was more horrific than anything Jerord had done since; merely because he had been manipulated into lying to the Lord Protector who had come to investigate. He remembered how he had stood there, sweating even in his light armour, being watched intensely by the lord's white-haired son who sat atop a magnificent black horse, and blamed the whole affair on a conspiracy between dragons, Watchers, and the neighbouring noble with a view to overthrowing Laden's Folly.

At the time, Jerord feared that the Lord Protector would simply pursue the matter with the Watchers and learn the truth, but it was not long before he learned that the man's son had talked him out of it. Balaam had decided right at that moment that he would ally himself with Dassan, and a year later, on the same night, the two of them had murdered their respective fathers, signifying their commitment to the cause and to each other. When Jerord's mother learned the truth about her husband's death, she was so infuriated that she set about trying to disenfranchise her son, which simply would not do. The woman had shattered his worldview, sullied his relationship with his father, and destroyed his innocence. In Jerord's twisted mind, she was the root of all his demons, and he told her as much as he smashed her head through the bedroom window.

'The Watchers have passed through Churchfield.'

Jerord turned away from the window, which he was convinced still had his mother's hair caught in the frame, and he blinked: 'What?'

'They'll be upon us in minutes,' said the young man. 'Your horse is saddled and the men are ready.'

'I presume everything is in place?'

'Absolutely, my lord. They should encounter the first wave any moment.'

'Good.' Dassan took one last look at the window. 'I didn't do all this to be stopped by those cave-dwellers!'

Ω

The defence took them all by surprise. The four walls of a huge barn ahead and to their right suddenly fell to reveal a row of four giant crossbows, and the bolts were released without delay. One of them struck the front of the lead ATV, the undercarriage collapsing

315

and flipping it over, and it started to burn as three survivors crawled away. Benjamin felt the whip of the bolt as it cut the air between he and Celeste, and he jumped up to the cannon without thinking, flipping up the trigger catches and opening fire. A bolt tore the wheel off Julieanna's ATV, and her arms were nearly torn from their sockets as she struggled to maintain control of the steering. The vehicle slammed into a stone wall at the edge of a farm, and she felt something slam against the back of her seat as Marianne, a twenty-two-year-old botanist, died with her neck broken. The fourth bolt was also off target, leaving four vehicles with the capacity to respond to the attack. They fanned out around the farms, cutting through recently sown fields and animal pens, their cage-mounted cannons cutting through the crossbow team with automatic fire. But as Julieanna gathered the fallen Watchers to herself, a second wave of attackers came at them, these ones on horseback and brandishing swords, spears, and bows.

Benjamin watched them gallop in as his ATV rounded back to regroup with the others. Celeste helped him latch another magazine into the cannon, and he gripped the handles with his now white hands with his fingers hovering over the triggers. Lucas had mounted his rifle on a tripod trap in front of him, and he was already taking pot shots at the riders. The foreleg of one of their horses was blown off by the explosive round, and a rider went tumbling through the air before smashing his skull on a wall. Benjamin could see that Julieanna and the others left on foot were being peppered with arrows by some of the dismounted archers, and she lost another two men, but once the rest of them gathered themselves, they returned fire and the fully automatic weapons made short work of the entire group of attackers.

The remaining ATVs came together around Julieanna and her group, and Lucas and some others helped them back into the vehicles. Lucas caught Benjamin's questioning gaze, but he shook his head angrily: 'Not a word!'

'Okay,' Julieanna shouted to address them all, standing at Benjamin's seat as he manned the cannon. 'We clearly underestimated these people. There's no way we'll make it to the Manor Home if we stay together. Zarifa, you're with us. You've an RPG. We'll take the east gate. Jinn...north, Harry...south. We'll meet at the centre and –'

'No!' Benjamin argued, shaking his head. 'Not the centre. The boy said that's where they killed the dragon. It's a killing zone.'

'So, where do you suggest?'

'Leave the ATVs at the gates. Use the streets and keep the Manor Home in your sights for soldiers. Once you're in the town, don't give them a chance to ambush you. That's what they're counting on.'

'Suddenly an expert?' Julieanna quipped.

Benjamin shrugged. 'I'm as surprised as you. What do you think?'

She looked around at the others, who clearly agreed with him, and she nodded. 'Let's do it. I want this white-haired son of a bitch before the sun sets!'

Ω

Of course, Balaam was not in Laden's Folly. He had taken a circuitous route around Churchfield to come at the outpost from the south. He was alone, finally away from the prattling townsfolk and sycophantic soldiers. The only man he had come close to respecting was Duke Dassan, mainly because of the man's ruthlessness. However, Jerord's scheming was only ever in service of his own enrichment, with Laden's Folly only benefiting incidentally. He was incapable of committing selflessly to the bigger picture, concerned solely with his own share in the outcome. Which was why Balaam had fed him to the wolves.

He imagined he could hear the sounds of fighting to the west, knowing that the Watchers had heavy weaponry, much more advanced than anything in Dassan's possession; but knowing also that the duke's soldiers had been training for years to fend off an attack from a superior force. The Watchers would meet the farmers and maybe some light infantry first, but that was nothing compared to what was waiting for them in the town. If nothing else, Dassan was at least creative.

Creativity was something the Masters possessed in great abundance, and Balaam had been entranced by their genius from very early on. He liked to imagine that they had known him from the womb, had even chosen him before he was born. And it was perhaps true, for the Masters had spent centuries studying the Network, accruing knowledge which raised them to rival perhaps

317

the Prophet himself. They manipulated people and dragons alike, and Balaam delighted in the fact that those he served held sway over the fates not only of the Great Dragons, but of Asherah herself, greatest of all…for now.

He drew rein on the team of horses and brought the wagon to a stop, looking at the enormous, isolated rock formation. Apart from its provocation of natural curiosity and wonder, it appeared as innocuous as the Watchers had designed it, but Balaam had seen them exit and re-enter here on numerous occasions. He knew which one of the giant boulders was not actually there. As he dismounted, he heard the slightest of animal roars on the wind descending from the north, and he needed no Lines to discern that the dragons were on their way. It was all coming together as the Masters had determined, and he felt a shiver of excitement rush through him as he looked up to the sky and goaded Asherah through gritted teeth: 'This way, you bitch!'

From under his robes, he took a leather satchel and unrolled it before climbing up onto the wagon and pulling the lid off the barrel which had been fixed upright with ropes. The ice had melted, and the human hearts were floating in the water, loose from their wooden housing. He lifted them out one by one and placed them in the satchel, beyond caring now as to their condition. They were still icy cold and would stay so long enough for him to complete his task. As he slung the satchel from one shoulder across his chest, he saw that the dragon heart would be a different matter, for it had sunk to the bottom of the icy water. With all his strength, Balaam tipped the barrel until it fell, draining its contents out across the wagon. The huge heart, almost as large as a human torso, flopped out in the flood, and Balaam stared at it for a moment, wondering how he was going to carry it. The satchel was not an option.

The horses were becoming unsettled, for the scent of dragons carried far, and Balaam decided to simply bear the heart in his arms and waste no more time. It was harder than he had expected, its texture unlike those in the bag, but this may have been down to the temperature. His fingers immediately felt like they would be frostbitten if he carried the organ too long, but he had to persevere. Jumping down from the wagon, he wobbled on his feet a bit before gaining his balance and walking towards the rocks. The sun was high, but the breeze took the edge off, which delighted Balaam, considering the perspiration rolling down his forehead and working its way through his long hair. He hurried towards the rock, three from the right, the one from which they regularly emerged to proliferate their insidious manipulation of the truth about this world. It was large enough to accommodate large vehicles and he might have been able to lead the wagon team through had he the patience to coax the horses through the optical illusion. But there was something about being on foot. Something true, natural, independent. And in a world where everyone was dancing to the same tune, any sense of freedom was welcome. He reached the rock face and took a deep breath as he stood with the massive heart in his hands, burning his fingers with its frost. And he stepped through.

The Masters had assured him that all but a skeleton crew of Watchers would be here, and as he found himself standing in a wide corridor with walls of probably the smoothest material he had ever seen, Balaam could hear nothing but his heart pounding in his ears. The air was cooler in here, but somehow the giant heart no longer stung his fingers. Perhaps they were numb, he thought absently as he walked on. Lights which hurt to look upon lined the ceiling, and every now and then he passed through a section of the corridor emitting a cool breeze from either side. The path was in decline all the way, and he soon came to a junction. There were three doors, but the one ahead was so large it was likely for the vehicles upon which the Watchers scouted the land. On the one to his left was an image of a staircase, while the one to his right showed a box with someone standing in it. Balaam was no idiot, and he had visited some of the large cities of Kiranis. The most impressive elevator system he had seen was in the Tower of Harbour's Gate in Neval, where a magnificent network of brass cogs, wheels and pulleys took passengers up almost a hundred feet to look out upon the natural splendour of Carver's Bay to the south, and the bustling conquest of reclaimed land that was Annalise City to the north. Balaam stepped towards the elevator door, which beeped before opening.

The dragon's heart was getting heavy now, and Balaam took advantage of the elevator journey to put it down. The Masters told him to which level he should descend, and so he tapped the numbers on the illuminated keypad as if this technology were second nature to him. The elevator car in Neval was an unwieldy curiosity compared to this one, and Balaam found himself leaning his head closer to the walls to hear or perhaps feel any sensation of movement. It was only when the elevator car had descended beyond forty levels that Balaam's senses were attuned to his journey, but not because the car rattled or rumbled. It was because something told him that this part of the world was different, and he closed his eyes and sought out the Lines with the release of a deep breath. They were faint and disjointed, and he felt a panic grip him at the thought of their absence. With an ethereal hand, he tried to reach out for them, but as he did, they all vanished. 'No!' he shouted out as he opened his eyes.

He heard the words of the Masters from his memory, as if they had been implanted for this very moment: 'When you are close, the Lines will be inaccessible. This is the work of the Watchers, for they protect their secret energy source in a way you wouldn't understand.' Balaam simply had to accept this. The Lines were not gone. They were just hidden from him down here. If the Masters were right, he would not need them, but the prospect of being completely alone after decades of connection with the Network was more than unnerving. The elevator stopped and the doors opened, revealing darkness ahead. Balaam calmed himself and picked up the dragon's heart, now also feeling the weight of the human hearts in his satchel. The iciness was gone from the larger organ, and probably the smaller ones, and Balaam felt the pressing nature of his task. He rushed straight out the doors and the lights came on as he headed down the corridor. He did not have far to go before he reached the door of the south antechamber, and for that he was thankful. A beam of blue light suddenly shot out from above the door, expanding to envelope him as it moved down his body, and he looked around with eyes wide. When it disappeared, an alarm sounded, and Balaam understood. They would come for him now.

He realised that the door would not open for an intruder, and he was forced to put the dragon's heart down again. Blood was now on his hands, and he wiped them on his robe before withdrawing one of the Mediator's guns from his belt. Haphory would certainly never use it again, and Balaam looked at it for a moment, admiring the craftmanship before levelling it at the entry control and pulling the trigger. It was a large calibre bullet, and it smashed the panel despite the recoil and Balaam nearly taking another shot at the ceiling. The door unlocked with a click, but still didn't open. Back up the corridor, the elevator door closed, called from above.

With a sigh, Balaam took the satchel off his shoulder and placed it on the floor. There was no handle on the door, and no depression for hands or fingers, but Balaam pressed his weight against the door and pushed it as hard as he could with his hands. Initially, the door moved less than an inch with each push, but eventually he slid it open enough to squeeze through, hearts and all. Once inside, he closed the door behind him, knowing the Watchers would be upon him within minutes. And so, he did not delay.

He knocked the existing Slave stone, the frozen heart of a Grey dragon, from its pedestal and replaced it with one of the human hearts, awkwardly bearing the larger heart in the crook of one arm. As he moved to the door at the end of the antechamber, he slammed a large blue button before exiting and closing that door behind him. As he turned back to look through the glass panel, a sustained blast of nitrogen from above began freezing the organ. Now he was in the containment room proper, the central chamber constructed to house the heart of a Great Dragon, the Reaper stone through which energy was drawn from the Masters knew where. At least, so Balaam believed.

He had been told there should have been a ritual, that creatures from another world revered this process and shared in its initiation, but there was no time for such things. They would be at the outer door now, and perhaps gaining entry simultaneously from the other antechambers. The Sensitive reached up to place the dragon's heart on the high pedestal in the centre of the arrangement and hurried to blast it with nitrogen at the door to the east chamber as he readied his gun for interruption and continued his work. Balaam had never felt so excited, so fulfilled and purposeful, and he wondered how his compatriots across the planet were faring as this great scheme was playing out in the backyard of all Dragon Killer settlements and cities. Not once did it occur to him that he had been lied to. He was part of a worldwide effort to return the people of Kiranis to the galaxy, and he could not have imagined a greater honour. But Balaam had no idea of the implications of what he was about to do. Because despite the secrets of the Watchers' outpost beyond Churchfield, real secrets were always kept in the darkest of places.

Ω

Robert had no idea how he knew the way to the levels below the outpost. He had long ago left the emergency staircases and subterranean exit tunnels above him, descending beyond what seemed like nothing but abandoned or unfinished excavation projects until arthritic stalagmites stood in pained stillness around pools of sulphuric water that had him wrinkling his nose and trying not to vomit. The wide beam of the flashlight cut a swath of revelation out of the living, breathing blackness around him, and Robert pressed on, feeling the decline in the stony ground as he avoided stepping in the pools.

At this point, he also had no idea where his courage was coming from. The twelve-year-old boy riding the duke's prize mare might have been brave in that regard, but this was something far beyond that. This was a world of men and monsters, and Robert had learned enough to know that the lines between the two were often blurred by mere actions. Deep in this fetid darkness, he did not know which of the two he would rather encounter.

He could hear a sound up ahead, growing as he continued down into the world until it sounded like a million nightflies in the putrid air around him. He remembered the first time he encountered nightflies, asking his mother as the two of them stood in the middle of the cornfield why they made that high-pitched buzzing sound. She had looked down at him in the moonlight, her smile warming him in the cold night as she whispered, 'You'll see.' Then the clouds had covered the moon, and Robert witnessed what he had believed back then to be magic. The nightflies lit up, thousands and thousands of tiny points of yellow-white light filling the sky above them. Now he imagined he could feel the grip of his mother's hand as the source of this buzzing was brought into view by his flashlight. Yet if this were magic, it was of the darker kind.

The pools of water were boiling around a central point, and silvery-black stalagmites were gathered, leaning inwards as if drawn by a singular force. Robert moved the light upwards until he saw him, the young man who was the source of this preternatural curiosity. His nakedness was mostly covered from below by the stalagmites which had embraced and grown around him, while his head was held fixed by stalactites drawn in at angles all around by the energy somehow being emitted. What skin could be seen was grey and calcified, but the man's eyes were blue and alive, almost glowing with a mix of fervour and anguish.

Robert stared, horrified, for a while, but eventually he managed to draw his attention away from the man to look around. The buzzing penetrated the rock, but the boiling waters revealed another secret of this place, for in these pools were piles of pale red stones. No, not stones, Robert realised. Hearts. Calcified dragon's hearts. 'What is this place?' he whispered, before looking back up at the man. 'Who are you?'

'His name is Cana,' said Naveen, almost reverently, as he appeared, startling the boy. Robert noticed that he was on top of one of the pools, but not in the water. And he realised that he was not really here as he continued: 'He's the reason you're all here. The reason dragons roam this planet.'

Robert stared at him for a moment without understanding, before looking back to the young man. 'Did you know him?' he asked.

'Not really, but I pity him. He was caught up in his own faith, and they used him.'

'Who?' Robert moved closer, seeing a red glow above Cana's head.

'They call themselves the Church of the New Elect.'

'*Call*?' Robert noted, turning back to Naveen. The Prophet nodded: 'They're here now, on Kiranis. And they've been preparing for this day for a thousand years.'

'What's his part?'

Naveen walked, and yet did not walk, towards Robert, looking up at Cana as he did so. 'The Sentience reached out to him, knowing that he'd end up here. It implanted an image of dragons in his mind and when he encountered the entities I'd brought here...well...you saw the results.'

'How is he still alive?'

'*Alive* is too simple a word for what he's experiencing, Robert. Too mundane. His consciousness reaches far beyond what you...or even *I*...would experience. Most of the dragons think he's dead, devoured by the one they call Leviathan. But something happened that surprised even me when I saw it.' He held Robert's gaze as he said, 'The Sentience saved him.'

'I thought the Sentience was just...you know...*there*.'

323

'So did I, for a…short time. But the Sentience likes to intervene, and I came to learn that it often works to fulfil its own prophecies. And because all time exists at once for the Sentience, Cana was left with memories of the future. Those who found him helped him to build and shape the Network to make sure that others could access those memories…to manipulate them so that the future he saw would definitely happen.'

'I don't understand. I thought the planet was *definitely* going back to the galaxy.'

'There's no definite without the Sentience. Kiranis will return because Cana *wants* it to. There's a society of creatures across Kiranis that the dragons call the Deep Dark Ones, but these creatures are the reverse of what the dragons became. They're humans who have subsumed their companion entity.'

'The New Elect?

Naveen nodded. 'Yes, the refashioning of the Church here on Kiranis. And they're powerful, Robert. They've been fixated on the return of Kiranis even more so than the dragons, and they took Cana a long time ago. In fact, they moved him here, but he may have orchestrated that by projecting it across the Network.'

'Why?'

'Because all he wants…all he's dreamed of since he was tricked into coming to Kiranis…is to go home. So, the Church fed on that, magnifying his desperation and pushing him to enhance his abilities as they came to learn that he was the key to getting what they wanted. They almost killed him, but he did it.'

Robert was fascinated, and the buzzing sound was nothing but background noise: 'Did what?'

'He reached out, Robert. Off the world, through the Cage.' Naveen looked up at Cana again, and it was clear to Robert that the Prophet felt enormous remorse. 'That's when I realised that the Sentience doesn't abandon anyone,' he continued, his voice tinged with passion. 'It just waits until they've learned how to get back in touch. It's amazing what a person can learn given enough time.' Naveen shrugged: 'But then that's the curse of mortality.'

'What do you mean?'

'Well, knowledge takes time, wisdom even more so. Don't you think that if we didn't die, we'd have a greater chance of perfecting our craft? Even if someone lived for centuries, imagine what they could achieve.'

Robert nodded. 'But if people knew they were going to live forever no matter what they did, they might not bother doing anything worthwhile. Or anything to help others.'

'That's true. Ultimately, Cana used what he's learned to help himself.'

'And what about you?' Robert asked shrewdly. 'Who benefits from what you've learned?'

Naveen smiled. 'You know, Cana could be considered a god. The Network he oversees represents the past, present, and future here on Kiranis. The difference is that his perception of reality is restricted by the limitations of the Network.'

'That doesn't answer the question.'

'No, it doesn't. But if learning as you go through life happens only in one direction, imagine what one could achieve if they experienced reality *across* time.' Robert could not really get his head around the concept, and it showed. Naveen laughed: 'For a start, it's how I'm here...and how I can also operate across the universe controlled by the Sentience. From my perspective, this is all the past, and yet it's all accessible to me at once. Cana *will* reconnect with the Sentience, but because he already *did*, I'm able to be both here...and there.'

Something more pressing was bothering Robert, and he looked up again at the red glow above Cana's head: 'I have another question.'

'I thought you might.'

'You said the Deep Dark Ones found Cana. But how did they keep him alive...or whatever this is?'

'They didn't do *all* the work. Look around you.'

Robert did so, making more now of the red stones in the bubbling pools. 'They brought him the hearts of dragons.'

Naveen nodded, but he also pointed up to the formation above Cana's head: 'And?'

Robert stared for a while; at the rock, the stalactites, the red glow, feeling awed by the scheme as he pictured the multiple levels of the outpost above and their secret use of bio-electrical energy. 'The Watchers!' he gasped. 'They've been feeding energy down here all this time!'

'The Watchers alive today have no idea about this, Robert. It was selectively forgotten over a number of generations, but in this outpost, Cana draws the Reaper stone from the crystal chamber.'

'But if the Reaper stone disappears from *above* the Slaves, how does Cana take it from down here?'

'You're fixated on a three-dimensional world. Even those up on the surface who learn about the power of the Lines think they flow underground. Humans are obsessed with ancient concepts of supernatural power as being either up in the sky or deep below ground. But the Lines are everywhere, in every direction, and they're always right beside us. Close your eyes.'

Robert took a deep breath and closed his eyes. At first, nothing but bright red filled his internal vision, and he imagined that he would be blind when again he opened his eyes. But gradually, Cana's dark form could be seen amidst millions of veins of red spreading out from him in every direction. 'Is this the Network?' he asked Naveen quietly. But trapped in his vision, Robert saw that Cana was suddenly alive with his cold eyes fixed upon him with an angry glare. '*I* am the Network!' he roared, as the vision of red vibrated. 'And I won't let you *destroy* me!'

Robert reeled from the fury, and his eyes opened. It took a moment for the blinding red to dissipate from his memory, but he was more panicked by the fact that he could not move. Stalagmites had gripped his feet and ankles, and they were somehow growing. The ceiling above was descending to welcome him, and he screamed, 'Help me, Naveen! What's *happening?*'

'You're his replacement,' the Prophet explained calmly. 'Cana's about to reach out to the Sentience again with enough power to grab hold of it, but he won't survive what I've arranged. He's been waiting for salvation for a thousand years, but while it just so happens that a redeemer is on its way, this is all designed to save someone else.'

'*Who?*' Robert cried, staring up at the descending rock.

Naveen smiled and said, 'Me,' as he vanished. The flashlight fell from Robert's grip and rolled away as the world continued to consume him. The light bounced off countless points of crystalline stone surrounding him, and his terror was diminished by a dream of stars which lulled him into unconsciousness. Robert dreamed. And a world dreamed of him.

Ω

Julieanna and the remaining Watchers had made their way as Benjamin suggested, splitting into pairs to skirt the centre of Laden's Folly and avoid an ambush. That was not to say there was no resistance to their presence, and they dealt rapidly and decisively with townspeople who felt it was their duty to protect themselves and their property. Objectively, the Watchers could not blame them, but subjectively they could not allow them to live, for they could raise an alarm that would see them meet an end likely planned by the duke.

Although they had moved through the town in pairs, still they came to a choke point beyond which a stretch of land led to the Manor Home. And they arrived there in time to see the duke and his soldiers thundering back towards the town centre. When it was determined that it was safe to converge, they came together, and Benjamin was the first to speak: 'The Sensitive won't have many men left up there to protect him. We should make a run to the Manor.'

'No,' Celeste argued, her expression hardening like the blood on her face. 'We should take the opportunity to do to them what they had planned for us.'

'An ambush,' Julieanna nodded. 'We *could* do that...'

'We *should*,' Lucas interrupted. 'We lost *friends* today. Good people.'

'*I* know who we lost, Lucas!' Julieanna snapped. 'You wanna waste time on *revenge*? There's a bigger picture here.'

'Yeah, well, I'm *done* with the bigger picture, Julieanna!' Celeste declared. 'We're all gonna *die* one way or the other. I'm *sick* of the games!' The others agreed, and they all waited as Julieanna looked around, exhaling as she took it all in before making her decision. 'Okay,' she said, nodding as she checked her gun. 'You want them to pay? Let's make 'em pay.'

INTERVAL 4
MOTIVATION

Pain makes us do terrible things, as if more pain in the world might allow us to be absorbed by it, or so overwhelmed by its prevalence that ours seems normal or fair by comparison. The retreat from pain may take many forms, not the least of which is a determination to avoid any good circumstance which might one day lead to its deterioration or loss. Yet it is pain which colours the world, making the experience of good circumstance recognisable for its value. Without pain, why would we feel so compelled to give thanks for its absence?

Anonymous, c. 330 NE

Heragon Orbit, 319 NE

Few people from Earth had been out at the Kiranis system since the Cage event, despite the immense curiosity surrounding the disappearance of the eponymous planet. While it was rumoured that the Jaevisk had allowed people to get close enough to carry out detailed reconnaissance of their vigil along the orbital path of the absent world, it was fear of encountering Kwaios scout ships which had gradually seen visitors from many worlds peter out. But Samuel Vawter was not a man to succumb to such fear, and since his brush with death the previous year, he had paradoxically adopted a philosophy of recklessness, almost as if he might test the Universe itself. After all, he had faced the Sentience and lived. No, Samuel Vawter did not fear.

Amara chided him these days for many things, not the least of which was not spending enough time with her. They argued so much more than before – so much, in fact, that it seemed as if they had always argued. He still loved her, but it was a love tainted by the knowledge of what was to come; and in his tortured soul, he convinced himself that she would suffer less pain in the future if he distanced himself from her. It was the logic of a fool, but it was because Samuel Vawter did, indeed, fear.

His outcraft had taken him farther into the system, launched from a ship called Argo, a prototype deep-space exploration vehicle still under construction by an army of bots and looking like a skeletal barracuda. He knew where he was going, and he had been told what to offer them. But the stakes were immensely high, the cost beyond anything he had ever thought possible. When the Kwaios ships began emerging from their crackling portals to surround him, his fingers had hovered over the engine controls as his mind screamed at him to turn and flee. But he felt the imagined weight of his father's hand upon his shoulder and pressed on, extending the docking clamp like a child reaching for a parent. There were a few minutes of inactivity, of indecision, but eventually the boarding process was initiated.

The scout ships, now eight of them – each one many times larger than the Argo's outcraft – joined together in an almost spherical configuration, manoeuvring to create a single vessel into which Samuel's craft was drawn. His heart was pounding but his resolve was unflinching, and he stood in the airlock as if awaiting a dinner guest. Of course, his outer airlock was like a child's door in comparison to the portal which secured itself on the Kwaios side, and he imagined that his door bulged before opening. There was darkness beyond the door, and he stepped through, leaving a universe of certainty behind him. He was in their domain now, their reality. But not in their control.

Gradually, soft blue lights illuminated hybritech surroundings, that melding of the biological and technological synonymous with Kwaios superiority. Somehow, he was standing on a floor he could not see that did not – contrary to what he recalled from his childhood adventure – run perpendicular to the hybritech pillars. Due to the configuration of the scout ships and the angle at which they had secured his outcraft, the pillars were leaning at almost forty-five-degree angles. Or so he thought. When the Kwaios came into view, three of them, they walked parallel to the pillars, as if occupying a variant floor. A communication cube dropped from directly above Samuel, not the Kwaios, hitting the floor at his feet in complete silence and settling without reverberation: 'Which one are you?' he was asked, the moment his hands touched it. He flinched from the audio shock through his skull but recovered swiftly. 'I'm Samuel Vawter,' he replied, 'owner of the Vawter Corporation.' He searched their faces in the blue half-light but had no idea to which one he spoke.

'You deal in weapons, as did your father.' It was a surprisingly accusatory tone from a species who moved into this area of the galaxy on top of the food chain. Samuel knew they would instantly search their databases for his pedigree, so it did not faze him. Instead, he smiled and said, 'I'm not here to sell any, if that's what you're thinking.'

If they were amused, it did not show: 'Explain your presence in our territory.'

'I'm here to make you an offer.'

'You have nothing to give us,' they argued. 'Your ship on the edge of the system has been built using our technology, but we have advanced since your people stole it.'

Bringing the Argo here had paid off, and they would likely pay it little attention from now on. Samuel felt his heart racing, saying his next words in his head before voicing them: 'I have humankind.'

There was silence, and he was equally surprised. It had been said. The foundation of the great scheme had been laid. 'Explain,' came the eventual response, as the communication cube vibrated in his hands.

'I've been working on developing an interstellar transport network,' he told them, 'but the transmission of organic material remains unstable. I propose that you both construct and operate the network, but without the knowledge of anyone on Earth.'

'To what end?'

'Two things.' Samuel stepped closer to them, finding himself tilting his head to maintain eye contact. 'One...I understand that your population of humans here hasn't exactly been...fruitful and multiplied. Probably because of what you're putting them through. And two...I know that you're close to perfecting the cloning of my species.'

The Kwaios exchanged information and opinions across their hybritech network before responding, 'You are well informed.'

'One needs to be in this business.'

'And what do you want in return?'

'Well, the same as you, of course. When you've achieved your goal, I want to reap the benefits.'

'You wish to achieve Transference?'

'That's exactly what I want.'

'We will need something else before we proceed. Your people call it...collateral. We need to be convinced of your commitment.'

'O-kay...what did you have in mind?'

'Your female. Amara. She will be returned unharmed...and unaged. You may share Transference with her if you like.'

Samuel was horrified. To hand Amara over to these...monsters. And yet...they were offering immortality for them both, and the Kwaios understood this as the ultimate desire. For most humans, it was, and so refusal would arouse suspicion. 'She'll be...what...in stasis?' He could not believe he was ironing out the contractual details, but inside he was furious, for the Prophet must have known the price.

'That is correct,' the Kwaios replied. 'Nothing will change for her.'

The irony was that if he had not initiated this scheme and had not begun to push her away, he might have felt the love of a year ago, that adoration that meant that the world could fall apart around them so long as they were together. Perhaps, if he had maintained the intensity of his love for her, he would not have given her up. Perhaps if he had loved her more than humankind itself. 'How do we proceed?'

PART 5
HERAGON

This great empire, this star-spanning phenomenon that even now struggles to keep the gods at bay, was born from that which has spawned many of humankind's great empires; namely, death on a grand scale. There were heroes, of course, but these fighters possessed ideologies and agendas and even minds which had not from the start been their own. Of the rest, and especially the millions lost through Kwaios Transference, these had not been in possession of a mind with which they might have made a choice. But then martyrs, given the choice or not, are often the vanguard of those who seek to build peace upon skeletal foundations.

Heragonnica 5, Data-Line 41a, Author Unknown, Decrypted 1113 NE

The space around the sixth planet was already filled with shipyards of destruction. The huge Garran armada was almost completely wiped out, but the Jaevisk control virus had taken its toll on their real targets, and many Kwaios vessels of various shapes and sizes were out of control, crashing into their counterparts or drifting aimlessly in the vacuum. Still, the Kwaios fought with the Jaevisk who were defiling their gods and perverting their beliefs, both here in orbit of the outer planet and down on the surface. It was truly a warzone...

THE SHIELD

Illeri Orbit, 230 NE

In a star system far removed from this chaos, there was a burst of crackling blue energy before a great fleet of Kwaios ships appeared in the space around a grey world of stone and sea, around which an astonishing feat of construction was underway. These fifty vessels moved into position, occupying pre-configured points of synchronous orbit as another vessel many times larger than these emerged from the still burning blue of Kwaios energy. Once it fully emerged and the energy field was deactivated, the Colony Ship gave the order, and the assault began. Centres of habitation on the planet Illeri were systematically devastated before shuttles launched and the occupation was initiated. It would not be a simple operation, considering that the Illeri's access to the Sentience made them relatively formidable foes in their own environment, but it would be a conflict worth considerable loss. On the Colony Ship, a giant Kwaios oversaw the proceedings, taking in the impressive section of the protective shield being built to protect from exactly this action. Turning his back on this marvellous and portentous object orbiting the doomed planet and the unfolding invasion, this Kwaios Master addressed twenty of its immediate subordinates: 'In their haste, the Jaevisk have failed to appreciate the true value of the humans. Our Magi have been studying humans for many years – dissecting them, implanting them, testing them in many contrived environments and circumstances. They have determined that the most significant aspect of human physiology is their brain.'

337

Many of the Kwaios in attendance had heard the rumours about the human triune brain and they clicked their triple-pronged tongues and cracked their long fingers to show their excitement as the master continued: 'Brothers and sisters, fathers and mothers, we have found the solution to the greatest concern of the Kwaios Council, that which has troubled our kind for generations beyond counting. As part of our plan to advance this revelation beyond the experimental phase of individual humans, we will initiate the incorporation of humankind on a species level. We have seen from the difficulties we are enduring in the Kiranis system that a direct assault on any world will be anticipated by the Jaevisk and is likely to be manipulated by the Prophet, for that is his domain. While the Jaevisk are by no means beyond defeat, there is no need for us to sacrifice so many of our brothers and sisters, fathers and mothers when we hope to embrace them all in this venture.'

Agreement was heard amongst the attendees. 'The first phase of this operation,' the master resumed, 'will set the stage for mass infiltration. We will use the species named Illeri for this, convincing the humans that they are a powerful race concerned with an alliance…against us.' The master turned back to the scene behind him, and the display changed to show a virtual expansion of the gigantic structure which the Illeri had intended for the defence of their own world. 'We will build this shield around Earth, completely controlling their world. In their naivety and desperation, they will find themselves at our mercy, and Transference may proceed without external interference.'

One of the attendees rose and bowed before asking a question: 'My master, the lifespan of a human is considerably less than ours, and even now their numbers are insufficient to provide for our needs.'

The master agreed. 'Once the battle at the Kiranis system has passed and the Jaevisk have retreated to their home, we will occupy Heragon and construct a Transference colony there. We have taken humans from the Cage, but the means by which we will continue our supply has yet to be confirmed. The timing must be right and the population precise and self-perpetuating. The shield we will construct at Earth will take many years, and I will not be alive to witness its completion.'

This was sobering indeed, that a master would initiate a plan which would continue beyond his lifetime, but this was the way of the Kwaios. They were nothing if not patient.

'Are we to possess Kiranis?' another of the attendees asked.

'The Prophet has ensured that we will not,' the master replied, 'and yet the Council has determined that we should not attempt it at this stage. Our time for confronting the Prophet will come. It is not this time.'

'What will follow this occupation of Illeri?'

'This occupation will continue until Earth is completely under our control and full Transference has occurred. This is the most important operation ever undertaken by the Kwaios and it will not fail. It cannot.' Another Kwaios entered the chamber, passing one of the hybritech pillars before bowing to the attendees and then bowing lower to the master. 'Have you located the human?' asked the master.

'Yes, my master. It is a male named Anev Tesckyn.'

'Connect me immediately.'

The connection was made and, on Earth, Anev Tesckyn was puzzled by an incoming communication the source of which his people could not identify. '*Who is this?*' he was heard to ask angrily, arrogantly.

'We are the Illeri,' the master replied, the Kwaios language corrupted and obscured as the attendees and the administrator looked on, suppressing their excitement. 'We wish to help.'

THE PLAN

A Century Later, Earth

'They won't know what hit them, will they?'

The conversation with Naveen had ended. Short and concise, the man had a habit of simply vanishing following what needed to be said. Samuel wished that many more of his conspirators would do the same. It would save a lot of time.

Tzedek came into the great room, looking around. 'He's gone?'

'For now,' said Samuel. 'I'm sure he'll turn up again when you need him.'

'So, I'll meet him?'

'You'll have to.' Samuel activated a panel on the interior of the door of the free-standing annex room: 'I'll be gone.'

Tzedek nodded and exhaled heavily as he came closer, the huge glass table just before him. 'And this is the only way?'

Samuel chuckled darkly. 'Do you really think I'd do it if there was another option?'

'No one in their right mind would do it, Samuel.'

The laughter was louder and genuine: 'Well, I never claimed sanity in any of this, Kai.' He moved to the table and poured himself some water before sitting. 'Is everything else in place?'

'God, I should hope so,' said Tzedek, joining him. 'The Kwaios are almost here.'

'The *Illeri*, Kai. The *Illeri*. Be careful how you think, or it'll betray you.'

There was silence for a while, and Kai stared out the giant windows before asking, 'What will you say to the child?'

'I'm not sure yet.' Samuel's face darkened. 'But that's the least of my concerns. I'll sedate her early and pretend she's asleep if I have to.'

Tzedek puffed again: 'I'll get the Argo out there. I promise.'

'You mean *he* will!'

'Well, yeah, but…if he doesn't. If something goes wrong…I'll find a way.'

Samuel forced a grin and put his hand on Tzedek's arm, keeping his emotions…and the truth…in check. 'I know you will.'

340

He stood up and stretched dramatically. 'Now, if you'll excuse me...I have an alien cloning colony to infiltrate.'

They embraced, before holding each other's gaze and nodding. 'Here we go,' said Samuel.

'Here we go,' said Kai. 'Vengeance.'

Samuel felt the rush of fear and excitement, and there was a hint of moisture in his eyes as he imagined what his father would have thought of this great scheme. 'Vengeance,' he said.

Ω

He had to sedate her. She kicked and screamed, calling for the nanny to help her. But the nanny was already out cold and would be for some time. Samuel's team bundled the child into the dark vehicle and used a nanoneedler to knock her out. She was still out when they arrived at the feeder post for the Mars station, and Samuel carried her, her arms round his neck like a loving child. The staff recognised him, of course, and they knew he did not have a child. 'My niece,' he said with a smile. 'So excited, she wore herself out.'

'Oh, I've been there, sir,' said the security guard as she took her from him and lay her on a child's pod-buggy. 'I'll just have to bring the dosage down. Don't want her exhausted at your destination.'

Samuel laughed internally at the absurdity of the explanation, but he was prepared. 'I've already set it,' he said, handing her a box containing two needlers. 'I like to cover these things myself.'

The guard looked momentarily confused, but she conceded. 'Of course, sir. What's her name? So I can match the booking.'

This was the part where he could not lie, for every Traveller was supposed to be scanned and their DNA had to match the booking profile. 'Hannah Saranne,' he said with a smile.

The guard did not recognise the surname, and Samuel's relief was almost too evident as the scanner in the buggy confirmed the child's identity. Then the guard turned to him: 'Ah...will I be scanning you, sir?'

It was flouting protocol to even ask, but he took advantage of it and said, 'No. I'd prefer to remain unrecorded at this end.'

If she was disturbed or curious, she was professional enough not to show it. 'Of course, sir. You of all people should have that option.' Samuel realised that she had seen his security detail, four black-clothed men, standing beyond the departure gates.

'That's very understanding of you...' he read her name tag, 'Lisa. I'll remember it.'

Samuel Vawter's personal gratitude was hard to come by, and Lisa smiled widely. 'Thank you, sir. Enjoy your trip.'

He forced a smile, considering there was nothing about the next week he was going to enjoy.

$$\Omega$$

He could have taken a ship through MEC, but he did not want to involve an entire crew in this madness. Sedated and unaware of their ordeal they might have been, but he would have to watch as they were delivered in sacrifice. He could have taken a small craft, secured the girl next to him and flown up to Mars. But he needed Captain Saranne at Arrivals in the feeder post, to see her daughter walking back out without him. He needed her to panic, to feel the horror. He needed her to question, to wonder...to suffer. And he hated himself for it.

Foot passengers were herded towards conveyor rows of 'beds' akin to lidless coffins. Adults lay in them, while pod-buggies carrying young children were transferred into them. Samuel's needler cartridges were snapped into his bed and inside Hannah's buggy, customising their experience. Everyone else got the standard jab from the integrated needler unit, meaning they would not be woken until end-user protocols were initiated. Samuel could not wait that long, for interaction could mean identification. His heart was pounding as he lay in his bed and the leg and arm clamps snapped into place. He closed his eyes as the needler cartridge aligned itself with an injection point on his left arm. Piercing his clothes and skin, it felt as if someone were simply pressing gently. Then he was out.

As the system registered full capacity, the beds began moving towards a blue light in the distance, their unconscious Travellers blissfully unaware of the terror to come. In rows of ten, the beds moved upwards on the conveyor towards the blue light, passing through to the enigma of MEC. From here, the beds were stacked to fill the feeder shuttle. It took off soon after that, drifting from the feeder post before a short thruster blast took it towards the monstrous MEC station lying in wait. The station opened as all of this newer generation of MEC allowed, its central gaping mouth twisting open to allow the passage of whatever size ship was approaching. And like every ship that went in, it was taken apart.

There had been no need to do it quite like this – and Naveen had warned him not to – but Samuel wanted to know. He had to know what happened when the sedative did not keep you unconscious through the whole process. As his eyelids lifted, he immediately wished he had taken a higher dose and waited until he got to the end of his journey. The upper bulkhead of the shuttle was opening wide – six rows of beds in front of him were all progressively raised, and he could see inside them. Four of them were already empty, and mechanical arms were descending towards the fifth row, working fast. It was terrifyingly silent inside this enormous chamber, which Samuel knew was the area into which ships passed to be stripped of their crew and passengers, before being reduced into nanoscopic pieces and reused for the reconstruction of other vessels. The ten arms took their unconscious prey from their beds and dropped them into tubes arrayed around and below, while the beds themselves were disintegrated by the unseen bots. Samuel braced himself as the clamps snapped open. Then he heard the girl scream and panic rushed through him: *Oh God, no! How is she awake?* 'Hannah!' he called out to her. 'It's okay.'

'Where am I?' she cried. 'Where's my mom?' She screamed again as the arms came down. Each person was grabbed around their middle, a pneumatic plate securing them at their chest. Hannah kicked and screamed, and Samuel was reminded of the arms which had taken her, even as he, too, was lifted. 'What have I *done*?' he asked, Hannah's terror infectious. He could not understand how her memory was intact. She should not even know who she was. Not yet.

'She's coming to get you, Hannah!' Samuel shouted as the arm lined him up with a tube. 'Be strong for her. Close your eyes.' He was dropped, splashing into the red liquid designed to induce stasis. The cold burned, and his tears froze as his heart slowed. Unlike all the others who would awake with no memory of this

343

ordeal, Samuel would. He would never forget it. Nor would the child he had kidnapped just to get the Argo where he needed it.

Ω

Shortly after a blast of energy emitted from the MEC station fooled observers into thinking that a molecularly disintegrated ship and its crew and passengers were racing across the stars towards a predetermined destination, a decidedly utilitarian vessel detached from the station and began moving slowly away. This vessel was ostensibly responsible for removing the spent fuel cells of MEC transportation to a sufficiently safe location, to be jettisoned and left for later generations to dispose of. Of course, this vessel did not carry spent fuel cells. None of them did. Because MEC was not real.

Instead, this vessel was full of human bodies stored within the cells, Samuel and Hannah amongst them, and it rapidly increased velocity until it was far enough away to activate systems designed to mask its disappearance into a spatial distortion enabling a very different means of transit. A crackle of disruption saw its arrival at Heragon, the gigantic Kwaios planet in the Kiranis system. It was escorted down to the night surface by monitoring automatons, its cargo unloaded. The cells were arranged so that the people inside were standing upright, or at least would be had the stasis fluid allowed their feet to touch the bottom. This was a small delivery. Feeder shuttles had a capacity of only two hundred, and so only six Kwaios jumped off the arriving vehicle – little more than a floating cage – to process the newcomers.

They moved along the rows with shoulder-mounted lights illuminating their work, as they deactivated and opened the stasis tubes and sloshed through the fluid spewing out to soak into the ground. They talked amongst themselves, these workers, and as Samuel found himself on his hands and knees coughing and spitting outside the open tube, he echoed the behaviour of others to ensure he did not stand out. Then he remembered the girl. She could get them killed. Luckily, she was in the tube next to him, and he reached out to her as she lay sobbing, assuring her without a word that all was well. She looked up at him and he smiled softly in the twilight, putting a finger to his lips to encourage her to silence. As young as she was, she might not have seen even an image of a

Kwaios, and they towered over the stasis tubes, intimidating even the hardiest of men and women. Of course, with one's memory gone, it was hard to be hardy.

That was the beauty of the MEC system, at least from the Kwaios point of view. The sedative administered to every Traveller deactivated the areas of the brain related to memory, stripping the Travellers of their identity. In short, it created empty vessels, hosts. But the needlers performed a dual function, extracting that same information by a method inextricably linked to what Vawter and Tzedek were attempting to do. The memories of the Travellers, translated into hyper-digital signal packets and shot across the galaxy, were transferred to their corresponding clones formed at the destination station, giving them the impression when they woke on their reconstructed ship or Feeder shuttle that they were the same people who had entered the system. It did not matter if one were a clone going in, and the system kept repeating this facsimile creation indefinitely, meaning that the Kwaios had a potentially endless supply...of empty vessels. Until these vessels were brought to their respective processing centre, the Kwaios had no idea whether any of them were clones of clones of clones; or they had just used MEC for the first time. And they certainly had no idea whether any of their new arrivals were aware of the journey they had just made.

Samuel edged closer to Hannah, who was silently trembling, still on her hands and knees with her head turned towards him. The droplets beneath her eyes may have been tears or stasis fluid, but they hung as if sharing her fear of movement. The Kwaios were paying little attention to the activity of their captives, accustomed as they were to their shock and terror, and it was only when someone got up to run away that Samuel took Hannah's head and squeezed it reassuringly as one of the Kwaios lashed out with a crackling whip of energy to blow the man's head off. Hannah's lips were trembling and she was about to cry, but Samuel met her eyes and shook his head slowly, a warning passing between them. She drew in a sharp breath and nodded almost imperceptibly, and they both waited until they were processed and herded on to the vehicle before taking comfort in each other's touch. Some of the silent and desperate captives looked to them as they travelled, and Samuel looked around the cage until he had the attention of every

345

human before him. 'Don't be scared,' he whispered. 'I'm here to end all this.'

Ω

From a Kwaios ship in low orbit, scores of MEC fuel ships were descending to Heragon with their cargo, delivering them to destinations around the Kwaios world predetermined by the re-population requirements of the respective colonies. It was a massive operation, and these colonies of human clones kept in check by their Kwaios overlords were spread out across the gigantic planet in a variety of environments ranging from the sublime to the hostile. The numbers fluctuated, depending upon the intensity of many experimental circumstances which led in some zones to fatalities reaching into hundreds of thousands. Towards the end of the second year of the MEC programme, almost three million clones were lost to a virulent outbreak of a Kwaios-manufactured zylobyte that had adapted to feed on human bone marrow. While its lifespan was rather limited and could not be entrusted to bring down the entire species, the results were still considered promising amongst a small contingent of the Council. Of course, with what was planned, preservation of such hybrid weapons was extremely risky for the future well-being of the Kwaios.

One of the fuel ships coming to ground had a faulty transponder, apparently damaged while transecting a rogue meteor shower on its journey away from its station. As a result, it had been commandeered remotely and brought to the surface outside an experimental intake facility on an island in the north-eastern quadra-sphere. Owing to the rarity of such an occurrence, it inevitably attracted considerable attention as it came to ground. Waiting for it, amongst sixty or more Kwaios, was a master who had made the journey down to the surface as a matter of security protocol. The Kwaios Master was fourteen feet in height and encased in a hybritech battle-suit, meaning that his personal guard and the rest of the Kwaios gathered here were under no illusions that this unprecedented arrival was to be taken seriously.

They waited as vehicle depressurisation completed, and the master made his way towards the descending ramp against the advice of his soldiers, his great palms held out to either side of his body as they faced the ground. Kwaios masters could access the Sentience, often harnessing the power of the Lines to perform telekinesis. This was done by drawing the extra-natural energy of the Lines up through their hybritech gauntlets until a gravitational field could be directed at proximate objects. It was said that some masters could even levitate and direct their movement above ground, but few Kwaios had seen such a thing. What was known and had been regularly observed, however, was the amassing of Line energy in anticipation of its need. This master was doing just that, unaware that he would have been better served reading his own Line and anticipating his fate. But this was one of many active temporal intersection points brought about by Naveen's activity, and the Kwaios had yet to understand the mechanics at work.

Before the ramp met the ground, an enormous human male, more than seven feet in height, leaped out towards the master wielding a massive plasma-blade. Weapons were raised by soldiers all around, but their reactions were not fast enough, for the human had already latched on to the gravitational field building up around the master, and he dragged the huge Kwaios through the air towards him with a raised grip, impaling him with his blade before the master exploded in every direction. The Kwaios soldiers first stared in horror at the blood- and gore-covered human, whose eyes were wild with righteous rage, but when they again made to fire, the man dropped to the ground as a score of armoured humans raced out with heavy and advanced weaponry to decimate the gathering. It quickly became clear that the Kwaios numbers and strength were too great to see these humans triumph, especially as air support began moving in, but those who could get close enough to groups of the huge aliens threw themselves at them and activated explosive material strapped to their bodies. As the explosions dismembered the Kwaios defence, the giant man took advantage of the chaos and ran faster than a normal human towards the intake hangar, managing to reach the doors in time to turn and see three air vehicles drop to train their weapons on him. He smiled...

And the fuel ship exploded, an immense release of destructive energy that not only took every attack craft out of the sky and incinerated every living thing outside the hangar; it tore through the hangar and brought the front of it crumbling down. This destruction of the intake facility marked the first of what would be numerous suicide attacks against the Kwaios on Heragon, and as such it struck at the heart of their most audacious operation in the most unexpected way. Considering the intended destruction of the fuel ship, some might have thought that the individual suicides were unnecessary. But the director of this opera was deeply aware of the hearts and minds of each of his cast members. Collectively, culturally, the Kwaios shared an immense fear of death. In light of their ongoing mission, this event was only the opening act of a production designed to chill them to their hybritech bones.

Ω

The journey had been relatively short, and Samuel and Hannah were being directed out of the floating Kwaios vehicle amongst the rest of the vacant-eyed, shuffling captives. He held her hand discreetly as she kept as close behind him as possible, and she gripped his hand thankfully as tears rolled down her face and she stole furtive glances at their Kwaios escorts. They pushed and prodded at the group with sparking batons, and as they crested a hill at the eastern edge of a seemingly endless expanse of wild vegetation, Samuel squeezed Hannah's hand a little more and gestured for her to look ahead.

Great towers illuminated the entire world, it seemed, as dark clouds roiled above and one of the engineered synchro-moons of Heragon monitored the situation. The towers were constructed of an organic black substance and shimmering metal married against their will, with blue garters of crackling energy climbing upwards until they exploded off into the air, some of them leaping so high they seemed to ignite the clouds. Hundreds of these enormous structures filled the landscape beyond the hill to shrink beyond the horizon, and countless people could be seen in their wake, shuffling around like sleepwalkers. The group came to a halt, stunned by the scale of the operation. Of course, they had no idea that the operation was under attack from their own kind.

As word of the attack on the Hakar-5 intake facility spread across the hybritech network, one of the Kwaios herdsmen snapped out something in its language, and many people jumped in fright. One man in the front of the line, however, took advantage of the confusion and screamed in terrific fury as he rushed the huge alien to grab its weapon. He was lifted from his feet by his neck and shaken until his spine snapped while people screamed and shouted and cried. Others began to rush the Kwaios, thinking to overwhelm them, and as Hannah made to huddle into Samuel, burying her face in his clothes, he pushed her back and asked, 'Can you run?'

A Kwaios head turned in their direction as Hannah looked up and nodded, and Samuel dragged her towards their right as the alien threw people aside to pursue them. They were quickly in the thick overgrowth at the beginning of the wild expanse, and it towered above them as they forced their way through. Samuel held his right forearm high as he pushed inwards, with Hannah's hand gripped firmly in his left. He could hear the Kwaios behind them, but his concern was taken up by the increasing thickness and sharpness of the vegetation through which they passed. Both he and Hannah took cutting swipes to their face and limbs, and the girl was crying as he dragged her onwards. It seemed that the lone Kwaios pursuer would catch them, and all would be for naught…until the ground gave way.

Samuel heard himself shouting out with fright and Hannah screaming with him, but they were sounds whipped away by the tumbling rubble and Samuel's desperate attempt to grab the girl as they fell down a steep ravine that had been obscured by the vegetation above. He could not get her, and she had stopped screaming as she fell. He reached the bottom first, tumbling head over heels until he came to a stop just short of a crackling blue energy field. He instantly turned…and grabbed Hannah before she continued farther. He looked into her eyes to confirm that she still lived before drawing her into his arms. Feeling her chest rise with a deep breath, he sobbed and held her tightly. There was no sound of anyone coming to take them. But that did not mean the Kwaios had given up. If Samuel understood anything, it was persistence.

'What do we do now?' Hannah asked. Samuel's heart lifted, and he let her go to look into her eyes again. 'The attacks have started,' he said. 'So, we hide. And we wait.'

'For what?'

He smiled: 'Not what…*who*. We're waiting for your mom.'

Ω

349

Kwaios society had evolved from one of hierarchical complexity to a state of relative simplicity. Despite the retention of a ranking system related to military service and a bureaucracy for civic duty, Kwaios society demanded the abandonment of any expression of distinction outside of these realms which might precipitate resentment or spread discord. In fact, every Kwaios maintained a secret identity within these spheres of society, returning to anonymity at the end of each tour of duty. This was not an easy life to maintain, as Kwaios individuality was also encouraged amongst this species-wide fellowship of equals. The solution to this was the incorporation into the hybritech network of any manifestations of individuality by way of their knowledge, insight, and vision for the future of their species, so that it might be disseminated to those in need of it at an appropriate time. Such circumstances ranged from the mundane to the world-threatening, meaning the capabilities of an entire species were available to each and every Kwaios at all times. But not all capabilities were shared.

The hybritech network, an advanced artificial intelligence merged with the evolving biology of the Kwaios, had been founded upon the realisation that the Sentience not only existed, but could be used; and it developed symbiotically in conjunction with the education of certain Kwaios individuals of variant physiology whose capabilities the network had chosen to share only amongst those same individuals. These were the Masters, Kwaios mutations whose connection to the Sentience was born, not learned. The network searched the species constantly for these mutations, calling them to it upon discovering their dormant potential. It then set about concealing their abilities at the same time as it both educated them and learned from them. In other words, they were only masters because the network chose them. When a master was killed, the network knew, and every Kwaios was informed of their failure to prevent it from happening. Like the Network on Kiranis, the hybritech network of Kwaios construction was a self-contained universe of interdependency. But unlike the Kiranis Network, its nature did not call for connection to the Sentience to realise its potential. Instead, its obsessive quest for immortality had infected the mind of every Kwaios to the point that it defined them. And so, like the Kwaios, the hybritech network feared the terminal nothingness of death.

The shock of a master's assassination at the Hakar-5 facility preceded the greater shock of learning of the means by which the destruction of the facility was achieved. This shock pervaded the network, with every Kwaios across the galaxy – and some beyond – sharing in the discussion:

'The fuel ship should have been destroyed. The risks at this stage are too great for complacency.'

'Where did these humans come from? How were they armed with such weapons?'

'Search and destroy clusters have been dispatched around the planet and beyond, but there have been no incidents at Central Containment, which means these were clones.'

'Why were these clones not secured in the cells of the feeder shuttle?' This was a disturbing question, and investigations were already underway, but it suggested that the MEC system was no longer operational. There were, of course, other issues to consider: 'These humans sacrificed themselves. How do we control a species who does not fear death?'

'We observed this when the Argo set a collision course with a Jaevisk warship. The humans are unpredictable and reckless.'

'Other attacks are underway across the planet as we speak. They are killing themselves to damage our operation.'

'These advanced clones must have been concealed amongst the harvest. Their non-conformity suggests that the entire supply could be tainted.'

Despite this error in judgement, this announcement changed everything. Suggestions as to how to remedy the situation filled the network, but there was limited time for the introduction of another layer to their complex operation. The most appropriate and efficient solution to the problem meant not only that millions of Kwaios might have to face their ultimate fear; but that the completion of their mission would have to be postponed for perhaps another turn of the God-Sphere. And with the times to come that the masters had seen in the Lines, the times that the Prophet had seen fit to bring upon this galaxy, many more Kwaios would die in the interim. It was as if individual Kwaios were unwilling to give the order, but the hybritech network was beyond individuality, and it spoke: 'Prepare the final Transference merge. Abandon the remaining stock and continue the operation from Illeri.' Despite being aware of the arrival of Kallon Raesa at the planet Illeri, the network could not have known what was about to happen there.

THE SLEEPERS

A Few Days Later, Heragon Orbit

Many attacks followed the crippling of the Hakar-5 facility, and another major blow to the operation had been sufficient to distract Arrien's hosts as they arrived in orbit of the massive world. The distraction worked for only the shortest of times, but such times were a gift for someone who had been waiting for many years to act. The Kwaios were generally hypervigilant, and even when one thought one was being ignored by the Kwaios, there would be some sort of readjustment of plans underway before one's presence was acknowledged. But Arrien was attuned to the Lines in a way the Kwaios did not expect. In their arrogance, they presumed that no human was anywhere near as connected as a master. And because humans did not have hybritech, the Kwaios were partly correct. For the other part – the one that overlooked Arrien's abilities honed over the decades he had been hidden from them – they completely underestimated him.

In the heart of one of the huge ships orbiting Heragon, he had been left inexplicably alone, but he had been watching the hybritech pillars since arriving here, and he knew that the current rushing waves of power through these arteries of the ship symbolised the transfer of massive amounts of information. Activity had spiked within the past few minutes, and he knew that something significant must have happened. He had to know what it was, and so he went straight to grip two of the many glass-like, twisting tubes running the height of the nearest pillar, squeezing them tightly and gritting his teeth as the material cracked and cut his skin until he could feel the slimy, organic material inside. And when he closed his eyes, he saw them…

The pillars were filled with Lines, hundreds in the centre of each, tightly intertwined like spiralling red liquorice. Arrien allowed his mind to leap out to them, but it felt then that they grabbed him, and he was overwhelmed by their desperation and fear. Instead of the chronological journeys which usually accompanied his interaction with Fate Lines, he was bombarded with images of various lives from different aspects of Kwaios society and inhabiting different parts of the galaxy. There were scenes and the

353

echoes of scenes from Kwaios memories of life, ranging from the most unexpectedly tender aspects of nurturing a child to dreadfully violent military encounters. Arrien fought for calm and control, until he isolated a single Line, and followed it. When he did, he rushed to one end, finding only pre-birth blackness. He rushed back along it to the other end, reaching the inevitable darkness at the end of life. He was reminded of what he had discovered when he tried finding Kallon Raesa, and he knew what this was. More than that, he knew what this entire ship was.

As a Kwaios soldier ripped him away from the pillar and shouted a horrible sound of fury, he knew he had discovered and damaged something sacred. As others approached, he looked up from the floor and shouted, 'This is a *cemetery*!'

Ω

Abigale was freezing cold, shivering in a world of darkness she could not recall entering. She could hear voices around her, the volume rising to a crescendo before fading away. At their peak, they cried, 'No! Please!', but that was not what disturbed her. It was the fact that all the voices were hers. They got louder as the scene cleared, but it was below her, and what she thought was mist all around began to clear until she realised she was somehow standing in the clouds, the land far beneath populated by gigantic towers probing the night sky. At their zenith, a crown of chrome fizzled with energy, visibly vibrating as circles of crackling blue light ascended the towers before snapping off into the clouds to illuminate and disrupt them as if they were silently exploding.

Abigale quickly discerned that the rising blue rings of energy coincided with the rising volume of her multiple voices, and she felt an emotional connection as she heard her own agony and fear and perceived her own death again and again and again. No sooner had the thought entered her mind than the snap of energy from the nearest tower whipped the cloud out from beneath her. And she dropped. Frantically, chaotically, she fought for control, plummeting helplessly towards a ground filled with people, stacked high in piles of misery. Hundreds, thousands, millions…arms reaching for her as if they might catch her, as she began to focus on individual faces. Her faces. She screamed silently, straining her

354

lungs and searing her throat while not a sound escaped amidst this tumbling hell. She slammed into their hands, bones snapping as her weight struck them. The impact crushed many, and Abigale was left broken in their wake, laying atop groaning bodies as others leaned in to take her. She screamed. And it was not silent...

She woke herself with that scream, but when she did, waking on the floor on the bridge of the Argo after passing through the MEC system, it was unlike before. For everyone aboard the Argo, it was unlike before. Many of the crew were vomiting, others walking around disoriented. Carenna had been sitting on the floor, scratching her head as if the answers were inside. But she looked over at Abigale and said quietly, 'You screamed.'

Abigale stared at her for a moment. 'Where are we?' she asked, getting up from the floor.

'In the Kiranis system,' Carenna replied absently. 'But we're *inside* an asteroid!'

Abigale struggled to recall what had happened as the rest of the crew gathered themselves and manned their stations. 'Why would the system put us inside an asteroid?'

'Because someone thought it would be funny to put a MEC station in here.'

'So, we go in through one hidden station and come out another,' Abigale noted. 'I'm thinking the Kwaios might not know about either of them.'

Carenna nodded and got to her feet, looking around at the rest of the crew as they began to get their act together. 'Which might explain why we all feel like crap,' she said. 'We didn't go through their network.'

'No,' Abigale agreed, 'we went through something else. Something...*real*. Maybe one that actually works the way we believed the rest of them did!' She stepped up to her friend and right hand and whispered, 'Did you have a nightmare?'

'I heard myself screaming and shouting and there were huge towers –'

'Me too!' a young man in earshot told them. 'I think they were dying.'

Abigale shook her head and explained as the rest of the crew took notice: '*We*...were dying. They were our clones. The product of Vawter's MEC network. We've been harvested for years and brought out here!'

'All due respect, Captain,' Carenna argued, 'but that's a bit out there, isn't it? I mean, how could we all see the same thing? And how could we possibly see our own clones being killed?'

'I've no idea,' Abigale admitted, 'but I believe what I saw.' She turned to activate the viewer, seeing nothing but rock. 'First things first,' she ordered. 'Get some walkers out there and see what's going on. I don't want us sticking our necks out from under this rock if the Kwaios are sitting on it.'

Ω

In powered EVA suits, four men exited the Argo and manoeuvred in different directions to investigate this clearly man-made hollow inside the asteroid. While three of them sought strategic exit points, one of them went straight for the MEC station, to the control area that no known human had ever been permitted to see. One presumed that Samuel Vawter had been inside, but all bets were off since his revelation to Captain Saranne. Every member of the crew knew of the clone story now, and it was a bitter and terrifying pill to swallow. How could one be sure of one's identity, one's memories, if one were a mere facsimile of an echo of a life once led?

Travis Miller was the man lucky enough to find himself blasting towards the strangely configured MEC station, the index finger of his right hand maintaining his momentum on the trigger. He pushed down – way down – any thoughts of not being who he thought he was, convincing himself that there was no other way to be, no other person to be, than who he remembered himself to be. The past was everything when it came to maintaining a grip on the present. It was the foundation of a building, the record of one's health, the childhood interactions, failings, mistakes, successes, and aspirations. Travis Miller knew who he was.

Next to what looked like the intake for a giant retractable appendage, there was an airlock, strangely accessible, as if waiting for human entry. Travis was about to discover that the opposite was true. He reported his position and opened the airlock, moving inside and making his way to the inner door. Inside the station, atmospheric readings were favourable, and gravity was perfect, so his suspicions were piqued. He retracted his protective visor and opened the helmet, allowing him to savour the oxygen-rich air, but

356

when the corridor before him was illuminated and he saw the rows upon rows of advanced EVA suits, his stomach warmed with uncertainty. 'What the hell's going on?' he asked, his voice carrying over the com.

'*What are you seeing, Miller?*' Carenna asked him.

'EVA suits,' he explained. 'Maybe a hundred. Never seen anything like these ones, though.' He moved towards one and activated the atmosphere generator, watching the levels balance out until stabilising to a mix he did not find appealing. 'They look like they're made for us, but they're not set for our atmosphere. I mean, we could survive a while, but this looks more like Garran levels, what they create on their ships to emulate Sieltor Prime.'

Abigale could be heard on the com: '*Or on the Promies facility?*'

Miller nodded. 'Yeah, I guess so,' he realised. 'So, they were sending people out here. But for what?'

'*Get to the main control room,*' the captain ordered. '*We need to figure this out...fast.*'

Miller did, on both counts. What he figured out was as exciting as it was mysterious, and he reported back while he tried to take it all in on the massive monitors above him. The control room was more like a war room, and he felt his heart racing as he shouted, 'They're on *our* side! They're *everywhere*!'

'*What are you talking about?*' asked Abigale. '*Who?*'

'Whoever they've been sending through this station from the Sieltor system. It's been going on for *years*! There are coordinates here...all over the planet. Strategic locations, by the looks of it.'

'*My God!*' Carenna exclaimed. '*Sleeper cells. They have to be sleeper cells!*'

Miller was quiet for a moment, nodding as if they could see him while something caught his eye. The profiles of the people sent here were displayed on a separate monitor, one of them showing a man over seven feet in height. Miller, starting to doubt his earlier affirmations of identity, activated his VR sender as the captain asked, '*You okay, Miller?*'

'There's something...*weird* here,' he replied. 'Look at this.' The VR sent real-time footage of what he was seeing, and holo-emitters brought the control room to life for the crew to see. 'See what I mean?' Miller asked them. 'There's only one *team*!'

'The same team,' Carenna said as they looked at the monitors. 'Clones...sent over and over again.'

357

Abigale nodded: 'But why were they being sent from a *Garran* facility?'

'Dunno,' Carenna replied, 'but what about Carak Tae Ahn and Anya Echad? Word was he had a vested interest in protecting her. And we just followed *Arrien* Echad to get here…like we were *told*.'

'So, where the hell is he *now*?' Abigale wondered.

It was an open channel, and Miller had been listening, which was why he figured the next discovery was the answer to her question: 'Ah…Captain?'

'*What is it?*'

'Take a look at *this*.' He focused the sender on a holo-image of the massive Kwaios world, rotating on the far side of the room. Hovering above one point of the planet, a collection of codes and designations indicated a landing point. 'These are our transponder codes…and GPS coordinates.'

There was silence on the bridge until another team member reported: '*I found us a way out. No sign of anyone around, so it should be a safe enough exit.*'

'This was all *planned*,' said Abigale, disgusted at how she had been played. 'Put Hannah through MEC, get her cloned and killed to lure me out here to find my *real* daughter. Tell me only Arrien Echad can help, and we happen to bump into him at what's apparently the only working MEC link in the galaxy…and there's a fuckin' X-marks-the-spot waiting for us at the end!'

'We're as much a part of this as those clones they've been sending through,' Carenna agreed.

'Yeah, well…let's just hope we're the cavalry,' Abigale added. 'Cos I've no idea what we're supposed to bring to the table here.'

Ω

Back in the Sieltor system, Elder Menalis watched closely as readings came in from the device Villon had secured to the inner walls of the Argo's engine housing. It was a simple device, with a Kwaios crystal at its core. The countless millions of bots and their flurry of activity as the engine powered up were like a swarm of the now extinct Teuvas hallerites, the device on the fringes like a sleeping lyracat. 'There'll be a significant delay,' Villon explained as he looked back to the Elder, who simply nodded. He was still visibly irritated by what Villon had revealed, and Villon needed to

358

get him back on side, especially now that his patron had been murdered: 'But we'll be able to see the effects relatively quickly.'

Menalis found his smile again, hidden beneath his fleeting distrust: 'I can't imagine they'll want to continue their arrangement with the humans.'

Villon nodded. 'Given the nature of the Argo's QUIC engine, the crystal should completely disintegrate.'

'*Should*? We're playing a dangerous game, Villon. *Should*...isn't good enough.'

'As soon as the engine initiates its intake process, it will find the crystal. The bots will see it as a fuel source...a part of the engine they'll work to process.'

'Are you confident of the results?'

'If you're asking me if this is going to disrupt the current human-Kwaios relationship, then, yes...I'm confident.' Villon grinned, but his enjoyment of what was to come was tainted, as he thought of how Carak was missing the culmination of his plans. 'Let's just say that it's a good thing we're in a different star system.'

Ω

'Why did you bring me here?' Hannah asked as she chewed on the tiny piece of protein track marking the end of Samuel's meagre food supply. They been hiding under an overhang at the bottom of a dark stone ridge, only slightly protected from the wind sweeping across from the west. Samuel looked down at the girl. 'Why have you waited so long to ask?' he countered. He had told her everything he thought she could understand, about the MEC system, the Kwaios, his mission. Of course, there were things she could not or should not know, but she was surprisingly clever, and he had enjoyed teaching her.

She shrugged: 'I don't know. I was scared.'

'You're not scared now?'

'Not as much,' she realised, continuing to surprise him. 'But I wish my mom was here.'

Samuel looked up at the sky. 'Arrien will be here soon. He'll find her.'

'What if he doesn't come?'

Samuel realised that he hadn't considered the possibility, so dependent he was on the integrity of the Prophet. 'He'll come,' he

359

assured her, doing his best to convince himself. 'And so will the captain of the Argo. She's coming for *you*.'

'So, that's why you brought me here? To get my *mom* here?'

'It's the Argo I need, not her.'

'Why?'

'I designed it for a very specific reason, Hannah. And I let the Kwaios get a look at it a long time ago in the hope they'd ignore it from then on. They might have figured out what could go wrong if the ship ended up out here.'

'I've no idea what you're talking about,' Hannah admitted, her tone conveying how little she was concerned.

'That's okay,' Samuel laughed, 'you don't need to.' They were far from any of the processing fields, but in the distant skies above the towers they could see, massive shapes were descending through the clouds. Hannah saw them, too, and asked, 'Is Arrien here now?'

His smile faded, for things would get worse for this child before they got any better. 'I think so,' he said. 'But you have to trust me on something, okay?'

Despite their slight bonding over the past few days, she was hesitant. 'What?' she asked suspiciously.

'I have to go,' he told her. 'I have to leave you here.'

'What? *Why*?' She pointed to the skies, knowing that many more Kwaios were descending. 'They'll *find* me!'

'Someone will,' he assured her, pressing a needler into her arm before she knew what was happening. He gently lowered her to the ground before rising with a lump in his throat. 'You'll be safer this way.'

Ω

Arrien was aware of parts of the plan. He was pretty sure the same was the case for everyone involved, but he doubted it was because the Prophet thought things could go wrong. Instead, it was more likely to protect each party to the scheme from the moral dilemmas they would face. Arrien had seen numerous future outcomes, and the one he knew to be most favourable to humankind was horrific. But then, the last time the Prophet intervened in anything on this scale, humankind decidedly lost out, so there was no way to know what his endgame was. Whatever way one looked at it, whatever way one read the Lines, there was a certain element of helplessness that made one question the point of making decisions in a galaxy overseen by an interventionist demigod...or whatever he was. Now, as the ship on which he found himself descended towards Heragon, along with hundreds of others, Arrien questioned the very nature of existence. This species had developed a unique way to prolong life. Surprisingly, and with a certain pride, a master had joined him to explain exactly what was happening: 'You were correct to call these vehicles cemeteries. They house the Fate Lines of our myriad dead.'

Arrien steeled himself against the pain of the voice in his head as he held the communication box. 'I'm guessing I'm about to see why.'

'The towers around which we have gathered human vessels with no sense of self are designed to ensure that they are ready for Transference. It involves the merging of our dead with these empty lives.'

Arrien was forced to pretend he had no knowledge of this. 'You're talking about fusing the Fate Lines of two completely different *species*!' he snapped.

'You know a little of this Universe, Arrien Echad, but not enough.' The massive ship was burning through the clouds of Heragon, the gigantic Transference towers waiting like penetrative organs for what was about to be brought to them. 'Beneath the lies of the flesh, there is no distinction between any species. Consciousness is merely borrowed by our physical forms and returned to the Universe after life. As such, we are all potentially compatible. The Fate Lines of our clones are disconnected from their past as a result of having their memories erased, and they risk the oblivion of absorption. We are saving them.'

'That's the ideology of every race who thought themselves superior,' Arrien argued. 'Thinking they could exploit or *murder* those deemed less significant. You're *killing* them, plain and simple!'

'They are not alive,' the master replied calmly. 'Without a past, there is no meaning to their existence.' All over the world, ships like this one were now directly above groups of Transference towers, some of the ships so close they could have connected by airlocks. In some parts of the world with particularly dense processing populations, they were like rooftops across continents.

361

'Not from *their* point of view! Their past was *stolen* from them. As was their *future*!'

'They have no point of view.' There was a delicate hum then, but as the intensity of the energy transfer from the Kwaios ships to the Transference towers increased to the point that only the hybritech pillars could be seen, Arrien could feel it in his bones and he felt as if he might either soil himself or vomit as the master said, 'And now they have no future.' But Arrien's was a mild suffering compared to those on the surface below.

Ω

Abigale could not believe what she was seeing. The viewer showed that every major Kwaios ship was descending to the surface, and the entire planet was alight with hybritech energy, crackling across the world and enveloping every enormous vessel in blue fire. 'What the hell am I looking at?' the captain asked of no one in particular.

'Whatever's going on,' Carenna put in as she stepped up next to her, 'this has to be the real reason for the MEC system.'

Abigale shook her head and then turned to the nav officer on duty. 'How long until we reach those coordinates?'

'Six minutes...if we can get through all that,' he replied.

'I've a feeling we will,' she said as she turned back. 'Anyone got any ideas as to how we find Arrien Echad in all this mess?' She did not want to ask about her daughter. The thought of her down on that world right now was terrifying. Carenna put a hand on her shoulder: 'Maybe that's what the coordinates are for. And not just him.'

Abigale nodded, feeling a small measure of hope. 'Maintain course,' she ordered. 'Ready all weapons and bring the QUIC drive to a travelling stop.' The officer on engine ops began punching in the numbers based on their current course and velocity, while the Kwaios ships below, their primary systems fully dedicated to Transference, could turn only auxiliary weapons towards this significant intrusion.

Ω

There was one sleeper cell remaining, with the work of all the others complete. The giant amongst them, who was always their leader, checked the time: 'Less than five minutes. Let's go.'

The forty-strong team, some of them duplicates and triplicates, carrying heavy weaponry and hardware on their backs, began the journey upwards from deep below the surface where they had lived for months, checking their weapons as they ran and prepared to fight, and die. This was why Elder Carak had created them. This was their purpose in life. They shared the memories of those who had come before them, and as he ran at the head of the team, the giant recalled the inspiring words of the ageing Garran when he had visited years before any of this team had been born:

'The Kwaios have held me in their grip for a long time. They threatened not only my family but my species. And while none of you are Garran, I consider you my family. You are born not only of my will to fight back, but of my purpose for living. With the help of others, I have been able to construct and conceal a MEC station that works as it is supposed to...as Samuel Vawter of Earth had intended it to. It has one destination...the Kwaios world in the Kiranis system. Over the years to come, you will be infiltrating the cloning facilities there, which they intend to use to invade Earth and ultimately consume humankind. Each team will have very specific instructions and timing is crucial.' He had looked around at the first batch of superhuman clones and smiled like a father: 'Are there any questions?'

The giant, the first of his perfected kind, asked, 'Will it hurt to die?'

Carak stared at him, momentarily bewildered by the innocence of the question. He smiled again, but it lacked warmth as he assured them all, 'You won't even know it has happened.'

They were less the innocents of the first batch, yet still the question was pertinent. Given the nature of the Kwaios operation, it seemed almost unfair that the answer to that question implied that the nature of human life and death was so very different to that of the enemy. The giant's reminiscing was interrupted by the alarm on his monitor. 'The Argo has entered the atmosphere!' he shouted back to them. They saw blue crackling light up ahead, and they exited the tunnel in a huge clearing directly in the centre of four Transference towers, each of them far away on the horizon, each of them glowing brightly as the terrible process was underway. They could see the distant masses of clones, thousands of them herded around the base of each tower. At this point, one could easily get confused about the mission, but there was no time for distraction. Directly above them, Samuel Vawter's prized possession was afire as it descended rapidly through the clouds, and Kwaios weapons were turning on it. Ten of the clones raced to the middle of the clearing, immediately snapping components off their backs and beginning construction of what looked like a huge weapon. Three Kwaios dropships moved in to surround and fire upon the clone team, while they in turn set ten gigantic Kwaios guns upon tripods and began the fight to protect the device in the centre, while a protective energy field pulsed active around them. The alien guns were used to ground the dropships before blasting holes in the nearest Kwaios vessels as the Argo continued its fighting descent. The giant turned to see the man they had been waiting for, looking decidedly out of place in his plain grey suit as he hurried towards the chaos. 'Is it ready?' he shouted.

'Yes, Mister Vawter,' the clone replied, gesturing towards the device in the centre of the clearing. 'And the Argo is almost in range.'

Ω

The Transference towers around the planet were pulsating now, blue rings of light crackling upwards, but this time snapping off to electrify the ships above. The towers were ready to create life, and their energy disseminated throughout the graveyard ships to ignite and excite the Kwaios souls interred within. Their Fate Lines snapped with renewed vigour and purpose, while on the surface, the human clones jolted and spasmed, even as they stood upright and raised tear-filled eyes to hybritech heavens. Their past may have been erased, but still they held tight to their present, their awareness of existence, even this painful experience informing them of their lives. Everything at that moment was past, present, and future combined, for nothing else mattered but their will to survive. It was a will, however, which could not last.

The invisible Fate Lines of the Kwaios dead were drawn into the towers, rushing downwards like snakes of Eden, punishing the spawn of those who had pushed too far, those who had wanted to know. At the end of the towers, still invisible to the naked eye, they leaped through reality to inseminate the clones. Bodies stopped spasming and they dropped to the ground, eyes glazed as the heavens rained upon them. The noise of the system was deafening, but the sound within the human minds was worse. It screamed and caused agony, irradiating identity second by second. Everything remembered from the moment of coming out of the MEC process and waiting in dread for this one was consumed, annihilated from then until now. Until Kwaios thoughts and memories and dreams occupied human minds. Across Heragon, Transference was occurring, but its hurried execution would leave millions of Kwaios souls without host bodies, their Fate Lines rushing back up to the hybritech pillars which would continue to keep them in quantum stasis.

Ω

While Transference was underway and he and the master stood in the half-light of a Kwaios cemetery ship, Arrien could feel through his connection with the Sentience the snuffing out of the short, remembered lives of the human clones, and as he felt their terror, he looked up to the shadowy master with fury and despair. 'This is *genocide*!' he hissed with tears in his eyes, raising the cursed box of communication. 'You're a race of *murderers*!'

'I have something to show you,' the giant Kwaios replied quietly. 'I believe it will change your perception of what is happening here.' The master brought up an image of people in square cells, maybe a hundred in each. As he caused the image to zoom out, it became clear that there were thousands of these cells, and they were spread all over the largest continent on the planet.

'What *is* this?' Arrien breathed.

'Preservation. These are the original humans taken here from each of their first journeys through the MEC system. Every single one has been kept alive and sustained since the inception of MEC. Deep below ground, they are protected from Transference. All of their memories are intact and not one has been harmed.'

'I don't understand.'

'As you can see,' said the master, gesturing towards the populated map, 'we are not the monsters you believe us to be. Not one of your people has died.'

At the same time as he knew that this was the reason he was here, Arrien forced his mind to work around their twisted logic. From their point of view, the clones were not people. They had no memories, no awareness of who they had been; and for the Kwaios, this made them worthless. But they had been aware of their existence, right up until the moment they had been consumed. 'You see life differently to us,' he said quietly.

'Perhaps,' the master agreed. 'But –' His head jolted up to one side, as if he could see something in the space above him. 'Impossible! Not during Transference!'

Arrien felt a chill, sensing that this was his moment. 'What isn't possible? What's happening?'

The Kwaios Master said a name, and it sounded as if the bogeyman had arrived: 'Samuel Vawter.'

$$\Omega$$

As the ship was coming down and suffering considerably under Kwaios attack, the officer on engine ops shouted, 'The engine's restarting!'

'What?' Abigale snapped. 'Shut it *down…now*!'

'I *can't*! The *intake's* been activated! There's a foreign body in the reactor!'

Carenna was already up next to him. 'Abbie…' she said simply, horrified as she looked at her friend with her eyes wide. Abigale looked at her for a second, before darting for the elevator. This was no doll that cried, but she had to see what was happening. Their lives, and that of her daughter, depended on getting down safely. But if the QUIC drive was taking in quantum energy in an atmosphere, all bets were off. From the elevator, she could see something flash red as its motion towards the centre of the living drive was illuminated by the mirrored bots, and she was astonished to see that the bots, in their self-replicating billions, were reaching out to consume it. She could not have known that a senior Garran officer had stroked her hair while planning this violation, but all that mattered now was shutting down the engine. '*We're almost down, Captain*,' a voice reported over her com as

366

she hurried to the override interface. *'But there's a heavily-armed force in our LZ and I can't figure out whose side they're on!'*

Engine staff were waiting for Abigale, the chief engineer with his dotkey in hand. 'Emergency shutdown?' he asked hopefully.

'Damn right!' she said, withdrawing her key and moving to the panel. But when they tried, it was frozen, giving an error sound and reporting, *'Manual override has been revoked.'*

'The *hell*...?' Abigale tried again, and as the ship was rocked by a blast from a Kwaios ship which tore through its belly and incinerated scores of men and women, a face appeared on the glass between the captain and the QUIC drive. 'I'm sorry it has to be this way, Captain,' Samuel Vawter told her, above the noise and confusion of the battleground in which he stood. 'But we have to see things through.'

Abigale was stunned: 'How the hell did you get *out* here?' She looked through him to the engine. 'And what are you *doing*? We're all gonna die if we don't stop the intake *now*! Somehow, there's another *crystal* in the engine!' The staff around Abigale had no idea what she was talking about.

'You're confusing me with someone else, Captain. But I'm sure he told you I have remote access. The intake will keep going, and the crystal has a job to do. Preferably before the Kwaios destroy you.'

The Kwaios attack was getting more intense on the ground and in the air, and Abigale screamed at Vawter, 'You *led* me here! You took my *daughter*! For *what*? To get me *killed*? It makes no *sense*!'

'My *clone* led you here!' Vawter shouted over the noise of the fighting. *'You're* a clone! Don't you *get* it? Hannah's not *your* daughter!' Abigale stared at him, speechless, her breath catching in her throat. 'And the *sense* it makes...' Vawter continued, 'is that we're all here to *end* this!'

Ω

Arrien could feel their confusion, their desperation. It was going wrong, and they were unprepared. This was it. He backed away from the master, whose connection to the hybritech was disoriented by the fixation on Transference, the discovery of the asteroid housing the only real MEC route in the galaxy, and the unexpected appearance and intervention of Samuel Vawter, with whom they had made this arrangement. This weak connection diminished his role as gatekeeper, opening a window of opportunity for Arrien. He felt it, an unravelling of the fabric of protection keeping him out of the hybritech network. And he pushed through...

This was not the Sentience, the pure consciousness of the Universe. Instead, it was an alien corruption of consciousness and technology, in seemingly perfect unison that defied distinction between the two. The red Lines of dislocated and contained fate, the trapped energy of the Universe powered by the relentless progression of time, were intertwined with the crackling blue lines of power generated by the Kwaios mainframe, itself a mere echo of the unknowable God-Sphere. In a moment immeasurable, Arrien took in his ethereal surroundings, the red and blue multi-layered grid of the hybritech network, which in this ship protected the souls of passed Kwaios, and he identified central power chords. Throwing his imagined self headlong at them, he sped towards one of the many control nodes, determining the means by which weapons were controlled. He felt the hybritech's awareness of the attack on the Argo and Samuel Vawter, and he grabbed hold of the twisted chords with both hands. In this place between realities, he was able to freeze the chords with just his touch. The chords snapped, the frost racing away in both directions...

$$\Omega$$

...and Kwaios weapons deactivated, the Argo no longer under attack from the cemetery ships. Ground troops and small aerial vehicles maintained the fight, and Carak's final sleeper cell was losing men and women fast, their protective shield gone and only four of the huge guns still standing. There was an impact too close to Vawter for comfort, the dust momentarily obscuring his vision as he clung desperately to the remote unit standing in the centre of an increasingly contracting last stand. He could feel the presence of the huge clone next to him, the man standing with his back to him as he protected him fiercely. He knew the giant had suffered numerous injuries, but he was a creation of prodigious strength and endurance, built especially for this mission and under the watchful eye of a Garran whose entire race had been threatened

368

by the Kwaios. Motivation was far from lacking in this enterprise, and Samuel's father was in his mind as he coughed and got back to work.

Samuel had run the simulation hundreds of times. Ten years of practice, but nothing could have prepared him for what he was about to do. Simulations were far from reality. 'What's going to happen?' Abigale snapped over the still open channel. 'You're tampering with a Jaevisk life engine, for god's sake!'

'The Argo was specifically designed for this mission,' Samuel replied absently as he frantically punched in the numbers based on the readings from the engine. There was nothing further he could do, but he wanted to confirm what was coming. He would have given anything to see his engine as it was now, as Abigale could see it, the central sphere of bots opening to unveil a platform containing four red stones. Four beams of energy created a red pyramid from which a single blast pushed the Reaper stone out of the Universe. 'The Kwaios saw it. Every time you went through MEC. They knew the Argo's QUIC drive was only the auxiliary housing of a life engine, but they figured it harmless. The Garran have used them for decades.'

'So where did the extra crystal come from?'

'We had someone in place amongst the Garran. Before they pushed you through the only real MEC route in the galaxy, they gave you a little upgrade.'

Abigale was horrified, but there was no time to dwell on her naivety and the trap into which she had led them all. 'This is insane!' she roared. 'A fifth feeder stone will disrupt the process. There's no telling what will happen!'

'I beg to differ,' Samuel replied. 'The QUIC drive bots are about to get back to doing what they were designed for – gathering fuel. And the new stone will give the Reaper a whole new purpose.'

'I don't understand,' Abigale replied as a chill went through her. 'What fuel? We're in an atmosphere!'

'Organic fuel,' said Samuel, looking at her directly. 'The new stone is a Kwaios heart.' He cut the channel. In the centre of the QUIC drive, and as Abigale and the engineering staff looked on helplessly, the extra crystal was being brought by the bots towards the life engine configuration, that which the Jaevisk used for their ships and had gifted to Governor Ben-Hadad of Sieltor Prime a century ago. The red pyramid began to shudder as the crystallised

Kwaios heart came closer, and the bots moved it across one of the lines, disrupting the sourcing process as they placed it on the platform in the centre.

Neither human nor Garran knew where a Reaper stone usually vanished to, but when it returned to the Argo's engine, it dropped upon the smaller stone, cracking it open to release molecules of blood which began floating around the life engine. What remained of this fifth stone, this Kwaios heart, was incorporated as part of the quantum sourcing, the four feeder stones connecting through it before once again pushing this now composite stone out of the Universe. What Abigale could not have known was that this new configuration inverted the purpose of the device, and the Reaper was now set to expel energy rather than draw it.

There was no time to do anything, and Abigale put her hands on the glass as tears ran down her face. 'Hannah,' she whispered, as the bots of the QUIC drive began assimilating these new parameters, gathering the spilled Kwaios blood as they worked.

Ω

The master turned with a roar and slammed Arrien's body against a pillar...

He knew it had happened, but there was no pain. Not in this place. To stop him now, the master would have to come for him. He could feel how much focus there was on this place now. Everything was going precisely as Naveen had said it would. And why not? The man was from the future. But to see every detail, to know how every single person in his grand scheme would play their role...

It was as if Naveen was writing the very past he sought to set in stone.

The master was before him, its hand at his throat. Arrien was lifted from his feet in this place between places, and Arrien struggled to keep thoughts out of his head which would damage the cause. Certainly, Naveen and Vawter had kept things from him, but Arrien could travel the Lines and had seen many things. He knew what was happening out at Phobos, and what the Vawter clone –

He was dragged out of the hybritech network, enraged black eyes glaring down at his damaged body. 'There is a *clone*!' the master snapped. Arrien could not understand him, but he did not have to. As he coughed blood, he sensed a pulse of information sent across the network, and he prayed to the Sentience that he had not ruined everything with his careless musings as the information was picked up by an unlikely recipient on a Kwaios ship in the Sol system. A ship out at Phobos, that moon of Mars where Samuel Vawter had hidden the Redeemer. The master before him waited for a response, some assurance that it was not too late. But what happened next left no time to consider such possibilities.

Ω

The Argo was less than a kilometre above ground and taking fire from Kwaios attack craft. The crew of the ship from Earth were defending themselves furiously, but multiple hull breaches and failed protective arrays heralded the obliteration of Samuel Vawter's prized possession. Before it exploded, however, Samuel tapped one key on the panel before him. One key, before the giant clone was torn apart by Kwaios fire and Samuel's head was blown off. That one key ejected the engine core, which collapsed into a metal sphere and shot up into the air, continuing to function. The countless bots of the QUIC engine escaped containment through the disconnected intake vents, exiting as if a hornet's nest had been cracked open. They streamed out into the atmosphere of the Kwaios world with an entirely new energy mandate, and with no immediate restrictions in this larger environment, they began multiplying to fuel their exponential population explosion. The hybritech network was too late to register the threat. With Transference occurring in every direction across the planet, where para-quantum echoes of Kwaios lives were being fused with the severed fates of humans, the towers were like power plants, beacons of purpose for the ever-multiplying bots of the QUIC engine, which sought only to fuel the life engine at their heart. But the Jaevisk design which had long infuriated the Kwaios had been corrupted, operating in reverse, and the disappeared feeder stone drew energy on a level of reality about which humankind had only theorised. It fed on the Kwaios Fate Lines, drawing them first from within the cloned humans, who dropped dead in their millions. But

371

the greatest horror of all for the Kwaios came when the bots began to disintegrate Transference towers, within which the unprocessed Fate Lines awaited fusion. Millions of disconnected Kwaios souls were consumed.

There were many easier targets, of course, and Kwaios soldiers and masters still on the ground were drained by the voracious bots. As their numbers continued to rise, and they moved like clouds through the skies, the bots were recognised by the hybritech network as a threat to its existence, even though the ships across which it was spread were above the surface of the Kwaios world. The cemetery ship within which Arrien lay in agony was amongst the first to fire its engines and raise itself out of the atmosphere of a planet suffering the consumption of its destiny. He cried not only for himself, but even for the Kwaios, for their horror and despair was overwhelming. He had seen how they had protected the original people taken from the MEC system, and he had allowed himself some measure of their perspective. They had worked towards this Transference process for a century, and now they were losing so many resurrected souls. The sensation of being in orbit came to Arrien, and he saw the hybritech pillars illuminate around him as he was left alone and they made a great leap across the galaxy. Yet they travelled to the planet Illeri, and the ship was immediately rocked by massive amounts of debris from a planet destroyed by its own inhabitants as punishment against its Kwaios invaders. In desperation, there was no choice but to make the leap to the final stage of their scheme. A blue and white planet called Earth.

INTERVAL 5
DESOLATION

Loneliness is not the way for most people. They seek the company of others, often to validate their own existence, to have their opinions and aspirations heard and shared and discussed. But often, the company of others overwhelms one's own voice, suppressing the sense of self. You must first know who you are, if you are to be anyone whose existence might one day be validated, and your opinions discussed.

An extract from the enigmatic *Teachings of Sansaya*, Lady Protector of the Dark Ruins of Einnor, 806 NE

Phobos, Mars Orbit, 320 NE

The Pegasus had brought him out here, cutting engines on the dark side of Deimos, the tiny outer moon of Mars, and its newly appointed captain, Gerard Hill, was relishing the secrecy and subterfuge. 'The workstations are on lockdown protocols,' he reported to Samuel as they stood on the bridge. 'None of the crew will be able to monitor or record your journey.'

'Good,' Samuel replied absently. Despite this assurance, he was calculating an approach path to Phobos which would keep him from being detected. The inner moon was currently on the far side of the planet, but it moved fast. Timing was everything if there were to be no deaths just to keep this meeting quiet.

'You can trust me, Mr. Vawter,' Hill added, concerned as to whether this was an issue. 'Truth be told, I'm quite...' He shrugged with a silly grin that was altogether unbecoming of a man in his position.

'Excited?' Samuel suggested.

Hill nodded. 'I know, it's ridiculous, but...I've always been a bit of a conspiracy buff.'

'You'll learn,' Samuel replied dismissively. 'You'll get tired of whatever secrets you think you know.' He walked away from the eager young captain, adding, 'Or they'll kill you.'

Samuel left the bridge and headed to the recon speeder he had taken for this mission. Amara was already there, waiting for him. 'Hey,' she said softly, unsure of the situation. 'Everything okay?'

He was about to give her away, handing her over to monsters so he could destroy them. But she was not the weapon, nor the bait nor lure. She was merely the price, a dowry for his adherence to the pact. His heart pounded and adrenaline coursed through him so much that his teeth chattered and anxiety rushed from head to toe; but he needed to hide it. He loved her still, despite his conscious efforts to retreat and convince himself otherwise so this would be easier. But Samuel Vawter was about to become the monster, and nothing would be okay from here on. 'Sure,' he replied with a soft smile. 'Had to get the timing right. You up for this?'

'A trip to Phobos?' she laughed. 'Of course! I hear it's fast. Two laps in a Martian day, right?'

He chuckled and kept tears in check. 'Something like that. We need a perfect entry path.' He turned quickly, feigning focus on the speeder as he slapped its hull: 'This beauty will get us right. Then we hop on a buggy to the forma plant.'

'Sounds like fun.' She came up to him, kissing him on the cheek before he could stop her. 'Thanks for this,' she said. 'We haven't done anything together for a while.' He was about to reply, moving into the shadow of the craft so she could not clearly see his eyes, but she cut him off: 'I know…you've been busy.'

He nodded and ducked under the speeder. 'Come on,' he said. 'Let's go.'

She stood for a moment before joining him, desperately trying to shake the feeling that something was wrong. He was stressed, she knew that. But still, she could not escape the idea that he had been avoiding her on the journey here. The speeder took them in towards Mars, adjusting course and slowing to prepare for the arrival of Phobos along its orbital path. At almost eight thousand kilometres per hour, Phobos was, as Amara noted, fast. 'Do you still remember the day we met?' she asked him, once he had completed the orbital match.

Despite himself, he smiled with genuine warmth. If he were aware that she was trying to figure him out, he set it aside. It would be a long time before they could once again reminisce, and by then he would be older, and she would likely despise him. 'Of course I do,' he replied. 'I remember that dress.'

She laughed. 'Oh, I'm sure you do. I'm surprised you didn't need your eyes put back in!'

He turned to her. 'You were so beautiful,' he told her. He held her gaze and his voice broke as he said, 'You'll always be beautiful.' And she knew: 'Sam…what's going on?'

There was a gravitational disturbance which rocked the speeder while its systems compensated to keep it steady. 'I'm sorry!' he pleaded, with his tears released. 'They gave me no choice!'

Amara was horrified, rushing to the port window to see an alien ship materialising. 'What the hell *is* this, Sam?' she shouted, swinging on him. He stood, saying, 'It'll be okay, I promise,' ostensibly making to embrace her and calm her down; but she delivered a sharp right to his left eye and he went back against the console. 'Get us *out* of here!' she roared. 'I'm not going to be a pawn in one of your games.'

376

'The deal is done,' he explained coldly as he righted himself, and when she looked at him and saw his dark determination, it was as if a different man were standing before her. 'They won't hurt you.'

'*Who*?' she snapped. '*Who* won't hurt me?'

He took a breath before saying, 'The Kwaios.'

'Oh, God,' she whimpered as she moved back from him, looking around as if there were some escape. She ran to the com console and slammed a key before shouting, 'Captain Hill! Get me outta here!'

'They're on lockdown.' Samuel came around from the control area as docking tentacles from the Kwaios ship latched on to the speeder: 'Amara, I'm going to save humankind from something terrible. *We're* going to.'

'What are you talking about?'

'The Shield isn't being built by the Illeri,' he explained. 'The Illeri never contacted us. They never had a part in this.' She stood and listened, stunned into resignation as he continued: 'The Kwaios occupied their world so they could infiltrate ours.'

'How?' The speeder came to rest inside the Kwaios ship.

'They're going to use human clones with Kwaios minds. Millions of them.'

'And you're going to let this *happen*?' She put her hand to her mouth. She knew him better than that: 'Oh, my *God*! You're complicit in this. You're *helping* them!'

He raised a hand. 'It's the only way.'

'The only way for *what*? For you to *survive*? To get *rich*?'

He shook his head sadly, realising that she did not know him at all: 'No, Amara. That's not what this is about.'

There was no time to get her answers. Power was shut down in the speeder, and Samuel passed her to head to the airlock. 'Will I…will I see you again?' Amara asked without turning.

He could not bring himself to look at her. With a deep and agonising breath, he raised his head to the imaginary heavens and gathered himself enough to reply, 'I hope so.' And despite the horror to which he was delivering her, he told her he loved her. But Amara, with tears streaming down her face, stalked defiantly towards the airlock, pushing him aside as she said, 'I seriously doubt that.'

PART 6
ASCENSION

The gods warned our ancestors, saying, "You may climb any tree here in Paradise, except the Tree of Ascension. If you climb to the uppermost branches of this tree, you will fall, and you will die." But the Sentience, in its wisdom, said, "You will not fall. Nor will you die. These gods know that when you climb to the uppermost branches of the Tree of Ascension, your eyes will be opened, and you will be like them, looking out upon the Universe and knowing its secrets." Then the gods said, "Look, humankind has become like us. They have climbed the Tree of Ascension and they know the secrets of the Universe. If we do not act, they will happen upon the Tree of Eternity, hidden in the shadows, and they will climb it, and they will live forever." And so, we remember to this day the guidance of the Sentience and the Tree of Ascension. For it was from that day that our eyes were opened, and we knew the Universe. And it was from that day that we learned a great truth – that even the gods fear us.

From the 'Observances of the Elect', documents concerned with explaining the ceremonies and rituals of a significant sect attached to the Omega Federation. There is great debate as to whether the 'Observances' should be dated to before or after the Day of the Prophet, considering the reference to the Tree of Eternity. Many scholars researching the 1ST Millennium NE suggest that this could not be a retrospective on the Day of the Prophet because of the tense used in reference to the gods. The problem, of course, is that the archives of the Omega Federation were destroyed by the Second Cen-Dith Incursion of 982 NE.

THE ATTACK

The Illeri Vessel, The Shield, Earth, 330 NE

'Red Squad, move to board hostile vessel. Blue Squad, enter monitoring station Gamma-5. Authorisation code Alpha 8-1-2.'

A bulky, heavily armed utilitarian craft was ascending through the clouds when orders for the soldiers on board came from the general standing at Tzedek's table. He told one team to board the hostile vessel which would within seconds be in their sights, while the other was instructed to investigate an old monitoring station on the interior of the Shield.

'Acknowledged,' the pilot replied, turning to look back at the team. 'You heard the man. Asses up!'

The men and women jumped to action, ten of them forming Blue Squad, twenty Red. Blue Squad were swift to move from the main hold into a smaller craft fixed to the starboard airlock. Once released, they could be seen from the cockpit window, heading up and away towards the monitoring station. Then, as the port sunshields opened like metal curtains, all eyes took in the black monstrosity to which they had been sent – the Illeri ship. The pilot changed course, heading for the sleek demon, his heart pounding as distance lessened and size increased. 'Hope you boys 'n' girls are ready,' he called. There was no reply, and he risked a glance back. Seated like zombies, none of them moved, staring yet not seeing, breathing yet not living. 'What the –?' He screamed as a terrible pain like piercing needles struck his brain. Holding his head with both hands, he lost control of the ship and it began to pitch to port. He never saw the concealed weapons of the smooth-hulled Illeri ship turning towards them.

Blue Squad landed at the monitoring station, their small craft rotating so the port airlock connected and pressurised. Through the tiny windows of the airlock passageway, one of them saw the flash in the distance, announcing the demise of Red Squad, but despite her shock, she did not call to turn back. There was no turning back. Snapping a mag into the breach of her rifle, she joined her squad, taking a deep breath as they took their first tentative steps into the station. There was no power here, and they needed their flashlights to navigate the tunnels leading into the main control area. The silence was unnerving, broken by the sound of the airlock door closing in the distance behind them.

The control area in the centre of the cubic station had been plunged into irreparable darkness, the reason coming to light as they stepped down to the main floor and into a pool of deep water. It was up to their knees, and black waves rippled in the flashlight beams. One of the soldiers gasped as something touched his ankle. He reached down and pulled it up, the eerie light revealing a black face with empty eyes. 'It's part of an Illeri biosuit,' another noted with fascination.

'There's another one here.'

'And here.'

They found four, reporting the same back to the general, along with news of Red Squad's demise. What they did not report straight away was what they realised next, as one of them directed his flashlight to the ceiling. A hatch was dripping water into the station, and they became immediately conscious of the immense pressure it must have been under. But more importantly, they realised that these discarded biosuits were evidence of an escape into the Shield itself; somewhere, as a certain red-haired Garran once said, there was a lot of water.

THE BARGAIN

Kwaios Colony Ship, Near Phobos, Mars Orbit

The Redeemer, still bearing Jena's shuttle by airlock, was suspended in blue light in a hangar, floating horizontally so that the occupants of the airlock could still stand. Vawter and Jena readied their weapons as the Kwaios began surgically cutting into the passageway to avoid rapid depressurisation. 'How powerful is this bomb you've rigged?' Vawter asked.

'It's not a bomb, but it'll feel like one. It'll immediately disable the Redeemer's safety protocols and set the propulsion systems into overdrive.' She held his glare: 'It'll happen fast.'

Vawter shook his head. 'You've no idea what'll happen,' he told her. 'The Redeemer is a one-off creation designed to travel along routes we can't even see.'

'Those...*Lines*?'

He nodded. 'They're sort of...beside the Universe, on a level we call para-quantum.'

Jena had nothing to say. She had plunged headlong into this venture, and now she was lost. 'So, what do you think will happen?'

'I'm not sure, but the Kwaios are likely to regret taking us in.'

'Maybe that's what Tzedek wanted.'

'What?' Vawter felt his blood go cold. Jena was about to explain when the Kwaios broke through and waited until the atmosphere equalised. 'Doesn't matter now,' she said, feeling the air change around her. 'Let's hope they want to keep us alive.' Her head was swimming and she felt sick.

'They'll want to keep *me* alive,' Vawter asserted as he placed a hand against the wall to steady himself. 'We have a deal.' The side of the airlock was ripped away and Vawter's blurred vision took in the huge Kwaios reaching out for him. As the air equalised and the two humans once again held their wits, and notably not their weapons, Jena stood next to the airlock and looked up at Vawter, who was struggling in a Kwaios grip around his throat. 'I think there's a new deal,' she remarked dryly.

An order was barked in the painful language and Vawter was released. On his knees, he hung his head as he caught his breath,

383

and a communication cube was thrown at his chest as he straightened up. He took his time retrieving it, and Jena leaned down to him: 'Want me to take it?'

He shook his head, angry with her, with Tzedek, the Kwaios, the Universe. 'You've done enough damage,' he said as he snatched the cube and brushed her away. He got to his feet and snapped at the Kwaios, 'I wasn't coming for you! I wasn't coming for *any* of you!'

'We know why you are here.' They pointed at the floating Redeemer behind him and Jena. 'But why did you come to retrieve this simple craft?'

'*Simple*?' Vawter snapped, with Jena only getting his side of the conversation. 'If you've looked closely, you've seen its engine.'

'You believe it has a para-quantum engine,' said a master, coming into view as the others moved aside to let him through. 'You believe it is the one you saw built by the Garran saboteur...the one who works for the man you call the Prophet.' Many more Kwaios had arrived to witness this exchange, but both Vawter and Jena knew that their itchy trigger fingers would be of no benefit.

'Of *course* it's that one!' Vawter argued. 'Look...I don't care about Naveen or his pet Garran. All I want...' Vawter's voice broke and he took a moment to compose himself. 'All I want is to get back to Amara. I can retrace my life with the Redeemer. It follows the Lines, so I can get back to before the accident. I can *save* her!'

The master exchanged glances with the other lesser Kwaios, and Vawter needed no extraordinary senses to feel their confusion. Given what they had observed in recent days, there were many concerns. 'How did this craft get here from the Illeri home world?' the master asked. 'We watched it descend into the planet, but it did not emerge.'

'What are you *talking* about? I've had it hidden out here for two years!' There was obvious consternation, and the master was intrigued by Vawter's conviction. Vawter felt a niggling pain in his head as a bolt of enlightenment told him that what he believed was not true. If he was not the real Samuel Vawter, what else about his sense of reality was a lie? He looked up at the master: 'You said you know why I'm here. What did you mean?'

'I will show you.' He turned away, sending the message throughout the network that the real Redeemer was likely still out there and had to be found, while the other Kwaios gestured that Vawter and Jena follow them. Jena met Vawter's invitation with an angry and imploring glare, just short of asking him if he were crazy, but he snapped, 'Got a better idea?' and walked on. She swiftly stepped up. 'What's going on?' she asked him. 'I mean...why *are* you here?' But Vawter remained silent as they struggled to keep pace with the huge aliens.

There were no tangible walls across the expansive levels of the Kwaios vessel, just fluctuating energy fields designating various areas of activity and operation. Theoretically, one could see the inner hull from every direction, if one had incredibly good eyesight to traverse such a distance. This arrangement meant that the only thing separating observers from seeing what they were waiting to see was distance, and Vawter saw it long before Jena, almost as if he had been programmed to. Up ahead and to their right, just beyond one of the liquid-like energy fields and blocked only by the movement of the master and the eight or nine Kwaios in front of them, someone was suspended in white light, a motionless crucifixion. Vawter hurried now, his heart racing, his subconscious explaining what he was seeing even as he lost sight of her while pushing through the leading Kwaios. The master let him pass, without the need for a communication cube to answer Vawter's question as he ran on. The Universe slowed to allow him to catch up with the truth, and he had no words as he reached her.

Clothed in white, angelic and peaceful as she was held in stasis, Vawter's past beckoned to him as every inch of Amara's form screamed at him that he had been used, manipulated, his memory altered. Ironically, it was this which kept him from accepting what was before him. The master and the other Kwaios soldiers had reached him, and Jena pushed through, rushing to her sister as she cried her name and Vawter turned to the Kwaios to snap, 'She's a *clone*! Amara *died*!'

The master took the communication box from behind the half-robe hanging from his left shoulder, but Vawter roared, 'You throw that *fuckin'* thing at me and I'll throw it back!' He stalked forward, pointing back at Amara as Jena reached her and stopped, suddenly unsure of herself. 'If she's real,' Vawter continued, 'how's she here? And if she's a *clone*, why would you bother keeping her like this? Why not use her like the rest of them?'

The master threw the box, and Vawter bared his teeth in anger as he refused to take it up. Jena was about to intercede, but the master had another idea. Gesturing towards Amara, he caused her head to lift, and her blue eyes stared in anguish through her long blonde hair: 'Sam? Is that you?'

Her voice cut through his doubt, and he turned with a heart-wrenching groan. 'Yes, Princess,' he replied. 'It's me.' She began sobbing, and he went to her, reaching up to hold one of her hands in both of his. 'How is this possible?' he asked her.

She did not answer him. Instead, she looked beyond him to the master, saying, 'He needs to know why you don't remember, Sam. You remember so much...but not about *me*. Not what you *did*.'

'What I *did*?'

'You gave me up to them, Sam. Part of your deal. Did you remove the memory?' Amara hoped that this was so, as if it might indicate some measure of shame or at least lead to redemption.

'I...I don't...' Vawter was confused, and his head was pounding. There was a buzzing behind his eyes, and he felt like his ears would explode. Jena glared at him: 'What the hell *is* this?'

He ignored her. The removal of memories would explain a lot, but... 'I remember them *telling* me you were dead,' he argued. 'Why would they *do* that?'

The master could have drawn his own conclusions, and he was already stalking forward with an outstretched hand when Amara's link to the hybritech network led her to intercept the information speeding across the galaxy from Heragon; information gleaned from Arrien's wayward thoughts. 'He's a clone,' she announced. The master grabbed and lifted Vawter by the head, immediately reading his Fate Line as Vawter went numb. The clone's history had in places been cleverly disconnected and re-threaded to conceal absent truths, a false legato of the past activity of Samuel Vawter. But new truths had also been implanted to become the basis of a subtly different identity, and the master growled as he swung around to throw the clone to the Kwaios soldiers. They dragged him to his feet as the master stared at Jena. She was horrified at this twist of fortune, and it was made doubly horrific by the knowledge of what she had brought on to this vessel holding Amara. 'I...I didn't know she was here,' Jena pleaded. 'She's my *sister*.'

The master regarded her for a moment before turning away. 'She is nothing,' he told the others. 'And she has nowhere to go.' They lifted Vawter, holding him horizontally, and he was too stunned to struggle in their powerful grips. The master placed his great hand on Vawter's face, so that he could communicate directly through his skull. 'You came to us many years ago,' the master explained, the words causing Vawter to scream as the sound burned like fire. 'You asked for something in return for our operation of the MEC system.'

The pain eased as the Kwaios stopped talking and Vawter replied between breaths, 'I...don't remember.'

The master made the fatal mistake of taking this at face value: 'You wanted to live forever.'

Vawter's death anxiety had developed as a direct result of losing Amara. The constant musings on the impermanence of life and the inevitable suddenness of death had escalated his spiralling selfishness. Now, as one eye caught a glimpse of Amara through the giant fingers of the Kwaios Master, he knew the appreciation of life he once had – if it were even he who once possessed it – would never return. Yet still he feared its end. 'I still want that,' he declared.

Amara screamed, 'Sam, NO!' but it was too late. The soldiers released him as the master took Vawter again by the head, his other hand reaching to the ceiling. Apart from the master, only Amara could perceive this rudimentary reversal of transference, this internment of consciousness. Vawter's Fate Line passed through the master and leaped up to the ceiling, passing through the hybritech interface to merge with the network. Vawter's body shuddered before falling still, and Amara screamed again and cried aloud. Amidst her terror and grief, she interpreted the messages which were suddenly disseminating across the network, and so she relished in vocalising them, hissing through gritted teeth, 'You've lost your Transference operation on Heragon, and the Illeri planet has imploded. *Millions* of Kwaios are *dead*!'

The master roared in fury, and Amara screamed in pain. 'Take us to Earth and disconnect her,' the master ordered, gesturing towards Amara. His shared thoughts with the hybritech network led him to become aware of the escape from Heragon of the ship which bore Arrien Echad, and his heart swelled as he declared, 'We will bring an end to this species!'

387

THE NEW ELECT

Senate Buildings, Tokyo, Japan, Earth

Standing in silence inside the annex room, with the glowing yellow portal on the wall behind him, Naveen recalled the day his world had changed; at least, in retrospect. What happened that day had simply laid the foundation for his outlook on life, for there had been more sadness to come. Yet it was strange how this day was the one upon which he mused more than any other:

He was a boy, a mere eight years old, a golden-haired child playing with his best friend in all the world, a small white dog with long, floppy ears, and a short snout that never failed to find its way into one of two things – food or dirt. Today, however, in their private retreat in the southern reaches of the Second Realm, where the rest of the world seemed like a distant rumour, Monty was enjoying the simpler things in life, as little Naveen threw with all his imagined might a ball which had seen better days. And all Monty had to do was collect it in his little jaws and bring it back. What could be more fun?

Again and again, with Naveen's father watching amused with a pipe in his mouth, Monty retrieved the ball, more chewed each time, and spat it out for the little boy to retrieve from the grass. The sun shone, there was a mild breeze, and the world was good. Agmirus decided to check on the hens as his son played, convinced that all would be well. Before a row of great trees, a gentle stream ran along the eastern border of their land, and Monty would often dip in to cool himself. Naveen had joined him on numerous occasions, and so he thought nothing of throwing the ball towards the water. He laughed aloud as the silly dog bounded desperately towards the stream, yapping and chasing the ball as it descended from the air. He even laughed as he yelped and lost his footing at the edge before tumbling down the sloping bank into the water, convinced that all would be well. He laughed further as he ran to the water, but he soon realised that there was no splashing, no indication that Monty was in there getting the ball. He stopped before he reached the edge, afraid to see his little friend. He stayed there until his father, a tall man who could see what Naveen could not, was by his side. Agmirus placed a hand on the boy's shoulder, saying, 'Wait here.'

He released a long breath as he came to the edge, where Monty had been speared through his belly by sharp branches displaced by the weather only days before. Monty was silent until Agmirus came to him, whimpering as he hunkered down to stroke the poor creature's head. Now Naveen was beside him, and he made a similar keening sound. 'Monty?' he asked the dying dog. 'Are you okay?'

'He won't make it, son,' Agmirus told him, drawing him close with a strong arm. 'The wounds are too bad, and there's no healer who could get here in time.' He held his son as he sobbed and patted Monty's head, and they both waited until the dog took his last breath. For a while, they stayed in silence, until Agmirus stood and lifted his son to take him back to the house. But Naveen struggled in his arms, crying, 'No! I want him back!'

Agmirus set him down again. 'I'm so sorry, Naveen,' he told him gently, 'but that's just not possible. The world doesn't work that way.' Little Naveen looked up at his father, barely able to see him through his tears. But when he looked back to Monty's body, his expression became fixed with the determination of a child who knew no boundaries, no limits. As if his future had found him...

While Naveen was older and wiser now, and he knew more about the way the world – and the Universe – worked, still he drew on the pain he recalled of that moment when Monty had breathed his last. For despite other horrors to come, that day had laid the foundations for his scheme. He unlocked the door of the annex room and waited until Kai Tzedek came to pour in some light for his guest. For a moment in which he forgot about the eyes of his interim Senate on his back – still reeling from the revelation about human bodies in MEC fuel cells – he stared at the portal on the wall as it dissipated and closed, unsettled by the technology which the Garran called Chaerakh had brought to bear to have his master here. 'You're supposed to be in Antarctica,' Naveen told him.

'And you're supposed to know I decided not to go,' the senator countered.

Naveen grinned: 'Omniscience has its limits.'

389

Tzedek hesitated. He was in no mood for mockery, especially with his subordinates around him. 'Are the Kwaios coming?' he asked, hearing the shuffling of feet behind him as the senators and military personnel moved to see what was going on. 'They've suffered Heragon and Illeri,' Naveen told him. 'They're coming.'

Tzedek gave a nervous laugh, his heart pounding in his throat. 'What's this all about?' he asked the Prophet quietly. 'I mean, right now…what's really happening? Why do you need the Kwaios *here*?'

Naveen's reaction was somewhere between condescension and exasperation, for there was so much happening that he would not know how to begin. 'I'm building the house in which I was born,' he replied cryptically. 'Now…if you don't mind…'

Tzedek moved aside and Naveen stepped out with all eyes upon him. 'I see you've gathered a pleasant bunch, Kai,' he teased. 'I hope for their sakes they're more sycophantic than the last lot.'

'Who in *God's* name are you?' the general demanded.

'If I were here in *anyone's* name, it certainly wouldn't be one of *them*!' Naveen replied, heading to the table to take Tzedek's place: 'Now listen carefully and don't interrupt, because we've been working for a long time to bring all this together. What we're about to do will lead to humankind dominating this part of the galaxy for centuries to come. I presume everyone's on board with that?'

Dumbfounded, they nodded, slowly at first, and Naveen was the only one unaffected as the building began trembling. 'Of all the times to have an earthquake!' Tzedek complained, moving to the window to look out confidently from his ivory tower.

'It's not an earthquake, Kai,' Naveen told him. 'The planet is on the verge of reconnecting.'

'Reconnecting?' one of the senators asked. 'To what?'

'To the Universe!' said Naveen, looking to Tzedek, who was equally concerned. 'Surely you're aware of what happened when Earth disappeared with the Cage a hundred years ago? The planet lost its position in the galaxy. We're about to move it back.'

'How?' asked Tzedek.

'With a very advanced needle and thread.' Naveen grinned. 'Didn't you wonder about sending Kallon Raesa all the way out to Illeri? *I* could have told you what was going on out there. And Cassandra's clone was *always* going to be leaving from Earth.'

As the others ignored Naveen's warnings about interruptions to ask pressing questions about mercenaries like Raesa, and cloning people like Cassandra Messina, Tzedek just stared and asked above the noise, 'So what was the *point*? Why sacrifice Raesa at *all*?'

They quietened to hear Naveen: 'The Illeri needed their *world* brought here, Kai. Not long after the construction of the Shield began, they started arriving, and they got stuck into modifying it to accommodate their own needs.' He laughed disdainfully: 'You think it's full of water to help with *climate change*? They've been living in it for *decades*.'

Tzedek raised a hand to stop the others interrupting, and he snapped, 'But I thought the *Kwaios* built it? This makes no *sense*!'

'The design was Illeri,' Naveen explained, shaking his head. 'Look, you're missing the point. The Illeri didn't just come here...they made a deal to ensure the consciousness of their *world* would be brought to Earth. So they could *live* here.'

The general drew his gun: 'I've heard enough!'

'Don't waste your time,' Tzedek told him. 'This is the man who orchestrated the Cage event. You really think that's gonna work?' The planetwide rumbling picked up and all eyes were raised towards the clouds, and beyond. 'This is what the Shield is really for, isn't it?' Tzedek realised.

Naveen nodded. 'The Illeri world was special. A tangible extension of the Sentience. The Redeemer just dragged that consciousness across the galaxy, and Earth needs to move to intercept it.'

'So, we...what...took their *god* from them?' asked Tzedek.

'No. They did this. They destroyed their own planet to release it. If the Redeemer hadn't been there, it would have been absorbed back into the Universe. For over a year now, a very special kind of shockwave has been racing towards us. The Illeri began building the Shield around their own world to provide a blueprint for their survival.'

'But that means they *knew* the Kwaios were...' Tzedek shook his head, while Naveen spread his hands and said, 'What can I say? I'm nothing if not thorough.'

Tzedek held his head with his hands. 'But the Kwaios came for us because of *you*! You've done...*all* of this!'

It was the general who noted that Tzedek was missing the point. Actually, he was missing a few points, but the most pressing one was, 'Did you say Earth's going to *move*?'

'I'm glad *someone's* paying attention,' Naveen congratulated him.

'But the Shield can't protect us from *that*! And even if it could, it's in a synchronous *rotation*. If the planet shifts position, the hydro pillars will slam into coastlines, not to mention the *waves* they'll bring up out of the oceans!'

'Two things are about to happen, General,' Naveen explained. 'The hydro pillars have already begun retracting, so the first will be quite a surprise for your guests.'

'What guests?'

The doors burst open, and shots rang out as masked assailants began taking out the Senate's last line of protection, men and women dropping to the floor as they sought to keep out this threat. Tzedek moved to the general and stayed his hand, shaking his head without looking at him. When the fight was over without any unarmed casualties, and only one of the intruders lay dead, Tzedek stepped up as a young woman with blond hair stepped in. 'Who the hell are you?' he snapped. 'Do you realise what you've just *done*?'

'My name's Harriet Messina,' the woman replied proudly. 'And that's an incredibly stupid question.'

Tzedek looked around for Naveen, who was for some reason still standing there. 'You didn't leave,' he noted. 'Did you know about this?'

'Two stupid questions in such a short time,' said Naveen. 'Miss Messina is a representative of the Church of the New Elect. They're here to take over this operation.'

'*What*?' Tzedek was incredulous. 'You had me do all this to hand everything over to these *freaks*?'

'And what exactly did you do, Senator?' Harriet challenged him as she came closer. 'We haven't seen you doing any of the *dying* in the past few days, that's for sure!' She looked around at the stunned faces of the interim government, remembering the man with whom she had concocted this plan: 'Unlike your friend out on Heragon.'

Tzedek looked back to Naveen. 'Sam's dead?' he breathed.

Naveen nodded: 'He knew it was a possibility.'

392

'But *you* knew it was inevitable!' the senator accused him. 'Did you tell *him*?'

'He needed to remain focused. He believed his fleet would come for him.'

Tzedek deflated, thinking of his friend dying on some alien world; but Harriet wasted no more time. 'You need to prepare for an attack, General,' she explained. 'We infiltrated a number of alien worlds and…caused a lot of damage. They're coming for revenge. All of them.'

'What are you talking about?' the general asked. 'What did you do?'

Harriet addressed them all. 'A Garran Elder was helping us. His facility grew clones to infiltrate the Sori, the Vesstal, the Cquaston…every major space-faring race in the vicinity. We attacked them all…they figured out it was us…and now they're coming to kick the shit out of us.' They were all horrified.

'We need to close the Shield!' Pritchard shouted. The others agreed, but Harriet shook her head as Naveen simply looked on. 'Not yet,' she said. 'That's not the plan.'

'So, what the hell *is* the plan, Messina?' Tzedek spat as he arrived back in the present. 'You people have been hiding from us for a *hundred years*, and you just show up and take *over*?'

'Pretty much,' she replied, nodding. 'If it makes you feel any better, hiding from *you* was never our priority. You just made it necessary.'

'So, who were you hiding from?'

'The Kwaios. If they knew we'd survived the Cage event, they wouldn't have spent so much time chasing Arrien Echad. And what they're about to attempt would have been so much easier.'

'Senator! The Kwaios are here! They've already started coming through!'

'What are the Kwaios here for?' Tzedek demanded, looking to Naveen as well. 'What are you *doing*?'

Harriet resented being stuck in the same category as the Prophet, but she held his silent stare as she replied, 'We're building our future.'

THE DEFENCE

Earth (Shield) Orbit

The Kwaios had arrived as one, more of their gigantic vessels than anyone had seen in one place; and with them, the mock Illeri ships they had planned on using to infiltrate Earth with their human-Kwaios hybrids. They pushed in towards Earth and from all around it, easily penetrating the open Shield and the minimal defences put into play by self-motivated militia groups and other world militaries not officially answerable to the Senate. On one of the overtly Kwaios ships passing through the Shield to move towards a predetermined parking space on its interior, Arrien felt the suspicion arising from the lack of defence, in particular the noticeably quiet Shield arsenal, but he knew that the rage of the Kwaios following the losses at Heragon and Illeri was now at odds with the logic of the hybritech network; and so, they pressed on with their plan as it should always have been. Certainly, they had less ships and their precise calculations to ensure the ongoing proliferation of their hybrids had been swept aside, but they could yet glean some measure of victory to justify the deaths at Illeri and the lost souls at Heragon.

Arrien was seriously injured, intermittent shocks from his spine piercing the back of his brain, but still his mind was strong enough to test their patience. As he lay on the floor of the cemetery ship, two Kwaios came to collect him, overseen by a master he had not seen earlier. Following the others as they dragged Arrien standing between them, this master touched his forehead to communicate, and Arrien groaned through gritted teeth as the Kwaios said, 'It is time for you to be the one. The beginning and the end.'

'Why are you doing this?' he snapped back against the fire in his head. 'Why do you need to use *my* people to keep yours alive?'

'This is not merely about immortality,' the master replied, keeping pace with the others. 'It is about ability. Humans have an innate physiological capacity for connection to the Sentience. Transference to human anatomy will allow us all to reach our potential without hybritech. We will all be masters!'

394

Arrien was horrified, but he envisaged a problem for their current sociological arrangement: 'So you want to escape the network?'

The master snapped his hand away from Arrien's forehead, but before he did, Arrien saw something that he realised he knew absolutely nothing about. It had not even been spoken of before, nor had the Jaevisk ever mentioned it in any intel-sharing over the past century. It was a great blue ball in space, spinning and generating energy, but it had a consciousness, and around it were six planetoids. He felt its name in his mind in that flash of information, and he spoke it aloud: 'The God-Sphere.'

The master glared at him, growling as if violated. They brought Arrien to a room and secured him in a coffin-like box of glass. 'You will never know the God-Sphere,' the master told him, this time needing nothing to communicate as it towered over the box. 'You are about to die.'

The cemetery ship had completed its docking procedure, but just as it did, it reversed engines and moved away from the Shield, releasing the coffin box from its hold. Inside, Arrien was strapped in, helpless, as he watched the enormous ship silently abandon him. It moved away to his right and he was eventually able to see the Earth below. And despite having faith in his destiny, an involuntary scream began deep in Arrien Echad's soul, growing until it was all he could hear.

Ω

Arrien was not the only human brought to Earth by the Kwaios, but Samuel Vawter had arrived in a very different way. It was dark where he was, unimaginably so, although he was not entirely sure his eyes were as wide open as he felt they were. He recalled what it felt like to have his eyes open, but this was not it, for he could not feel his eyes in this place. There was a tingling sensation, but it was everywhere, as if he were very slightly burning, or perhaps remembering what it was like to be burning. Intermittent waves of relief passed through him, as if he were bobbing in a burning sea next to an outlet pipe for cold water. The pleasure these waves brought gradually helped him to accept the tingling burning as part of his reality, and he found that the heartbeat he imagined having simply faded to allow a blissful belonging to envelop him. And it was then that he knew.

It was more than just the knowledge that his consciousness had left his body. Instead, it was the gradual knowledge of having access to everything the Kwaios knew. Vawter was in the hybritech network, the great techno-consciousness that was the mainframe of Kwaios intercommunication. And unlike so many beings who lived and grew and died, Vawter knew why he was here. He knew what he was, why he had been cloned. He understood the meaning of his existence. And it was a revelation as bittersweet as life itself. As if an encoded switch had been flipped, Vawter imagined a light at the end of a tunnel, a beacon of purpose signifying his value. But at the same time as he imagined this light, a blue glow appeared behind him, and a snapping chord struck his mind. He screamed without making a sound, and the blue glow pulsed as it grew, becoming a Kwaios head of light that completely enveloped him. He felt the pressure of his circumstance as the hybritech network sought to consume him, but Vawter had seen the light. And with a mouth that did not exist, he smiled as his consciousness was absorbed by the Kwaios mainframe.

Ω

As the Kwaios were positioning themselves strategically around the Earth on the inside of the Shield, everyone else began arriving; and because they were in such haste to perform surgical strikes on the Shield in retaliation for the attacks on their respective worlds, they immediately began moving into tight orbits which brought them into the range of the Shield's now activated weapons as it began a rapid emergency closure. The battle began without delay, the Sori engaging the Shield with scores of razor-sharp destroyers which were likely to have come in from motherships farther out in the system. The Vesstal came at the Shield from six different directions, launching and firing everything at the metal world, while the Axcebians launched continent-sized nets of drill-cannons from their high orbit ships to work on piercing the Shield before moving in any closer. Manodderi ships came in, and a rapid deployment of their raiders saw them setting out on coordinated bombing raids all around the Shield. Their motherships launched magnificent flurries of countermeasure projectiles which rendered huge arrays of the Shield's weaponry network ineffective. The hidden architects of the Shield, however, those who had occupied its interior since its inception, had an entirely unexpected method of defence. This was something the attackers could not combat, something they could not destroy or intercept or deflect. Operating from within control and communication centres all over the interior of the Shield, thousands of Illeri worked together to expel Earth's most precious resource into space, waiting for the hydro pillars to completely retract. As soon as they did, the Illeri released the water.

The vacuum of space gorged on these giant waterfalls streaming from outlets all over the Shield, freezing them even as it hungered for more, and sheets of ice hampered enemy strategies even as they doomed those unfortunate enough to crash into them. The only ones who were not so easily led into the trap were the Cquaston, whose seventeen awkward-looking ships – each resembling a small, industrialised city – kept their distance just short of the moon. These were power plants of destruction with great range to their violent weaponry, and they began launching hundreds of long-distance missiles as the war machine of Earth – now under the auspicious control of the Church of the New Elect – oversaw the emergence from the planet's defences of thousands of fighter craft of all shapes and sizes. It was a madness of metal, a world of fire and ice, and the Illeri still had one last card to play. The release of the water into space served a secondary purpose, one which was of the utmost importance for this species that had lived in communication with the Sentience for countless generations. Because of the symbiotic nature of the planet and the Shield, releasing water into space reduced the overall mass of this biotech world, and this great expulsion was occurring in preparation for an existential shockwave on its way from the implosion of the planet evacuated by the Illeri. Mere seconds lay between the shunting of Earth back into its relative galactic position.

Inside and around the interior of the Shield, the Kwaios had positioned their mock Illeri ships holding tens of millions of human-Kwaios hybrids, as well as their cemetery ships and every other vessel they had brought; and they wasted no time, activating their neuratech network to connect them all. This sent a paralysing blast of energy around the world, which not only knocked out all power across the Shield; it also caused every hybrid to collapse unconscious in preparation for the final stage of their ultimate Transference. The box in which Arrien was strapped, staring down at the world, was a focal point of this network, his brain the fuel for Transference. For a century they had sought him, realising that while he represented the next stage of human evolution, so too could he be the answer to theirs. They had taken him at the facility at Sieltor Promies, and while they knew now why there had been a MEC station hidden there, still they did not question whether his presence there had been orchestrated to distract them from the complex scheme unfolding across the galaxy. For just as Arrien Echad had been plugged into the neuratech network, the Kwaios realised that a virus was spreading throughout the hybritech network, that which controlled all subordinate operations. This virus had a name, but not the one it once had held. For now its name was Vengeance.

THE REDEEMER

South Polar Research Facility, Antarctica, Earth

The Earth was rumbling violently. The Redeemer materialised in the chasm under Samuel Vawter's Antarctic Facility, thrown up and out of the reality beside the Universe by the red lines of the Sentience, Kallon Raesa's decaying body breaking old bones as it was thrown off the medical bay trolley. The craft came to rest rather precariously on the edge of the transparent platform, sitting lifeless and patient until a small team arrived to engage it. This team was led by Chaerakh Tae Ahn, the Garran whom many representatives of many species knew as the World Killer. For his reputation preceded him.

He directed the bewildered team of specialists – one of whom was pushing in a wheelchair the heavily-bound clone of Cassandra Messina – towards the Redeemer, barking orders at them: 'Move! We're on the clock here! And keep her head up! We can't damage the implant!'

The module had never been fully reconstructed since the accident over a decade ago, although the ground had been cleared to allow access through the tunnel track. Since the World Killer became involved and told Tzedek and Vawter why he was there, there had been little need to maintain the facility beyond anything requiring more than a minimal security detail. Chaerakh had come and gone over the years, not always arriving in chronological sequence, and he had gradually helped them to put all this together. Naveen's dependence on a different means of travel to Chaerakh meant that the latter was often required to put in place those very means. There were times when Tzedek or Vawter picked up on something of Chaerakh's story, depending on the Garran's mood, but it was difficult to figure out exactly what he was doing in the larger scheme of things. From their perspective, this would have been his first time in the Antarctica Facility in years; but from his perspective, he had not been here before. Also, from his perspective, it was best that they were not here today, for they would surely suffocate him with questions to the point that he would probably have shot one of them in the face.

Chaerakh accessed the Redeemer, and Cassandra was brought towards the descending ramp. She was silent and disconnected, with no idea of who she was or what she was doing here. She was aware, but it was an awareness lacking memory and, as such, identity. All that was about to change, and Chaerakh found himself contemplating the bliss she was about to leave behind. He envied her that state, as he did with all clones prior to the memory dump. If a good life was said to be charmed or blessed, Chaerakh's was cursed. Many times he had threatened to leave Naveen's service, and many more times he would do the same, but in truth it gave him a sense of purpose that nothing else could. And Naveen knew all the secrets, the lies, and most of all he knew Chaerakh's future. The Garran had to trust his master when he promised that he would end up with the one he loved, but Chaerakh had learned enough to know that nothing was set in stone, and he knew that with Naveen overseeing his destiny, it was open to being erased or re-written at the Prophet's will. So, he continued to serve.

Cassandra was taken aboard the sizeable craft, and they took her directly up the short corridor to the flight deck. 'Where's the pilot?' asked one of the team.

'Long gone,' Chaerakh replied, in a tone which ended conversations. 'Now turn that chair around. She'll be looking into the past, after all.' They did not care for the joke, but they placed the clone with her back to the console while Chaerakh got down on hands and knees to locate the release mechanism beneath. A panel moved aside and a hidden console was revealed, dotted with scores of holes. Chaerakh got to his feet with a crack in his knees that got the attention of the others. Wisely, they made no comment and kept any expressions of amusement to a minimum. 'Get her strapped securely and jab her,' he told them. 'She has to maintain the course.'

'You think she'll fight it?' one of them asked.

'Wouldn't you?' Chaerakh countered. 'Everything will come back to her as soon as the Redeemer's launched. Once she gets past her initial disorientation, she'll do her best to break free. It may be this one's first time going to Kiranis, but as soon as she connects, she'll feel like she was there before.' He moved away while they strapped her head, arms, and legs, saying, 'Which is, of course, the point.' He stopped in the centre of the flight deck and once again got to his hands and knees. He opened a panel to reveal a large circular mechanism hidden in the floor, about a metre in diameter. 'What's that?' he was asked by someone not focusing on their own work.

'A door to the future,' Chaerakh answered dryly. 'Well...*from* the future. Don't worry, I'm switching it off.' That invited more attention than the crack in his knees, but he ignored them and deactivated the portal. This one would no longer be needed, and neither he nor Naveen could risk anyone or anything else gaining access to it. He rose slower this time, watching them as his knees straightened. But there was no sound from his tired bones. 'Time to go,' he ordered, as a micro-needler was withdrawn from the back of Cassandra's hand. He waited while they gathered their equipment and passed him to make their way back down the corridor. Cassandra's head was strapped at the forehead, and in her emptiness, she stared at him. She judged him, as he judged himself. 'I'm sorry,' he told her. 'This is all in the service of the bigger picture.' He withdrew a rectangular device from his pocket. 'You're going to hate us for what you're about to experience, but I want you to remember that what you become is our doing, too.' He held her accusing, soulless glare: 'Remember it, Cassandra. Remember that we created your empire.'

He turned his back on her and tapped in the activation codes on the controller. As he approached the exit, he heard her scream as the tendrils of the remade Jaevisk implant in the back of her head pushed out, snapping out to connect with the advanced console of the Redeemer. As the ramp drew itself back into the craft and the door closed, her scream was one of fury. And as Chaerakh and his team backed swiftly away, the Redeemer's engines activated, lifting it upwards towards the ice of Antarctica. But it did not need to travel any farther in this reality, for its path was a different one. As Cassandra Messina relived her escape from Earth and her fateful journey to Kiranis, the Redeemer vanished, taken by the Lines of her Fate.

Ω

Arrien forced himself into a dream, a place of gentle warmth and blissful air, where mothers kissed their children and fathers held them high. Here, aspirations went unchecked and disappointments dissipated like Summer clouds. His body was strong and still in this

401

place, so disassociated from the broken writhing thing he had become at the hands of the Kwaios. 'What would you like, Arrien?'

He turned to see his mother holding iced treats on this glorious day, his father looking into the distance where hopes were in flight. And he realised they were on a world untouched by the madness brought by the Prophet, a world which did not – could not – exist. 'I'd like time,' Arrien replied involuntarily. 'I'd like to spend forever here.' The treats melted in his mother's hand, collapsing into an ooze running down her arms until she dropped screaming to the ground, his father silently bursting into flames before falling dead. Arrien screamed first in terror and anguish, but it became a thing of agonising fury as he realised his mind was drawing him back. He could see the shaking Earth beneath him, watching volcanoes blast and fault lines snaking their violent destruction. Yet even amidst his agony and fear, while the neural fire spread and the para-quantum energy of his connection with the Sentience was gathered against his will so that the Kwaios could feed his abilities to their hybrid creations, he could feel the gentle reassurance of the arriving wave of power. As the release of consciousness from collapsed Illeri was introduced to Earth.

In the chasm of the Antarctic, the furiously seeking Lines of Earth's dismembered fate were lashing out as if their mother, too, were coming to bring them treats. But the Sentience was here to do more than that. It was here to redefine them, to give them purpose. As it struck the Earth and the planet's position in the galaxy was restored, the home world of humankind was for the first time in a century not only connected to the Universe; it was inhabited by a species with the ability to take full advantage of that connection. Arrien felt it wash over him in a way which brought new tears to his eyes.

A coldness began inside his head, and he imagined it as an expanding piece of ice in the centre of his brain. He fed on the relief it brought, and his surety helped it grow. On every Kwaios cemetery ship, masters overseeing the Transference process knew there was something wrong. But for the first time in thousands of years, they could not communicate with each other, for the virus coursing through the hybritech network rendered the great biotech server ineffective. Some of them tried to draw power from the Lines, but their hybritech interface was disrupted. Without the ability to fight back, their terror was complete.

Arrien drew on more power than he had ever imagined, so much that he knew he would not survive its purpose. A voice came into his head, a familiar voice that could have been his mother's, had he not seen her burned to death by the relentless Face in the Flames. 'You can set them free,' this voice told him. 'They can be human again.' And he knew why he was here. Not to be used by the Kwaios. Not to be tortured or tested for the advancement of others. But to be the catalyst for evolution. 'No more hiding, Arrien,' his mother told him. 'You'll be free, too.' The pain of her death arose in him anew, and he cried like a child at her breast at the same time as he pushed out with all his mental might until the glass box exploded, all air was sucked from his lungs, and all the para-quantum energy the Kwaios were seeking to draw from him was sent back across the dying neuratech network with human memories and emotions. Enough to overwhelm.

Kwaios consciousness was dissolved amongst the millions of hybrids on the mock Illeri ships, and humans awoke with a sense of who they had been. But more than that, they now had an awareness of the Sentience and the ability to connect with it. In a heartbeat, they had evolved. The hydro pillars were descending again, and hundreds of thousands of Illeri were using them to make their way down to the seas and rivers of Earth as horrified Kwaios Masters removed the ships they still controlled from inside the Shield and fought their way out of Earth's now growing sphere of power and influence. Shocked by this rapid change of circumstances, what remained of the multi-species attack on Earth began retreating, until only two species were left anywhere near Earth. This was an unprecedented victory which would alter the course of human history, but most people on Earth had no idea what had just happened. Millions had died in the geological upheaval wrought by the shifting of the planet, and it would take many years for humankind to recover. In Tokyo, where many of even the hardiest architectural wonders had been shaken to the core, one building still hosted the most powerful people on Earth...

Harriet had allowed the interim Senate members to leave, for they were deadwood at this point. General Tellin had demanded he stay, and Harriet saw no reason to deny him. While the Church's hired guns kept watch around the room, Tzedek was sitting at the head of the table, looking at Naveen. 'What happens now?' the

403

senator asked, offering a perfunctory glance of recognition to Harriet, who might also have the answers he required.

'What would you like to happen?' Naveen asked simply, as if talking to a child. 'You've just sent the Kwaios and half the galaxy running with their tails between their legs, and the Illeri are in your waters with invaluable knowledge about how to use this new connection to the Sentience.'

'I don't want them here,' Tzedek replied, to which Harriet nodded in agreement. 'I'll arrange for them to be rounded up and removed.'

'That won't be easy,' said Naveen. 'They're a formidable species.'

'So are we,' Harriet interjected. 'It's high time we stopped pandering to these other races.'

'Indeed it is,' the Prophet agreed. 'And your people can now evolve beyond the hunted rats they've become.'

'We'll bring the clones into the fold,' she said, nodding. 'They'll have an entirely different understanding of the Sentience that'll help us become even stronger.'

'Do you *seriously* think...' Tzedek began, rising from his seat, 'that I'm going to let you people reap all the benefits here?'

'Why shouldn't we?' Harriet countered. 'We were as much a part of this as you! And in case you've forgotten, *we* were decimated by the Cage event...not you.'

'You're *all* human!' Naveen snapped. 'Get your house in order before you go any further.'

'What do you mean?' asked Tzedek.

'The clones are already moving out,' Naveen told them both. 'They're not for your exploitation.'

'*What*?' Harriet demanded. 'Where are they going?'

'The Kiranis system,' the Prophet explained. 'There's someone waiting out there to meet them. To lead them.'

Tzedek could feel his plans falling apart, sensing a betrayal by the Prophet that he always knew had to happen: '*Who*? *Who's* waiting for them?'

Naveen regarded them both. 'I think you both know the answer to that.'

404

THE NETWORK

Laden's Folly, Jala-Bakor, Kiranis

In the centre of town, lying next to a great pit in which the butchered form of a Great Dragon was reverting to its human host, Haphory's still-living body was being tested by hungry dogs, with no false prophet around to oversee his end. His mind was clear, his resignation even more so. Retreating inside himself to disconnect from the pain, his human memories from his time on Earth bled into shape. His name had been Wojciech, and he had been married for a time, fathering a son and daughter who were as proud of him as he was of them. The marriage had not worked, but mutually so, and no animosity had arisen from the separation. It was a rare occurrence, yet they came to corrupt it, projecting the stresses of their separate lives upon each other when it came to sharing time with their wonderful children – who only ever wanted their parents' love. Wojciech recalled the heated arguments which should never have begun, and the path he had taken towards the Church to soothe his troubled soul. He recalled it with the resentful wisdom that only retrospect could provide.

Church leaders convinced him of his superiority to others and of his destined contribution to and participation in a momentous shift of power which would see the Church dominate the affairs of humankind. His relationship with his ex-wife became increasingly strained, and he eventually lost the respect of his children. Yet still the Church called to him, and he answered their call, becoming immersed in conspiracy and subterfuge and the conviction that he was a paragon of righteousness in a world of godless anarchy. And then the Cage came. Wojciech recalled the day he had submitted to the implantation of the Jaevisk device, loath to question the leadership of Mannix Relland. And, of course, he recalled the journey across the galaxy to become merged with an entity who did not even belong to this time. Now, once again, almost as if the Haphory entity was volunteering its own retreat, Wojciech was awake. Yet he heard a voice calling his other name:

'Haphory!' It was a man's voice, a man he had seen in the Lines but had not met in life. Wojciech opened a swollen eye and looked up at the duke. He could hear others shouting at the dogs as they

405

kicked and warned them away. 'That *is* your name, isn't it?' Duke Dassan asked him.

'Not anymore,' Wojciech managed to say, his throat parched. 'He's gone.'

The duke looked surprised: 'I didn't know that could happen. It must be a relief.'

'I feel…weaker,' said Wojciech, as the duke directed that water be given.

Dassan hunkered next to him as soldiers raised him to drink. 'Well, that could be from any number of things that white-haired madman did to you,' he observed. 'Do you know where he went?'

'I thought he served *you*.'

'Let's just say I've realised it was the other way around.' Dassan looked furtively around the centre of town, a place he barely recognised. 'I knew this place was a Dragon Killer, but to see it in action…' He shook his head.

'You've no idea what he's planning, do you? What these places are for?'

'Do *you*?'

Wojciech coughed, still leaning against two men. 'He probably told you it was to bring this world back to the Universe,' he said.

'It had been suggested, yes.'

'Do you know what the hearts are used for?'

'Power,' the duke replied, nodding.

'The hearts of what you call *dragons* are used for power,' Wojciech corrected him. 'Human hearts are different. When it comes to the Universe, human hearts are made for *connecting*. It's one of the reasons we merged so well with the creatures waiting here for us.'

'*Connecting*?' Dassan was unnervingly aware of his own heart pounding: 'What would Balaam want to connect to?'

Wojciech took a deep breath and looked up as a score of dragons flew overhead, the urgency of their cause ignoring the scene below. 'Something even *they're* afraid of,' he told the duke as all eyes were upon the monsters in the sky. 'Something that's been kept away from this world for a thousand years.'

Dassan looked back down at the dying man, and he felt a surge of rage. He dragged him to his feet and spat, 'I'm sick of this cryptic nonsense! Tell me what –' A bullet seared his shoulder and Wojciech found himself atop the duke's shocked form as the soldiers were under attack. The small band of remaining Watchers emerged from streets around the town centre, and this time they had the upper hand. With automatic weapons, they cut through the duke's soldiers, over forty of them who tried their best to fight with inferior weapons. With the soldiers caught in the killing zone at the centre of town, it was all over within minutes.

'What are you doing here?' Wojciech groaned as they turned him over.

'We came for Balaam,' Julieanna told him, looking at the duke, who lay silently staring at the sky, expecting the worst. 'But I was convinced to double back for...you,' she lied.

Wojciech shook his head. 'Balaam's not here...*anywhere* here,' he told them. 'You should have stayed at *home*!'

'What are you *talking* about?' Benjamin snapped. 'Where the hell *is* he?'

As dragons were heard roaring in the distance from the direction of the Watchers' outpost, the ground began to shake. It had begun.

$$\Omega$$

In the lower levels of the outpost beyond Churchfield, Balaam had completed his task, placing the final human heart in the last of the four antechambers. But the world was shaking, and mere coincidence led Balaam to believe he was responsible. 'It's happening,' he whispered zealously, desperate to reconnect to the Network and inform the Masters. He needed to get back up. There was a loud bang and he looked back through the outer window of the antechamber, seeing smoke in the containment room. For some reason, they thought he was still in there. They could have doubled back and come around the entire housing to stop him on his way out. 'Idiots,' he chuckled, as he backed away and turned to find another way out, checking Haphory's gun. There was only one bullet left, and he cursed his stupidity, recalling the number of shots the Mediator had managed to get off before the pikemen lifted him from his horse. Balaam had taken the wrong gun.

There must have been another way out, he thought to himself. These people had been here for centuries. Surely they had prepared for countless scenarios in which their usual means of egress were compromised? He pressed on into an increasingly

407

dark corridor, conscious of the walls changing from evidence of the Watchers' technology to the hand of lesser developed men. These passageways, hewn from stone, descended into the world beneath the outpost, and Balaam felt his heart pounding in his ears as the air became stale and heavy. Dust and debris were being shaken lose by the vibrating planet, and Balaam knew that he had to get out of here soon. He splashed through pools of water from which terrible odours leaped to curse his curiosity, and soon he saw a light up ahead. He hurried towards it at first, and the shaking and breaking was getting worse down here, but he was not fool enough to maintain such a pace. Slowing as the tunnels began to widen, he eventually came to an opening, a cave in which he felt an immense thrum of energy. 'The Network,' he whispered, blinded by a light emanating from the floor which kept him from taking in his surroundings.

The Sensitive held a hand up to his face and moved forward to pick up what looked like a black club emitting a strange light. As he used it to illuminate the cave, he let a short sound of shock. A grey, almost stone-coloured young man, whose body could barely be seen, was glaring wide-eyed at something just over Balaam's shoulder, and the Sensitive took control of his breathing before slowly turning to see another, younger boy, being consumed by the rock in much the same way as the other one. This younger boy was staring upwards, his mouth open in terror as the cave itself held him in place. 'Can you hear me?' Balaam asked, mystified by the circumstances. There was no response, but something was happening as the world continued to shake. And the stone holding both prisoners in place was starting to crumble.

Ω

Cana could feel the Sentience. Crystallised tears burned his eyes as he recalled the dream which had become a nightmare. He had seen himself as a beast which he had come to create en masse, populating an alien world with creatures which should not have existed. And worst of all, despite being so far from Earth, he had still ended up a slave to the agenda of the Church. The only thing which had kept him going was the certainty that one day he would get home, a certainty provided by the Sentience itself. Everything had come full circle, for the passage of time was nothing to the soul of the Universe. And now that soul was calling for his. The Cage began to groan as the Universe existing alongside its place of residence demanded its return, fighting against its programming and infrastructure. On the planet, the land shook and sea levels began to fluctuate, but the destruction was limited by the dynamics of the Cage, even while it was being shaken to its mechanical bones.

Cana was aware of the boy next to him in his chthonic lair, but Robert was no threat. He knew comparatively nothing of the Lines and could do nothing but watch and feel as the heart of the Network reached out for its host body. Yet Robert heard the same voice, recognising it without ever hearing it before. It was Cana's grandfather, a wise and warm man whom Cana had loved with all his childhood heart. Robert felt that same love, and his heart swelled as Cana was called: 'Come back to us, little man. We miss you.' Cana fought to reach him, willing the words 'Coming, Pops!' to leave his sealed mouth, but still the Cage could not pierce the ethereal curtain between realities, the membrane of the Universe from which it had taken Kiranis.

Robert felt a fire in his brain as Cana struggled to get home, a searing anger that rushed through his veins, and he perceived that the place they were fighting to leave was desperately trying to hold on to them. The darkness which had held Kiranis for so long did not wish to release it, for darkness enjoyed company. But Cana had been building his strength quietly, learning everything about his circumstances and gathering the knowledge of every single creature which had inhabited Kiranis since he arrived here. He was a master of darkness now in the grandest possible way. For he was using it to return to the light.

The contractions of the Universe caused ripples of gravitational distortion which were immediately picked up by the vigilant Jaevisk, whose warships were waiting in their thousands for this very occurrence. Cana focused his mental strength on the perception of his grandfather, despite the deeper layers of his psyche being fully aware that this was merely a desirous projection of the Sentience. The Universe with which he sought to connect had been communicating with him on an emotional level where images, names, and places were irrelevant and only feelings registered, but the human psyche needed tangible representations of its emotions to make deep connections, and so the Sentience

409

offered Cana's grandfather. Cana imagined himself reaching out his hands, and calcified matter began crumbling around his shoulders and arms. 'There's only one way this will work, Cana,' his grandfather told him.

'What do you mean, Pops?' he asked, as they stood facing each other in a place that did not exist.

'You've been living in a place outside time,' Pops explained. 'To come back now means returning to the natural progression of time.'

'Will I die?' Cana asked.

'You should have died a long time ago, my boy,' said Pops gently. 'They sustained your body, but only your hunger to get home really kept you alive.'

'But I *won't* get home, will I?'

Pops shook his head sadly: 'I'm afraid not. But if you choose to stay alive, the Cage will remain in the darkness and Kiranis will be trapped forever.'

Cana hung his head and began sobbing. 'I…never wanted…any of this,' he cried. 'I thought I was serving the Church.'

'I want you to serve yourself, Cana. That would be best. I don't need anything else from you.'

'You mean…' Cana looked up. 'You're letting me go?'

'I'm setting you free, Cana. That's all I want for you.'

Cana nodded. 'I think I'd like that. I also think I'd like that for you.'

'My freedom is for another time. For now, there's a small vessel trying to get inside the Cage. Its engine follows the Lines, and its pilot needs you to bring it in. But *you* can use it, Cana…to *leave*!'

Cana imagined his arms stretching far beyond capacity, pushing through the amniotic division between realities, until he found the Redeemer, waiting as if on a weighbridge for appraisal before resuming its journey. His imaginary appendages touched the hull of the vessel, and he was immediately inside, looking at the woman staring at the floor who was tethered to the operations panel by threadlike tendrils protruding from the back of her head. He looked around the control room, but the woman was staring at him when he looked back to her. 'Get me out of here,' she demanded.

'She came from Earth,' Pops told him. 'She belongs to *your* time.' Cana rushed to the engine, understanding instantly the mechanics of its unique para-quantum entanglement drive. 'It connects particles in this Universe with their counterparts between dimensions,' he whispered in awe. 'It's like a magnetic track system.' He placed his hands on the engine housing and focused on his desire to return.

'The Lines are always there,' said Pops. 'Everywhere.'

'I *found* it!' Cana cried exultantly. 'I can feel my *past*!'

Pops appeared and placed his hand on Cana's shoulder: 'Then come home, my boy. Let go.'

Cana's cry of anguish shook the Cage as his memories of Earth forced it to pierce the veil of time and space, a huge chunk of its northern hemisphere appearing in the Universe which it had left behind. At the same time the Redeemer emerged inside the Cage, with Cassandra screaming as the tendrils disconnected and she was thrown to the floor. Cana's consciousness was propelled along the Lines which Cassandra had travelled, but he was not free to leave his prison, his symbiosis with the Cage securing his fate. Robert felt more pain in his soul than he had ever imagined possible as Cana realised that he had to let go. Of everything. The underground cavern far beneath the Watchers' outpost suddenly exploded with blinding light, and when it dissipated, Robert was left standing, free of the stone around him. He could move as before, but where Cana had been, only dust filled the empty space. Robert coughed, but as he gathered his senses, he realised that someone else was there, shining a shaky flashlight in his direction...

The Cage pushed fully through the aperture, emerging into the Universe. Hundreds of Jaevisk warships were caught up in the sudden gravity shift, drawn spinning towards the Cage to either smash against its world-spanning arms or pass through into the atmosphere of Kiranis. The rest of them backed away, retreating to a safe distance from which they could better assess the situation. If anyone had been watching, they might have been surprised to see this retreat expanding, with thousands of warships setting course for the Kiranis sun. It was a mystery which would not be answered for centuries – Kiranis was home, yet those who had watched it for a century had simply left. The Jaevisk who had been pulled down through the Cage, however, descended towards the surface, desperate to once again plunder their ancestral world. Caught up in their fervour, they failed to account for the position of the planet.

411

For though it had dissipated over the years, and though the Kiranis star had moved on, a residual echo of the rift in space through which the World Killer had arrived had somehow maintained its relative position along the orbital path. And a great scheme was underway to regenerate it.

Inside the Redeemer, Cassandra was getting to her feet. The tendrils streaming from the back of her head were the mark of her Medusan will, and so this time her scream was not one of pain. But one of fury.

The white-haired Sensitive also took a moment to gather himself, but when he did, he was swift to set his course. 'You're the boy who stole the duke's horse,' he stated as he levelled his gun. 'What's happening?'

'You're the Sensitive...Balaam,' Robert replied, still coughing. 'What are you doing down here?'

'I asked you first!' Balaam snapped, stepping forward with the threatening weapon as the shaking got worse. Robert closed his eyes and tilted his head like an inquisitive bird, seeing through the now expanding Lines the collective energy from all over the planet forcing open the dormant rift in the space alongside the world. 'You set beacons,' he realised. 'You're calling it back.'

'What are you talking about? Calling *what* back?' Balaam shook his head: 'We returned Kiranis to the *Universe*. To connect the Network to the *Sentience*!'

Robert shook his head: 'No, that was already in hand. The Prophet had seen to that.'

'*Damn* the Prophet!' Balaam shouted, raising the gun again. 'He's *nothing* compared to the Masters!' He pulled the trigger, but not before Robert had gripped his Line and whipped him from his feet. Balaam lay winded, staring at the dark ceiling and blinking in confusion as the bullet was heard ricocheting against the stone walls of the cave. How could this boy have learned how to do such a thing in such a short time? He got to his feet and was stunned to see that hundreds, *thousands* of Lines were creeping like serpents from every direction to connect with the boy. The thrum of energy he had initially felt was all around them now, and Balaam stumbled back, reeling from the power wielded by this child. 'How is this possible?' he snapped. 'Who are you?'

Robert smiled a wicked smile. 'I'm the future of Kiranis,' he told the bewildered Sensitive. 'And the Prophet won't be damned by the likes of *you!*' He ripped Balaam's Fate Line from his body and the white-haired man dropped dead.

Ω

Asherah and a score of other dragons had descended upon the Watchers' outpost, immediately starting to dig and burn their way into the facility. She was set on finding the boy Cana, whom Naveen had arranged to have brought here so long ago. She doubted that the boy was malevolent in any real sense, but she appreciated the majesty of madness which surely consumed someone taken from their home and manipulated for the ends of others. Asherah found an entry point and she changed to her human form with a cry of agony. Immediately she thought of Haphory, and she sensed his recent presence here. Taking a short moment, she raced swiftly along his Line towards Laden's Folly, groaning when she saw him dying with the Watchers around him. It was a scene which confirmed her suspicions about these people, and she swore to see them pay.

Some of the dragons had found fleeing Watchers at various entry points around the huge subterranean site, and they dragged them out with claws and teeth, showing little concern for the bigger picture as the planet continued to tremble violently. There was a terrible cracking as a snaking fissure opened to consume a fire-breathing dragon. Asherah thought twice about taking her first steps down into the facility, but a boy approaching from her right sought to set her straight. 'You don't belong here,' he told her. 'You should leave before you're all killed.'

'*Killed*?' Asherah snarled, steadying herself on the rumbling ground. Perhaps it was time to change back to dragon: 'By who? *You*?'

Robert shook his head and pointed to the sky, where a black and silver ship was passing through the clouds. Asherah was horrified, realising that she had not even noticed Kiranis returning to the Universe: 'The Jaevisk!' She turned and ran, leaping to the air to sprout wings and become dragon in one horrifying, bone-crunching motion. She roared at the others to retreat, but it was too late. The warship opened fire, screaming guns and multiple

413

salvos of missiles raining from the still-burning sky. The first blast sent Asherah spinning through the air, but Robert was unharmed, liquid flames going under, around, above him. He was watching intently the beams of para-quantum energy corrupted by Balaam and Sensitives all over the world. Every Watchers' outpost was now the potential site of return, but Robert knew it would be this one. Moving away and closing his eyes, even as the Jaevisk warship engaged with the dragons rising from the flames, Robert saw the shimmering rift in space through which Kiranis had begun to pass. He imagined he could hear the Cage groaning in protest, for it was the only thing keeping the planet from being consumed. But the giant red eyes at the edge of the rift were not a thing of imagination. They were very real.

The bellowing roar of the black beast from the rift was heard before the creature was seen, and the Jaevisk attack wavered as uncertainty struck the world. This was Cana's monster, the first he had seen, the first he had created. This was Leviathan, whose form had been trapped in a place beyond places, separated even from the temporal stasis into which Kiranis had been moved. This thing of darkness and rage blurred in and out of existence amidst the madness, materialising too late for the Jaevisk to do anything about it. It took to the air and threw itself headlong at the warship, and despite the vessel being many times larger than Leviathan, the impact of this massive dragon crippled the warship, and it plummeted to the ground far from the site. Leviathan prepared to join the fight, but it blurred again…and vanished.

Robert watched the rift collapsing in upon itself, and heard echoing across the Network the maniacal screams of the Masters as their plans came to nought. He walked away, finally free of the destroyed outpost and of the ignorance of his childhood. Yet with the Masters learning more and more of the world around them – and with them now assured that they could call upon the beast when the time was right – this first magician of Kiranis would come to learn that his was a freedom fraught with condemnation.

Ω

Cassandra took the Redeemer down to the surface, coming to the shell of a mountain in which she had found herself a century earlier. No, not her, she realised, all awareness now at hand. She

414

knew she was a clone, that she had been created to bring the Redeemer through the Cage. But she longed for more reason to her life, and she knew there was only one person who could give it to her. 'Where *are* you?' she called as she set foot outside the Redeemer, the cold wind whipping her words into uncaring oblivion. Dragons circled in the air, but the one with whom she would speak was considerably more fearsome than such creatures. And he appeared before her. 'We meet again,' he said casually. 'You look well, Cassandra.'

'What…considering I've been dead for a hundred years?' she replied. 'Yeah, I imagine I look great. Now, are you gonna tell me what the hell I'm doing here? Because I'm sure they didn't have to engineer *me* to get the Redeemer here. There were *millions* of others brought here whose DNA would've been on file!'

'That's my girl,' he toyed with her. 'You're starting to get it now, aren't you?'

'There's always a bigger picture,' she said, nodding. 'Now get to the point.'

He smiled: 'How would you like to rule an empire?'

She grinned despite the ordeal he had just put her through. 'You know, I can't figure out whether you're a god or a devil. What *is* this…my wilderness trial?'

Naveen laughed aloud. 'You think you're a messiah?' He laughed again: 'Even *your* ego won't go for that, Cassandra!'

The tendrils at the back of her head were lashing out as if to reach him, and she snapped, 'Get to the *point*, Naveen. I'm not getting any younger and it's *freezing* here!'

'I'm going to take you to Heragon.'

'Heragon?'

'It's currently a Kwaios world, but…they won't be needing it anymore.'

'And why would I want to go there?'

'A lot of people out there are waiting for you. Waiting to be guided…taught.'

Cassandra sighed, knowing that being cryptic was part of his game. 'Taught what?' she asked, resigned now to his scheme.

His cloak was billowing, as much from the downward-spiralling dragons as the wind in this ever-cold place, and he extended his left arm as his own dragons played on the black fabric. '*Magic*, Cassandra,' he told her. The frozen ground next to him started to crack and shuffle, pieces leaping up until she saw lots of red lines sprouting like weeds, before straightening and shooting towards his hand. As he gripped them as if to gather string, he looked her in the eye and told her what she had longed to here in another life: 'You're going to control the fates of millions!'

PART 7
AFTERMATH

In extremely arid conditions, it is fascinating to observe what are generically referred to as 'Resurrection Plants'. These plants generally appear desiccated, as if life has abandoned them. Some are blown across shifting deserts, uprooted wanderers destined to be forgotten. Yet seemingly dead plants, devoid of water for years at a time, are revived within hours when the rain finally comes, taking immediate advantage of the situation to spore and propagate.

Ancient Earth Almanac, Author Unknown

THE BOOKS OF BALAAM

Laden's Folly, Jala-Bakor, Kiranis

Robert had not yet gone home. While he was eager to see his parents again, despite the possibility that he would find it difficult to connect with them, there was something more pressing calling him to Laden's Folly, a sentient tugging at his Fate Line that he was compelled to heed. This must have been what holy men spoke of when they said they were called to service, despite being misled by their socio-religious context into believing it was the god of their books who demanded their obeisance. For the Universe itself called to these people to recognise it apart from the falsity of their doctrines and dogmas. Theirs was not true knowledge of the Sentience, but given that they were on the road, it was not beyond belief that a Damascus could set them right. Robert's Damascus had seen the world crumble around him before being rebuilt for his appreciation. And he had a destiny to fulfil.

Laden's Folly was decimated and silent, except for some looters here and there, and small groups of people returning to the town to survey the damage to their homes and businesses. Robert stopped and took in for posterity's sake the scene in the centre of town, where the hybrid dragon-man, Haphory, lay in ruins, and dogs and birds were gorging themselves on the dragon laying in the pit. There was no pain here that Robert could feel, so the Lines were silent, and he pressed on. Up the hill towards the Manor Home he went, seemingly indifferent eyes regarding his journey in case they might later need the information. He nodded to some cautiously and respectfully, some remnant of his boyhood manners assuring them that he cared for their plight. But they thought little of this boy walking towards the duke's residence, perhaps thinking that he would find only death.

The door of the great Manor Home was wide open, and he did not flinch even as a shot rang out inside the house. He entered in time to see a looter tumble down the stairs with a hole in his chest as silverware and trinkets went flying. Robert passed the dead man without a concerned glance and made his way up to the duke. 'I'll kill anyone who comes up here!' shouted Jerord Dassan. 'I'm not afraid of any of you!'

419

'I'm not here for you,' Robert replied as he continued ascending. 'Nor your valuables.'

With blood still pressing through a hastily applied bandage at his shoulder, Dassan was at the top of the staircase with a gun brandished: 'Who are you?'

'I'm the boy who stole your horse. You sent men to kill me.'

Dassan looked at him for a moment. 'And what...you're here for *revenge*?' he mocked. 'How will you stop a bullet?'

'You have none left,' said Robert. 'But it's okay. You don't need any.'

'I have knives and swords, boy. What will you do?'

Robert was a mere five steps from the man now. 'I'll walk past you and go to the rooms you allowed the Sensitive to stay in.'

'Will you, now?'

Robert nodded. 'And you can go back to your room and drink. No one else will come for you.'

Dassan took a deep breath and nearly cried. 'I was a fool,' he realised.

'Yes. But we are all fools. The game is not ours.'

'The Prophet,' said Dassan, nodding. 'He controls it all.'

'Maybe not,' Robert suggested. 'I'm here for Balaam's books.'

Dassan looked at him again, before turning and heading back to his room. 'He told me once that there was so much to learn,' he called back. 'Time might be on your side, boy.'

'Time is on no one's side, my lord,' Robert assured him as he headed for Balaam's rooms. 'Which is why we must beat it at its own game.' But Dassan was not listening, and Robert came to the ransacked rooms of the Sensitive, looking around for the books. There was no sign of the ones he wanted, and he closed his eyes, focusing on finding one single Line amongst numerous possibilities for him in this place. It was brighter than the others, warmer and more potent. It wanted him as much as he wanted it.

Behind a panel in the wall, revealed by a simple button in the eye of a painted lady nearby, were seven books, a different symbol on the spine of each. Robert found a satchel, slightly torn and stuck under a chair leg, and he filled it with the writings of Balaam, the scriptures of the Sensitives. These were works they had not yet come to fully understand, works which the Masters had relayed to them in the hope that one day they might triumph; a reality more cogent with their release of Leviathan upon the world. But now, in

420

the hands not only of a human, but of the First Magician of Kiranis, they were works that would see them brought to their knees.

THE EMPIRE

Jones' Quadrant, MEC Captive Holding, Heragon

Almost seven years had passed since Abigale had first travelled through the MEC system. But, of course, she had never done so. The original crew of the Argo had been taken to the Kwaios world, there to suffer their disconnection from reality in the company of an ever-growing population of abductees whose subterranean habitation seemed to stretch across the world. To add to their confusion and frustration, those who had spent so many years here began to suffer a reconnection to their past, as the effects of the Kwaios memory suppressant were gradually overwhelmed by a subconscious struggle to rebuild identity. They could not have known that this was the effect of their Fate Line fighting back, repairing its essence so that past, present, and future once again existed in harmony and the Line was a viable candidate for return to the Universe when the host body died. The Lines of clones were different, for there was no historical identity through which the Universe could determine familiarity and ownership. It was as if their Fate Lines had been acquired without permission, and they were truly facsimiles of existence.

So now, seven years since Abigale had seen her little girl, she could remember their last conversation:

'Momma?'

As she finished packing the last of her suitcases on her bed, and the others were stacked on the floor next to it, Abigale looked down at her three-year-old daughter, the most beautiful thing she had ever seen and the most wonderful thing she had ever done. 'Hello, Glitterbug.' She lifted Hannah up to sit on the suitcase. 'What is it?' These were the moments she loved and hated in equal measure, for she knew what was coming: 'Where you goin', Momma?'

The tears came, as they had done with every new deployment since Hannah was born. But this one would be different. Longer. Farther than before. 'Will you miss me?' she asked the child, choking through the words.

'Uh-huh!' Hannah nodded emphatically. And Abigale held her close. 'Me too,' she said. 'But I'll be back before you know it. And you and Karolina will have lots of fun.'

'Don't want you to go!' Hannah sobbed, burying her face in Abigale's breast. Abigale raised her head to the ceiling and took a deep breath to compose herself. 'I know, sweetheart,' she said, 'but this will be the last time. I promise.'

Hannah got there first, raising her hand without even drawing back from her mother, her face still hidden. Her pinky finger was up, slightly curled and waiting for the proof. Abigale felt she might suffocate, but she linked her pinky finger with Hannah's and repeated, 'I promise, Glitterbug. Last time.'

That seemed to please the child, and she smiled up at her mother before turning to point at the window and saying, 'Show me.'

Abigale laughed through her tears, and she nodded as she lifted Hannah and took her to the window. There, she pointed to a random star and said, 'That one there. That's where I'll be.'

Hannah smiled: 'It's pretty.'

'Just like you, Glitterbug,' said Abigale, kissing her hair. 'Now let's get you to bed.'

She had not risked waking her that morning, leaving without kissing her goodbye for fear of upsetting her further. In truth, of course, Abigale's fear had been for herself. And as she had boarded the Argo for the first time and set out upon its inaugural deep space mission, she could never have anticipated the horror of being taken to the Kiranis system and left to languish in confusion and disconnection amongst millions of captives. Perhaps, she thought, as she walked the makeshift streets of what the people had come to call Jones' Quadrant, it was best that the early years were spent in ignorance.

Over the years, as the humans began to exponentially outnumber their Kwaios captors and the delivery of food and services became automated, resignation to the circumstances led the people in this vast subterranean habitat to do what humans always did. They formed groups and societies defined by everything from language, ideologies, beliefs and aspirations to the perception of shared histories. Some groups fuelled their call to arms using their shared concessions to their fate on this alien world. A decade was not a long time, but humans were always swift to create reasons for segregation and alliance rather than maintaining bonds of unity to move towards freedom.

Abigale had tried to avoid becoming assimilated by any of these cliques, many of whose influences reached from one end of the underground world to the other. It was difficult to remain neutral when indifference to anyone's plight marked you as favourable to that of someone else. Despite this, Abigale had somehow found herself in a position of influence amongst Jones' society; she became a mediator of disputes and a legislator of sorts. People respected her, and she found that she enjoyed it. It was almost enough to make her appreciate her life here. Almost.

Walking these streets, she had become accustomed to people calling her name, for there was always some situation unfolding that required her attention. But today, the voice was not so much calling as it was demanding her presence, and that she was not accustomed to. She angrily stalked towards the source of the shouting voice, which she could hear was that of a woman. But as a great crowd up ahead parted to let her through, she felt the weight of their stares and her heart pounded as she anticipated encountering whatever shocking circumstance they knew awaited. A woman stood beyond the crowd, blood on the shoulders of her dusty white outfit and metallic fibres hanging like extensions from her hair. She held the hand of a filthy-faced girl in tattered clothes, and she looked directly at Abigale as she said, 'I believe this is yours.'

Abigale's world paused in that moment, for as her eyes returned to the girl, there was no crowd around them, no underground prison, no Kwaios, no alien planet. The Universe itself could have been removed from around them, and all Abigale would see was the girl her little Hannah had become. 'Mom?' she heard her ask tentatively, almost as if she were afraid of the response.

Abigale put her hands to her mouth, desperately trying to stop the sobbing that brought her to her knees. Hannah came to her, cautiously at first, as if there were more deceits to be suffered. But Abigale managed to reach out one trembling arm, and Hannah screamed 'Mom!' as she ran to her embrace.

Cassandra looked at the ever-growing crowd, addressing them with the authority she knew she would come to wield – had to wield – if they were to survive: 'We'll be joined soon by very powerful people who will bring their ships to the surface to create cities across the planet. The surface is now open to you, and it's completely devoid of Kwaios. All of you...*all* of you...will become more powerful than any Kwaios and we'll build something out here that will make the galaxy tremble!'

'What are you talking about?' Abigale asked, wiping tears from her face as she rose and held Hannah close. 'How do you expect any of that to happen out here?'

Cassandra came swiftly towards her, the metal tendrils seeming to come alive with determination. 'This world was being used to merge Kwaios consciousness with human clones,' she explained. 'To make hybrids with Kwaios souls and human bodies. But we're going to exploit the technology they left behind. We're going to use hybritech so we can do everything they could do...and more.' She looked around at their faces. So many faces – unsure, afraid, weakened by their experience. And she gave them a wicked smile of assurance to lift their downtrodden hearts: 'We're going to build an empire!'

EPILOGUE

Kiranis Orbit

Naveen had come to the Jaevisk in his human form at the first signs of Kiranis returning, as Cana was battling with his desire to live and lose or die and win. The Prophet stood before their most senior guardians, four Old Ones who had overseen the vigil since the most recent days of water and rust had begun, when the Warlord Krell had led them to retake Kiranis. He had failed, yet he had triumphed, for the Jaevisk Society valued failure in a cloak of valour more than success in the tattered robes of blind fortune. Now the Old Ones regarded this harbinger of great change in much the same way as one might acquiesce to the arrival of the End Season – such things were inevitable, a part of life that was less about death as it was an opportunity for palimpsestic reassessment. They even inclined their blackgem-encrusted golden heads in a gesture of respect. For the Old Ones were wise. 'Why have you come amongst us again?' one asked.

Naveen appreciated their reception, and it showed. He was neither smug nor condescending, but this was partly because of what he had in store for this great species. 'I want you to abandon Kiranis,' he told them, adding, 'temporarily.'

'Why would we do this?' another asked. 'Our destiny awaits below.'

Naveen shook his head. 'This isn't your destiny. Kiranis is mine.'

'We have fought and died for this world,' a third disagreed. 'Our entire species has been dedicated to its possession.'

'I need you for something else,' Naveen said bluntly. 'To be the vanguard of this galaxy's defence.'

'Against what?' the fourth asked. 'We've watched your scheme against the Kwaios. They are about to fall at Earth. We need Kiranis to survive your people.'

'It's not my people you need to fear. The Station Masters are on the move…jumping across galaxies to lay waste to ours.'

They were clearly disturbed by this news. 'This is *your* doing, human,' the first accused him. 'Why would you bring such an enemy to our shores?'

426

'I'm doing only what I did,' Naveen replied. 'Destiny is what it was.'

They were silent for a time, as the rest of Kiranis returned to the Universe and hundreds of Jaevisk ships caught up in the gravity of the planet made their descent to the world of dragons and stones, unaware of the horrors that awaited them. 'Which star?' the second Old One asked eventually. 'We will not waste our supply on multiple jumps.'

Naveen nodded. 'I understand.' He waved a hand, and walls and floors vanished around them until they were standing in the darkness around Kiranis, where warships could be seen passing through the Cage. 'Stars know each other,' the Prophet explained, 'even across galaxies. Their Lines are the most powerful of all. But when they cast their Line out into the emptiness, only one other star will take hold. They're like lovers across the Universe…the ultimate long-distance relationship.' He smiled, always enjoying the sound of his own voice. 'Guess which one is bonded to the one I need you to visit.'

In the distance, they saw the burning sun of the Kiranis system. A short time later, as thousands of Jaevisk warships headed towards this portentous star, heading into the unknown to defend their galaxy against the armies of a god, the Old Ones did not feel so wise.

BONUS CONTENT

From Kiranis Book 3
Secrets of The Universe

PROLOGUE

Sighing seas of blackness lost drew the Shoal of the Starmaster closer to the Abyss. His Journeymen were now each of three across the Ranks, and so the course was hampered still. Onwards pressed the harried crews, their faithful hearts glowing for blissful atonement. But the Metal Demons crossed the horizon soon, their molten hearts brimming for chaos.

From *The Odyssey of the Resounding Sea*, a Jaevisk Epic discovered in hundreds of parts, engraved upon the solidified bodies of thousands of Cen-Dith fused to the hulls of scores of ruined warships. The debris field corresponds with Jaevisk records of an encounter with the flagship of Aphestan.

Galaxy NGC 6503, Constellation Draco, 583 NE

Aboard the Jaevisk warship, its name in English akin to the Cursed Jump, Mryra Yln had served as a Journeyman for thirty-eight cycles of the Core. His role on the Jump meant that he spent most of his time either with his three Brothers, or on his own. In this isolated galaxy perched on the edge of a death-filled darkness, those who oversaw the odyssey of their race were dependent upon each other for their very survival. Journeymen were not trained or educated in their role; they were born with the ability to navigate the Lines. They absorbed the harmony of the Sentience with every breath in every waking moment; and as they slept, the Lines whispered in their ears, assuring them of their significance in the Resounding Sea even as they taunted Journeymen with their fate. For only through their dreams could their future find them.

Yln had dreams of a different nature, aspirations of plotting a course to their home galaxy and returning his people to the world of Kiranis. It was said that the ancient gods of the Jaevisk Society lived on that mystical planet, but Yln had seen so much in this galaxy that the concept of gods had become somewhat skewed. The Old Ones referred to their great enemies as Station Masters, but it was an enigmatic term for numerous reasons. Firstly, they appeared to be both hunting and evading the subordinate species of only one of these creatures, whom the Old Ones called Aphestan, and no Jaevisk with whom Yln had ever spoken knew of any other. Secondly, there was no apparent reason for their mission, for ancient Jaevisk lore bore no reference to these Station Masters. And thirdly, the name of these enigmas suggested that a route was being monitored or protected, but no Jaevisk knew anything of either the existence or nature of such a route.

There had been reports of engagement with the vessel of Aphestan, but they had no sooner been transmitted than contact had been lost. Incomplete images and corrupted readings had been received by fleets too far away to come to the aid of their outmatched brothers, and the Lines would pulse with the loss of every Journeyman whose heart was returned to the Core. Yln experienced these deaths as if fleshhooks were teasing his muscular frame, promising him an infinitely slow and painful journey across the Resounding Sea before finding rest in the Core. And now, as he hooked himself into his restframe to enjoy some respite from the endless war, he felt the irony of the alignment of sleep and death. For only by his dreams was a border raised between these brethren realms.

With the last of the sleep-hooks connected to the piercings at his ankles, hips, and shoulders, he was drawn upwards to hang from the ceiling. His head hung back, and he felt his breathing slow and his heartrate diminish as his eyes fixed upon the circular porthole of his cell. But something slammed against it from outside and his inbound slumber was unceremoniously diverted. Hanging from the ceiling with his great heart pounding, Mryra Yln stared at the circle of black eyes watching him. They were set within a hexagonal head of silver and gold, and they were unblinking. Perhaps this had been one of Yln's kills, one of the many he had dismembered when last the Cursed Jump had been boarded by the enemy. But it was impossible to say, for these Cen-Dith – vanguard of the Station Master Aphestan – all looked the same. These formidable soldiers of a mysterious god were made of metal, with six semi-autonomous appendages centred upon their head section, the one now glaring at Yln through his cell window.

Yln held its glare for some time, as his heart slowed and he relaxed again. The great cold of space kept these prisoners of war from reforming, and they had been broken apart and spread randomly around the hull of the warship like a vast display of trophies. It would take a long time for them to solidify, and experience what the Jaevisk presumed was their equivalent of death, so the warship was protected by a shield of living Cen-Dith warriors, whose bodies always held out for some time against the onslaught of their kin.

Content in this ironic protection from the greatest enemy the Jaevisk had ever known, Yln drifted off to sleep. His home was a fleet of two hundred warships sailing the Resounding Sea in an alien galaxy, with living Cen-Dith fused to their hulls. The captive aliens watched the blackness for any sign of rescue...their arms flailing...their eyes unblinking...

For more Bonus Content, including:

Pieces of Kiranis #1: The Barrier

Visit the (Dis)Members Area
templedarkbooks.com